...ry Colburn, Conduit Street.

Thomson & Hall, sculp.t 14, Bury Str.t Bloomsb.y

GEORG HEINRICH von LANGSDORFF

REMARKS AND OBSERVATIONS ON A VOYAGE AROUND THE WORLD FROM 1803 TO 1807

VOLUME ONE

THE VOYAGE FROM COPENHAGEN TO BRAZIL, THE SOUTH SEA, KAMTSCHATKA AND JAPAN

AND

VOLUME TWO

THE VOYAGE FROM KAMTSCHATKA TO THE ISLAND OF ST. PAUL, UNALASKA, KODIAK, SITCHA, NEW ALBION, KAMTSCHATKA, OCHOTSK AND THROUGH SIBERIA TO ST. PETERSBURG

Dem Freunde gezeichnet von L. Bojanus Profess. in Wilna. Gest. v. F. Lehmann in Darmstadt 1809
G. v. Langsdorff.

Alaska History No. 41

REMARKS AND OBSERVATIONS ON A VOYAGE AROUND THE WORLD FROM 1803 TO 1807

VOLUME ONE

by
GEORG HEINRICH von LANGSDORFF

Translated and Annotated
by
VICTORIA JOAN MOESSNER

Edited
by
RICHARD A. PIERCE

THE LIMESTONE PRESS
Kingston, Ontario : Fairbanks, Alaska
1993

Box 1604
Kingston, Ontario
Canada K7L 3N6

U.S. Office:
The Limestone Press
c/o History Department
University of Alaska Fairbanks
Fairbanks, Alaska 99775-0860

International Standard Book Number 1-895901-00-6

Publication was funded in part by the Alaska Humanities Forum, Anchorage, and the National Endowment for the Humanities.

Translation from Georg Heinrich von Langsdorff, *Bemerkungen auf einer Reise um die Welt in den Jahren 1803 bis 1807*, Frankfurt am Mayn, Friedrich Wilmans, 2 vols., 1812.

Production: J. Ketz, Pauline Higdon

CONTENTS

VOLUME ONE

CONTENTS

VOLUME TWO

CONTENTS

TRANSLATOR'S INTRODUCTION

A generous and elevated Mind is distinguished by nothing more certainly than an eminent degree of Curiosity, nor is that Curiosity ever more agreeably or usefully employed, than in examining the Laws and Customs of Foreign Nations.

— Samuel Johnson
Father Lobo's Voyage to Abyssinia, 1735

Strenge Wahrheitsliebe ist kein Vorzug, sondern Schuldigkeit eines jeden Reisebeschreibers (The rigorous love of truth is not a priority but rather the duty of every travel writer).

— Georg Heinrich von Langsdorff

Georg Heinrich von Langsdorff's life encompassed a period in which new ideas and discoveries were quickening the pace of intellectual life in Europe and laying the foundations of modern scientific disciplines. At the same time, revolutions and economically motivated exploration and competition for territory and markets at the farthest corners of the globe were beginning to change the political face of the earth. Langsdorff was a son of his age: restless, curious, thirsting for new knowledge, eager to leave his mark on the world in the form of natural historical collections and new scientific information. He was highly educated and widely traveled. He shared with his contemporaries a passion for investigating and collecting the new and the unknown and shipping it back to Europe. He felt angry and frustrated when his efforts, from his point of view, were misunderstood and thwarted by the pettiness of those around him.

In addition to collecting specimens and information, Langsdorff wanted to test and evaluate the information available to him from earlier travel accounts and to establish objective truths about societies and natural phenomena around the world; yet he, like his contemporaries and those traveling before them, remained culturally bound and viewed the world from their narrow European background. They often were, as Adelbert von Chamisso (1781-1838), the German poet and naturalist on board the *Riurik* (1815-1818) said, like cannon balls hurled "round the world . . . to collect pieces of rock, dried plants and animal skins."[1] Langsdorff could admire the organizational ability and handicrafts and workmanship of other cultures and tried to describe them objectively as well as to debunk fallacies in older literature, but he remained convinced that only Europe was truly civilized and, therefore, was culturally superior to the rest of the world.

Langsdorff was born April 18, 1774, at Wöllstein, Rhinehesse into a baronial family that traced its descent to the fourteenth century. His father was mayor of Wöllstein and later vice-chancellor of the superior court for the Grand Duchy of Baden at Karlsruhe (Carlsruhe). Langsdorff first attended school in Buchsweiler (French: Bouxwiller), Alsace, and then the *gymnasium* (secondary school) in Idstein, Nassau. In October 1793, he matriculated at the University of Göttingen in order to study medicine with an emphasis in gynecology and the natural sciences. He left Göttingen with a deeper interest in anthropology, ethnography and natural history and with a greater desire to earn his living through scientific research than through the practice of medicine. Johann Friedrich Blumenbach, professor of medicine and comparative anatomy and the founder of modern anthropology, had deeply influenced Langsdorff's concept and practice of scientific research. Like Blumenbach, whose philosophical base lay in Kant's writings, Langsdorff sought deeper causes for behavior and scientific phenomena, rather than simply listing and describing them superficially and indiscriminately.

Soon after completing his studies at the University of Göttingen in 1797, Langsdorff left for Lisbon as the personal physician to Prince Christian of Waldeck, who had been named a general in the Portuguese army. In 1798 Prince Christian was fatally wounded. Before his death on September 24, 1798, he interceded with Prince D. Joáo VI on Langsdorff's behalf so that Langsdorff could remain in Portugal. From 1799 to 1800 he served as a doctor at the German hospital "Irmandade de São Bartolomeu" in Lisbon and introduced the vaccination against smallpox discovered by Edward Jenner three years earlier in England. From 1801 to 1802, he served as surgeon-major with the English Regiment de Castrier, which fought in Spain until the Peace of Amiens, March 27, 1802. During his time in Portugal, he undertook scientific research and established contacts with members of the Academy of Sciences in St. Petersburg. In 1802 he offered the Academy the results of his scientific work in Portugal and sent to St. Petersburg a report and a crate of insects and fish which he had identified and classified.[2]

After the Peace of Amiens, Langsdorff returned to Göttingen by way of Paris and London. He was working on his natural historical collections when he heard through Russian friends about a forthcoming voyage around the world, the first to be undertaken by Russians. Langsdorff thereupon turned his Iberian collections over to the museum and, as he describes in the introduction to his *Remarks and Observations*, hurried to Copenhagen to entreat the expedition's commander, Adam Johann von Krusenstern (Russian: Kruzenshtern), and Chamberlain Nikolai Petrovich Rezanov (Resanoff) to let him join the expedition as a physician and natural scientist. His powers of persuasion — perhaps because he had excellent medical and scientific credentials and spoke Portuguese — prevailed, and he was invited to go on board the *Nadezhda*. He could not have failed to note that the small, crowded ship boiled with malice, most of which was directed toward Rezanov.

In order to fill in details of the controversy surrounding Rezanov, one has to turn to other sources, specifically the published accounts of Captain Krusenstern and Fedor Ivanovich Shemelin, a Russian-American Company clerk who sailed on the *Nadezhda*, as well as Rezanov's letters and other documents. Ewert von Krusenstjern's *Weltumsegler und Wissenschaftler: Adam Johann von Krusenstern* (Circumnavigator and Scientist) contains an extensive discussion of the atmosphere aboard the Russian ships, as well as a secret report written by Johann Caspar Horner to Franz Xaver Freiherr von Zach and excerpts from Hermann von Löwenstern's (Levenshtern's) diary.[3]

The discontent and animosity among the leaders of the expedition had begun to ferment even before the *Nadezhda* and *Neva* set sail from Kronstadt. Krusenstern had labored for ten years to convince St. Petersburg officialdom of the value and necessity to finance a Russian voyage around the world. Tsar Alexander I finally rewarded him with a letter dated August 7, 1802, appointing him commander of an expedition to the Northwest Coast of North America. Iuri Lisianski, with whom Krusenstern had served in the British fleet during the American Revolution, was made second in command. Krusenstern sent Lisianski to Hamburg to purchase two vessels. He found nothing suitable there so he went to London, where in February 1803 he purchased two ships, the 450-ton *Leander*, three years old, and the 370-ton *Thames*, 15 months old. He took them to Kronstadt, where they were renamed the *Nadezhda* (Hope) and the *Neva*. The former, under Krusenstern, was to have 85 men on board and the *Neva*, under Lisianski, 54.

But by then Krusenstern's expectations had been dashed. In January 1803 Krusenstern was informed that an entirely new project had been added to the original plans for the voyage and that he would no longer be the first in command. The *Nadezhda*, under the leadership of Rezanov, a high court official and executive of the Russian-American Company, was to carry an embassy to Japan under the pretext of returning five Japanese, shipwrecked on Russian territory some years earlier. The hope was to establish trade and diplomatic relations with Japan, which had been closed to Europeans for two centuries except for one Dutch ship a year which was granted permission to put in at Nagasaki (Nangasaki) Harbor. This news arrived quite late in the preparations for the voyage, making Krusenstern's resentment quite understandable. He was already well along with the selection of personnel when he found he had to make room for the Ambassador, his five-man retinue, and the five Japanese. In addition, cargo, including nine months of rations, had to be off-loaded to make room for cases of porcelain, mirrors, glassware, and textiles intended as gifts for the Japanese Emperor and his officials and a library of 500 volumes destined for the settlement of Paul's Harbor (now Kodiak) in Russian America.

For Rezanov, meanwhile, the matter was clear. "Two merchant vessels, purchased in London, have been placed under my command," he wrote in a letter of April 1803.[4] The expedition sailed from Kronstadt on July 27, 1803. In a report to the Board of Directors of the Russian-American Company, Fedor Shemelin, supercargo on the *Nadezhda*, wrote that "unimaginable disagreement and riot instigated by the naval officers reigned on the ship *Nadezhda*. Their circumspection, zeal, good will, and loyalty to the Company disappeared as soon as the anchors were weighed in Kronstadt harbor . . . " According to Shemelin, Krusenstern and the others wanted to discharge him at Copenhagen and install a man of their own choosing from Reval (present-day Tallin). Rezanov, who found Shemelin satisfactory, refused, "and it began with that." Shemelin accused the naval officers of disrespect toward Rezanov, disloyalty, criticism of the government, atheism — "they have no God other than sails" — and debauchery.[5]

After Copenhagen, Krusenstern made no effort to hide his resentment; his subordinates followed his lead with taunts, insults and threats. Lieutenant Count Fedor Ivanovich Tolstoi, a member of Rezanov's retinue who at the age of 22 already had a reputation as a duelist, eagerly joined in the persecution. Rezanov, accustomed to the polish and tact of court circles, was apparently unable to cope with the situation. Neither patience nor attempts to ignore the insults did any good. At St. Catherine's (Catharina), Brazil, Rezanov, on May 17, 1804, wrote to Chichagov, the assistant Minister of the Navy, expressing hope that Chichagov might spare some time from state affairs "to look into my circumstances which are causing me anguish and constraint." He wrote of his "sufferings" and his inability through mild and humane measures "to put a stop to this turbulence" and that "I am ashamed to repeat what I have had to endure. Now I feel fully the consequences of the disorder that began even when this expedition was being organized."[6]

Shemelin writes that he often wept because of the officers' treatment of him as a hireling of the Company. Lieutenant Romberg threatened to throw him overboard. Count Tolstoi succeeded, writes Shemelin, in spreading hatred toward Rezanov from the *Nadezhda* to the *Neva*. Tolstoi stirred Captain Lisianski with the gossip that Rezanov had recommended that the Company cancel a provision for a 10,000-ruble bonus to the officers of the expedition. "It would be hard to find another man as corrupt as the Count; he is an atheist, an ingrate and an insolent calumniator of his fatherland and all that is sacred. By him you may judge Krusenstern, who chose him as his tool."[7]

The other side of the imbroglio is found in a secret report dated January 28, 1804, which Johann Caspar Horner sent to Franz Xaver von Zach from Brazil. Horner asserts that Krusenstern was the originator of the expedition and agreed to take Rezanov along to please the Tsar so that his embassy would not have to go overland. Horner himself had become well acquainted with Rezanov's character on a trip through England. Rezanov had proved himself not only to be "weak of spirit" but "bad as a matter of principle." Before they reached Teneriffe, he had done his best to turn members of the party against Krusenstern. He went too far, causing Krusenstern to remonstrate "gently" at Teneriffe, whereupon Rezanov pulled out "underhanded" instructions signed by the Tsar, which "he, out of fairness, should have made public in Kronstadt. I say underhanded instructions, for Tsar

Alexander would not desire to offend someone like Krusenstern, to tear away the fame of his own work and give it as booty to another . . . " Krusenstern explained "that the Tsar had been deceived and that he intended to write St. Petersburg in order to complain about this injury to his honor. But Rezanov begged sincerely for forgiveness, that the matter be put aside and nothing written about it, which the peace-loving Krusenstern promised and also did." Horner ends his report by saying: "In Kamchatka (Kamtschatka), hopefully we will be delivered from this rare fellowship."[8]

Matters nevertheless became worse as the voyage continued, culminating in Kamchatka where an appeal to Major General Koshelev (Koscheleff), commandant of Kamchatka, restored order. Krusenstern had to apologize, lest it affect his career. The other officers were told to mend their ways. Lieutenant Tolstoi, of Rezanov's suite, was sent home. (There, he continued duelling, keeping a score which eventually numbered eleven men, and became a social lion known as the "American," because he sometimes dressed in imaginary native costumes and provided listeners with colorful accounts of regions of North America he had never seen.)[9]

After returning to Petropavlovsk from the fiasco in Japan, Krusenstern prepared to continue the voyage back to Europe and Rezanov to sail by way of the Aleutian Islands to Kodiak and Novo-Arkhangel'sk (now Sitka) aboard the *Maria*, a vessel belonging to the Russian-American Company. On Rezanov's promise that he would be able to collect natural history specimens, Langsdorff decided to accompany him to Russian America. Shemelin writes that he and Lieutenant Golovachev, the sole officer on the *Nadezhda* who had not taken part in persecuting Rezanov, were the only ones to see the ship off.[10]

In his *Remarks and Observations* Langsdorff is reticent about the winter of 1805-1806 in Novo-Arkhangel'sk, except for his intense joy when he could no longer see Mt. Edgecumbe as he sailed toward Kamchatka on board American Captain John D'Wolf's tiny vessel. If Langsdorff had tried to explore, collect, and work then as he did later in Brazil, he could only have been intensely frustrated and angry. He blames Rezanov and other company officials for not rationing food properly and for disregarding the welfare of the promyshlenniks. He praises Davydov (Davidoff) and Khvostov (Chwostoff) but says nothing about the latter's part in a winter-long carousal described by Rezanov in a letter to the Board of Directors of the Russian-American Company, written in Novo-Arkhangel'sk on November 6, 1805. Rezanov writes that A. A. Baranov (Baranoff) was "more than once" in tears, because the foreigners Captain D'Wolf and "my doctor [Langsdorff] found here a drunken republic . . . " In another letter to the Directors, dated February 15, 1806, he states that Lieutenant Sukin "sits in his room all the time; his only recreation is drink and sleep," and that Lieutenant Mashin, who was also a heavy drinker, was costing the Company a good deal of money and required discharge. The worst of all, however, was Khvostov, who was the main participant in all the escapades. He tried to take part in company business affairs and to blacken the reputations of other employees. With the onset of winter, Khvostov began a three-month drinking bout to the point where even his bosom friend, Midshipman Davydov, avoided him; and he was making drunkards out of other company personnel, notably the young ship apprentices Koriukin and Popov, who would have to be sent out of the colonies.[11]

After his return to St. Petersburg with 16 crates of specimens on March 16, 1808, Langsdorff remained in the country that had made his round-the-world voyage and research possible. He was now at the peak of his career. The Tsar honored him with the title of Knight of the Order of St. Anne, Second Class, and Privy Councilor. He was elected a member of the Academy of Sciences. Through his stay in Portugal, he spoke Portuguese and, as his *Remarks and Observations* indicate, he was enchanted with Brazil: he lamented having to leave "the most beautiful and richest country on earth. The memories of my stay in Brazil will remain unforgettable all my life." Langsdorff entered Russian state service September 24, 1812, on his appointment as Russian consul in Rio de Janeiro. Two days before this appointment, he married Friederike Luise von Schubert (Russian: Friderika Luiza von Shubert, 1791-1842), the daughter of the mathematician and astronomer Friedrich Theodor von Schubert (Russian: Fridrikh Teodor von Shubert), who had taken part in a Russian expedition of 1805 to Kiakhta and Mongolia. On April 5, 1813, she set sail with Langsdorff for Brazil, where they arrived 67 days later. In 1815 she bore him Wilhelmine, the first of two daughters.[12]

Rio de Janeiro had become a hospitable stopping place for diplomats, artists, scientists, merchants, adventurers, and even musicians from all over Europe. Langsdorff soon became one of the best known personalities in Brazil. He helped almost all European scientists and artists passing through Rio de Janeiro by sharing the hospitality of his home or providing connections and information about the countryside or by giving them duplicates from his extensive collections of minerals, plants, birds, butterflies, insects and artifacts obtained from aboriginal tribes. The Langsdorff home became a lively evening salon for all of the Europeans in the area and their visitors. Langsdorff's wife Friederike enchanted the gatherings with music of high quality. She continued her musical studies begun in St. Petersburg with Sigismund Ritter von Neukomm, one of Haydn's favorite students who was Court composer in Rio de Janeiro and an avid entomologist and botanist.[13]

F. P. Litke (Lütke 1797-1882) has left a description of both Langsdorffs as seen in 1817. He describes Langsdorff as a man of "about 45, small, lean, with a rather insignificant face. He loves to speak Russian but finds it very hard to explain things. Trying to help us pass the time, he showed us among other things an unrivalled collection of insects he had made here. According to him there were over 6,000 species either undescribed scientifically or wholly unknown. He has already sent one such collection to Petersburg and will soon send this one." Friederike Luise von Langsdorff was "a woman of wonderful qualities; a tender mother and a loving wife, she does not forget that there are also social obligations, and fulfills them . . . She speaks good Russian, although with mistakes like all our Petersburg Germans, but even this appears astonishing if you remember that from the time that she left Russia her sole practice with the Russian language has been a three-year old daughter . . . "[14]

Soon after his arrival in Rio de Janeiro, Langsdorff began sending reports to the Academy of Sciences in St. Petersburg. In 1814-1815 he and the German botanist Friedrich Sellow explored Serra do Orgáo and Serra d'Estrella near Rio de Janeiro. In 1815 Prince Maximilian zu Neuwied visited him and met Sellow and G. Wilhelm Freyreiß with whom he then undertook an extended expedition to Bahia. In 1816 the Count of Luxemburg arrived with a French entourage, including the botanist Auguste de Saint-Hilaire. At the end of 1816, Langsdorff and Saint-Hilaire, at the invitation of the Brazilian botanist Antonio Ildefonso Gomez, traveled to Minas Gerais to visit W. C. von Eschwege (head of Brazilian mining, 1810-1821) and to the estate of Gomez's parents. Saint-Hilaire describes the excursion and Langsdorff's influence upon him in *Voyage dans les Provinces de Rio de Janeiro et de Minas Gerais*: "In the company of Mr. Langsdorff, the most active and indefatigable man I have ever met, I learned how not to waste a minute of my time on a scientific expedition, to ignore deprivation, to accept cheerfully all possible discomforts. My travel companion went here and there, became excited, called first this person over to him and that one, gave commentary; he ate, wrote in his diary, put his butterfly collection in order — all at the same time. He walked quickly, his head and arms — thrust forward — seemed to admonish the others for their sluggishness. He spoke quickly, causing him to lose his breath like after a long hike."[15]

Langsdorff tired of a diet of city life and longed for his own land to explore and develop according to his own theories. On September 28, 1816, he purchased an estate, "Mandioca" (tapioca or cassava), at the foot of the Serra d'Estrella. It could be reached by a day's sail from Rio de Janeiro across the Bay of Guanabara and then a day's ride through the luxurious landscape. It had 30-40,000 coffee trees and many workers, including 40 slaves. From "Mandioca" he conducted consular business, entertained many foreign visitors, including Russian circumnavigators, and carried out his scientific research. In 1817 Johann Baptist Ritter von Spix and Carl Friedrich Phillip von Martius visited "Mandioca," as did the English merchant-explorer John Luccock. Spix and Martius have given us a colorful description of their trip to "Mandioca" and of one of the side efforts of collecting Brazilian artifacts: "The first American aborigine we saw here was a boy belonging to the Botocudos, a cannibal tribe in Minas Gerais. He was in the home of our friend von Langsdorff. Conde da Barca, the former Portuguese minister of state, had requested that the district commander for the Indians in Minas Gerais provide an Indian skull for our famous fellow countryman, the Honorable Privy Councilor Blumenbach. Since he was unable to acquire such a specimen, he sent the Count two living Botocudos, whom his soldiers had taken prisoner in a sudden raid. Mr. von Langsdorff got the one whom he soon came to like so much that he served not only as a living museum-piece but also as a collector of natural curiosities."[16]

In 1818 Langsdorff sent 13 crates of animal skins, as well as an extensive report of his observations and research, to the Academy of Sciences in St. Petersburg. He also requested of the Russian government an 18-month leave in Europe so that he could, among other activities, visit museums in Paris and Munich, further efforts to attract German and other immigrants to Brazil, and seek support for his long-desired, grand expedition deep into the interior of Brazil.

In 1819 Langsdorff's wife bore him a second daughter, Elise, but soon after Elise's birth — no reasons are given in published sources except that she could not bear the climate — Wilhelmine von Langsdorff left him and returned to St. Petersburg with both of their daughters. T. von Leithold, a Prussian officer visiting Rio de Janeiro in 1819, has left us a hint in his description of a ball Langsdorff gave at "Mandioca" in honor of the members of two Russian expeditions, whose ships were anchored in the harbor: "Gentlemen and ladies from Russia, Prussia, Austria, England, France, Spain, and Portugal, as well as Brazil danced at the ball; and the ladies presented the observer a splendid view of feminine charm from all of the nations represented there. By eight o'clock, however, the arms, shoulders and backs of the ladies, who were dressed in the prevailing style, i.e., in low-cut dresses, had been so bitten and sucked over by mosquitoes that they appeared no less red than soldiers flogged by the whip. May I be excused for the perhaps tasteless comparison; but it does not exaggerate the truth . . . and then the unbelievable heat from which all the people suffered in the restricted confines of the room."[17]

Soon after his arrival in Europe in October 1820, from Paris Langsdorff wrote the botanist Carl Bernhard Trinius in St. Petersburg that he would be traveling to St. Petersburg by way of Lahr, Munich, and Vienna and that in St. Petersburg he would be turning over his extensive Brazilian collections, as well as his "Catalogoue génerique des insectes apportés du Brésil." In the spring of 1821, he arrived in St. Petersburg and turned over his collections and report. In addition he begged he be granted permission and support to explore Brazil's interior. Ever restless and while waiting for the Tsar and his councilors to reach a decision, Langsdorff joined a caravan going to Bukhara. He had reached Orenburg when news arrived that the trip had to be postponed but also that he had been nominated to head the scientific expedition into the interior of Brazil and funds for that purpose would be placed at his disposal. Thereupon, he returned to St. Petersburg and on July 3, 1821, set out for Germany to carry out preparations for the expedition, as well as for the transport of immigrants to Brazil.

To provide information about conditions awaiting immigrants in Brazil, he had written *Memoire sur le Brésil* published in Paris (the German translation appeared in 1821 and the Portuguese in 1822). He hoped to establish farms and estates modeled after "Mandioca." In the German edition Langsdorff states: "I have written this especially for those who desire to settle in Brazil. My intention is in no way to encourage the immigration of my fellow countrymen but only to call to their attention an almost unknown land that is as large as Europe . . . " He lists the advantages (climate, eternal summer, and the availability of products from the rain forests) against the disadvantages (high prices, no good roads, thus making it difficult to get products to market, and tropical diseases and insects) in Brazil, "the best and most beautiful of all the known countries in the world." Brazil is better than the "cold, ungrateful North America (the United Free States)," where many have "sacrificed their freedom . . . to be able to buy infertile land deep in the interior after years of hard labor." In his *Remarks and Observations*, based upon his visit in 1803, he castigates the inhumane treatment of slaves, but seemingly as the illogical management of valuable property. A decade later, however, in his *Memoire sur le Brésil*, he openly defends slavery: "The English may preach as much as they want against the slave trade, but in the end they will have to admit that they have damaged themselves with their campaign. I consider it a great service, more pleasing to God to convert barbarous Negroes to Christianity and to make useful citizens of them, than to leave them barbarous heathens in Africa. Therefore, Brazil offers a special advantage that one can buy slaves who are viewed as the main investment capital of the owners of estates and have been well raised physically and morally for the owner's own use."[18]

On March 5, 1822, Langsdorff arrived in Rio de Janeiro on board the *Doris* (a ship he had chartered in Bremen) together with 29 German colonists and their families, a total of 94 German immigrants. Langsdorff's party also included his natural son Karl Georg (born in 1809 in Rennrod, Germany), his cousin Heinrich, his aunt Johanna, and her daughter Wilhemine, Langsdorff's second wife who was to bear him four sons and a daughter between 1822 and 1830. In addition, the party included the German artist Moritz Rugendas, the French naturalist C. Ménétriez, Baron de Drais, Chamberlain of the Grand Duke of Baden, and F. Mack, Langsdorff's personal servant. Langsdorff also carried with him an authorization from Emperor Alexander I to undertake the long-awaited major expedition.[19]

From 1822 to 1825, Langsdorff undertook shorter expeditions. Finally, in September 1825, he and several companions set out deep into the interior.[20] For two and a half years all went well. In the provinces of Rio de Janeiro, Espirito Santo, Minas Gerais and São

Paulo, he and his associates collected quantities of bird, animal, and insect specimens, plants and minerals, compiled vocabularies of Indian tribes now long extinct, and made many drawings and paintings. Then, in April 1828, Langsdorff was stricken by a virulent form of malaria which attacked his nervous system and brain, leaving him delirious, hallucinating, and deathly ill. He was brought back to Rio de Janeiro in March 1829, and in 1830 he and his family returned to Europe, accompanied by Major Anton Adolf Friedrich von Seveloh. At first the family lived with his sister Countess von Sponeck in Baden Baden but then moved to Freiburg im Breisgau. On Sunday June 26, 1831, the following comments appeared in the *Freiburger Zeitung*: "For the past four months we have had the pleasure of the presence of the famous traveler G. v. Langsdorff, Imperial Russian Privy Councilor, in our midst. Until now we have remained silent because of the sad news we had read in several public sources: that he was a complete senseless imbecile. We were not able to judge this earlier. But now that we have been able to observe him and have perceived an apparent lack of truth in the rumors, we see it as our duty to tell the world that Mr. v. Langsdorff is anything but imbecilic or absent, that he had suffered greatly on his significant expeditions, but even this fog has become significantly abated since his arrival here, that we may hope that he will soon be completely well in our temperate, friendly climate. We, his fellow countrymen, wish him this from the bottom of our hearts and hope that we may retain this generally esteemed scholar and honorable man in our midst for a long time to come."

The Russian Academy of Sciences granted Langsdorff a pension. He remained in Freiburg until his death June 29, 1852, at the age of 78. His tombstone, shaded by the foliage of huge trees, is fixed in one wall of the quiet, dignified old cemetery in the center of Freiburg; in tune with Langsdorff's character, it has impatiens blooming in front of it.

Despite Langsdorff's illness, numerous crates of specimens collected on the ill-fated expedition were shipped to St. Petersburg, but for a century his diaries and many other materials from the expedition were considered lost. It was not, however, until 1973 that a complete descriptive listing of the archival materials was published. Slowly, these materials are being published or being made available to scholars on microfilm with the help of the Langsdorff International Studies Association.[21]

Langsdorff's two volume *Remarks and Observations on a Voyage around the World* (London, 1813-1814) belongs to the large body of scientific travel literature of the period and is considered his most important written contribution to knowledge. Scholars consider his observations on Polynesia, California, and other areas the expedition visited reliable and essential. By contrast, in 1886, the American historian H. H. Bancroft, who accepts Rezanov's reports and letters without taking Rezanov's character, position and intentions into account, judged Langsdorff very negatively: "As a savant he was superficial; as a chronicler he was biased . . . His statements as to the condition of the natives and the promyshlenniki appear to be greatly exaggerated. They are not indorsed by any of the Alaskan annalists, and though Lisiansky gives some color to them, they are strongly at variance with the reports of Rezanof, who was a keen and impartial observer."[22]

Even though Krusenstern's *Voyage round the World in the Years 1803, 1804, 1805 and 1806* (London 1813) is quoted or referred to more often, in part because it is a more readable, more English-sounding translation, it can best be understood in conjunction with Langsdorff's *Remarks and Observations* up to the time when Krusenstern sailed from Kamchatka for Europe and Langsdorff for Russian America.

During Langsdorff's lifetime travel books such as his belonged to one of the most important international literary genres. The travel book was considered a subspecies of history and a branch of learning. Men like the English historian John Adams at the end of the 18th century advised young people to read travel literature because "one is struck by the differences between the customs of his own country and those of other nations. Then penetrated by that difference, one seeks the reason for it, and there for him is the beginning of political, commercial, and moral combinations."[23] Unlike our modern guide books, the travel accounts written by scientists were expected to be serious, intellectual documents with important information to contribute to the advancement of the sciences, though not necessarily devoid of humor. Translations of travel accounts made the thoughts and observations of other nations accessible to men like Montesquieu, Rousseau, Goethe, Sir Charles Sloane, Humboldt, Blumenbach, and Voltaire, who were in turn influenced by them.

As the list of subscribers to Langsdorff's book and the all too quickly done translations of his works into other languages indicate, a large, international audience was waiting to buy new, entertaining, informative descriptions and engravings of exotic and little known places and people. Readers, including those like Langsdorff and his traveling companions, were dependent upon travel books for information about places they would be visiting. In his *Remarks and Observations* Langsdorff clearly assumes that his readers have read a great deal of the older, as well as contemporary, travel literature and are aware of the controversies about the veracity of some of it. He assumes his readers will have read Krusenstern's book, which appeared just before his, and apologizes for using material from it to make his *Remarks and Observations* more complete.

For the modern reader his *Remarks and Observations* read more like slightly reworked and polished diary entries than a serious scientific discourse. Langsdorff has difficulty in portraying scenery and events plastically in words. His style is mostly pedestrian and wooden, though not without subtle humor, but then he was trained as a scientist and not as a writer. He had no aspirations to be the Goethe of circumnavigatory literature. He was writing at the beginning of modern scientific disciplines when the boundaries between scientific and non-scientific discussions were less rigidly defined than today. He writes in a generic pattern developed in the 18th century for such travel literature. He apologizes for duplication from other sources and for extended descriptions which might bore the reader. He explains the divergence of his views from those of his fellow travelers on the voyage in order not to offend them and also to help establish his observations as those of an accurate, truthful and perceptive observer in an age of travel frauds (for example, the gold and silver islands purported to be near Japan). He carefully selects his data and usually refers to older sources in footnotes so that he primarily supplies information that cannot be found in other accounts. His contemporaries considered his work scientific, though not of the same level as treatises on specific subjects published in Latin. His chapter on Kamchadal sled dogs and their use was considered exemplary in 19th century Germany.[24]

Unfortunately for modern readers, the conventions of Langsdorff's time required the narrator not to be self-centered, but rather to suppress most personal feelings and reactions and to report objectively.

Also noteworthy with Langsdorff and other writers of this voyage, and indeed with others of that time, is the scant mention and characterization of shipmates and associates. Langsdorff mentions Shemelin only once; Shemelin mentions Langsdorff about eight times, but only in passing, as when naming the members of a shore party. On the voyage from Sitka to Okhotsk (Ochotsk), K. T. Khlebnikov, a young company official and writer of the future "Notes on America," an encyclopedic account of Russian America, was taken aboard the small vessel, but Langsdorff makes no mention of him, whereas D'Wolf praises him. A writer was not expected to be chatty, to gossip and relate "trivial" or personal information about interpersonal relationships, i.e., the tensions and disputes among expedition members, although Langsdorff cannot suppress all of his frustrations with Rezanov, particularly in Russian America and California where his scientific activities were curtailed and specimens wantonly destroyed. Whenever Langsdorff does give his own personal reactions, we wish for more because they are among his liveliest passages. This is why a contemporary English reviewer spoke more positively of Langsdorff's *Remarks and Observations* than of Krusenstern's book:

> To the general reader it will probably be more amusing than Captain Krusenstern's, because it is less grave, and, with the exception of a storm or two, without which a voyage would be nothing, divested of all nautical matters. Doctor Langsdorff is a German of a far more lively caste than most of his philosophic countrymen, whose ponderous labours we are occasionally doomed to encounter; he even attempts to be witty, and occasionally manifests a disposition to be waggish.[25]

As mentioned above, an international audience desirous of new and entertaining information about little known or unexplored parts of the world was willing to buy works such as Langsdorff's. Therefore, such works were quickly translated into other European languages, usually with the inclusion of engravings, sometimes altered from the originals to make them suitable for the intended audience. They were also edited for youthful readers, as was the case with editions of Langsdorff's *Remarks and Observations* in 1816 and in 1819. If one reads many of the translations from the period or compares them to the originals, one quickly realizes how poor many of them are. Surprisingly, contemporary reviewers of translations, like the one quoted from the *London Quarterly Review*, do not tend to be critical of the translations nor to comment upon deletions or mistranslations. August von Kotzebue, however, did publish a critique of the English translation of Krusenstern's book in German. He excuses mistranslations resulting from ignorance but faults Hoppner for his arrogant assertion that he knows German when he does not.[27]

Sometimes the name of the translator is given, as in the case of Krusenstern's *Voyage*; otherwise, the translator remains anonymous, as in the case of the 1814 publication of Langsdorff's *Remarks and Observations*. *Allibone's Dictionary of English Literature and British and American Authors* attributes the translation to Anne Plumptre, novelist, travel writer, and translator of August von Kotzebue's plays and H. Lichtenstein's *Travels to Southern Africa, 1803-06*. However, a comparison of translations under Plumptre's name and internal evidence in the translation of Langsdorff's work indicate that she did not do it. Discrepancies indicate that at least two women worked on the translation, for certain words are translated correctly in one section and mistranslated in another. Readers of the period were quite aware that travel accounts had often to be taken with more than a grain of salt, that they had to be compared with each other. As reviews and other comments, including Langsdorff's, indicate, travel writers were held suspect of falsifying what they did and saw, even those who strove to be truthful. In Langsdorff's case the first translation into English contains significant inaccuracies. At that time great freedom was taken in editing and translating. Langsdorff's first English translators followed Elizabeth Helme's tradition. She "softened . . . a few passages . . . which would ill accord with the delicacy of a female translator, or indeed with the temper and genius of English readers."[28]

Thus, Langsdorff's fairly graphic passages describing nudity below the waist, 12- to 13-year-old boys in Brazil with syphilis contracted from slaves and prostitutes, circumcision or subincision on Nuka Hiva, wives on Nuka Hiva bribing their husbands to let them have affairs, the wish that European women be educated like Tlingit Indian maidens at puberty, references to the bloody excesses of the French Revolution, and other "indelicate" observations are "softened" or deleted without telling the reader even in the preface. In Langsdorff's description of San Francisco, the translator does not translate *Lustseuche* (venereal disease) but uses "other diseases" and, yet takes the liberty of adding, "which some traditions assert to have been first introduced into Europe from this quarter of the globe" without telling the reader that this is not Langsdorff's opinion.

The extensive list of subscribers to the German edition, which could be the envy of many a modern travel writer, is excluded in the first English translation. It certainly is of interest to modern readers for the information it gives about his readership, which ranges from the royal family of Prussia to the Queen of Sweden to the royal family of Russia to Mr. John Quincy Adams, Minister of the "United American Free States."

Why is a new translation of this book worth publishing today? Langsdorff's *Remarks and Observations* are an indispensable source, for example, for the history of Russian relations with Japan, and the state of the Russian-American Company holdings, including the influence of Baranov and Rezanov on events of the period. It is valuable as an accompaniment to other accounts of the voyage, as well as of worth in the history of science, including botany, zoology, and anthropology, and even women's studies, since Langsdorff, as a specialist in gynecology, inquired about birthing and women's health wherever he stopped.

A more accurate and readable translation of Langsdorff's work is long overdue, since his *Remarks and Observations* are important for several disciplines and non-German reading scholars have been dependent upon a faulty translation for almost 200 years. The old translation might be in part what prompted Bancroft's negative assessment of Langsdorff, Gertrude Atherton to portray him so negatively in her novel about early San Francisco as "dry and crusty," and Hector Chevigny to call him "the little slipper-nosed German naturalist" in his semi-fictional account of Rezanov's life,[29] instead of finding him, as did the *Quarterly Review* in 1813, of a "far more lively cast than most of his philosophic countrymen." Unfortunately, Atherton's unfair assessment has been the more accepted one among English readers.

Each page of the first translation contains not only incorrect grammar but mistranslations that distort the intent of the original. The present translation aims for readability and accuracy. Langsdorff's paragraphing has been retained, except when inordinately long, as well as his careful use of the German "von" to denote members of the nobility. Long, unwieldy sentences, however, have been divided and active voice used in preference to his awkward passive sentence structures. Most of Langsdorff's spellings of personal names and places have been retained. They are found in his other works and in secondary literature discussing the period. They give the reader an idea of names and usages as Langsdorff understood them and the changes that have taken place in spelling conventions or names since that time. Langsdorff himself mentions several times the variations possible due to differences in hearing perception. Certain variations in the spelling of names in this introduction and works written in English, e.g., Krusenstern (Kruzenshtern), Kronstadt (Kronshtadt), Löwenstern (Levenshtern), are the result of a name having been transliterated into Russian and then transliterated from Russian into English. I use contemporary English spellings of names in this introduction with Langsdorff's spellings, as they appear in the translation, in parentheses. Also see the index. In *Remarks and Observations* it is also not always clear which language was Langsdorff's base, since in addition to his native German, he knew Latin, French, English, Portuguese, and Russian. The German *w* is pronounced *v*, *j* = *y*, *v* is usually *f*, *st* = *sht*, initial *s* = *z* and *z* = *ts*. As far as possible, the index provides alternate spellings or modern names.

The book is in two parts, the first relates to the voyage from Kronstadt to Brazil, Kamchatka and Japan, and the second to the Aleutians, Kodiak, Sitka, California, Kamchatka and, cursorily, the overland journey across Siberia to St. Petersburg. The first volume is dedicated to the Emperor Alexander I, the second to Krusenstern. Each part has its own pagination. Chapter headings are as Langsdorff had them. For the reader's convenience, the long list of subscribers to the work, of significance en masse because it indicates how avidly a book of this sort was then received, has been moved to the appendix at the end of the second volume.

The footnotes are Langsdorff's. The translator's notes are at the end of each chapter. The English translation of 1813 and 1814 omitted some of the engravings which were in the German edition. All of the engravings from that edition have been placed in one section at the end of the second part, with explanatory comments. Some of the original drawings, a number signed by Langsdorff, others by the young shipbuilder Koriukin (an excellent draftsman), may be seen in the Honeyman Collection at the Bancroft Library at the University of California, Berkeley. The "Brasilan Air," the "Song of the Natives of Nukahiva" and the map of the world (end papers) have been taken from the English translation of 1813. A glossary of weights and measurements and an index have been included. Langsdorff changed his weights and measures as he moved around the world, since he did not have a generally accepted international system to use. As the appendix "Weights and Measures" indicates, a *zoll* is not necessarily an inch or a *klafter* or *faden* an English fathom. Therefore, I have left most of Langsdorff's weights and measures as he uses them instead of giving inaccurate English equivalents, i.e., inch for *zoll* and pound for *pfund*. Therefore, I translate mile or German mile but leave *zoll*, *pfund*, *arrobas*, *pud*, *ri*, *toise*, *unze*. The reader should consult "Weights and Measures" for equivalents.

May I express my gratitude to all those who have helped me with this translation, especially Rae Ammons Jones and Doris Nichols, and to the Alaska Humanities Forum for the grants which helped support work on this annotated translation.

NOTES

1. F. P. Wrangell, *Russian America: Statistical and Ethnographic Information*, translated by Mary Sadouski and edited by Richard A. Pierce (Kingston, Ontario: The Limestone Press, 1980), p. xiii.

2. Hans Becher, *George Heinrich Freiherr von Langsdorff in Brasilien* (Berlin: Reimer, 1987), p. 65.

3. Ewert von Krusenstjern, *Weltumsegler un Wissenschaftler: Adam Johann von Krusenstern* (Circumnavigator and Scientist: Adam Johann von Krusenstern) (Gernsbach: Katz, 1991).

4. Pis'mo N. P. Riazanova k I. I. Dmitrievu (Letter from N. P. Riazanov to I. I. Dmitriev), *Russkaia starina*, cols 1331-1335.

5. Draft of a letter, Fedor Shemelin to the Board of Directors of the Russian-American Company, n.d. (probably end of 1803). Yudin Collection, Box 2, Folder 28, National Archives, Washington, D.C. (Hereafter cited as Shemelin.)

6. [P. A. Tikhmenev], *A History of the Russian American Company*, translated by Dmitri Krenov and edited by Richard A. Pierce and Alton S. Donnelly (Kingston, Ontario: The Limestone Press, 1979), vol. 2, p. 144.

7. Shemelin, *op. cit.*

8. Ewert von Krusenstjern, *op. cit.*, p. 282f.

9. Shemelin, *op. cit.*

10. *Ibid.*

11. Tikhmenev, *op. cit.*, pp. 172, 191, 192-195.

12. Becher, *op. cit.*, p. 67.

13. Becher, *op. cit.*, p. 5.

14. L. A. Shur, *K beregam novogo sveta. Iz neopublikovannykh zapisok russkikh puteshestvennikov nachala XIX veka* (Moscow: Nauka, 1971), p. 97; Richard A. Pierce, *Russian America: A Biographical Dictionary* (Kingston, Ontario: The Limestone Press, 1990), p. 291.

15. Auguste Baptist de Saint-Hilaire, *Voyage dans les Provinces de Rio de Janeiro et de Minas Gerais* (Paris, 1830), vol. 1, p. 129f.

16. Johann Baptist von Spix and Carl F. P. von Martius, *Reise in Brasilien in den Jahren 1817-1820* (Travel in Brazil in the years 1817-1820) (Stuttgart: Neudruck, 1966), vol. 1, p. 96f.

17. Becher, *op. cit.*, p. 24f.

18. *Bemerkungen über Brasilien mit gewissenhafter Belehrung für auswandernde Deutsche* (Remarks about Brazil with conscientious instructions for German immigrants) (Heidelberg: Groos, 1821).

19. Becher, *op. cit.*, p. 26f.

20. Becher, *op. cit.*, p. 28ff. Becher's book contains detailed maps of the routes traveled.

21. *Materialy ekspeditsii akademika Grigoriia Ivanovicha Langsdorfa v Braziliiu v 1821-1829 gg. Nauchnoe opisanie.* Izdanie podgotovili Berttel's, D. C.; Komissarov, B. N.; Lysenko, T. I.; Leningrad, 1973.

22. H. H. Bancroft, *History of Alaska, 1730-1885* (San Francisco: Bancroft Publishing Co., 1886), p. 442.

23. Percy G. Adams, *Travels and Travel Liars* (Berkeley: University of California Press, 1962), p. 13.

24. *Allgemeine Deutsche Bibliographie*, vol 17, p. 690.

25. *Quarterly Review*, London, 9(1813): p. 453.

26. "Bemerkungen über die Englishche Uebersetzung von v. Krusenstern's Reise um die Welt, von Hoppner, Esq." in *Allgemeine Geographische Ephemeriden*, vol. 43, January 1814, pp. 124-135.

27. Preface to François le Vaillant's *Travels from Cape of Good Hope into the Interior Parts of Africa* (1790).

28. Gertrude Atherton, "Nicolai Petrovich Rezanov," *The North American Review*, 189(1909):658; Hector Chevigny, *Lost Empire: The Life and Adventures of Nikolai Rezanov* (Portland, Oregon: Binfords & Mort, 1937), p. 100.

DEDICATED
TO

HIS IMPERIAL MAJESTY ALEXANDER THE FIRST

Most gracious Emperor!

The first Russian voyage around the world is one of the most remarkable events in the annals of your Imperial Majesty's glorious reign. Every contribution toward more detailed knowledge of this great undertaking commands the interest of the entire civilized world.

The observations which I, as the fortunate companion of the first Russian circumnavigator, had the opportunity of collecting, have the most valid claim to the attention conferred upon them, since I may place at their beginning the most illustrious name of your Imperial Majesty and publicly display this new sign of your highest favor and magnanimity toward my humble efforts.

May it please your Imperial Majesty to grant indulgence to this little token of unbounded gratitude and veneration and to accept graciously the most reverent sentiments which will accompany me till death.

Most Gracious Emperor
Your Imperial Majesty

Your most obedient servant and subject

G. H. von Langsdorff

AUTHOR'S PREFACE

Some people may consider it presumptuous of me to present the public my observations of one of the most interesting voyages around the world when the expedition's illustrious commander has already published part of his description. In answer I can only say that the main reason for my undertaking is that my duties as a doctor and a naturalist directed my eyes to other things than those of interest to that learned, scientific navigator and that I left his expedition in 1805 in Kamtschatka. As a result my journey had a completely different route, since I visited the Aleutian Islands and the Northwest Coast of America and then traveled by land through Siberia back to Russia.

Every observer has his own point of view from which he contemplates and judges new objects, his own sphere into which he tries to bring whatever excites his curiosity, knowledge and interest. The reader, therefore, will perhaps find I touch upon things which are not found in Krusenstern's description, or are presented in a different way, or not at all, in his universally esteemed work.[1]

It was not my intention to write a nautical description of the voyage, or of the political or mercantile purpose of the expedition, or the plans for the voyage, or the appointment of crew and outfitting of the ship. That would be superfluous and out of place after the appearance of our worthy commander's work. I have attempted to emphasize objects of general interest, the customs and habits of the various peoples, their ways of life, the products of their countries, and the general historical course of our voyage, and to present in a popular narrative such events as I can assume will be new, informative and welcomed by a reading public of all classes. How well I achieve my goal I must leave to the judgement of others.

The strict adherence to truth should not be a matter of preference but rather the duty of every traveler describing his journey. In reality I have no need, given the extensiveness of such a voyage, to invent adventures and tales since the voyage of itself offers such remarkable, interesting observations that I find it difficult to include everything and omit nothing.

Since I think that scientific, natural-historical descriptions of plants and animals do not belong in a book offering general information intended for readers of all classes, I have removed them from the body of my work and shall publish them separately. I have done this already with the plants, since this is the most popular branch of natural history at present. Contributions to the knowledge of insects, fish, birds, etc., will gradually be published, if time and strength permit.

In order to make traveling worthwhile, one needs to a certain extent a special fortitude that one properly cannot acquire other than on earlier journeys. I was fortunate to be able to prepare myself for this greater voyage by earlier, shorter journeys. After completing the degree of Doctor of Medicine and Surgery in Göttingen in 1797, I accompanied Prince Christian of Waldeck to Lisbon, where he became commander-in-chief of the Portuguese Army.[2]

The study of natural history has fascinated me since my youth. Blumenbach's instruction gave my inclination a more precise direction, and in Portugal I found a wide range of observations satisfying to my thirst for knowledge.[3]

My occupation as surgeon did not interfere with my favorite inclination to study natural history. I found in the person of the Prince, himself a man of learning and friend of scientific knowledge, someone who gave me all possible support and encouragement.

In the spring of 1798, I accompanied him on a military tour of several Portuguese provinces. Unfortunately, he did not live much longer but died in that year of dropsy in the chest after he had lost an arm.

Upon the advice at that time of the Portuguese Minister Luiz Pinto de Souza Coutinho, I decided I would rather begin a career as a practical doctor in a beautiful climate in the midst of a friendly circle of educated, amiable people in Lisbon than return to Germany. Soon I had acquired an extensive circle of friends and members of German, English, and Portuguese homes who had confidence in my medical knowledge, so that I was left little time, only a few hours a day, to investigate the many natural products new and unknown to me. This induced me to accept an appointment as surgeon major to the English auxiliary troops stationed in

Portugal at the time, i.e., the Regiment de Castrier, because I would have sufficient income and could dedicate myself to my favorite pursuit in my free time. I took part with those troops in the campaign against the Spanish in 1801. When, after the Peace of Amiens in 1802,[4] we were dismissed from service and shipped to England, I used the opportunity to return by way of London and Paris at the beginning of 1803 to my fatherland.

In the meantime, I had my large natural history collection sent from Lisbon to Hamburg and Göttingen, where I went in order to prepare an account of my travels in Portugal.

The friendship shown me by the foremost natural scientists of France, i.e., Hauy, Olivier, Bosc d'Antique, Latreille, Geoffroy, Prognart, Dumeril,[5] etc., and the honor the Imperial Academy of Sciences in St. Petersburg bestowed upon me at almost the same time in naming me a corresponding member, which gave me the courage and, at the same time after my arrival in Göttingen, excited the ardent desire in me to go on a longer voyage solely for natural-historical reasons. No better or more desirable opportunity could offer itself than accompanying the first Russian circumnavigator.

As a corresponding member of the Academy, I thought I would, to a degree, be justified in asking directly for their support of my plans. I therefore wrote them. Even though the honorable Councilor of State and Knight von Krafft and Collegiate Councilor and Knight von Adelung did everything possible in support of my request, I received a letter in Göttingen on August 18, 1803, in which the former said he regretted not having known about my desire earlier because time was too short;[6] the ships (*Nadeschda* and *Neva*) were sailing with the first wind and would stop over in Copenhagen for eight days at the most; and besides Dr. Tilesius had already been appointed the expedition's natural scientist and was to join it in Helsingör.[7] I probably would not want to undertake the journey in view of this uncertainty at my own expense. Therefore, nothing concrete could be promised me in regard to my request, etc.

I nevertheless remained true to my plans and did not want to give them up until I was completely convinced of the impossibility of carrying them out. Therefore, I quickly decided to leave that very same day for Copenhagen. On the morning of August 21st, I arrived in Lübeck and found a ship in Travemünde ready to sail to Copenhagen. We weighed anchor in the night of the 22nd to 23rd and with a favorable wind reached Copenhagen early on the morning of the 24th.

I went to Mr. Rau's hotel where to my greatest joy and satisfaction I found most of the officers belonging to Krusenstern's Expedition, an event that renewed my courage and that I took for a good omen. Indeed, the result met my expectations. I entreated Ambassador to Japan and Chamberlain von Resanoff to allow me to become a member of the voyage.[8] Since the illustrious Captain von Krusenstern, the actual head of the expedition, supported my petition, he finally granted me permission.

I wish to thank our worthy leader Mr. von Krusenstern, whose service is generally recognized far and above any praise I may give. I wish here publicly to express my grateful indebtedness for his kind support and the friendship shown me on the voyage and afterwards.

I owe no less thanks to my friend and traveling companion Councilor Tilesius, who unites extensive scientific knowledge with rare artistic talents and has given me not only some of his sketches but has also promised to enrich the second part of the description of my voyage with more sketches. We owe to him and not to the expedition's painter all of the historical plates in von Krusenstern's *Atlas*. In addition, he has a very large collection of sketches of natural-historical objects which he is gradually preparing to complete and publish for the scholarly world.

The scientific part of my work, the geography of Japan and the language of Tschoka have been helped considerably by the valuable remarks of Councilor Julius von Klaproth. This learned friend and colleague was kind enough to give me the translation of several interesting remarks about Japanese maps and geographical works. I am indebted to the kindness of that talented artist Mr. Alexander Orloffsky for the portrait of the Frenchman Jean Cabri and several other sketches and to the ship's master builder Mr. Ivan Petrowitch Korükin for highly exact and beautiful plans and descriptions of all of the vessels used in the countries we visited.[9]

Here publicly I wish to express my deepest, warmest thanks to each one of these valiant men for their friendly help and kindly assistance.

St. Petersburg
June 12, 1811

G. H. Langsdorff

PREFACE

NOTES

1. Adam Johann von Krusenstern, Russian: Ivan Fedorovich Kruzenshtern (1770-1846), was the captain of the *Nadeschda*. He was born in Estonia and trained for the sea in Kronstadt. He became a Russian admiral and was famous for his knowledge of the world's geography. See: *Voyage round the World in the Years 1803, 1804, 1805 and 1806 by order of His Imperial Majesty Alexander the First on board the ships* Nadeschda *and* Neva, trans. from the original German by Richard Belgrave Hoppner (London: Printed by C. Roworth for J. Murray, 1813).

2. Christian August, Prince of Waldeck (1744-1798), rose to become a Cavalry General. He served in various capacities all over Europe before going to Lisbon in 1797, where he died a year later.

3. Johann Friedrich Blumenbach (1752-1840) was a professor of medicine in Göttingen. He is considered the father of anthropology and was the first professor to hold lectures on comparative anatomy.

4. Peace of Amiens, March 25, 1802, which was concluded between Great Britain, France, Spain and Holland. It provided three years of peace but did not prevent French hegemony.

5. L'abbe-Réné Just Hauy (1743-1822) was a mineralogist who gave crystology its mathematical base.

Guillaume-Antoine Olivier (1756-1814) was a doctor of medicine, entomologist and explorer in the Ottoman Empire, Egypt and Persia.

Louis-Augustin-Guillaume Bosc d'Antique (1759-1828) was a physician and naturalist. The German text lists "Bosc, d'Antin." Since neither d'Antin or a variation of the name is given in *Académie des Sciences Partis: Index Biographique des Members et Correspondants 1662-1939* (Paris: Gauthier-Villars, 1939), I checked other sources. There is undoubtedly an error in the German text since the translator in 1813 corrected the name to read Bosc d'Antique.

Pierre-Andre Latreille (1762-1833) was an entomologist.

Etienne Geoffroy Saint-Hilaire (1772-1844) was a professor of zoology and comparative anatomy. Between 1798 and 1804 he took part in Napoleon's Egyptian expedition.

Prognart: This in undoubtedly an error in the German text; Langsdorff probably means Alexandre Brongniart (1770-1847), who was a mineralogist, geologist and paleontologist.

Andre-Marie Dumeril (1774-1860) was an anatomist and zoologist.

6. Wolfgang Ludwig Krafft (1743-1814) went to St. Petersburg in 1767 to become a professor of astronomy and remained there until his death.

Friedrich von Adelung (1768-1843) was a linguist who published Old German poetry contained in the Vatican Library. In 1803 he went to St.

Petersburg to become the tutor of Alexander I's brothers. Later he was director of the Oriental Institute.

7. Dr. Wilhelm Gottfried Tilesius (1769-1857) studied medicine in Leipzig. He became known for his drawings of rare animals and plants. In reward for his service, the Tsar raised him to the nobility as Tilesius von Tilenau. He published his observations of the voyage in St. Petersburg in 1813: *Naturhistorische Früchte der ersten kaiserlich-russischen, unter dem Commando des Herrn von Krusenstern vollbrachten Erdumsegelung* (Natural historical observations from the first completed Imperial Russian Circumnavigation of the world under the command of von Krusenstern).

8. Nikolai Petrovich Resanoff, Russian: Nikolai Petrovich Rezanov (1764-1807), was one of the founders of the Russian-American Company and plenipotentiary envoy to Japan.

9. Julius Heinrich von Klaproth (1873-1835) was a famous orientalist. From 1805-06 he traveled as part of a Russian expedition through Russia to China, collecting Chinese, Tibetan, Manchu and Mongolian works. From 1807-08 he traveled to the Caucasus and Georgia. He published extensively on Asiatic languages.

Jean Cabri appears in Chapter 4.

Ivan Petrovich Korükin, Russian: Koriukin (fl. early 1800s), was a shipwright on the *Neva*. Resanoff describes him as a very good draftsman inclined toward drunkenness and wildness. He took part in the raids on Japan and was arrested in Okhotsk in 1807 with lieutenants von Chwostoff and von Davidoff, whose untimely deaths are described in Volume Two. Korükin's fate is unknown.

Chapter 1

Departure from Copenhagen for England. Stop in Falmouth. Sea Voyage to Teneriffe. Description of that Island and the Pic. Voyage to Brazil.

September 1803

Even though we weighed anchor on September 8, 1803 in Copenhagen, we had to postpone the start of our voyage for several days because of contrary winds. We were only able to depart from Helsingör on September 15th. During the night from the 18th to the 19th, we were greeted in the Skagerrag by a heavy storm which made most of the gentlemen on board, including especially the ambassadorial gentlemen, extremely seasick. The ship bounced about terribly and warm meals were out of the question.

The violence of the wind, the waves first hitting and then breaking around the ship, the ringing, rattling and clattering, the screaming and hubbub of the people on board — all that was for many on board a new and unaccustomed show. On the evening of the 19th, we all eagerly watched an exquisitely beautiful display of the northern lights. Pillars of fire rose on the west-northwesterly horizon. Individually, they more or less alternately were darting rapidly or becoming first brighter then paler. The refraction or vapors of the columns became surrounded by brightly arched light which gradually spread out and rose to the zenith, until it became paler and paler and finally dispersed in the atmosphere.

After being subjected to changeable weather, to stormy winds, calms, rain and sunshine, early on the morning of the 28th, we entered the harbor at Falmouth, where Captain von Krusenstern acquired more provisions, instruments and other necessary items.

Falmouth

Falmouth, at the southwestern tip of England, has a very good harbor protected by a castle fortress on one side and a little fort on the other. Its location and anchorage ground make it one of the best harbors in England.

The town is small and unimportant. All packet boats to Portugal and the East and West Indies put in and out there. This regular ship traffic and a fishing trade of considerable importance are the main sources of livelihood in the area. Irrespective of the fact that the capital city is over 700 English miles away, the village contains very important warehouses filled with all kinds of goods.

Falmouth in the County of Cornwall is distinguished from all other English counties by its barren, dry, and infertile appearance — but in reality it hides its treasures in its bosom. Cornwall is one of the richest and most interesting provinces in England. It produces quantities of the best quality tin and the most excellent copper, and some silver and hard coal.

Mineralogists have found very rare minerals there, i.e., arsenate of copper ore, wood tin and tin gravel. The nearest copper producing mines to Falmouth are in Redruth.

Only a few miles (English) from Falmouth is the little village of Menacan, which takes its name from menacite or titanium sands. Pure titanium is obtained by washing it laboriously out of the sands.*

The shafts and tunnels of the mines around Penzance and other villages in Cornwall probably belong to the most remarkable on our earth, since they are worked at a considerable depth under the waters of the ocean.

The coastal waters are rich in fish, crabs and oysters. The fish market is always abundantly filled with many varieties. I observed during my stay principally the following: *Raja Batis*, *Raja Rubus Gmel*, *Esox Belone*, *Mullus barbatus*, *Muraena conger* and several types of *Perca*, *Labrus et Pleuronecties*.[2] *Squali* or sharks are sometimes caught, but not brought to the market and are only used as bait.

Trigla lineata is only found in Cornwall. I found especially interesting *Clupea Pilchardus*, a very peculiar and little known kind of herring. This fish is caught in great quantities along the coast and

---

*Privy Councilor Klaproth of Berlin, whom Sir John Hawkins sent a complete collection of minerals from Cornwall, has determined their composition.[1]

is valued on the tables of both the rich and the poor. It is pickled in large quantities and sent, in particular, to Gibraltar and the Mediterranean.

October 1803

After acquiring the best of provisions, and in the belief that we had everything on board needed for our long, important voyage, we saluted the fortress and the guard ship on the 5th of October and left the European coast accompanied by beautiful weather and favorable winds.

We were all looking forward to the experiences before us. Most of us could not suppress the emotions in our hearts caused by the thought of being cut off from the rest of the world at the mercy of winds and waves, and by the prospect of being away every hour of the day for at least 6 to 8 months from our parents, brothers and sisters, relatives, and friends, in short, of being at an ever greater distance from everything we loved and held dear.

Captain von Krusenstern chose Teneriffe instead of the Island of Madeira for our first port of call because on Madeira landing and provisions of all kinds are by far much more expensive. Thus, we sailed straight for the Canary Islands. The English coast was soon lost from sight and the great Atlantic Ocean lay before us.

Many people err in believing a long sea voyage* must be extremely boring because one sees nothing but water and sky every day. They believe that the eternal monotony fatigues the spirit. This, however, hardly ever or never happens and then only with those who are easily bored on land if they are not entertained by the theater, balls, concerts or card-playing.

With an expedition like ours, a society of numerous scientists and men thirsty for knowledge, it was almost impossible to be bored. Each individual probably did not have as much time to take advantage of the opportunities available as he might have wished.

I want to attempt to describe the course of a typical day so that the reader can better judge things for himself.

---

*I mean a voyage as commonly understood, for a crossing from Dover to Calais or Cuxhaven to London is not what is being discussed here.

The men who got up somewhat later in the morning took tea or coffee no later than eight. Conversation generally consisted of relating the events of the night, how wind and weather had changed and how far we had traveled.

After breakfast everyone turned to his own private affairs. It was not difficult to find interesting reading, given the selective but large library on board containing, in particular, travel literature and maps, which Captain von Krusenstern in his own polite and friendly manner invited all of us to use. Thus, we spent mornings reading, writing, drawing, and charting the sun's altitude and the distance to the moon.

The Canary Islands, where we hoped to arrive in a few days, naturally occupied us. We mainly read the descriptions given by previous visitors to the islands. All of us had already studied their discovery, history, location and products, and the way of life of the inhabitants. We made comparisons of the various accounts kept by voyagers, of the state of past and present governments, of battles, and the aborted attack of the English in which the valiant Nelson lost his right arm, etc., etc.[3] All of this provided material for scientific controversy, for pleasant and instructive conversation, and for fun and jokes. If the discussion became somewhat heated, we went on deck for a short walk to breathe the fresh air and cool off. The schools of dolphins (*Delphenus Delphis L.*), bonito (*Scomber Pelamys*), flying fish (*Exocoetus evolans L.*), and floating seaweed (*Fucus*); sharks following the ship; many sea birds we had not seen before; whales; a poor little land bird that had been driven off course by strong winds and found a safe harbor on the ship; a foreign ship on the horizon; the expectations of landfall — all of this and thousands of other things occupied, enlivened and entertained us, so that I am inclined to claim that a sea voyage is just as entertaining as one on land, provided that one does not stop at all the stage stops and in every little town. Why should such a lifestyle be more exhausting than a scholar's? Why more boring than a craftsman's? Thus mornings passed, filled with all kinds of activities and diversions. Daily, around two o'clock, 22 of us sat down to a table covered with good food. After the meal we worked until teatime. Everyone was keeping a diary and the day ended with merry conversation around a *Bowle Punsch*[4] which, drunk moderately in the moist air, indeed on a sea voyage, is very healthy and to be recommended as highly beneficial for almost everyone. Several of our traveling companions were music lovers and sometimes on a beautiful, quiet evening they played duets and quartets.

The weather remained quite favorable. Each day brought us closer to a better climate, and on the 19th of October, a clear day, we sighted Pic's world famous silver-white head on Teneriffe at a distance of about two degrees latitude.[5]

Teneriffe

On the 20th we dropped anchor at Santa Cruz in the eastern anchorage ground in 36 *fadens*[6] at 28°27′33″ N latitude and 16°15′50″ W longitude from Greenwich.

Santa Cruz on the northeastern side of the Island of Teneriffe has a rather good bay which, however, offers little or no protection against winds from the east or southeast. The little town consisting of several hundred houses situated some distance from the shore is very attractive. Most of the houses are two-storied, a few have balconies; and most of them have wooden shutters on the windows as is the custom in Spain and Portugal. The streets are straight, clean, and well paved with lava. They have sidewalks on both sides or wide, slightly elevated stones for pedestrians. It is a pleasure to find such a well built little town under skies so distant from our home. The interiors of the houses, the clothing, the customs and habits of the area are so similar to the Spanish that one could think one was in the mother country. The streets are always filled with people, more women than men, and evenings especially with shameless, disorderly prostitutes and rabble of all kinds who look more like bandits than civilized human beings. In addition, there are crowds of beggars in torn clothes, half naked, with the looks of thieves and rascals who nauseate all visitors by their repulsive skin diseases.

The place flourishes thanks to the shipping trade. Close to shore are 15-, 20- and 50-faden anchorage grounds. Ships, especially if they arrive a month earlier than we did, can buy very good provisions cheaply. Grapes, peaches, pears, lemons, apples, bananas, almonds, chestnuts, dates, melons, potatoes, onions and other kitchen plants are produced there in abundance and brought into the town from the surrounding areas. Some grain is also grown on Teneriffe and even more on the neighboring islands. There is not enough salt; therefore, I was told, that from time to time it is imported from Portugal. Wine is one of the principal branches of trade on the Canary Islands and costs half as much as Madeira wine. This is most likely the reason why in England, France and Germany Teneriffe wine is frequently sold for Madeira. A prominent merchant claimed that the quality difference comes mainly from the addition of small amounts of French brandy that could not be procured in Teneriffe. There are no real inns there, therefore the greater the hospitality, as Mr. Armstrong most obligingly showed us. The lower class seems to suffer from great poverty; many do not even have baked bread to eat but grind grain into flour between two stones and eat it after kneading it in their hands together with milk or water. Sometimes they subsist also only on roasted grain.

The fish market was well supplied. During our stay I did not see a great variety in the kinds of fish being sold — large quantities of mackerel (*Scomber Scomber*) were brought to the market everyday. The poor eat shark. I saw two varieties of ray (*Raja*) whose tails had been cut off, probably because there, as in Europe, the thick tail spines are thought to be poisonous. One species appeared to be *Raja Aquila*, the other one was completely skinned and had a very sharply pointed head. I did not try to identify it from such an imperfect specimen. In addition I recognized several other species: *Esox Belone*, *Muraena Helena*, *Sparus*, *Labrus*, *Chaetodon* and one specimen of *Salmo*.

Most fish are caught on a line. Instead of string line a brass wire imported from Cadiz is used. To catch mackerel, 6 to 8 people go out in a little boat in the evening. As soon as it is dark, big tar fires are lighted on both sides. The lines are not dropped deep into the water, and almost continually fish are taken from the line. Fishing often continues the whole night. It is pleasant to see so many bright fires on the water in the darkness.

In Santa Cruz there are two monasteries. The town has several open squares and one public promenade, which is seldom used, except on Sundays. A monument of white marble honoring the Virgin Mary of Candelaria stands in the market square. A Candelarian nobleman commissioned it in Italy and had it erected on the square. The donor is said to have spent most of his wealth on it and, in so doing, neglected the economic needs of his household.

The town, the seat of the government, and the island are protected by forts and bulwarks guarded by a regiment of soldiers.

The island has steep, almost inaccessible mountains and cliffs which bear witness to its volcanic origins. No matter where one looks one sees various types of lava. All the houses and forts are built from it and the streets are paved with it.

I made an excursion along the seacoast to the northeastern tip of the island. After a good hour I reached the little village of St. Andrés. In the nearby mountains I observed volcanic products containing much obsidian, schorl and pyroxene. In various places on the island on the more distant mountains I found some looser, more porous lava mixed with more or less burnt ferriferous clay. Here and there I saw large shapeless masses of smaller and larger basaltic balls, as they are called, and in other spots a clayish stone, partially streaked and crusted with calcspar. About one-half hour from St. Andrés the lowest part of the mountains forms a true trap into which the lava flowed. In a deep valley nearby I saw a mixture of finely grained schorl and granite. There are several grottos or underground caves in which the first inhabitants of the island, the Guanches, are supposed to have lived in earliest times.[7] This much is certain: quantities of human bones can still be found in many of the caves, granted extremely seldom, and occasionally dried-out cadavers sewn in leather. The National Museum in Paris has one of these natural mummies. We were lucky enough to obtain another one for the Museum in St. Petersburg.

We were unable to obtain any exact or satisfactory information about the first inhabitants, the Guanches. We were told that there are some families on the island, still without Spanish blood in their veins, who can be considered the descendants of the Guanches. We also saw men of very repulsive appearance who looked coarse and wild rather than civilized. Their dirty, yellow-brown skin color, their poverty, bad clothing, and unsanitary living habits all contributed to making a bad impression upon us Europeans and led us to consider the majority of the inhabitants Guanches rather than civilized Spaniards.

The climate is so mild that even in winter one can run around in the lightest of clothing. We saw many naked children playing in the streets and 12- to 14-year-old boys without any clothing whatsoever busy on the beach. The temperature during our stay was generally 18° to 22° Réaumur.[8]

There are several windmills in the area. As already mentioned, the poor man grinds his grain between two round stones. The smaller top stone is light and porous, and the bottom one is larger but of a solid, thick lava.

Santa Cruz is not totally devoid of social life. Our group found pleasant entertainment every evening at Mr. Armstrong's, an English trader. This friendly man suggested and then helped several of our fellow travelers to make a little excursion into the interior of the island, specifically to the north-northwestern part, to Porto de l'Orotava. From Santa Cruz it takes about 8 to 9 hours or 4½ German miles. Usually such excursions are made on donkeys, mules, or very small horses. Ambassador von Resanoff, Major von Friederici, Dr. Laband, Councilor Tilesius and I chose horses.[9] We left on our trip early on the 21st. The road goes through La Laguna, La Matança, La Victoria and Santa Ursula. After about an hour we arrived in La Laguna. The road goes mostly uphill over lava and offers a rather bare and not very enjoyable view. La Laguna is the capital of the island. It lies in a very fertile area where a great deal of grain is grown. The town itself is orderly, clean and pretty, but with worse streets by far than Santa Cruz. There are two nunneries and two monasteries.

We visited the Dominican Monastery where several monks greeted us very courteously. They betrayed in their conversation the greatest lack of knowledge, and therefore we learned absolutely nothing about the locality. They did not even know the origin or the history of their monastery. The library contained only a few religious books and hagiographies of famous saints. We tried to visit a convent, but were turned away most politely at the gate by an old housekeeper who smiled mysteriously. However, we had the impression that we probably would have received a more friendly answer from the good lady towards evening. Tired from the heat of the sun and all the walking around, we tried to find an inn, but to no avail. We had to ask a total stranger for hospitality. We rested awhile in his house, ate some fruit and boiled eggs which he sold us, and then continued on our way.

A short distance from the town of Laguna is a beautiful, wide valley where grain is grown. The soil of weathered lava appeared to be exceedingly fertile, even though to our eyes it looked empty and weary with hardly a bush or shrub around. Cactus, figs and mulberry trees were about the only things we saw there. After 1½ to 2 hours we exchanged that fertile area for a stony, hilly one covered primarily in vineyards. The closer we came to La Matança, La Victoria, etc., the more vineyards we saw. We arrived in Santa Ursula, a rather substantial little village, after nightfall. The entire village and people from the surrounding area had come together to celebrate St. Ursula's Day.[10] For that reason many booths had been set up where all kinds of trifles and refreshments were being sold right against the church and in its vicinity. Now and then we saw groups of men and women dancing and singing crudely to the music of a guitar. The dance consisted of a more or less very slow, swaying motion, so that the people hardly moved from their initial places and, at the most, formed a *demie-chaine* once in awhile. In the dark of the night the crowd of people looked more like a carnival than a church celebration. We still had 3 hours ahead of us to Porto de l'Orotava so we hurried on as soon as we had satisfied our curiosity.

The path from Santa Ursula was bad, stony and uncomfortable. We turned our attention to a high peak that appeared to be very close to us even though it was probably five German miles away. Most of our companions did not trust the insecure footing of our horses in the dark and dismounted while descending the mountain. In the bright moonlight at its foot, we could see the town of Orotava, where we finally arrived about 9 o'clock, tired after making our way down the winding path. We went to the home of Mr. Barry, Mr. Armstrong's partner, who had been told ahead of time about our arrival. He offered us the very friendly hospitality of his home.

Porto de l'Orotava is a small town that has grown with the addition of several fishers' cots and become the place of residence of the richest merchants on the island. Most of the streets are wide, clean and rather well paved. The bay is by far not as good and secure as the one at Santa Cruz. Near the shore there are many rocks and much heavy surf. The town and its surroundings enjoy the most beautiful location. Since it lies on the northern side of the Pic, it is less hit by the burning heat of the sun. This is where most of the island's vineyards are, and that is why ships often lie anchored far from the shore in order to load wine. They, however, must sail out to sea when strong winds arise.

The most interesting thing in the town is probably a beautiful botanical garden started in 1795 by the Marquis de Nava, a rich man living in Laguna. As a friend of science, he had presented a plan to the Spanish Court for cultivating plants from all over the world there. An attempt was to be made to gradually acclimate some useful plants from hotter areas of the world to the colder European climate. The plan was approved and the government promised to support the venture. The Marquis did everything he could to see the project through; he advanced the government considerable sums of money. For several years he has been trying to receive a reimbursement for his very major expenses, but unfortunately in vain; so it is highly probable that this memorial in honor of a private citizen and a country will soon fall into ruin. That is even more regrettable since about 3,000 of the rarest types of plants, mainly from Mexico, Peru, Chile and the Cape of Good Hope, and planted under the direction of a skillful gardener, who was brought from England, are grown in splendid array. He also has made an effort to cultivate plants native to the Canary Islands in the garden. It will all end soon, because the Marquis finds his financial situation much reduced, and the State does not seem to want to be part of it.

The dragon's blood tree (*Dracaena Draco L.*) is native to these islands. The inhabitants, although they know its uses, make little effort to take advantage of them. About an hour from Porto de l'Orotava is a villa of the same name, where a dragon's blood tree stands next to Don Pedro Franchy's house that is said to be 42 feet (English) across. We did not have time to see that unusual natural curiosity. On the 23rd we returned to Santa Cruz. In the meantime, Captain von Krusenstern had purchased water, wood, wine and other provisions for the voyage. We heard from our officers that they had given a ball on board the *Nadeschda* while we were in Orotava.

The crew was invigorated and we were all ready to sail on October 26th.

Pic

Before I leave the island I should probably say something about the world famous Pic of Teneriffe. It certainly is one of the best known of all the high mountains on earth. According to Borda's best geometric measurements, it is 1,905 *toises*, according to others only 1,901 toises.[11] Now that we know the New World better, that Chimborazo is 3,357, Cayambe Urku 3,030, l'Antisana 2,993, and Cotopaxi 2,952 toises high and that there are many other mountains much higher than Pic, it has lost much of its former reputation.

Our party would have liked to climb it very much but the length and uncertainty of our stay prevented us. In addition, the inhabitants assured us that at that late season of the year we would not be able to overcome the obstacles and would have to turn back — so we had to give up our plans. Since, however, Mr. Cordier,[12] who is well enough known for his zeal and knowledge, especially of mineralogy, had visited that extremely remarkable mountain the previous spring, I would like to tell my readers the results of the newest information recently made public by this scholarly traveler in his manuscript.

On April 16th he left Porto de l'Orotava to climb the Pic. He found the plain (Las Faldas de las Canadas), from which the mountain rises 1,100 toises above sea level, covered only by glassy lava and pumice. Large quantities of broom (*Spartium supranubium*) are found together with several varieties of lichens on the large desert. The barometer read 19° *zoll* 9.05 lines and the temperature +4°.09 Réaumur warmth near Stancia de los Ingleses. According to corresponding observations, the Stancia is 1,529 toises above sea level. Broom is still found at that height, although very stunted. On the 19th at 4:45 the thermometer fell to +3°, but the cold was very bearable. He reached the summit of Pic in three hours. To get there one has to climb over piles of vitreous lava, consisting of very large, coarse and sharp pieces. The steep slope leading to the peak is covered with crushed pumice and is exhausting to climb because of its tendency to slide. In mild, clear weather one could only see the islands of Hierro, Gomera, Palma and Canaria. The inside walls of the crater are steep and higher to the north. One can only descend through 3 clefts. The crater is elliptical, about 1,200 *fuss* in circumference and 110 deep. The steep slopes leading to the depths of the crater consist of a white earth that is decomposed vitreous lava. Sulfur crystals of the most beautiful color and the liveliest shine decorate the inner walls. Hot steam, rising frequently from all sides, had undoubtedly been rising for several hours from the depths and made a thermometer held in a crack climb to over 80° R. The steam consists of sulfur and traces of tasteless water. It is curious that along with incrustations of sulfur, which the steam quickly accumulates, are found opals of various shapes.

At 8 o'clock Mr. Cordier was still 1½ toises from the peak. The barometer read 18 zoll 4 lines, the thermometer -6°09. At the same time in Porto de l'Orotava the barometer read 28″5‴06, the thermometer +19°.09. The elevation of the last observations was 7 toises above sea level and increasing the result of the total by 8½ toises makes Pic 1,901.02 French toises high. The needle of the magnet continually pointed more than 5° toward the South Pole.

Mr. Cordier found incorrect and very exaggerated the reports of others about the keenness of the cold, alcohol becoming weak, breathing difficulties and the appearance of the disk of the sun. The cold was very bearable, liquors did not lose their strength, the hydrosulphuric steam caused no breathing difficulties, aside from forcing him to stop rather often as he approached the summit. Even though Mr. Cordier's observations are different from those of previous travelers, theirs still could be correct, for it is well-known that in the Swiss Alps the temperature often changes within an hour. Mr. Cordier was very lucky to climb Pic at an exceedingly favorable time. He left that interesting spot after a stay of 3½ hours. Ascending he very soon reached the *Narices del Pico* or Pic's nostrils, two vents at the foot of the peak which continually eject steam. Nearby is the cave known as *Cueva del Gelo*.[13] There are thousands of tales told about it. One can get an idea of it by imagining a grotto formed by flowing lava when it explodes over empty space. The floor of the grotto is usually well filled with water-soaked snow. In the summer, however, it dries out periodically. The various kinds of lava one finds on this trip are marked by a transition from obsidian to pumice.

There are several other volcanoes: the crater of the volcano that filled the harbor of Garachico with lava is 5 hours from Orotava, the new volcano is 7 hours from Irod de los Vinos. The three openings that poured lava onto the plain de las Canadas are one above the other on the steep slopes of the mountain de la Chahorra, which itself is a huge extension of the foot of Pic on the southwestern side. It is 1,200 paces in circumference, the rim about 1,300 toises above sea level. One can only descend down the other two. There is a little sulfur and the steam is almost totally insignificant. While climbing the heights of the mountain de la Chahorra, Mr. Cordier discovered a new crater not noticed before. It is about 1,600 toises above sea level and more beautiful than all of the well-known ones. It is about one and one-half hours in circumference and very old. Its steep walls show the clearest traces of the most terrible fire. The Pic has a free standing cone.[14] The uncertainty until now about this beautiful phenomenon results from the fact that it is impossible to climb the Pic's cone on the northern side.

The volcano Guimar is 670 toises above sea level on the steep slope leading to La Cumbre. After a mass of lava more than one hour's journey and square in size had built up on the steepest slopes, it spread across the Plain of los Barraneos at the foot of the steep hills. Part of it reaches as far as one-quarter of an hour from the ocean and two and one-half hours from the crater. The lavas are gray petrosilex mixed with crystals of augit and crysolites. The slag is now decomposing and producing a fine sand which possibly could be made productive through cultivation.

On the morning of October 27th, we weighed anchor amidst the thunder of cannons to set out on our voyage to Brazil. The weather was unusually clear, and on the morning of the 29th at six o'clock, we could still see the Pic at a distance of more than one hundred sea miles. We had a voyage of about two and one-half months at sea ahead of us. Even though many would think it terribly boring, we all found it very entertaining.

A few days after our departure we found ourselves in the tropics. Favored by trade winds, we had the most pleasant sailing. The thermometer showed mostly 20° to 22°. By wearing thin clothing, especially of nankeen, we sought to make the heat bearable. The ship sailed through the waves so quietly that only the occasional gusts of wind reminded us that we were on an ocean voyage. Nights were cool and often damp. Captain von Krusenstern kept a watchful eye out to make sure neither officers nor sailors went lightly dressed at night or even slept uncovered on deck. Indeed, some thought him too strict since they thought the cool of the night strengthened them. But the happy result of the regulation, that everyone on board was healthy, showed that we all were indebted to this excellent man for his prudent attention.

Most of our northern travelers found the warm climate very pleasant and agreed that 20° to 24° cold froze ears and noses, but that the same degrees of warmth were not detrimental to their health. The riches of southern lands where nature, almost without help from man, has brought forth fruits and foods of all kinds, where man does not have to worry about either warm housing and wood or warm clothing, proves adequately that human existence in milder climes is the natural one and in colder climes artificial. No doubt for exactly this reason can higher civilization by far be found where need compels our minds to exert themselves more and where mutual activity has as its purpose obtaining food.

Only one Russian, whose constitution had previously been shaken, complained that the heat was unbearable.

Daily we found new scenes and sources of entertainment of various kinds:

We often saw tropical birds (*Phaethon aethereus L.*), flying fish (*Exocoetus et Trigla volitans*), bonito and tunnies (*Scomber Pelamys* and *Scomber Thynnus*), etc., in these regions. Occasionally one or the other fish was taken by harpoon. For us the hunt was less often successful than for other travelers who tell of catching large quantities of fish. Several times we also caught small sharks (*Squalus coeruleus L.*) which the sailors, for want of fresh food, ate with relish and then admired their usual companions (*Echeneis remora* and *Gasterosteus Ductor*), the ship sucker or sucker fish and the pilot fish. During calms, we also sometimes watched how difficult it is to catch a Portuguese man-of-war (*Physalis pelagica*). The peculiar shape of this creature, which resembles a small bladder with many little tentacles hanging from it, its beautiful colors and novelty, delighted us all. The individual little sucker tips of its tentacles caused sharp pain when touched and a strong inflammation of the skin, as if a plaster of Spanish fly had been applied. In good weather boats would be sent out now and then in order to check the clearness and temperature of the water or the current, or else to fish for mollusks, or to make a formal visit to our traveling companion the *Neva*. Such little excursions on the open sea have a great deal of charm. Every time there were always more admirers than seats in the boat.

November 1803

The closer we came to the equator the more changeable the weather became. Calms, strong gusts of wind from every direction and rain showers alternated frequently with thunder storms, cloudy skies and sunshine. The heat was bearable and seldom over 22° Réaumur.

On the morning of November 26th, 1803, we crossed the Equator at 24°20′ W longitude from Greenwich. All Europeans found this event of to be of sufficient interest to note in their diaries. That particular day had to be more noteworthy for the Russians, since the ships of that great nation had never up to then navigated those waters. Our ships were the first to approach the southern half of the globe. A feeling of national pride awakened in every breast. Even the hearts of us foreigners beat faster for having part of the honor of laying the basis for active Russian trade, which could produce results of the greatest importance.

Every last person was happy. For everyone it was a day of celebration. At about ten o'clock in the morning when we crossed the equator, both of our ships (the *Nadeschda* and the *Neva*) hoisted their Russian flags. An old tradition dictates that anyone crossing the equator for the first time should be dunked in water, or at least drenched. We of course observed this tradition on board our ship. One sailor, filled with natural gaiety and liveliness, had dressed as Neptune to make the whole thing more impressive. That god of the seas was dressed as if he lived on either the North or South Pole. It is hardly possible that he ever appeared at the equator in such strange clothes. Instead of a trident, that Nordic Neptune had a harpoon in his hand that we used for fishing. He was incredibly active as he filled one bucket after another with water and doused all those standing around him. Considering the fact that we had temperatures between 22° and 23° Réaumur, it is easy to imagine how hot that sailor became under his mask, wrapped in thick furs, jumping around for several hours on the deck in order to carry out his lofty role for the pleasure of his audience.

The Commander of the other ship (the *Neva*), Captain Lisiansky, had his ship turn at the moment when the Russian flag greeted the equator, and then pass close by us in full sail with his yards manned and a threefold Hurrah. We returned the Hurrah with equal ardor and joyful hearts.

Our god of the sea executed all kinds of acrobatics. Ambassador von Resanoff, so that he, as well as the rest of the ship's crew, would remember this remarkable day in the history of Russian navigation, had all of the sailors solemnly assemble on deck and had each one step forward to receive a piaster (a Spanish dollar). Meanwhile, mealtime had arrived and we all sat down at the table in the happiest of spirits. During the meal, to the shots of cannons, we toasted the health of *His Imperial Majesty*, Our Most gracious *Monarch*, the Benefactor of His Subjects, the Promotor of navigation and trade, and member of a great Imperial House. We toasted the Minister of Trade, Count von Romanzoff and Minister of the Navy Tschitschagoff, the President of the Academy of Sciences in St. Petersburg, von Novosilzoff, the Directors of the Russian-American Trading Company, our brave Commander von Krusenstern, Ambassador von Resanoff and all of our friends, relatives and participants.[15] We had just arrived at that degree of merriment, which can only be felt and not described, when we got up from the table to go on deck where the jubilation began anew. Captain von Krusenstern, the Ambassador and all of the officers were hoisted up one after the other, with cries of joy and Hurrah!, and swung on hands. This is a Russian way of showing the greatest respect and honor. We capped the joy of that noteworthy day with a *Bowle Punsch*.

The heat below the equator, and in general between the Tropic of Cancer and the Tropic of Capricorn, is by no means so intolerable as is generally believed. In order to understand my conclusion I have to admit that I find the heat of a quite hot summer day in the most northerly parts of Europe far more oppressive than the continual warmth day and night below the Tropic of Cancer, because in that area a day seldom passes without a cool thunder storm and rain, refreshing all of nature.

In the north people protect themselves against the cold by wearing warm clothing and a fur hat. In warmer climates people protect themselves from the sun's heat by wearing extremely light, thin clothing and large, light straw hats.

Our Neptune, wearing a mask and a thick fur coat and continually jumping around for several hours in 22° to 23° Réaumur, indeed, had to endure a very unusual degree of heat. Perhaps the custom and practice of taking Russian steam baths helped a lot to make his present situation more tolerable. Indeed, if we compare the present regulations for ships with the older ones, we find them silly when judged in terms of present precautions. In 1670, for example, B. Narborough*[16] said that he "took the precaution of bleeding his people often in warm zones and experience showed him that high fevers could be prevented in this manner." That navigator must have had a very healthy crew. I could, indeed, prove to him that there are very good reasons why exactly his precautions would be sufficient to weaken every single one of his men and cause petechial putrid fever, scurvy, etc.

Captain Cook's and von Krusenstern's experiences are far better.[17] They gave their crews good food, careful treatment, good water, cleanliness, a little glass of grog (a mixture of brandy and water), wine or punch at the proper time and in moderation. The entire crew, without being bled often, crossed the equator four times and returned to Europe healthy.

The poultry we had along from Europe and Teneriffe could not stand the heat nor the long sea voyage very well. All but a few of the chickens went blind and became noticeably emaciated. I cannot venture to say what might have caused this. Labillardiere,[18] who noted the same disease among chickens, ascribes it to the influence of the air. Perhaps it is caused more by sea water, since the ship is often washed by sea water in the strong winds and considerable amounts of sea water unavoidably get into their food and water barrels.

On a voyage like ours every little thing, even though often apparently a trifle, provides diversion. That is why I have to mention a ship

---

*See *Histoire des navigations aux terres Australes* [History of Navigation to Australia], Vol. II, p. 5.

we saw on November 22nd which appeared to be sailing for Europe. Von Krusenstern sailed over to it and then sent an officer with letters on board. I was permitted to accompany him and I mention this because such an excursion in a little boat on the wide ocean does not happen every day. We were told that the ship came from the United American Free States and was heading for Batavia.[19] The captain, like many others, was making this long voyage without much knowledge of astronomy and without a chronometer. In reality he was three degrees farther west than according to his calculations. He was very grateful to von Krusenstern for pointing out to him his correct longitude and he corrected the ship's course immediately.

Captain von Krusenstern used December 7th and 8th to try to visit the problematic Island of Ascençao,[20] whose existence has been questioned by the most recent navigators, e.g., La Pérouse. We headed west. Toward evening we were located at 20°42′ S latitude and 37° longitude, that is 2°1′ farther west than that unlucky navigator, without sighting an island. If the island truly exists, then it is not at the location given by geographers on the maps up to now.

Entrusted to the winds and waves, we had been swimming on the wide ocean for several weeks (since October 27th), when finally on December 12th, we sighted Cape Frio, the long-desired coast of Brazil. This land, rich in gold and diamonds, along with its splendid towns and wealth of products, had been for weeks the object of our attention, our daily conversations, our curiosity, and our longing. Several of our ship's company had wanted to visit Rio Janeiro, the large port city near the Cape. Captain von Krusenstern, however, was concerned with the difficulties we would have to overcome. He knew very well that we would be unnecessarily subjected to strict controls, an exact customs inspection and especially, as in all large towns, considerable expenses and loss of time. That is why he chose to sail to the Island of St. Catharina, a few degrees farther south. It has many advantages over other ports of call and refreshment and had been visited by the immortal La Pérouse. We contented ourselves in the meantime with observing the many new objects found in the waters near land. We were sailing about 25 to 30 sea miles from land when we saw several fishing boats near our ship. They sailed past totally ignoring us, probably because they had nothing they could offer for trade or sale.

Even at that distance we could recognize the riches of the country. The sea seemed filled with life. In forty fadens we fished for dorades, and gold dorades (*Coryphaena Hippurus*) which have an excellent taste. We saw at the same time unusual numbers of salpae, beroes, medusas and other slime-like, gelatinous, transparent creatures known by the general name of zoophytes and mollusks. It was especially striking that wide stretches of the ocean in several places were completely red in color. Closer inspection showed us that the color was caused by an indescribable number of small crustaceans swimming on the surface of the water.

We fished out several shiny silver onisei (*Ligia Fabric*) we had spied at a greater depth in order to admire and inspect them. They seem to have obtained their rich silver appearance from their nearby motherland.*

On December 18th we sighted the Island of St. Catharina. At a distance of 60 to 80 sea miles from land, we were welcomed by several butterflies on board our ship, which probably had been driven from land by a strong wind. The weather was beautiful, the horizon clear, and we headed toward the coast. The wind blew gently into the sails. About half past four in the afternoon, we were so close to the shore that we could distinguish trees, rocks and other objects. We were imagining ourselves lying at anchor that same evening, or at the latest the following morning, and enjoying the most marvelous fruits Brazil has to offer, when suddenly a heavy thunderstorm with gusts of wind and rain forced us to sail away from land and the many greening islands ahead of us and to seek safety to the southeast in the high waves of the open sea. That brisk wind continued longer than we would have liked. Only on the 20th did we dare to approach the coast again to sail into the harbor.

Notes

1. According to the *Dictionary of National Biography* (London: Oxford, 1968), Langsdorff means John Hawkins (1758?-1841) and not Sir John Hawkins (1719-1789). John Hawkins was a man of considerable means who devoted his life to the study of literature, science and art. He was a fellow of the Royal Society. Most of his papers on scientific subjects discuss the geology of Cornwall.

Martin Heinrich Klaproth (1743-1817) was a professor of chemistry at the University of Berlin. He is best known for his exact chemical analyses which

*See Cook's *Dritte Entdeckungsreise in der Sudsee* [Third voyage of discovery to the South Seas], March 1778.

caused German scientists to reject many prevailing theories. In 1789 he discovered zirconia and uranium.

2. Langsdorff classified animals, plants, etc., according to Johann Friedrich Gmelin's (1748-1804) revision of Carl von Linné's (Carolus Linnaeus, 1707-1778) *Systema naturae per regna tria naturae, secundum classes, ordines, genera, species, cum characterbus, differentis, synonymis, locis*, ed. 13 (Leipzig: G. E. Beer, 1788-93).

3. Horatio Viscount Nelson (1758-1805). Langsdorff is referring to Nelson's abortive attack on July 24, 1797, against Santa Cruz. As Nelson was getting out of the boat, a bullet shattered his right elbow so that his arm had to be amputated.

4. *Bowle Punsch* is a cold drink usually made from fruit or herbs, sugar, wine and champagne or mineral water. *Bowle* derives from the English word bowl.

5. Pic: Pico de Teyde or Teide. Together with its supports and spurs it occupies nearly two-thirds of Teneriffe, the largest of the Canary Islands.

6. See the appendix of weights and measures.

7. The Guanches are an ancient Berber people, now extinct, who were conquered by the Spanish in the 15th century.

8. René Antoine Ferchault de Réaumur (1683-1757) was a French physicist and inventor, who constructed a thermometer. Zero degrees represents the freezing point and eighty degrees the boiling point, an accident caused by the dilution of the alcohol he employed.

9. Major Hermann Karl von Friederici (1779-1869) was born in Estonia and entered the Russian military service in 1796. He became the Commandant of Pavlovsk in 1826 and General of the Infantry in 1848.

Dr. Moritz Laband was the *Neva*'s doctor. He is not listed in any of the national bibliographies.

10. According to legend, St. Ursula, a Cornish princess of the 4th or 5th century, was martyred together with eleven thousand other virgins by the Huns at Cologne.

11. Jean Charles Borda (1733-1799) authored jointly with Jean René Antoine Verdun de la Crenne *Voyage fait par ordre du roi en 1771 et 1772* (Voyage by order of the King in 1771 and 1772) (Paris: Imprimerie royale, 1778). All of the mountains mentioned by Langsdorff are in Ecuador.

12. Langsdorff is probably referring to Pierre Louis Antoine Cordier (1777-1861), who worked on the geology of Spain.

13. Narices de Pico — Las Narices del Teidecueva de gelo — Cueva del Hielo.

14. Pictures of the mountain and maps indicate "*Der Pic steht auf seinen Rändern auf*" as "The Pic has a free standing cone," rather than the literal rendition "It rises from its supports."

15. Captain Lisiansky (Russian: Iurii Fedorovich Lisianskii, 1773-1837) and von Krusenstern prepared and led the expedition. The *Neva* was the first ship in history to make the return voyage from Canton to Portsmouth without stopping.

Count von Romanzoff (Russian: Nikolai Petrovich Rumiantsev or Rumiantsov, 1754-1826) was a statesman and patron of the arts and of exploration. Under Alexander I he was appointed Minister of Commerce. He helped plan the expedition around the world.

Tschitschagoff (Russian: Vasilii Iakovlevich Chichagov, 1726-1809), educated in England, was an admiral, who led the first expedition seeking a northern sea route from Europe to the Pacific.

Novosilzoff (Russian: Nikolai Nikolaevich Novosiltsev, 1761-1836) was a statesman under Alexander I and Nicholas I.

16. Sir John Narborough (1640-1688). *An Account of several late Voyages and Discoveries to the South and North . . .* by Sir John Narborough, Captain Jasmen Tasmen, Captain John Wood and Frederick Marten (London: printed for S. Smith and B. Walford, 1694).

17. Captain James Cook (1728-1779), the famous British navigator, was sent in 1768 and again in 1772 to explore the South Pacific Ocean and to chart New Zealand and Australia. On the 1772 voyage he lost only one man out of 118 to scurvy. He was killed in 1779 in Hawaii. The descriptions of his voyages were translated into German soon after their appearance in English.

18. Jacques Julien Houton de la Billardiere (1755-1834), a French geologist and naturalist, took part in the expedition from 1785-1788 commanded by Jean François de Gallaup, Comte de La Pérouse (1741-ca. 1788). La Pérouse was the commander of a French expedition sent out in 1785 to discover the Northwest Passage and to collect information on the fur trade in North America, as well as on whaling in the South Pacific. On January 26, 1788, he arrived in Botany Bay. After that, nothing more was heard of him. In 1826 Captain Peter Dalton found the wreckage of the two ships on the reefs of Vanikoro, an island to the north of the New Hebrides.

19. Batavia was the capital of the Dutch East Indies on the Island of Java, present-day Djakarta.

20. Ascençao — Ascension Island — lies at 7°57′ S and 14°22′ W.

Chapter 2

Arrival in Brazil, Stay at St. Catharina. Villa Nossa Senhora do Desterro. Customs and Habits. Dance of the Negro Slaves. Excursion to the Mainland. Arts, Science and Public Institutions, Train Oil Factory, Medical and Natural History Observations.

From a great distance, the view of the landscape lying ahead, all decked in the most beautiful of green and colorful flowers, promised us the most pleasant of stays and abundant refreshment. The Island of St. Catharina and the part of the American mainland opposite it consists of highlands, although even the highest mountains are only of medium height with their peaks covered by tall trees. They are mostly steep and intersected by several valleys. Along the coast we saw a great many bays and islands watered by a large number of springs, creeks, mountain streams, rivers and swamps. Some of the shores are sandy, others inaccessible and still others bounded by granite rocks, which make them impossible to approach in the raging surf.

The sight of land after a voyage of two months, even of the most barren rocks, is always a happy moment. And how much happier that moment is when the land has been so very blessed by nature in every way, a land filled with all imaginable beauty and charm. A magnificent landscape rose from the ocean's shore intensified by the green of the mountains bordered in the golden red of the setting sun. We saw several ships in the straits we were gradually approaching. On the 21st we dropped our anchor near the little fort of St. Cruz on the Island of Atomeri.[1]

My imagination was filled with so many beautiful pictures that I could hardly await the return of the sun in order to visit that nearby paradise. I admit that my imaginings were grandly exciting. Nevertheless, the closer I came to land the more I saw that reality had outdone my expectations.

The colors, shapes, forms and varieties of many flowers filled the atmosphere with a mixture of pleasant smells that strengthened our bodies and cheered our dispositions with every breath.

Large butterflies, which I had only ever seen displayed as rarities in our European collections, fluttered around many magnificent luxuriant flowering plants never seen in our greenhouses, or if present, only stunted. Glittering gold hummingbirds hovered around the honey-rich flowers of the banana groves. The echoing songs of birds I had never heard before rose from the water-rich valleys, delighting my heart and ears. Dark, shadowy paths wound from one peaceful hut to the next and exceeded in beauty and charm, in variety and simplicity all of the plans of our European gardens, no matter how well executed. The newness of everything I saw amazed me and left an impression that can only be felt and not described. In the evening I enthusiastically returned to the ship with a rich collection of plants and insects that everyone admired because of the numbers of objects I had collected and because of the size, variety, magnificence and mixture of colors of the butterflies.

The Island of Santa Catharina forms the smaller part of the province of the same name. It is 25 miles long and three to four, in parts, eight to nine miles wide.[2] Its north-northeastern point lies at 27°19′10″ S and 47°49′20″ W according to von Krusenstern's and Dr. Horner's observations.* It is separated from the mainland by straits that, at the narrowest point, are not over 200 fadens wide. All entrances are guarded by forts, artillery and soldiers, but in case of enemy attack they could not be defended for very long. Smaller ships, for example, cutters, brigs, etc., can reach the outpost through the southern entrance to the straits; larger vessels, however, must choose the excellent, safe northern entrance. It is defended by two small forts or fortifications. The one on the northwestern tip of the Island of St. Catharina is called Forte da Ponta Grossa and the other, close to the mainland on the little island (Atomeri), is called Forte de St. Cruz, where ships coming in can find a secure and convenient anchorage.

The main city on the Island and of the Province, the residence of the governor, is called Villa Nossa Senhora do Desterro.[4] This little town is found in the southwestern part of the Island of St. Catharina, about ten sea miles from the anchorage mentioned above,

---

*Upon Zach's recommendation, Dr. Horner of Zürich was appointed astronomer for this expedition. In his book Captain von Krusenstern comments with the utmost justification upon this excellent man's activities and knowledge. He won the respect and friendship of everyone by his honesty, integrity and excellence of character. He distinguished himself most advantageously on several occasions.[3]

at the foot of several moderately high mountains on a gently sloping hilly spit of land. It has between 400 and 500 houses.

The number of inhabitants on the whole island is supposed to be around 10,000, and in the province around 25 to 30,000 souls. There are quite a few people who are well-off but few or none who are rich. In general people are well-off without being wealthy. All of the houses are made of stone and crushed or dried clay. The streets are mostly regular. There are all kinds of merchants, or rather shopkeepers, and craftsmen. A great quantity of provisions and food are brought to the market from the surrounding countryside every day. In the numerous stalls I found almost everything from Europe necessary to make life comfortable, e.g., iron wares, glass, porcelain, silk and cotton goods, cloth, mirrors, candlesticks, paper, etc., as is easily imagined, all very expensive. The inhabitants of the entire province are kind, friendly and polite. They are very hospitable and sociable. In the evening little family groups come together and they dance, laugh, joke, sing and play in the typical Portuguese way. The usual instruments played are guitars and dulcimers. The music is expressive, tasteful and enchanting. The content of the songs is moral, usually a repetition about love and maidens, about Amor's wounds and bleeding hearts, about sighing and yearning. But perhaps many of my readers will find a Brazilian air more pleasant than my empty description, so I am including one here.

The female sex is not ugly. Among those of the upper class we saw several who, even in Europe, would have been justified in claiming to be beauties. They are mostly of middle stature, well built, with brownish skin color (*basané*). Even though some are very white, they have heavy, black hair and dark, burning eyes. In addition, that beautiful sex greets guests very politely. They live much less restricted and confined than they would if they were in their motherland, Portugal, where ladies are shut up the whole year and hide behind doors from where they observe the arrival of a stranger through a keyhole or a crack in the door. As small as the place may be, it still has its many little love intrigues. Presents of European trifles, sequins, ribbons, earrings, etc., are accepted very gratefully.

Both sexes wear European clothing, except that everything is made from the thinnest and lightest of cloth and materials. Muslins, fine linen, nankeen and silks are often worn.

The province was created recently. It extends from the Rio Grande at 32° S to the province of St. Paul at 23°, from where it is supposed to obtain most of its population. The Portuguese government has granted them many privileges, e.g., foreign as well as Portuguese ships entering and leaving the harbor pay far less than in other Brazilian harbors. The province is fertile and all necessities of life are very cheap. Nature provides everything without a great deal of help or care. There is a superabundance of diverse kinds of fruits, e.g., oranges, lemons, bananas, pineapples, peaches, sweet melons and watermelons, figs, coconuts and other nuts, grapes, legumes, Turkish rye, rice, and many edible and useful roots such as batatas[5] (*Convolvulus Batatas Linn.*), onions, yams (*Dioscorea alata et sativa*) and many more. What the Brazilians call tapioca (in other places it is called mandioca or manhiocca or cassava root), *Jatropha Manihot Linn.*, is the principal food of the inhabitants here and is used instead of bread. They call the finer kind tapioca, a true white sago, the coarser *Farinha de pao*, which is eaten by the lower classes and poor people. I saw little rye or white bread, only in the homes of the richest and best off people. The manduni plant (*Arachis hypogaea*) is also commonly raised. After blooming, its hypanthia bend toward the ground, giving its ripened fruit to the earth. I have heard that they are also being grown in several places in Southern France.

Almost all of the landowners have a great many domestic animals, i.e., oxen, cows, pigs, horses, ducks, geese, turkeys, etc. For this reason meat is to be had in quantities at low prices. An entire steer weighing at least 400 *pfunds* costs eight Spanish dollars at the most, a good milch cow 12 to 16 Spanish dollars, a fat pig weighing 200 pfunds ten piasters or Spanish dollars, a fat chicken one-half of a Spanish dollar. Fish, mussels and crabs, especially a kind of very large shrimp, are to be had in quantities. They, however, are relatively more expensive than other foods because the people living on the coast take care of their own needs first and bring only small amounts to the market. Negro slaves usually do the fishing.

A large, fertile country estate several hundred *ackers* in size with woodland and grazing land costs 300 to 400 Spanish dollars. If one owns such an estate and several good slaves, one can live like a well-off man, free of want and with a superabundance of products. Cleanliness distinguishes the inhabitants here very decidedly from the dirty Portuguese. Soldiers, peasants and the poor people observe great cleanliness not only in the care of their fine, good clothing but also in the rest of their housekeeping.

The greatest part of the Province of Santa Catharina is, in reality, coastal, since it can only be settled six to eight German miles inland, that is, to the west. At only a distance of two hours or one German mile, one finds isolated huts of poor country people widely separated from each other. They live mainly from cattle. They own countless herds of cattle fenced in on vast grazing areas. Without further attention the cattle run around free the entire year and reproduce without the owner being able to determine how large his herds are. These wild, or rather feral, animals cost on the spot only from two to three Spanish dollars and are driven in large numbers to the coast and to the town of Nossa Senhora do Desterro. The hardest work involves catching one of them out of the herd. Several men on horseback and on foot surround an animal and lasso it around the horns or a foot. The animal becomes tired in a little while and can be thrown on the ground and forcibly tamed in this manner. Then it can be driven to the main town on the island. Transporting such a herd is also wrought with many difficulties. For this reason, the price of an animal at least doubles before it reaches the Island of St. Catharina.

The inhabitants of the most distant outposts toward the interior of the country are not only the poorest of the province but, from time to time, are subjected to raids by the aborigines, the Indians, who are called *Gentio brava*, wild peoples, or *Caboccolos*. During our stay, there was such an incident and the governor had to send out a detachment of soldiers to help. Such incidents are said to be common.

As far as the climate is concerned, we found the heat of the sun not as unbearable as we had been led to expect. During December and January, which in the southern hemisphere can be compared to our summer months, the thermometer usually showed from 20° to 22° Réaumur warmth in the country in the shade. The highest temperature was 26°. The governor told us that he had experienced 10° warmth in the winter, something highly unusual. In that country that is the coldest it becomes.

Scarcely a day passes in the warm season without rain and thunderstorms towards evening. Nature's winter, as I have just mentioned, comes in the southern hemisphere during the summer months of the northern hemisphere. It is, according to the inhabitants, the most pleasant season — one continuous, delightful spring.

The air is always moist. The higher chains of mountains eternally covered with green, attract the clouds, which then descend into the valleys to nourish and refresh the animal and plant kingdom and to supply new spring water for the creeks and rivers. The warmer or hotter the day, the more one can count on rain or thunderstorms in the evening. The moisture, together with the continual heat, correctly can be viewed as the source of the great richness and variety of plants and animals. A naturalist, however, must overcome great obstacles when trying to preserve specimens. The insects, crabs, heavy-bodied butterflies and moths, grasshoppers, large spiders, etc., which dry out easily for us at home, here mostly begin to rot if one does not take great care in storing them in closed, dry places in order to prevent to some extent that unpleasant circumstance. Unfortunately, due to my ignorance of the climate's influence and my resulting lack of necessary precautions, I lost the greatest part of the plants I collected in the beginning. I had left them for several days in order to make an excursion into the interior. Upon my return I found most of them were mouldy.

The nights are especially damp. Despite this, the climate does not seem to have any ill effect upon the health of the inhabitants. Indeed, this province (with the exception of the northern part called Sao Francisco) is considered very healthy. In the area just mentioned, a great many swamps and a lot of stagnant water are said to give off vapors very detrimental to the health.

The customs and habits of the country are in general not very different from those of Portugal. They differ mainly due to the difference in climate and products, which cause a change in the way of life and customs. Thus, for example, the warmer clime requires little clothing. For this reason, the female sex at home wears a very simple costume consisting of a blouse and a thin skirt. Wealthier women wear blouses of fine linen or cotton embroidered beautifully all around. In addition, they also wear muslin scarves. For evening parties the ladies wear European clothes decorated with many ribbons and sequins. The brighter and more colorful their dresses are, the more elegant they believe they are dressed. The men also dress in light clothes almost totally in European styles. The Negro slaves go almost without any covering. The men wear half breeches, the women only short skirts and at the most old blouses or rags hanging from their shoulders over their breasts.

The quantity of Negro slaves of both sexes seen here no doubt astonishes every European unaccustomed to such a sight. A totally new, outraged feeling grew in me the first time I went to Nossa Senhora do Desterro and caught sight of numbers of these miserable, helpless human beings lying exposed, naked in front of the doors on the cross streets for sale. At first only their genitals were covered with old, torn sackcloth and then, several days later, with pieces of new, coarse blue material. It is well-known that yearly large shiploads of Negro slaves are sent to Brazilian ports from the Portuguese possessions in Africa, especially from Angola, Benguella, Mozambique, etc. These are the circumstances under which these miserable creatures had recently arrived in Rio Janeiro and from there had probably been sent here in order to be sold for higher prices. These people are offered for sale like goods. Depending upon whether old or young, strong or weak, healthy or sickly, male or female, they sell for more or less money. Even though recently many respected men have defended this trade, it is my opinion that the way it is done here would shock the refined feelings of every cultivated European. The buyers inspect especially to see if the slave on sale has already survived smallpox, in which case, far more is paid. During the transport from Africa to Brazil, most of them die of smallpox, putrid fever and homesickness or depressed emotions or melancholy, from which, once stricken, they usually die. In Brazil a young healthy Negro costs about 100 to 150 Spanish dollars. Once he is used to field work or has perhaps learned a trade and understands Portuguese, his price increases according to the skills he possesses. Many of them are a valuable investment which produces many thousand percent profit every year, if we remember that everything these slaves earn as skilled workers or day-laborers goes not to them but rather to their masters and that their owners rent them out for an appropriate price by the day or week for field work, rowing, hauling, construction, etc., just as we do with animals.

These unfortunate people have to do most of the cultivation of the land and the hardest work of all kinds. How wealthy the inhabitants here are is usually judged by the number of slaves they own. The slaves can consider themselves lucky if they fall into humane hands. Woe be to the ones who are cast under the control of strict masters. They are sometimes mistreated very inhumanely. That is why the desire for freedom in these oppressed people comes alive and they secretly escape their cruel masters by fleeing into the remote mountains. They would rather subsist by hunting and from plants, fruits and roots than by serving a tyrant. Under such circumstances, they sometimes join the savages in the interior and take part in the raids upon isolated settlements as mentioned above. In rare cases, the extreme mistreatment of slaves has caused them to murder their masters. Such a case happened just before our arrival in St. Catharina.

Since the Brazilian coast is very thinly populated, the annual increase in the number of industrious slaves would be a true benefit and considerable gain for the population and culture of the country. Therefore, it would behoove the government to pay more attention to insuring that they are treated humanely. Unfortunately, it seems as if the government itself has never considered their relief. Very creditable people say that, indeed, the slaves working in Crown establishments, i.e., in sugar refineries, on whaling ships and in mines, are treated the most harshly and brutally of all.

The products of this country are highly varied and could become an inexhaustible source of very profitable trade if it were not subject to many restrictions and mostly dependent upon Rio Janeiro, since the inhabitants are only permitted to sell their goods there. If these excellent areas become more populated and less neglected by the government, then by grace of the products flowing almost by themselves from Nature's cornucopia, this could become in a few years one of the most important trading areas of Brazil. The cultivation of coffee and cotton would produce great profits. Rice and sugar for export abound. Despite that, there is not enough rum and arrack. Indigo, pepper, vanilla, copaiva balsam,* and numbers of other products could be harvested without difficulty, but there is a lack of industry.

The finest and most varied kinds of wood for building ships and making furniture grow in the nearby forests and could be an immediate source of profitable articles for trade, if their export were not prohibited.

In the southern part of the province, that is in Rio Grande, one finds most of the products grown in the milder parts of Europe, but almost no one cultivates them. Given this and similar facts one can judge the condition of the rest of the province.

Anyone with a more intimate knowledge of Portugal would be surprised to discover that in this province, where there could be so much affluence, there are so few monks. They have often petitioned the Portuguese Court for permission to build a monastery here. The present governor, Colonel Joaquin Xavier Curado, however, has prevented such an establishment every time by giving reasoned arguments about its impracticality, most recently just before our arrival. Despite

---

*The tree that produces copaiva balsam (*Copaisera officinallis*) is called *Oleo breto* (black olive) here. It abounds in the forests, but despite this very little use is made of it. I was told that the moment one makes an incision into the tree to obtain sap (which has to be done in the middle of summer) it rushes out, making a loud noise not unlike the one made when bleeding a human. *Relata refero.*

this, I suspect that with an increase in population and wealth the monks will in the end manage to slip in.

I will try to mention some of the best, most unique customs and habits I had an opportunity to observe during my stay on St. Catharina.

The inhabitants here often drink a tea brewed from leaves called *herba do matto* (wood herb). Most of the people are as accustomed to using this drink as many Europeans are to drinking coffee, tea, etc. I could not obtain any of the plants used to brew this tea.* It does not grow on the island but in the most northerly part of the province, that is in São Francisco. The leaves are collected and put into longish baskets holding some two to three pfunds and then brought here. When used, hot water is poured over them and sugar added. This is the way they are presented to guests. So that guests do not get leaves in their mouths, they drink through a little straw about the size of a tobacco pipe, about one-half fuss long and widened at the bottom end into a shape like a watering can with many small openings woven basket-like from fine wood fiber. One drinks the tea through this. The drinking vessels of the poor called *cuja* are very simple. They usually are made from coconuts or a kind of gourd (perhaps *Cucurbita Siceraria*) or also baked clay. They are served on and with colorful napkins like those used in England with dessert. This is done so that the tea vessel, heated up by the hot water, can be held comfortably. Affluent people have very carefully carved or also painted and lacquered coconuts. Others I saw had cups and straws nicely made from silver and, instead of napkins, little plates of the same metal.

I was told that this drink had been introduced from the Spanish possessions and had been in general use for a long time.

Instead of guns and firearms, the inhabitants use a kind of bow (*Betocca*). They do not shoot arrows, but small stones or hardened balls of clay. It is surprising how accurately even the smallest boys can use these weapons. They can kill just as well at considerable distances as we can with our firearms. They are not just play things for the boys. I was told that there were experienced archers who always brought home from the hunt as many large birds as clay balls they had taken with them. I did not find this exaggerated and all the more probable since the small boys who often accompanied me on

---

*Judging by the texture of the leaves, it is probably *Ilex* and perhaps somewhat similar to *Ilex vomitoria* (Paraguay tea).[6]

excursions shot with the greatest accuracy. I watched a ten-year-old boy on my request shoot at a little butterfly sitting on a flower about six paces away so forcefully that its body and wings immediately burst into a thousand pieces. I observed another one who ripped an orange, which had been pointed out to him, by its stem from a tree with one shot and also killed several hummingbirds hovering at flowers in this fashion. Since in Brazil a good gun counts as an expensive, valuable import from Europe and gunpowder cannot be bought even with money, this method of hunting is all the more important. From a natural historical and especially an ornithological point of view, this method should be more generally used. All birds, including the smallest hummingbirds, shot for me in that manner were not damaged in the least but rather killed by blow of the clay ball.

Another custom practiced all over the country is to wash one's feet with warm water every evening before going to bed. Both sexes from the wealthiest landowners in the most splendid houses to the lowliest slaves in the poorest huts observe this custom. The only difference is that the slaves have to wash first the feet of the fathers of the house and their masters and last of all their own. The main reason for this custom is caused by the fact that the common man frequently goes barefoot. Day laborers and slaves returning home in the evening, tired out from the day's work and covered with sweat and dirt, necessarily seek refreshment and strength in this custom and protection, especially from the effects of harmful, noxious insects which have fastened themselves to or buried themselves under the skin. For example, sand fleas (*Pulex penetrans*), which make themselves at home in careless or dirty people who go barefoot and often cause chronic abscesses on the feet, are not uncommon here.

In Villa Nossa Senhora do Desterro we were struck by the long fingernails, especially on the thumb, worn as decorations by higher class people. Here, as in many places in the East Indies, this is a sign of wealth. It indicates that these people do little or no work with their hands.

In our European cities we ride in luxurious coaches for state inspections or visits and to celebrate marriages or baptisms. In the small towns of the New World on such occasions, they use a kind of sedan chair called *cadeirinhas* (little chairs), in which the wealthy have themselves carried very majestically by their Negro slaves. Unlike ours, these sedan chairs are not closed in with glass windows and doors but resemble an armchair with a fixed, straight back and a bright canopy, usually scarlet red bordered by a rich gold fringe. When the curtains are left open, they resemble a prince's throne.

We had the pleasure of celebrating New Year's 1804 there and of taking part in the entertainment accompanying the occasion. Negro slaves, who are forced to work hard the whole year, are permitted several days of freedom solely at the New Year. They enjoy themselves in their own way by practicing once again their national dances during this time. They are very interesting to watch. Even though I can at the most give an imperfect description of these dances, I will try to describe at least several of these scenes.

Usually the Negro slaves reel in the streets very impetuously and noisily. That time, however, it rained so much that they were forced to celebrate their bacchanal in several miserable huts, in public taverns and bars. The dance was easy to find in the place because the music and shouts of the dancers could be heard from a distance. I say music, even though I could not hear a single one of our European wind or string instruments, not even a bagpipe. A monotonous shouting, a wild, loud, yet measured, sort of drumming, cymbals clanging and clattering, a rattling and clapping of hands announced from afar where the assembly was. Upon entering that hall of joy, the evil smelling cloud streaming at us from the many wildly dancing and jumping Negroes sweating heavily in the confined space sufficed to satisfy the curiosity of most of us, or rather to scare it away. If, however, one overcame his aversion and approached somewhat closer he had the pleasure of seeing African aborigines dancing in America. The king or leader of the dancing horde stood out from the rest by virtue of this body size, height and appearance. As a hero of his people, he led those gathered in a circle around him. Instead of a steel blue helmet, his head was ornamented with shiny gold paper and colorful feathers. Instead of an iron breastplate, little mirrors, gold fringes and silver spangles glittered from his body. Quantities of suns and stars made of gold and silver paper had been fastened all over him. The hero held a cane about two fuss long in his left hand, decorated with many notches placed close together. He continually rasped a little stick down it with his right hand. The rest of the dancing chorus had similar little canes, rattles and bells — in short all kinds of sound-making instruments. Instead of musicians, several Negroes sat in a corner on the ground beating with their hands on an ox hide stretched over a hollow tree trunk. This was a drum. Most of those present at the ball were almost without any covering except for loincloths or half-breeches and decorated with many bright feathers, silken ribbons and diadems made of gold paper. Several wore masks, others had smeared themselves horribly and frightfully with red, white and other contrasting colors. Negroes and Negresses, as already mentioned, had formed a circle around their leader. Then, more or less, depending upon how agile they thought themselves, they would do solo dances in the middle. In doing so they made the strangest and most unusual movements. The rest sang or rather screamed several incomprehensible African songs in accompaniment. They moved their hips and pelvic bones unbelievably fast in a horizontal circular motion. The upper part of the body seemed to stand still and at the same time to be balanced on the furiously moving part below. Similarly, they shook their necks, shoulders and shoulder and back muscles in such a indescribable way that they seemed to have every individual muscle under control. A half-naked Negress displayed the greatest agility. She united an extraordinary speed with the most vigorous muscle and hip motions, while moving her feet in the most unnatural manner. In addition, distortions of the facial muscles, blowing up of the cheeks and other horrible gestures, contributed an essential part to the completeness of the dance.

Many of the shadings in the colors smeared on those black bodies caused by their dripping sweat should be seen rather than described in words. The main object of the dance is to present the typical events of life, for example, catching fish, hunting, war, etc. They are represented with so much fidelity that they could offer our European ballet dancers suitable new material for the better presentation of similar subjects. If we take into account the warmth of the climate and the numbers of human beings closed up in a small room, we can easily imagine that their bodies, overheated by such unnatural exertion, nearly dissolved in sweat. All the more, this makes us have to admire the length of the dances, which often continued for an entire hour.

In the night before the feast of Epiphany, it is the custom for a lover to serenade his beloved and a friend to serenade his friend, in short, for each to serenade the other. We did not know about this custom and were suddenly awakened in the quiet of the midnight hour by the soft, sweet harmony of melodious songs accompanied by flutes and guitars. Everyone knows the effect of enchanting music, especially in the night. It is superfluous to describe the pleasant impression made by the languishing, charming transitions of sounds in minor keys upon our ears, half overcome with sleep. Only the next morning did we hear that this was a sign of the goodwill and friendship we had acquired among many of the inhabitants there during our stay.

It was a very unexpected pleasure for me to learn from the governor that there was someone who had been catching insects here for many years. I sought to take advantage of this rare and favorable opportunity by asking the governor to introduce me to the man. The problem, however, was that he was not on the island itself, but lived on the mainland of America about one German mile away, and his exact place of residence was not known for certain. The governor sent out people to look for him. Several days later I had the pleasure of his visit. The first thing I did was to ask him to show me the area richest in insects and to take me along on some of his excursions. He immediately offered to do this, in a friendly and eager manner.*

On the same afternoon on which I became acquainted with this man, I accepted his invitation and left Villa Nossa Senhora do Desterro and followed him to the mainland on the other side of the straits. We arrived at his home about five o'clock in the evening.

He and his family lived in a small house in a charming and fertile spot several hundred paces from the shore. The considerable tract of land he owned provided him with the means to produce ample foodstuffs. Three slaves, eight cows, several pigs, chickens, ducks and turkeys made up his household. Several fine, alert dogs were delegated to guard them. His wife, an industrious woman and good at woman's work, was the head of a girls' school. She had the house full of young pupils. Upon entering, I saw young girls seated on straw mats spread on the ground. One was spinning, another sewing, a third knitting, a fourth learning to spell and read, a fifth making lace — in short, all were busy so that the whole scene left a very vivid impression upon my mind and filled me with the highest opinion of the industriousness and activity of my new companions. I was welcomed in the friendliest manner and treated in the customary way of the country and as well as the couple could.

Two grown daughters, quite well educated for their station, sang at the end of the day's activities at my request several pleasant and expressive arias. Even though they played no musical instruments, they accompanied their songs, rhythmically marking time by shaking a mussel shell with a little stone inside. They shook the shells so that the simple rattling sound, similar to Spanish castanets, produced a very nice effect.

---

*The name and address of this kind gentleman: Sr. Matheos Cardoso Caldeira, nos carreiros, Freguesia Sao José, Governo da Ilha St. Catharina.

After this pleasant entertainment, they excused themselves for a short time. Cheerfully the one brought me some figs, the other some flowers which she had just picked in the nearby garden. Their demeanor was replete with rural innocence full of charm. It was a beautiful moonlight evening. Their father suggested we take a short walk to the nearby seashore. I accepted with all the more pleasure because we were accompanied by both daughters.

Upon our return we found an excellent supper waiting which the mother had been preparing in the meantime. Cooked bananas,* which I ate for the first time prepared this way, tasted very good. The evening passed very pleasantly. Our larger excursion was set for very early the following morning.

Before going to bed, a slave, according to the custom mentioned above, brought me a warm footbath to my bed. As soon as I put my feet into the water, the man washed, rubbed and massaged them so that, I have to admit, this treatment was so extraordinarily soothing that, on that day and in the following days, I found its use each time refreshing and pleasant. During this pleasant ritual, I remembered the ailing Forster[7] who sincerely claimed that the best means to return elasticity to his tired, weary muscles was to have the daughter of his host, who surpassed all Tahitian beauties in graceful demeanor, light color and pleasant facial features, gently rub his arms and thighs with her soft hands, as well as gently massaging his muscles between her fingers.** I readily admit that I would very gladly and with pleasure rather have the daughter of my host perform this ritual than a Negro slave. The effect of the treatment is little different from that of animal magnetism.

At daybreak the following morning, after a good breakfast of bananas and milk (because I had turned down coffee), we began our natural history walk. We went hardly a German mile from the house and returned long before evening with a large number of insects and

---

*The banana, *Musa sapientum* and several other types, is a fruit only found in warm climes. It can be had all year round. It is a benevolent gift of nature, a good tasting, healthy and nourishing food, whose taste can best be compared to a mixture of flour, sugar, butter and eggs. It can be eaten raw or simply cooked in water or cooked and fried in butter, since they then acquire completely the taste of a good omelette or pancake.

**See *Geschichte der Seereisen und Entdeckungen im Südmeer* [The History of the Voyages and Discoveries in the South Seas] by Georg Forster. Berlin, 1778, vol. 4, part 1, p. 266.

butterflies. For my part I caught everything that crossed my path. I filled four rather large catch boxes, carried by a small boy, full of the most excellent and, at home, rarest of butterflies and insects. My companion had only one box full, captured more discriminatingly. After our return and after I had refreshed myself with food and drink, I expressed the desire to return that same evening to Villa Nossa Senhora do Desterro because I had no empty catch boxes for a future excursion. Then I asked my friendly host to arrange this for me. He immediately sent one of his slaves to the shore and had his own canoe prepared to take me across. Indeed, he accompanied me to the island even though he had no immediate business there.

Instead of describing the several excursions we undertook together, I will only mention one to the mountains Sertão das picadas and one to the large stream Ribeirao about two and one-half German miles inland. My guide assured me these were the principal habitats of rarer and larger butterflies, among them especially the *Papil. Adonis Crameri*, *Pap. Epistrophus Weber.*, *Pap. Helenor. Cram.*, *P. Lysimnia*, *P. Februa Hoffmanseggi*, *P. Thoas*, *P. Archidamas*, and many others awakened my curiosity.

We would set out before daybreak. A bright Portuguese lad, whom I took along, carried the collection boxes and necessary refreshments. I carried a trap, a net, botany and insect boxes, pins, knives and other tools. Hardly had I put the areas behind my back I already knew along the nearby sea coast, which had up to then provided such a rich harvest, and reached unknown woods than with every step forward I was continually surprised and stared, charmed and sighing deeply, at the multitude of new objects before me.

Bewitched and drunken with joy by the beauties of nature, I had us stop often to let me take a few minutes delight in them. My companion could not understand how it was possible for his common, everyday objects, the variety and growth of tree trunks crowned with flowers, the fragrance in the air, the new shapes and colors of fungi, the size and wonderful variety of the ferns,* could cause such joyous amazement in me. Instead of cocoa and banana trees, instead of coffee, sugar, rice and cotton fields, instead of tapioca and ground nut

*I could not get more than the names of them. To obtain leaves of the trees we would have had to chop down every single tree. A botanist, who will have to stay there not just days and weeks but years, will undertake excursions with ax and hatchet and be rewarded by the discovery of quantities of new genera and species of plants.

(manduni) fields, whose sight along the coast had enchanted me, I now saw dark, richly shadowed, impenetrable woods: *Beroba*, *Oleo*, *Figueira*, *Garabisi*, *Garaberi*, *Garaxuba*, *Garabrura*, *Cedra*, etc.,* all of them the tallest, thickest and most slender trees my eyes have ever viewed. The tall trunks, whose crowns were full of shadows and whose branches were covered with flowers and fruits, made a very spontaneous impression upon me, just as did the various vines, *Bouchinia*, *Aristolochia* and other plants winding their way up to the towering tops of these magnificent trees, from which hang thousands of varieties of parasitic plants forming, first here and then there, groups of the most beautiful garlands.

Luxuriant nature, far exceeding the highest idea of her fertility, of her variability of colors and beauty in the type of trees, of her imaginable charms and riches, also animates the woods with an unending variety of various creatures; mammals, birds, insects and amphibians, which we Europeans only rarely or never get to see in large natural history collections either stuffed or in spirits, excited my attention continually and vivaciously.

To my right, parrots in all kinds of sizes and colors shyly and quickly flew past, screaming loudly. To my left, a large-billed, red- and yellow-breasted toucan (*Ramphastos*), unaware of any danger, was eating the fruit of a nearby tree I had never seen before. Deeper in the woods arose the cries and roars of monkeys. At my feet were the opening to the dens of armadillos (*Tatu Dasypus Linn.*), then a bright butterfly larger than a bird (for example, *Pap. Idomeneus*) fluttered majestically from flower to flower, then again a magnificently beautiful hummingbird whirring as it sucked sweet honey from the fragrant smelling flowers. Here a poisonous snake gliding straight across the small footpath frightened the foreign hiker, while the heavenly harmony of the colorful bird songs filled his ears and heart with ecstasy and delight. Wandering through such pictures and similar ones that seemed to me like dreams, we reached the ridge of a steep hill made of damp, red argillaceous earth. Suddenly, I was surprised anew by the view of a wide, open valley before me. We exchanged the cooling shade of the forest trees for an open area subjected to the burning rays of the sun. We had been hiking around for several hours when our stomachs demanded tribute. Along the path we had taken for more

---

*See *Plantes recueillies pendant le voyage des Russes autour du monde par Langsdorff et Fischer* [Plants collected during the Russian Voyage around the World by Langsdorff and Fischer], *Fol. avec des Figures* [Fol. with pictures], Tübingen: Cotta, 1810.

than a German mile, we had only seen up to then one single miserable little hut. We asked its inhabitants in vain for some milk or some other refreshments. Farther down the valley into which we were ascending, we came upon another small hut around ten o'clock. There we found no European kitchen, but indeed an excellent watermelon, which they gladly and hospitably gave us for nothing, even though it was the only one in the hut, along with a gourd full of tapioca meal. Our meal was completed with a swallow of brandy and a piece of bread which we had brought along as provisions. At our departure we gave our hosts, who wanted no payment for their refreshments, a small loaf of bread which they gratefully accepted, since the common man rarely has bread but always eats instead meal from mandioca.

Sufficiently fortified, we took up our hike again and pushed farther into the valley. When we reached the goal of our trip for that day, the stream Ribeirao, my companion asked me to take off my boots and stockings and hide them in a nearby bush and then follow him. Even though I did not like his suggestion very much because I had fresh memories of poisonous snakes, I had no other choice to satisfy my curiosity, since it was impossible to penetrate into the thickest and most impenetrable swampy woods any other way than by following the stream winding through it. Boots and stockings were left in nearby bushes awaiting our return. We then waded along up to our knees in the crystal clear stream. We had hardly gone ten steps when sparkling butterflies of the most beautiful colors appeared in indescribable swarms. My companion became totally occupied with pinning my captured heroes. Since it was not our intention to collect objects in such difficult and distant places which we also could collect near the sea coast, though granted neither so easily nor in such quantities, we turned to our primary goal. Like hunters lying in wait along a woodland path, we waited with extended nets a short distance from each other for brilliant, rarer butterflies to appear. Very soon beautiful *Adonis* and *P. Epistrophus Weberi* appeared. The former, the epitome of all butterflies, climbed rapidly high into the air. Their satin or rather shiny metallic wings flashed over wide distances. The latter, mocking the frivolousness and arrogance of the others, hovered slowly and majestically over the stream's crystal waves.

The sun burned oppressively hot from almost straight above the parts in our hair while our bare feet were first subjected to the cool water of the woodland stream and then the hot puddles left from overflow and the swamp.

My guide was more used to this manner of capturing butterflies than I. After we had spent several long, grueling hours that way, I had the most painful of feet. While going barefoot and wading in the stream, the sun had burned them badly and the hot water in the puddles had scalded them red at the same time, so that in their infected condition they began to swell considerably. We had gone there intending to spend the following day also in that rich area. I had to give up the idea because I was afraid that I would not be able to walk the next morning. We immediately turned back. The manifold beauty of the many new objects I would be able to admire once again softened my pain. Despite the ever increasing swelling of my feet, I turned back happy and richly rewarded and late in the evening reached the home of my guide, whose guidance that day had made it one of the most remarkable of my entire stay there.

The country folk are always hospitable, friendly and obliging. Every family I approached was most generous in offering me some of their food to quiet my hunger. Once in a while I was able to get a chicken, some eggs, milk, fish or also bananas, oranges and watermelons. At other times I had to be satisfied with tapioca and dried beans. I found confirmation in the old adage that hunger is the best cook.

Since at that time of year it rains almost daily, sometimes a thunderstorm or shower overran me and soaked me to the skin so that I had to seek roof and refuge in the nearest hut. The people, voluntarily and without being asked, offered me a change of clothing, hurriedly washed any dirty garments and dried them while offering me food for refreshment and comfort. Sometimes when I could not reach the ship or my assigned quarters in Villa Nossa Senhora do Desterro before dark, I was always offered very clean quarters for the night, sometimes better sometimes worse, depending upon the circumstances of the people. Frequently they consisted of one or two thin straw mats spread on the earth and covered with a clean blanket and a soft pillow in a light cotton case, or instead of that, another blanket. As hard and as uncomfortable as such a bed was at first, I soon got used to it. These opportunities showed me how very little man really needs and how much he is spoiled by higher culture and luxury, for the simple straw mat, a bed I was at first not used to and from which I would get up feeling as dashed to pieces as when I had gone to bed, indeed often came to strengthen and refresh my tired limbs.

The same straw mat that serves as a bed, or a similar one, is spread out in the middle of the room at meal times and covered by a table cloth. The entire family lies down around it, the men stretched out with one arm usually supported by a little pillow, the women cross-legged in Oriental fashion, approximately in the same way tailors like to sit among us. The use of chairs in the country is almost as little known as the use of tables. Instead of the former, one sometimes sees a kind of small footstool made of two small boards whose seat is not horizontal but angular.

I have previously mentioned the mandioca root (*Jatropha manihot Linn.*) which the common man generally eats instead of bread. At this point I wish to note how it is eaten there. One-half of a small, dried gourd shell filled with the meal, along with several wooden spoons, is brought to the table. Instead of bread, it is either eaten alone or mixed with the food on the plate. In Nossa Senhora do Desterro I was struck by the sight of an upper class lady, who, as is customary there and without thinking she might be doing something impolite, mixed this meal made from roots with the food upon her plate and then raised it to her mouth with her fingers.

The dexterity of people who eat mandioca dry instead of bread is worthy of not a little admiration. Using their fingers or spoons, they can deftly throw the kernels into their mouths from a considerable distance without a single kernel falling outside. The custom of eating with the fingers causes another one. After every meal, water is brought so that all can wash their hands and mouths. I observed this custom without exception even in the most miserable of peasant huts and even when knives and forks were being used and not the hands.

The peasants' houses are small and comfortably furnished, usually situated in beautiful, pleasant spots. Inside they usually have a living room, one or two other rooms and a kitchen. Often there is a special building nearby containing a small room which serves the Negro slaves as place of residence and sleeping quarters. Among well-off landowners the main room has a wooden floor; among the poor this is not the case. Only a few homes have tile roofs: the large majority are covered with palm leaves from a kind of palm tree probably as of yet unidentified. There are few or absolutely no villages as we know them. The houses stand by themselves with greater or lesser distances between them. Every countryman has his possessions and fields around his hut. Most of the houses along the sea coast stand in orange groves surrounded by coffee, banana and cotton plantations. Near every hut one usually finds a crystal spring shaded by orange trees.

The small canoes, made from a single tree and used by the inhabitants for fishing and water communication, are usually 24 to 32 fuss long and about three fuss wide. They are pulled up and left lying along the riverbank unattended and not tied down, protected by a roof from rain and the sun's rays. All over I was met by harmony, well-being and hospitality.

Rarely are these people only knowledgeable in one handicraft. Each one, like a true cosmopolitan, is his own craftsman. They slaughter their animals themselves, are carpenters, joiners, tailors, fishermen, hunters, etc., and many, among other occupations, are also weavers.

Naturally one cannot expect much in the areas of the arts, science and public institutions. Tools, mechanical instruments and implements used in the household and in agriculture are poor and wanting. All of the inhabitants groan under the pressure of a kind of government whose *raison d'etre* is not to enlighten its subjects, so that they, as a result, are not powerful enough to want to offer resistance to the small Portuguese kingdom and throw off its oppressive yoke.

The activities and industry of anyone, who through assiduity tries to distinguish himself from the rest of his fellow citizens, have the greatest obstacles thrown in the way instead of help and encouragement. This was the case, for example, of a man who wanted to start an indigo factory, and with this in mind, had established a large indigo plantation, which, due to lack of governmental support, fell to ruin.

The manner of making brandy and the distilling equipment, which I did not personally see, must be very wanting, since the rum is quite bad. Rice, as far as I know, is not even used for producing arrack. Both could and should be used to produce a superabundance of goods excellent enough for export. Indeed, brandy is even imported from Lisbon and sold under the name of *aqua ardente do reino*.

For separating cotton from its seeds, they use a very inconvenient machine, which needs two people to turn two cylinders rotating in opposite directions.

Weaving looms are in their infancy and the mills unsatisfactory. With so many imperfections I have to mention the very excellent pottery produced in Nossa Senhora do Desterro. Fine red and black clay is found in quantities and processed very well. Part of the pottery is even shipped to Rio Grande and Rio Janeiro. There is also a very good tile works.

I have no particular information about the sugar works. Whaling and train oil works in the province desire special attention and mention.

Formerly they were leased to a company as a monopoly and were very profitable. In recent years, however, the government itself has taken them over. Perhaps the lessor, due to the yearly decrease in the number of whales, found no great advantage in continuing; perhaps the government also hoped, by taking over, to increase the gains. Be that as it may, the whaling and train oil works are very extensive and feed several thousand souls, especially many Negro slaves, who have to earn their daily bread the whole year by doing the hardest of work.

The various establishments for whaling from south to north are:

1) Armação da baleia da freguesia de villa nova, i.e., the whaling warehouse in the parish of Villa nova.

2) Armação de Garopaba.

3) Armação de baleias na ilha. A warehouse on the southeastern side of the Island of St. Catharina.

4) Armação do baleias na entrada. A warehouse at the northern entrance to the straits.

5) Armação de rio do Gravato. A warehouse on the River Gravata.

Warehouse number four at the northwestern point of the Island was the closest to our anchorage. Therefore, some of my fellow travelers and I took the opportunity to visit it. In the preceding winter of 1803, only ten sperm whales (*Physeter macrocephalus Linn.*) were taken. The overseer assured me that no other species of whale had ever been taken there. The largest one according to him was 35 fuss long; most of them were seldom more than 24 fuss long. Whaling here is very easy and comfortable. Two and two boats are sent out to hunt in the morning. They return to the works in the evening. They never go out farther than the nearby Island of Alvoredo. Sometimes the whales even come into the straits. When the works were first established, they caught up to 400 sperm whales in a winter; the largest number is said to have been 500. The fact that they were able to boil up such numbers in one single winter gives an idea of the numbers of kettles, stoves and storage containers found there. The earnings of a single works from 500 whales is about 346,000 *reichstaler* [imperial dollars]. Every year the number of whales taken, and, thus, the earnings, have been decreasing, especially since the English and the speculative heads of the United American Free States have begun to hunt in the area, in particular around the Falkland Islands. Can one reason for the decrease in the number of whales taken be due to the fact that the management has passed from private hands into those of the state? Everyone knows how active individual merchants are is seeking their own advantage and how indifferently the same institutions are often run, if with good pay, the choice of directors unhappily falls to people who are more interested in the correct payment of their salaries than the advantage they could and should bring about for the government.

In addition to the five warehouses mentioned above, there are also several along the Brazilian coast south of the Rio Grande. I was unable, however, to ascertain the number.

The following remarks about medicine are of course only general, cursory observations. No fair judge expects to obtain detailed histories of diseases which often have very exact connections with the climate, economy, style of life, customs and habits of the country. A foreigner staying only a few days or weeks in a place cannot immediately win the confidence of the inhabitants, who unfortunately only all too often hide or distort the truth. For this reason I confine myself to the following small number of facts.

The medical authority for the Island and the entire province is the regimental surgeon, who lives in Nossa Senhora do Desterro and is in charge of two hospitals there, i.e., a military and a civilian hospital. Despite their being well situated and rather roomy, if putrid fever and other malignant diseases were unfortunately to break out, then they suffer from the same mistake that is found in most European hospitals that too many sick people are crowded together in a relatively small room. Thus, through the influence of the contaminated air, the sick infect each other. In one ward of the military hospital, hardly big enough for fifty beds, they were crammed together so that eighty beds fit. The great cleanliness which I had almost always found all over among the natives was missing where it was most necessary. Even though the province is generally praised for being very healthy, a few years ago there was an infectious disease which killed several thousand people. According to the information I could collect about it, it seemed to have been dysentery connected with putrid fever. The loss of many thousands is considerable and irreplaceable for a small colony with so few people. Nevertheless, the Portuguese government was not sufficiently moved to send a scientifically trained doctor.

The only remedies used by doctors there are vomiting, purging and bleeding. The common man frequently uses home remedies which often are just as damaging as bad medical help. In Nossa Senhora do

Desterro there are three houses called apothecaries whose owners claim to have a supply of medicine. Not even homegrown medicinal products were in them. I asked for a single *unze* of copaiva balsam or ricinusol in vain. Smallpox is a dreaded and devastating disease here. Whenever a smallpox epidemic breaks out, it takes the lives of many thousands and is especially dangerous for the Negro slaves. Nothing is known about vaccination for smallpox and even less about the God-given gift of protective pox.

As is the case in all warmer climates, one finds all kinds of skin diseases and in many forms and modifications. Scabies and scabies-like rashes are found in the distinguished families and in almost every peasant's home. They do not, however, seem to be passed on by contact, since none of our crew became infected.

The venereal poison is also very widely prevalent. As in all warm climates, the sex drive awakens very early there. Twelve- and thirteen-year-old boys, who, in order to gratify their sensual needs, use their slaves and other dissolute prostitutes, skulk around with that terrible disease.

A common pest here is *Bicho dos pés* (*Pulex penetrans Linn.*) or the sand flea. It is a small insect that eats into the skin and flesh of people going barefoot. It makes its presence known by an itching, stabbing pain and sometimes chronic sores on the feet. The slaves doing field work barefoot are the main ones subjected to this pest. Most of our traveling companions who went about in thin silk stockings or sometimes barefoot became infected. In two cases the itching pain only appeared weeks later after we had left Brazil and had already sailed around Cape Horn. If this little animal, which immediately builds a nest under the flesh and even soon multiplies, is dug out like a splinter, no bad results can be expected.

It is peculiar that most of the women there had dead and rotten teeth, since native Portuguese are especially characterized by their beauty. Many fourteen- to sixteen-year-old girls had one or more front teeth missing. Is mandioca meal, the most common food here, possibly a cause? For headaches a red clay dampened with water is used. It is smeared on the forehead and temples. A Negro's face painted in this fashion, as I often observed, is a very funny sight.

There is even less possibility of help from a trained midwife than from a trained doctor. Help at delivery is given by a woman who has already given birth several times or by a girlfriend. I concluded from the stories of several credible housewives that abnormal births are not unusual and that many women die from the resulting hemorrhages, indeed, that there are far more unnatural and difficult deliveries than have been observed in other warmer climates. In various places separated by a distance from each other, I brought the subject up. Every housewife could tell me immediately about several examples of unfortunate deliveries. By the way, the fertility of the women, as in Portugal and several provinces in Spain, is very high. It is absolutely not uncommon to find families with fifteen to twenty children. All of the streets are filled with them. The population of Brazil is increasing rapidly. Considering the fact, as explained above, that the people here can provide themselves with a rich basis for life without working very hard and have no other more important business than to fulfill their conjugal duties, thus, this and the warm climate may be the main reason for such large families. The children are fed bananas from earliest childhood. Many mothers, however, try to nurse their children and keep their milk as long as possible. That is why I often saw three- and four-year-old children nursing. This was done, as several women admitted, for the sole purpose of preventing an increase in the size of the family, since it is a known fact from experience that as long as a mother nurses her baby there is usually little hope that another one will follow.

Since true natural history has been excluded from descriptions of our voyage, I will only relate several things I believe are of general interest.

As charming as the beautiful woods are, as enchanting as the countryside is, which I have described earlier, there are quantities of poisonous snakes and carnivorous animals that make walks dangerous for the hiker.

The Cobra Coral (coral snake) and the *xiraracca* (schiraraka) are among the particularly dangerous ones. Whenever inhabitants talk about them, they usually add with fear and terror — certain death. These snakes move very slowly by propelling themselves forward with motions to the side in the manner of our blind-worm (*Anguis fragilis Linn.*). In open fields and on the shore, it is easy to get out of their way or to kill them. I often did this myself. They usually try to escape when a human approaches. Inhabitants are only in danger of being bitten when cutting wood barefoot in the thick, impenetrable forests and stepping on one of them hidden in the thick underbrush. Examples of their having caused deaths are not rare. The usual results of a bite are: sudden swelling of the entire body, blood streaming from the nose, ears, eyes and finger tips. They seldom are longer than one and one-half *ells*. The xiraracca is also considered very poisonous. Many people have died from its bite, but it is not totally as fatal as the bite of the former. They sometimes obtain a length of 2 to 3 ells.

When I asked if an antidote was known, I was told that various people could give a blessing and that this was the best antidote. Rational people help a great deal by cauterizing the wound.

Often in the evening, especially in low damp areas, there are places of two to fifteen paces in circumference filled with a true musk smell. I noticed this often and made inquiries each time. The general belief among the people is that the smell comes from xiraracca. If and in how far this may be true, I have to leave for future natural historians to describe on their trips. Perhaps nature warns people by this odor, just as the highly poisonous rattlesnake makes its presence known with its rattle. I myself killed several xiraraccas and skinned them without ever being aware of the otherwise penetrating odor ascribed to them. Why should the odor only be present in the evening and not just as well during the day? It is my opinion that the answer lies somewhere else than in the vicinity of the xiraracca.

The bird spider *Araa caranguexeira* (*Aranea avicularia Linn.*) is common all over. Councilor Tilesius drew a very accurate picture of one in nature. They are called bird spiders because it is claimed that they sometimes attack and eat hummingbirds. This rumor is absolutely false.

These spiders spin no web but rather live in burrows in the earth which they only leave — at the most a step away — when the sun is shining very warmly. They live almost like crabs (pocket crabs). That is the source of their Portuguese name *caranguexeira*, i.e, crab spider. I myself caught three and fourteen others were brought to me. Each time I asked for exact information about their way of life and food. Whenever I asked country people if these spiders sometimes ate hummingbirds, they always answered no while smiling. They assured me that they ate nothing but all kinds of insects, for example, large flies, ants, bees, wasps, bugs, etc. My own observations confirmed that. The construction and characteristics of the mouth totally contradict the old prejudice. They are indeed true sucking instruments. At the most they could only suck the blood of such animals. Hummingbirds fly rapidly from one flower to the next. How are a bird in the air and a spider on the ground to get together? The crab spider is in addition slow and rather sluggish of movement. For this reason it would be impossible for them to catch a fast flying hummingbird. It is hard to explain the origin of the idea that this spider's main source of food is a bird. Its bite is neither dangerous nor fatal, but can, however, cause a bad infection. The hair covering its entire body falls off at the slightest touch and causes an unbearable itching and stabbing pain under the skin, as I discovered various times when preparing them for preservations. The spider seems to use very little muscle power against enemy attack. Like many other animals, plants and insects, it is not found on St. Catharina but frequently, however, on the mainland, especially in an area *os barreiros* that is heavily planted with Turkey wheat.[8]

At first, and during the summer, only a few small butterflies of various kinds appeared; the largest and most beautiful appeared only after the hottest period was past. Even though I was very satisfied with the collection I made there, my Portuguese guide, Sr. Caldeira, told me it was no comparison to the beauty of the species which came out in February and March, and, indeed, the last days of our stay were the most interesting for capturing butterflies. The nature and way of life of these magnificent butterflies is in many ways as different from ours as is the climate. They rise up into the air in part in light, quick flight and flutter around the flowers of tall trees, quite shy and restless. They settle down so seldom on flowers that I had to catch them in flight most of the time. If I tried to use the typical European butterfly net, I would return home for sure not very satisfied. Large nets fastened to long, light poles are utterly necessary. I remembered a butterfly net I had seen at Mr. Latham's in London several years before and hurriedly had a similar one made that served excellently. On my excursions I was most surprised to observe a particular species (*P. N. Februa Hoffmanseggi*) which made a very loud, clear clapping sound (probably with its wings) when it flew away from a tree or a male followed a female. It lives in thick orange groves, lands with spread wings on the trunks and is hard to recognize because of its color being similar to the tree trunk. If one approaches, it flies up with a clapping noise while one is still far away. *P. E. T. Archidamas* is a butterfly that gives off a gentle, not penetrating, but rather, if I may say so, honey-sweet, musky odor. It lives on flowers, is hardy and tenacious, and flies high and fast.

I became aware of another remarkable phenomenon with a butterfly (which I took for *P. Catilina Crameri*). From a special opening in its breast plate, it emitted a foam-like moisture, probably to ward off the attack of its enemies, something like the caterpillar of the *P. Machaon* does.

Several different species of the most common butterflies — *P. Dan. Philea*, *D. Trite*, *D. Alemeone*, *D. Sennae*, *D. Eubule*, *D. Argante* and others — live together in great numbers, by the hundreds, indeed by the thousands. Their favorite spots are in low, sandy and, at the same time, damp areas near rivers and streams where they collect in swarms on the damp sand. When I caught one of these butterflies, pinned it, stuck the pin in the ground and stood quietly next to it, I was sure I could catch at least forty to fifty in less than an hour with the butterfly net.

The inhabitants have enemies we do not know in Europe, not only on land but in the water. Near the Island of St. Catharina, around Alvoredo and the other nearby islands, there is supposed to be a large species of sepia called *Polvo*. Fishermen told me they sometimes were larger than a man and had endangered lives by embracing bathers or people fishing, so that they could not free themselves unless someone came to their rescue by chopping the body of the animal into pieces; otherwise, death was inevitable. I admit that a very large sepia could be dangerous to humans in this manner, but that there is a species that has encircled three-masted ships and sunk them is certainly a fairy tale, which recently indeed has been warmed up again in France.*

Few fish were taken to the market during our stay, probably mainly because the burning heat at that time of year causes them to spoil very quickly. In particular I saw *Coryphaena hippurus*, *Silurus Bagre*, *Scomber Trachurus*, *Squalus Zygaena*, *Trichurus Cepturus*, *Salius argentinus*, *Scomber Pelamys*, several species of *Chaetodon* and *Fetraodon*, *Sparus*, *Diodon* and many others. Councilor Tilesius has catalogued their names.

The large numbers of still unidentified animals, the observations of their life cycles in a stretch of heaven so distant from our own, the wealth and variety of the plant world could occupy hundreds of natural scientists for years. Our short stay and the minimal support which Councilor Tilesius and I received for natural historical undertakings and purchases forced us to be satisfied with the few things we had an opportunity to obtain using our own means.

**Histoire naturelle des mollusques* [Natural History of Mollusks] by Denys-Montfort, Paris, An. X. 8, Parts I-IV. See Part II, p. 256, Plate XXVI, *Le poulpe colossal* [colossal sepia].[9]

Notes

1. The Island of Atomeri — Anhatomirium.

2. "Twenty-five" indicates that Langsdorff means German miles. It can be assumed that where Langsdorff does not indicate otherwise he means German miles.

3. Franz Xaver von Zach (1754-1832) was an astronomer who published numerous papers about geographical subjects. He also was the editor of three valuable scientific journals.

The physicist and astronomer Johann Caspar Horner (1774-1834) was born in Zürich but studied in Göttingen. In 1798 he was planning to return home at the time of the French invasion of Switzerland, when Zach offered him employment and support for scientific research, and helped him enter the Russian service as an astronomer. He was named Privy Councilor and member of the Academy of Sciences. He returned to Zürich in 1809 and continued his work there.

4. Modern Florianopolis stands where Villa Nossa Senhora do Desterro once stood. It was renamed after General Floriano Peixoto, president of Brazil from November 1893 to November 1894.

5. Batatas — sweet potatoes.

6. Paraguay tea is also known as mate or yerba mate. It is a beverage steeped from the dried and ground leaves of Brazilian holly (*Ilex paraguayensis*).

7. Johann Georg Adam Forster (1754-1794) was born near Danzig. His father, Johann Reinhold Forster (1729-1798), was a pastor there. The family is saïd to be of Scottish extraction. In 1765 Empress Catherine commissioned his father to inspect the Russian colonies in the province of Saratov. He took his son along, thus giving the younger Forster an opportunity to learn Russian and the elements of scientific research. After a quarrel with the Russian government, the elder Forster obtained a professorship in England but later lost it, and he and his son had to earn a living from doing translations in London. They were then invited to accompany Cook on his second voyage. Georg Forster published *A Voyage round the World in His Britannic Majesty's Sloop Resolution commanded by Captain James Cook during the years 1772, 3, 4, and 5* (London: B. White, 1777), which was later translated into German. He based the work on his father's journal. In addition, he wrote what is considered some of the best travel and scientific literature of the 18th century, which influenced among others Humboldt, Goethe and Herder.

8. Turkey wheat: Indian corn, Guinea corn, Crimean wheat.

9. Pierre Denys de Montfort (born 1768), *Histoire naturelle, générale et particulière des mollusques, animaux sans vertèbres et à sang blanc. Ouvrage faisant suite aux Oeuvres de Leclerc de Buffon, et partie du Cours complet d'histoire naturelle rédigé par C. S. Sonini* (Paris: Impr. de F. Dufart, an X-XIII [1802-1805]).

Chapter 3

Departure from Brazil. Voyage around Cape Horn. Easter Island. Arrival at Nukahiva, one of the Washington Islands. First Impressions.

The ships were ready to sail again by the end of January. We all had refreshed ourselves from several weeks of eating the most excellent food. The crews of both ships were healthy. Captain von Krusenstern, who had his ship provided with a large store of all kinds of fresh provisions, gave everyone living in Villa Nossa Senhora do Desterro orders to go on board February 1st. Thus, we had to leave the richest and most beautiful country on earth. My memories of my stay in Brazil will remain unforgettable all my life.

On February 2nd the governor, who had been very hospitable during our stay, came to see us off. He came on board together with a large group of both sexes to wish us goodbye.

Captain von Krusenstern thought it necessary to hurry our departure from Brazil as much as possible, because the prospect of sailing around Cape Horn so late in the year was not the most delightful.

Admiral Anson's dreadful descriptions, the reminders of the great difficulties Captain Bligh, Wilson and others had to endure, and whose descriptions constituted our daily discussions, hovered in our minds, thus making the departure from Brazil even more painful.[1]

We were scheduled to leave on February 3rd. A storm from the north was raging so strongly that Captain von Krusenstern thought it advisable to remain in harbor and wait for more favorable weather conditions. On February 4th in the forenoon, the anchor was raised when a strong south wind arose. Toward evening both of the expedition's ships were under sail. The weather was overcast. It rained almost continually on that day and the following ones. A continuous south wind soon carried us away from the Brazilian coast. Using an east wind, we sailed very rapidly toward the south so that on February 9th we were already on a level with Rio de la Plata, in whose vicinity a little ship on the southeastern horizon caught our attention. It would have been senseless to pay for our curiosity by losing time; therefore, we continued on our way, taking advantage of the favorable wind. All kinds of new objects occupied and entertained us in that southern stretch of the heavens.

Flying fish, bonitos, porpoises or dolphins, dorados, tropical birds and other objects of warmer climes had now disappeared. We had albatrosses (*Diomedia exulans*), stormy petrels (*Procelaria*) and whales for daily company. At 40° S latitude we frequently saw seaweed (*Fucus*) of a special kind, even though we were 600 miles from the nearest land. On February 20th the *Neva*'s crew was left more than a little frightened, for the ship suddenly received such a strong blow that everyone on board thought that they had hit a rock or at least a sandbank. Alarmed, all of them ran on deck to find out what had happened but were quickly relieved to find out the whole thing had been caused by a dead or live whale.

Enjoying variable but mostly favorable weather up to then, we found ourselves on February 25th in the neighborhood of Staaten Land. The sight of that rough, uninhabited island, whose steep, pointed, rocky cliffs marked our southern horizon, gave us in clear skies many a change of scene. We saw Cape Sao Joao probably about 33 sea miles away. This headland, 63°47′ W longitude, has to be of utmost importance to every seafarer, because its location has been determined so exactly that the greatest difference among the best trained astronomers and seafarers is only a few minutes. Every merchant seafarer without instruments can use this Cape to establish his longitude and as a trustworthy landmark in order to correct his ship's calculations.* This is doubly important in an area where sailing is dangerous and where sailing safely around Cape Horn can frequently depend upon establishing the exact degree of longitude. The numbers of albatrosses and stormy petrels increased the farther south we sailed. The fountain-like spray of whales, which were sometimes taken at night for surf on some unidentified island, had become so common that we hardly paid attention to them anymore.

Now and again we saw large stretches or areas of the ocean marked from a great distance by their smooth surfaces and few move-

*Remember the American who was three degrees too far to the west.

ments of waves. These areas are caused by the oily, fatty parts cast into the water when whales breathe and blow and by their excrements. It is a known fact and remarkable how little oil is necessary to spread over an unbelievably large area of water. This is the basis for the suggestion (I think from Franklin) to pour oil on the water during a storm in order to quiet it.[2]

An almost continually favorable wind, with which we had sailed from St. Catharina so quickly to this location, enlivened our wishes and animated our dreams of sailing around that so dreaded Cape Horn in the most beautiful weather. This joy did not last very long. We had just barely sailed around Cape Sao Joao and reached the latitude of that infamous headland on the morning of February 26th, when a violent storm with fierce blasts of wind and hail and rain came up from the south-southwest, letting us know which regions we were sailing in.

We were so used to the warm climate and to a continually moderate temperature that we had seldom observed temperatures under 12° warmth until we arrived one noon at 54°12′ S latitude. On that day (the 25th) the thermometer in rain and storm fell to eight degrees warmth, which we all found very severe. On February 27th the weather cleared somewhat. At noon we took readings of 57°19′ S latitude and 5½° warmth. The waves from the previous day's storm were still rolling very high, making us and the swaying ship tired. The hope of a quieter sea, with which we had been flattering ourselves, soon came to naught, for on the 28th arose the most dreadful of fog, rain and hail storms accompanied by southwest winds. It lasted more than twenty-four hours until finally on March 1st the storm slackened when the wind shifted more to the north. During the whole thing, the water poured into the ship almost all over.

March 2nd was one of the most beautiful days we had experienced after so many in those southern latitudes. The reviving rays of the sun warmed us that day more than ever before. Since the continual fog, the rain and the unpleasant, melancholy weather had kept almost everyone who did not have to be on deck from breathing fresh air, everyone tried to take advantage of the break in the weather. For the first time in three days, the height of the sun was established. Our happiness was partially destroyed when we found out that we had only sailed southward during the period and not eastward at all.

Our most longed for wish, to get out of that cold, stormy region, finally seemed to be heard by a weak, northeasterly wind that arose in the afternoon and became so brisk toward evening that we sailed ten sea miles an hour to the west. On the morning of March 3rd, we had the pleasure of hearing from our excellent leader that we had sailed around Cape Horn. We conveyed to him our most heartfelt good wishes and deepest thanks.

Since February 17th, the thermometer had been showing usually from one and one-half to three and one-half degrees warmth. During the night of March 1st, it was only one degree above freezing.

The lowest point on the barometer came on February 28th during a storm at 28″5, and the highest point on March 2nd at 20″50.

We had just entered the South Seas when the northeasterly wind left us, and instead a not very favorable westerly wind was blowing, forcing us to head farther and farther south, so that on March 5th we found ourselves at 60°, the farthest south we reached on that voyage.

After sailing around Cape Horn, despite the fact that we were sailing farther south, it became warmer every day the farther to the west we went. From March 3rd to 13th, the thermometer was usually 4°, the lowest 3° and the highest 5° above the freezing point.

Calms, fog and sun accompanied us at first with moderate easterly winds and then from the 12th to the 16th with strong north-northwesterly winds.

On the night of the 17th, between three and seven o'clock, the mercury in the barometer fell from 29″10 to 28″45. This reading, which up to then we had not observed, made us once again afraid of a storm, the likes of which we had not yet experienced. Despite this, on the 18th we had the most beautiful of weather. It was almost calm, the sun shone warmly, and at noon the thermometer was 7° warmth in the shade. A number of albatrosses (*Diomedia exulans*) swam like geese around the ship (55°46′ S latitude, 89°51′ W longitude). We tried in vain to shoot several of them. As soon as a shot was fired, several of them tried to fly away. They could only rise up with great difficulty. At first they ran for a long stretch over the waves of the sea before they had gained enough wind to rise up on their narrow, long wings. This was a new and very desired scene for us.

Despite our frequent attempts to hook the birds as other seafarers have, we were not so fortunate and only snagged one. Captain

Bligh reports: "The method used by sailors to catch albatrosses is to attach bait one or two feet ahead of the hook. When the bird came to the bait they jerked the line suddenly, thus hooking the bird by the foot or in the body. Albatrosses and other birds caught in this way are then caged and fed and thus acquire a taste comparable to that of geese."*

The following week was pleasant. Until March 24th nothing especially noteworthy happened. On that day a very strong north-northwesterly wind arose which continued until the end of March. On that day in a thick fog, to our sorrow we became separated from our loyal companions up to then — on the *Neva*.

In such a case, our Commander von Krusenstern had designated to Captain Lisiansky Easter Island as a meeting point, so we now turned our attention to sailing there.

All of the previous seafarers' excellent descriptions of the island were pulled out and made us curious to compare the present conditions on the island with older ones in order to see if the presents La Pérouse had left there had helped improve the lot of the unfortunate inhabitants.**

The history of that island, lying totally isolated in the midst of the ocean, and the changes which it must have experienced in a short span of time are exceedingly remarkable. Special circumstances and contrary winds caused Captain von Krusenstern to change his mind about visiting the Island, even though we were only 500 sea miles to its east. Cook's, Forster's and La Pérouse's works give descriptions of more recent conditions on this island. I, however, cannot avoid quoting several places from the less known descriptions of its first discoverer, which show the exaggerated claims made back then.

Roggeween discovered the island on April 6, 1772.[4] Among other things a work describing his voyage states: "The savages do not go naked but are clothed in cotton garments. The most remarkable thing about them is their long ears which are considered great decorations. Some of them have such large holes that a hand could comfort-

---

*See Bligh's *Voyage to the South Seas*, p. 39.[3]

**These consisted of goats, sheep, pigs, lemon trees, cotton, Turkish wheat and all kinds of seeds. See *Voyage de la Pérouse*, etc., Part II, p. 94.

ably be stuck through them. Up to this point my story is believable because it contains nothing unusual. But now I have to add that all of these savages are *more than giant size*, the men are *more than twice the size and shape of the largest of our people*. Most of them are *12 fuss tall, so that we very easily* — who would not be surprised — *could have walked between the legs of these sons of Goliath without bending over*. All of them are well proportioned so that each individual could be called Hercules. None of the women are as tall as the men. None of them was over ten to eleven fuss tall. I suspect that most people reading this will not believe my story and will call it an invention or a fairy tale. Therefore, *I repeat again that I am writing down nothing but the pure truth* and that these people, after the most exact examination, are indeed bigger than normal, as I have written."* Mr. Forster says of the inhabitants of this island: "We did not find a single individual we could have called large; indeed, they were skinny. The women were small and delicately built."

That is how much earlier descriptions differ from newer ones. We all deeply regretted not being able to visit that small, interesting island.

In the meantime we had gradually sailed through stormy weather into warmer zones. On April 1st the wind subsided. During the following days, clear weather alternated with rain showers and calms. The thermometer climbed from 13° to 15°. On the 5th such a strong west wind arose that the ship rocked and rolled so much that the side of the ship was over three zolls in the water and the foresail took water. On the 17th we crossed the Tropic of Capricorn. After the tiresome, difficult trip up to then, we found the continuously warmer weather very enjoyable and bearable. A few days later (the 22nd) the trade winds set in (18°45′ S and 114°50′ W). We were approaching the Marquesas Islands in clear, beautiful weather with temperatures from 18° to 23°. At daybreak on May 6th, we saw the island, which Cook had named Hood's Island, some 30 sea miles in the distance.

The brief description of the new Marquesas or Washington Islands[5] left by Hergest, Marchand[6] and others seemed in general so advantageous and promising that Captain von Krusenstern expected to be able to acquire provisions in abundance on Nukahiva, the largest

---

*See *Twes Jaarige Ryse rond onde Wereld*, etc. [A two-year voyage around the world], Dordrecht by Joannes von Braam, 1728, 4, I.

one. Therefore, he chose it instead of nearby St. Christina which is otherwise often visited.

An unusual number of birds, large schools of little fish similar to herring (probably *Scomber scomber Linn.*) announced that land was nearby on May 5th.

At daybreak on the 6th, we had the pleasure of sighting Fetugu, or Hood's Island according to Cook. It resembles a steep rock rising out of the sea and appears to be, at least on the northern side, bare, desolate and infertile. At about seven o'clock, somewhat farther to the southwest, we saw the islands of Dominico and St. Pedro on the fog-covered horizon. Around nine o'clock Riou's Island (Uahuga) came into view. Its bare appearance and steep, abrupt, peak-shaped cliffs did not provide us with any great pleasure. We noted a quantity of birds. Large pods of porpoises (*Delphinus phocaena Linn.*) were swimming around the ship. In the evening at five o'clock, we caught sight through the fog of our desired port of call, the Island of Nukahiva. Almost at the same moment, rain showers and blasts of wind came up; therefore, with the arrival of darkness most of the sails were hauled down in order to keep the ship as far as possible from land in the rather strong wind and rain. Early in the morning, just as the fog dispersed, the Island of Nukahiva became visible again. The closer we came to it, the more our curiosity grew. We surveyed through our telescopes the quite close southeastern coast with the greatest of attention. Longingly, after our long, tiresome voyage, we sought those fertile, South Sea island valleys filled with excellent breadfruit trees, coconuts and bananas so highly praised by Cook, Forster and others. We were already imagining eating the most magnificent fruits, despite the fact we were only seeing bare, desolate cliffs. Here and there we could see some traces of cultivation and people in the deep, rocky valleys. During the night it rained heavily. Now a lot of waterfalls, some of which were at least a thousand fuss high, tumbled over the dark cliffs into the stormy surf and breakers, enlivening that dead, poorly blessed landscape — a scene that in our eyes put the island in an even more pleasing and agreeable light, since we had been suffering for several weeks from a great lack of water and had been placed on a daily water ration.

The land ahead of us was of moderate height. Steep, suddenly ragged, rocky masses alternated with pointed ones jutting up as well as slanting, bare masses of stone which were completely irregular, as if simply thrown there. We thought we were once again at Teneriffe.

In outward appearance it had been scorched in the same way. A first impression divulged a similar origin with all other volcanic islands. I only saw a bush or shrub here and there decorating the top of the dark, rocky pyramids or a tree clinging to an almost black rock barely covered with earth. The few gently rising hills were covered by a charming carpet of grass. As inviting as the landscape appeared to be in the beginning, it soon became boring to my eyes because of its eternal sameness, since it was enlivened neither by human beings nor by some kind of grazing herd on the slopes of a mountain.

The heavy surf caused by the foaming waves against the rocks gradually became more visible. We had already come so close to the shore that we were attempting with the utmost care to discover some inhabitants or a canoe, who, enticed by the novelty of a European ship, would be hurrying toward us from a nearby bay. To no avail. A few times we spotted individual rocks jutting out of the water in the excited expectation of a canoe. Finally, we had almost given up all hope of being welcomed at sea by the inhabitants; therefore, Captain von Krusenstern had two shallops lowered in order to inspect the dead coast nearby and scout for the harbor. In the meantime we spotted some islanders fishing on the rocky shore. As far as we could see, they stared at us with complete indifference as we sailed past. A short time later, to our great joy, we finally saw a canoe with a white flag approaching. It contained eight naked people rowing toward the shallops we had lowered. We tried to observe them at some distance. We were boundlessly happy when we saw one of these savages, totally without hesitation, jump from their canoe into our shallop, which immediately returned to our ship. There was a lot of guessing. We were more than a little surprised when all at once we caught sight of not a South Sea islander but of a European dressed in the manner of the island jumping on deck. He was bare but for a small loincloth. An English sailor named Roberts — and God knows by which opportunity or chance he had arrived there — stood before us, assuring us in rather good English that he had been living on the island for several years.[7] He differed little or not at all in skin color from the rest of the islanders. That is how great an influence the climate had had on his skin. Various letters of reference from other ship captains attesting to the man's honest and helpful service, which he showed us, naturally had to instill in us a greater trust for him than his seedy appearance. We were very happy all at once totally unexpectedly to have a European pilot on board who could give us exact news about the island and its inhabitants.

He was plied with thousands of questions. Everyone wanted to be the first to get an answer to his own question. When we asked about the chief or head of the island, he said a king ruled there. His brother had come with him in the canoe traveling alongside our ship. That seemed ridiculous to us, so we immediately permitted his royal majesty to come on board. A well built man, tattooed over his entire body, climbed on board. Like the rest of his companions, he was completely naked. He had no special appearance, no special distinguishing marks. He was so stupid and shy that we were all struck at finding in such a strong, muscular, robust man such childish timidity and fearfulness. In the beginning he refused to shake the hands offered him. A very few moments later he snuggled up to anyone who showed him a friendly face. He hardly had enough courage to stay alone by himself for a moment.*

After our unusual guests had shyly looked around the ship for a while and wanted to return to their canoe, they were presented with some nails, knives, red cloth, and other objects. They then happily jumped overboard and swam rapidly to their vessel.

In the meantime, we had reached the harbor with our pilot in the midst of all kinds of questions and answers. At about one o'clock in the afternoon, we dropped anchor at a distance of about one-half sea mile from land.

Everything on the nearby, mostly sandy shore still seemed dead. It did not take long, however, until a number of people of both sexes appeared. From a great distance most of the women could be distinguished by their mainly yellow garments made from the paper mulberry tree, which they had flung around themselves.

Now a lot of islanders came swimming to our anchorage from the opposite northwestern shore about three sea miles away. At first we could only see a large number of black-haired heads sticking out of the water. A short time later we saw the rare spectacle of several hundred naked men, women and girls swimming around our ship. Most of them had brought coconuts, bananas and breadfruit to sell.

---

*The strange fear can possibly be explained by the strife which the *Daedalus*, a supply ship for Vancouver, had had with the inhabitants when it was anchored at the harbor (Port Anna Maria) in February, 1793. It had come from the Northwest Coast of America. The initially friendly intercourse was interrupted by a row between a sailor and an islander. The latter hit the former. Immediately after he had jumped overboard, the sailor shot him dead. The commander of the ship, Lieutenant Hansen, was forced by the islanders' hostile behavior to leave the harbor. That death, as we consequently heard, of a person from a respected family seemed to be a fresh memory, and the basis for his fear.[8]

The noise, laughter, and romping of those eternally happy people were indescribable, and everyone of us had his own impression. Only a few of the islanders whom the Englishman Roberts declared genteel were allowed on board ship. The others cheered while swimming like sirens around the ship. The continual noise was greater than at the largest of our fairs. We could hardly hear ourselves think at our meal. The young girls and women, totally naked like the men and not there in any lesser number, were exceedingly loud and talkative, and at the same time, according to our European views, brazen. They let loose a loud, joyous laugh at our every movement or action. Since we did not understand even one little word of the many beautiful things they were telling us, they soon made clear the charms they were offering through the most immoral and improper gestures and pantomime. Several pointed disdainfully at their larger playmates and sought to gain advantage by shouting repeatedly in loud voices "*wahine iti-iti*," that is, "little girl," and trying to give their offers emphasis with "*huka-huka.*" Others showed their bodily dexterity by doing somersaults in the water, turning on their backs and swimming. They were beside themselves with joy if they saw that one or the other of their poses had aroused the attention of a spectator. It is almost impossible to imagine any indecorous position that they would not have tried their best to do for us. The men who had swum out with them seemed not to be the least bit jealous. On the contrary, the husband seemed to promote the virtues of his wife, the brother of his sister, the father of his daughter, and the lover of his beloved.

Toward evening most of the islanders, at our urgent request, returned to land after several of them had tired our ears out no little bit by their continual shouting and noise for at least four to five hours.

The women and girls, there as almost everywhere, proved to be more stiff-necked and even less obedient than the men. Perhaps they also knew, spoiled by earlier visits from Europeans, that the newly arrived strangers and good-natured men would not, in the end, give a negative answer. Enough. The island beauties insisted so persistently that they be allowed to come on board and were so pushy and loud that it was finally decided, in order to simply put an end to the noise which was in part very piteous begging, to permit at least a few of them to come on board. Now these lovelies appeared in all their nakedness. Even though they never leave land without tying on a little green leaf, most of them were missing that careless covering from swimming around so long and from their manifold antics. Only a few of them had that little bit of foliage still in place. It was their good luck that we had no goats or sheep on board.

They probably would have undoubtedly craved for the leaves as much as we did for the bananas, coconuts and breadfruit brought us. We would have to say with Wilson, "The roguish goats caused a lot of mischief with the beautiful young girls, since the goats did not even leave them with green leaves. They attacked them from all sides so that they were quickly defoliated, totally naked."*

As willing as the island girls and women were in the distribution of their favors, as willing as they were to follow any sailor who reached out his hands to them, still they had a certain modesty about them. All of the ones who had lost their leaves were more than a little bit concerned that one might see part of their otherwise hidden charms. In order to prevent that, they were taking small steps, barely putting one foot in front of the other, bent over with their knees and thighs pulled in and held tightly together while they were trying to use their hands to replace the leaves. Their position, resembling the Venus de Medici, offered a philosophical observer of mankind a beautiful spectacle. The ones who still had leaves hanging on them were busy with every movement trying to direct them back to their proper locations.

We were more than a little surprised to see among the girls who had rushed aboard of their own accord several who were barely eight or nine years old. They had to be considered children in every way, given their bodies which would not mature for a long time. Nevertheless, they were gay, happy things, taking their youthful charms to market, enjoying themselves as much as their older playmates. By expressly asking, I learned from Roberts that these supposed children had not had that which one should suppose for a long time. Indeed, he assured me that it would be considered a disgrace for girls if men despised them and they could not distribute their favors. The more lovers an unmarried girl has had, the more highly she is prized. Another child, at the most ten or eleven years old, was, according to our informant, the acknowledged wife of an islander.

We were not able to engage in our philosophical observations for very long. Soon one siren after another disappeared with a sailor in hand to the inner parts of the ship, and the goddess of the night with her dark veil covered everything that might have happened.

**A Missionary Voyage to the southern Pacific Ocean, performed in the Years 1796, 97-98 in the ship* Duff *commanded by Capt. James Wilson*, London, 1799, 4, with maps, charts and views.

Thus ended the first day of our stay, with new, wonderful scenes we had never before experienced. Early the following morning one beauty after another hopped overboard and swam with various gifts nimbly to the nearby shore.

The sailors, who really had very little to offer, gave their lovers bottles, broken pots, porcelain, bright little pieces of cloth, etc., which seemed on the first day to cause a lively expression of joy. One of the sailors, who in his hurry did not know what to give to show his gratitude, ripped the cord from a pair of old worn-out trousers and decorated the neck of his beauty with it. She, richly rewarded with such a rare gift from Europe, hurried home prouder and happier than many a knight with the ribbon of an order, while thinking to herself: "*Honni soit qui mal y pense.*"[9]

NOTES

1. Captain, later First Lord of the Admiralty, George Anson (1697-1763) sailed around the world from 1740 to 1744. He lost 5 of his 6 ships and 1,051 men out of 1,955, mostly to scurvy. The account of his voyage was very popular and appeared in many editions. It was translated into several languages. The German translation was published in 1749. See *A Voyage round the World in the years 1740-44 by George Anson, Esq., commander-in-chief of a squadron of His Majesty's ships, sent upon an expedition to the South Seas, compiled from papers and other materials of the Right Honourable George Lord Anson and published under his direction by Richard Walter* (London: Printed for the author by J. and P. Knapton, 1748).

Admiral William "Breadfruit" Bligh (1754-1817) was Captain Cook's sailing master on his second expedition between 1772 and 1774. He was sent in 1787 as captain of *H. M. S. Bounty* to introduce breadfruit into the West Indies from the South Sea Islands.

James Wilson, *A Missionary Voyage to the southern Pacific Ocean in the years 1796-1798 in the ship* Duff (London: Printed by S. Gosnell for T. Chapman, 1799). Wilson (1760-1814) was the captain of the *Duff*, which was commissioned by the London Missionary Society to carry Christianity to the South Pacific. It carried a number of missionary tradesmen, e.g., a butcher, weaver, hatter, carpenter, tailor, harness-maker, who were to preach the Christian message and stimulate economic ventures.

2. Langsdorff probably means Benjamin Franklin (1706-1790), who sponsored two voyages from Philadelphia to the Arctic in 1753 and 1754. Franklin was also most interested in voyages of discovery and in the new lands they found. See his remarks to Bishop Shipley, August 19, 1771, in Alexander

Turnbull Library, Wellington, as quoted in Lynne Withey, *Voyages of Discovery* (New York: Morrow, 1987), p. 171fn.

3. See *A Voyage to the South Seas undertaken by command of His Majesty for the purpose of conveying the breadfruit tree to the West Indies* (London: Printed by G. Nicol, 1792) or *A Narrative of the Mutiny on board His Majesty's ship Bounty* (London: Printed for G. Nicol, 1790). These works were published in several European languages as well as in Ireland and America.

4. Jacob Roggewein (Roggeween) (1659-1729) was Dutch. At the age of 62, he left the Netherlands to search for a southern continent. In 1772 he visited and named Easter Island. Andrew Sharp, ed., *The Journal of Jacob Roggeveen* (Oxford: Clarendon Press, 1970).

5. The Washington Islands are the seven northwestern islands in the Marquesas, of which Nukahiva is the chief island. Historically most of the islands have each had three or four alternative names. In 1791 an American, Captain Ingraham, sighted them and named them after George Washington. See R. Gerard Ward and Ernest D. Dodge, *American Activities in the Central Pacific, 1790-1878* (Ridgewood, N.J.: Gregg, 1967), vol. 5.

See also Chapter 4 where Langsdorff gives additional information about the names they have been given.

6. Richard Hergest of the *Daedalus* — see Langsdorff's footnote later in this chapter.

Étienne Marchand (1755-1793) was a French explorer and navigator who arrived at the Marquesas in 1791 and named them "Revolution Islands." See Charles Claret de Fleurieu, *A Voyage Round the World by Etienne Marchand* (London: Longman and Rees, 1801), 2 vols.

7. Roberts, Edward Robarts (ca. 1771-1832), deserted from the whaler *Euphrates* in 1798. On Nukahiva he became a self-appointed mediator for vessels calling there. He left in 1806 because of impending civil war. He spent most of his time in India, where he lived in poverty until his death. His autobiography is a major source of Marquesan history during early Western contact. See Greg Dening, ed., *The Marquesan Journal of Edward Robarts* (Canberra: Australian National University Press, 1974).

8. Captain George Vancouver (1758-1798), *A narrative or journal of a voyage of Discovery to the North Pacific Ocean and round the world in the years 1791, 1792, 1793, 1794 and 1795* by George Vancouver and Lieutenant W. R. Broughton (London: Printed for J. Lee, 1802). As becomes apparent in later footnotes, Langsdorff used the French translation even though a German one had also appeared in 1799.

9. "Disgraced be he who thinks evil of it" is the motto of the Crown of England and also of the Order of the Garter. The motto is said to refer to the campaign against France, which Edward II led in person and which terminated in the Battle of Crecy, August 26, 1346.

Chapter 4

Description of Nukahiva. Introduction. Short overview of the Marquesas and Washington Islands. Description of the Island. Climate. Location. Population. Products. Inhabitants.

Instead of relating events as found in my journal, I find it more practical to summarize the results of the observations I made during our stay on Nukahiva. In this way I can present a general view of the archipelago and its inhabitants along with their customs and habits. With this in mind I find it necessary to make the following introductory remarks.

As mentioned previously, we were met by an Englishman named Roberts. He immediately told us that we would also find a Frenchman on the island. He, however, described him very negatively and at the same time warned Captain von Krusenstern not to get mixed up with the man. Had the Frenchman been lucky enough to be the first to come to us, he certainly would have said the same things as his archenemy Roberts. Be that as it may, even though this Englishman tried to prevent our associating with the Frenchman, the Frenchman was clever enough to come to our ship immediately after our arrival in the company of the so-called king. He was named Jean Baptiste Cabri, born in Bordeaux.[1] Because of the friendly nature of our honorable Commander von Krusenstern, who tried in every way to promote peace, quiet and unity between the two parties, they seemed truly to become reconciled with each other. During our stay, they both offered us a helpful hand — especially the Englishman Roberts, whose orderly behavior led us to have a higher degree of trust in him since he conducted himself the entire time in the most unselfish and irreproachable manner. He tried in all ways within his power to satisfy our desires.

The two Europeans had been living on first one island of the chain and then another for several years. Both of them, especially the Frenchman, had learned the language. They were able to serve us as interpreters and give us the best information about the islands, habits,

habits, customs and manners of their inhabitants in so far as they understood them. It is a pity that we could only take advantage of such a rare opportunity for so few days.*

The following remarks are not simply conjectures based on philosophical judgements about an unknown chain of islands but rather a true portrayal of them according to the information given by two people who had been living among those peoples for several years. They did not have the slightest reason for hiding anything from us. They themselves were also not enlightened enough to think of telling us meaningless tales. I tried, in as far as possible, to obtain information from both of them. I only assumed a fact was true if it were confirmed by both of these men, who were basically hostile toward each other. I have to confess, however, that I placed less value on the Englishman's information than on the Frenchman's, because the latter had been living there longer. He was so very much like the savages that I can say that I found only very little difference between his habits, way of living and thinking and those of the natives. He had almost forgotten his mother tongue. In the beginning he only repeated to me *parler français* as proof of his home country. He was tattooed over his entire body, including his face. He swam just as well as the islanders. He lived with the daughter of one of the lesser chiefs or propertied men of the island. He dealt with her family and the rest of the Nukahivans on an exceedingly intimate footing. The Englishman Roberts, in contrast, lived more apart from the natives. As far as we could see, he did not speak the native language very well. In my opinion, he was less acquainted with the native customs and even seemed rather indifferent toward them. He, however, was of better character and more native intelligence, far better educated. By means of his good conduct, he seemed to exercise a great deal of power over the natives. Perhaps this was only the case for the time being, because the natives soon noticed that we had more confidence in him, trusted him more and that he was our actual business agent and interpreter, the Frenchman, in contrast, only secondarily.

The influence, which the former alleged to have obtained through his marriage, indeed contributed little to his reputation, since he was living with a girl of low descent and only under the protection of a respected chief. He wanted to claim kinship with him even though he had only exchanged names with him, which here and in many other places in the South Seas creates a kind of kinship or a

---

*We spent only ten days at Nukahiva.

definite religious connection something akin to a baptismal sponsor with us.

The first part of Captain von Krusenstern's trip has already appeared in print. His interesting remarks are, in part, different from mine. The apparent cause is that he has used Roberts more as an informant, and I, in contrast, used Cabri. My difference of opinion and individual facts is not an intentional or even deliberate attempt to insult our valued von Krusenstern, without whose support I could not place these observations before the public. No impartial judge will think that I am blaming him for particular untruths or openly speaking against him. I find it necessary, in order to be correctly understood and not to appear in the wrong light, to publicly assure this man, to whom I owe everything and for whose friendship I entertain the warmest feelings of gratefulness, that I have no base intentions or desire to contradict him, but rather differ from him simply because I used another informant. When I, for example, say that mothers nurse their children, that there are marriages and jealousy, then Jean Cabri is at fault for these and other contradictions. Thoughts are duty-free. These and similar minor facts are truly not important enough to jeopardize my friendship with a man whom I will always admire and whose merits are recognized all over Europe. The divergences will rather show my readers the difficulties standing in travelers' paths to ascertain truth and facts about foreign lands and peoples. Thus, each reader may decide for himself to accept Roberts's or Cabri's opinion.

Brief Overview of the Marquesas and Washington Islands

The Marquesas were discovered in July 1595 by Alvaro Mendana de Neyra. He named them in honor of the Marquis Mendoça de Canete, who was viceroy of Peru at the time and who had sent him out with four ships to take possession of the Solomon Islands, which Neyra had discovered. Afterwards, the Marquesas were first visited by Cook in 1774, who discovered the Island of Fetugu or Fatauga and called it Hood's Island. Since then, they have been visited by Le Marchand in 1791, Hergest in March 1792, Brown in June 1792, Captain Roberts in 1793, Wilson in 1797 and many other seafarers especially of the United American Free States.[2]

Captain Roberts, an American, visited Tahuata (St. Christina) for three months. He built a small vessel with which to sail to the Northwest Coast of America to engage in fur trading.

The Marquesas or Washington Islands were discovered almost simultaneously by Ingraham and Le Marchand. Readers interested especially in detailed and exact descriptions and geographic information about the islands should look in Le Marchand's, Vancouver's, Wilson's and especially in von Krusenstern's voyages for detailed and exact descriptions. I am contenting myself with a general overview of the Islands.

Description of Nukahiva

The Island's coastline is mostly steep, a bare black mass of rocks that owes without doubt its existence to a volcano. They rise up almost perpendicularly from the ocean. The closeness of the equator, only a few degrees away, indicates a very hot climate. The thermometer seldom shows less than 18° to 20° warmth. Marchand noted 27° in the month of June. In May we usually had 23° to 25° and that on board ship. A stay there is supposed to be very healthy, something the two Europeans clearly proved to us. They hardly had known any diseases except for wounds and other accidental injuries.

The winter, as at most places between the Tropics of Cancer and Capricorn, is characterized by frequent rain showers. If, however, as sometimes happens and unfortunately did happen the year before our arrival, not a drop of rain falls for nine to ten months, famine causes not only a great many deaths but also the most abhorrent and outrageous behavior which I will talk about later.

The dominant winds are eastern trades; especially in the autumn they are the strongest and called *tiutin*. The islanders call the southwest winds *tuwatone*.[3] They are said to dominate the winter and are used for sailing to neighboring islands. Navigation is in poor condition. They usually need three days to reach the nearby Island of St. Christina. In the spring and summer a northwestern wind called *tukuahu* blows. For the west or northwest wind, no special word is supposed to exist in the language of the area because they say this wind blows exceedingly rarely or not at all. Thunderstorms occur only rarely.

The island is about fifteen German miles in circumference and consists, as previously stated, of naked, craggy, mostly inaccessible mountains with small, very fertile, water-rich valleys here and there between them.

On the southern coast are several secure harbors:

Tabular View of the Older Marquesas

	Correct Name	Older Name	Named by		Landing Place	Latitude (S)	Longitude (W)
1.	Fatuiwa	Ohitatoa	La Magdalena	de Neyra 1595	center of island	10°25′	138°49′
2.	Montane	Onateaya	St. Pedro	—	—	9°47′	138°55′
3.	Tahuata	Ohitau	Santa Christina	—	Port Madre de Deos	9°55′	139°08′
4.	Hiwaoa	Ohiwana	La Dominica	—	eastern point	9°39′	138°21′30″
5.	Fetugu	Tihboa	Hood's Island	Cook 1774	center	9°27′	138°29′30″

Tabular View of the New Marquesas or Washington Islands

	Correct Name	Older Name	Named by		Landing Place	Latitude (S)	Longitude (W)
1.	Nukahiwa	Nuahiwa	Federal Island	Ingraham 1791	southeastern point	8°57′	139°32′30″
			Isle Beau	LeMarchand 1791	southern point	8°58′40″	139°44′30″
			Sir H. Martin's I.	Hergest 1792	northwestern point	8°53′30″	139°49′
			Adam's Island	Roberts 1793	—	—	—
2.	Uahuga	Ruahuga	Washington's I.	Ingraham	western point	8°58′15″	139°23′
			Massachusetts's I.	Roberts	double peak	8°55′58″	—
			Riou's Island	Hergest	center	8°54′30″	139°09′30″
3.	Uopoa	Ruapoa	Adam's Island	Ingraham	—	—	—
			Isle Marchand	Le Marchand	northern point	9°21′30″	139°09′
			Jefferson's Island	Roberts	—	—	—
4.	—	—	Lincoln's Island	Ingraham	—	9°29′30″	—
		—	Isle Platte	Le Marchand	—	—	—
		—	Resolution Island	Roberts	—	—	—
		—	Cevel Island	Wilson	—	—	—
5. }	Motuaiti	—	Franklin's Island	Ingraham	—	8°37′30″	140°20′
6. }		—	Blake's Island	Roberts	—	—	—
7. }	Hiau and	—	Knox and Hancock	Ingraham	southern point	7°37′30″	140°13′
8. }	Fatuuhu	—	Masse et Chanal	Le Marchand	—	7°50′	140°06′
	—	—	Freemantel and Langdale	Roberts	—	—	—
	—	—	Robert's Island	Hergest	—	—	—

1) The harbor and Bay of Tayo-Hoae or Taïo-haïe or Tiohai,* which Hergest called Port Anna Maria.

2) Home, Hoome, Siume, Tscho-ome, named Comptroller's Bay by Hergest.

3) The new harbor Hapoa was named Port Tschitschagoff by Krusenstern.

4) Captain Brown on the *Butterworth* claims to have discovered several good harbors with numerous inhabitants on the northwestern side of the Island. No one, as far as I know, has carefully investigated them or described them.

5) The *Neva* at its arrival noted an inhabited bay on the northeastern tip of the Island.

6) The southwestern side appears to have low, gently rising land. Probably bays and secure anchorages could also be found there.

Since the islanders alternately fight with each other and live in continual hostility, we could obtain little information about distant areas of the island. Rivers and mountains mark the boundaries of their territories.

Inhabited areas in the neighborhood of our anchorage are the first three harbors mentioned above and the bordering valleys, which altogether have about 3,000 battle-ready men.

We were told that the area around Comptroller's or Home Bay is one of the most populated parts of the island and consists of three valleys.

I was told the largest river on the island and a very populated valley named Jacapa are on the western and southwestern side.

Captain von Krusenstern was told of another named *Hotty schewe*** that can field around 1,200 warriors.

---

*The reader can see from this and the following variant pronunciations how difficult it must be for a foreigner to convey the correct sounds. I would have written *Tiohai* but use instead Captain von Krusenstern's spelling *Tayo-Hoae*.

**The Englishman probably pronounced this poorly. The word does not seem to me to be Nukahivian.

The valley near the harbor of Tschitschagoff (Hapoa) is called Schegua and another one bordering on it nearby Ihanahui.

Mauday, the son-in-law of the chief of Tayo-Hoae, is said to rule a valley in the interior of the country that also has around 1,200 warriors.

From this information and other untrustworthy information, the population of Nukahiva can be set at about 18,000. I think this figure, however, is too small, judging by the area of habitation we got to know and the many, probably even larger number unknown to us.

Wars kill fewer people than do famine and the detestable practice of eating human flesh to still their hunger. According to our interpreter, during the previous year in the valley of Taio-Hoae hundreds of people lost their lives, so that now there are four men for every woman and very few children remaining.

In how far the way of life contributes to depopulation will be elucidated in the discussion further below.

It is possible and highly probable that the island at one time was more highly populated and will recover again in a few years. Hergest, who visited the harbor twelve years before we did, claims to have seen around 1,500 inhabitants on the shore. At our arrival 800 to 1,000 at the most collected.[4]

The products of the Washington Islands are essentially the same as those discovered by Cook and others on the well-known Marquesas, as well as on the Friendship and Society Islands. The breadfruit tree (*Artocarpus incisa*), whose fruit, according to the Forsters, is larger and better tasting there than any place else, coconuts and bananas, taro or Indian kale (*Arum esculentum*), yams (*Dioscorea alata*) and batatas (*Convolvulus Batatas et chysorrhizus Sol.*) are the most common foodstuffs from the plant kingdom. Sugarcane is also common, even though little used. The Tahiti chestnut (*Inocarpus Forsteri*) is used here as there for light, the casuaren wood (*Casuarina equisetifolia*) for spears, billy clubs and other weapons.[5] The bast of the paper mulberry (*Morus papyrifera*) is used to make the cloth for the only clothing they have. They build their houses from bamboo (*Bambusa arundinacea*), calabashes probably from *Crescentia Cujete*. They use coconut shells for water and drinking containers.

Most of the plants the Forsters found on St. Christina I found again on Nukahiva. I will include a few new species in my botanical notebooks. Tahitian apples (*Spondias*), which that famous natural scientist noted was missing from the Marquesas, are found on the Washington Islands, although sparingly.

In addition to the foodstuffs listed above, there are some other fruits and roots which the inhabitants collect in time of famine in order to stay alive. Since these grow only in the high, inaccessible mountains, I could only get the names of some of them from the natives: *wahinei*, a very good fruit that tastes like chestnuts (probably *Aniotum fagiferum*); *tefah* or *tipah*, a red fruit that is only eaten in time of need; *tih*, a fat root, obtainable the whole year but only eaten in time of famine; and *cape*, a good, nourishing food, probably the same as the Tahitian *ape* and the *kappe* of the Sandwich Islands (*Arum macrorhizon*).[6]

The land would be capable of very intensive cultivation of several useful crops, for example, of sugarcane. We gave Roberts some orange seeds. He will certainly try to grow this excellent fruit there.

According to the information of all the seafarers who have visited the Friendship and Society Islands, the inhabitants of the Marquesas and Washington Islands exceed the inhabitants of all the other South Sea Islands in size, bodily beauty, regularity of facial features, color, etc.

The men[*] are almost all strong, tall and well built. Few of them were as fat and clumsy as the Tahitians of high rank, none as thin and emaciated as the Easter Islanders. I saw not a single cripple or deformed person, but mainly beautiful people whose regularity of features aroused our admiration. Many a one could have been compared to the masterworks of ancient art and certainly would have lost nothing in the comparison.

Their beards are shiny black and usually thin because they pluck out a lot of their hair. Their hair is usually long, curly, thick and black; a few, however, have lighter hair.

Above all, a certain Mau-ka-u or Mufau Taputakaya caught our attention because of his strength, the proportions of his muscles and all of his individual parts. He was 20 years old and six fuss two zolls Parisian measurements tall. Councilor Tilesius, with his knowledge and eye for

---

[*]See Forster's *Reise um die Welt* [Voyage around the world].

art, had never seen proportions more beautifully united in a living body. He made the effort to measure exactly all of his individual body parts and their relations to each other. After our arrival in Europe, he communicated his observations to Councilor Blumenbach in Göttingen. This worthy scholar, who has earned so much recognition for his history of the human race, compared Mufau to the Apollo in Belvedere. He discovered in the evidence given him something no one suspected — that this masterpiece of Greek creative art, uniting everything admired as the ideal of male beauty, has the same proportions and relationships as our Mufau, an inhabitant of Nukahiva. We were told that the chief on the neighboring Island of Upsa has the most regular of proportions but is a head taller than Mufau. He would then be at least seven *schuh* tall if our Roberts and Cabri's information is true.

This object seems to me interesting enough to give again Mufau's measurements as taken by Councilor Tilesius and published in *Voights Magazin der Naturkunde* [Voight's Journal of Natural Science], vol. 12, part 6, p. 495:

Height	6′2″ Parisian measurement
Width of shoulders	19″2‴
On the periphery	40″
Width of chest	15″
Length of arms from shoulder to the finger tips	22″4‴
Height of head from forehead to the chin	10″
Circumference of the head across the forehead just over the ears	23½″
Circumference of the chest	42″
Periphery of the abdomen in Hypochondria	32″
Periphery of the large pelvis, measured over the hips	42″
Periphery of the thigh	25″
Periphery of the calf	17½″
Periphery of the shin, measured a zoll above the feet where it is smallest	10″
Length of the foot	12½″
Widest part of the foot	5½″
Circumference of the upper arm	13½″
Circumference of the forearm	13¼″
Circumference of the hand	11¼″
Length of the hand	9″
Circumference of the neck	16″

Distance from the part to the navel	31½″
From the navel to the division of the thighs	10½″
From the division of the thighs to the soles of the feet	38″

The facial features of these people are pleasing, open and full of life. Their black eyes are not without expression. Most of them have such charming and pleasing traits that we, like Cook and Forster, would have left there with the insane notion of having found a hospitable, obliging and good people if our European interpreters had not taught us something else.

In general, the women are much smaller than the men but of very proportioned build.* Several resembled in build and physiognomy the beautifully built women of high rank on Tahiti.

In 1797 Captain Wilson visited that island, which was formerly famous for its enchantingly beautiful girls, and then sailed to the Marquesas. He had a Tahitian woman on board. He writes, "even though our Otahitan was quite beautiful and good, she was, indeed, put in the shade by the very well proportioned women here. She seemed to feel her weakness to no little degree, but she was amiable and possessed more of the kindness and gentle feelings of her sex than they."

The women** have well formed heads, full, more round than long faces, large sparkling eyes, glowing facial color, very pretty teeth, expressive, symmetrical facial features, and black, mostly curly hair. Several of the low class women who hung around the ship every day had small bodies without good posture, their stomachs disproportionately fat, their walk sluggish. This was not the case with the ones of higher rank who came on board rarely or not at all. They have a more pleasing build, slimmer figures and are very lively, so that in this respect they may be called beautiful. I convinced myself of this truth on walks when we, Major Friederici, Councilor Tilesius and I, sometimes met girls of high rank and women from some of the more distant valleys. They are prettier by far than all of the others from near the harbor. They were taller with a great deal of decorum. They were always covered and did not want to talk with us but rather sought their distance bashfully, shyly and reservedly. Even Captain von

*See Forster's *Reisen* [Voyages], pp. 16 and 23.

**See Krusenstern, p. 170 [English translation, p. 153f].

Krusenstern admits that the daughter and daughter-in-law of the chief on Tayohoae and Roberts's wife were so beautiful that even in Europe their beauty would not have been denied them and that they found the women in the Valley of Schegua better built, indeed many of them could be called very pretty. They were not any of the common girls who visited us on the first day. As much as all of the seafarers praise the beauty of the female sex in the South Seas, I am still inclined to think that the beauty of females on Nukahiva exceeds them by far. If we had not convinced ourselves by seeing individual examples of well built, beautiful women, prevented from having contact with us, and if we had only been visited by members of the lowest class, it would have seemed physiologically remarkable and inexplicable how those weak, small girls, hindered by early dissoluteness of growth, could produce the gigantic body of a Mufau and many other similar men. It is most probable that we saw only a few of the many beautiful women and mostly only slovenly wenches of the Island. I do confess that I find the shape and figure of a well built Negress more pleasing and more perfect according to our European concepts of beauty and proportion than those of the women on South Sea Islands. To be sure, we found a Belvedere Apollo on Nukahiva. The question remains whether an attentive observer after us would be able to discover the original of the Venus de Medici on the African coast or in the South Seas.

The natural skin color of the islanders is almost as white as the European. Influenced, however, by the climate and the effects of burning rays of the sun, it gradually becomes brownish. This is especially the case with members of the lowest class who barely wear a loincloth for covering and, as a result of their work, are continually exposed to the sun. Wilson states that some women, who, at their arrival, were almost as white as Europeans, came on board ship and, as a result, often exposed themselves to the sun's heat until finally they acquired a very dark appearance. The newborn children we saw had skin that was almost as white as the skin in Europe. Women of higher rank are just as concerned about keeping their lighter skin color as are our beauties. In order not to spoil it, they live withdrawn and seldom expose themselves to the influence of the sun's rays. They cover themselves with cloth made from mulberry bark. If they go out they carry green tree branches or banana leaves instead of parasols. By doing this they keep their natural color to the degree that they very much resemble European brunettes. The desire to please has already reached such a high degree among the women that they have invented a preparation which makes sunburned skin white again within a few days. They use it for a period before large folk celebrations and public games so that they can arouse more approval and admiration on these occasions. For this reason, they cover their entire bodies with the juice obtained from the leaves of various plants they call *epapha*, *hoko-kuh* and *ohue*. At first it makes the skin become very black. People wanting to regain their beauty in this way dare not leave their houses for five to six days and have to avoid the sun even more. After this period, usually a day before the celebration, they wash off the black color of the plant juices with fresh water, causing their natural whiter skin to appear.

Another habit of both the men and women is to cover their whole bodies with coconut oil, which they consider very pleasant smelling. For beauty's sake, they mix it with various yellow-colored plant juices (especially of *Hibiscus populneus Linn.*). Along with the shiny oil, this yellow color, in the opinion of some islanders, especially of the male sex, intensifies their physical beauty, makes the skin soft, pliable and especially prevents strong perspiration, which, in so hot a climate, weakens the constitution very soon and would lead to the greatest disadvantage. It also contributes a great deal to making swimming easier.

Even though we Europeans could not consider this evil-smelling, shiny smear pleasant, the old women and young girls considered it a great adornment and intensification of their charms. Many a one thought they could achieve a conquest by the art of the toilet and were very surprised when we tried to make them understand that the natural condition of their skin was more beautiful.

Nukahivans also think it proper to have a completely smooth body devoid of all hair. For this reason, they pluck it out on and under their arms, on their chests, in short, everywhere. They consider the neglect of this habit great sloppiness. The chief or the eldest man in the Katanuah Valley stopped, totally surprised, in front of one of our naval officers. Using signs he asked him to stand still. With pointed fingers and nails he wanted to pull out a little hair from the inside of the officer's nose. The hair in this location is probably doubly unbecoming because on those islands, instead of kissing as proof of love and friendship, they press their noses together.

NOTES

1. Cabri, also Cadiche or Joseph Kabrit, Cabrit. He died in 1818 or 1822 in France. See "Extract of two letters from Captain von Krusenstern,

Commander of the Russian Expedition to Japan, dated at the Harbour of St. Peter and St. Paul, July 19 and August 20, 1804," *Philosophical Magazine* 22:3-13, 115-23. See also Nikolai N. Nozikov, *Russian Voyages around the World*, translated from the Russian by E. and M. Lesser (New York: Hutchinson, 1945).

From Kamtschatka, Cabri ended up in St. Petersburg by way of Moscow. He exhibited his tattoos and performed Marquesan dances and was appointed swimming instructor to the marine cadets at Kronstadt. Later he was forced to earn his living at the fairs of Brittany and Paris. After his death, there was talk of preserving and exhibiting his skin for posterity.

2. Alvaro de Mendana de Neira (ca. 1542-1595) left Spain for the New World in 1567. In that year he sailed from Peru in search of the Pacific islands of Incan legends filled with gold and silver and returned two years later. In 1595, he again sailed from Peru and on that voyage landed on the islands he named Las Marquesas de Mendoza. See William A. Amherst and Basil Thompson, eds. and trans., *The Discovery of the Solomon Islands by Alvaro de Mendana in 1568*, 2 vols (London: Printed for the Hakluyt Society, 1901) and Celsus Kelley, ed. and trans., *The Voyage of Petra Fernandez de Quiros, 1595 to 1606*, 2 vols. (London: Printed for the Hakluyt Society, 1904).

Captain William Brown of the *Butterworth* sailed out of London. He is mentioned by James Colnett in *A Voyage to the South Atlantic and round Cape Horn into the Pacific . . .* (London 1798), by James Wilson, who says he visited the Marquesas June 1, 1792, and George Vancouver, who met him at Nootka in September 1792. Captain Josiah Roberts of the *Jefferson* in other sources is listed as being there in November 1792. See his article "The Discovery and Description of the Islands called the Marquesas . . . ," *Collections of the Massachusetts Historical Society* 4:238-46.

3. Since in the vocabulary list I am leaving all spellings as Langsdorff has them, I am doing the same thing in the text. That means that Langsdorff most probably pronounced this word "Tuvatona" and "hotty schewe" as "sheva." See Langsdorff's own comments about pronunciation in this chapter.

4. Early population figures, as Langsdorff himself points out later for the Aleutians, are very difficult to estimate accurately. Given Langsdorff's, Krusenstern's and Robarts's figures, it seems clear that between 1800 and 1887, the date of the first census, that the population fell dramatically. The 1887 census shows the population of the Marquesas was 5,245.

5. *Inocarpus edulis Forsteri*, also known as Fiji chestnut, Ota-heite chestnut, Taheite nut.

6. I could not find this in *A Dictionary of Plant Names* by H. L. Gerth van Wijk (The Hague: Nijhoff, 1911) or other sources. *Arum* is a family of plants, many of which yield an edible starch. Langsdorff would have pronounced "ape" and "kappe" approximately "apa" and "kappa". Kapa, tapa, toppa is the cloth from the mulberry tree. Possibly *macrorhizon* is a typographical error and should be *maculatum*.

Chapter 5

Tattooing. Clothing. Food. Breadfruit Tree. Housing.

Tattooing or puncturing is the South Sea islanders' most curious and interesting way of beautifying their naked bodies. This adornment, used by so many peoples of the earth, deserves greater attention from travelers than has been the case up to now. I am surprised that Forster's acute eye so indifferently passed over this practice, since it is, without contradiction, very striking that among nations lying very distant from each other without any mutual contact or, to our knowledge, ever having had any contact with each other, one and the same custom is practiced.

Among Europeans, namely pilgrims to the Holy Sepulcher and sailors of almost all European nations, on the Aleutian Islands, the Northwest Coast of America, on the Sandwich, Friendship and Society Islands, on Easter Island, among the New Zealanders and other nations, in short, in the northern and southern hemispheres, in east and west, in the Old and New World are found sometimes more, sometimes fewer, traces of the custom which serves either as a souvenir of some place or even as the concept of physical beauty.* Among nations on earth probably the art of tattooing is nowhere practiced to such a high degree of perfection as by the inhabitants of the Marquesas or Washington Islands.

The most symmetrical marks and decorations with which the men on Nukahiva cover their bodies from head to foot serve in a way as a substitute among those people for clothing, with which they can completely dispense because of the hot climate. Many of them try to obtain recognition through symmetrical tattoos in just the same way as many among us do with expensive clothing. Thus, members of the

*Perhaps and most likely, tattoos over the whole body in warmer regions of the earth contribute to reducing perspiration through the scarring of so many skin pores and replaces in this way, so to speak, the need for using ointments.

upper class especially do it, since they alone have the means to pay for it.

The business of tattooing is left up to some individuals whose sole employment consists of practicing this art. I suspect that the man who displays the most taste and the greatest dexterity in execution also has the most work, approximately like a good tailor among us, only with the difference that the choice cannot be made so indifferently, since, if the tattooed clothing has a single mistake, it has to be worn for the rest of the person's life.

For tattooing they use the wing bones of the tropic bird (*Phaë-ton aethereus*), which is cut comb-like and pointed on one end or formed into half-moon shapes, or straight, wide or small hooks or tattoo points, depending upon how the artist needs to use them to carry out his intentions.

These comb-like, pointed bones are stuck at a pointed angle into a finger-thick piece of bamboo. The tattoo master can hit it with another little piece of bamboo so gently and cleverly that its point barely breaks the skin. The lines on the skin of the figures to be tattooed are first drawn with the same color which is rubbed into the lines afterwards. At the same time they serve as guides for the various forms to be pricked in. After this is completed and blood and lymph have oozed through the fine pricks, then they have charcoal from the Marquesan oil or candle nut (*Aleutites tribola*) mixed together with a little water to form a thick paint rubbed into them. As a result, a slight infection and scabs form on the tattooed areas. When the scabs fall off several days later, the bluish or blue-black tattooed shape appears. As soon as a Nukahivan enters puberty, tattooing begins and this is one of the most important events in his life.

The artist who does the tattooing is given several pigs before and afterwards. The number given depends upon the wealth of the individual. During our stay on the island, Chief Katanuah's son was tattooed. As the son of one of the ranking families in the country, he was isolated, put in a special house for this purpose for several weeks as long as was needed for the tattooing, and was taboo, which means he dared not leave it and nobody dared to visit him except for the people excluded from the taboo — his father, for example. All of the women, even his mother, were forbidden to visit him. The best food-stuffs, which the person being tattooed and the tattooist needed during the time of tattooing, must be provided ahead of time. As long as the tattooist is working, he receives them daily in superabundance. The first year he only tattoos the basis of the main figures on the chest, arms, back and thighs. He does not begin the next figure as long as the scabs of the first one have not dried up or fallen off. Each individual drawing, therefore, requires three to four days. The first session usually takes three to four weeks.

During the period of the first operation or of the taboo, the boy may not drink much. They believe this prevents bad infections. He may not eat even early in the morning, but only at noon and in the evening. Once the process has begun, then every three or six months, and sometimes after even longer periods of time, secondary figures are added and the main figures are improved, so that 30 to 40 years can pass until the entire body is totally tattooed. We saw several elderly men of rank who were so completely covered with tattoos that we could just barely distinguish one figure from another, thus causing their bodies to have a very negroid appearance. According to their ideas, this shows the high degree of perfection possible in physical adornment, possibly because it costs so much and the cost of the numbers of pigs needed reveal how well off a man is. It is striking that the rich men seek beauty in a negroid appearance and women, to the contrary, in the retention of their natural white color!

Tattooing of the less well off takes place in common taboo houses specially furnished for this purpose. They belong to the tattooists and serve both as boarding houses and as tattoo workshops. Eight to ten people can be housed in each one of the houses belonging to a tattooist. The tattooist who often visited us on board had three. They then had to pay him for their tattooed clothing according to how laborious and artistic the figures were to be tattooed.

The poorer islanders with not many pigs for slaughter, who mainly must live on the fruit of the breadfruit tree, have themselves tattooed by beginners and amateurs whose work is not particularly of special merit. Even a stranger can very soon recognize examples of it.

The lowest and poorest class, for the most part fishermen (we saw only very few of them), do not have enough to pay for such clothing even if done by apprentices. Therefore, they are not tattooed at all.

According to our interpreters, there is no honor or privilege associated with tattoos in general or with the shapes of any individual figures. Whoever can pay the master tattooist well gets his skin adorned according to the amount paid. Women on Nukahiva are seldom tattooed. This distinguishes them from all other women in the South Seas. Tattoos on the hands, which are only done from the fingers to the wrists, produce the same effect as if they were covered by beautiful gloves. Our glove makers could borrow a pattern à la Washington from the printed gloves of the women on that Island.*

The feet, which only a few have tattooed, resemble brightly knitted, high-top shoes. In addition, one sometimes sees women with long stripes on their arms and rings like the bracelets used by our European women. Only a very few also have tattoos on their earlobes and lips to the gums inside of their mouths.

Women are not tattooed in a taboo house like the boys and men but are tattooed without any ceremony in their own houses in the presence of their relatives, or wherever else they want to have it done.

Sometimes a rich islander puts on a feast out of generosity, ambition or love to honor his wife, which consists of slaughtering a pig. He also allows her to use this opportunity to have an earlobe tattooed or a bracelet or some other figure tattooed. He tells the male and female friends he has invited the reason for the feast. Sometime afterwards, they, in turn, return this courtesy by letting the women they love have the same figure tattooed as their friend's wife.

This is one of the few opportunities for women to eat pork.

During a very dry year when famine comes and breadfruit, pigs, roots and other foodstuffs are rare, then the person with the largest stores, usually the headman, gives his hungry brothers something to eat. Thus, for a period a certain number of the poor devils have free board. At that time all of those present are tattooed with a particular figure denoting the party. By virtue of a taboo, all of the brothers afterwards must help all of the others with foodstuffs, if they are able to, during a period of famine in the future — help and help alike: one of the most logical orders of free masonry on earth.

Our interpreter, Cabri, who had been tattooed poorly and irregularly all over his body (by a quack), had gotten a blackish-blue (tat-

*See *Voigt's Magazin der Naturkunde* [Voigt's Journal of Natural Science], vol. XI, Table V, for a picture of Queen Kätänuäh's hand.

tooed) eye on one such occasion. Roberts had only a small square about six zolls long and four zolls wide tattooed on his chest. He assured us that he never would have submitted to being adorned with a cuirass if the famine the previous year had not forced him to become one of the 26 guests accepted by Kätänuäh (the headman in the Tiohai Valley) and fed, thus saving their lives.

It is possible for a person to be a member of several of these societies. The priest or magician (*Taua*) has to be sent a portion of every dish served, even if he himself is not a member of the society. At dance festivals similar eating societies are also formed.

Sometimes during times of famine, several men who have been tattooed in this way join together and share anything they have, can rob or kill, and thus form true robber bands.

The figures or drawings themselves are chosen with care and suited to each individual part of the body. They portray animals, as well as other kinds of objects related to the way of life of the islanders. Just as on the Friendship Islands, every one of them on Nukahiva has its own name.

When one examines the tattoos carefully, one finds rows of points or spots, curved lines, diamond and other designs which have the greatest similarity to the designs known by the name à la Grecque.[1] The most perfect symmetry is adhered to all over the body. Each individual section of a man's head is tattooed; the chest, however, usually is decorated with a shield-shaped design. Several sometimes narrow, sometimes wider stripes are so cleverly tattooed on the arms and thighs that one could suspect that these people had studied the course and placement of the muscles. A wide cross runs down the back beginning at the nape of the neck and ending at the last vertebrae. On the front of the thighs are usually figures intended to represent the human face. The knees have special decorations. On both sides of the calf are oval figures which produce a very good effect. In short, the whole thing displays much taste and skill. Even the most sensitive parts of the body, e.g., the eyelids, are also tattooed.

The islanders' clothes, as I have mentioned above, consist of a loincloth; the men's are called *tschiabu* and women's *teweu* or *teuweu*. The women usually cover themselves with large pieces of cloth made from the bark of the paper mulberry tree (*Morus papyrifera Linn.*). They do this less from a sense of modesty than to prevent sunburn. When we bartered with them, some of them would have gladly traded their coverings for a piece of iron or a knife, if their houses had not been so far away and they had not been afraid of losing their white skin in the burning rays of the sun.

Only a few of the men had cloth or woven mats hanging very carelessly down their backs and fastened together on their chests or under their chins.

Their main source of food comes from the plant kingdom and consists of the natural products already mentioned above: breadfruit, coconuts, bananas, etc.

Breadfruit, as on almost all of the South Sea Islands, has the same importance as grain and potatoes in Europe, tapioca or cassava roots (*Jatropha manihot*) in Brazil or rice in the Orient.

The breadfruit tree (*Artocarpus incisa*) is native to the South Sea Islands. It was mainly first called to our attention by the great English seafarers. The discovery of its importance and usefulness caused the English government in 1787 to outfit an expedition under the command of Captain Bligh, which was to transport that healthy, excellent source of food to English colonies in the West Indies. This first attempt failed, so Captain Bligh was ordered as a result to sail to Otahiti[2] a second time, from where he finally successfully transported this God-given gift to the West Indies. Since 1792, they have been flourishing there.*

Breadfruit is about the size and shape of a coconut or melon. It produces a tall, thick-trunked tree which provides good shade. Its leaves resemble those of an oak, only with the difference that they are far bigger — one to one and one-half fuss long. Like potatoes, this fruit cannot be eaten raw but must be eaten cooked, roasted or fried. The taste differs according to the method of preparation. In general the taste can be compared to that of bananas. It, however, is not as sweet and not as fatty and greasy, so that it is closest in taste to rolls or white bread prepared from the best flour, butter, eggs, milk and sugar. The breadfruit's texture is looser and mealier than the banana's.

---

*"Voyage to the South Sea for the Purpose of Conveying the Breadfruit Tree to the West Indies" by L. W. Bligh, London, 1792, 4; and *Voigts Neues Magazin der Naturkunde* [Voigt's New Journal of Natural Science], Vol. 1, Part 2, p. 110.

The usual method for roasting them is to line a hole in the ground with smooth, wide stones and then to start a big fire there. As soon as the stones are hot, coals and ashes are cleaned from the hole and replaced with bamboo sticks and leaves. The breadfruit, wrapped in banana leaves, is covered with pieces of bamboo, hot stones and earth. The dish is left in the ground as long as thought necessary. Breadfruit, when roasted tender in this manner and eaten together with milk pressed from coconut meat, is called *waikai*. It is very popular and tasty. Once, the headman in Taiohai Valley brought us this dish as a present as an example of the cookery there. We all found it very tasty.

After the breadfruit has been roasted over a fire, its outer hull is scraped off. It is then mixed with some water, or as people of higher rank do, with milk pressed from coconut meat, so that one obtains a good-tasting dish called *akuh*.

Fresh, ripe breadfruit keeps for only a few days. During the time they are superabundant, they are cut up into little pieces and thrown into a pit lined with wide stones about eight fuss long, four fuss wide and five to six fuss deep. They soon begin to ferment and true sourdough forms that can be kept for months. The inhabitants call this foodstuff *popoi** and carry it all over, rolled together into lumps, as the most common food.

When sourdough (popoi) is mixed with water, one obtains a drink which tastes exactly like good, fat buttermilk. It is very cooling and refreshing. I was unable to obtain any exact information about the particular preparation of other dishes in various situations from a mixture of taro and yam roots, from bananas, coconuts and other fruits.

The islanders' animal foods consist of human flesh and pork, fish and chickens — the last two hardly count. Pigs, on the contrary, along with human flesh, play a leading part in the economy and in politics.

No birth, no marriage, no funeral, no tattooing of a high ranking man, no dance, feast or other ceremony takes place but that sometimes more, sometimes fewer pigs are slaughtered. They are eaten

---

*Probably *popoi* means food in general because the eating house is called *popoi taboo*, even though mainly pork is consumed there.

after being roasted in hot pits filled with hot stones, usually without salt. The islanders are not used to using salt since they, at most times, use sea water.

Fish and crabs are not highly prized. Chickens, especially roosters, are kept more for their feathers than as food.

They try to remedy the lack of variety in animal products by enjoying or eating enemies they have killed, i.e., human flesh. I will describe the importance of this more extensively below.

During a period of famine they are happy to eat anything and are satisfied with rats, jellyfish (Medusa) and other things they do not eat at other times.

We did not observe the common custom on the other South Sea Islands of drinking an intoxicant, a cava drink, made from pepper root (*Piper latifolium*), even though the inhabitants are acquainted with the plant and the drink made from it.[3] Probably abstinence from using this unhealthy drink contributes greatly to the beauty of the species of humans there.

Nukahivan houses vary in size. From the outside they resemble little, one-storied European houses without windows and cut through length-wise in the middle. The back wall is by far higher than the front one. The former one is three to four fuss, the latter ten to twelve fuss high. Such a house is about 25 fuss long and six to eight fuss wide. It is held firmly in the ground by four heavy posts driven into the ground with horizontal poles lying on top of them. The side walls are made of thin bamboo slats of equal thickness placed perpendicularly about one-half zoll apart, in part, quite nicely done. Inside, they are lined with coconut palm leaves and several types of ferns in order to prevent drafts. The roof is covered with several layers of leaves from breadfruit trees, which protect the inhabitants during the heaviest of rain showers.

The entrance is in the low, front wall. I think it is a curious fact that not only in Nukahiva but also in the houses of all raw, uncivilized peoples, it is so relatively low and small. In cold climates inhabited by relatively small people one could see the reason in the fact that larger openings would permit the cold to penetrate more easily. I cannot understand why these generally tall people in a warm climate make entering their houses more difficult by having such low, small and narrow doorways.

The good houses are built on platforms made of large, square-rounded stones or on elevations which sometimes jut several fuss wide in front of the houses, thus undeniably providing drier houses and freer views. We have to admire the skill, given their situation, with which the inhabitants put together such large stones, which ten to twelve men can barely carry or roll, so artfully and beautifully without cement or mortar that they represent true Roman walls which would do honor to a European architect.

When a new house is being built, one neighbor helps the other. They often build houses for the fun of it. Wealthy people have similar houses, or rather huts, which can be built in a few days at several locations in their valley.

Larger houses intended for the common use of a large family are built with the help of men as well as of women. If the men haul in the stones needed for the foundation of a house without the help of the women, then the house built on that foundation becomes taboo for the women, i.e., they never dare to enter it. Every well-off islander has at least one of these taboo houses, which usually stands somewhat isolated from the living quarters. He builds it completely according to his wishes and especially as his dining hall, so that he may enjoy his pork in uninterrupted peace, alone, without the presence of his wife. Women get a piece only on rare occasions and then as a favor or generous gesture on the man's part. Such a taboo house is called popoi taboo.

A taua, or priest, magician, sorcerer, has to consecrate every newly built house. He gives a speech and then speaks in a language which none of the natives understands. He has to be entertained with pork and other good dishes for which he performs a lot of very curious ceremonies and sleeps in the new house the first night. By doing this the house will be protected from all the evil spirits which might appear.

At certain times in their domestic lives, women also use houses meant only for them. Thus, for example, a young girl showing signs of maturity and a woman ready to give birth are isolated in distant huts built solely for this purpose.

The interiors of their houses are clean, since the inhabitants are bound by taboos or laws to maintain a high degree of cleanliness. A beam placed the length of the interior of the house divides the floor into two unequal parts. The smaller front part has only the bare stones on it. The back part is strewn with soft grass that is covered by straw mats. These are used by the inhabitants without sexual distinction as beds.

The walls are hung with utensils, for example, large and small calabash gourds (*Crescentia Cujete*), coconut hulls, fishnets, spears, slingshots, stilts, battle axes, hatchets, various ornaments, drums, etc.

Notes

1. A fret is ornamental work in relief. It is done by cutting, carving or embossing and was much used in Greek art and copied with modifications in later periods.

2. Tahiti.

3. Ava, kava, kawa pepper and the drink made from it.

Chapter 6

Social Organizations. Religion and Laws.

It was so difficult in the few days that we were there to obtain correct information about the islanders' social organizations, wars, religion, character and way of thinking that I hardly dare write anything about them. The knowledge and judgement of our interpreters were also so limited that, usually as soon as we tried to generalize information, they would then contradict themselves.

In reality we saw no kind of government at all. Roberts, an Englishman, always had a king in mind. He designated the most distinguished man in Tihohae Valley named Kätänuäh by this title, even though he did not appear to have even the power of a chief, let alone that of a sovereign. He probably belonged to one of the oldest families. Perhaps as the distinguished head of a household, he has the most extensive kinship ties and the greatest possessions. He did not, however, seem to exercise any political supremacy. He was not in the slightest way distinguished from his fellow citizens either in outward marks of distinction or clothing, except that he was somewhat more tattooed like many of the other rich people. His body was well nourished and awkward. He undoubtedly could not have functioned advantageously as a leader in disputes where agility is of essence. They laughed at his orders and commands. He had so little influence over the other inhabitants that, at Captain von Krusenstern's request, he could not even keep the crowd of people away from our anchorage or make it taboo. Sometimes he arrived with other islanders in a canoe. At other times he would swim out with his fellow citizens and come on board. We could not note any difference or respect for his rank caused by his presence. According to our interpreter, every district and every valley on the island has a king. That means that this island, which is 16 German miles in circumference, has ten to fifteen or more kings. The ones we saw have less power over their subjects than the village judge over the peasants among us. That is why I maintain that Roberts and Cabri have made a king out of Kätänuäh. Neither he nor the other elders, neither the rich nor the poor, have any concept of political supremacy, of government or governmental institutions.

This headman, the so-called king of a valley, owns and probably inherited many breadfruit trees and coconut and banana groves. As a result, he is in a position to feed many people who, for this reason, place themselves under his protection, but still, so that each person is his own judge, the behavior of all of the islanders is determined by taboos.

If one of them kills another — something that probably happens quite often among such highly passionate people — then the dead man's family unites against the murderer. It comes to an open fight, which usually does not end until either the murderer or a member of his family is killed. As soon as a man or woman, a boy or girl is dead, all hostilities cease and the best of harmony returns between the parties. Sometimes during such family battles, there are a great many spectators from neighboring houses who watch without anyone attempting to bring about reconciliation or friendship.

Every islander lives according to prejudices and customs. His passions are kept in check by deeply rooted superstitions and the fear of invisible spirits and ghosts (all of which are denoted by the word taboo). This is the source of their laws and what we would call religion among them.

Knowledge of all their taboo laws would make it possible to explain their institutions, way of life, customs and habits. Had Roberts and Cabri been educated, we probably could have collected more important contributions to the subject. I have to confine my remarks instead to the few observations I collected by chance.

1) The person of the priest or taua* and all of his possessions, i.e., adornments, calabash tools, canoes, etc., are taboo, meaning they are considered sacred and no one except the owner may wear them or touch them.

At first we could not understand why some of the islanders, who did not in any way appear to be different from the others, did not want to trade their head ornaments or other normal utensils for important presents until we understood the meaning of the word taboo.

---

*Since the word priest or high priest quickly calls to mind a religious idea, I call the magicians or sorcerers here and later taua, as in the language of the country.

2) The persons of the ranking members of the society and of the rich are taboo, i.e., no physical force may be used against them without offending the invisible spirits and arousing their hatred.

3) Any man, even if he is the lowliest in the valley, who kills an enemy or the first one in battle, is taboo for ten days as a result of his heroic deed. In other words, during this period, he may not associate with his wife. He is given pigs as presents. He is treated like one of rank. During this period, fire is taboo for him. As a result, someone else has to build his fire and cook for him. Perhaps by such special, honorable treatment he and others are encouraged to perform further deeds of valor.

4) The *morai* or cemetery is taboo for the female sex. No woman is allowed to visit the place.[1] If she is in its vicinity, she has to cover herself with a large piece of cloth. If she is naked, she has to make a wide detour.

Every islander has a cemetery near his house. Here or not far away is the popoi taboo, or tabooed eating house, where men can enjoy pork in peace and quiet.

The morai of the taua stands completely isolated from all of the houses. Usually, this is where dead enemies are eaten. This taboo, therefore, prevents women from enjoying pork and the even greater delicacy of human flesh. Only men who are taboo, the tauas, the country's men of rank, their relatives of the same name and the battle heroes may partake in the feast.

5) Human flesh is taboo for women. That means they get nothing from that delicacy. Sometimes, under certain circumstances, exceptions are made, but I have no exact information.

6) The wife of the headman is taboo for his friends and anyone who bears his name. That means his friends and namesakes may not take any special liberties with his wife.

7) An islander's head is taboo. That means no one may step over the head of another while he is asleep, even a father over his son's. No one may even put his hand on the head of another. At our arrival we wanted to run our hands over the heads of some of the handsome men. They became afraid and embarrassed and told us about this taboo.

The basis of these laws seems to be a concern for personal safety. No one may attack another while he is sleeping or even only take hold of his head.

8) Every child immediately after birth receives at least one breadfruit tree from his parents which is taboo even to the father and mother. If the parents are so poor that they cannot spare a breadfruit tree, then they plant one for the child. In this way the child is provided for, since one or two breadfruit trees suffice to feed a person year round.

9) The large calabashes (*Crescentia Cujete*) used for holding water and liquids are taboo for every individual of the opposite sex. Women may never touch the man's, not even to hang them up in the house. This is undoubtedly an expression of property rights.

10) If someone has something stolen, for example, a pig — and suspects who did it — for revenge, he puts a taboo on the thief's pigs and other property. He gives the pigs or trees his own or somebody else's name. Then, according to the islanders' beliefs, the objects become bewitched and enchanted. They believe that a dead person's spirit, or a living person's (*natetu*), is in them. This practice is often enough to force the thief to leave his possessions and settle somewhere else. Pigs, which are natetu, i.e., bewitched, may not be slaughtered.

Every inhabitant, whether of male of female sex, can bewitch the best of his trees and make them taboo, thus rendering his property secure.

11) All loincloths are taboo, which means no one may use someone else's or that they may not be hung up in the house next to other articles but have to be hung on a stick in the corner or put on the ground. The purpose of this is cleanliness.

12) The house is taboo for water or water is taboo for the house. No one may wash in the hut or pour a drop of water on the stones or mats. This custom always keeps the house dry and clean.

13) The best runners on stilts, who perform at public dances, are taboo for three days preceding a dance. They do not go out, take care of themselves well and do not associate with their wives, probably in order to gather more strength.

14) The part of the dance area used for the music, i.e., ten or more drums and a lot of singers and screamers, is taboo for the women because these gay, restless creatures might easily disturb the musicians with their liveliness.

15) Men's fires are taboo for women, which means they may neither cook over fires started by men nor eat any of the food prepared over them. Men, however, can eat as much as they want from women's food.

16) If a man buries a dish made from bananas and coconuts in the evening in the hot stone pit so that it roasts overnight, then he is taboo. He has to stay away from his wife that long, otherwise his food will not be cooked.

17) If a pig is sleeping anywhere, lying straight across a footpath, it is taboo. No one may step over it or wake it up but must go around it, probably so that good animal's peace and quiet are not disturbed.

18) As I have already said, pork, in general, as well as human flesh, is taboo for women, i.e., they are not allowed to eat any of it, although there are exceptions. For example, if a man gives his wife a pig (this is an extremely rare event), she may cook it herself so that she and her girlfriends may eat it; or if a man gives his wife a piglet which she alone feeds and raises, slaughters and cooks, then such a pig is taboo for the man. She may then do whatever she wants to with it without any further approval. In individual cases feasts are given where women get to eat pork.

19) Almost all fish, e.g., *Perca*, *Choetodon*, *Dioden*, *Muraena*, *Raia*, *Squalus*, *Scomber*, etc., are taboo during the time when most of the breadfruit are green. As a result, they may not be eaten. They believe the superstition that disobeying this law causes young breadfruit to fall off of the trees, which would cause famine. The connection between breadfruit and fish is incomprehensible. Are they perhaps at this time unhealthy and the inhabitants are prevented from eating them by this taboo? Or is it perhaps the spawning period and the observation of such a law prevents an increased reduction in the small number of fish there? It is a curious fact, at least, that, as soon as the breadfruit are ripe and they are available in the greatest of abundance, the fish taboo stops and they may then catch as many as they desire.

20) During the time a woman is preparing coconut oil,* she is taboo, that is, for five or more days. She must also avoid contact with men; otherwise she gets no oil.

21) The coconut oil that a women prepares is taboo for a man and vice versa.

Anyone breaking a taboo is a *kikino*, a bad fellow. He cannot escape just punishment for his offense, i.e., the immediate or later influence of the spirits, *Atuan*, and the priest, Taua. Disease or sudden death is the inevitable result.

If anyone speaks unfavorably of the tauas, they know about it immediately from the spirits serving them. Sudden death for the wagging tongue is unavoidable.

From this we can conclude that people sometimes suddenly die without having been ill, that is, they die of apoplexies. I find this all the more probable since, according to the ideas there and information provided by Roberts and Cabri, sometimes after breaking a taboo, their faces become distorted by the spirits and lameness appears in their hands and feet.

These and similar concepts and prejudices serve as a basis for the institutions, religion and laws of the inhabitants of that group of islands.

Notes

1. Here, as elsewhere in Langsdorff's work, we find abundant evidence, indeed some unintended humor, which modern feminist scholars might use to support their theories of sexism in general and in language in particular. Langsdorff does not ask about or consider the disposal of dead women. For another example of this, see his description in Volume Two of burial practices on the Aleutian Islands where women become nonexistent with a shift of a pronoun.

*For preparation see further below.

Chapter 7

Customs and Habits of Nukahiva. Anthropology.[1] *War. Birth. Marriage. Burial. Magic. Circumcision. Dances. Music. Running on Stilts. Swimming. Ornaments. Utensils. Toys. Canoes. Short Remarks. Samples of the Language.*

I now come to the customs and habits of the Nukahivans. I believe that by describing individual events I can give a somewhat better view of that uncivilized nation's character and way of life.

There is no creature on earth in all zones and climates that rages against its own species as much as man.

We only need to take a look at the history of the earth. In the most barren steppes and in the most infertile lands, on the smallest islands and on the largest continents, in short, all over the world, among savages as well as civilized peoples, man eternally seeks to destroy his species. All over the world man is cruel and harsh by nature! Observing the inhabitants on those newly discovered islands, who, to our knowledge, had not had any contact with any civilized nation and can be considered primeval children of nature in their original condition provide curious examples which prove my hypothesis.

I have, unfortunately, seldom observed the gentle, tender feelings of affection and love, of friendship and attachment, even of parents for children and vice versa among brutal, uncivilized nations.

The African hordes market not only their enemies but also their own children and relatives. The Kirghiz, the Kalmuks and some tribes on the Northwest Coast of America do the same thing. Even on Nukahiva a woman would have given us her nursing child without any second thoughts for a little piece of iron we offered her in jest.

Our passions are held within bounds by higher culture, i.e., by reason, refined customs and mainly by religion. If these and conscience are missing, then man is harsh and in this primeval condition capable of everything, even the most despicable behavior without being conscious of having done anything wrong. That is why from this standpoint I can easily explain how it is possible that the Nukahivans can eat, like many other nations, their slain enemies and that men during famine can slaughter and eat their wives and children. The custom is an old and deeply rooted one, inherited from the father and grandfather, which they consider so little detestable or reflect upon as we do when eating a piece of beef and, indeed, some Asiatic nations consider this a matter of conscience. Before talking about the anthropophagy* of these islanders, I would like to make several general remarks because the subject seems important enough to me to dwell upon it longer.

Several famous men have doubted without basis that cannibals existed. It is undeniable that almost all peoples have been guilty of this vice. As unbelievable as it sounds, there have been and still are peoples, especially in South America and the interior and western part of Africa, who eat human flesh only for its good taste and simply as a delicacy. These peoples eat not only prisoners but their own women and children. Indeed, some of them openly buy and sell human flesh. We can thank these peoples for the news that whites taste better than Negroes and the English are supposed to taste better than the French. Further, the flesh of young girls and women, but especially the flesh of new-born babies, is supposed to taste far better than the flesh of the most handsome youths and men and, finally, that the palm of the hand and the sole of the foot are preferable to all other parts of the human body.

The motives which cause men to behave so unnaturally seem to be in the main the following:

1) Extreme need: if, because of a total lack of food, hunger is so great that life can only be sustained by this means.

This is the most general motive and seems innocent if only the flesh of corpses is eaten. A corpse does not care in the least whether it is eaten by worms, animals or people. Still, despite this, the following

---

*During my stay in Lisbon (1797-1802), I had an opportunity to study a manuscript of J. de Loureiro, the well known author of *Flora Cochinchinensis*. I have no second thoughts about combining some of his interesting and new observations about the subject with my own, while at the same time calling the reader's attention to Professor Meiner's meritorious work in Göttingen: *De anthropophagis et diversis ejus causis*. See *Göttingen Anzeigen von gelehrten Sachen* (Göttingen Reports of Scholarly Matters), 153 St., 26 September 1785.[2]

behavior cannot be excused: In India Loureiro observed during a long famine, which caused several hundred thousand deaths, that the streets and roads were covered with the dead (because there were not enough people or ones with the strength to bury them). Many people decided to stay alive by eating this abhorrent food. A very few, after the famine had passed, not from necessity but rather from an irresistible desire for human flesh, waylaid and killed people in order to eat them.

Among others, there was a man living in the mountains who hid in a wood near a road. He threw a loop around the necks of passersby, pulled them into the bushes and ate them. He continued to do this until he finally was discovered, arrested and executed.

At the same time and for the same reasons, there was a woman who captured children who had strayed away from their parents' homes. She filled their mouths and noses with clay to suffocate them. She admitted that in the beginning she had eaten them from hunger when fresh but later for their tastiness, and salted part of them for later use as food.

These and other examples show that human flesh is so tasty and appealing that, once people have tasted it and gotten used to eating it, they can only stop with difficulty.

This is the reason why the eating of corpses is forbidden, even at times of greatest need and greatest hunger.

Several undeniable examples of cannibalism not only among barbarians, but also among civilized people have been noted.

One of the most remarkable, because of its age as well as the number of people involved, is probably what Herodotus relates in his third book, *Thalia*: "Cambyses, King of Persia, wanted revenge for the contemptuous answer sent by the King of Ethiopia in consideration of his envoys' ichthyophagy. He immediately placed himself at the head of a large army and headed toward Ethiopia. Since the path went through a long, sandy desert, his army suffered from a lack of supplies. His desire for revenge had been so strong that he had not taken the time to provide for his troops. In the beginning they slaughtered their horses and draft animals. Then they ate grasses, herbs and plants found along the way. Since there are none in Africa's burning deserts, they finally were driven by extreme need and despair to eat every tenth soldier. In that way one man ate the next and most of the army was destroyed. King Cambyses was forced to abandon his plans and return home with the small group of soldiers remaining."[3]

According to our informants Roberts and Cabri, on Nukahiva when famine comes, many of the men kill their women and children in order to nourish themselves with their flesh. Only the most extreme circumstances bring them to this act. The rich islanders, that is, those who have foodstuffs, appear not to exercise such extreme measures. At least during a famine that lasted several months before our arrival, no one in Kätänuäh's family died or was eaten. On the contrary he fed 26 people. I almost suspect that tattoo and festival societies were formed in order possibly to keep in bounds those basically extremely unnatural and horrid actions.

2) A second reason for cannibalism is unusual, unregulated human lasciviousness and lickerishness.

Americans, particularly in Mexico, certainly did not suffer from a lack of food when they were continually offering up large numbers of human sacrifices and, even though the pretext was used that they were placating their gods in this way, they, indeed, did it in order to gratify their hunger more pleasantly. This is the only reason — without any religious pretext — for Tabunas in Brazil to eat this food. Other peoples in South America, in order to titillate their palates, customarily fatten the unfortunate victims of war that fall into their hands for a few months before killing them.

The Jaygas, a savage people in Africa, have a similar custom which is found all over the deserts from the borders of the Hottentots to the Cape of Good Hope. The Anzigos, likewise an African people living on the borders of the Kingdom of Congo, kill and eat not only prisoners taken from other peoples but even their own people, whom they feed for a period with many delicacies in order to make their meat tastier. Afterwards they sell it at public markets.

Pliny writes of Asia (*Lib.* 7, c. 2) that most of the Scythians and Tartar peoples are cannibals.[4] The most recent travelers tell us that almost all of the inhabitants of the South Sea Islands, i.e., of New Zealand, of the Fiji, Navigator, Mendoza, Washington, Solomon, Sandwich Islands and most probably of the Friendship Islands, eat human flesh with great relish.

As far as we know, it does not happen any more in Europe, not even in any single part, even though, as Pliny writes, it was the case among the ancient Italian people, the Lestrigons. Strabo (*Lib.* 4, p. 192) says this of the ancient inhabitants of Hibernia, whom we commonly call the Irish,[5] and Coelius Rhodriginus (*Lect. antiq. lib.* 28, c. 2) says this of the Scots, their neighbors. It is, indeed, most likely that all of our ancestors in those periods when they were on the lowest step of civilization were cannibals.

3) The third motive is the most curious, since it seems to contradict nature and reason: under the pretense of humanity, man is inhumane; convinced he is acting out of loyalty and love, he is hostile and disloyal.

What is of more value than life? To whom do we owe life more than to our parents and relatives? And yet the Massagetae (an Oriental people living on the other side of the Caspian Sea against whom, according to Herodotus, Cyrus undertook a campaign during which he died) knew nothing of this innate duty of nature. Herodotus says of these barbarians in the first book of his history (*Clio*) that when some of them reached frail old age, their sons and other relatives united to kill the poor old man.[6] They mixed his flesh together with the entrails of other animals, and they then put on a large feast. They were very happy since they claimed that by burying him in their own intestines, they were giving him the most honorable and happiest of deaths.

Ancient writers confirm this information, for example, Pomponius Mela.[7] He says, when speaking of the Scythian people, the Essedones who lived near the Lake of Maeotis: "*Essedones funera parentum laeti et victimis no festo coitu familiarium excipiunt, corpora ipsa laniata et caesis pecorum visceribus immixta epulando cusumunt.*"*

The Massagatae and Essedones have the same customs in so far as they eat their nearest relatives with delight at a banquet.

The question can be asked whether our German saying "to eat some one up for love" does not originate in such a tradition in primeval times, since our ancestors observed the same custom as the Massagetae and Essedones.

---

*"The Essedones rejoice at the death of their parents. They feast upon their bodies at a banquet with their friends. They cut them into pieces and mix them together with the intestines of animals."

4) The fourth motive for cannibalism is hate, revenge and contempt.

In Cochin China a law declared that all rebels, if found guilty, should be put to death and their flesh eaten by faithful subjects, particularly those immediately under the king.[8] When J. de Loureiro was in the country, such an execution took place. If the guilty person was a man, he was beheaded; if a woman, she was stabbed to death. The soldiers guarding the palace then hurried to the corpse. Each used a pocketknife to cut off a little piece, put it into a green lemon and swallow it raw. Since the size of the piece was not prescribed and the country has an aversion to such dishes, the most clever of the soldiers would let the piece of flesh slip between their fingers and only swallow the lemon.

At almost the same time the Cochin Chinese were warring against some mountain people called Mois (they lived to the west and often undertook vicious raids upon the kingdom). Their general, with an army, marched into the mountains. Since he could not reach the enemy due to its inaccessibility and was filled with rage and desire for revenge, he ordered two prisoners to be killed and made the soldiers eat them.

In 1777, while Loureiro was on board an English warship in the harbor of Teirao waiting to leave Cochin China, a troop of rebels arrived who had joined the party of a mighty warlord named Nhae. They captured and killed various people and confidants of the king and, among others, one who had done a great deal of damage and offered a great deal of resistance. As proof of their special hatred for him, they ripped his liver from his body and ate it.

The Cochin Chinese prove their inclination to this perversion by saying: "I want to eat the liver or flesh of this person" to express their hatred of him.

Among many other peoples the desire for revenge is expressed by the wish to drink the enemy's blood. Our German expression "to be bloodthirsty" perhaps originates from that period when our ancestors stilled their thirst for revenge literally with the blood of their enemies and not of grapes.

When at the beginning of the French Revolution desire for revenge and rage of the various parties reached its high point and to gain freedom, equality and fraternity, they persecuted each other enthusiastically and to the extreme; now and again we saw that even in the most civilized nations of Europe man took on his primeval form by thoughtlessly casting off the veneer of higher culture and showing his true character as a child of nature. At that time — and that is only a few years ago — it is claimed that people ate Princess Lamballe's heart from a fanatic desire for revenge.[9] Almost at the same time we were reading in public print that people in Lyons and Naples ate their enemies at public squares.

Sometimes man's natural inclination to brutality breaks through even in the customs and culture of the most educated of nations. As difficult as it is for man to climb to the highest level of education, it is nevertheless very easy for him to crash down again to the lowest by making one single mistake.

The Frenchman Cabri, whom we met on the Island of Nukahiva and who, granted, only had the education of a sailor, provides curious proof of this assertion. All traces of his European upbringing had disappeared. Physically and morally, he had gone wild. He claimed he had never eaten a slain enemy. He had always traded them for pigs. Roberts supported his claim. Despite this, I am convinced that a man who in all his sensibilities has become very much a native, who himself admits that he goes hunting to kill people in order to trade them for pigs and really enjoys this amusement, is just as capable of eating his take in the company of his brothers. He would have made himself look absurd if he had let his comrades eat his laboriously acquired delicacy all alone. Roberts's statement freeing him of all guilt is not convincing because Cabri is clever enough not to tell his enemy about the feast or invite him to it. As a result, he could not know anything about it.

The Nukahivans undeniably eat their friends if pressed by hunger and by their enemies from hatred or custom. The tauas do even more by often lusting for human flesh from lasciviousness and lickerishness. They deliberately act as if a spirit has possessed them (they do this, of course, in places and on occasions where many people have gathered). Using tricks and pretended convulsions, they seem to sink into a dead sleep for a short period of time. They then wake up suddenly and tell the spectators what the spirits in their dreams have inspired and dictated to them. Sometimes the inspiration is that a woman, a man, a tattooed or untattooed man, a fat or thin man, a young person or an old man from the next valley or the other side of the river has to be captured. The spectators then hide in the bushes near a footpath or a stream abounding in fish. The result is that one person or another somewhat resembling the figure from the dream is captured and eaten in the taua's morai in his taboo friends' company. It thus often depends on the magician, sorcerer or taua to determine who, or how many enemies, are to be killed.

If one of the tauas is ill, depending upon the severity of his illness, one, two or more inhabitants of a hostile valley are captured to be consumed as sacrifices for his recovery. If, as a result, the taua recovers, this is good; if not, the sacrifice is repeated. If he dies in the end, then the whole valley participates and war breaks out. That means that they attack their neighbors not from ambush but openly with a large retinue. The neighbors are considered enemies solely because they live on the other side of the river. If they kill a single man or woman, they return to the morai with their take and consume it.

The victor or hero who has killed the enemy receives the head. He immediately severs it from the body, widens the opening at the back of the skull and drinks the blood and eats the brain.

The skull is cleaned of all flesh, and decorated with pig bristles. The lower jaw is ingeniously fastened to the skull by a ribbon made from coconut fibers. During our stay, we had the opportunity to trade for several such skulls.

Deeply rooted prejudices and lasciviousness for human flesh are the main causes for wars and hostilities. In general, however, I cannot imagine their being horrible, since the two parties fighting with each other are seldom large. Desire for conquest, pride of ancestry, claims to a whole valley or a piece of land seem to be seldom or never the cause of war.

During open hostilities, the islanders decorate their hands and feet with lots of feathers. Around their heads they wear slings woven from coconut fibers, which to a foreigner look more like an adornment than armament. The most distinguished heroes fasten the skulls of enemies they have slain around their ankles and hips. In their hands they carry lances, javelins and clubs made from casuarina wood. During the battle, they jump and hop and make all kinds of movements in order to try to avoid being hit by stones or spears. Often they leave the battlefield as soon as a single enemy is lying on the battlefield. Judging by the stories of the Frenchman, who tried to explain the military spirit of these islands to us, it seemed to me that the battle had some similarities with the war games our boys play in the streets.

When they ambush a single enemy, they do it mainly when the weather is bad or on days when it is raining because at these times a larger number of people go fishing. The enemy also cannot see far and cannot easily hear the sound of the hero hidden in the bushes.

I do not know if these islanders also prey upon their enemies during a famine. It would seem strange and, at least for me, unexplainable if, during periods of extreme need, they would rather slaughter their own women and children than ambush their hostile neighbors.

When a woman is near childbirth, a little taboo hut is built near her home for this purpose. Cleanliness is obviously the reason for this custom. The mother or another close female relative manages the business of delivery. Only some women and no men may be present. A large piece of cloth made from the inner bark of the paper mulberry is placed on the ground and another is used to cover the expectant mother. The father usually waits some place near the birthing hut. As soon as he is told that his child has been born, he hurries over and cuts off the umbilical cord about a foot from the child's navel with a sharp stone. To prevent bleeding, it is then knotted and left until it falls off of its own accord. A sharply protruding navel, almost like a hernia, which we observed here and on the Sandwich Islands, is probably the result of such treatment.

Immediately after birth the mother moves about. Her first excursion is to the next stream in order to wash. The baby is also carried by another person for this purpose. Fortune requires that at least one pig be slaughtered at this event and a second one when the umbilical cord falls off. The first pig is usually eaten only by the father; good friends are invited to join in with the second one.

Delivery is said to be easy. Usually it takes one-half hour to, at the most, one hour. Sometimes, however, there are difficult deliveries caused by an unnatural position of the child or in cases with some part of the child's extremities. Every mother generally nurses her own child. Sometimes if she is busy, she will give it to a good friend for a short while. There is no set time for a child to be nursed. Most of the children are not weaned until they can walk alone and some only when they can already talk. Many of them are given other food very early, consisting of popoi and, a few months after birth, raw fish.

Young, unmarried girls may give in to their carnal urges, happily, unhindered, unpunished and without dishonoring themselves or their families. But, as soon as they have chosen the state of matrimony, that is, being the wife of one man, then, according to the laws, all free association with other men stops. As the slave of her husband, she is punished by beating for infidelity or driven off. Her seducer is punished as the husband sees fit, secretly, publicly or not at all. This plainly proves that true ties in marriage and jealousy are present, even if Cabri's information is correct.

As soon as two people have mutually agreed to live together, the bridegroom gives the parents-in-law presents and receives presents from them. The marriage lasts as long as unity and mutual harmony exists. If one or the other wants out of the bonds, he is free to do so. The children find food everywhere and remain either with the father or with the mother, depending upon their parents' agreement. In general, I think this is seldom an issue because complete indifference exists between parents and children.

When a man of high repute's daughter marries, a great many pigs are slaughtered and all the family's friends and acquaintances are invited to a feast. If the bride agrees, every wedding guest has the right, along with the groom, to partake of the joys of the wedding night. The feast usually lasts two to three days or as long as it takes to eat all of the pigs that have been slaughtered. Afterwards, the young wife has to break off all relations with other men and live only with her husband. At least, she dare not give into her inclinations at will, unless her husband is made indulgent with gifts or she is forced against her will to submit to another man.

Rich men may have as many wives as they want or can feed. Monogamy is, however, the most common form of marriage.

When someone dies, the body is washed immediately and placed on a bier made from bamboo covered with a new piece of cloth. It is covered with several new pieces of cloth. At least half of the pigs owned by the deceased's family are slaughtered and roasted. Then the taua and other taboo persons are told of the death and invited to the funeral the following day. Upon the arrival of the guests, behind the bier on which the deceased lies a piece of cloth is stretched and some little stakes erected which are decorated with little, fine, white pieces of cloth.

This is the symbol of the taboo or taboo place. The taua brings along at least four large drums and performs the funeral ceremony. It consists of his babbling a long speech in a totally incomprehensible language, which takes place amidst continual drumming, perhaps in order for noise to prevent evil spirits from harming the deceased. Then the guests begin to consume the pigs, the popoi and breadfruit. They do not stop until there is nothing left. The taua receives the pig's head as his part and the headman, who is always invited to funerals in his valley, receives the pig's hindquarters. If he does not come, it is sent to his home. That is why he usually finds it to his advantage not to appear. The closest relatives have to guard the deceased day and night and rub the body daily in coconut oil. The business takes weeks and months to protect the body against decomposition and finally turns it into a true mummy. Finally, the corpse is wrapped in pieces of cloth which has been soaked in this oil and placed on a special scaffold in the morai or family cemetery, which is taboo for women.

Similar concern for the dead is found almost all over among uncivilized peoples among whom one otherwise finds no trace of religion. It is remarkable that these people display such great veneration and respect for their dead that one might almost suspect that they possess a dark feeling for life after death. The enemies in neighboring areas try to steal each other's dead from the morai. They believe they have performed a heroic deed if they are successful. As soon as they suspect an enemy attack, to prevent it the bodies are taken from the morai and buried someplace nearby.

Among the many types of magic practiced by the islanders, as well as the tauas, is the art of making someone ill by means of magic. An instrument called a *kacha* is used for this purpose. Its preparation is one of the islanders' greatest secrets. The following are supposed to be some of its most important requirements: the person wanting to prepare a kacha must carefully clean his entire body. He may not eat for three days. He may drink very little and must not associate with the female sex. He has to spend the entire time for its preparation at a taboo place, for example, a morai or popoi taboo. The kacha itself is a little purse or bag woven from coconut or other fibers. The skin of a freshly skinned lizard, various kinds of plants, some little stones with a certain shape, a piece of bamboo cane and a number of other things are tied together and put in it. The important thing is to have in it something belonging to the enemy whom one wants to make ill, or something that was somehow connected with him, and keep it with the mixture in the bag. For example, some of his hair, scraps of his food, dirt he had spit upon or urinated on, a little piece from his loincloth, etc. Without this ingredient the kacha does not work. Usually three of these magic purses are prepared. When they are all finished and well smoked, they are buried individually in some remote spot. If a short time later the intended effect occurs and the charmed person becomes ill, he has to try to find out who caused it (especially with the help of a taua). Due to the power of a taboo, this person is required to confess, that is, if a person (whom the ill person suspects) really did weave the magic knot, if asked, he has to admit it because a denial breaks another taboo and immediate death would be the consequence. The ill person immediately brings the magician or enemy a gift of one or more pigs so that the charm is lifted. This consists in digging up the kachas in the presence of several people. If the first gift of pigs is not large enough and the ill person does not become well, then he has to give the enchanter more presents. He then digs up the second kacha and under similar conditions the third. If the enchanter is sufficiently rewarded, the ill person recovers; if not, there is no saving him. The spirits support the just revenge of the enemy and demand the death of the ill person who, depending upon how the kacha has been prepared, must die sooner or later.

Fear of magic and the influence of spirits controls and keeps within bounds the behavior of the inhabitants on that group of islands. The Englishman Roberts told us that he threatens the Nukahivans very often with the influence of his spirit and that they sometimes only obey him because they are afraid that his revengeful spirit could call in European ships that would put an end to their existence on earth.

The tauas are also able to explore the causes of many diseases with their extensive knowledge of magic. If someone does not feel well, he sends for the taua. He examines the ill person or has already had someone else do it. During his visit, he strokes the patient's chest three times and acts as if he has caught his spirit (about like we catch flies). He presumably uses this opportunity to perform some magic tricks and ceremonies. Cabri, the Frenchman, told us in all seriousness (so deeply had superstition taken root in his mind) that he himself had heard the spirit of an ill person in a taua's balled fist and it sometimes whistled loudly and even, in answer to the question why the ill person had to suffer that way, answered in unintelligible language only understood by the tauas. Then the secret was discovered that the ill person had broken a taboo, had stolen breadfruit, coconuts or something else from a taboo tree. He immediately also determined the punishment and the number of pigs necessary to atone for breaking the taboo and restoring health. The pigs offered are then taken to the taua's morai and eaten to restore the ill person to health. The tauas have the advantage of increasing the number, depending upon the wealth of the individual.

Circumcision or the slitting and expansion of the foreskin is a universal operation and is generally performed when a boy reaches puberty. A small stick wrapped in a little piece of cloth is pushed under the foreskin, which is then slit with a sharp stone. The juice of a plant (*pahpa*) is rubbed into the wound. Even though sometimes a rather serious infection develops, this is generally supposed to be over in about ten to twelve days. The operation can be performed by anyone but the father. The person performing the operation is taboo. He has to remain in the patient's house until the infection has disappeared. During this time, he feasts upon pork. In addition, when he leaves, he is rewarded with a pig. Cleanliness is clearly the reason for this operation.

Male modesty consists of a man's carefully hiding his member under its foreskin. That is why it is always kept covered and tied with a string. It is not improper to go totally naked. If a man, however, were not to bind his foreskin, he would be brazen according to the islanders' beliefs.

Given the plentifulness of food, these ever-happy people have a penchant for all kinds of amusements. During the season when the largest numbers of breadfruit are ripe, the headmen or chiefs of a valley sponsor festivals for which they have collected and saved pigs, coconuts, bananas and several kinds of roots for a long time. That way they can distribute them even more lavishly among their people.

Dances are one of the most preferred public festivals. The participants jump about making all kinds of gestures while rapidly swinging their hands and arms without moving much from one spot. It looks as if the people of Nukahiva, like other peoples, are trying to express through dance various activities of their way of life, fishing for example, using slingshots, walking on stilts, and swimming.

All of the people present at these balls come dressed in the most valuable adornments they own. The adornments made from the tail feathers of a tropical bird are particularly important. They are rings decorated with six feathers and worn on the dancer's middle fingers. They help improve the swinging movements infinitely. Along with these finger decorations, they have others ingeniously woven from hair and feathers on their hands, feet, around their hips, on their heads, around their necks and in their ears.

Even though women of rank, as I have mentioned before, always wear at least loincloths at all other times, they must come to dance festivals totally naked. This rule leads to a lot of indecencies permitted everyone on this occasion, to the amusement of the crowd. Cook observed the same thing at dances on Otahiti. The Frenchman Cabri claimed that only young girls, women or widows whose lovers and husbands had either been taken prisoner or died in war danced, that on that occasion they tore at their skin with little stones and their dance could be considered an act of mourning or sorrow. If we remember that, contrary to their usual circumstances, they have to appear totally naked and subject themselves to the laughter and mockery of the crowd, then it is clear that they stand under pressure at the dance.

The places used for dancing are found in the most level areas of the valleys. Large, smooth stones, which are several feet across, are placed tightly and cleanly next to each other so that one almost has to think that European craftsmen had laid such an area at least 100 fadens in length with paving stones.

Places used for dancing are taboo. During the great festivities, all of the hostilities within the various valleys cease so that their inhabitants can take part in the amusements. Despite the taboo, however, the foreign, basically hostile guests are ever on the alert. They never come unarmed and stay together and gather only on one side of the dance area, so that if trouble starts they can better defend themselves if the need arises. Usually they are armed with slingshots, which are very light and bound around their heads. They look more like head ornaments than defensive weapons.

In reality the guests coming from other valleys are not always safe from attack or other hostilities, since sometimes such occasions are also used as cunning ambushes to entice the enemy into a trap in order to be more sure of catching him. It only takes one taua to become possessed by spirits and to dream, thus ending the festivities and beginning the feud.

The music at the festivals consists of wild screaming, the beating of drums, some of which are very large. They have the approximate shape of an upright cylinder or keg. Measured from the ground they are four to four and one-half fuss high. They are one and one-half to two fuss in circumference and of very good workmanship. They have a sharkskin stretched over them. The place used by the musicians is taboo for the women.

Councilor Tilesius, who combines extensive scientific knowledge with rare talents in several branches of the fine arts, was so kind as to share with me the following remarks about the islanders' music. I was all the happier for them, because I am not a votary of Apollo.

It is remarkable, says this scholar, that almost all music of uncivilized peoples, and even in the musical art of the less educated European nations, arises from minor keys. It is characteristic of the Nukahivans' songs that they hover around quarter tones and do not extend beyond the minor third from E to G, except for sometimes dropping to D. The songs are sung in unison. At the most, boys whose voices have not yet deepened, or, women (which is rarely the case), sing an octave higher. Their songs sound sluggish and droning, dark and melancholy and conclude like our choral music. It resembles in many ways the melody of the litany: Kyrie Eleison, which is still sung in many German churches as well as in monks' monotone horae. I have noted the rising and falling from E to G and G to E in half tones, i.e., with F and F sharp. They should, however, be quarter tones. Even though the savages drone out the song, one still notices that distinction. At every break in a word or a line, which I note with the symbol for a rest 𝄐, they pause several seconds and then continue again, gradually decreasing sound from sustained G to E, which I have expressed each time by a diagonal line.

The penchant of these Nukahivan cannibals, those rough, wild children of nature, who certainly are without all trace of musical or any other culture, to love the minor third and the minor key certainly derives from no other cause but that they are the easiest and most natural for them to sing. Where one should look for an explanation for this preference for the minor key is beyond my knowledge and I have read no satisfactory explanation in the works of musicologists. In the songs of Russian sailors, which sound so happy and pleasant at a distance, I have observed a preference for the fourth with three to four beats to a measure. It is clear that they also are artistic, because, even though they contain many minor keys, one still hears occasional apparent transitions to the related major keys, which, even though they return to the minor key after two or three measures, in its totality conveys some happy and comforting feeling. Since, however, these songs are art and are harmonized for several voices and are sung in a lively, quick tempo and the singers themselves betray more musical culture and good ear, they cannot be compared to such uncouth singing. Despite their minor tones, they do not make a sad or melancholy impression. Indeed, their unique quarter-time and the fire with which they are sung lend them rather, in general, life and a sense of joy which is the source of the music.

It is a very different case with the single melody of the savages' national music on Nukahiva. It is used at funerals, marriages, dances, battles, for drinking songs, etc. It is sung at every occasion.

In the few lines I have written about the text's meaning in the following paragraph, I am only trying to explain its genesis, to point out some of the contrasting feelings present in these savages' characters which have given rise to their national music. Since some of the proof lies in what I suspect is the Nukahivans' psychological make-up and is reflected in the meaning of the text, it is possible, if my remarks about the national character and state of affairs of these uncouth, uneducated islanders are correct, that my remarks will be accepted as confirmation of this.

In the beginning the Nukahivans probably sang songs only after returning from battle, especially after victory in which they had lost no more than one or two people and their enemy ten. Probably it was simply hunger or the need for fortification after having asserted themselves, or the imitation of their enemies, or the desire for revenge which led them to the idea of their right to retaliate and thus began the practice of human sacrifice and cannibalism. Their priests (tauas), the craftier and more clever members of the nation, then openly demanded similar feasts, made use of it at every religious and profane opportunity, encouraged the others' simplicity and propensity for superstitions and miracles and demanded human sacrifices also at other times. The savage became accustomed to the idea, and thus soon took on the horrid form of a cannibal.

They accompany their songs at numerous get-togethers and folk festivals by a regular, very loud sound, which they produce by holding their naked left arms tightly against their bodies and hitting the cavity formed between their ribs and the inner side of their elbows with their right hands. These blows mostly produce the following rhythm:

At the same time others clap their bare, hollow hands in eight-time rhythm. Especially if the dance or feast is solemn, drums are added and beat in the same rhythms as with the hands. After this grotesque music, which is accompanied by the basically melancholy song, choral-like in minor tones, the whole group begins to dance at a spot reserved for it. The drums are made of hollowed-out tree trunks, with sharkskin stretched over them. Along the length of the narrower end, holes have been bored as in a stringed instrument's sounding board. Depending upon the degree of tension and the size of the drum or cylinder, the tones are tuned to various heights and depths or pitch, not, however, according to any specific rules or principles. They are mainly used at funerals at which there is singing but not dancing. The drums, together with war trumpets, which together with the troops' war cries send them into battle, are these savages' only musical instruments. The war trumpet is made from a large shell, the triton's horn (*Murex tritonis*), which has been decorated with the hair of a slain enemy. On its lower point (which is its end point as well as an opening into the inner empty chamber), they fix a little coconut shell or the hull of an oil nut as a mouth piece. It sounds something like a herdsman's horn and is blown, inasmuch as I could ascertain, only during war excursions.

Councilor Tilesius has made the following remarks about the text of a song:

The song's point is to present a war scene. At night a savage sees a fire on an enemy island and asks his companions, where is the fire? They answer on the island of Montane (St. Pedro) or on Tauata (St. Christina). They think about the right of retaliation practiced upon prisoners or slain enemies. They demand a fire in order to roast the enemy who has been chosen for the meal. They rejoice in the heroic deed and all of the circumstances associated with it. At the same time, though, come the feelings of sympathy and humanity about the sad results and impression left upon the wife and children, the parents and family of the slain person. The number of days given at the end possibly indicates how many days worth of human flesh is available. I think this text contains a great deal about the national character of these people, of its strange mixture of good and bad united in the savages, of lust for human flesh, cruelty and sympathy.

Singing the song at night, together with their rhythmic clapping and the sight of the fire they are lying around, makes, from a distance, such a wild, partially melancholy, partially despairing, impression upon the listener that he could believe he was hearing his funeral knell.

During the night I spent on land, I found that the continual singing of these generous appearing people left me with a not much more pleasant feeling than those mentioned above. The strong hollow sounds made by the hand hitting the angle formed by the arm pressed against the chest take the place of a death bell. Those people enjoy dancing, which consists of nothing more than arbitrary and artless hopping and jumping while making alternately fast and trembling motions with their extended arms, hands and fingers.

A Nukahivan Song together with Music, Translation and Critical Notes

I obtained this song from the Frenchman Cabri. As far as the text is concerned, it may be correct. I discovered, however, in his translation, after I had studied the Nukahivan language and then a literal translation of the text and compared this to the vocabulary collected on Nukahiva, many things which are wrong, incorrect and defective. If my literal translation is correct, the proof of which is to be found in the text itself and my critical remarks, then I cannot agree with Councilor Tilesius's judgement about the islanders' way of thinking and the mixture of good and bad, the feelings of cruelty and sympathy which he thinks are expressed in this song. I am more of the opinion that they have no sentiments or feelings of sympathy, at least not in this case where they have no sense of having done anything wrong, but rather totally rejoice in the joy of having slain an enemy and are now able to roast and eat him instead of being roasted and eaten themselves.

	Nukahiva Text	Cabri's Translation	Critical Translation
1.	Hia-t-eama äh?	Where is the light?	Where is the light?
2.	I Tauata oh.	On Tauata	On Tauata
3.	t' eama äh?	Why or for what purpose the light?	The light, for what purpose?
4.	tau enata oh.	To roast the enemy.	Here is a man.
5.	Hia ehahe, äh?	Let's start the fire.	Where is fire?
6.	Tai eama oh.	We have fire.	Here (is) light.
7.	Tau enata äh	We want to roast him.	Here is the man.
8.	enata oh.	We have him.	The man.
9.	Ōtĕmăō.	He wanted to escape.	The flying fish.
10.	ah mate mate äh	Now he is dead.	Is he dead?
11.	itŭētŭĕ äh	The sister is weeping.	Is he weeping?
12.	titi hei äh	His parents are weeping.	Is he angry?
13.	mate moi äh	His daughters are weeping?	Is the daughter dead?
14.	Atahi äh, etc.	1st, 2nd, 3rd, 4th, 5th, 6th, 7th, 8th, 9th, 10th day	

Critical Remarks about Each Line

1. *Ihea* or *hia* means where; *eama*, the light. The "t" seems to be inserted for the sake of obtaining a pleasant sound; *äh* is often used to denote a question. See vocabulary.

2. Tauata is the Island of St. Christina, one of the older Marquesas Islands.

3. This is basically a repetition of the first line and could also mean where is the light or the fire.

4. *Tau* has to mean to roast. Unfortunately, I do not have this word in my collection and therefore cannot say with certainty what it means. *Enata* means the man, human being. Perhaps *tau* and *tai* mean the same thing. The latter means here: thus: here is a captured man already or an enemy. As soon as the islanders have killed someone, naturally the next idea is to roast him.

5. *Hia* should probably be *ihea* as in the first line.

6. *Tai* here (see line 4) *eama*, the light.

7. Perhaps this *tau* should be *tai*: here is the fire, here is the man, who, of course, has been captured for roasting and eating.

8. The repetition undoubtedly intensifies the joy.

9. Symbolically, just as the flying fish is often captured when fleeing, so now we have this man as our booty.

10. This can mean: he is dead or is he dead? I prefer the latter because of the following questions.

11. *Ǔě* or *ŭwäh* means to cry, to weep. Probably the slain enemy is meant and not his relatives. At different times Cabri translated this line in various ways. One time: the stone got him and another time: the man is a prisoner. In both cases it is natural that the unfortunate man weeps. Nothing is said here at all about a sister (*toăhine*), but rather about weeping. This most naturally can refer to the enemy and can also serve as a contrast to the tenth line, that is: Is he dead or is he alive? If the stone hit hard enough, then he is most likely dead. Weeping then follows.

12. *Titi* is supposed to be a male name. *Hei* means angry, angered. The enemy who has been wounded by a stone or spear, it appears, is often captured and perhaps sometimes tries to save himself by fleeing or using his strength.

13. *Moi* means the daughter; *mate*, dead; *äh* could again indicate a question. Perhaps *moi* actually means the female sex and the question is whether the victim on the battlefield is male or female.

14. Numbers follow: here, from one to ten or whichever are chosen. I do not know what they truly mean. I could not find out whether they indicate the number of enemy killed in battle. They sing from one to ten. See the numbers.

Running on stilts is as great an amusement as dancing. The inhabitants of the Washington Islands have perhaps more dexterity in this sport than any other nation on earth. They put on races during their large public festivals. One tries to get in the other's way and, while balancing on one leg or stilt, tries to throw his opponent off balance. The one who falls to the ground is subject to general laughter and mockery. The execution of the sport caught our attention all the more because the dance-place used for it is covered by smooth stones which must make running more difficult. Eight- to ten-year-old children are accustomed to using them. Pleasure seems to be the main reason for this exercise. If we were to assume that frequent floods and the need to maintain contact with each other gave rise to their use, then we would have to admit that naked people, who often spend days in the water, would certainly not be afraid to get wet feet on occasion and, as a result, are not forced to use such things.

We admired their swimming ability above all. It surpassed anything we could imagine. They could easily make an observer think that we human beings were born to live in water.

They can do everything in water. They can almost remain standing in the same place by using their feet so that one could only see their heads and shoulders. They cracked coconuts open in the water and ate them, brought various articles for trade tied to a long pole which they carried above the water to keep them from getting wet. Often they swam with small children on their shoulders, dived from high, steep cliffs into the ocean and preferred to swim to the opposite shore rather than take the long way around the bay on foot over sharp stones. We saw some islanders who spent almost the whole day swimming around the ship without seeming to tire. Mufau, who had never been on a European ship, climbed the big mast several times of his own accord and jumped for fun and to the astonishment of the spectators into the ocean. Captain von Krusenstern had him called back when he was about to jump from the top yard. We could not stand to watch him without shuddering in amazement as he balanced for several seconds at such a height with his feet pulled in tight against his body in order to keep his head up, and how the force of his fall and the weight of his body caused him to dive so deeply that he only appeared again on the surface of the water several seconds later.

Their manifold adornments do not appear to have any special significance, to be worn as a mark of class or distinction. They decorate their heads with headbands as well as ornaments made from feathers mixed with mother-of-pearl and other trimmings. Usually they shave their heads except for two small round spots just above the ears and bind this long hair into a high bunch so that they look as if they have horns. The same custom is almost universal among Chinese children.

The holes in their ears are so large that one can comfortably stick an object through them which is three to four lines thick or about the size of the little finger. A mussel weighing about an unze with a somewhat ground-down pig's tooth fastened to its back, or a light, oval piece of breadfruit wood is the largest decoration put in their ears. They also stick in their ears or hang from strings in their ears large iron nails, little black wooden sticks several lines thick and about two zoll long and other trifles.

They consider a kind of gorget in the shape of a horseshoe the most beautiful necklace. It is made from several rows of small bands of light breadfruit wood. They fasten red and black seeds (*Abrus precatorius Linn.*) to these using resin obtained from the same tree from which necklaces are made for women in Europe.[10] One often sees necklaces made of rows of pig's teeth and some pieces of bone or thick, rounded, longish mussel shells fastened to a string neatly woven from coconut fiber. Some of them, for lack of objects of art, had hung around their necks or stuck in their ears little fish, crabs, flowers, mussels, fruit or even a present from us (a nail, a knife or some other object), which they wanted to carry on their persons.

Red or any naturally bright feathers (they learned very soon to recognize artificially colored ones) seemed to be valued very highly. Kätänuäh, who was not very generous with his pigs, wanted to trade us one for a small parrot we had brought from Brazil. Cabri as well as Roberts told us that he wanted to make a platonic man of it, that they plucked roosters and other colorful birds very often in order to use their feathers as ornaments.

The *hopemoa* is the most valuable ornament. It is a bunch of long, curly hair the men cut from their wives' hair and tie behind them. Certain rings made of tropical bird feathers, worn on their fingers during dances, are the next most valuable. In order to get them, the inhabitants climb steep cliffs at night, capture the sleeping birds and pluck their tail feathers without killing them so that they can repeat the process when the feathers have grown in again. In addition, we saw another kind of feather jewelry worn on the arms and feet and strings of little *conchylia*.

The preparation of clothing or cloth from the inner bark of the paper mulberry tree differs little from the methods described by Cook. Women solely and alone are responsible for making it. The men's main occupation is making tools, utensils and weapons. The latter are tastefully and carefully made. One man carves lances, slingshots and war clubs. Another man decorates them with the neatly braided hair of an enemy slain in war. Beautiful, sturdy slings are woven from coconut fibers and those of another plant, which I did not get to see (probably a kind of nettle or *Phornium tenax Forst.*). They make stilts industriously and well. There are figures at the morais intended to represent human beings. They clearly show that these people have not made much progress in the fine arts. They spend more time making fish nets than hooks. The latter are simple and made from mother-of-pearl shells without any barb. Sun or wind fans are woven skillfully and well. Utensils consist of calabashes decorated with human and other bones and surrounded by nets and smaller and larger eating vessels resembling troughs with poorly carved human faces and fish and birds for decoration. Coconut shells are used for drinking cups.

Among their toys we got to know one made of a small, long stick about a zoll thick and as long as a shoe. It had an opening at one end. A five- to six-zoll long peg pointed at the lower end was stuck through it. They stuck a ball of loosely woven coconut fibers onto the point. If they hit the stick with another stick, the ball stuck to the peg was shaken off. The trick was to catch the ball in the air before it hit the ground, thus creating a kind of yo-yo.

It is highly probable that the islanders have some other games and amusements, but we heard nothing about them.

In comparison to the inhabitants of other South Sea islands, the Nukahivans are very backward in shipbuilding. Their canoes are twenty to thirty fuss long, only one fuss wide and hold at the most six to seven people. To prevent them from capsizing they use a balancing pole or outrigger, as is also common among many other peoples. The whole canoe is poorly built. The boards used for the sides are sewn together with coconut fibers. Openings and joints are stuffed with moss and painted with resin from breadfruit trees. In case the boat capsizes or becomes very leaky, they all jump out, swim next to it and bail it out in a few minutes with their hands so that they can climb in again without the danger of sinking, and continue paddling on their way. Paddles and rudders are made with more care than the canoe.

Miscellaneous Remarks

Bread, sugar, rusk, in short everything we offered these people, they smelled like monkeys. Several times I had the opportunity to observe that they have a very strong sense of smell. They were very fond of sugar but did not like salted meat at all.

Since they have no clothing and carry no bags or purses, they often carry little things in their mouths. One day an inhabitant, who saw me looking for little common crabs along the beach and under stones, accompanied me and pulled six living crabs he had caught out of his mouth.

They are very adroit in many physical exercises and activities. They can climb the highest trees with indescribable dexterity — not as we usually do with our knees pressed together, but rather like monkeys with their toes extended. Probably their strong nails also help. They climb the steepest cliffs with ease, but they are clumsy when running fast.

If they want to give a negative answer or say no, they stick their tongues out.

Threatening with the index finger is a sign of friendship on the island.

If two friends meet, they press the tips of their noses together instead of kissing. They know nothing about that sweet sentiment.

The upper class there, as in many other Asiatic countries, grows very long finger nails in order to show the others that they do not have to work with their hands.

They can move their toes freely and arbitrarily. When they were on board the ship, they would often reach a comrade swimming near the ship a piece of iron they were holding in their toes so that they did not have to bend over.

In order to make coconut oil one scrapes the meat from several coconuts onto banana leaves which are placed in the sun for four to five days. Then juice from as many freshly scraped coconuts is poured on it and again left lying in the sun for two or three days. Coconut oil is then obtained by pressing this and stored until used in a hollow piece of bamboo.

Here, as well as on the Sandwich Islands and other South Sea Islands, shark teeth from the upper jaw are used for cutting, indeed even for shaving. The lower teeth are used for drilling. They are fastened to a stick and whirled by hand.

Small pieces of coral, madrepore and millepore serve as rasps in making tools and working on hard casuarina wood. They work like a wood file. Shark skin is used to polish weapons. Bows and arrows, which are used by so many peoples, seem to be totally unknown there.

Kätähnuäh's father, an elderly man, is said to have a great deal of medical knowledge. Drinking sea water is said to be the prescription he prefers.

According to Cabri, the birth of twins is not very rare there.

Pigs and rats are the only native mammals on the island. The inhabitants catch the latter with their bare hands and feed them to the pigs. During periods of famine, they also serve as human food and are supposed to taste quite good.

We saw enough pigs the size of our European ones, especially in the Schegua Valley. Their owners, however, did not want to trade or sell them, at least not at the price we had set.

The Englishman Roberts had two dogs, which the inhabitants called pigs, probably because they had hardly ever seen another animal. A billy and nanny goat (probably called horned pigs) are supposed to have been brought to Nukahiva from St. Christina. Since we were in another valley, we did not see anything of them.

There are neither domestic nor wild cats there, probably, however, feral ones in uninhabited areas that feed upon rats.

Not many chickens are raised. Roosters, however, with beautiful feathers are highly prized for these. From time to time they are plucked bare. There are no fleas whatsoever there.

The above are about the most noteworthy things I observed during our ten-day stay on Nukahiva. Readers, especially interested in the Marquesas and Washington Islands can find in Cook, Forster, Vancouver, Marchand, Wilson, von Krusenstern and others many interesting observations which I have left out in order not to be repetitious.

With Roberts' and Cabri's help I had the rare opportunity to collect some samples of the language.[11] Although incomplete and less entertaining, I still find them important enough to list.

Vocabulary from the Island of Nukahiva[12]

German	English	Nukahivan
	-A-	
Aal (Fisch)	eel (fish)	puchi
Abend, diesen	evening, this	achi, achi
Abbrechen	to break off	wĭwāh
Ich breche in Stücken	I am breaking into pieces	wiwah ïaoë
Abhauen	to fell	koti
Laßt uns Bäume abhauen, oder Holz machen	Let's fell trees or make wood	koti te wehīe
Abbeißen	to bite off	anē-nahu
Beißt ein Stück Schweinefleisch ab	bite off a piece of pork	anē-nāhu te buaca oë
Abkühlen, d.h., Wind mit dem Fächer machen	to cool off, i.e., to make wind with a fan	tahi te tukuanu
Nehmt einen Fächer um euch abzukühlen	take a fan in order to cool yourselves off	ata oë tahi maï-oë te tukuanu

German	English	Nukahivan
Abkratzen, abschaben, abreiben	to scrape off, grind off, rub off	awau
Schabt Cocosnüsse und preßt den Saft daraus	Scrape coconuts and press the juice out of them	awau oë tĕēhi ŏōe toco ehi
Absegeln	to sail away, to set sail	watē ĕ
Das Schiff ist abgesegelt	The ship has set sail	te waka watē-ĕ
Abkürzen, abschneiden, (ein Stück von etwas)	to shorten, to cut off (a piece of something)	kokō ŏti pōōtonōa
Alter Mann	old man	koūha
Alte Frau	old woman	bachaïo
Angel	fishing tackle	medau
Ankleiden, sich, d.h., das Stück Zeug nehmen	to dress, i.e., to take the piece of cloth	ătō te kachu
Anführrer	leader	aïki
Ankommen	to arrive	watātā
Ein Schiff ist angekommen, d.h., eigentlich: großes Canot nahe	A ship has arrived, i.e., in reality, a large canoe nears	te waka nui wātātā
Antworte mir	answer me	apëa maï-oë
Anzünde, z.ß, das Licht	to ignite, for example, the light	apūhi, tĕama
Arme (die)	arms (the)	ehima
Arm, nicht reich	poor, not rich	kikino
Atmen, erhitzt sein	to breathe, to be heated, flushed	kaï-kaï
Auge	eye	matta
Augenbraunen	eyebrows	tuke hāë
Aufwachen	to awaken	u-a-aï
Ausschnitzen	to carve out, cut out	ēhū
Aufhängen (das) des Leichnams im Morai	The hanging up of the corpse in the morai	hakatu des
Aufhängen an der Wand	to hang on the wall	akikitiïuka
Aufdecken, aufmachen, (ein Gefäß)	to uncover, to open (a container)	apepeho
Auslöschen (das Licht), d.h., tot Licht	to extinguish (the light), i.e., dead light	matte tēama
Ausruf für den Geist eines Verstorbenen, dem man etwas opfert	call for the spirit of a person for whom one is offering something up	natetu
Austern	oysters	uchi
Axt	axe	toki

-B-

German	English	Nukahivan
Baden, waschen	to bathe, wash	kaukau

German	English	Nukahivan
Bach; eigentlich: viel Wasser	stream; in reality, a lot of water	wai nui
Bananen	bananas	meiga
Bald	soon	eppo, or heppo
Bart	beard	kumi
Bauch	belly	koopu, ecopu
Bataten	batatas, sweet potatoes	tekuma
Befehlshaber	chief	aĭki
Beil	axe	toki
Beide zwei	both, two	tau
Begräbnissplatz	burial place	mahai
Beischlaf	cohabitation	uka-uka, titōi
Beine	legs	waĭwaĭ
Beissen	to bite	nahu
Binde, die Vorhaut mit einem Schnürchen	to tie up the foreskin with a little string	ehunatibuna
Binde, Schamgürtel	protective wrap, loincloth	eūte
Binde (von grobem Zeug)	wrap (of coarse material)	tiābu
Binden	to bind	ahumu
einen Schädel um die Hüften	a skull around the hips	ahumu te opogo tēhōhĕ
Blut	blood	tooto
Blume	flower	puamomono
Blitz	lightening	teū-ĭ-ĭa
Blatt eines Baumes	leaf of a tree	tehōŭ
Bohnen, rote (*Abrus precatorius*)	beans, red	boniŭ
Brotfrucht	breadfruit	mähie
Sauergegohrene	sour fermented	maa
Brotbaum	breadfruit tree	tĕmŭ mēi
Boden, Erde, Grund	ground, earth, dirt	whennōa, hennūah
Brust	chest	huma, huma
Brüste, weibliche	breast, female	tehu, ehou
Bringen, bringe mir	to bring, bring me	tukukumaĭ
Bruder	brother	tunane eteine
Brennen, verbrennen	to burn, to burn up	etutu teāhi
Böse	bad, evil	whahāi
Busch	bush	teita

German	English	Nukahivan
	-C-	
Canot	canoe	hwaa, wahah, wakah
Coconüsse	coconuts	nīu, aehie, teehi
Corallen (Glasknöpfe)	coral (glass buttons)	pipi
	-D-	
Daumen	thumb	maga magaïma
Donner	thunder	hatu piki, hatuti
Du, oder Ihr	you or ye	oï
Dieb	thief	ekamu
Dolch	dagger	cohe
	-E-	
Eisen	iron	tokï
Essen	to eat	akaï
Gib mir zu essen	give me something to eat	kaï-maï
Ehemann	husband	medua, motūa
Vater	father	(motūa)
Er, sie, Ihr	he, she, ye	oë
Erde	earth	hennua
Es ist so, es ist wahr	that is the way it is, that is true	ehoï
Ellenbogen	elbow	hima
Eidechse	lizard	ekaka
Eltern	parents	teamutu
	-F-	
Fächer	fans	tahi
Fächer mit geschnitztem Handgriff	fans with carved handles	tahikatu
Fangen	to catch	amu
Felsen, Insel	rock, island	moto, mŏōto
Feuer	fire	eachi, eahi
Feuer machen (reiben)	to build a fire (to rub)	eika teahi
Feuergewehr, Flinte	firearms, musket	pūi
Federputz, Kopfschmuck	feather adornment, head ornament	beue
Eine andere Art	another kind	beigūa
Federn von Hähnen	rooster feathers	teūhū

German	English	Nukahivan
Federschmuck für den Hintern	feather ornament for the backside	hopemoa
Fechten, streiten	to fence, fight	toūa
Fersen	heels, tracks	tuki te waïwaï
Fisch	fish	ika
Fischen	to fish	tanaï ika, peke teika
Fische, eine besondere Art schwarzer	fish, a particular type of black ones	pahūa
Fischangel	fishing hook	medau
Finger	finger	magamagaima
Fliegen	to fly	eōhna
Fliegender Fisch	flying fish	māŏ, ŏtemāo
Fliege, die	the fly	tika-uē
Flöte (von zwei Röhren)	flute (with two pipes)	buchoche
Fuß	foot	tewaï-waï
Freund (eigentlich: gut)	friend (actually: good)	taï
Freundschaftlicher Mann	friendly man	enata mitaï
Wir wollen Freunde sein	we want to be friends	mitaï ane-u-tau
Frau	woman	wehine
Frau eines Ehemanns	wife	wehanna
Furcht haben	to be afraid	hametau-oë
Ich fürchte mich	I am afraid	hamatau-aü
Ich fürchte mich nicht	I am not afraid	aoë hametau-au
Folgt mir	follow me	mamūï maï
Fremder	stranger, foreigner	manehih

-G-

German	English	Nukahivan
Geben	to give	tukemaï
Gib mir etwas	give me something	tukumai, taïtaï
Gib mir zu trinken	give me something to drink	eïnu maï
Gebären	to bear, give birth	aïa-teama
Gefäß für Wasser (Kalebassen)	vessel for water (calabash)	hūĕ
Gefecht	fight, battle	toūa
Gestern	yesterday	enenahe
Geschenk	gift	taïtaï

German	English	Nukahivan
Geschwür	abscess, running sore	memāï, mamaï
Gewand der Frauen um die Hüften	women's hip-wrap	teiwēu
Geruch (guter)	smell (good)	kekāa
Geist des Verstorbenen	dead man's spirit	wahinehăi
Geist (der verfolgt) das Gespenst (Auch der Geist der Lebendigen, der bei dem Tahbu wirkt)	spirit (that pursues) ghost (Also the spirit of the living that is active in taboos)	tetūa
Gelb (vieleicht auch die Wurzel welche gelb färbt)	yellow (perhaps also the root that dyes yellow)	ĭ ĕga-mōa
Gelähmt	lame	mohoi, cowi
Genug	enough	ĕtōe
Glaskorallen	glass beads	pipi aï
Gut (dies ist)	good (this is)	mei tahi-mitāki
Gras	grass	mugu, totoë buaga
Groß (und viel) sehr groß	large (and much) very large	nui nui-nui
Groß, lang, großer Mann	large, big big man	hōa enata hōa

-H-

German	English	Nukahivan
Haar	Hair	whu oho
Sehr langes Haar zum Tanzschmuck	very long hair for adornment while dancing	hobemōa
Halten	to hold	koiteima
Halt an	stop, check, hold	ākăēa
Hand	hand	eïma
Hals	neck	kaki, kăkĕihe
Halsband von roten Bohnen	necklace of red beans	teha tefa
Haus	house	ohāāï, tehāĕ
Haut des Menschen	human skin	kūko
Harz von der Brotfrucht	breadfruit resin	eipāu
Haifisch	shark	mōno
Herz	heart	tĕ ā te
Heute	today	kabo

German	English	Nukahivan
Herabsteigen	to climb down	amaï ahēke
Hintere (der)	the man at the back	papa titōhe
Hinaufsteigen	to climb up	amei ahiti
Holz	wood	wahie
Hoden (die)	testicles	comāi
Hoch	high	ōă
sehr hoch	very high	ōă nūi
Holen, hole es mir	to fetch, fetch it for me	atu, utio-oë
Hügel	hill	pūfi
Hund	dog	buaka nūohĕ
Huhn	chicken	mōha
Husten	to cough	ehapu
Hungrig sein	to be hungry	eoue

-I-

German	English	Nukahivan
Ihr	you	ooë
Ich	I	āu, wau
Insel, Land	island, land	whennua
Insel, Felsen	island, rocks, cliffs	mooto

-J-

German	English	Nukahivan
Ja	yes	àh
ist im Frageton; auch als Frage, wie das französische *est-ce* zu gebrauchen	is an inflection, also a question, which is used like the French *est-ce*	

-K-

German	English	Nukahivan
Kamm, Läusekamm	comb, comb for lice	kōhĕu
Kalt	cold	ĕānŭ
Katze	cat	pōtŭ
ist nicht *pŏhōtu*, einem schönen Mädchen, zu verwechslen	is not to be confused with *pŏhōtu*, a beautiful girl	
Kahn, ein Canot	boat, a canoe	waga
Keule, Streitkeule	club, war club	kăāu-tōa
Kinn, Kinnlade	chin, jawbone	Cohu-āï, Coufai
Klein	small	iti
sehr klein	very small	iti-iti
Kleiner Knabe	little boy	tama iti

German	English	Nukahivan
Knie	knee	mōë
Kommt her	come here	ĕtămāi, bimai, ïutamaï
Kopf, Schädel eines Menschen	head, human skull	oopocho obogo
Kratzen	to scratch	tube
Krebse	crabs	epōōto, pēhū
Krebse fangen	to catch crabs	aheke pēhū
Küssen mit Nase	kissing with noses	ehoni teīhu, onaichu
	-L-	
Lachen	to laugh	bucata, whacata
Lahm	lame	cowi
Lanze (schwere, lange)	lance (heavy, long)	pakehu
Lanze, leichte	lance, light	kēbu
Laß sehen	let's see	aï
Laß mich allein (im Unwillen)	leave me alone (annoyed)	tume aha
Licht	light	eama
Lieben, das Weib	to love, a woman	wehine nau
Lippen	lips	kĭ nūtu
Das Tätowieren der Lippen	the tattooing of the lips	koniho
Legen in die Erde (vergraben)	to put in the earth (to bury)	etōmi
Leibbinde, ein Netz oder Tuch um den Leib, worin sie während eines Gefechtes einen Steinvorrat schleppen	a body sling used for carrying a supply of stones during battle	katu
Lüge, die	lies, falsehoods	tichoë, tiwāwa
L. m. i. A. ein ziemlich europäisches Schimpfwort	k. m. a. a rather European swearword	tororo
	-M-	
Mann	man	enata
Ein magrer Mann	a skinny man	hua-mocca
Mann, fetter, großer	man, fat, large	enata nui
Männliches Glied	penis	ĕūĕ, komaï
Matte von Stroh	straw mat	moïca
Meer, das	the sea	tăi
Das Meer ist still, ruhig, d.h., es ist tot	the sea is quiet, calm, i.e., it is dead	mate tetaï
Messer	knife	koche

German	English	Nukahivan
Machen, was macht ihr	to make, do, what are you making, doing	ehata oë
Machen (ein Haus i.d. bauen)	to build a house	eata tehae
Menschenfresser	cannibal	kaïnata
Mond	moon	mahine
Neumond, d.h., der Mond welcher kommen wird	new moon, i.e., the moon which is coming	mahine etamai
Vollmond, d.h., großer Mond	full moon, i.e., big moon	mahine nui
Morgen, der	the morning	oï-oï
Morgen früh	tomorrow morning	oï-oï tika
Mutter	mother	ĕkūhi
Mund, eigentlich Lippen	mouth, actually lips	henutu
Muschel, die, womit man Coconüsse schabt	shell, with which ones scrapes coconuts	tū-ū-aï
Perlmuttermushel	mother-of-pearl shell	uchi

-N-

German	English	Nukahivan
Nabel	navel	pitu
Nagel, eiserner	nail, iron	pūïpui
Nägel an den Fingern	fingernails	matugu
Nahe kommen, kommt mir nicht nahe	to approach, don't approach me	auhāhăgă pīmāï
Name, wie heißt ihr	name, what is your name	oaïtoichoa, oaïtouhoa
Naß, viel Wasser	wet, a lot of water	nuï nüi waï
Nähen das Zeug	to sew the material	tuïtuï cacho
Nehmt dies weg	take this away	akawe
Nehmt dies	take this	aï-ïa
Nein	no	ăŏë
Nordwind	north wind	tukuahu

-O-

German	English	Nukahivan
Ohren	ears	buaĭna
Oberhaupt	chief	a-ï-ki, e-i-ki
Öffnet die Coconuß, d.h., Wasser der Coconuß	open the coconut, i.e., coconut milk	wahi teēhi
Ostwind	east wind	tiutiu

-P-

German	English	Nukahivan
Packt euch fort	get out of here, scram	atā-oē
Packen, zusammenpacken	to pack, pack up	appa
Pech, S. Harz	tar, see resin	

German	English	Nukahivan
Pisang	banana	meika
Pfeiffen	to whistle	mahpu
Priester	priest	atūa, etua

-R-

German	English	Nukahivan
Rauch	smoke	uwaï
Regen	rain	eūa
Reinigen, eigentlich mit weißer Farbe bestrichen	to clean; actually, to coat with white color	tawaīhĕ
Rot	red	kua
Ruder	rudder	ehoh
Rücken	back	matetua
Rufen	to call	apewau
Rufe den Mann	call the man	apewau tenata
Riechen (gut) von einer Blume	to smell (good) of a flower	kekau

-S-

German	English	Nukahivan
Sagen	to tell, say	peau
Ich sage Euch	I am telling you	peau, maï oë
Ich sage	I am saying	eata-oë
Sagt mir den Namen des Landes	tell me the name of the country	ahaki maï oë te hennūa ăh
Saamen	seeds	kakanaï
Salz	salt	tāi
Sand	sand	enutai
Bring mir Sand	bring me sand	tukamāi enutāi
Schlecht, nicht gut (von Essen)	bad, not good (of food)	vhau-vhau
Schwanger sein	to be pregnant	ētŭbŭtāma
Schenkel	thigh	puwha
nicht mit *pucha*, Corallen zu verwechseln	not to be confused with *pucha*, coral	
Schwester	sister	tōăhine
Schlagen	to hit	pēhi pēhi
Schwarz	black	keke
Schlafen	to sleep	emōĕ
Schlafe mit mir, d.h., beide schlafen	sleep with me, i.e., both sleep	emoë taua
Festschlafen, schnarchen	to sleep soundly, to snore	matekāuhiĕmōĕ
Schwein	pig	buaca
Schiff der Europäer, d.h., großes Canot	European ship, i.e., large canoe	tewaka nui
Schön	pretty, beautiful	metaki
Schneiden	to cut	kokoti

German	English	Nukahivan
Schulter	shoulder	bowhei
Schreien	to scream	wewau
Schmutz	dirt, filth	ēĕpo
Schwitzen	to sweat	tuchuanu
Stinken durch Ausdünstung	to stink from perspiration	tuchia
Schlechter Kerl, armer Teufel	bad guy, poor devil	kiki-īnŏ or kikinŏ
Schneidende Instrumente aus Muscheln oder Austern	cutting instruments made from mussel or oyster shells	uchi
Schönes Mädchen	beautiful girl	poŏtu
Schwimmen	to swim	ĕkāu
Schmerz, Es tut weh	pain, it hurts	hemimaï
Schnecken, eine Art großer	snail, a large variety	butata
Setzen, setzt euch	to sit, sit down	noho oë
Segel auf dem Canot nicht zu verwechseln mit *tevha* ein Halsschmuck	canoe sail not to be confused with *tevha*, a neck adornment	tēa
Sehen, laßt	see, let's	aï-aï
Sehen	to see	tioche
Seele des Verstorbenen	dead man's soul	nătĕtū
Seil, Tau	rope, hawser	vhau
Dünne Schnur	thin thread	iti-iti vhau
Setzt euch	pull	noho
Singen	to sing	caba
Singe etwas	sing something	caba mai oë
Singe, das, der Priester bei Toten	the priest's singing for the dead	ewanahna
Sonne	sun	ūmăti
Sohn, kleiner Knabe	son, small boy	etama iti
Sogleich nicht zu verwechseln mit *eepo*, Schmutz	immediately not to be confused with *eepo*, dirt, filth	eppo, heppo
Spiegel	mirror	ehakatta, uhatta
Springen	to jump	hobu
Sterben	to die	mate-matte
Stehlen	to steal	makamu
Sterne	stars	evhetu
Stirne	forehead	hāi

German	English	Nukahivan
Stille	quiet, peace	tuitui
Macht keinen Lärmen, d.h., mir schmerzen die Ohren	don't make noise, i.e., my ears hurt	maï nia te buaina
Stock	stick	mihu
vielleicht auch ein Stück Holz dieses Namens	perhaps also a piece of wood with this name	
Stein	stone, rock	ekiwa, kiwa
Stück (Teil eines Ganzen)	piece (part of a whole)	pōðtonoa
Stinken	to stink	pĭāu
sagen *peau*	pronounced *peau*	
Stinken	to stink	tuchia
Schimpfname, ein, wörtlich: Schlafe deiner Mutter bei	a pejorative name; literally: sleep with your mother	titoitokui
L. m. i. A.	k. m. a.	tororo*

-T-

German	English	Nukahivan
Tag	day	uateu, watea
Tätowieren	to tattoo	pīkipātu
Tätowieren der Lippen	to tatto the lips	conīo
Tanzen	to dance	ehaka, wehaka hobu
Oder den Tanz springen	or to leap the dance	te coika
Tanzschmuck	adornment for the dance	hobumoa, hopemoa
Tot	dead	mate, matte
Töten	to kill	womate
Tote aufhängen im Haus	to hang the dead up in the house	hakatu
Tochter oder Mädchen	daughter or girl	moï
Testikel	testicle	comāï
Tuch, Zeug	cloth, material	kahu, kachu
Trinken	to drink	aïnu, eïnu
Trommel	drum	epachu
Trocknen	to dry	waïwēi
Das Land ist trocken	the country is dry	hennua weïwēi

-V-

German	English	Nukahivan
Verboten	forbidden	tahbu

*It is remarkable how this thought, the most common pejorative among the Russians, is found here on Nukahiva.

German	English	Nukahivan
Verheiratet sein	to be married	noho te wahanna
sitzen oder stehen mit einem Weib	to sit or stand with a woman	
Vogel	bird	emānu
Vater	father	motua
Verletzen	to injure	bohōhĕ
Verwunderung (Ausdruck der)	surprise (expression of)	ehōōōh

-W-

German	English	Nukahivan
Was ist das	what is that	ĕhātĕmeanēi
Warm	warm	weawea
Heiß, außer Atem	hot, out of breath	kaï kaï
Warum	shy	iwawa
Wartet	wait	eppo
Wasser	water	ewāi, ewahi
Wahrheit	truth	tiătohu
Waisenkind	orphan	enata tubenōa
Was wollt ihr	what do you want	ehata oē
Wachsen	to grow	ŭătūbū
der Brotbaum wächst	the breadfruit tree is growing	uătubu te mei
Waschen	to wash	cokau
Weib	woman	wahine
Weib, Frau eines Mannes	woman, wife of a man	mahui
Weinen	to cry	uwäh
Wehtun	to hurt	hemimaï
Weggehen	to go away	tăhatăchōĕ
Wegnehmen, tragen	to carry away, to bear	hakawe or wahio
Weiße Farbe, wahrscheinlich Kreide oder Muschelkalk	white paint, probably caulk or shell lime	pūī-o
Wer ist dies	who is this	ehate-ēï
Wind	wind	metāni
Wind lassen (einen)	to let wind	ēhū
Wieviel	how much	ehīa
Wir beide	both of us	tehua
Wo	where	ĭhēa
Wofür	for what, why	ehata
Wollen, ich will eigentlich groß und vielleicht: auch sehr	to want me to, I want to; actually, large, or perhaps also very much	nui
Ich will nicht	I do not want to	koë nui
Ich will trinken	I want to drink	eïnu-nuï
Wollen	to want to	teāki

German	English	Nukahivan
Wollt Ihr (als Frage) dasselbe heißt auch ich will. Es kommt auf die Aussprache an, ob fragend oder bejahend	do you want to; the same thing means I want to. It depends upon the pronounciation whether it is a question or an affirmation	äh
Wund werden	to become chapped, raw	bohŏhĕ
Wurzel (*Arum macrorhizon*)	root	happeh

-Z-

German	English	Nukahivan
Zähne	teeth	niho
Zeug von Maulbeerbaum	mulberry cloth	cachu
Zeigt mir	show me	aï-aï
Zerbrechen	to smash to pieces	tŭwāh
Zuruf (Ausdruck des)	shout, cheer (expression of)	ēhōh
Zunge	tongue	ĕēho
Zuckerrohr	sugar cane	tĕtō
Zwillinge	twins	mahaka

Zahlen, numbers

German	English	Nukahivan
Eins	one	botahai
Zwei	two	bohua
Drei	three	botou
Vier	four	boha, bofa
Fünf	five	bohima
Sechs	six	bohono
Sieben	seven	bofiddo, fiddu
Acht	eight	bowahu
Neun	nine	bohiwa
Zehn	ten	boohu, ongofulu
Zwanzig	twenty	hua fulu
Dreißig	thirty	tolu, (tou 3.) ongofulu
Vierzig	forty	fa ongofulu
Fünfzig	fifty	hima ongofulu
Hundert	one hundred	tehau
Zweihundert	two hundred	uatehau
Dreihundert	three hundred	tou teha, etc.
Tausend	one thousand	afeï

NOTES

1. The original German is *Anthropologie* (anthropology); however, Langsdorff discusses anthropophagy in this chapter.

2. Juan de Loureiro (1715-1796), *Flora cochinchinsis*, edited by Karl Ludwig Wildenow (Berlin: Haude and Spener, 1793). De Loureiro was a Portuguese botanist. He spent 36 years away from Portugal, traveling in the Far East, the Indian subcontinent and Africa. Cochin is on the Malabar coast. The Portuguese first established contact with India in 1498. The Dutch drove them out in 1662 and they, in turn, were replaced by the British at the end of the 18th century.

Christoph M. Meiners (1747-1810) was a professor of psychology, aesthetics and the histories of philosophy and religion in Göttingen. He suffered from a monomania to clarify historical periods and cultures, which led him to publish quantities of hastily written books and articles of questionable validity.

3. Although born a Persian subject, Herodotus (ca. 484-425 B.C.) is the Greek historian called the Father of History. His education was thoroughly Greek and he was well versed in literature available at his time. He traveled through Asia Minor and European Greece probably more than once and visited most of the important Greek islands. Ancient and modern commentators have questioned the accuracy of some of his accounts.

Cambyses was the King of Persia (ca. 529-522 B.C.). He was the son of Cyrus the Great.

4. Pliny the Elder, Gaius Plinius Secundus (ca. A.D. 23-79), was born in Comum. Only his *Naturalis historia*, a work consisting of 37 books, has survived to our times. Book 7 is concerned with anthropology and human physiology, Book 4 with geography and ethnography.

5. Strabo (born ca. 63 B.C.) was a Greek geographer and historian. He traveled a great deal, including to Rome and Egypt. His *Geography* is the most important scientific work we have from antiquity. The work consists of 17 books dealing with Europe, Asia Minor, India, Persia, Egypt and Africa.

6. Langsdorff's grammar is inconsistent. He begins his sentence by speaking of some frail, old people and shifts to one old man.

7. Pomponius Mela was a geographer of the early first century A.D. See Pliny, *Nar.* 1.3.

Lake of Maeotis — Sea of Azov.

8. Cochin China — the southern-most state of Indo-China, capital Saigon (Vietnam).

9. Maria Thérèse de Savoy-Carignan, Princess de Lamballe (1749-1792), was an intimate friend of Marie Antoinette. She was incarcerated in LaForce and turned over to a revolutionary mob that, after beheading her, placed her head on a pike and paraded it in front of the Queen's windows.

10. Langsdorff is referring to the jequirity, the scarlet and black seeds of Indian licorice which are used for rosaries and necklaces. They also have been used as a standard of weight.

11. A comparison of Edward Robarts's "Vocabulary of the Marquesas Language" shows little concordance with Langsdorff's. A letter dated 12 September 1989 from Herve Marie Le Cleac'h, Ancien Eveque des îles Marquises, says that Cabri's and Roberts's vocabulary indicate that they were not of the upper classes and that some of the words are mistranslated or do not belong to Nukahiva but rather to other islands.

12. I have changed the German to conform to modern orthography but have left the Nukahivan untouched since it is unclear how it would be pronounced, although we might assume, since Langsdorff is writing in German, that the transcriptions should have many things in common with German, e.g., *w* = *v*, *j* = *y*, *s* = *z*, *z* = *ts*.

Chapter 8

Departure from Nukahiva. Arrival on Owaihi. Remarks about the island. Separation from the Neva. *Voyage to Kamtschatka. Arrival and Stay.*

May 1804

During our stay on Nukahiva, we unfortunately had only been able to get a few pigs by barter, partially because the inhabitants demanded too high of a price and partially because they did not like to do without them at their frequent feasts and other amusements. We procured instead quantities of coconuts, breadfruit, bananas and nourishing roots. We left the island in the best of health and with the pleasant expectation of obtaining ample compensation for our lack of meat on the Sandwich Islands.

During our stay, we had brought on board as much wood and good water as Captain von Krusenstern thought necessary. Roberts, Cabri and a number of the natives helped us a great deal with this business. The latter were well paid with several pieces of iron hoops about a zoll long from old casks and the former with canvas, knives, axes and several other objects they could use. We were on the best of terms with the islanders from the first day of our arrival and, as I dare assume, had instilled in them respect and trust for all of us, which perhaps will be transferred to seafarers after us. At departure we found no reason to complain about the behavior of these, according to our standards, repugnant, cruel, yet kind-hearted, generous people.

On May 11th to our great joy the *Neva*, from which we had become separated near Cape Horn on March 24th, arrived in Nukahiva and brought us the news that they had waited for us near Easter Island for three days. They had been prevented from landing by a strong west wind. Except for some batatas and bananas that the islanders had brought out in a little canoe, they had obtained no fresh supplies.

On May 16th preparations were made on both ships to head to sea. On May 17th, since everything was ready for departure, anchor was weighed. Little gusts of wind were coming in from the nearby high mountains surrounding the bay. They were almost continually changing direction, causing the ship to tack so often that we made little headway. Around ten o'clock a strong gust of wind came in from the sea, rolling waves ahead of it with such force into the harbor that our ship was overpowered by the current and gradually approached the southwestern shore. Our situation became very dangerous when we were carried to within 120 fadens of some steep cliffs. Luckily we found anchorage. This and the ability of our excellent leader and the activity of the officers and crew saved us from the obvious danger of shipwreck on the nearby rocks on this island inhabited by cannibals. Our sheet anchors were cast out. After signaling, the *Neva* sent her shallop over to us in order to help get us more safely and quickly away from the dangerous rocks. A large crowd of natives had gathered on that terrible shore. Many of them appeared to be armed. Probably they were little aware of the danger we were in because one of the spectators, accompanied by a girl, dived from a steep cliff into the boiling surf where the water crashed up about twenty fadens, and as usual offered us the favors of the person (perhaps his wife). Another woman came happily swimming up. When no one paid any attention to her, she swam back to land with a banana twig that had happened to fall overboard.

Around four in the afternoon, we were again in the middle of the bay at a safe anchorage freed from danger. The unpredictable weather, rain showers, continual gusts of wind and the fact that the crew had been working continually since daybreak in 22° to 25° temperatures led Captain von Krusenstern to give them a night's rest.

Jean Cabri came toward evening in order to say goodbye once again and asked for some European trifles for himself and his wife. He told us that our ship's position had looked very dangerous from the eastern side of the bay. The rumor had spread through the valley that we could not escape being shipwrecked. That is why so many islanders had gathered on the shore with the sole intention of immediately saving us and all our valuables from the expected shipwreck.

Toward evening we took leave of Roberts, who was taken ashore in a small boat. We gave Cabri the friendly advice that he also should use the opportunity to leave since we would possibly sail in the night if a favorable wind arose. Despite this he stayed on board and assured us he could very comfortably swim to the nearby shore at our departure.

Early on the morning of the 19th, the anchor was weighed. We had just sailed between the two islands at the entrance to the harbor when suddenly a strong, uneven gust of wind arose accompanied by rain. All at once the whole crew had to set about raising more sail and trimming cable of the sheet anchor. At this critical moment Cabri asked to be taken ashore by boat because it had become impossible to swim to the island in such high seas. Everyone was so concerned with the ship's safety that little notice could be given his request. He also asked in vain for a large piece of board to use to swim to land. In a few minutes he was forced to remain on board and to leave this fairy island because of the increasingly high seas and the fact that we were already a considerable distance from land. Thus, Roberts was freed of his enemy and Cabri separated from his wife and child.

He soon seemed to be reconciled to his fate. He was useful as a sailor but a vile man. He was more than a little inclined to steal, lie and cheat and capable of carrying out these arts with more than a little cleverness.

We set our course toward the Sandwich Islands and Kamtschatka. The wind was rather brisk. After a few days, that is on May 25th in the afternoon, we sailed across the equator at 146°31′ W longitude from Greenwich. On that day the temperature by day was 22°, by night 21°.

On May 27th, we saw a branch with green leaves at 2° 10′ N latitude and 146°50′ longitude and at the same time many tropical and other sea birds as well as some fish. We noticed small changes in the trade winds. We most probably were near an undiscovered island that we were not fortunate to find.

On June 7th, the eastern point of the Island of Owaihi (19°34′ N) came into view at about a distance of 36 sea miles. This, the largest of the Sandwich Islands, is best known in history as the place where the greatest navigator of recent times met his death. Vancouver, his worthy student, produced a detailed map of these islands a few years after Cook's death.

Captain von Krusenstern planned to arrive in Nangasaki,[1] a large trading center in Japan, before the end of September. By speeding up his trip he hoped to avoid the change of the northeasterly monsoon that often takes place in that month.

In order to gain time he did not anchor in Karacacua Bay on the Island of Owaihi but instead followed the example of other seafarers, who had traded advantageously with the islanders along the coast without stopping. In a few days he obtained a large store of pigs and all kinds of other provisions.

For this reason he continued to cruise along the southern tip of the island until the 10th. He discovered, however, to all of our regret, that the few inhabitants who visited us during this period and brought provisions wanted so much for them that he decided not to stay, since prospects of success were so uncertain but rather to leave the island and sail for Kamtschatka. He was better able to do this because the crew was enjoying the best of health.

The islanders we had an opportunity to observe were naked, unclean, not well built, of middle stature, and with dark, dirty, brown skin covered with rashes and sores, probably the result of drinking cava or of venereal disease. Most of the men had no front teeth. According to them they had been knocked out by stones in battles. Many of their navels stuck so far out that the swelling was not unlike a hernia. They were good swimmers and tattooed on their arms and legs with lizards, billy goats, muskets and other rhombus-shaped figures, which in no way embellished their bodies, as on Nukahiva, but rather distorted them. The bad impression these people made upon us was even greater because we had just left (May 17th) an island a few weeks before whose inhabitants' stature and body proportions correctly make them count as some of the most beautiful on earth. The Sandwich Islanders, probably because of more frequent contact with Europeans, seemed more adroit than the Nukahivans. Our Frenchman Cabri liked the members of both sexes so little that he could not make up his mind to remain among those ugly people and asked Captain von Krusenstern, who wanted to put him ashore there, to take him to Kamtschatka, which he did. Cabri, who fully understood the Nukahivan language, tried time and again in vain to speak with the inhabitants of Owaihi. We were sometimes able to make ourselves understood using some English words.

The canoes the people use in order to venture several miles out to sea are light, very cleanly and beautifully built. They show that they have made greater progress by far in the art of navigation than the Nukahivans.

The coast we saw looked friendly and highly cultivated and had lots of coconut and banana groves. We were particularly attracted to the majestic mountain Mowna Roa.[2] According to older measurements, it rises 2,578 toises from sea level, according to Dr. Horner, our illustrious astronomer, 2,254 toises.

This lofty mountain, which is 300 to 400 toises higher than the Peak on Teneriffe, rises as gradually from sea level to its high peak that it is a very remarkable phenomenon, a very pleasing sight. Probably nowhere can one climb such a high mountain with so few difficulties. The warm climate contributes greatly to the fact that the highest peak, despite its considerable height, barely reaches the snow-line of mountains below the equator. When we were there, the summit was totally free of snow.

How many unknown plants might be discovered there, how many contributions to geography and natural history could be gathered there! We can only hope that a natural scientist would choose to spend at least a year researching it.

We left Owaihi on June 10th without obtaining any information about the present conditions on the island. While wintering on the Northwest Coast of America in 1805-06, I had an opportunity of learning something about them which I wish to include here.

The Sandwich Islands, which are very handy for ships sailing to the Northwest Coast of America, the Aleutian Islands or Kamtschatka, have safe bays, a superabundance of pigs, breadfruit, bananas, coconuts, taro and yams, batatas, salt, wood, water, etc., and excellent places for refreshment. Ships from the United American Free States visit them every year on their way to the Northwest Coast, where they exchange iron ware, cloth, knives, axes, kitchen utensils, rice, molasses, rusk, gunpowder and weapons with the inhabitants for furs, for sea otter pelts (*Lutra marina*) which the Chinese prize so highly. They then take them to China. The trade has prospered since the English as well as the Spanish left Nootka Sound and gave up their former outposts there. The trade must be very profitable, since almost annually six to eight ships cruise from 50° to 57° N latitude, i.e., around Nootka, Queen Charlotte and Norfolk Sounds. If in a given year, they do not obtain a sufficient cargo of sea otter pelts for Canton, they sail to the Columbo River[3] in October or November or more frequently to the Sandwich Islands, where they winter and plan their voyage so that they reach the Northwest Coast at the beginning of March and can begin to trade again.

The numbers of ships arriving at Karacacua Bay and frequent trade has had such great influence on the culture of these islands that this nation has taken giant steps forward in its civilization and, faster than any other place in the South Seas, will be transformed into a civilized trading country.

Because of the continuous contact with seafarers of the American Free States, and especially with Messrs. Young and Davie who have been living for years with him and are his ministers, King Tomoomo has introduced European customs, the English language and habits, so that the most active inhabitants of the island now speak English.[4] Tomoomo succeeded in conquering all of the islands in the chain and is now their sole ruler. Through the continual trade and exchange of goods, he got to know the value of silver after a few years. He prefers to sell his country's products to ships for good hard cash in Spanish dollars or piasters. As soon as he had collected enough money, he bought a ship from an American. He manned it with his own sailors as well as foreign sailors — at present there are many of them living on Owaihi. The superabundance of natural products available for little labor and beautiful girls suits the sailors from the United States so well that almost every ship sails away leaving not one but several members of its crew behind. The King only lets people of good character stay who have good letters of reference from their captains. The natives have become so accustomed to life at sea that they have become excellent sailors. On the Northwest Coast of America I spoke with inhabitants of these islands coming from Owaihi and working as sailors on ships from Boston who earned ten to twelve piasters a month.

They have become so skilled in making cordage, fishing nets, ropes, hawsers (perhaps from the fibers of *Phornium tenax Forst.*) that seafarers outfit their ships there and consider wainscoting from the Sandwich Islands more durable than European.

Tomoomo carries through all of his dealings with a great deal of understanding, energy and clear-sightedness. In a short period of time, he has increased his sea power considerably. In 1806, he already had fifteen vessels, including some three-masters, brigs and cutters. In the same year he sent a message to the business agent Mr. von Baranoff of the Russian-American Trading Company in New Archangel (Norfolk Sound) that he had heard that the Russian outpost on that coast sometimes suffered from lack of provisions and other goods.[5] He therefore offered to send a ship annually with salt, pigs, batatas and other supplies, indeed, even with European products, if he would sell him sea otter pelts for cheap prices with which he wanted to speculate in China.*

---

*This trade, as I have learned since returning to St. Petersburg, has actually begun. The Imperial Russian Trading Company sent a ship from Norfolk Sound to Owaihi and bought not only provisions but also a cutter from the King with which they returned to the Northwest Coast.

The King, among other things, is very interested in shipbuilding. He is said to be able to find and judge very well the strengths and mistakes in a ship. The tools and equipment needed for shipbuilding are the best articles of trade. Sailors who are carpenters are very welcome and are given land and special privileges.

Several years ago on Owaihi an extremely useful kind of wood for shipbuilding was discovered. Ship or bore worms (*Teredo navalis Linn.*) found in these waters absolutely do not attack it. The otherwise usual practice of sheathing ships with copper plating is totally unnecessary if this discovery turns out to be true.

Among the products of these islands is sugar cane. If its cultivation were perfected and planted most advantageously, then in time Kamtschatka and all of Siberia could be supplied with sugar from there.

War and the political situation in Europe in recent years have drawn merchants' speculative ventures from this area and they have become solely engrossed in Europe. When once again freedom of the high seas and shipping are established, then the advantages of trading with this region, as Cook, La Pérouse, Meares, Portlock, Vancouver, Marchand, Broughton, Krusenstern and many others have clearly demonstrated, will not go unused.[6]

On the evening of the 10th at six o'clock, we took leave of our companion ship the *Neva* after mutual hurrahs. Captain Lisiansky was sailing to Codiac and the Northwest Coast of America. He was less pressed for time than we were. He had decided to anchor in Karacacua Bay for his crew's sake. Captain von Krusenstern decided, however, it was necessary to sail straight to Kamtschatka, since we had not been able to obtain provisions in four days along the coast and it was uncertain whether we would obtain any by taking the time to anchor in that Bay.

Nothing special happened during the first days of the voyage. Our food was simple. The officers' food, like that of the sailors', consisted of salted meat and rusk. The latter was very tasty, but a little bug (*Dermestes paniceus*) had built so many nests in it that we had to knock them out before putting a piece of bread in our mouths.

Unusual numbers of birds, which we saw at 17° N latitude and 169°31′ longitude, caught our attention and awakened our hope of discovering an unidentified island, which, as several times before, disappeared again. A geographer could do a great service if he would study the expanses of empty ocean from the western coast of America to Japan and its southern islands or from 24° to 45° N latitude and produce a map showing all of the known ship routes along with signs observed in the vicinity of land. There is no doubt about the fact that there are some undiscovered islands some place there, but where? That will be the subject of future research. I know of no navigator sailing between Canton and the Northwest Coast of America who has not observed here and there signs of nearby land. As far as I know, between 18° and 26° latitudes only low, sandy islands have been discovered which are very dangerous for shipping. After comparing all of the routes known up to now, one could set a new course and in this way most probably make new discoveries.

During my voyage from Norfolk Sound to the coast of New Albion[7] in 1806, I observed almost daily signs of nearby land from 37° to 39° N latitude and 227° to 22° longitude.*

We found June 22nd noteworthy because it offered many diversions. On that day at 181°56′ W longitude we passed the Tropic of Cancer when the sun was at its zenith. The temperature was 21° to 22°. In an extraordinary calm Captain von Krusenstern had a boat lowered onto the mirror-smooth sea. He permitted Dr. Horner and myself to use it. Dr. Horner took various physical observations of the water's temperature, transparency, currents, salt content and I noted natural history observations.

According to Dr. Horner's observations the barometer at the surface of the water read 20°5 and at 125 fadens only 13°3. The difference in temperature from the surface to 25 fadens was 1°, to 50 fadens 3°2, to 125 fadens 7°2.

I was astonished by the quantities of zoophytes and mollusks, beroes, medusas, salpae, sea squills, *Cyclops Muelleri*, *Zoëa latifer et pelagica*, *Bosea*, *Gamarellus*, *pedunculatus* and many other microscopic objects which Dr. Tilesius will describe in more detail in Krusenstern's *Atlas*.[8] I also found innumerable schools of *Physalis pelagica* and *Medusa velella Linn.* In my opinion they differ from the ones in the Atlantic only in their small size. They were just barely a zoll long.

---

*More details are found in Vol. II.

Very early in the morning we saw a large shark (*Squalus Glaucius*) near the ship. Even though it appeared to be hungry and followed the ship in order to grab up garbage thrown overboard at first it did not want to take our baited hook. Finally it could not resist and bit and was pulled on board amidst shouts of joy. It was seven and one-half fuss long and weighed 200 pfunds.

While we still were enjoying this first show and this amazing animal, a second one of the same size and species appeared. Immediately it gobbled up our baited hook. We were all the more happy about our good fortune because we had acquired some fresh meat. Even though shark meat is hard, dry and tasteless, we ate heartily from it that very evening. Everyone enjoyed it very much. Some sailors, however, began to vomit a great deal. I am inclined to attribute this to their having overeaten or some other accidental cause than to the nature of the fish, which I very frequently saw poor people buying for food in Lisbon and Teneriffe at the public markets.

At 21° N latitude the trade winds left us and with them the pleasant sailing between the Tropics. Foggy weather, brisk variable winds and unpleasant weather accompanied us the rest of the way to Kamtschatka. At 30° N latitude on the last day of the month, we saw such a number of dolphins that from a distance we thought we were seeing surf against some rocks.

July 3rd when we were at 36° N and 191°13′ longitude, Captain von Krusenstern directed our course to the west in order to look for the Islands Rica de Ora and Ricade de Plata or the Gold and Silver Islands, which are located on the best maps in various places and have been hunted repeatedly in vain. The sky was overcast. In the afternoon a strong favorable wind arose, which, however, soon turned into a storm. With reefed sails we headed straight to the west at nine miles an hour in a night that was so dark that we could barely see a ship's length ahead of us. Very fortunately for us we did not run into any gold or silver rocks or cliffs.

On the following day (July 4th) the wind changed. Despite this the weather remained very foggy. Since Captain von Krusenstern counted the time lost as more valuable than uncertain success, he decided it was more advisable to abandon that doubtful excursion. I can only add to the comments this worthy navigator makes about the islands in his excellent book on pp. 227 to 229 that the Dutch interpreters in Nangasaki, whom I repeatedly asked about the islands, had heard their names and of their existence.[9] They said they were four to five days voyage east of the southwestern coast of Japan. Since the Japanese know little about longitude and latitude, it was very difficult to obtain any more specific information from them.

On July 5th at 38°32′ N latitude and 194°50′ longitude we saw a turtle without noting any other signs of land nearby. On the 6th at 40°34′ N latitude and 195°35′ longitude, we saw numbers of whales, on the 7th ducks and an old log. After that the signs of nearby land increased almost every day. On the 11th at 49°16′ N latitude and 199°49′, we saw large flocks of sea gulls (*Larus*), auks (*Alca*), large and small storm petrels (*Procellaria*) (because of their long, narrow wings they somewhat resemble larks or swallows, but not in flight) and albatrosses (*Diomedea exulans*) near our ship.

On the morning of the 13th, landfall was announced from the top of the mast. This little word sounded heavenly in our ears after a voyage of more than five months — finally to go on land again and, in certain respects, our native land. The following day we were becalmed. We gazed longingly at the promontory Schibunskoy Noss at 53°06′ N latitude and 200° longitude ahead of us. Nearby lay the long-desired harbor of St. Peter and St. Paul.

The high mountain ridges, peaks eternally covered with snow, and active volcanoes give the country a very unique appearance. Since it was already so late summer, we doubted whether it was really snow covering the upper half of the mountains.*

As much as we were at first repelled and depressed by the view, because of the bad reports generally coming from Kamtschatka, we cheered up the closer we came to the coast. On the morning of the 15th, a rather brisk, favorable wind arose and the low mountains covered with green woods surprised us with their beauty and charm. Since leaving Brazil, we had seen no landscapes which smiled such friendly greetings as this Peninsula of Kamtschatka with its undeserved, bad reputation. The beautiful birch woods and hills thickly carpeted with grass in the foreground resembled a European landscape in so many ways that we were already imagining we were in our fatherland with the Alps in the background — the mountains, which yesterday had made such a bad impression on us, today we admired as the distinguishing features of the country.

---

*Since snow-line at 46° in Europe is 1,460 *toises* above sea level, I think we can assume that the average height of these mountains in Kamtschatka is 1,000 *toises*. Some peaks on the peninsula, e.g., in the Glutschefskaia, I estimate are over 2,000 *toises* high.

Around noon we arrived at the mouth of the large Bay of Awatscha. Using the very good charts made by Cook and Saritscheff, we sailed into it without any difficulties.[10]

The thousands and thousands of sea gulls (*Larus*) living on the rugged rocks along the shore seemed to be calling a friendly welcome. Since the bird's call resembled the human voice in many ways, some of our crew thought at first they were hearing one of the inhabitants from the nearby hills.

Besides sea gulls we saw countless numbers of auks (*Alca cirrhata et alca arctica*) ducks, pelicans (*Pelacanus Urile*) diving birds (*Colymbus*) and many other birds we had never seen before. We had just entered the large Bay of Awatscha, when we spied a boat with an officer rowing toward us. As soon as he heard who we were, he told us that St. Petersburg had long ago informed them about our voyage and probable arrival in the harbor. He quickly returned to St. Peter and St. Paul. We were then welcomed with cannon salvos, which we returned from our ship with an equal number. We dropped anchor at one o'clock after a 35-day voyage from the Island of Owaihi.

Petropavlovsk is situated at the northern end of the Bay of Awatscha in a short, narrow valley with a long, freshwater lake to the north. It has a harbor on the shore of a little inlet which is separated from the Bay by a tongue of land, so that it is completely protected from wind and storms.

The town has thirty houses, all of wood as all over the Russian Empire, built of logs or tree trunks laid one on top of the other. About 150 soldiers and an artillery battalion, some Cossacks and the Commissioner of the Russian-American Trading Company live there, also a priest, even though there is no church. According to all navigators, the harbor is one of the best. It is most probable that St. Peter and St. Paul will become a trading center and a very flourishing town with increased industrialization and trade with China, Japan, America, the Aleutian and other islands in the South Seas. Kamtschatka's climate is better than that of similar latitudes in Siberia, but in the Harbor of St. Peter and St. Paul it is rawer than in other northern areas of the Peninsula.

The harbor is open seven to eight months of the year, from April to November. Parts of the Bay freeze over very rarely, the whole Bay never. Near the harbor there is generally more snow than in other areas so that the very low houses sometimes are completely covered by it.

However, it melts early and is quickly soaked up by the earth which freezes slightly. They can count on spring at the end of April, at the latest in very bad weather at the beginning of May, when they put their few head of cattle out to pasture. Very little land is cultivated there. They claim the sea air is bad for grain. I think this is an excuse for laziness because potatoes, turnips, radishes and other garden plants, which thrive there despite this, are only planted sparingly. I was told that agriculture in the country's interior around Virchnoi Kamtschatka and Glutscheffskaia have progressed farther, that agriculture and the raising of cattle has been increasing every year.

The commander of Petropavlovsk, Major Krupskoy, gave us as good a reception as the situation and circumstances permitted.[11] Major General von Koscheleff, the commander-in-chief of the peninsula and commander of the battalion, does not live there but in Nischney-Kamtschatka, the capital of the province about 700 *versts* away. The ambassador to the Japanese Court, von Resanoff, who urgently needed to speak with the General, had a messenger sent immediately with orders for him to come to the harbor as soon as possible. This situation, as well as the travel time involved due to the distance, caused an essential change in the continuation of our voyage.

Captain von Krusenstern began to have the goods from Kronstadt intended for Kamtschatka unloaded so that only the goods intended as gifts for Japan remained on board, so that in that otherwise mistrusting country not even the slightest suspicion could arise that we were there to trade.

Part of the soldiers and inhabitants of the place lent a helping hand so that the ship could be more quickly unloaded and readied to sail. Another group, upon orders from Major Krupskoy, went hunting and fishing in order to provide officers and crew with all kinds of fresh provisions.

Councilor Tilesius and I had not made much progress in learning Russian. For the first time during our trip, we felt how disadvantageous it is to be in a foreign country without being able to understand the language. Even though we often asked the Ambassador to provide us with a guide so that we could undertake an excursion into the interior or some distance from the harbor, we were not once lucky enough to have our wishes fulfilled. He could not actually give the soldiers orders and most of them were busy on board ship. There were only a few Kamtschadales and Cossacks there and they were employed hunting and fishing to get provisions. We dared not go out alone any distance from town without a guide. The numbers of bears and wolves, the almost impenetrable grass taller than a man, swamps, mountains, brush-filled woods were obstacles enough to frighten us off. That is why we had to stay near the harbor where there was little of scientific interest. We did visit in the company of some of our traveling companions the little village of Awatscha about twelve versts from Petropavlovsk. It has five houses and about thirty people. Two disabled soldiers live there and Kamtschadales, who hunt and fish for a livelihood. The village of Paratunka, whose priest and inhabitants are sufficiently well known from Cook's and La Pérouse's descriptions and had lived at their time in the greatest of affluence, had died. It existed only as a name and unfortunately has shared this fate with many other places on the peninsula.

Politically, conditions had also changed a great deal since those worthy navigators had been there. Nischney-Kamtschatka is now the capital instead of Bolschoiretsk. Instead of a civil government, there is now military rule.

Tsar Paul wanted to control the Peninsula's increasing depopulation.[12] About ten to twelve years ago he ordered a battalion of 800 men from a regiment in Irkutsk to go there as a kind of country militia in order to promote agriculture. His intentions were the best. As is often the case, they were frustrated by a number of extremely unfortunate circumstances.

It cost a great deal to send the troops there, and even more since then for their maintenance. They are supplied with provisions, clothing and arms from Irkutsk (a distance of about 6,000 versts). They have nothing to do but guard duty or to guard the supplies stored there. Lazy, slothful, undependable and totally without knowledge of agriculture in the few years they have been there, they have done by far more damage than good and become the greatest of burdens for the Kamtschadals. They are sucking these poor people completely dry and laying the foundation for the moral and physical destruction of this nation. If the government does not soon prudently follow other paths, these poor, kind natives, whose numbers have shrunk from about 10,000 to 3,000 souls, will be gradually totally destroyed.

Finally on August 12th, the long and impatiently awaited General von Koscheleff arrived at Peter-Paul Harbor. He was accompanied by his younger brother, Captain Feodoroff, and sixty soldiers, whom Ambassador von Resanoff had desired to see.

The continuation of our voyage to Japan — rendered doubtful because of our long stay and the change in the monsoons expected to occur soon — was finally decided on August 20th. Three of our traveling companions, Lieutenant of the Guards of his Imperial Majesty Major Count Tolstoi, the Ambassador's physician Dr. Prikin and Mr. Kurlandzoff, the painter accompanying the expedition, who up to then had not drawn a single interesting sketch of our trip, were tired of the sea and preferred to return by land rather than subjecting themselves any longer to the stormy waves. In their stead General von Koscheleff's brother and Captain Feodoroff were to act as ambassadorial cavaliers. In addition, eight soldiers were to go along as a military honor guard.

St. Paul's Harbor had become far livelier and gayer with the General's arrival. Instead of lots of fish, which we were getting very tired of, we were given meat. Cattle were slaughtered and wild sheep (*Ovis Ammon*) and reindeer killed. We were happy to find in the person of the General a man who enlivened our society and told us interesting information about conditions on the Peninsula and kindly procured provisions of all kinds for us with the utmost willingness. Through his kind help we obtained several head of livestock and a large supply of salted fish, among them *tschavitscha*, an exceedingly tasty kind of salmon. Vegetables, reindeer, salted geese and other products were brought to us from other areas and convinced us that Kamtschatka is not as poor as is usually assumed.

The General put on a ball for us in a tent which Ambassador von Resanoff had set up. Except for Major Krupskoy's wife, the only other women present were the women of non-commissioned officers and soldiers and some Kamtschadals, who, in Russian fashion, wore silk, chintz and nankeen. We had an opportunity to watch Kamtschadal dances which imitate bears, birds and dogs.

General von Koscheleff deserves our utmost gratitude for his care, attention and willingness to help us.

By the end of August everything was ready. The ship sailed out of the harbor into Awatscha Bay, where contrary southerly and easterly winds and thick fog detained it. On the morning of the 7th, we left the harbor in order to proceed on our embassy to Japan.

Notes

1. Nangasaki — Nagasaki. From 1640 to 1859 it was the only town in Japan where foreigners, i.e., the Dutch and Chinese, were permitted to enter and conduct trade.

Karacacua Bay (also spelled Coracacua in the German text) — Kealakehua Bay on the Island of Hawaii.

2. Mawna Roa — Mauna Loa.

3. Columbo River — Columbia River.
Norfolk Sound — New Archangel, modern Sitka, Alaska.

4. Langsdorff undoubtedly means John Young and Isaac Davis. They were forced to remain on the island after the infamous visit in 1788-90 of the American Captain Simon Metcalfe of the *Eleanora* and his son on the *Fair American*. Both Young and Davis were natives of England. Both adapted to the life there and advanced in influence and rank until they became equals of the most powerful chiefs. They advised King Tomoomo (Kamehameha) (1736-1819). Kamehameha II, called Liholiho (1797-1824), abolished taboo and idolatry.

5. Von Baranoff (Russian: Aleksandr Andreevich Baranov), 1746-1819, was the chief manager of the Russian-American settlements in North America from 1790 to 1818. He grew up in northern Russia. In 1780 he went to Siberia. In Irkutsk he established a glass factory and distillery and engaged in contracting and tax-farming as well. In 1788 he and his brother with government aid established a settlement on the Krugovoi Main from which fur and walrus hunting as well as whaling could be promoted. In 1790 he signed a contract to become the manager of the Russian-American Company's North American enterprises.

6. John Meares (1756?-1809), *Voyages from China to the Northwest Coast of America; Voyages made in the years 1788 and 1798 from China to the northwest coast of America, to which are prefixed an introductory narrative of a voyage performed in 1786 from Bengal in the ship* Nootka; *observations on the probable existence of a north west passage and some account of trade between the Northwest Coast of America and China and the latter country and Great Britain* (London: Printed at Logographic press, 1790). Georg Forster translated Meares's books into German, the first printing in Berlin, 1791. A French translation appeared in 1794 or 1795. Langsdorff does not indicate his actual source here.

Captain Nathaniel Portlock (1748-1817), *A Voyage Round the World; but more particularly to the Northwest Coast of America performed in 1785, 1786, 1887 and 1788 in the* King George *and* Queen Charlotte; *Captains Portlock and Dixon* (London: Printed for J. Stockdale and G. Goulding, 1789).

Georg Forster in 1791 published in German translation a history of travel since Cook to the Americas by Meares, Dixon, Portlock, Coxe, Long, etc., which includes many maps and etchings. A French translation appeared in 1794-95. Langsdorff does not indicate his actual source here.

William Robert Broughton (1762-1821), *A Voyage of Discovery to the North Pacific Ocean in which the coast of Asia from latitude 35° North to latitude 52° North, the Island of Insu* [commonly known under the name of the land of Jesso], *the north, south and east coasts of Japan, the Lieuchieux and the adjacent isles, as well as the coast of Corea, have been examined and surveyed;*

Performed in His Majesty's sloop Providence *and her tender, in the years 1795, 1796, 1797, 1798* (London: Printed for T. Cadell and W. Davies, 1804). This work was translated into German in 1805 and into French in 1807.

7. New Albion — California.

8. *Voyage Round the World in the years 1803, 1804, 1805 and 1806 by order of his Imperial Majesty Alexander the First on board the ships* Nadeshda *and* Neva *under the command of Captain A. J. Krusenstern*, in 2 Volumes, trans. by Richard Belgrave Hoppner (London: Printed by C. Roworth, 1813) does not include the *Atlas* which accompanied the Russian and French editions.

9. "His Excellency Count Romanzow had given me particular instructions, previous to my departure from Russia, to look out for an island, that had been formerly repeatedly sought by the Spaniards and the Dutch. As to the first discovery of this land the world is completely in the dark, and it rests upon ancient, perhaps fabulous reports. The Spaniards, who had heard that an island, very rich in gold and silver, had been discovered to the east of Japan, sent a ship there in 1610 or 1611 from Acapulco with orders to take possession of it. The Dutch were equally allured by the supposed wealth of this land, and sent two ships under the command of Captain Matthias Kwast for the same purpose. But this undertaking did not succeed better than that of the Spaniards. The attempt made by the celebrated Captain Vries on board the *Castricom* in 1643, and La Pérouse in 1787 to discover this land, proved equally unsuccessful. Of modern navigators La Pérouse is indeed the only one who has really made this attempt, since neither Cook, in his voyage from Unalaschka to the Sandwich Islands, nor Clerke, in proceeding from these islands to Kamtschatka in 1779, nor indeed Dixon, Vancouver or any others have ever renewed it. I do not know any work in which the parallel followed by Captain Kwast in search of this island is mentioned; but it is probably the same in which Vries was directed to look for it, i.e., that of 37°30′ which he followed from 142° E longitude to 170°. La Pérouse continued to 179°31′, one point from 13°41′" (pp. 204-205 of the English translation of Krusenstern, *op cit.*).

10. Gavriil Andreevich Sarychev (1763-1831), *Account of a Voyage of Discovery in the Northeast of Siberia, The Frozen Ocean and the Northeast Sea*, trans. from the Russian (London: Printed for R. Phillips by J. G. Barnard, 1807-08), 2 vols. in one.

11. Major Krupskoy, also Krupski.

12. Paul I (Pavel Petrovich, 1754-1801) was Emperor from 1796 to 1801.

Chapter 9

Introduction to the Envoy. Departure from Kamtschatka. Sea Voyage. Coronation Celebration. Terrible Typhoon. Arrival in Japan.

September 1804

Politically and geographically the embassy to Japan was the most interesting part of our expedition.

The Japanese, about whom we still know little and that almost only from Kämpfer, Thunberg and Charlevoix, have shunned almost all contact with Europeans and other countries for nearly 200 years.[1] They have permitted only the Dutch very limited trade.

Since Japan has no other European neighbor but Russia, it is natural that this empire would claim rights of friendship. The importance of trade with Japan did not escape Empress Catherine's astute mind. As soon as she was told that a Japanese merchant named Kodai and some other people, who had been shipwrecked on the Kurile Islands several years before, were in Siberia, she used the opportunity to show the foreigners the high value Russia places upon hospitality.[2] She had Kodai brought to St. Petersburg at her expense. After showing him all the splendors and treasures of the capital city and the brilliance of her court and heaping honors and kindness upon him, she offered him a ship to return to his fatherland. He then traveled to Okhotsk. In 1792, Naval Officer Adam Laxmann, son of the well known naturalist, took him to Atkis, a port on the northeastern coast of Matmai. The governor general of Siberia sent a letter with Laxmann for the Emperor of Japan, in which he, in the name of his great Empress, declared the reasons for the voyage and requested future neighborly friendship and the building up of mutual trade between the two countries. He also sent along some gifts of not very great value to be presented to the Emperor in Jedo, the capital of Japan.

Kodai, a very intelligent and comprehending man, had learned Russian during his stay. Partially from gratitude, partially perhaps in his own interest, he used his influence to promote Russia's trading interest.

He served as interpreter during their stay in Atkis. After several months had passed, Laxmann received a kind of order instead of a letter or answer addressed to the Empress or the Governor General.

It had approximately the following content:

"The law in the Japanese Empire has remained the same from ancient times to the present and it can never be changed. Laxmann, coming from his Empire with people who happened to have been shipwrecked on foreign shores, unknowingly had not sailed to Nangasaki but rather to an unusual port in the Japanese Empire where foreign ships are not allowed.[3] This had never happened before in Japan.

"It is the law that all ships, and no matter how many, are immediately placed under arrest, all the more if they are armed.

"The Dutch, as a friendly nation, have been coming since ancient times with their ships to the Harbor of Nangasaki but not into the interior of the Empire. He, together with the Japanese entrusted to his care, dared to do this on an armed ship without the slightest knowledge of Japan.

"The result should be to prohibit him from ever returning to his fatherland. As a foreigner, however, not knowing anything of their laws and not intending to carry out any illegal actions, he will be permitted to return. This is being done in consideration of the subjects of their Empire entrusted to his care by his government and because of the care and effort with which he has carried out his mission as well as his ignorance of their laws.

"Letting him return home is excusable, but only under the condition in the future that he not sail into a forbidden harbor.

"Since Japan has never had friendly ties with Russia and as a result has no knowledge of the degree of dignity accorded the Russian Empire, and the translation of an individual sentence or a letter does not permit an assessment of whether it is large or small, also does not convey information about customs and habits in Russia, it is therefore not known how closely the ways of expressing the concepts of honor or of contempt of the two empires coincide.*

*Here the Japanese government is alluding to the fact that it is forbidden and extremely disrespectful to have addressed a letter to the Emperor. Lieutenant Laxmann was expressly informed of this law at the time orally and even in writing. According to Japanese law,

"For this reason and lack of information, we cannot answer the letter delivered from Russia in any other way than to assume that it was written for the benefit of the people who chance had brought there. Further discussion of the matter is not desired.

"Any further discussion of future friendship cannot take place in this harbor (Atkis). No permission is granted to go to the Capital Jedo.

"Furthermore, it is the law that all armed ships, no matter at which harbor or anchorage, are to be treated with the greatest strictness. No negotiations are to take place with them and no excuses are accepted."

The last point of the message means:

"By showing the permission given you (Laxmann) by us, you may go to the harbor of Nangasaki, if this is not produced, then it is also forbidden to go there."

The permission reads approximately as follows:

"One ship from the great Russian Empire is permitted to enter the harbor at Nangasaki. As we already have stated, foreign ships are strictly forbidden to land at any other place. We also repeat that we do not tolerate the Christian religion in our Empire and therefore require during the stay in our country that no church services be held in case of any future agreement. Our laws are stated above. We deliver to Adam Laxmann the necessary papers for this purpose."

The disturbed state of affairs in Europe was probably the main cause why so many years had passed without their having taken advantage of the Japanese grant of permission or having outfitted a ship to sail there.

It was left to the glorious reign of our gracious Monarch Alexander I and the efforts of his illustrious Minister Count von

---

no one, not even if he were Emperor of the World, may write directly to the Emperor of Japan. The minister of a foreign power has to go to the Governor in Nangasaki and he then reports to the minister of the Japanese Emperor. The Governor General of Siberia in writing directly to the Emperor of Japan thus obviously committed high treason and *crimen laesae majestatis*.

Romanzoff to organize a voyage of discovery around the world and to combine this with an embassy to Japan.[4] They had reason to believe the latter would meet with success since they were convinced of the good will of the Japanese permission to sail into Nangasaki. In addition in 1796, a few years after Laxmann's return, another large Japanese vessel had run aground on the Aleutian Islands and now they had a new pretext: to return subjects rescued from the storm to their mother country.*

Mr. von Resanoff was chosen as ambassador. He was provided with valuable art works and manufactured products of all kinds.

Thus equipped, we left the harbor of St. Peter and St. Paul on September 7th full of expectation for Nangasaki.

We had rather favorable weather for the first days of our trip. On the morning of the 11th, however, a strong east wind arose and by two o'clock in the afternoon had turned into a violent storm that raged the whole night. The waves ran higher than we had seen on our entire trip up to then, even including Cape Horn. Only on the following morning (September 12th) did the wind suddenly die down so that the ship, like a cork, was tossed and buffeted by highly irregular waves and restless seas. The rocking made us all weary. Not since leaving Europe had we experienced such a bad storm. Despite the ship's having been carefully caulked in Kamtschatka, it began to leak so much that the pumps had to be continually kept working.

A partition in the cabin and the chimney collapsed. Continuous fog, fine rain, and water leaking in through the breach prevented us from drying our wet books, papers and clothing, thus making our unpleasant situation even more unpleasant. We saw numbers of little land birds and whales almost every day now.

On the 15th at noon, when we were at 39°57′ N and 208°7′30″ W, the weather changed to our relief. We felt a noticeable change in the

---

*These Japanese, who had been living in Irkutsk for several years, were taken to St. Petersburg and received there very hospitably at the time the expedition was being prepared. After they had been given money, clothing and watches, the ones who had not become Christians were given the choice of returning to their fatherland or staying in Russia. Of the fifteen, five decided to return, the others voluntarily went back to Irkutsk, the capital of Siberia. One of them, Nicolau Kolstichin, is now a professor of the Japanese language at the *Gymnasium* [secondary school] there, where he is paid to teach six to eight young people.

climate. Instead of wet, damp fog we now had clear, dry days and warm moonlit nights. The thermometer, which had rarely been showing more than 10° warmth, rose to 18°. A constant, brisk, favorable northeast wind, which on the 17th was accompanied by violent rain, carried us so fast that we forgot all our fears that we might sail into that infamous stormy sea so late in the year. We seldom sailed less than eight to nine miles an hour.

According to various maps, we were now in the vicinity of the Island of Vulcano, whose existence and location Captain von Krusenstern wanted to determine precisely. As a result of his research we can now maintain with certainly that the supposed Island Vulcano, located at 37° N and 214° W as well as Islas nuevas del anno 1716, Islas del anno 1664 and Penia de los Picos and others in the vicinity, if they really exist, are at least not to be found where they have been placed on maps.

Correcting old mistakes and proving that supposed islands do not exist is just as important for geographers as discovering new ones.

On September 27th, we celebrated the anniversary of the crowning of our beloved monarch, his Imperial Majesty Alexander I, in these regions so remote from his Imperial Capital. The Ambassador, who commanded his mother tongue at its finest, used the opportunity to give a solemn speech to the crew on deck. As proof of von Resanoff's ability to speak beautifully, I have no second thoughts about including here a translation of his speech, even though much of the power of the original language has been lost.

> Russians!
>
> We finally find ourselves on this voyage around the world in Japanese waters!
>
> Love of the fatherland — dignity — skillfulness — defiance of dangers — perseverance — subordination — mutual respect — gentleness — these are the characteristics that mark a Russian seaman, these are the virtues which Russians possess in general!
>
> (To the Officers):
>
> Tested officers of the *Hope*,* you have earned the gratitude of your fellow citizens! You have ac-

---

**Nadeschda*, i.e., *Hope*, was the name of our ship.

quired renown of which even the jealous can never rob you!

(To the envoy's cavaliers and the scholars):

You, my worthy companions and associates, will carry out just as brilliant deeds and discover new sources of wealth and knowledge! And (to the sailors) cherished children of the navy, rejoice at the happy success of your industrious work!

We have long since united our hearts and souls to fulfill the will of our monarch who has sent us out, of a monarch whom we venerate. Now may our gratitude for our magnificent ruler stimulate all of our senses.

Today is a solemn day for all the sons of our fatherland. It is all the more solemn for us because we have advanced to the borders of the Japanese Empire and are watching our glorious Russian flag wave for the first time in waters of Nangasaki.

As ambassador of our *most gracious Emperor* and witness to your great exploits, I have found it just as flattering to share your worries and dangers as now solemnly to acknowledge the gratitude which awaits you all in the bosom of your beloved fatherland.

I am celebrating the anniversary of *Alexander I*'s coronation in Japanese waters and am making this day forever memorable for you as a reward for your services. Here you have a portrait of your great Emperor. Wear it as an ornament testifying to your diligence and zeal. Remember this moment, that you are all the more duty-bound to remain very true to those virtues of which your ancestors were so proud. On the crest of fame bless the times when the merits, services, even of the least among his subjects in the remotest places of the world never go unrewarded before the throne of our *Just Monarch*.

Then von Resanoff decorated all of the sailors with medals with *His Imperial Majesty's* portrait made in honor of his coronation. The heavens favored the ceremony with calm and clear weather.

During a happy meal we drank to the health of our august Emperor. On this occasion the thunder of Russian cannons resounded for the first time in Japanese seas.

The heat was oppressive, little different if not at all, from that at the equator.

On the 28th, we finally saw the Japanese coast about 36 miles away. Toward evening the wind became somewhat stronger so that we could approach it. The headlands in front of us, lying according to the most exact of determinations at 32°38'30" N and 226°43'15" W, appeared to be the southern tip of Sikokf.* Contrary winds and cloudy skies with heavy rain showers prevented us from sailing closer to land.

Captain von Krusenstern, an excellent navigator and geographer, determined our exact location hourly in that unexplored area which has hardly been visited by European ships. His description and contributions to the more complete geographical knowledge of Japan are so important that this section of his work will be read with the greatest of interest. We found Arrowsmith's maps, acknowledged to be the best available, very defective and inaccurate.[6]

At daybreak on the 29th, we again caught sight of land. Our joy was short-lived because murky skies soon followed by rain showers and a violent northeaster made the vicinity of an unknown coast so dangerous that Captain von Krusenstern thought it better to stay as far away as possible and wait out the night. Soon, however, we had 24 hours of almost continuous stormy weather. Only on the 30th in the afternoon did it abate somewhat. For the first time in several days the sun shone. For three days it had rained and stormed almost continuously. As a result, on the morning of October 1st when the wind died down some, we had reason to believe we would see a change in the weather. At noon it cleared. Cheered by the sight of the sun, we determined our location at 31°7' N and 227°40' W and set our course again westward to reach land.

Uncommonly high waves from the southeast, a continually falling barometer — at noon 29 3½ zolls — gave us little hope of good weather. That is why Captain von Krusenstern again sailed southward while hoisting as much sail as the ship could bear in order to carry us away from land. A prudent precaution, as the following shows, that probably saved our lives.

---

* According to J. von Klaproth this promontory in Japanese is Scheissui-saki, i.e., the Cape of Clear Water.[5]

Just after noon the weather underwent great changes.* The barometer fell noticeably. The southwesterly wind gradually became stronger. At one o'clock it had increased so much that only with the greatest exertion and danger could we haul in the top and lower sails. Even though most of the ropes were new, the force of the wind ripped them apart. The sailors, with undaunted courage, defied the apparent danger, tied sails down and lowered the upper masts. Until three o'clock the storm sails held out, then the fury of the storm increased boundlessly and shredded the strong ropes and new sails in a few seconds. The barometer stood at 28″3‴.

The waves rolled furiously. Black-grey clouds streaming just above us like arrows, darkened the pale, foreboding sun so that around 4:30 we were enveloped in deep, frightening night.

The rudder had long since been tied down and was without any guidance. It was completely impossible even to set a double-reefed storm sail. As a toy for the unruly, outraged waves, we approached the threatening danger. We lived in the constant fear that we would see creaking masts go overboard. All of the axes were held ready to cut the shrouds. Every blow from a wave seemed to want to put an end to our existence. The wind roared hideously through the riggings. The ship rolled more than ever before. Water rushed into the ship from every direction. The crew was more than a little tired from continually manning the pumps.

The barometer was still dropping. After five o'clock the mercury disappeared below the scale that was divided at 27″6‴. At first it appeared now and then four to five marks above and below the middle with the highest and strongest rolls of the ship. Soon we were even deprived of this consultation when even with the greatest of rolls we saw no mercury, so that we had to assume that it was at its lowest point, that is, 27″ or perhaps even less without assuming too much. During this period the typhoon raged beyond all description. All of nature seemed outraged and in an uproar. In short no words can describe the scene forcibly enough. Officers and crew worked frantically to ward off damage continually happening on the ship. Large weapons chests were swimming on the deck. The noise and pounding had no end. The speaking trumpet could hardly be heard three steps away.

*The following is a concise description of a typhoon, something that has rarely been described. For the sake of completeness, I am including some remarks from von Krusenstern's *Voyage* with my own.

Everyone was splashing all over with lanterns. The ship could hardly withstand the might of the elements. The impetuous seas were united with the heavens. There were no boundaries between air, sky and water. One monstrous wave after another washed over the ship and then seemed to cast it into the abyss from which it had just ascended. All of the tools and equipment were scattered and smashed. The ship's bulkheads flew off. The cannons on the forecastle touched the water. The hope of staying alive totally disappeared with the thought that we were being driven toward land at three English miles an hour and that if the storm continued we would wreck on the nearby coast without hope of rescue.

We all seemed to say a last goodbye to each other and place ourselves in the hands of God. After eight o'clock, when the hurricane was raging at its height, a sudden five-minute calm occurred. This was used to raise a reefed storm sail on the mizzen mast. It was not quite up when the wind started to rage just as violently, only this time from the west-southwest instead of the east-southeast. At this sudden change a monstrous wave smashed into the back of the ship, ripped away the left side of the gallery, broke through the double wall of the captain's cabin and flooded it with three fuss of water. Valuable books, chairs, tables, maps and presents intended for Japan, mathematical instruments, and clothes were swimming together around the cabin, a foretaste of our coming destruction. The sailors were encouraged to stop the leak any way possible, but no one was thinking anything else but: "In vain! We are doomed!"

The wind's sudden, unexpected change of direction, its raging from the opposite direction with equal violence, seemed to have rescued us from the danger of smashing on the coast, but the typhoon's violence still seemed to be pronouncing our sentence of death. The storm raged, whistled and roared frighteningly through the shrouds. The masts were still trembling and creaking and the foaming billows flooding the ship when, to our no small joy, after ten o'clock the mercury in the barometer appeared again with the highest rolls of the ship.

Every flicker of the dying lamp of life brings hope. We regarded the return of the mercury like the arrival of an old friend whose presence consoled us. It was the most certain indication that the storm's continuing rage was decreasing. Toward twelve o'clock it indeed began to abate. We had just observed the hopeful change in the barometer when our sole comforter was smashed by a violent shock.* This loss prevented us from recording the barometer's climb and comparing it with the abatement of the storm. The turbulent waters gradually quieted down. Our fear of death disappeared with the subsiding wind.

Early in the morning we were all enchanted by the majesty of the sun. Never had the golden rays of this returning god seemed so beautiful to us mortals as he now arose in all his shining glory on the expanse of the horizon. His blessed, reviving rays instilled in us the most intense feelings of gratitude for our preservation. We cried with one voice.

Lord, how great thy works!

The ship actually had not suffered as much damage as we had assumed. The rigging needed a lot of repair and all of our possessions were more or less damaged. A lot of equipment had been destroyed. Clothing, valuables, charts and important papers were soaked. Several gifts for the Japanese Emperor and even a Letter of Credit packed in a double chest were wet, instruments and weapons damaged. The expensive draps d'or, velvets and silk materials had to be dried. There was hardly a spot on deck that was not being used to warm us up in the warm rays of the sun or to dry our belongings.

It was not until around noon on the 22nd that we could set sails again. Toward evening at a distance of 45 sea miles to the west-northwest we sighted land. On the afternoon of the 3rd we were within 15 to 20 miles of the Japanese coast of Kiusiu. Captain von Krusenstern named a high promontory at 32°14′15″ N and 228°18′30″ W Cape Tschirikoff and another farther south at 31°51′00″ N and 228°33′30″ Cape Cochrane.**

The land seemed fertile and afforded a variety of charming views. At nightfall we saw a number of fires along the coast not very far apart from each other. We took them for signals. Upon our arrival in Nangasaki this supposition was confirmed.

---

*Dr. Horner used the first opportunity to repair it with a tube that he had taken the precaution of bringing along from England.

**Both are in the Japanese province of Fiun'ga, the latter is called Whossiro in Japanese. — Julius von Klaproth

On the 4th we sailed through the Van Diemens Strait. The important detailed geographical descriptions and determination of this part of the southern coast of Japan can be found in Captain von Krusenstern's excellent work along with maps.[7] We followed the southern coast of the Provinces of Oosumi and Satzuma. We sometimes came so close to land that we could distinguish buildings and people. Of the numbers of small vessels and fishing boats not one tried to approach us, even though our Japanese often called to them loud enough to be heard.

The southeastern side of Satzuma is especially charming. The area appeared to be very well cultivated and highly populated. We gained a good idea of Japanese industriousness and culture. In this respect the nearby coast left nothing to be desired. The hills were being cultivated on terraces up to their very summits. Avenues of tall shade trees lent the fertile landscape an uncommonly friendly appearance. On the 6th we reached a spacious bay. A calm and the sight of a number of islands and rocks on the western horizon caused us to give up an attempt to sail through it. We therefore turned back to the south and sailed around the Island of Meac Sima.

A large number of boats we saw in the bay avoided most carefully coming near our ship or entering into conversation with us in accordance with Japanese law.

On the 7th, we headed north. Early in the morning we saw the Goto Island.* In the afternoon we came within three miles of the southwestern coast. It was not wooded as in Satzuma but cultivated to the highest degree possible, so that we were unable to see any uncultivated spots. The southwestern tip of these islands lies at 32°34′50″ N and 321°16′00″ W. The wind permitted us to sail to the northwest in the night. Early in the morning of October 8th, we sighted mountains and the part of Kiusiu with its long wished-for harbor of Nangasaki nearby. At daybreak we saw a fishing boat and hailed it. The fishermen in it were naked except for bands of cloth around their heads and hips. They do this, take their clothes off, so that they do not spoil them. They came, despite it being illegal, drank the brandy we offered them and told us that they had received word in Nangasaki by means of night fires of the approach of a three-masted ship, that on

---

*According to Klaproth *Go-to* means five islands in the Chinese dialect common to Japan. In reality the group consists of five large islands and a lot of small ones. Firando, lying to the northwest, is not counted as part of them. — Julius von Klaproth

the nearest hill at the entrance to the harbor an observation post had been set up. At the present time two Dutch ships had been in Nangasaki since July. They then showed us the direction to the harbor. Using a weak wind we slowly sailed ahead and arrived in the vicinity of the mouth of the harbor around one o'clock. Soon after a signal was given, a little vessel came out carrying a white flag with a blue cross-stripe and various Japanese characters. The two officers in the boat refused to come on board, but demanded that our Japanese go into their boat and inquired about the smallest of events. They had frank open faces and appeared to receive us with polite friendship. Among other things they asked us who we were? Where we came from? Our intentions, whether the envoy was only to Japan? Whether and how many cannons, muskets and swords we had on board? How long we had been underway and what was our last port of call? What flag were we flying, etc.? They requested the letter of permission, copied it and asked: why we were now using it twelve years later. Its existence had been publicized for four years after having been granted all over the Japanese Empire and they had expected the arrival of a Russian ship. One of the Japanese who had returned with Laxmann was still living in Nangasaki and was to serve as interpreter upon the arrival of the Russians.*

The main point of all their inquiries was to be convinced whether we really were Russians. For this reason when leaving they demanded a note written in Russian; its content did not matter. Around two o'clock we sailed with a very weak wind into the bay before Nangasaki. Between five and six another boat with two officers arrived to show us our anchorage as ordered by the governor. It remained with us until we dropped anchor in 33 fadens of water about ¾ of a mile from land around six o'clock in the evening at the entrance to the Bay of Nangasaki near Papen Mountain, the Island of Iwo Sima and Cape Facunda.

The officers sent by the governor did not want to leave us until we had provided them with written proof that they had carried out their orders and showed us our anchorage. When told that we could only do this in Russian, they assured us, as had the first officers, that there were people in Nangasaki who knew Russian.**

---

*We were unable to confirm this information later.

**Either they were pretending that the Japanese brought by Lieutenant Laxmann were still living in Nangasaki or else they wanted to conceal their location from us.

NOTES

1. Engelbert Kämpfer (Kaempfer) (1651-1716) was a German physician and historian who had studied in Germany, the Netherlands, Poland and Sweden before becoming the secretary of a Swedish embassy to Persia in 1683. Kämpfer then entered the service of the Dutch East India Company, going first to Batavia in 1689 and the following year to Japan by way of Siam (Thailand). In 1690 he reached Nagasaki where he was the physician at the Dutch factory. He stayed two years. His *Geschichte von Japan* (History of Japan), translated into English by J. G. Scheuchze, 2 Vols. (1727-28, repr. 1926), contains many mistakes because Scheuchze was a Swiss without an adequate command of English to translate the work accurately.

Carl Peter Thunberg (1743-1828) was a Swedish physician and botanist, who visited Japan in 1775. He had studied medicine and botany with Carl von Linné (Carolus Linnaeus) at the University of Uppsala. He became a doctor with the Dutch East India Company. In 1775 he arrived in Nagasaki and stayed one year, during which he collected specimens of flora and lectured on Western medicine, botany, zoology and astronomy. After returning to Sweden, he taught at Uppsala. He wrote several books about Japan, including *Flora Japonica* (1784)

Charlevoix was a French Jesuit historian, who traveled for his Society to various countries including America. Among his works are *Histoire de l'etabliasment, du progres et de la decadence du Christianisme dans l'empire du Japon* (Rouen, 1715), English trans.: *History of the Church of Japan* (1715) and *Histoire et description generale du Japon* (1736), which went through several editions. It is chiefly a compilation from Kaempfer.

2. Catherine II (Ekaterina, 1729-1796) deposed Peter III in 1762 and ruled Russia from 1762 to 1796.

Kodai, Kaikokuya Kodayu (1751-1828), was taken in 1791 to St. Petersburg, where he was granted an audience with Catherine II. He returned to Siberia the following year and then, accompanied by two other Japanese seamen from the original party and Adam Laxmann, he returned to Japan. He was 41 at the time. The shogun and other high shogunate officials thoroughly cross-examined him the following year. After that, he had to live until his death in mild confinement in Edo on the grounds of a garden for medicinal plants.

From 1792 to 1793, Adam Laxmann (Adam Erikovich Laxman, 1766-1796?) led the expedition to Japan which had been organized by his father, the noted Finnish naturalist Eric Laxman.

3. Jedo — Edo; after 1868, Tokyo (Capital of the East).

4. Alexander I (Aleksandr Pavlovich, 1777-1825) was Emperor from 1801 to 1825.

5. Von Krusenstern spells the name "Sikofk."

6. Aaron Arrowsmith (1750-1823) made himself famous in the 1790s by his large chart of the world on Mercator's projection: *Chart of the World on*

Mercator's Projection Exhibiting all the New Discoveries to the Present Time (London, 1790). He and his family became important map and atlas makers.

7. See Adam J. von Krusenstern, *Voyage Round the World in the Years 1803, 1804, 1805 and 1806* (London: Printed by C. Roxworth, 1813), Vol. 1, pp. 219-221.

Chapter 10

Stay in Japan. Roadstead before Nangasaki Harbor. Anchorage in front of Papen Mountain. Change of Anchorage. Events from October 8th to 17th.

The importance and rarity of Russians spending six months in Japan will excuse, at least for most readers, my becoming now and again somewhat long-winded about even the minutest details. Even if I may seem nevertheless boring to some, I am still convinced that others will find it very interesting to learn more about the spirit of this nation, about which we have so little information, through one or the other unimportant-appearing events. As much as I know how unpleasant it is to be put to sleep by a boring book, as much as I have tried to avoid repetition, I still find it necessary to do so. I can give my reader one consolation that he may leaf through or skip over in a few hours experiences we were forced to collect in six months.

We had just anchored around seven o'clock on October 8th when, as before, some officers appeared asking again the very same questions.

Night fell. About twenty large and small vessels, which we could only consider guard boats, stationed themselves about 50 to 100 paces away around our ship. One after another they raised melon-shaped, colorful paper lanterns. Since there were so many of them, they had a very pretty effect.

Around ten o'clock we saw a number of boats, each equipped with a lantern, rowing toward us. One of them was distinguished from all others we had seen by its size and beauty as well as two bright lanterns decorated with transparent coats of arms.

At first they said the governor of Nangasaki was coming. Soon afterwards we heard that it was an important man, ordered in the name of the governor along with his secretary, sent out to welcome us and to seek our permission to do this. After he received this permission, several officers and Dutch interpreters* were taken into the cabin where we received important guests, *groote Heern*** or *Opperbanjos* (as the Dutch interpreters would say).[1]

A short time later they appeared with a large entourage, including several interpreters, and were received with drum roll and an honor guard of seven armed men. They immediately went to the Ambassador's cabin where all of his ambassadorial cavaliers and naval officers had gathered.

The Opperbanjos*** with a secretary sat down on the sofa and crossed their feet. Several servants, even though the cabin was well lighted, placed a lantern and paraphernalia for smoking, which consisted of a bowl filled with glowing embers and another for tobacco and a spittoon, before each of them. The interpreters knelt in a semicircle around the sofa.

We very soon noticed that these *great men* had not come for any special business. They had come rather to ferret out information from us than to welcome the Imperial Russian Ambassador. They repeated most carefully the questions asked by various officers that day which we had already answered until weary. Our answers were carefully written down. Among other things they wanted details of the voyage from St. Petersburg to Nangasaki. Whether from Kamtschatka we had sailed between Korea and Japan or along the eastern coast of the island and how many days we had needed for the trip? The answer to the last question seemed of great importance for them. They also even wanted to see the original document of permission and told us about some Japanese customs, for example, that we had to turn over our gunpowder, cannons, muskets and swords until our departure. They promised us fresh supplies by the next day.

---

*The Dutch interpreters are Japanese, whom the government has had learn Dutch. There are around 60 to 70 of them. The Dutch factory abroad cannot undertake anything, whether in trade or otherwise, without them.

**All over Asia, where the Chinese culture dominates, *great man* or *human being* is the title of high state officials. In Japanese it is *dai-sin*; Chinese, *da-schin*; and Manchu, *amban*. — J. von Klaproth

***The title *banjos* has the same meaning as *groote Heern* or high statesman. I was never able to find out what kind of word it really was. As far as I know, it is neither Japanese nor Dutch.

The Ambassador requested an early audience with the governor in order to show him the letter of permission. He preliminarily agreed to relinquish possession of our gunpowder and those weapons not belonging to the uniforms of the officers and soldiers. We also requested a safe anchorage within the harbor because we were very exposed to the wind. We were promised an answer the next morning.

After we had spent over an hour with questions and answers the *great man* asked us to permit the head of the Dutch factory, Mr. Doeff, and some of the other people there to visit us.[2] We were not a little surprised to discover that these people, who had been sitting in a nearby boat during the entire discussions, had waited more for the Japanese to give them permission than for us.

Mr. Doeff, together with his secretary and the captains of the two ships (Mr. Musquetier and Mr. Bellmar) lying at anchor in the harbor, had barely entered the cabin when they were announced one after the other by the interpreters in order to pay their respects, *compliment*, before the Opperbanjos or great man. They had to bow very low and remain in that bent-over position until the interpreters said the *compliment* was finished. Whenever the interpreters kneeling on the cabin's carpet were to speak with a person of high standing, they threw themselves on their hands and spoke with bowed heads. As soon as they had finished their speech, they drew in or caught their breath with a hissing sound. Their superiors spoke so softly that it seemed to us it would be impossible to hear or understand them. They spoke in such a quiet whisper that it barely reached our ears. The interpreters' usual answer consisted in a loud ay, ay, which I understood probably meant yes as far as I know. They all returned home after midnight. On October 9th in the forenoon nothing of importance occurred. We talked about the number of boats decorated with all kinds of flags surrounding us. On some of them we saw bows and arrows and imperial Japanese sailors, who were distinguished by their clothing with blue and white cross-stripes. In the afternoon a little boat brought us fresh provisions — chickens, ducks, radishes, rice and fish. Soon afterwards the Japanese Dutch interpreters arrived and announced the arrival of very *great men*, i.e., the treasurer, who is said to have the same rank as the governor, a secretary of the governor and a banjos, who had all been sent in the name of the Japanese government to welcome us. Around five in the evening, we saw a large vessel decorated with many flags and signs of distinction and with blue and white awnings being towed toward us by several small boats rowed to the stroke of drums and rhythmic cries. Upon arrival the *great men* sent word that they would not come on board until they had been welcomed by the Ambassador, the Captain and several officers of our vessel. Mr. von Resanoff answered that this offended his honor, that if they expressly desired him to, he could send some of his cavaliers in his name. After a little discussion they were satisfied if the Ambassador would come out to the forecastle to meet them. Several officers then welcomed the great men with European bows and returned to the ship. In the meantime the Ambassador had gone to the forecastle to receive the high state officials with all military honors to the accompaniment of drum rolls with all military honor. After going into the cabin, the treasurer and secretary took seats on the sofa, the banjos in an armchair. Unlike the day before all three did not sit with crossed feet but in the European manner but with similar tobacco paraphernalia and the interpreters kneeling or lying before them in a half circle on the floor in order to await their orders.

The reasons for their visit mainly concerned the following points.

1) The Japanese required, on the strength of an ancient law, that all arms, i.e., cannons, muskets, pistols, swords and sabers immediately be delivered to the Japanese government for safekeeping until our departure.

Von Resanoff agreed with the following restrictions:

(a) that he and his officers might retain their swords as an essential part of their uniforms whose removal would dishonor them. Granted.

(b) that for the same reasons an honor guard of seven men should retain their arms since the Emperor of Russia had given them to the Ambassador as an honor guard without which he was not to appear.

This condition caused the greatest of difficulties. The interpreters urgently asked von Resanoff to forego this condition, since it was totally against their country's laws and even the first princes of the empire were not permitted to appear anywhere with open firearms but always had to carry them covered. The Japanese offered him the largest honor guard of their kind and assured him that even the people would be astonished to see armed foreigners entering their country, that such a thing had never happened before and that this condition could not possibly be well received at Court. When von Resanoff, despite this, insisted on retaining his entire honor guard with muskets and swords and uncovered bayonets, this condition had to remain unanswered until further orders were received. For this reason a courier was undoubtedly sent to Jedo.

2) In the name of the governor they required Laxmann's original letter of permission. Granted.

3) They requested the Russian Emperor's letter to the Japanese and informed us that our ship could not enter the Harbor of Nangasaki until the Governor had been informed of the letter's exact content. Von Resanoff gave a copy of it to the banjos and interpreters so that they could inform themselves of its exact content. He also stated that his monarch had enjoined him to give the original himself to the Japanese Emperor and the copy to the Governor of Nangasaki.

The *great men* read the letter which was written in Russian, Japanese and Manchu and then said they could not read or understand it because it was written in the vernacular and with such bad handwriting that the Governor himself would have to have it in order to be informed of its exact content and the intentions of the envoy. Von Resanoff requested again an early audience with the Governor with the assurance that he would tell him orally and in writing the content of the documents and the reasons for his arrival. In response to the express desire to know the content of the letter, he told them that the sovereign of Russia wished to establish friendship and trade with Japan and for this reason was sending the Ambassador with some gifts for the Japanese Emperor. They immediately asked what the conditions of alliance were. He responded that the Ambassador was mandated by his sovereign first to take into consideration the conditions in Japan and then to conclude an alliance in the name of the Emperor. This seemed to make a great impression upon them.

The request for a safe anchorage was repeated with the additional assurance that if the Japanese government distrusted us and did not want to receive the envoy, we would set sail immediately. But even in this case we did expect for the time being a safe anchorage as an act of friendship since we were forced to make repairs to the ship which had been damaged in the recent violent storm.

The Japanese then permitted us to anchor to the west near Papen Mountain as soon as they had our gunpowder and arms.[3] This happened within the hour since a number of little boats had been standing ready for the purpose.

Since it was dark the government officials went back to their vessel to eat dinner during the time the gunpowder was being unloaded. Afterwards they issued the order that we should be towed by a sufficient number of boats to the western side of Papen Mountain. We were most surprised by the way this was accomplished. About sixty boats were lined up in five rows. Each one was attached to a tow rope. Thus was our boat towed at least a mile in two hours in the most orderly fashion.

The head of the Dutch factory, Mr. Doeff, the captains of both ships, Messrs. Musquetier and Bellmar, and a Dutch traveler, Baron von Pabst, were allowed to visit us. Since they could speak German, English and French and we only poor, broken Dutch, they helped us considerably with our negotiations.

When Mr. Doeff entered the room, he immediately wanted to go to the Ambassador to greet him. The interpreters took him most politely by the arms, turned him gently around and said he first must "den grotten Heeren een Kompliment maaken." According to our ideas, this was done in a very demeaning way. He had to stand for a time in front of the *great men* with deeply bowed head holding his arms perpendicularly. He dared not raise his head. When it however seemed to him to take too long, he turned his head to one side and asked one of the interpreters: "kann ik wederom opstaan?"[4] A similar *compliment* also had to be made before the secretary and the banjos. Only then was he allowed to greet the Ambassador.

Around eleven o'clock in the evening, these distinguished guests departed. The Dutch had to repeat the ceremonial *compliment*.

Baron von Pabst, who had already mentioned how embarrassing it was to see Dutchmen being subservient, tried to sneak out of the cabin to escape having to perform the *compliment*. One of the interpreters called immediately: "Heh! meyn Heer Pabst, err je weg gaat, moet jede groote Heeren een Kompliment maaken."[5] He had to return and submit again to the accepted custom.

That was the only opportunity we had of enjoying the company of those cultivated Dutchmen. We never again were given permission or opportunity to speak with them. Around one o'clock they departed in the company of the banjos who pointed out to us our new anchorage.

The morning of the 10th found us a short distance west of Papen Mountain. The surrounding area was extremely charming. The hills were under cultivation from the bottom to the very top. The most fertile fields were on terraces on the slopes, interspersed with green areas, little groves and bushes. Several villages and individual houses added variety to the scene. The industrious peasants' activities enlivened the charming landscape. On the nearby shore we saw several earthen walls with houses behind them decorated with awnings and varicolored flags. We were told these were batteries or forts. We had 35 guard boats or vessels in our vicinity. Three of them had been ordered to stay close to our ship to serve us in case we needed provisions, interpreters or something else.

Around five o'clock in the evening, we again caught sight of the Japanese flotilla being towed toward us to the sound of muffled drum beats and rhythmic cries, i.e., a large garland boat with a lot of little boats. A head banjos, his secretary and some interpreters arrived, in all fewer people in the entourage than normally.

The main reason for the visit was to ask for exact information about the document intended for the Japanese Court. Since von Resanoff had said he intended to hand the governor of Nangasaki a copy personally the day before, the interpreters requested they be acquainted with its contents word for word because a courier was to be sent to Jedo to report the intentions of our visit. After von Resanoff had handed the banjos the copy of the letter to the Japanese Emperor to read, he stated that it was poorly written and for the most part unintelligible. The interpreters wished to know the precise meaning of the main points in order to avoid misunderstandings, ambiguities and other difficulties and get them out of the way. They wrote down every sentence and repeated them two or three times in order to be as true to the original text as possible. Its contents were approximately as follows: "von Resanoff had been sent by the sole sovereign of all Russians as his ambassadorial representative to the Japanese emperor in order to thank him for granting permission to come to Nangasaki and to offer him continuing friendship. The Russian Emperor wished to draw up a trade agreement for the benefit of his subjects, especially those peoples bordering on Japan, i.e., inhabitants of the Kurile and Aleutian Islands, of Kamtschatka and America. For this reason he also wanted to grant the inhabitants of Japan all freedom of trade in his great empire. He had also issued orders for them to be received hospitably all over his empire. In addition Japanese who had been shipwrecked on the Russian coast and wished to return to their fatherland were being returned. The Emperor of Russia was grateful for the courtesies extended Lieutenant Laxmann in 1792 and was sending the Japanese monarch some gifts manufactured in Russia, which, though of no great value, could serve for them to judge the state of arts and crafts in his empire and to determine which of them in the future might be useful and desirable for Japan."

The best of these gifts were: a very artistic clock in the shape of an elephant in the oriental style with many precious stones and mechanical objects, two large mirrors, each made from a single piece of glass fifteen fuss long and six fuss wide. A number of other bigger and smaller mirrors. An excellent precious black fox coat. An ermine coat. Vases of fossil ivory from Archangel. Beautiful guns, pistols and sabers. Fine steel products from Tula. Magnificent chandeliers, vases, table service and other glass and china from St. Petersburg, carpets and other embroidered pictures. The portrait of the Russian Emperor by Madame LeBrun.[6] Marble vases, damasks, velvet and silk materials of all kinds. Fine chintzes, clothes, furs, gold and silver pocket watches. A complete electrical machine.* A beautiful microscope. Galvanic plates, etc.[8] All of it worth about 300,000 rubles in Europe.

After the translation was finished, we found an opportunity to complain about the conduct and behavior of the Japanese we had brought with us. They had refused to carry out their duties since we had anchored in Japan. The banjos sent for them. He reproached them severely and told them they were acting most ungratefully. They had been supported in Russia for many years and enjoyed all kinds of benefits and were being returned to their fatherland at considerable cost. Their behavior brought shame upon their fatherland.

When the main business and instructions on the governor's part were finished and the Japanese *great men* had shown themselves to be very courteous and polite in their questions, answers and behavior, the Ambassador offered the banjos the copy of the letter to the Japanese emperor, which he had so persistently refused to hand over the day before and that day, so that they could deliver it to the governor for his perusal. This caused an inexpressible joy. Satisfaction could be read in all of their faces. The preceding ceremonies seemed to have been converted into confidence and closer friendship. The interpreters inquired about various objects considered for trade. For this purpose they had a number of questions drawn up in a little pocket book. I

---

*This attracted the Japanese's attention and admiration more than anything else. A *banjos* or *great man* rarely came who did not ask to feel the effect of the Leiden bottle[7] or to do some experiments.

cannot say whether from personal curiosity or upon the governor's request. Among other things they wanted to know: what products Russia could and wanted to trade? What articles of trade Russia wanted from Japan? Whether Russia would trade sugar, rye, furs, medicine and other goods and how many ships she would or could send to Japan every year? Whether four, five or even more? Where the ships would sail from? Whether from Kamtschatka? or from Europe? How long the ships would have to be underway? Which was the best time of year for navigation to Kamtschatka? etc. On the Russian side all these questions were only answered in general terms. When we told them that we could not immediately agree to anything and that the matters would be the subject of subsequent talks, they were satisfied and changed the conversation to small talk. Among other things, whenever possible, they appeared very interested in the geographic situation of Japan and Kamtschatka. It seemed totally unknown to them. They appeared not to know that Russia also had possessions in America. They asked for a map and proved in part to have quite good knowledge of geography. On a general map of the world, the head banjos used his finger to draw the route we had indicated to them we had followed and finally asked why we had sailed to the east of Japan to Nangasaki and not through the Korean Sea?

The Ambassador used the opportunity to show them a small pocket globe (from Adams in London) that excited a great deal of pleasure.

The Japanese knew that the world was round, but seeing it so represented seemed at least new to the banjos. He had a short face and wore a bad pair of glasses. He was offered a better English pair which he did not accept by saying he first had to get the permission of the governor. It is forbidden to accept any gift even of far less value. In the meantime he asked the Ambassador to keep the glasses until he obtained the permission he planned to try to get.

Some interpreters who were not needed for official business began to learn Russian. The first Russian expression they learned was: What is that called in Russian? As soon as they knew this, they began to ask for the names of various objects, of the numbers, good and bad, good day and goodbye, best wishes. Soon afterwards they were making use of their lessons. We were amazed by their scholarship, memories and thirst for knowledge. Finally the banjos told us that the following day on the 11th was a holiday (the Dutch said *kermes*).[9] For this reason no one would be coming to us. The day after the next, the Governor of Nangasaki would be replaced by another one expected from Jedo. We would have to remain at our present anchorage until he arrived and both would discuss the matter and decide on measures to satisfy our wishes. If, however, we wished to insist at the most upon immediately unpacking and checking the damaged gifts, they would bring a large Japanese boat for the purpose up to the side of our ship. That request remained unanswered. Around eight o'clock in the evening, the banjos said, since they had disturbed our peace, quiet and comfort for several evenings now, they would not bother any longer. Thereupon they went on board their vessel and were towed away amidst the usual ceremony and a number of little boats lighted by lanterns.

On that day (as we already had heard the day before) there was a large festival (kermes), so the Japanese did not visit us but left us totally alone to our devices. We thought we saw more guard boats than usual. We speculated about this nation with which we now had connections and admired their serious strictness. Their every step was taken thoughtfully and carefully. The most minor mistake, even of upper class people, would probably have cost their lives. Every thought, every question, every word was weighed and appeared to have some kind of intention.

At daybreak on the 12th, five Chinese junks that had laid at anchor on the other side of Papen Mountain set out to sea. They were towed by Japanese boats quite close to our anchorage. The shouts of the large crew, its clumsiness, the time and trouble needed to raise a single heavy sail sewed together from mats as well as the ponderous, poor workmanship of the boats themselves gave us the clearest proof of how far behind the Chinese are in the art of navigation. They could only sail with the wind. They therefore had to return to the harbor twice when it changed slightly, something European vessels could have used to advantage, before they finally succeeded in heading to sea with a constant northeast trade wind.

Around eleven o'clock we caught sight of a *great man's* boat decorated with many flags and accompanied by a drum roll and a number of little boats being towed toward us. The governor had sent two state secretaries to return the copy of the letter addressed to the Emperor of Japan, which they had received with so much pleasure two days before with the greatest of apologies and at the same time to request a true, literal translation of it into Dutch. They said that the letters and words were indeed Japanese but the letter itself was unintelligible* and no sense could be made of it. To save ourselves any further delay, we explained each sentence of the letter as best we could, for in the whole expedition there was not a single person who knew Dutch. The interpreters' great ability to comprehend helped us to the utmost.

After the translation was completed in many bits and pieces, the Japanese had another view of our envoy. For example, in the Japanese letter, the Ambassador, an Actual Chamberlain, was compared to and given the name and title of an official in the government of a little country prince.** After they knew the Ambassador's actual rank and importance they very carefully studied his key of office and ribboned orders and asked very naively whether the Emperor of Russia sometimes conferred such orders on a foreign monarch, for example, the Japanese Emperor? They indeed seemed now to have a totally new and higher concept of our Ambassador's rank. Finally they inquired about the intent of the imperial seal and Alexander I's signature. They were not a little surprised that the Emperor himself signed the letter, something the Japanese Emperor never does. The name of the reigning emperor is the greatest state secret in the whole country. His subjects only learn after his death what kind of emperor has reigned.

Then the Japanese we had brought from Russia were presented to the *great man*. They were wearing silk clothing in Japanese style sewn in Russia. Each one of them showed him the silver watch and twenty ducats he had received from the Russian Monarch. The banjos thanked us for all the acts of kindness and help given their Japanese subjects. The interpreters asked us to instruct them in Russian and offered to teach us Japanese of their own accord. The Japanese of rank display fine, very courteous behavior in all of their actions. Except for the language and clothing, we might have thought we were among the most cultivated of Europeans.

Around five o'clock all business was completed. The next day, the 13th, was again kermes or a Japanese festival. According to the interpreters, no one would visit us. They assured us that the day after tomorrow we would receive answers to our various inquiries.

---

*A Japanese in Irkutsk had translated it from Russian into Japanese. The translator was a former fisherman. Of course, no great correctness of style could be expected from him.

**Probably the fisherman who translated it had never heard of a higher official in the province.

Because of contrary winds, the Chinese junks returned again to their old anchorage in the harbor that afternoon.

No one came on today's kermes. We were surrounded by a number of vessels. We noticed, when the guard was relieved in the morning, the men arriving in civilian clothes exchanged them for the uniform of the crown sailors, which led us to conclude that they were only worn during actual service.

Around eight o'clock on the 14th, a north wind arose which gradually grew in force. It forced the small open guard boats to leave us and seek shelter behind Papen Mountain. The great amount of shouting and noise led us to suspect that their lives were in danger. Some trading vessels used this favorable wind to sail into the harbor, perhaps also to seek shelter. Because of the strong wind we received no fresh provisions but had again to be content with salted meat and ship's food.

The morning of the 15th, with a great many apologies for not bringing provisions the previous day, we got turnips, sweet potatoes, radishes, pork, fish, bread and rice. Around eleven o'clock in still beautiful weather, the banjos came with a small entourage. The Ambassador, tired of the frequent repetition of the same talk, greeted the *great men* rather coldly that day and said he did not feel well. The banjos brought news of the governor's arrival. Along with the former governor, he promised the Ambassador to come to the harbor soon and that in the future we would not suffer from lack of provisions. They both assured the Ambassador of their friendship and respect and asked him to be patient a little longer. If he had been a *little man* like, for example, Lieutenant Laxmann, he would have long since been in the harbor. For such an important man, they had to await instructions from Court on the manner in which he was to be received and to make necessary preparations in Nangasaki for a suitable reception of a man of his rank and dignity. The Ambassador insisted upon quickly receiving a completely safe anchorage, partially because of his illness and partially in order to repair the ship. The interpreters promised to bring the governor's answer the following morning.

During the general discussion, the interpreters said that the two governors had a very clear idea of an Imperial Russian Ambassador's greatness and dignity. Therefore they had sent out an order to all of the country's princes, the inhabitants of Nangasaki and the surrounding areas, not only to make known the arrival of such a *great man* from Russia but also to order everyone to treat this great man and all Russians with the utmost respect and deference and to avoid any situation leading to misunderstanding. All of the princes and people of rank would be called together in order to be present at a reception for the Ambassador. The city of Nangasaki would also be cleaned for the occasion.* At the same time they claimed the numbers of boats surrounding our ship were an honor guard. Around noon they left us and promised to return the following day with an answer to von Resanoff's earnest request for a change of anchorage.

The weather was clear and beautiful. We saw an indescribable number of pleasure ships and little boats without flags, mostly filled with women, apparently of rank, drawn by curiosity to gape at our ship from a distance. They all had to stay outside of a boundary formed by our honor guard. The Chinese junks, that had tried to leave the harbor again that day, returned in the afternoon.

Very unexpectedly the Ambassador's half-feigned indisposition had very good results. At nine o'clock in the evening, the interpreters arrived with both governors' answer that we would be given a better anchorage early the next morning. They had been sent in the evening in order to relieve the Ambassador of all his worries and to express the governors' endless regret upon hearing about the Ambassador's indisposition.

At about eight o'clock on the morning of the 16th, we caught sight of about one hundred small tug boats, all with the same flags, rowing toward us. Gradually they joined one or another of the large boats in our honor guard and awaited further orders. Around ten o'clock several banjos arrived amidst the usual ceremonies. In the name of both governors, they expressed their regrets at the Ambassador's indisposition and offered him all possible services, even *the services of Japanese doctors*,** if he wished. At the same time they brought the news that the ship was to be towed to a safe anchorage on the eastern side of Papen Mountain that day. They gave as an excuse for not towing it into the inner harbor, as the Ambassador had already requested several times, that it would not be showing proper respect to anchor an Imperial Russian warship with such a high personage

---

*I do not know what they intended to say by this remark, since the streets in general, as well as the nation as a whole, are very clean.

**This offer, as I will explain, is worthy of remark.

aboard among merchant ships. The Dutch would soon be setting sail and he could then have their anchorage all alone. Since this reason did not make sense to us and in reality seemed ridiculous, the interpreter said that one of the country's great princes, who had been summoned to receive the Ambassador, had not yet arrived. He wanted to give a further explanation when one of the others stopped him with a hardly noticeable sign. It is also worth mentioning here that at almost every visit, as also that day, one or more new people, banjos as well as interpreters, came to us. The government's distrust was mainly at fault. In this way it sought to make sure that the requests and answers were not connected to secret business agreements because in this way a new officer and unfamiliar interpreter acted as guards for each other.

Around twelve o'clock the anchor was weighed. At least one hundred tugboats towed us to the other side of Papen Mountain, where we caught sight of the City of Nangasaki for the first time several miles in the distance. The banjos stayed with us while we were changing anchorage. They appeared to be especially interested in geography. As on all previous visits, they wanted to know more about the locations, lands and people in the great Russian Empire. They followed our voyage on a map and asked for the exact distances from one place to the next. They wanted to see the small pocket globe, which was much talked about in society parties in Nangasaki. They inquired about the various Russian art and manufactured goods of which we showed them samples. They admired our astronomical instruments, even though they did not understand how to use them. Out of curiosity they still wanted to look through them at the sun. I mention this because it is incorrectly believed that religious beliefs forbid the Japanese from looking at the sun or the stars.

We anchored around one o'clock. Soon afterwards the banjos left us. An unbelievable number of large and small vessels filled with sometimes larger and sometimes smaller numerous families and parties of both sexes, especially however of the fairer sex, came from the city that afternoon to satisfy their curiosity about the large Russian ship. Not a single one of them dared to venture inside the boundary marked by the honor guard. To the right on the slope of the mountain, we saw a house hung with awnings and surrounded by palisades. We were told it was an Imperial guard post. As night was falling, the vessels surrounding us and the Imperial guard house were lighted by large numbers of lanterns — a very beautiful illumination.

NOTES

1. *Nagasaki-bugyo* was the title of the official in charge of the administration of the town of Nagasaki, overseeing the Dutch and Chinese trade, and the defence of the neighboring coasts. The title was first granted in 1603. *Bukjo*, *bugyo* originally meant to receive orders from a superior and carry them out, but in time it came to mean the person who bears chief responsibility for some activity.

2. Hendrik Doeff (1777-1835) was the director of the Dutch Factory from 1803 to 1817. He was also known by his Japanese name Dofu. During his stay in Japan, he went as ambassador to Edo three times. Upon returning to the Netherlands in 1819, he wrote his memoirs, *Herinneringen uit Japan* (Memories of Japan), (Haarlem: Bohn, 1833).

3. Papen Mountain is the mountain on the Island of Takabogo west of Nagasaki Harbor. The Dutch called it Papen (Priests') Mountain because hundreds of Christians were said to have been thrown from its heights at the beginning of the 17th century when Christianity was liquidated in Japan.

4. "Make a Complement to the *Great Men*." "May I stand up again?"

5. "Heh, my dear Mr. Pabst, before you go, you have to make a *compliment* before the *great man*."

6. Elizabeth Vigée-Lebrun (1755-1842). She was a favorite of the aristocracy and Marie Antoinette and, thus, had to leave Paris in 1789 at the outbreak of the French Revolution. She went to Italy, Vienna, Berlin and then to St. Petersburg, where she lived for five years. For reasons of health, she left St. Petersburg in 1801 and returned to Paris by way of Berlin and Dresden. From 1802 to 1805, she was in London and from 1808 to 1809 in Switzerland. After her return, she bought property in Louveciennes near Marly and remained there for the rest of her life. She is known primarily for her portraits of women, including seven paintings of Marie Antoinette.

7. The Leiden bottle is named after the city of Leiden. It is also called a Kleist bottle. It is the oldest electrical condenser. In 1745 P. van Musschenbrock (1692-1761) in Leiden and E. J. von Kleist (1700-1748) in Cammin, Pomerania (modern Poland), built it independently of each other.

8. Luigi Galvani (1737-1798) was an Italian physiologist and physicist who discovered galvanism, the production of an electrical current from chemical action.

9. *Kermes* means festival. The festival of the Nagasaki Suwa Shrine is also called *Okunchi* or *Nagasaki Okunchi*. The word "okunchie" is a variation of the word "okuniche," which means "ninth day" and refers to the ninth day of the ninth month in the lunar calendar. This is the traditional starting date for autumn festivals.

Chapter 11

Roadstead behind Papen Mountain. Events from October 17th to November 9th. Anchorage before the Imperial Guard and Negotiations. Departure from Anchorage and Entrance into Megasaki.

Nothing special happened from the 17th to the 21st. Pleasure-seekers from the city came out every day to look at the Russians. The Prince of Fisen's[1] boat was distinguished from all of the others by its outward splendor. It was decorated with many insignias of honor, flags, staffs, bows and arrows and muskets in cases. We could hear a large muffled drum and the sailors' rhythmic shouts from a considerable distance.

When beautiful weather lured vessels filled with curiosity-seekers from the city, they were no less entertaining for us than we for them. Sometimes a whole boat full of 10- to 14-year-olds would come out. It looked to us as if they wanted to show an entire school the Russian ship. In other boats we saw women who, judging by their rich clothes, belonged to the upper class, mothers nursing babies, girls with stringed instruments, still others with telescopes, which were passed from hand to hand — in short, old and young, married and unmarried. We could easily recognize the former by their blackened teeth, which, to our horror, they showed quite often when unconstrainably gay or laughing. As long as a girl is unmarried, she does not stain her teeth.

The nearby shore had also become very lively. Groups on excursions from the city frequently went there or visited a little temple at the foot of a mountain near our anchorage. It was no less entertaining for us to observe these groups on land. They frequently ate the rice or other food they had with them from beautifully lacquered little bowls with two little chopsticks instead of forks and then gathered in groups to visit the temple or walk along the shore, etc.

We had only 10° warmth on the 21st. We found this temperature made us very sensitive to the cold, since we had been used to warmer ones. Even though the weather was clear and fine, only a few vessels came from the city to observe us.

An interpreter came in the afternoon. Since he had no banjos along, he was not permitted on board. He requested someone from our boat to go on his so that he could carry out his orders. He then pulled a paper from his chest and informed us of the governor's instructions as follows: (1) Since the Dutch ships would be leaving their anchorage and it had been customary since the olden days for them to salute the Imperial Japanese fortress on that occasion, they wanted to tell us this so that we would know why so many cannons were being fired. (2) We were requested not to send a boat or vessel either to a Dutch ship or to any other nearby or uninhabited island. The Dutch had been given the same instructions. (3) Any provisions we wanted would be delivered free of charge. We were not permitted to purchase anything with money. For this reason (4) the Governor asked the Ambassador to forgive him for not having yet sent the Japanese tobacco pipe he had requested a few days previously. In accordance with Court instructions, he was not allowed to let a foreigner buy even the smallest trifle and had to recommend that we be patient until an answer came from Jedo. According to the interpreters, this could take 25 to 30 days. Finally, the Ambassador instructed the interpreter to request permission of the governor for one of the Dutch sea captains, who were setting sail soon, to come to us or for one of us to go to the Dutch in order to send letters to Europe.

The Dutch ships left Desima the same day and anchored closer to us. At unequal intervals each ship saluted the Imperial Japanese fortress with 150 cannon shots. Strangely, the Japanese did not answer with even one single shot. This led us to suspect that the Japanese had no cannons.

The fine weather and the movement of the Dutch ships undoubtedly led thousands of people to come out for enjoyment that day and numbers of curiosity-seekers, especially beautiful women, to visit the nearby temple. When the nights were very dark, the illumination of the harbor, of the guard boats and of the guard posts on land was a beautiful sight. Every evening I counted 400 lanterns in the surroundings. The Ambassador sent word to the Governor on the 23rd that he wished to speak with a banjos the following day.

The comings and going of boats filled with girls, women and pleasure-seekers continued. Around noon on the 24th, two interpreters arrived with as many civil servants or banjos in order to listen to the Ambassador's requests. He then explained:

1) He wished to meet with the Dutch ship captains or at least request permission for Captain von Krusenstern to visit the Dutch, who were soon to set sail, since he considered it his duty to use the opportunity to notify his monarch of the envoy's safe arrival in Japan.

2) He was displeased to hear that the Dutch merchants fired a cannon every morning and evening but a Russian warship was forbidden to do so under the pretext that it was illegal. Since the Dutch were permitted to do so, this constituted an insult to the Russian flag. He, therefore, demanded the same rights as the Dutch.

3) He was, indeed, very grateful for the offer of providing provisions free of charge. But he wished not to accept such favors because we had been receiving provisions extremely irregularly and often — for example, the day before — not at all. He would consider it an act of friendship if we were allowed to pay for provisions and always receive them at a predetermined time.

4) He was, moreover, very hurt and embarrassed to have been almost totally forgotten for 8 days. They were not showing him the courtesy expected of the Japanese toward His Imperial Russian Monarch, whose Ambassador he was. Neither he nor any other Russian would have come there, if they had suspected such treatment since, after safely surviving the great dangers of the voyage, he was being treated in Japan not as a friend but rather the same as a criminal and state prisoner. He had been at sea for 14 months, lived in a totally unaccustomed way, causing his health to suffer greatly. Therefore, he was again earnestly entreating them to permit him and his officers sometimes to visit land, even if only an uninhabited island so that he might get some exercise, as his doctors were recommending.

5) He was again repeating the request to be given a house in which to unpack, dry and clean the gifts intended for the Japanese Emperor and also a suitable place to repair our ship which had been damaged in the terrible storm.

The interpreters gave in answer:

Both governors had instructed them to tell the Ambassador that he must think they did not have any ears. They were sufficiently acquainted with the Ambassador's desire to live on land, unpack the gifts and to repair the ship. They, too, found themselves in a most embarrassing situation and could not act contrary to the laws prescribed to them. He would, therefore, have to be patient until an answer arrived from Jedo from where they expected orders about each individual point, rule and act.

The interpreters wrote down all of the above points. The meeting ended with the Ambassador's wish to be visited by the Japanese from time to time so that he could at least inquire about the governors' health.

The interpreters acknowledged the justness of our understandable displeasure and attempted to blame everything on their Empire's singular system of government and the unchangeable nature of their laws.

Upon being asked for an honest assessment of when an answer from Jedo would arrive, they said that couriers had been dispatched on October 11th and 13th and they would have to wait at least 27 to 30 days for an answer.

We were astonished by the length of time. That is why we requested even more urgently permission to go on land at least in the vicinity of our anchorage.

The interpreters asked among other things when the Ambassador planned to turn over the Japanese he had on board. In answer he said he planned to do this personally as instructed in his orders during his first audience with the governor.

They now requested to know the size and number of letters intended for Europe. That afternoon (the 25th) we observed a beautiful, large, high vessel with 36 or 38 rowers being towed past our ship by several large towboats. It was only decorated with one large, dark-red flag with a round white spot in the middle and a few honor staves. The sailors were all dressed in dark blue uniforms with a white and blue horizontal stripe across their chests and backs. According to our guard ships, the Japanese Emperor's nephew Prince Tschingodsin[2] was on board. The vessel was accompanied by several others. The procession was grand and impressive. The number of workers and rowers was considerable and their rhythmic cry could be heard at a distance.

Our provisions did not arrive until 8 in the evening after we had sent word to Nangasaki that we wished to speak with the interpreters. Many excuses were given while delivering the provisions for not coming sooner. Prince Tschingodsin had arrived. Everyone, including our people, had been occupied with his reception ceremony.

Around two o'clock on the 26th, the interpreters arrived accompanied by two officers. They brought the answer to the points made at the meetings two days before, that is:

Even though it was expressly forbidden and totally against the laws for foreigners of different nations in Japan to correspond with each other or with other nations and as a result the Dutch could not sail to Europe in Chinese ships or they with Dutch, the governor would permit the Russian Ambassador, as a token of special respect, to send two unsealed letters to Europe with the Dutch.

The Ambassador refused the offer and explained to them the impropriety of sending his Emperor an open letter. It was then decided that the letters would first be perused by the Governor of Nangasaki. A banjos would take them from him back to our ship. In the presence of a Japanese civil servant, the Ambassador would seal them and then they would be returned to the governor who would finally hand them over to the Dutch for further transport.

The letters were to be ready for the Governor to read by the next morning when they would be picked up.

In answer to the request to go on land, we were informed that all foreigners were forbidden to set foot on Japanese soil without the special permission of the Emperor. But because of the Ambassador's illness, an exception was being made. The governor, as an act of special respect, would permit him to use a small spot on nearby land for walks. The interpreters immediately brought for this purpose two well marked maps of small areas that could be seen from the ship. He should choose one of them. After a choice had been made, they asked for a delay of two to three days. Since the spot belonged to a large island, it first had to be made ready, also a little house and a palisade of bamboo stakes, so that the Ambassador in case of rain had shelter and the bold crowds would not disturb the Ambassador. It was in reality to keep the Russians from going outside the limited space allotted them.

They asked to be forgiven for the irregular delivery of provisions with the promise that in the future we would have no grounds for complaint. In the meantime, we had heard by chance that the previous day's excuse about Prince Tschingodsin's arrival was a story. Only his court had arrived. He himself was not expected to land for several days.

They promised the answer concerning permission to fire our cannons the next day. Meanwhile, we noted that the Dutch had fired no cannons that evening.

At daybreak on the 27th, we saw a lot of people working at the place designated for us. The interpreters came in the afternoon to pick up the letter. They also asked for an exact description of the contents and wrote down a translation. They promised to return the original the following day so that the Ambassador could seal it in the presence of the banjos. Then it could be delivered to the head of the Dutch factory, Mr. Doeff.* Ambassador von Resanoff had prepared an exact copy of the letter and included it of his own volition for the governor. We were also informed for the time being that the spot intended for our use would be ready the next day and we would receive permission to go on land.

Two banjos with several interpreters came the following afternoon to give the Ambassador the letter so that he could seal it. It was brought in a totally new, finely crafted box, made only for it and bound with a silk ribbon bow. A small strip of paper around the bow substituted for a seal. The bow could not be opened without tearing it.

The letter for His Imperial Russian Majesty lay in the little box in paper with a red seal. The seal was cut and taken along as proof that the letter had been returned to the governor and accepted. The governor was thanked especially for the copy of the letter he had sent. The letter was then sealed in the presence of the banjos and handed over for further consignment.

The *great men* told us after business was concluded that the spot chosen by us would be ready in the evening or at the latest the following morning. They assured us that the fence was an exception

---

*Only one single letter was sent to Europe after many difficulties and before we had set foot on Japanese soil. A year later, however, letters dated from Nangasaki describing Japanese customs and habits appeared in various German magazines. That these letters or compilations from Charlevoix, Thunberg and Kämpfer were foisted on the public as originals is indeed a bit much and carrying the *Licentia poëtica* too far.

and should be considered as special respect shown the Ambassador, considering his weakened health.

Beginning the day before and even in the night by bright fire-light, we had observed continual work at the spot meant for us. Early in this morning to our great surprise, we saw a little wooden house which had been built in the night.

Our officers were permitted to take swords but not guns to shoot, for example, birds on land with them. The last condition seemed all the more curious to us since they had already taken all of our gunpowder and guns.

On the afternoon of the 29th around four o'clock, two banjos with interpreters arrived in order to bring us the happy news that the Ambassador's exercise area on land was ready and they would be glad to accompany him there. Afterwards he could visit there unhindered at any time by telling the guard officer ahead of time, so that he could assure that the area was clean. Basically this precaution was taken so that he could gain time on land in order to post the necessary guards or to double their numbers. A requirement, clothed in the form of a request, was that the Ambassador never take more than nine officers with him; the sailors were not to go on land and no one was to spend the night there. With the Governor's permission, the banjos also brought a letter from Mr. Doeff for Ambassador von Resanoff in which he wrote he had received the letter for Russia. He added the assurance that he would send it in the securest way by way of Batavia to Europe.

The Ambassador together with several officers then descended into a shallop to touch Japanese earth. The sailors manned the shrouds and accompanied him with a threefold hurrah. The head banjos, several guard ships and a lot of little Japanese boats followed us.

Upon approaching the spot, which was about 10 minutes away, we found it small, contrary to expectations. The area about twice the length of our ship intended for walks was surrounded all around by a bamboo fence. All plants and grass had been dug out, the ground leveled and partially filled with sand. A small wooden summer house, open in front, was to serve as shelter in case of rain. The inside was raised about two fuss and covered by soft red felt rugs.

The Ambassador, following Japanese customs, had had the Imperial Russian standard with its double eagle carried before him.

He sat down in the little house on a chair brought from the ship. Then several banjos welcomed him in the name of the governor and conveyed a Japanese courtesy or compliment from him. It was made from a perhaps three-finger-wide strip of folded white paper tied with a bow made from red and white paper string. Little pieces of fish or gut hung out from both ends. At the same time they brought a new little inlaid box sealed by the governor. It contained various sweets for the Ambassador's enjoyment. A number of people had gathered on a nearly hill to gape at us. The banjos left us soon afterwards with the repeated request not to stay the night. Since we found no special pleasure in walking for long around a small, bare, fenced and guarded piece of land, containing by chance three trees, we soon returned to the ship.

On the 3rd, the sky was overcast and rainy the whole day. We remained alone on shipboard where nothing special happened.

We had an agreement with the Japanese that when we wanted to go on land in the future we would indicate this with a red flag so that the officers on guard would be informed of our intentions. That day (the 3rd), after giving the signal and several guard boats had been readied to go to Kibatsch (that is the name of the place), several officers including me went on land without the Ambassador. We found a lot of people busy attaching a little house — for certain needs — to the larger one. Little 12- to 13-year-old boys were working as carpenters, planing, sawing and nailing boards. Their tools — planes, saws, chisels, etc. — looked different from European ones. They probably were superior for the most part. They are most concerned with saving wood. The Japanese were very friendly and polite. Dr. Horner established the height of the sun by means of an artificial horizon. The people standing around watched with the greatest of curiosity and respect. They were careful not to disturb him at his work. Later they thanked him very much for his giving them permission to look through the sextant. Many of them asked us to write our names on their fans.* They expressed their thanks by bowing with the signed fans held to their foreheads.

Some of them indicated by pantomime that we should make the letters so large that they covered the whole fan. They told us the

*A Japanese always carries a fan, pipe, tobacco pouch, writing mate-rial and paper. He uses paper instead of a handkerchief, since he considers the custom of putting a handkerchief with such dirt into his pocket indecent and unsanitary.

Japanese for all of the objects we asked to know and we were just as informative with the Russian.

A few hours later we returned to the ship and learned that in the meantime several banjos with interpreters had been there. The Governor had sent them to ask why the Ambassador did not go on land more often. They wanted to know if something were wrong, if the number of people present or the people on the other side of the palisade were offensive and bothersome or if something were missing? The Ambassador replied he had no complaints about the spot. He would, however, have liked it better if they had at least left some grass so that he would have more enjoyment form the beauty of nature. The main reason for his not going on land again was that he was still tired from his first big walk. The interpreters smiled, made excuses for the governor and the small size of the spot. They offered immediately to do everything possible in their power to make our freedom less restrictive.

Immediately after dinner, two other civil servants together with interpreters arrived. They said that the governor was offering all possible help and support so that our ship could be repaired. For this reason he was informing us about a large Dutch ship that had been repaired in Kibatsch 6 years previously. Since it might still take a long time to receive an answer from Jedo and the governor did not have the authority to permit the ship to be repaired in Nangasaki, he wished to know if it might not also be repaired in Kibatsch. In case it could be, he would give us several Japanese vessels in which the gifts, cargo and guns could be stored and another on which the Ambassador could live. Everything was being taken into consideration and the answer postponed until later. Then the banjos once again inquired about the reason for the Ambassador's going on land so rarely and whether he would rather have the little place enclosed instead of open on one side? Or if he had any other complaints about it or remarks? Von Resanoff replied he would prefer the little Island of Nesidesima or Rat Island offered in the beginning because it still had some grass and woods on it. Not knowing the area, he had chosen Kibatsch. He asked for permission to visit the uninhabited Island of Nesidesima once in a while. They answered that the governor had had a lot of trouble getting us the spot in Kibatsch. He had had to seek the counsel of two of the country's princes, Fisen and Tschingodsin. This would again be the case. They doubted the request would be granted because everything would have to be cleaned ahead of time, perhaps all of the trees chopped down and the spot covered with sand.

On November 1st, Captain von Krusenstern went on land with several naval officers and Dr. Horner to take a reading of the sun's altitude and to see if the ship could be repaired in the Bay of Kibatsch. He measured the greatest depth to be 5 to 6 fadens. The Japanese did not prevent him from sounding the bay; on the contrary, they looked on with eager curiosity. Since the day before, they had been busy making improvements to the little summer house on land. On the front side they had installed moveable walls made from very regular lattice work sections covered with paper, whose exactness and cleanness of workmanship could probably not be obtained in Europe.

On the 2nd, the interpreters came with the news that probably the numbers of poorly dressed curiosity-seekers displeased the Ambassador. The governor had, therefore, issued orders that no one was to come to our spot at Kibatsch. There seemed to be more to the order than that, since for the next two days now not one single boat could be seen near our ship. Thus, we were also robbed of the pleasure and entertainment of observing new, strange things. Since the Ambassador also did not want to go on land, the Japanese asked if he could give orders for anything else that would make the place more to his taste.

Various officers of ours went to Kibatsch and found the Japanese very friendly and trusting. They showed our gentlemen their guns which are fired with a burning lint instead of flint and steel. They took out their pocket books and showed them maps of the surrounding areas, their medicine boxes, etc.

On the 3rd, the Ambassador went on land accompanied by a few Japanese barks where there were only a few subaltern officers. There was nothing new to see in Kibatsch. It also was not possible to go for much of a walk. Therefore, the Ambassador returned to the ship about one-half hour later. No curiosity-seeking guests from the city could be seen near our ship.

Even though the sky was overcast on the 4th and it was raining some, I went on land with some officers. Our conversation with the Japanese was somewhat colder than usual and there were few of them. A young man who was talking to us alone was called away, which led us to suspect they had been ordered not to become confidential with us.

Finally, after a long absence, on the 5th, the interpreters arrived with the news that the Dutch ships were ready to set sail. We could take their anchorage after their departure. They said concerning repairs to the ship that the loading of gifts onto several Japanese ships would be troublesome and time consuming. Therefore, the governor was offering us a Chinese junk. The Ambassador could transfer all of the gifts and provisions onto it as well as live on it himself. Finally an agreement was reached that as soon as the Dutch set sail, the governor would receive an answer. If they set sail later than within ten days, he would then rather wait the ten days because he was expecting an answer from Jedo within the next three weeks and permission to live on land.

That day we received a refusal to use little Rat Island (Nesidesima) as discussed on October 31st. Since the Japanese had been treating us rather coldly for several days and we had not seen a single excursion boat for a long time, von Resanoff alluded that our one pleasure, the sight and variety of pleasure barks, was being denied us. The interpreters ascribed this solely to chance. Nothing noteworthy happened on the 6th and 7th.

Early, around eight o'clock on the 8th, the Dutch weighed anchor. We greeted them as they sailed past and wished them a safe voyage. They did not answer us. The following day, Mr. Doeff excused their behavior by saying the captains had been expressly ordered by the governor not to answer. The ships had not even reached the other side of Papen Mountain when a calm forced them to drop anchor.

In the afternoon the interpreters brought us the news that two boats would pick us up the next day around noon and tow us to the place the Dutch had left early that morning. Iron ballast was not to be taken on land but rather on board a Chinese junk. The governor would do everything possible on his part to repair the ship.

On the afternoon of the 9th, two banjos with several interpreters arrived to accompany us to our new anchorage right in front of the Imperial Guardhouse. In the evening after dark, towed by many towboats, we arrived at the place and anchored in 15 fadens about 3 versts from the city of Nangasaki, which we could see clearly for the first time the following morning.

The banjos accompanying us were very polite, pleasant and sociable. They were occupied most of the afternoon with maps and etchings which afforded them a great deal of pleasure. On the 10th, preparations were finally made to un-rig the ship.

The masts, yards, beams and other things belonging to the ship were taken to Kibatsch. The governor promised to place them under special guard.

The interpreter sent that day spoke more freely than any before him. He considered all of the Japanese government's strict regulations extremely ridiculous, regretted being Japanese and wanted very much to see and travel in foreign countries. He deplored his fellow countrymen's short-sightedness, blamed it on the education of Japanese emperors and state servants. He maintained that the subjects were blind simply because their leaders themselves had no clear ideas and were not able to develop any for themselves. He said man is not born just to eat and drink but also to become educated. He interwove his philosophical remarks with Japanese proverbs, e.g., a man can live to be one hundred, fame is forever. Man's life is short; his name can be endless. He regretted the unpleasantness to which the Ambassador was being subjected, tried to console him by comparing an intelligent man to water: an intelligent man has to know how to adjust to his surroundings in every situation just as water takes on the form of the vessel or container into which one pours it. The Dutch left the harbor that day.

Our sailors transported the masts and yards to Kibatsch in shallops on the 11th. About 40 of our people went on land without seeing more than the usual number of Japanese.

On the 12th, several officers went on land. During their stay, they did not see a single Japanese. The weather was very fine. For the first time in a long time, several boats with inquisitive women appeared to eye the Russians.

On the afternoon of the 13th, several interpreters appeared whom we had requested in order to obtain the governor's permission to have bread baked in Nangasaki from the rye flour we had with us. They promised to bring us an answer in a few days. They also announced that in 2 or 3 days a Chinese junk would be brought. They were waiting for high water to float it.

During the night a very strong wind was blowing, causing the water to rise high enough to float the junk. The interpreters came around four o'clock with permission to bake bread and requested one of our anchors for the junk since the Chinese one was of wood and could not be trusted at all. They transported the heavy anchor on a very flat boat that at first appeared to us to be too small. They promised to deliver the junk the next morning.

Since Kibatsch was too far away we requested a place in the vicinity to unload our iron ballast, the cannons and other things that were too heavy to transport.

On the 15th, they brought the junk and asked Captain von Krusenstern to go on board in order to ascertain whether it would suit our needs. Several officers accompanied him and were not a little astonished to discover that the cabin intended for the Russian Ambassador was a low, poor, windowless room. Light could only enter through the door. There was room enough for provisions, gifts and other things. Captain von Krusenstern immediately expressed his indignation and said it surprised him very much that it was possible for such reasonable people as the Japanese to offer the Russian Ambassador such living quarters that would have been unsuitable even for his servant. He went on to explain that we could only begin repairs to the ship when the gifts were unloaded and the Ambassador had been assigned suitable living quarters. He could not use it for that purpose and would await the governor's answer. On that day they already had an answer to the previous day's remark that Kibatsch was too far away for transporting the iron and other ballast and our desire to have a place closer to the ship. The governor had given orders for a good spot near the ship to be cleared and prepared for storing our ballast.

Several officers went on board the junk in order to inspect more closely that clumsy, heavy vessel. The interpreters informed us that it was not within the governor's power to assign the Ambassador living quarters in Nangasaki or any other place before receiving an answer and permission from Jedo. He hoped to receive this in 7 to 8 days. It was decided to send the junk away again and to wait on board our ship for the answer to arrive from Jedo in a few days in the hope that the gifts could be taken to a suitable warehouse and the Ambassador could move into living quarters suitable to his rank. Early on the morning of the 17th, the junk was towed away again and a short time later our anchor was returned.

Nothing noteworthy happened until the 24th. We were quietly waiting for an answer from Jedo. With each passing day the cold of the approaching winter had been increasing noticeably and we were all very affected by it. The temperature usually ranged from 4° to 12° warmth. The poorer Japanese on the fishing boats and the sailors on the guard boats seemed to be shivering more than a little bit mornings and evenings. Thin cotton clothing was their only covering. At night they slept in almost open boats on straw mats with their clothing for covers. During the day we saw many of them who were totally naked except for a loin cloth. In the afternoon the interpreters came for the first time in a long time of their own accord to inquire in the name of both governors about the Ambassador's health. At first they talked for a long time about very insignificant things. There appeared to be no special purpose for their visit. The main topic of conversation was the present cold weather. They said that it would become much colder and stormier shortly and informed us that it was, indeed, unhealthy to live so long on shipboard at that time of year. We were more interested in the long awaited arrival of a courier from Jedo than the weather so we asked about it. We were more than a little taken aback to hear that post had arrived from Jedo the day before but nothing about our concerns. At the time of their departure no one had known anything about our arrival. They concluded with the very unpleasant and expected conjecture for us that the courier might easily need 15 to 20 days.

When the Ambassador became somewhat impatient, the interpreters made the following suggestion. In their opinion a small living quarters at the edge of Nangasaki would be better than staying on the ship. They suspected that if the Ambassador earnestly insisted upon having the use of small quarters until the courier's arrival and gave as reasons the advanced season of the year, the bad weather, his weakened health, the unpacking and checking of the gifts and the necessity of repairing the ship, then the governor would, indeed, probably consent to giving him quarters on land from special respect for the Russian Court. They were convinced that he would give him roomy housing commensurate with his rank and honor upon receiving an answer from Jedo. It was easy to see that they had been instructed to get the Ambassador to come around for they added he would achieve his goal sooner if he left the soldiers in his honor guard on shipboard for this period or at least took them on shore without their guns. It was not customary in Japan to appear in public armed and with uncovered weapons as we had certainly been able to observe on the ships around us where all of the guns were in their cases. The Ambassador found the suggestion, to be sure, acceptable, but did not want to be without his military honor guard. At the most he would agree to taking them along without bayonets on their guns.

The interpreters then left us with the promise that everything we had discussed would be conveyed as a proposal from us to the governor under the conditions mentioned.

We could easily suppose from the whole affair that the previous day's courier had brought the governor a perhaps not very satisfactory answer and he was only trying to gain time in an acceptable manner so that he could have us wait longer for the arrival of a second courier. Everything the interpreters had offered us that day of their own free will was exactly what we had been trying to obtain for so long and to which the governor answered so often, and for the last time on the 16th of the month, that it was not within his powers to undertake anything without permission of his Court.

On the afternoon of the 25th, the interpreters brought us the news that the governor would very much like to grant the Ambassador's request, but he would be taking upon himself a great responsibility. To justify his actions, he, therefore, requested the Ambassador to state in writing that due to the storm the ship needed repairs and that due to the Ambassador's health and the bad weather, etc., he requested living quarters on land. This was done and the interpreters seemed very satisfied. They repeated once again that it was against the law, that even the highest princes of the land always had to appear unarmed before the governor. They requested that he do without his honor guard or reduce their number and place cases over their guns. But the Ambassador insisted upon taking his honor guard with him on land. He could just as little do without them as his officers without their side arms, because this would be an offense to the Ambassador's honor. The interpreters shook their heads and said they would convey the Ambassador's words to the governor. Then they drew out a plan of the spot to be used as the Ambassador's living quarters along with a storehouse for the gifts. Von Resanoff was satisfied and only asked in general how many people were supposed to live on land.

The interpreters did not visit us the following day. By using our telescope, we could see a lot of people working at the spot meant for the Ambassador.

On the following days they were occupied with preparing the place. On the 30th, we could already see a high bamboo fence.

The interpreters had not appeared for several days. Their absence was making us impatient and bad tempered. The cold, stormy, unpleasant weather was intensifying our gloomy spirits.

On the evening of December 1st, we saw Desima, the Dutch quarter, greatly illuminated. As far as we could tell from a distance, it was tastefully and very effectively illuminated with several hundred bright, colorful paper lanterns. The interpreters told us that the Dutch factory did not miss an opportunity for demonstrating the East India Company's reputation publicly, even if they now have very little trade.

On the 2nd, they were still busy on land getting the Ambassador's quarters ready. Longingly we awaited the interpreters with news that everything was finished. Because they had not visited us since the 25th, we invited them to visit us the following morning. That evening Desima was illuminated again. On the 3rd, we anxiously awaited the interpreters' arrival but they did not appear.

Finally on the following day (the 4th), one interpreter arrived, as usual he was very polite and courteous. Along with many regards from both governors, he inquired with concern about the Ambassador's health and that of the rest of the gentlemen. He brought news of the reception of the Ambassador's letter in which he stated his reasons for wanting living quarters in Nangasaki. He also assured us that the courier was expected daily but had not yet arrived and it was taking an unusually long time. Despite this, the governor had taken all of the circumstances into consideration and was willing to give the Ambassador a small place to live. He hoped the necessary preparations for turning it over could be completed in 4 to 5 days.

Even though we could already see the high bamboo fence on the spot intended for us, we asked jestingly if this spot, as in Kibatsch, would be properly fenced in with bamboo, so that the great gentleman could not be disturbed or, indeed, seen by the common people. The interpreter laughed and answered that he, too, felt the Japanese government's precautions were very small-minded, but they were the country's customs. He concluded by asking about our various household needs, how we wanted the kitchen furnished, whether with Japanese or our own equipment. He told us the Japanese have no tables and chairs and as a result we would have to provide our own. At his departure, we asked him to visit us again soon and to free us from ship arrest.

We waited in vain for a long time for news of the courier's arrival and were not visited by the interpreters. Finally, on the 10th, with happy expectation we watched them climb on board. We hoped for an answer from Jedo or at least the news that everything on land was ready for our arrival. As usual upon arrival, they began with inquiries from both governors about the Ambassador's health and at the same time their regrets that the living quarters intended for him were not quite ready. The interpreter's own objective opinion was that he should be able to move into the quarters in 4 to 5 days. In answer to the question if a courier really had not arrived, he answered the usual no.

During the preceding visit (on the 4th), we had requested some planks to repair the ship. Instead of bringing them, they now came with small samples of two kinds of wood to let the Captain choose which one would suit his purpose.

There was no one on board the *Nadeschda* who was not filled with impatience and indignation. Even the Ambassador could not keep himself from voicing his displeasure. He told the interpreters that we had already lost so much time unnecessarily through all of the delays that our ship would have to depart from Japan in four months at the latest in order to return to Kamtschatka. If it had not arrived there by July of the following year, it would be assumed in Russia that something had happened to us. Ships would perhaps be sent out to look for us. If they still continued to hesitate for a long time, there would not be enough time for him to travel to Jedo. Therefore, he found it finally necessary to request a final decision. The interpreter answered that he understood everything very well and had already often made it clear to the governor, but he could not do anything without receiving an answer from Jedo. He added, "it is ridiculous that Japan, a small country, a small island, sets so many conditions and is small in all of its behavior and is even small in its way of thinking." "Russia," he continued, "is a big country, therefore, all of the ways, thoughts and actions of her inhabitants are great and noble."

When we remarked that it was highly unlikely and almost impossible that no courier had returned from Jedo and that we knew from Kämpfer's and Thunberg's descriptions of Japan how long a courier needed from Nangasaki to Jedo and back (21 days), the interpreter said that this was, to be sure, true, but such an important affair required the entire council of state to meet. Therefore, a courier could not be dispatched again so quickly. It was already dark when the interpreter took leave of us with his usual empty promises. He assured us we would soon go on land and we would receive the planks we had ordered in a few days.

Nothing in particular happened in the following days (11th to 15th).

On the 15th, the interpreters brought us the news that the house was finished, the Ambassador would be expected on land in two days.

They, however, wanted to know ahead of time: (1) whether the Ambassador would come in his own shallop or whether he wanted to use the vessels belonging to the Prince of Fisen? Answer: the latter would be preferable. (2) How many officers and other persons would be accompanying the Ambassador on land? Answer: About 10 officers and 15 other persons, among others seven soldiers and the four Japanese to be returned by us. (3) Whether and what kinds of goods and other things we would want to take on land? Answer: Nothing except clothing and the gifts intended for the Emperor of Japan. (4) When were the gifts to be taken on land? Answer: Immediately after he had moved into the living quarters. (5) Which vessels would be used? Answer: He requested Japanese help.

After this was finished, von Resanoff suggested that some of his officers be allowed to go to the place intended for him the next day to ascertain whether he could live there or whether it perhaps resembled the Chinese junk. The only mention of the soldiers was that they would go along.

In the afternoon we saw several hundred people on a hill very close to the spot meant for our use. They were busy erecting little houses covered with curtains. These serve as forts in that country. We, therefore, suspected that probably our Japanese honor guard was to be moved there.

As promised, the interpreters arrived around noon (on the 16th), bringing the answer that several officers would be permitted to inspect the quarters early the next day at seven o'clock and if everything was in order the Ambassador would be expected in the afternoon. But von Resanoff objected, saying it would be difficult for him to move into quarters the next day because, even if everything were so good, tables, chairs, kitchen utensils, etc., would have to be taken there. Only after that, when everything was in order, would he go there. His words surprised the interpreters very much. They said the governor had made plans for receiving the Ambassador the next day, all of the gentlemen of the country and the city of Nangasaki had been informed and he would be very embarrassed if the Ambassador postponed going on land. The objection, that he had been embarrassed for a long time already and had had to wait a long time for permission to go on land, was felt so keenly that the interpreters in the end earnestly entreated him to consider it a special favor and forbearance if he went to Megasaki (that is the name of the spot intended for the Ambassador) the next afternoon. The governor would order a vessel with sixty rowers and a number of towboats for that purpose.

At daybreak we watched a number of large and small Japanese boats gathering around our ship. Around eight o'clock two head banjos and interpreters arrived. The former were greeted with the usual ceremonies and conducted into the cabin, where they formally turned to the Ambassador and said that the governor of his own accord, out of special respect for the Russian Ambassador because he was not well, had without having received a letter from Jedo had living quarters and several ware or storehouses prepared for the gifts. The spot was small and at the water's edge but could not be changed because the living quarters of all foreign nations in Japan (i.e., the Dutch and Chinese) were also at the water's edge. As soon as an answer came from Jedo, he would receive better, more spacious quarters.

According to the previous day's agreement, several officers, whom I accompanied, were sent to inspect the house meant for the Ambassador. We used our shallop accompanied by Japanese boats to go to Megasaki, where several interpreters met us. They immediately showed us our new quarters. It was a one-storied house with nine rooms. The floors were covered with straw mats. There was no furniture except for some large yellow copper braziers instead of stoves. The window panes were made of thin, unoiled paper stretched over a finely crafted framework. The storehouses appeared to be so spacious that one-half of one of them could comfortably serve as quarters for the soldiers and the Japanese we were returning. Upon finding everything very satisfactory and conveying this in the Ambassador's name to the two head banjos we found there, we again returned to the ship. Here a list was made of all the things to be transferred to Megasaki. Immediately after our meal the Ambassador together with his retinue and military honor guard went on board the Prince of Fisen's vessel. Even though it was made for 60 rowers, not a one was used. A lot of little boats towed it — that denoted more respect according to their customs.

That extremely magnificent 120-fuss long barge had two stories or compartments. On the outside of the lower one were lilac silk curtains decorated with the Prince of Fisen's coat of arms; the upper one had multicolored canvas awnings which lent the whole vessel a colorful, unique appearance. The inner walls of the various rooms and compartments were very beautifully lacquered. Part of the floors were varnished and part covered by costly rugs. The main room was in the lower story, about in the middle of the boat. The Prince of Fisen's coat of arms was crafted in gold — mosaic-like — on the mirror-smooth, black-lacquered walls. Shades were covered with tasteful, expensive wall papers. The Ambassador sat in the room in an armchair from our ship. In front of him stood a little table with our Letter of Credit lying on it. The Russian soldiers, one of them holding an Imperial standard, had been stationed on the upper, back part of the vessel, where there was a kind of gallery or deck.

That is how we, surrounded by an unbelievable number of Japanese vessels, proceeded to Megasaki. As we were passing the Japanese guardhouses and imperial fortifications in front of our anchorage, we saw that they had been hung with new cloth and the usual number of awnings increased. The hills in front of the fortifications had soldiers stationed on them, some holding muskets, others flags, standards and other insignias with symbols of honor. The interpreters called them to the Ambassador's attention and explained that they were there in his honor. The nearby shore was covered by thousands of people who followed our vessel to its destination, from which they were carefully kept at a distance.

Near Megasaki the water is very shallow. Therefore, the Ambassador had to transfer to a smaller boat which was also very finely and beautifully built and most magnificently lacquered.

His honor guard and envoy officers went on shore first. The Ambassador followed accompanied by several head banjos, interpreters, a number of Japanese who filled the little place. Here his honor guard welcomed him with ceremonial honors. The Ambassador found the apartment rather good and sent his thanks to the governor.

The kitchen at our arrival was in the best of order. A fire was burning, water boiling, beef, poultry, duck and rice had been provided for us.

About an hour later the Japanese *great men* and their interpreters had departed and several of our naval officers had returned to our ship, so the gates to our new living quarters were closed and locked from inside and outside and guards were posted on every side.

Notes

1. Prince of Fisen: Prince of Hizen, a province near Nagasaki.

2. Prince of Tschingodsin: Prince of Chikuzen, a province near Nagasaki.

Chapter 12

Our stay in Megasaki.

Our party was now divided into two: Ambassador von Resanoff, Major von Friederici, Councillor von Tosse, Captain Foederoff,[1] Lieutenant Koscheleff, Schemelin, Commissioners of the Russian-American Trading Company and I, the honor guard, the four Japanese we had brought along and several servants were living on land. Our spot was surrounded on three sides by water, on the fourth it was connected to land, thus forming a kind of small rectangular peninsula. The inner courtyard about forty paces long and thirty paces wide was enclosed on three sides by buildings, i.e., the Ambassador's house and two warehouses, the fourth side, which could have offered us a beautiful view over the water, had been blocked by a high double fence of bamboo which made it impossible to see anything.

The courtyard had two gates — one opened towards the water. This one was guarded by the Prince of Fisen's guard boats — already so familiar to us. Before the other one opening toward the city was stationed a double guard, i.e., an imperial civilian guard and a military guard provided by the Prince of Omuru. The former sat three paces in front of the entrance to our courtyard and had also taken up positions at another more distant gate. The latter guarded a hill rising immediately behind the civilian guard and were able to see our entire courtyard as if from a tower. Both gates to our living quarters were regularly locked and bolted every morning and evening.

Until the 21st nothing in particular occurred. The gifts were gradually being transported to the storehouses at Megasaki from the ship lying at anchor before the imperial guardhouse. On these occasions several banjos and interpreters were always present. They checked everything carefully against the list of things sent from the ship so that there was no fraud or anything stolen.

On the 22nd, interpreters brought the news that an answer had been received from Jedo the day before and that a great man would come that day in the name of the Governor in order to communicate it to the Ambassador. There had been long negotiations about how the Ambassador was to be received because, as the interpreters alleged, he was to communicate the Emperor's words. Von Resanoff turned down all of the suggestions for a special ceremony and declared that he would receive the head banjos with every possible politeness and honor and not depart from friendly practices followed up to that point. It was finally agreed that the Ambassador would receive the *great man* in the European manner. During the negotiations the latter would sit in a large armchair and the former upon a sofa.

The interpreters also mentioned provisionally and, at the same time casually, the ceremony the Ambassador would be expected to observe during his audience with the governor. Since ancient times all ambassadors had had to follow the Oriental custom of kneeling before the governor during an audience. As proof, they produced copies of official papers dating from the earliest Portuguese embassies. In answer, von Resanoff replied that he would return all acts of politeness from the governor in the same way and would conduct himself in accordance with the country's customs.

Finally the *great man* appeared wearing an extremely meaningful expression on his face. In the name of the governor he proclaimed the courier's arrival from Jedo with the important permission from the Emperor of Japan that the ship from Russia had permission to go to Nangasaki.

As a result, on the following day the ship was towed into the harbor and anchored about one and one-half versts from Megasaki, our living quarters. At the same time the curtained guard posts on the nearby hills were torn down. We later learned at the Emperor's express command.

Despite the numbers of guard posts and ships, they put a lot of obstacles in our way. They did not even want us to communicate freely among ourselves, i.e., between the ship and Megasaki. They had ordered us to notify the governor about everything ahead of time if someone wanted to go on land or return to the ship. We remonstrated and objected to such illogical precautions. The next morning we received permission for freer connections. They now ordered us to indicate with a red flag to officers standing guard our intention to go on land or to the ship. After this signal they came at once to open the doubly locked doors (that is, on the side to the courtyard and on the side to the water). They had one express condition, that the number of people living on shipboard and the number of people living on land should not be changed. We, therefore, had to stand inspection every evening. On the 25th, since Lieutenant Koscheleff had some business on the ship and wanted to spend the night there, we were forced to have a sailor come from the ship before the gates were locked in the evening in order to have the correct number of people on land.

On the 30th, the Ambassador sent for some interpreters and told them that we needed copper plating, nails, planks, beams, etc., to repair the ship. He also requested of the governor a small spot on the nearby shore where our tackling could be repaired. The interpreters promised this ahead of time and said the government felt responsible for providing us everything we needed free of charge.

On the evening of the 31st, the Dutch celebrated the New Year. Almost all of the interpreters were feasting in Desima, which we saw was grandly illuminated. In Megasaki we continued to endure and, as all the other days, sought comfort in a philosophical, small glass of punch as the gates were shut and locked.

In the night from the 1st to the 2nd of January 1805, it froze. The temperature was 1° below the freezing point.

On the 3rd, the interpreters brought us samples of copper plating and copper nails we had requested for repairing the ship which met our specifications. Confidentially, they told us that on the day before the governor had issued an order for the vessels belonging to Prince Tschingodsin to return to their province because Japan was on the best possible terms with Russia. We saw, indeed, that at least 40 vessels before the harbor were under sail that day and that the Fisen guard boats were now unarmed.

In answer to the question why it was taking so long for an audience or an answer about our envoy, they said the temporal emperor did not want to decide alone about our envoy. He, therefore, had called upon the Dairy or spiritual emperor to advise him. He had not yet answered.

Half a month passed without our hearing any news or hope about our envoy being accepted. The cold, unpleasant weather had a detrimental effect on Ambassador von Resanoff's health. Upon learning this, Mr. Doeff had a beautiful Japanese padded nightshirt made. When he wanted to send it to the Ambassador, the governor denied permission because it was a Japanese product. He, then, reimbursed Mr. Doeff and had the nightshirt delivered to the Ambassador in his name.

Early on the morning of the 16th, there was an unusual rebellion. We were suddenly informed that one of the Japanese to be returned had tried to slit his own throat. He had thrust a razor down his throat but had been caught in time by one of the bystanders. A lot of blood was streaming out his mouth. The Japanese civilian officers on duty did not want me to examine the wound or to give medical assistance. The incident was reported to the civilian guard post, who immediately sent for a banjos and doctor. They did not arrive until in the afternoon. They wrote down the entire sequence of events and conducted *Procès* verbal and sealed it.

The wound did not look dangerous. The doctor was brought a beautifully lacquered medicine chest. He immediately chose the medicine he thought necessary from his portable apothecary. He mixed various herbs and a soluble powder in gargle water.

This event caused the Ambassador to request of the governor that he take over the returning Japanese from us in order to prevent any similar incidents in the future.

On the forenoon of the 17th, head banjos, several interpreters and some other Japanese arrived. The governor sent word that he could not take over the returning Japanese at that time. Earlier, in the beginning, when he had asked to take them over the Ambassador had not agreed to it. Now he would have to wait for an answer from Jedo to the report he had already sent. The Ambassador tried again by putting the request in writing to the governor but with no better success.

The banjos and officers instituted an extensive investigation into the incident. They only established that the Japanese wanted to take his own life because he was afraid he would lose his freedom forever after returning to his fatherland.

At 8 o'clock in the evening, quite unexpectedly, our gates were opened and we were visited by a number of Japanese. The interpreters with him said the banjos wanted to see if everything was in order. He also had the same job by the Dutch and Chinese. We could not in general, for the life of us, make sense of the visit.

Since the 18th, the second gate, under the command of civilian guards that leads to a small, open, oblong spot fenced in by bamboo about 100 paces long and then from there into the city, was left open. The officers on duty did not interfere with our desire for freedom. We used the opportunity to go for walks in that desolate little spot that at least offered us a free view of the water. We ascribed our expanded freedom to the governor's reproach of the banjos some days before that our living quarters looked more like a prison than an Ambassador's residence.

Late on the evening of the 19th, just as two days early, a banjos arrived in order to inspect our quarters. This time he honored the Ambassador with a visit and said he was there on orders of the governor, since the Japanese who had attempted suicide had gone out of his mind.

On the 22nd, we sent for the interpreters to order various things needed to repair the ship. We told them among other things that we had been enjoying fresh air for the last few days and going for walks at the little spot in front of our gate. They then told us this was being allowed without the governor's consent and that this freedom we had taken upon ourselves could result in grave consequences both for them and the guard officers. They promised to report it to the governor and procure permission for us.

The interpreters brought us an answer on the 23rd. We were to have everything we had requested to repair the ship and also permission for the Ambassador and the officers of his entourage, but not for his servants and soldiers, to go for walks at the small spot behind our living quarters.

The ill Japanese was now being visited every day by a doctor and a surgeon and his assistants or apprentices. The former was distinguished by a cleanly shaved head, the latter by a full head of hair. Civilian and military personnel had only the hair along their parts shaved off, the hair on the sides of their heads and necks were left.

The interpreters told us that the governor hoped soon to be able to give us good news. On the other side of the bamboo fence around our new promenade, we saw a lot of people gather to watch us the same way we in Europe go to the circus to see the wild animals. Men, women and children of all classes, especially a lot of mendicant monks, came to gape at us. They, like the doctors, had their heads completely shaved.

On the 24th, several interpreters, who had come to us on various business, told us confidentially that it was taking so long for an answer from Jedo because the temporal emperor had sent one of his most important Imperial councilors to the Dairy. They were not in agreement about receiving the Ambassador and were negotiating. They thought a decision would arrive in about 15 to 20 days.

The Ambassador sent for the interpreters on the 27th and instructed them to inform the governor that his patience and endurance had reached their greatest limits. He wanted to receive a definite answer or at least to know the reason why they were letting him wait so long with empty promises from one day to the next. The interpreters on that day told us a great secret. An imperial council had been assembled in Jedo to discuss trade connections with Russia, thus causing such delays.

Since the next day was the beginning of the Japanese New Year, two fir trees were planted that day (the 29th) by each gate and the trunks surrounded by pieces of wood. Above the entrance a straw wreath consisting of a boiled lobster, an orange, a piece of charcoal, a lot of little pieces of dried fruit skewered on a little stick, two special little cornets with salt and rice, a little piece of seaweed (*Fucus Saccharinus L.*), and bamboo cane with leaves and ferns.

The lobster, because of its beautiful red color and its power of reproduction — whole body members (claws and feet) will grow again — is considered a symbol for health by the Japanese.

Orange in Japanese is *dai dai*, the same word used for descendants, an allusion to the hope for increase in their numbers in the new year.

Charcoal in Japanese is *sumi*; this word also means wealth, for which it is a symbol.

The other things are indispensable necessities for the Japanese. They probably all have similar allusions attached to them.

In the evening the Ambassador received a very beautiful new year's gift according to Japanese taste. Similar gifts are sent from one Japanese to another in accordance with rank and character. The one the Ambassador received was a rarity even in Japan because its kind can only be sent among the highest ranked, most distinguished people of the empire. It consisted of the following individual pieces.

On top of a finely crafted new wooden box were two large round rice cakes. On the topmost one was a lobster, an orange, a piece of seaweed (*Fucus saccharius L.*), salt and rice, a chestnut, figs, grass, various leaves, straw and then an honor strip.

Toward evening the interpreters arrived with the governor's answer to our question from two days previously. He wished to inform the Ambassador that he regretted unendingly having disappointed his expectations. The only reason he could find for the long delay in receiving a definite answer from Jedo was that reigning emperor's uncle, brother and another close relative had been summoned from over 200 miles away in order to consult with him about the Ambassador's reception. He considered this unexpected delay a sign of the desired successful conclusion in the matter because a negative answer would have probably arrived long ago.

January 30th was the Japanese New Year's Day. People called on each other until late in the evening and left visiting cards. This lasted three days. On this and other very solemn occasions the Japanese wore ceremonial dress, i.e., every Japanese from the emperor to his poorest subject has festive dress which is worn over his normal clothing. It is made of a light blue-grey cotton material, obtainable in the entire empire in one and the same quality, one and the same color, one and the same style.

On February 1st, an interpreter arrived in ceremonial dress, sent by the governor to wish the Ambassador a happy new year. He told us that a courier had again been dispatched to Jedo the day before to speed up the answer.

On the 2nd, the last day of the festival, the heads of anchovy on stakes were placed at the entrance to both gates. At the same time we received a new little box full of peas. They were cast into all the corners of the house in order to drive out the devils and evil spirits.

On the 4th, all of the new year's decorations were removed and replaced by little branches of fruit, a sign of approaching spring.

Since, on the 5th, the condition of our ill Japanese was very grave, yet a third Japanese doctor was called in.

Japanese paper is thin, light and strong, extremely suitable for constructing a *montgofier*.[2] I had decided to build one about 10 fuss in diameter and over 15 fuss high. Some interpreters and several Japanese happened to be visiting us on the 6th when I sent up the first balloon in Japan. It climbed to a considerable height, developed a little tear on the top end and fell into the city of Nangasaki. The balloon began to burn after landing because of the burning spirits hanging from it. The quantity of smoke coming from it caused the Japanese to think it was a fire machine. The fire brigade hurried over and extinguished the burning balloon, which was taken to the governor. The interpreters explained to him what had happened. If we had been dealing with a less reasonable man, I could have caused a lot of unpleasantness. The result was that I was asked in the future if I wanted to send a balloon up to choose a time when the wind was blowing out to sea and not toward land.

On the 8th, several interpreters arrived to take leave of us. They were preparing to leave for Jedo in order to take the emperor gifts from the Batavian Company. Either the Company considers the trip too expensive or permission for it has been refused in more recent times. We received a message from the governor saying that a high state servant had departed from Jedo. He would arrive in Nangasaki in a month with a definite answer about the Ambassador's mission to Japan.

We now had a rather well founded reason for doubting we could travel to Jedo. We were given all possible assistance with the ship's repairs. They started inquiring more often about the work and now even volunteered, if needed, a larger place for doing the repairs.

On the 12th and 13th, the various articles from the New Year's gift in the middle of the door, i.e, orange, the lobster, the straw, seaweed, etc., were burned and replaced by a delicate, round figure made from wood shavings intended to prevent all illnesses from entering the dwelling.

Nothing special happened until the 20th. The Ambassador felt quite ill. He complained of rheumatic pains and chest pains. He naturally was also annoyed as Ambassador of a great monarch to find himself so confined and treated like a state prisoner, this causing his ill health to worsen. The governor had been sending interpreters and banjos often to inquire about the Ambassador's condition and health. That day he sent for the Japanese doctor who happened to be there to visit the ill Japanese, told him about his ailments and asked him for advice and medical help.

The doctor examined his new patient carefully. The most striking part of his examination was his careful examination of the abdomen with his hands and instead of taking his pulse, he laid his head against the chest to check the heart beat. The Japanese officers were present and consented to the doctor's giving the Ambassador several remedies from his portable apothecary. They were edible herbs which he ordered made into a kind of chest tea to promote perspiration.

On the very same evening other officers arrived (they said they had been sent by the governor) asking the Ambassador to return the medicine he had received from the Japanese doctor and to request in writing ahead of time his desire to be treated by a Japanese doctor.

The following morning an interpreter, whom the Ambassador had asked orally the day before to request the governor's permission for the Japanese doctor to visit him, arrived with the answer that the importance of the Ambassador's personage obliged the governor to act very carefully in such a case. If the illness led to a fatal outcome, the Russian Emperor would perhaps demand retribution from the Japanese. For this reason he asked him most kindly to put his application to the governor in writing.

Major von Friederici then wrote a letter in the name of the Ambassador saying that his pain prevented him from writing himself. In the evening some interpreters and officers arrived demanding not to speak with the Ambassador but rather with his ambassadorial officers and with me, his doctor. They had been instructed by the governor to tell us that he found it very strange of the Ambassador to seek medical help from a Japanese doctor, since it was generally known how many advantages European pharmaceutical science had over the Japanese. Since three doctors medicinae were members of our expedition (Dr. Espenberg, Dr. Tilesius and I), he had to suspect the danger was so great that we were taking last extreme measures. Thus, he could not possibly give his permission for a Japanese doctor's services, unless the Ambassador's doctor and the ambassadorial chevaliers declared in writing that it was absolutely necessary to take this step. Neither I or anyone else could sign such a document in all good conscience, something that at first caused some difficulties, since the interpreters did not know which answer they should take to the governor. After my assurance that the crisis could be expected in the night and we, therefore, wanted to wait until the next morning, they were satisfied.

Early on the 22nd, his Excellency felt so much better that it was not necessary to ask for the Japanese doctor's advice again.

After a great deal of effort, several of our officers obtained their good fowling pieces for a few days in order to have them cleaned and saved from rusting completely.

On the 27th, the interpreters came on board ship to inquire about Captain von Krusenstern's health. Their real reason for coming, however, was to learn if we had been working industriously on repairing the ship and if it would soon be in condition to set sail. From talking about the ship, they turned to the Ambassador in order to ask about his health.

Among other items of interest, they said the governor had received a letter from Jedo six days before containing the news that the Emperor had ordered a high state official, who was being sent to Nangasaki because of our business, to depart from Jedo on February 18th. Then von Resanoff said he was greatly surprised at their deceiving him so often with falsehoods, since the governor had sent word on February 8th that the *great man* had already left and would arrive in a month.

On March 1st, the rest of our hunting muskets were brought for cleaning and polishing without our having to ask for them.

A private conversation with the interpreters led us to assume that everything dealing with future trade with Russia had been decided and the courier from Jedo would bring all of the official papers so that there was no prospect of our being able to travel to Jedo.

We had had almost no contact with the Japanese for a long time; only an interpreter came sometimes to ask about the Ambassador's health and the progress being made on repairing the ship. We were unable to learn anything about the outcome of our mission. Finally on the 12th, an interpreter told us that he doubted we would be able to travel to Jedo and that the *great man* arriving in about 10 days would probably wrap up all of our business in Nangasaki so that we could set sail again in April or May as we wanted to.

In the following days we made serious preparations for our departure. The tackling was transported on board again and readied to sail. Concerning provisions, the interpreters told us we would receive free of charge quantities of rusk, rice and salt because the government felt obligated to replace in some measure the provisions we had used on the voyage from Russia to Japan.

On the 26th, there was a heavy storm accompanied by rain showers. The west wind was so strong that our ship, despite being moored by two anchors, was driven almost 50 fadens and was in danger of being put on a sandbank. The third anchor had just been dropped when the wind died down. A violent thunderstorm put an end to the terrible weather. Turbulent weather seems to dominate that season of the year, since that had already been our fourth very stormy day since the 17th of the month.

Notes

1. Foederoff — Feodoroff. Langsdorff probably bases this on the German pronunciation spelled with an "e."

2. Joseph M. Montgolfier (1740-1810) and Jacques E. Montgolfier (1745-1799) were French inventors who sent up the first practical fire balloon or hot air balloon in 1783.

Chapter 13

Summary of Previous Events. Announcement of a Messenger's Arrival from Jedo. Preparations for Audience. Ceremonial Audience. Business Audience. Farewell Audience.

We spent several months in Megasaki, the place assigned to us, under lock and key. We had almost no contact with the Japanese. Even the interpreters were permitted to visit us only with the governor's express permission. They came rarely and only if they had business. We were mostly occupied with clearing the ship, taking the gifts on land, unpacking and cleaning them during that period. We then began to repair the ship and strangely enough, we could request anything we wanted for it and we got it. A request for the slightest trifle, aside from food, we either did not get at all or only with the greatest of difficulty. They even denied us the pleasure of a live bird or tobacco pipes. Provisions of all kinds which we requested were delivered free of charge at anytime. They put us all off from one month to the next by promising us all possible freedom as soon as an answer arrived from Jedo and permission for connections between the two countries had been granted. After about two months, we were notified of the arrival of a *great man* or a *courier* messenger from Jedo who would bring the Emperor's answer. The whole business affair seemed now to be taking a different course. Our hope to be able to travel to Court lessened with each passing day. The interpreter began to inquire all too often about the progress of ship repairs and finally we were left with the sole hope of being able to establish trade connections.

Anyone who can put himself in our shoes can at least have an inkling of the inconveniences and unpleasantnesses of all kinds we had to endure during the last months.

After surviving storms and hardships, we had reached an interesting foreign country. We were not, as we had hoped, treated as friends, not even as foreigners of distinction and importance, but rather as criminals or state prisoners locked up in a spot, at the most, a hundred square spaces in size for an undetermined length of time and guarded from all sides. That was hard and unjust.

Spring was approaching. All of nature was coming alive. They had even blocked our view of a charming scene by a high bamboo fence. We found ourselves cut off from all contact with the natives and unarmed in the hands of an extremely distrusting country, denied any means of doing scientific work and our spirits dulled by the unaccustomed loss of freedom. Only the fish delivered for our table provided us with a subject for scientific investigation. By secret promises we were finally able to have our Japanese supply master bring different kinds of fish every time. They provided Councilor Tilesius and me with a pleasant and informative way of spending our time. They went so far as to forbid us to purchase anything or to give a Japanese even the smallest trifle. We were all secretly able to get some little things, e.g., India ink, a couple of pictures, fans, tobacco pipes etc., from trustworthy interpreters. They were subjected to a search every time. If anything were discovered, they probably would have paid with their lives.

On March 27 the governor, to our joy, informed us in due form that he expected the arrival in Nangasaki of a high state servant from Jedo with the Emperor's answer in two days. On the 30th we learned through our guards that that messenger had actually arrived days before. But by April 2nd we still had not received any notification and for the previous 5 days we had not been visited by any interpreters.

Finally on the 3rd of April interpreters appeared to announce to the Ambassador the arrival of the *great man* from Jedo and at the same time to invite him to an audience at the governor's house the following day and to agree upon the necessary ceremonies at the reception.

When the Ambassador asked what form the audience would take, they answered: Early the next day around eight o'clock a head banjos would come to accompany the Ambassador to the governor's house. Since the shortest route was by water, he would be taken a large vessel belonging to the Prince of Fisen as far as a landing called the mussel stairs or the great stairs (Ochatto), where he would be met by military and civilian guards. From there he would be carried in a large *norimon* or sedan chair to the governor's house accompanied by a lot of *great men*. Only *he* would be so honored. The other officers had to go on foot. They assured him that the norimon was very spacious and comfortable and its use was reserved for Daimio or the most distinguished men of the empire. Upon arrival at the governor's house, he would go into one room and the ambassadorial cavaliers in another nearby and rest (they undoubtedly did not want to say wait) until the audience was announced. This was being done from special respect since it was customary for *great men* always to be separated from lower civil servants. The Ambassador declined this distinction and insisted upon his officers remaining in the same room with him.

Only the Ambassador, continued the interpreters, could be in the audience hall because it was reserved only for the most distinguished men of the Empire. The Dutch were not even permitted in the anteroom intended for the officers. The Ambassador gave several objections to these arrangements and after an exchange of words the last two points were written down for the governor to decide.

The Japanese, as a sign of respect, expected the Ambassador to follow Japanese protocol by kneeling before the Japanese Emperor's messenger and the governors and bowing his head in the same manner they did. Von Resanoff refused to do this by explaining that he wanted to greet these gentlemen according to European protocol just as he would his Monarch, the Emperor of Russia. After a great deal of effort and long exchange of words, he was finally conceded this point. In addition the interpreters wanted to know what kind of position the Ambassador would take during the audience. Since in Japan, according to Oriental customs, they had no chairs but rather kneeled on rugs and mats, they hoped the Ambassador would find it convenient to comply with this courtesy, to which the first princes of the empire were bound just as the courier from Jedo and the governors. They would kneel on soft padded straw mats. Von Resanoff refused. At first he wanted to stand in the European manner just as he would before his Emperor. After repeated attempts at persuasion by saying this was absolutely the most disrespectable thing he could do, he decided to lie with his feet stretched to the side. The interpreter also implored the Ambassador not to take his sword with him into the audience hall and assured him, even though all *great men*, as we knew, usually wore two sabers on such occasions, they would be appearing without any sidearms. After several objections by one or the other side, the Ambassador said he would comply with this demand only as proof of his respect for the Japanese Emperor.

The persons selected to attend the audience were: Ambassador von Resanoff, Major von Friederici, Councilor von Fosse,[1] Captain von Foederoff, Lieutenant Koscheleff and I. The Japanese once again refused permission for the honor guard with muskets to accompany us. They would permit a soldier to carry an imperial Russian standard behind the Ambassador as a sign of honor. In addition another servant could be along during the procession in Nangasaki.

In the evening the interpreters came with the governor's answer that the ambassadorial cavaliers could stay with the Ambassador in the antechamber and two could accompany him in the audience hall.

April 4th in the morning around eight o'clock, the banjos and interpreters appeared. The Prince of Fisen's magnificent boat decorated with flags and cotton and silk curtains received the Ambassador and his entourage. It was surrounded by numbers of little boats all flying the Fisen flag.

We left the vessel at the wide and comfortable stairs (Ochatto), where we were greeted by a lot of high ranking Japanese. Opposite the stairs or landing was a large imperial civilian guard station with a lot of honor insignias placed in front of it. Several rows of officers were kneeling behind each other. The houses facing the water, as well as surrounding the square, were all decorated with rows of royal Fisen and imperial hangings so that we could not be seen. Now and then we caught sight of some curious heads behind the hangings. Basically, however, the natives could not see us and at the same time we were led blindfolded through a very large part of the city because in all of the streets we passed through the same measures had been taken. Whatever the hangings did not cover on the houses and cross streets were covered by bamboo straw mats. The interpreters said the reason for these measures was to prevent the unworthy common people from seeing such a personage as the ambassador face to face.

As soon as we arrived at the large square of Ochatto, our procession was arranged as follows: In the front were about 40 persons of various rank, among others some banjos, each followed by his servants and people, then 6 imperial soldiers, holding long poles instead of muskets. They were followed by the Ambassador's norimon carried by four men. It was closely followed by the Russian soldier carrying the imperial Russian standard, then the ambassadorial cavaliers surrounded by a number of civil servants and interpreters, after them a commando of 16 to 20 Japanese soldiers along with an officer on horseback and a large number of state servants, lesser officials and servants.

This procession traveled through a number of streets whose names, in the order in which we traveled through them were: Hokowra-

Mass, Omura-Mass, Mottofacata-Mass, Foru-Mass, Honkose-Mass, Bungo-Mass, Sakura-Mass, Kaschijamma-Mass, Jooscha-Mass, at the end of which was the governor's house. Standing along all the streets were sometimes larger, sometimes smaller guardhouses decorated with garlands, some with civilian and others with military guards. The streets are wide and clean with wide gutters on each side to carry off the water, but not all are paved. Some had a single row of small stones and others of large square stones down the middle. We could see little or nothing of the houses. Most of them are single-storied, made of wood with lattices on the doors and windows.

At the governor's front door we all had to remove our shoes, even the Ambassador, so that we did not dirty the beautiful lacquered floor and straw rugs. It is customary for them always to remove their straw shoes upon entering a house. This no longer surprised us because the banjos and interpreters had been coming into our rooms in Megasaki without shoes for months.

A large number of officers guarded the governor's house both inside and outside. We were conducted through a long, wide corridor with a beautifully varnished floor and into a room whose floor, like ours in Megasaki was covered with straw mats. We saw no signs of furniture, i.e., tables, chairs, benches, etc. The walls were covered by wallpaper with quite pretty landscapes. All of the work around the doors and windows was finely polished. The light entered the room from the corridor. There are no glass windows in all of Japan; instead the window frames are covered with fine paper. Beautifully lacquered tobacco utensils — pipes, spittoons and tobacco box. Another large china spittoon stood in a corner. As soon as we had positioned ourselves around the tobacco utensils, we were served unsweetened tea. The cups were made of good china, but thick, heavy, poorly shaped and even more poorly painted. We all found the tea not especially good. After about one-half hour the Ambassador was called into the audience hall. Major von Friederici and Lieutenant Koscheleff accompanied him.

The courier from Jedo and both governors were kneeling almost in the middle of the room. Behind each of them stood other men holding their swords crosswise high over their heads.*

The Ambassador together with his officers paid their respects according to European customs. They then placed themselves about 6

*They had indeed lied to the Ambassador.

paces in front of the governors. The interpreters were kneeling on both sides. The knights or men of rank of the Empire were seated around the audience hall.

The first question the governor asked the Ambassador was: why and for what purpose had he come to Japan and why had the Emperor of Russia written to Japan, since they had very explicitly told Lieutenant Laxmann that this was strictly forbidden and broke Japanese laws and offended Japanese customs and sense of propriety. Next he asked if Lieutenant Laxmann had failed to carry out these instructions and whether he was still alive? Then the governor declared that the document we had brought along to Japan contained permission for a merchant ship to come to Nangasaki in order to negotiate trade (connections), but there was no mention of a mission. Finally he wanted to know why we were only now taking advantage of this document so many years later.

The audience ended around one o'clock and we returned to Megasaki in the same order as we had come in the morning.

Interpreters came in the evening to tell the Ambassador that he could have a second audience the following day if he so desired.

The proposal was accepted. About 7:30 the next morning it was raining so heavily that we thought the audience would have to be postponed. But around nine o'clock the weather cleared and the head banjos and interpreters came to escort us to the audience. We were ready to leave, but von Resanoff remarked that his officers could not go on foot as they had done the day before because the rain had made the streets very dirty and it was a very long way to the governor's house. At first the head banjos objected, but then in the end sent several people to inform the governor and to have norimons sent for the ambassadorial cavaliers while we were going by water from Megasaki to Ochatto. After arriving at the large stairs we had to wait on the conveyances for almost two hours before the news arrived that five norimons were ready for the officers. In the meantime a heavy rain shower with thunder had set in again. The vessel was so well covered that we could wait for it to end while smoking tobacco and drinking unsweetened tea.

The leader or captain of the Prince of Fisen's vessel was very polite and courteous. He wrote down the names of his unusual guests as a souvenir for himself and his family. We were no less observant of our surroundings than the Japanese. Among other things we saw a man hiding behind his fellow countrymen who was busy drawing. We tried to gain his confidence and asked him to draw anything he found of interest and then let us see his work. We had to admire his ability more than a little bit. In a short time he had sketched on paper everything he saw on and around us, for example the Ambassador's three-cornered hat with feathers, star and order ribbon, the various insignia on each officer's uniform, sabres, swords and scabbards, buttons, scarf, chancellory keys of office, watch chains and seals, etc. The quickness and dexterity with which he once again up close sketched all of these European objects he had never seen before was beyond the ability of most European artists. He outlined them in India ink on fine Chinese silk paper. What sureness of stroke, what lightness of brush must be required to give the proper expression to fine lines from the first insoluble stroke on delicate blotter paper. The few hours we had to spend waiting on those conveyances probably were of the utmost importance for this man.

Around twelve o'clock we finally heard that the norimons were ready, so we again set out on our procession like the day before, except that the officers were being carried in little sedan chairs.

The square, the houses and streets were still covered by hangings, cloths and mats. We had barely arrived at the governor's house and again camped around the tobacco apparatus when the Ambassador, together with Councilor Fosse and Captain Foederoff, were taken to the audience. Very soon he returned to us. There he had been ceremonially handed a large roll of paper with the request to have the interpreters explain it to him. They raised the roll bowing and full of reverence to their foreheads, opened it with a kind holy veneration and said: "This is a *groote beleftheit* (great favor) from the Japanese Emperor to the Russian Ambassador. This paper contains nothing but friendship. Since however it is written in the Japanese language, we have been instructed for the moment to explain its main points to the Ambassador orally. Then, however, we will provide a precise written translation so that everything will be understood precisely. This is no small or easy task for the paper is profound, i.e., written with great deliberation and great scholarship."

They then told us of approximately the following main points: "In the most ancient of times ships of all foreign nations had been allowed unhindered to visit Japan and Japanese citizens and ships had been allowed to visit foreign lands. For about the last 150 years the emperors had issued a ban to apply to all of their successors, by which no Japanese might leave the empire and only the Dutch, Chinese, the inhabitants of the Island of Riukiu (Likeern) and the Koreans were permitted to come to Japan. Trade with the latter had stopped many years ago, and only the first two still had permission. Since then, foreign powers had tried several times to establish trade and friendship with Japan. Each time they had been sent away immediately without consideration because of the long standing ban. It is very dangerous to form ties of friendship with unknown, unequal powers."

Here the interpreters paused for a special explanation. "Friendship," they said, "is like a chain, which, when formed for a specific purpose, must be made of equally strong parts. If, however, one of the parts is very strong and the other disproportionately weak, then the latter is predestined to be destroyed by use. The chain of friendship can therefore only be forged to the disadvantage of its weaker link.

"Thirteen years ago," they continued, "a great Emperor had sent Lieutenant Laxmann on the first Russian ship and now an Ambassador on the second one to visit Japan. The former's kind reception and the latter's friendly welcome are permitted. The Emperor of Japan is willing to do anything possible as long as the laws of the Empire are not broken. Thus, he is able and willing to consider the arrival of a second Russian ship as proof of the Russian Emperor's great friendship for him.

"This wealthy monarch had sent an ambassador and many costly gifts. In accepting them, the Emperor of Japan according to Japanese customs, which are considered the law, would also have to send an ambassador and comparable gifts to the Russian Emperor. Since it was strictly forbidden for either ships or people to travel outside of Japan and Japan was so poor that similar gifts could not be obtained or given, neither the mission nor the gifts could be received.

"Japan has no great needs and wants. Therefore it also needs only a very few foreign products: those few to which the country has become accustomed or which are sometimes in short supply. The Dutch and Chinese are already supplying these in sufficient quantities. He does not want to introduce luxuries. It would also be very difficult to control more extensive trade because it would be impossible to prevent the common people from having contact with the foreign sailors connected with the business trade and this contact was very strictly forbidden."*

The Ambassador made all kinds of remonstrations that he had not come in order to demand gifts in return for his. Since nothing helped, he insisted he wanted to pay for all provisions and all of the materials for repairing the ship. The Japanese replied that these were not gifts, but the first were necessities and the other assistance in time of need. It was the

---

*Probably contraband is meant.

duty of the government to grant both. They informed us at the same time that the Emperor in addition had issued a special order to deliver a two-month supply of all of the kinds of provisions we considered necessary or desired and to give us 2,000 30-pfund sacks of salt, 100 150-pfund sacks of rice, 2,000 pieces or bundles of the finest Japanese raw silk, the former for the crew, the latter for the officers. The Ambassador refused, saying if gifts were not accepted he could not accept the provisions and silk. During these negotiations, we were brought pipes to smoke and unsweetened tea and sweets as refreshments. The latter lay on a separate piece of paper and consisted of two slices of sugar cake, several small sugar rolls with a ribbon of sugar on top, i.e., sugar worked into the shape, form and color of colorful striped ribbon.

After the interpreters had explained precisely the Japanese Emperor's intentions, they brought another small roll of paper, addressed to the Ambassador from the governor. It stated in the main that our ship, as soon as it left the harbor, was to leave the Japanese coast. It was very dangerous to approach because there were many storms and rocks. In the future any Japanese shipwrecked on the Russian coast who wanted to return to their fatherland should be turned over to the Dutch in Europe so that they could be transported by way of Batavia to Japan.

Our audience was now over. Around four o'clock in the afternoon, we were carried in norimons without much entourage to Ochatto and then from there to Megasaki by water.

The cloudy sky and some rain increased our dejected mood.

Since they could not know ahead of time whether we would perhaps be in the audience until late in the evening, they had taken measures to illuminate all of the streets we used. Every 4 to 5 paces there was about a two fuss high post with a lantern fastened to it.

On the 6th the interpreters came in the name of the governor to talk about our accepting provisions. They said the governor could make no decisions in the matter and had to carry out the Emperor's orders. In case the Ambassador refused to accept the supplies and silk, he would have to send a courier to Jedo which would prolong our stay for at least two months. The Ambassador would have to accept them in order to obtain our freedom soon.

The interpreters then asked whether it would be agreeable for him to go to farewell audience the following day or whether he wanted to go on another day. Von Resanoff chose the next day so that we could leave Japan as soon as possible.

Around noon on April 7th, we again proceeded through the streets decorated with hangings and posted with guards to our farewell audience. It was raining quite heavily again on that day. When we arrived in Ochatto, we were each given a new umbrella and then carried in norimons.

The audience consisted of the reciprocal exchange of compliments and friendly words of farewell. Afterwards they showed us the 2,000 bundles of silk, the gift from the Emperor, in an anteroom. The interpreters assured us it would have been the greatest disaster if the Ambassador had not accepted the gifts intended for the officers because it would have been assumed that they had translated and interpreted the Emperor's orders badly. Therefore they too were expressing their very special thanks for his having accepted the gifts.

This is then how our extraordinary mission to Japan ended. There was nothing else to do but to pack the gifts intended for the Japanese Emperor as soon as possible and take them back on shipboard and then return to Kamtschatka. While preparing for the voyage, we once again tried to obtain permission to visit the Dutch in Desima or a temple in or around Nangasaki — all for nought.

After a great many often repeated attempts, von Resanoff finally received permission to give seven of the main interpreters some trifles for all the effort and trouble they had expended on us. In the end both governors sent a request for the little pocket globe of the world, some maps and illustrations of all of the Russian nations as souvenirs.

After that, every day had no other purpose but to get the ship ready to sail. I am convinced that the Japanese were more than a little surprised when we announced on the 16th we were ready to sail.

Notes

1. In this chapter in the 1812 edition, the name "Councilor von Fosse" appears. Earlier, "von Tosse" is used. This is probably a printer's error. Krusenstern lists him as Nadvornyi sovetnik (Aulic Councilor) Fedor Fos.

Chapter 14

Departure from Japan. Voyage from Japan to Kamtschatka Cape and Strait of Sangaar. Description of the Western and Northwestern coasts of Matmai or Jesso. Stay in Aniwa Bay. Description of it and the southeastern coast of Sachalen or Tschoka. Voyage from Tschoka to Kamtschatka. Arrival there.

All activities were now directed toward a quick departure. The ship was almost ready to set sail. The main thing left to do was to repack gifts brought from Russia and to fill the water casks as well to stow the provisions of Japanese rice, salt and rusk on shipboard. This work was done very quickly. On April 16th, after von Resanoff had received a copy of the Japanese documents together with a translation into Dutch, our single desire was once again to obtain our freedom of movement and to leave Megasaki that long ago had become our prison.

Captain von Krusenstern was now ready to set sail and to receive the envoy on board. On the following day, the 17th, we went on board. Many of the interpreters, especially however many of the civilian officers, seemed very moved at our departure in Megasaki and to be infinitely sorry that the hope of trading with Russia had come to nought.

Our departure was without any further pomp and ceremony. A few days before, the local ruler, Prince Tschingodsin, had taken over the duties of guarding the Harbor of Nangasaki. He had one of his official boats take us to our ship. As soon as we and all our possessions were on board, one hundred small boats towed our ship to the western side of Papen Mountain. Banjos on guard duty and interpreters accompanied us. In the meantime the Japanese had returned all of our gunpowder and guns, the latter were rusty. This time as we sailed past the imperial guard houses they were decorated only sparingly and not with new hangings. We also did not see, as at our entrance, any soldiers with muskets, flags or honor standards. Even the Prince of Tschingodsin's vessel with its colorful silk curtains we were using was far less splendid that the Prince of Fisen's.

Very early on the 18th we set sail. Our hasty departure undoubtedly left the Japanese with no bad impression of Russian navigation. The day before the interpreters had thought we still needed a long time before we could sail. They said they thought, like the Dutch ships, we would probably remain at anchor for about another 8 days and still need to finish a number of things before setting out on our distance voyage. Without our asking, they had promised in the name of the governor to provide us daily with fresh food and water during our continued stay even if it were for weeks.

The sails were set late in the night and early the next day. Early in the morning before even the guard boats or so-called honor guard, which had not yet left us, knew what was happening, we were already under sail. Some of them tried to accompany us for awhile. As soon, however, as a brisk east-southeasterly wind hit our sails they had to remain far behind us.

Captain von Krusenstern had decided to return to Kamtschatka by way of the Korean Sea along the western coast of Japan in order to map the Strait of Sangaar and the western and west-northwestern coasts of Matmai or Jesso and to continue the exploration of the eastern coast of Tschoka undertaken by the late La Pérouse.

The voyage whose description begins here is one of the most remarkable, since so very few Europeans have ever sailed on the Sea of Korea. Captain von Krusenstern is the first to make the Strait of Sangaar, the northwestern coast of Jesso and the eastern coast of Tschoka or Sagalin to the mouth of the Amur River the goal of scientific investigation.

The exact knowledge of our earth and its geography obtained through the efforts and attention of this learned navigator makes us all indebted to him for giving us knowledge of a part of the globe never visited before. Even though the second part of von Krusenstern's *Voyage around the World* was published while I was working on this chapter, I hope my readers will not hold it against me if my geographical description of this voyage is somewhat more detailed than by others and if I intertwine my own comments among the most notable astronomical points and data of that learned navigator and if I refer interested readers to the correct maps in von Krusenstern's *Atlas*.

Toward evening on the 18th, a very brisk southeasterly wind came up. By night in foggy rainy weather, we sailed through a 32-mile-wide strait between the little islands Asses Ears and Cape Gotto.

At daybreak on the 19th, we headed north and northeast in high seas. In the evening we were already in the vicinity of the Island of Tsus,* which we caught sight of on the 20th just at day break. Its northern tip lies at 34°40′30″ N and 230°30′30″ W.

Contrary winds, fog and rain prevented us from continuing to follow the coast of Japan lying to the east of us, which we caught sight of toward evening. Two days later on the 22nd and 23rd we were able to see it again for short periods of time in the following locations: 35°15′, 35°45′, 227°40′ W, 36°01′, 36°15′ N and 217°10′ W.

On April 30th Captain von Krusenstern again approached the western coast of Japan in order to determine the location of Cape Sangaar. The following day we discovered at 39°50′00″ N and 220°16′00″ W a very high Cape,** which we named Promontory of the Russians.

On May 2nd in clear weather we found ourselves near land. We could clearly see a city (40°50′ N and 219°54′ W) and small ves-

---

*The Japanese call this island Tsu-ssima, the Chinese Tui-ma-tao, i.e., island with horses standing across from it. On the western side it has a very deep bay beginning at the two promontories Kukuissaki and Ossaki which runs very deep into the island. This bay is connected to the sea on the eastern side of the Island by a canal (that has been dug) called the Ship's Canal which divides the island in two. To reach the Harbor of Kokuyan-noura (Fou-us-ura) on the island's northern side, the Japanese usually sail from the Harbor of Karazu in the Province of Fisen to Island of Iki, 13 Japanese miles (*ri*) away and from there they travel 48 miles to the Harbor mentioned above, Tsu-ssima. From the Korean Harbor of Tooscha (called Tshosan on von Krusenstern's map) on the River Fusan is another 48 miles. Jata, the main town on the island, lies on the southeastern tip. Very close to it is the large, convenient Harbor of Oo-ura, both at the foot of quite high mountains. The southernmost foothills on Tsu-ssima are called Oo-ssaki and the northernmost Tayo-ssaki. The latter lies between the Islands of Kaito and Oonoscheto.

— Julius von Klaproth

**In Japanese this large peninsula is called Votoko issika ssima, i.e., stag island; the mountains on it, Joo-moto; and its southwestern promontory, Nankaba or Kamo — on von Krusenstern's map this is called the *Promontory of the Russians*. On May 2nd the ship was near the plains and woods at the mouth of the Nossiro-gawa, called Nodai on other Japa nese maps. The snow-covered mountains we saw divide the Province of Dewa from Ooschin and have no common name. On the western side of the Province of Ooschin, which we passed on May 3rd, are the two important promontories of Nangasaki and, farther north, Torii-saki. Behind them is a high mountain called Iwaki-jama and to the east the important city of Jumenai, situated on a river that flows into the sea almost at the northwestern tip of Japan. — Julius von Klaproth

sels lying at anchor. It had a bay with long, flat, sandy shores bordered by high mountainous points of land. The city seemed rather large and the surrounding countryside very fertile, judging by the colors of the plough fields and meadows and woods beautifying the area. The harbor, if present, is probably formed by the mouth of a river and presumably only navigable by Japanese vessels, i.e., for small, *low-draft* vessels because, at a distance of 3 miles from land, the water was not more than 25 fadens deep.

Behind this charming landscape in front of us, especially on the northern coast, high mountains raised their snow-clad heads. Up to then we had seen whales and all kinds of seaweed around the ship every day, but especially here in the vicinity of land.

Four boats rowed out to us toward evening, each one with 15 to 20 men. Even though we were friendly and invited them on board in Japanese, they did not want to come near our boat. The construction of their boats and the shape of their oars, indeed even their way of rowing, was different from Nangasaki, so that we could hardly believe they were Japanese.

The next morning the wind was blowing very favorably. We sailed along the coast at 8 knots an hour. We discovered several bays and inlets and to the north a quite high point of land projecting far into the sea (40°37′40″ N and 220°11′30″ W), which was named Cape Gamaley. A very high snow-covered mountain (40°40′40″ N and 219°49′ W) lying to the northeast of the Cape received the name Mount Tilesius.

Finally in the afternoon we caught sight of our long-awaited Cape Sangaar (41°16′30″ N and 219°46′ W). Together with another one straight to the north at the southern tip of Jesso (41°25′10″ N and 219°50′30″ W), it forms the entrance to a strait with the same name, which we called Cape Nadeschda after our ship.

Later we approached the southwestern coast of the Island of Jesso, where we caught sight of the large city of Matzumai (41°32′ N and 219°56′ W)* situated on an open bay which offered very little

---

*Matzumai is the name of the island's capital city and means City of Fortress. The island itself is not called Matmai in any language. The Japanese call it Jesso and the Chinese *chia-y*, which means crab-shrimp (*chia* are little sea crustaceans called *Garnelin* in German, *camarones*, in Spanish, and shrimp in English). The Harbor of Matzumai is

protection for the ships lying at anchor. By using a telescope we could see the houses and temples clearly. Somewhat to the southwest of this city are two islands, the one farthest west (41°31′30″ N, 220°40′45″ W) is called Oo-ssima, that is, the big island, and the other (41°21′30″ N and 220°14′00″ W) Ko-ssima, the little island. They serve as characteristic landmarks for the Straits of Sangaar, which is 18 sea miles across between the capes.

Here Jesso lies quite high. Most of the surrounding mountains were snow-clad. They look volcanic, are desolate and barren with irregular, jagged, steep rocky cliffs. The interior of the island, where it is more protected from the severe winds and cold, may have some very fertile valleys. The immediate vicinity of the city of Matzumai, however — judging by its size and outward appearance larger than Nangasaki — is sandy and desolate, making it difficult to understand the source of livelihood for the large population if we had not learned in Nangasaki that not only the inhabitants of Jesso but also a large part of northern Nippon lives from whaling. We saw lots of little vessels sailing in the bay and some others anchored near the city and at docks but were unable to determine where a harbor might be.

Early on the 4th we sighted the Strait of Sangaar. Because of the strong current flowing through it, we had to keep our distance. We headed toward the most western of the little islands (Oo-sima), which is about 6 miles in circumference. We steered northward through a 20-mile-wide channel between it and Ko-sima. Both islands are small, steep, uninhabited, rugged and, from appearance, of volcanic origin.

Toward noon we sighted a third island, Okosiri. This is lower than the other two. It is situated west of Jesso and north of Oo-sima (42°09′ N and 220°30′ W) and is much larger by far — about 11 miles long and 5 wide. At its southwestern end it rises gently from the sea and has an inviting, pleasant, fertile appearance and is covered with

---

neither convenient nor safe for Japanese vessels. Before it, lies the small Island of Besaiten. The Japanese consider it sacred and have therefore built a temple on it. Southeast of the city is the southernmost promontory of the Island Ssirakami-ssaki and east of it two convenient harbors for small vessels. Even farther east is the Harbor of Chakadade with various Japanese settlements. Not far from it farther inland is the home of the Kurillion interpreters. Along the entire southwestern side of the island is found quantities of seaweed (*Fucus*), called *Kombu* by the Japanese and used as food. — J. von Klaproth

woods. It seemed nevertheless to be uninhabited, since we neither saw boats nor houses nor smoke anywhere along its coast.

After we had sailed around this island, we once again approached the Island of Matmai on the morning of the 5th. In the foreground behind a hill, we caught sight of thick smoke rising out a valley and, in the background, of a long chain of snow-covered mountains. A high promontory in the vicinity (42°38′ N and 219°59′ W) was given the name Cape Kutusoff.* We had an almost complete calm. In the otherwise very beautiful weather, we drew parallels between several European areas lying at almost the same latitude and this area. At this time of year in Europe, everything is in bloom, and one has all kinds of the best fruits. Here even the lowest mountain ridges of fields are still covered by snow.

On the 6th we caught sight of another high promontory, Cape Novosilzoff, and behind it a wide, deep bay which could easily have been taken for a passageway.** Filled with uncertainty and expectant hope, we began looking for a passageway. On the southeastern shore we saw a volcano sending up a lot of smoke and several other conical peaks. We were struck by the fact that smoke was only rising from a small insignificant mountain and that the nearby high peaks displayed no signs of volcanic activity. We named the highest and most important peak Mount Rumoffski. It is situated at 42°50′15″ N and 218°48′30″. On that day we were unable to sail very far into the bay but had to tack about the whole day because of a contrary wind from the south.

On the morning of the 7th, a favorable southwest wind came up so that we could sail farther into the bay in clear weather. We,

---

*The Japanese call the promontory Chokossenossaki. On its southern side is the last Japanese settlement on the western side of the island. To the north are the settlements of the natives (Aino) and even farther north a promontory named Cape Novosilzoff that the Japanese call Komoinossaki.

**According to Japanese maps, there is no passageway here but rather at the end of the Bay. The mouth of a wide river whose source is a magnificent large lake, Issikari, 4 Japanese miles (*ri*) in circumference. It is formed by the junction of various little streams. It is separated by a low ridge from two other lakes which empty into the sea on the east side of the island. South of this bay is a high mountain, Mount Ssiribetsu. A little stream, whose source is at the foot of the mountain, flows into the sea north of Cape Chokossinossaki. To the northeast is another mountain, Mount Yuuben, which runs to the eastern side of the island. — (Julius von Klaproth)

however, had to give up our hope of finding a new passageway. The shores grew closer and closer together toward the southeast, the depth of water decreased gradually with each drop of the lead, the water gradually tasted less salty, and finally we had no choice but to turn around and sail back disappointed. We then headed toward the northern promontory bordering on this gulf. We named it Cape Malaspina (45°42'15" N, 218°41'30"). Wind permitting, from there we set our course northward.

On the morning of the 8th, we caught sight of two small islands to the northeast,* Teurire and Janikesseri (the former 44°27'45" N and 218°43'15" W, the latter 44°28'45"), about 10 miles from the Island of Matmai or Jesso. We sailed close to its coast until May 10 when we sighted its northwestern tip. Here we caught sight of a high peak which we soon realized was Mount de Langle,** which La Pérouse located on the northwestern coast of Matmai. This conical snow-clad mountain visible from a great distance, now lay straight ahead of us.

It is not part of Matmai, as La Pérouse believed, but a separate island lying to the west. The wind was very favorable. Before noon on the 11th we reached the extreme northwestern tip of the island called Soya by the natives. Captain von Krusenstern named it Cape Romanzoff (45°25'50" N and 218°25'30" W). We had just realized that it is inhabited when a little boat left the shore and headed toward us. It held four people with long, heavy, lank hair and heavy, long beards. They were wearing loose dirty clothing. They rowed up close to our ship but turned down our invitation to come on board. After observing us for a short time, they again rowed home. Around ten o'clock we discovered behind Cape Romanzoff a large open bay to the north. We anchored there two miles from shore in 10 fadens of water.

---

*The island lying farthest west is called Teumu-ssiri and the other one Anke-ssiri in the language used there. According to Japanese maps, they are 10 *ri* apart. On another Japanese map the former is called Feure, perhaps its Japanese name. To the east of this island on Jesso is another high mountain named Mount Yullbetsu.

— Julius von Klaproth

**The natives of Jesso call Mount de Langle Rii-ssire. It is 20 *ri* from Teumu-ssiri. On the western side of Jesso opposite Mount de Langle is another high mountain, Mount Akanuno. To the north of Mount de Langle is the Island of Rebu-no-ssiri or Refuno-ssiri and to the northwest of it another island named Issigorotan or Isschoroton. Next comes the southwestern tip of the Island of Tschoka called Ssari by the natives of Jesso. They call the southeastern tip Karafuto and consider it a separate island.— Julius von Klaproth

A thick fog had blocked our view of the mountain and surrounded us a short time before. It did not take very long until several small boats similar to the first one were heading toward us. Some of them immediately accepted our invitation to come on board. They greeted us by rubbing the palms of their hands together and next by raising their palms several times slowly toward the heavens and stroking their beards from their chins to their chests and then exactly in the Japanese fashion falling to their knees. This greeting ceremony was repeated once again. They all appeared friendly and good-natured, had quite large eyes, rather high cheek bones, prominent chins, deep-set and somewhat compressed noses. Most of their cheeks and skin were covered by heavy, long, thick beards. They had their own language, but understood some Japanese. They said, as far as we could understand, they were not Japanese and did not belong to Japan. They called themselves Aino or Ainu.*

When we asked about Matmai, they pointed to the south. We concluded that they did not use the name for the island in their area but only for the City of Matmai or Matzumai. The brandy we offered them they drank without making a face. They poured the last drops in the cups on their palms, raised their hands to the heavens and then ran them over the lower end of their long beards and chests. After we had given them various small objects — knives, mirrors, needles, etc. — they returned to land and indicated we should visit them there. Accordingly, a party went ashore in our shallop and boat.

Since so many wanted to go on land and there was no room for me, I stayed on the ship. The boats had just landed on the eastern side of the bay when we saw a large boat resembling a Japanese boat being rowed toward our ship from the west. Four Japanese were really in it. Judging by their outward appearance, they belonged to the lowest class, probably fishermen. They came on board and were very

---

*Aino or Ainu means man, human being in the language of all Kurillian peoples. This is what they call themselves. The Kurillions in Kamtschatka call themselves Ainu and the ones on the Kurile Islands Ainuh. The ones on Jesso or Matmai, on Tschoka or Sagalin, Aino, and the ones along the coast of the continent near the Amur River, Ainuh. According to my linguistic research, this nation is spread from the southern tip of Kamtschatka to Japan, on all of the Kurile Islands, Tschoka and the entire coast of what is incorrectly called Chinese Tartarej and the lower Amur up to the mouth of the Ussuri-Ula. The Giljaki on Russian maps, the Yui-bi and Gedsheum of the Chinese belong to the same group. That's why the area is incorrectly called Tungusi. The Kurellians living on the continent call themselves and their language *Fiatta*. — Julius von Klaproth

uninhibited in their behavior. Out of curiosity they asked who we were and gave us the names of all of the surrounding areas and islands. A little later a better dressed Japanese arrived in another boat. He too was just as uninhibited in his behavior. Since we had only recently left Megasaki, it all seemed strange to us. He told us he was a merchant and offered to sell us or perhaps to trade us various Japanese goods. These included lacquered wooden drinking bowls, razors, tobacco, pipes, books with obscene woodcuts, which the Japanese are forbidden to sell to foreigners on pain of death but are rather well known in Europe as Chinese Bibles.

Very early the following morning, I went with a group on land. The surf was quite strong along the flat sandy shore. That's why an Ainu living close by picked us up from our shallop in a little boat. It took us to his miserable hut supported by logs with walls and roof of straw. At the back and in the front of the entrance were several poles and trees with leaves and wreaths, probably they had been erected for some religious purpose. The inside of the hut contained a room with a fire burning on the hearth in the middle with the whole family sitting around: an old woman, a young girl and several males. An iron kettle hung over the fire with fish cooking in it. I did not stay very long, but walked along the shore where I found a number of varieties of seaweed (*Fucus saccharinus*, *F. perforatus*, *F. gramenoides*, *F. siliquosus* and other kinds I did not recognize). Among some shell remains I saw the remains of *Nautilus papyraceus*. I even found several large nuts, which resembled completely our Italian nuts (*Nux Juglans*). I could not find out where they grew or where they came from or what kind of nut they actually were. The main rock on the shore was hardened clay, in which tunneling mussels had settled. The plants were very stunted in their growth. Among others I saw *Caltha palustris*, *Angelica* of unusual size, *Fumaria*, *Equisetum*, *Allium*, burrs and many more. A swamp with short, thin, weak reeds stretched out along the entire shore toward low mountains nearby with snow still lying here and there at their foot. Firs and birch were the main trees found in the area.

We saw a lot of dogs all over resembling the ones in Kamtschatka, only much smaller. Later I heard they too were used as draft animals and hitched to sleds in the winter.

In almost every hut we found young bears. They are fed, raised, slaughtered and eaten as delicacies. Among the furs, I saw small whitish-grey ones from an animal I do not know. These, as well as bear and dog fur, were the source of the people's warm clothing. On shipboard during my absence, sea otter pelts were offered for trade. They are probably found there just as on the other Kurile Islands.

The houses stand not very far apart on one street about one German mile long. I counted 7 large living areas with 15 to 20 adult men. Usually if I approached the houses the women ran away when they saw me at a distance. A few hid behind their men in order to stare at me as much as possible. The men were stocky, at the most 5 fuss tall, but very muscular and quite strong of constitution. The women were smaller. Their thick, black hair hung down. They had dark, bluish lips but I could not tell whether they were dyed or tattooed. Some of my traveling companions claim they saw tattoos on the women's arms.

Japanese live on the extreme western tip (Soya) of the island. A civilian officer lived there under command of the governor to guard the coast. As part of his duties as an officer, he came on board our ship with two sabers at his sides to inquire who we were and why we had come there? At first he did not want to believe we were Russians because our hair was cut and unpowdered. All of the Russians in Laxmann's time, whom he claimed to have met, had powdered, braided hair. He requested, or rather ordered, us as soon as the weather cleared and the fog dispersed to weigh anchor. In case we did not, he was obligated to notify the government of our presence which would immediately take serious action against us. He refused even the smallest present and did not even want to drink Japanese rice wine (Saki) we had brought from Nangasaki. He was a reasonable man and, as far as we could judge, well informed. He had quite good knowledge of the geography and gave Captain von Krusenstern a great deal of information about the locations and names of nearby islands. He knew the name and location of Kamtschatka and spoke of Ochotsk and America.

He called Tschoka or Sachalin* a Tartar island, separated by a strait from an Island he called Karafuto north of Jesso. He claimed of the latter that Japanese only live on the southern part.

---

*It is incorrect to call the Island Sachalin because the natives call it Tschoka. The Mandschu, because they did not know its name, called it Saghalen-ann'ga-chada, i.e., Black Mouth Island, since it lies opposite the mouth of the Amur, which they call Saghalen-ula or the black river. Thus Saghalin means black and is not the name of the island. We should not spread such mistakes. The island is also not under Chinese control at all as usually believed, since it is not included in the large national Chinese geographical work called *Fai-Zirn-y-tunn-dschi* that appeared under Kin-henn. — Julius von Klaproth

We learned from him that only part of Matmai inhabited by the Japanese (the southern part) is called Matzumai or Matmai (perhaps he only meant the city of that name) and that Jesso is the area inhabited by the Ainu. Most likely the entire island was called Jesso in former times. Since the Japanese had driven the Ainu farther north and had completely settled the southern part, now only the northern part retained the older name.

While out on my excursion, I came upon the home of the Japanese merchant who had been on shipboard the day before and wanted to trade with us. Hundreds of thousands of herring were hanging all around to dry. He said every year he brings the Ainu rice, tobacco, pipes, lacquered wooden eating and drinking bowls, kitchen utensils, some coarse cotton cloth and several other necessities. In turn he is paid in smoked, salted and dried fish and furs. He assured me at the same time that he visits all the nearby and distant islands, even the Kurile Islands, i.e., Urup and Iturup. From all I could see, it seemed to me that the Japanese are very sparing in their care of the Ainu. They are so poorly dressed and hardly possessed the most essential utensils and necessities, especially knives, kettles, tobacco and pipes, fishing nets, some rice, cotton cloth, etc.

They shot game by bow and poison arrows. The poison, made from thickened plant sap — (probably from an *Aconitum* that is common there) — is said to be so strong that the blood of a wounded animal breaks up after a few minutes and flows from its mouth, nose and ears. This is how they kill bears, wolves, fox, sea otters, etc.

Even though the Japanese visit the northern part of Jesso, southern Tschoka, i.e., their Karafuto, and the southern Kurile Islands and seem to have very close ties to the Ainu, just like any other nation, the Ainu are not allowed to visit actual Japanese possessions, indeed, not even the capital of their mother country Matzumai.

In comparison to other countries of the same latitude, the climate there is much colder; the plants had hardly begun to sprout; very few were blooming. Snow was still lying in many spots at the foot of the hills whose tops were still totally snow-covered.

On the morning of May 6th the Réaumur thermometer showed 2°; at noon 6° above the freezing point.

In several spots crystal-clear streams cut across the shore not far from the nearby houses.

At daybreak on the 13th, we weighed anchor. The weather had cleared, and we could clearly see all of the tips of land and islands around us. We were primarily interested in the island called Karafuto on all of the Japanese maps which lay on the northern horizon. We had just left our anchorage when it became clear that there was no doubt about our location. The information given by the unfortunate La Pérouse and our own observations clearly proved that the Island of Karafuto lying to the north and Sachachalen or Tschoka were one and the same. Our original assumptions were completely confirmed toward noon when we compared the location of Cape Crillon and the rock La Dangereuse.

The weather was beautiful, the wind very moderate. We gradually approached Cape Crillon. As night fell, however, we headed somewhat away from it, carefully trying to avoid La Dangereuse.

The wind was very favorable. La Dangereuse (45°47′15″ N, 217°51′15″ W) was about 5 sea miles north of us. We observed a spacious passage between it and Cape Crillon, through which we had seen a Japanese vessel sail very early on the morning of the 14th.

When we approached that rock, we heard a continual very loud noise. At first we thought it was caused by the waves hitting against it and the breakers. Soon afterward, armed with telescopes, we could see very clearly indescribable numbers of sea lions, common seals, sea calves (*Phoca*). At that distance it was not possible to determine their species.

The masses of bodies were camped in part on the rocks, in part sticking their round heads out of the water, and by the thousands bellowing frightfully.

Cape Crillon (45°54′15″ N and 217°17′21″ W) was to our west. Far to the east on the horizon we saw the tip of Tschoka, Cape Aniwa, which we at first thought was an island because the more northerly part which we sighted later is lower.

The wind had increased some. Soon afterwards we sailed into the Gulf of Aniwa at 7 to 8 knots while keeping more to the western side of Cape Crillon.

Around four in the afternoon, we finally were able to distinguish the very low, flat land which connects both spits of land. Toward evening we dropped anchor in 9 fadens in ever shallower water at the northwestern part of the gulf called Salmon Bay by the Dutch. Not too far away was a single-masted Japanese vessel. On land we saw several Japanese-style houses. The Japanese ship, which we had seen sailing ahead of us at Cape Crillon early in the morning, had already anchored in a little inlet on the eastern promontory.

Late in the evening I heard that Lieutenant Ratmanoff planned to go on land early the next morning at four o'clock in order to cast nets wherever possible. I therefore requested permission to accompany him. On the 15th nine of us in a small shallop set out toward land. In the hopes of finding a river, we headed toward the northern and northeastern side of the bay. When we were several miles from the ship, we discovered the surf along the shore was so strong that it was impossible to land. After several attempts we realized our shallop was in the greatest danger of being smashed to pieces.

We followed the entire northern and most of the northeastern coast at a distance of about a sea mile from the shore. We mostly found 2 to 3½ fadens water. We discovered the mouth of a river on the northern shore, which we were unable to approach because of the surf. We were surrounded by a number of whales, gulls, ravens and wild ducks. We had gone around 8 sea miles from the ship and reached the northern part of Cape Aniwa when suddenly, to our joy, we found a shallow spot we could safely wade through. Since we had gone that far, we decided to visit the spot where we had seen the Japanese ship ahead of us anchor the day before. Our sailors were ordered to follow along the coast in the shallop.

The shore was very flat. A few hundred paces from it the nearby hills were wholly inaccessible. Along the way we saw a number of the natives' miserable huts standing not very far apart from each other.

They were probably only intended for use in the summer fishing season, since most of the people we saw were grown working men. We saw very few women and children. Our supposition was strengthened by the fact that we noticed at several spots heavily used footpaths winding through the valleys and nearby hills into the interior. The few women we saw were occupied with cutting open, cleaning and preparing fish for drying. The intestines are thrown away, but the roe are carefully dried in fresh air. They were all sitting in the open, only sheltered on the windward side by a wall made from straw mats fastened to several oars and poles. Just like on Jesso they wore long, full gowns or coats open in front with wide sleeves (a kind of nightgown). When we were passing their houses and the places where they were working, the men would usually get up and take a few steps toward us. They would greet us in the friendliest of manner with gently smiling expressions in exactly the same manner as the Ainu on Jesso. The women stayed quietly seated behind their straw mats. Even though our appearance had to strike them as indeed very foreign, they acted as if we were very familiar to them and not in the least foreign. Several men accompanied us at most a few steps for politeness sake and then left us again. We were able to continue on our way unhindered and unbothered by these people's curiosity. After we had gone about a German mile, we reached a place where some Japanese vessels were anchored. Our walk had been very varied and not strenuous, because we had followed on a much-used footpath along the coast. The slopes of the nearby wooded hills consisted mostly of steep clay walls. Now and again we saw pleasant valleys watered by little streams which flowed into the nearby bay. Over three of the somewhat larger ones had wide, thick planks laid across them instead of bridges to make them easier to cross.

As we approached the houses, we saw two Japanese officers, each with two sabers at their sides and dressed in silk, coming toward us. They greeted us in a friendly manner and sat down in the open on a straw mat. Without requiring us to sit down, they began questioning us officially: Who were we? Where did we and the ship come from? They wrote down our answers. They then stood up and requested us to go to their nearby house for some refreshments. We were all the more glad to accept their invitation, since it was about noon and we had had nothing to eat since four o'clock that morning.

The Japanese settlement consisted of 6 large houses and several small ones standing around a courtyard or open place. It was not unlike a European farmstead. Most of the buildings probably were intended to be used as storehouses. We were directed into the first house. It was made of wood, one-storied and furnished in the Japanese manner, i.e., with a gallery, in front of it lattice work and, instead of window glass, a framework delicately covered with paper.

The anteroom was large. Around it were little open rooms or compartments containing goods of various kinds. Then a step higher was a spacious room that also served as the kitchen. A fire burned in the middle of it. Next to the fire opposite the entrance were spread fine straw mats where we were invited to sit down when we apologized that our dirty boots would soil the fine beautiful new mats. They took them away and asked us to sit on the ones below them which were less fine but also very clean.

Since we were unaccustomed to the Oriental mode of sitting and seated ourselves rather awkwardly with our legs stretched uncomfortably sideways, our hosts had some little barrels brought in and laid a plank on them to make a bench so that we could sit quite comfortably in the European manner. Each one of us was given a square wooden plate with a small lacquered wooden bowl filled with the best rice well cooked as well as a saucer with cooked fish. Each one of us also was given two small, new, wooden chopsticks to use instead of a fork. Despite the fact we had just come from Japan and had lived there for 6 months, that day on Tschoka we ate our first meal with a Japanese family.

During our stay the Japanese wanted various kinds of information from us and we from them. One Japanese officer said he had been living on the island they called Karafuto for six years and another for eight years. They thought it was about half the size of the Island of Jesso. They were totally unacquainted with the northern part. The original inhabitants on this part of the island were also Ainu. Together with the inhabitants of Jesso and the Kurile Islands they form one tribe. We were told they have their own chief or headman on Jesso.

These officers seemed to have very little knowledge of Russia and neighboring countries whose borders they knew. They also talked a lot about Kodai and Laxmann. They did not even know the name Kamtschatka. They asked for permission to inspect one of our hunting guns and were more than a little surprised by its lock,* which they had never seen before. Before examining the gun, they asked anxiously whether it was loaded. They were so afraid of the gunpowder that they refused to set on fire a few grains on the touch pan. I am convinced that they had no other weapon to defend their settlement than probably some bows and arrows.

I counted 22 Japanese who attentively observed us and our movement with the greatest of curiosity. I assume that a lot of them were sailors on the five little ships anchored there whose stay is probably limited to a few days or weeks. At other times, especially in winter, there are probably only a few Japanese there. The large front

*Japanese muskets are fired by burning matches (mêches) which are carried to the touch pan by a trigger.

room was filled with a lot of Ainu upon their knees in complete submissiveness. One single glance showed that they were ruled by the relatively small numbers of unarmed Japanese. They had barely satisfied their curiosity for a quarter of an hour when they were once again driven, in part beaten with sticks, back to their work. It consisted in cutting open and cleaning fish, salting them and hanging them up to dry and in turning the half-dried ones over in the sun. Of the several hundred Ainu we saw, only a few individuals had extremely heavy hair all over their bodies (as occasionally is the case with Europeans, only perhaps less often). That this entire race of men is covered all over with hair is a fiction of unreliable travelers' imaginations.[1]

Near the houses on a little hill stood a Japanese temple which we were allowed to visit on the condition that we took off our boots before entering it. We would have liked to have visited it if we had not been afraid of losing too much time. It was already four o'clock in the afternoon. Our shallop and sailors, whom we had been expecting to arrive long before, were nowhere to be seen. The wind and tide were unfavorable and Lieutenant von Ratmanoff was afraid something might have happened. He decided to look for our boat without further delay. After thanking our hosts for their hospitality, we said goodbye. We returned along the shore and found our boat about a half hour later.

In a moderate, unfavorable wind we tried to sail straight across the bay to our ship anchored 14 sea miles away. We had just left land when a stormy wind rose. The waves increased in size and strength. Our small shallop carrying 9 men had a hard battle with the wind and waves. With our lives in danger the whole time, we reached the ship in the evening just before eight o'clock, I can say, to the great joy of all present who had had to watch fearfully and anxiously as we were tossed from one foaming wave to the next in defiance of the rebellious elements.

Our ship was anchored at 46°41′15″ N and 217°28′00″ W.

At daybreak on the 16th we weighed anchor. Using a brisk southeasterly wind we reached the cape of Aniwa (46°02′20″ N and 216°29′40″ W) toward evening. The following morning we sailed around it. Soon afterwards the wind died down and in the afternoon it was completely calm. Large numbers of whales played around the ship, usually in groups of 2 and 3. Toward evening we saw a canoe with 6 people rowing toward us about 7 miles from land. The outward appearance of the boat and men was in no way different from that of the rest of the Ainu. Undoubtedly nightfall caused them to return again to shore.

We continued to follow the coast. On the 19th we approached a bay bordered on the south by Cape Tonyn of the Dutch (46°50′00″ N and 216°27′ W). Because of its bad anchorage, it can only serve as a shelter in time of need. It offered little shelter from north and northeast winds.

From there to Salmon Bay is about 20 to 30 sea miles and is only separated from it by a low ridge of hills. This bay is only thinly inhabited by Ainu. Good water and wood is available in abundance. We saw countless numbers of whales and seals. In the afternoon at 47°33′ and 217°14′ N, we caught sight of a high, rounded mountain. We assumed it was the one the Dutch named Spenberg and La Pérouse Mount Bernizet.

On the 20th several places along the coast appeared friendly and inviting. The weather was rough. Due to snow flurries and ½° warmth, the following days were overcast.

On the 22nd we found ourselves in what the Dutch call the Gulf de Patience. The following day we sighted the mouth of a river. Due to a calm Captain von Krusenstern decided to drop anchor there to inspect somewhat more closely the pleasant-appearing, low, wooded coast.

A shallop was lowered so that several officers could go on land. They returned in the evening bringing a quantity of tattered seaweed, smashed mussel shells, dried fish roe, a large salmon and thorn back (*Sygnathus*) along with the news that they had found a river filled with fish, firs and birch wood and juniper bushes and few people. The weather was overcast and threatened to become stormy. After our navigators established the northern border of the gulf at 49°19′ N, Captain von Krusenstern turned south in stormy weather. It was dangerous to be near land and particularly near Seal Island which, according to the Dutch, was nearby. Toward noon of the 24th, we sighted the dangerous reef of rocks surrounding the island. According to Captain von Krusenstern's determination, it stretches from 48°28′ to 48°36′ N and from 215°27′ to 215°50′ W. We then headed south and southwest in order to sail around both Seal Island and Cape Patience.

On the 26th we were presented with a new as well as unexpected spectacle to the west, i.e., a great many ice floes, some individually and some formed together into extensive, endless fields, forcing us to head to the east in order to sail past the outer edges at some distance.

Around four o'clock on the following morning, we caught sight again of giant fields of floating ice. Given these conditions it was impossible at that time of year to explore the northeastern coast of Sachalin any further. We had a choice to cruise about in uncertainty for several weeks farther south while waiting for the ice to melt or sailing without delay to Kamtschatka to drop off Ex-ambassador Resanoff, who had little interest or none at all in investigating the geography there, and then return immediately to pick up our observations where we had left off. It was decided to do the latter, so we headed straight east toward the Kurile Islands.

On the afternoon of the 28th, the wind increased to the point that it turned into a storm by evening. Our situation in the night was all the more dangerous because according to our astronomical observations we were not very far from the Kurile Islands. The wind raged the whole night, the waves rolled so high that the rolling of the ship was almost unbearable.

At daybreak on the 29th, we sighted land to the southeast that soon disappeared into the fog again and then later a high mountain peak to the east-southeast. While cruising around trying better to gain our bearings in that unknown region and to wait for the fog to disperse, we sailed to within a few miles of the peak. Then, however, the winds became so weak that the strong current carried us to the west. The peak in front of us had been smoking almost all day long. It threw up a light or yellowish-grey smoke that we could clearly distinguish from the dark grey of the fog. We could also clearly distinguish its crater on the western point. At a distance of 3 sea miles from its foot, the peak's height was observed to be 2° above the horizon. In the evening there was heavy snow. The air was cold. During the day the thermometer usually showed 6° and at night only 1°.

Early on the morning of the 30th, we sighted an island we took to be either the 10th or 11th of the Kurile Islands. We headed northeast and thought as soon as we had the island behind us that we would be in the Sea of Kamtschatka. Toward noon, however, we sighted 4 small rocky islands and farther to the northeast yet another high island through the fog. In that overcast weather a strong east wind had arisen and gradually increased so much and became so violent that Captain von Krusenstern dared not tack any longer among unknown islands and rocky reefs. He decided therefore to return again to the foggy darkness and impetuous wind, which was carrying us at 8 miles an hour. The storm continued the whole night and only died down toward the morning of the 31st after heavy snow flurries and a temperature drop to 1½° below the freezing point. We woke up (on June 1st) more than a little surprised to discover the deck covered with several zoll of snow. The weather cleared during the day. Once again we headed northeast toward the Kurile Islands. A lot of whales, including some very large ones, were our companions on that day.

A thick fog dispersed somewhat toward noon so that we caught sight of the high peaks on Onnekotan, one of the most northerly Kurile Islands, quite close. We were in a complete calm only a few miles from land. Only toward evening did the horizon completely clear so that we could see the lower coastal areas of the island rather clearly. The mountain ridges and higher areas were mostly covered with fog. Only occasionally could we catch sight of the high conical peaks we had seen in the morning.

With the help of a fresh wind we sailed through the 8-mile-wide strait between Onnekotan and Charamukatan around ten o'clock in the evening. Early on the 2nd we found ourselves in open Kamtschatkan waters and set our course for Kamtschatka. The morning was clear and provided us with a view of most of the Island of Poromuschir with its high snow-clad mountains.

On the following days we sailed along the southeastern coast of Kamtschatka, where we admired several, in part, very high peaks.

On the 4th we saw the Peak on Awatscha in the distance. The nearby shore and surrounding areas did not have the same friendly pleasant appearance of the previous year, since all of the mountains were still covered with snow. The following afternoon around five o'clock we anchored safely in the Harbor of St. Peter and St. Paul, where we, to our joy, immediately received letters from our friends and relatives.

Of all the information from newspapers we received, indisputably the most important and most unexpected was that first Consul Bonaparte had been named Emperor of France.

NOTES

1. The Ainu have been called "hairy people" or "covered with hair like a bear" since ancient times. The bear served as the supreme deity of the Ainu and they had bear houses and reared bears for sacrificial purposes. The men customarily grew long beards which accentuated the abundance and waviness of their hair.

Chapter 15

Vocabulary of the peoples called the Ainu, living along the northern coast of Jesso, the Island of Tschoka, the Kuril Islands to the southern part of Kamtschatka.

German[1]	English	Ainu of Kamtschatka	Ainu of Kurile Islands	Ainu of Jesso	Ainu of South Side of Tschoka	Ainu of NE Tip of Tschoka
Himmel	sky	nies	kandŏ	—	nischiuro	—
Sonne	sun	tschuppu	tschūpŭh	tonotschu	tombi, tschukfkamoi	—
Mond	moon	tschuppu	tschūpŭh	tschu	tombi, tschukf	—
Stern	star	keta	kitta	nodschu	keda, nodsi	—
Wolke	cloud	uuràr	ūrătăk	nischi, nishcikuri	urari	—
Regen	rain	ssirugen	ssyrūyhn	apto	apto, apftu	—
Hagel	hail	kaukàch	—	kawukawu	kawukawu, kaukaubass	—
Schnee	snow	úpasch	ūpāss	ubaschi	upaschi, obbas	nito
Wind	wind	keera	rāhrā	dida	dirra, rera	—
Donner	thunder	um	kāmŭighumpf	kannokimoí	kannakamoi	—
Blitz	lightning	kamùissiuuné	—	—	kamoinibigi	—
Feuer	fire	apì	āpĕh	undshi, abe	abe, undshi	undshi
Wasser	water	pi	pēh	waka	waka	wachkaa
Erde	earth	kotàn	kūdăn	toi	toi, tui	—
Berg	mountain	othùr	tāpkŭp	nuburi	kinda, noburi	—
Rauch	smoke	ssuipuja	ssupūjah	pa	sschubuja	—
Stein	stone	poinà	poīnăh	—	schiuma	—
Sand	sand	otá	—	ota	ota, oda	—
Ton	clay	teinitoi	doi	toi	toi	—
Meer	sea	atuika	ādŭikă	atui	atui, adui	—
See	lake	sso	—	—	to, geschi	—
Fluß	river	pet, mem	peth	piz	pez, bez	—
Mensch	human being	ainù	āinŭh	aino	aino, guru	uru
Ehemann	husband	kokaiò	mamăth körgŭr	chobu	chobu, chogu	—
Ehefrau	wife	kamtschi	gmātschi	mati	mati, maz	—
Vater	father	mitschi	grupnainu	—	eischiwa	—
Mutter	mother	áapu	grūpnĭ tschimăt	—	chabu	tschokkara
Son	son	kpúhu	ōkăi jĕnŏ bōmpŏ	—	poo	—

German	English	Ainu of Kamtschatka	Ainu of Kurile Islands	Ainu of Jesso	Ainu of South Side of Tschoka	Ainu of NE Tip of Tschoka
Tochter	daugther	kpómmatschi	mātnĕbōmpŏ	—	mazpu, mazenebu	—
Kopf	head	paóp	gpa	nanu	nanu, schaba	—
Ohr	ear	ksar	gsāhr	kischara	kischara	toko
Auge	eye	ssik	ssik	schiki	schiki, schigi	keremante
Nase	nose	etù	āhdūm	ito	idu	teneschi
Mund	mouth	tschar	tschar	zaro	paro, paru	—
Zunge	tongue	achù	aūch	barumbi	au	—
Zahn	tooth	imak	—	jumaki	nimaki	—
Hand	hand	tek	dēk	amoini	undi, tegi	kematiké
Fuß	foot	kemà	kēhmmă	uzkami	kema	kamko
Fleisch	flesh	kam	kām	naschi	kam	—
Blut	blood	—	kēhm	kem	to, kim	—
Fett	fat	—	pījĕp	ke	ke, kiū, schium	—
Herz	heart	ssampe	sāmpĕh	—	schambi	—
Rücken	back	ssetur	ssedur	schedru	schedaru, scheduru	—
Nagel	nail	—	āhm	am	am, ami	—
Haus	house	tsche	—	—	zisse	kee
Messer	knife	epirá	epȳhră	magide	magiri	bakiro
Beil	hatchet	—	mūkăr	—	mukar	ukari
Kraut	herb	mun	muhn	mun	mun	kīu
Robbe	seal	—	thoar	—	tukari	—
Seeotter	sea otter	—	kjakko, kothōnăp	—	raku	—
Krebs	crab	—	chaū īng	takaki	takaki	—
Hund	dog	stapu	stahpu	cheta	scheta, scheda	scheta
Maus	mouse	ermu	ārmūh	irimo	irimo, pon irimo	—
Fuchs	fox	kimutpé	kymothpĕh	schumari	schumari, schiumari	—
Bär	bear	kamui	kāmiŭ	hippari	chugujukf, ziramandi	—
Wolf	wolf	orgiù	storkhyg	—	uschi kamoi	—
Vogel	bird	—	tschirpu	tschika	tschikapu zkapf	—
Gans	goose	kiutàp	kūitūp	—	guitu	—
Ente	duck	tschirpu	—	kobettscha	kobettscha	—
Ei	egg	noki	nōhk	nuki	zapfnuku	—
Fisch	fish	ssūtschip	tschep	tschep	tschep, zma, zepf	iroki
Rochen	ray	omà	hóma	—	chuma, zepfchuma	—
Baum	tree	ni	nyh	ni	ni, niī	appec

German	English	Ainu of Kamtschatka	Ainu of Kurile Islands	Ainu of Jesso	Ainu of South Side of Tschoka	Ainu of NE Tip of Tschoka
Blatt	leaf	niep	—	—	nĭ-chamu	—
Wurzel	root	ssiurit	—	—	schyndshiz	—
Birke	birch	tanni	tah-nyh	—	karīmbanīĭ	—
Salz	salt	ssippù	—	abi	schippo, schipo	—
Milch	milk	toopi	dōpĕh	—	too	—
Groß	big	porogò	bōrūkŭr	poro	poro	—
Klein	small	moiogò	mŏĭjop	pon	ponno, pon	—
Hoch	high	triĭva	rihärujewa	ri	ruino, riuwa	—
Niedrig	low	oramua	—	tam	chaukino, uramua	—
Weiß	white	rétanoo	—	detara	tetara, tedari	—
Schwarz	black	ékururoko	—	kunne	kunni	—
Rot	red	úratatkiwa	hūrĕp	kure	furi	—
Essen	to eat	ĭschama	īppăh	amama	ebe, annuwa	—
Trinken	to drink	kpekreigina	pēhkŭh	ogauni	ĭku, igu	kagai
Schlafen	to sleep	kmokonrossiva	mōkor	mogoro	mokuru, moguru	—
Ich	I	ka	gānū	—	tschogai	—
Du	thou	éa	eānny	—	itschogai	—
Er	he	—	tăăngūr	—	tada ogai	—
Eins	one	ssinep	ssyhnāp	schinep	schineni, schnepf	—
Zwei	two	tuup	dūph	toopu	toni, tup	—
Drei	three	rep	rāch	reepu	reni, repf	—
Vier	four	inèp	yhnāp	inepu	ine, inipf	—
Fünf	five	assik	ahssīk	aschiknepu	aschikine, aschiki	—
Sechs	six	ivan	yhgŭähn	iwanebe	iwanbe, juwambi	—
Sieben	seven	aruuàn	ārŭahn	aruwanbe	aruwanbe, aruwambi	—
Acht	eight	tubis	dūhpyhs	tobischanbe	tobischanbe, tubischambi	—
Neun	nine	ssinepĭs	ssyhnahpyhs	schnipischanbe	schinpischanbe, schnebischambi	—
Zehn	ten	uupis	ūpyhs	wanak	wambe, wambi	—
Elf	eleven	ssinepikamua	ssynapikas maŭă	schinepu ikaschima wanbe	schnepu, iga-schima wambi	—
Zwölf	twelve	tuuptsch ikamua	duphīkās maua	toopu ikaschima wambe	tupu ikaschima wambi	—
Zwanzig	twenty	tuampè	dūāmpītschi, hoth	chozu	schnechoz, choz	—
Dreißig	thirty	reuampè	rauampitsch	wanbeitozu	wambi idochoz	—
Vierzig	forty	ineuampè	dūgōth	togozu	tochoz	—

German	English	Ainu of Kamtschatka	Ainu of Kurile Islands	Ainu of Jesso	Ainu of South Side of Tschoka	Ainu of NE Tip of Tschoka
Fünfzig	fifty	assikneuampè	uampöhrä hoth*	wanteniregozu	wambi irichoz	—
Hundert	one hundred	uánuampe	ahssik nä hoth**	aschikenegozu	aschikinichoz aschikinischine	—
Tausend	one thousand	uanotnékampe	—	—	wano choz	—

The Ainu call the Japanese *ssitscham*. The Ainu call Jesso *Inssu*.
— Julius von Klaproth

NOTES

1. I am including the German, since some words can have more than one translation into English, but I have changed the orthography to conform to modern practices. I have left the Ainu untouched since it is unclear how it would be pronounced. Since Julius von Klaproth was German, we might assume that the transcriptions should have many things in common with German pronunciation, e.g., $w = v$, $j = y$, $s = z$, $z = ts$, etc.

— End of Volume One —

*I.e., ten less three times twenty.

**Five times twenty.

GEORG HEINRICH von LANGSDORFF

REMARKS AND OBSERVATIONS ON A VOYAGE AROUND THE WORLD FROM 1803 TO 1807

VOLUME TWO

THE VOYAGE FROM KAMTSCHATKA TO THE ISLAND OF ST. PAUL, UNALASKA, KODIAK, SITCHA, NEW ALBION, KAMTSCHATKA, OCHOTSK AND THROUGH SIBERIA TO ST. PETERSBURG

Adam Johann von Krusenstern

Alaska History No. 41

REMARKS AND OBSERVATIONS ON A VOYAGE AROUND THE WORLD FROM 1803 TO 1807

VOLUME TWO

by
GEORG HEINRICH von LANGSDORFF

Translated and Annotated
by
VICTORIA JOAN MOESSNER

Edited
by
RICHARD A. PIERCE

THE LIMESTONE PRESS
Kingston, Ontario : Fairbanks, Alaska
1993

CONTENTS

VOLUME TWO

CONTENTS

As a Small Token of his Gratitude and Esteem,
the Author Dedicates this Second Volume

to the

FIRST LEADER OF THE RUSSIANS AROUND THE WORLD,

to the

Prudent and Dauntless Seafarer,

to the

Expert, Scientific, Studious Navigator,

to the

Humane, Solicitous, Paternal Commander,

to the

Compassionate, Considerate, Sincere Friend of his
Traveling Companions,

to the

Noble, Upright, Worthy Man,

to

UNIVERSALLY REVERED von KRUSENSTERN

INTRODUCTION

Soon after our arrival in the harbor of St. Peter and St. Paul, important changes were made in our travel plans. The mission to Japan had been completed, so Chamberlain von Resanoff had decided to travel immediately overland to St. Petersburg to give His Majesty the Emperor a personal report. He, however, received several letters which caused him suddenly to change his mind again and to go as plenipotentiary of the Russian-American Trading Company to visit the Aleutian Islands, the Northwest Coast of America, and especially the best and most distant Russian possessions and outposts.

Councilor von Tosse, one of the gentlemen of the embassy, was consequently sent as courier with the report to St. Petersburg. Captain von Krusenstern, as soon as he had put the Ambassador on shore in Kamtschatka, had the ship quickly cleared of all unnecessary cargo (especially the presents intended for Japan). With the ship lightened as much as possible, he planned to undertake the previous plan, abandoned on May 26th, of studying the northern coast of Tschoka as far as the mouth of the Amur and then to return to Kamtschatka in order to take on enough supplies for the trip to Canton.

Captain von Fedoroff and Lieutenant von Koscheleff, together with an honor guard, stayed in Kamtschatka, where they took up their previous positions. Major von Friederici, who was more interested in exploring more closely the province remote from the capital than mapping the coast of Tschoka, together with Lieutenant von Koscheleff (the brother of the commandant) had decided to go to Nischnei Kamtschatka in order to explore the interior of that remarkable peninsula until the ship returned and then to travel with Captain von Krusenstern back to Europe.

Ex-ambassador von Resanoff was concerned because he did not want to travel without a doctor to the rugged, uncivilized and inhospitable regions of Northwest America. He made me the most advantageous offer if I would accompany him. It was my decision whether I would sail with our amiable leader von Krusenstern by way of Tschoka, Canton and St. Helena back to Europe, or accept von Resanoff's very promising proposal and signed promises and go with him to visit the settlements of the Russian-American Company, that is, the Aleutian Islands and the Northwest Coast of America, and then to go overland through northeastern Asia, through Siberia back to Europe.

My choice, made difficult by other considerations, was finally for America because I felt I owed it to scientific knowledge to undertake this very unusual and rare voyage under such seemingly favorable conditions.

The friendship and harmony between Captain von Krusenstern and those under him on board the *Nadeschda* would probably not have been so easily established on another expedition of this kind. So with a sad heart I took leave of him. I cannot leave my traveling companions without publicly expressing my gratitude for their friendship, especially Captain von Krusenstern, Dr. Horner, Dr. Tilesius, Major von Friederici and Dr. Espenberg, for their extensive confidence and support of me on many occasions.

Before describing our new travels, I wish to make some general comments, so that my readers will understand the point of view from which they should regard my surroundings and descriptions.

During the first part of my trip, I did not have to concern myself much with the Russian language and did not have the time. Before joining von Krusenstern's expedition, I had never been in Russia* and during the expedition my daily contact had been with men who spoke German, French or English. In addition, I was occupied with so many activities that I hardly thought about learning a language which at the time seemed to be of little practical use to me.

But now the situation had changed; knowledge of Russian became an almost unavoidable necessity, because in Kamtschatka, as well as on the Aleutian Islands and on the Northwest Coast of America, there are not only Russians all over but also natives of those regions and islands who now speak a rather pure and correct Russian, with the exception of some provincialisms. My lack of knowledge of the language caused some gaps which are easily recognized in the following pages.

---

*See Preface to Volume One.

INTRODUCTION

Upon our return we found the Russian-American Company's brig *Maria* in the Harbor of St. Peter and St. Paul ready to sail to Kodiak. Lieutenants von Chwostoff and von Davidoff, two quite well informed naval officers who had joined together to sail to America to see to it that the Russian-American Company's shipping line was in good order, to build ships and to train sailors, etc., had arrived the previous autumn by ship from Ochotsk. They were sailing from St. Petersburg to Kodiak for the second time. They gave us favorable reports about the outpost there and, thus, played an important role in my decision to undertake the voyage.* I am exceedingly grateful to those decent men, especially to Mr. von Davidoff who often good-heartedly and patiently satisfied my craving for knowledge and who, using French, took the trouble upon himself to act as my interpreter at every opportunity.

In this second volume, I have decided to include more nautical and geographical observations as well as more information about natural history than in the first volume because simple descriptions of desolate regions would probably be of little interest and quite boring. I considered it my duty to study every event and object that came my way on land and at sea. Furthermore, I will now adhere to the Julian computation of time as generally used by the Russians in order to make fewer mistakes in the future.

The following works contain much valuable information about the early history, the geography and the living conditions of the inhabitants of the Aleutian Islands, etc., which I have decided is unnecessary to repeat here.[1]

Müller's *Sammlung russischer Geschichte* [Collection of Russian History], Vol. 3, Parts 1, 2, 3.

Fischer's *Geschichte von der Eroberung Sibiriens* [History of the Conquest of Siberia].

---

*In 1808 these two excellent men, who had twice traveled to America, returned to St. Petersburg from their last voyage together. In 1809, they served with distinction in the war against Sweden. At the end of that year, these two inseparable friends were lost to the world. On a very dark night they wanted to cross the raised drawbridge across the Neva. They tried to jump to a barge, missed, and were swallowed up by the fast-flowing river. Mr. von Davidoff's account of his travels has gone to press and probably contains many interesting observations.

INTRODUCTION

Pallas's *Nordische Beyträge* [Northern Essays].

Billings's *Travels to Northern Regions of Russian Asia and America from 1785 to 1794*. Published [in German] by Sauer.

Gavrila Sarytschef's *Eight-year Journey in Northeastern Siberia to the Polar Sea and the Northeastern Ocean*, translated [from Russian] into German by J. H. Busse.

Journal von Rußland [Journal from Russia], published by J. H. Busse in St. Petersburg between 1794 and 1798.

The history of the Russian-American Company, whose outposts I am now going to describe, its laws and statutes are probably so well-known from Councilor of State von Storch's *Journal* and the introduction to Mr. von Krusenstern's *Reise um die Welt, I. Theil* [Voyage around the World, Part I], that it seems unnecessary to repeat this information. I mention these reports so that my readers know where to find information about the Company — what it could be and should be. Circumstances often do not permit me to mention certain things directly.

I, however, believe that I live under a wise and upright monarch who takes every opportunity to promote the well-being of his subjects and am duty-bound to point out unknown abuses, since it is impossible for him, as for every other ruler, to bring about improvements if he does not know the problems of his individual subjects. I would feel doubly responsible if I were to remain totally silent about conditions of the Russian-American Company in America.

Sauer* has described at different places in his book several scenes in very pale colors, which von Davidoff will probably paint more forcibly and I myself cannot totally pass over in silence.

It is true that in recent years the Board of Directors of the Russian-American Company in St. Petersburg, through the support and care of its last elected Director, Commercial Councilor Benedict Cramer, has undergone several advantageous improvements. The most upright man, however, cannot, even with the best of intentions and utmost exertion, swim against the current.

---

*See Sauer's *Reise . . .* , p. 165, 177, 215.

INTRODUCTION

NOTES

1. The following is a list of the English translations of the works Langsdorff refers to or the complete bibliographical references for those that have not been translated into English:

Gerhard Friedrich Müller (1705-1783), *Voyages from Asia to America, for completing the discoveries of the northwest coast of America. To which is prefixed, a summary of the voyages made by the Russians on the Frozen Sea in search of a northeast passage. Serving as an explanation of a map of the Russian discoveries published by the Academy of Sciences at Petersburgh*, translated from the High Dutch of S. [sic, G.] Müller by Thomas Jefferys (London: T. Jefferys, 1761).

Johann Eberhard Fischer, *Geschichte von der Eroberung Sibiriens* (History of the Conquest of Siberia) (St. Petersburg: Hartknoch, 1768).

Peter Simon Pallas (1741-1811), *Newest Northern Contributions to the Study of Physical and Human Geography, Natural History, and Economics* (St. Petersburg: J. Z. Logan, 1781-1793), 6 vols.

Martin Sauer, *An Account of a geographical and astronomical expedition to the northern parts of Russia, for ascertaining the degrees of latitude and longitude of the mouth of the river Kovima; of the whole coast of the Tschutski, to East Cape; and of the islands in the eastern ocean, stretching to the American coast. Performed . . . by Commodore Joseph Billings, in the years 1785, etc., to 1794.* The whole narrated from the original papers by Martin Sauer (London: T. Cadell, 1802).

Gavrila Sarytscheff (Russian: Gavriil Andreevich Sarychev, 1763-1831), *Account of a voyage of discovery in the north-east of Siberia, the frozen ocean and the north-east sea*, translated from Russian (London: Printed for R. Phillips by J. G. Barnard, 1807-08), 2 vols in one.

Johann Heinrich Busse, ed., *Journal von Rußland* (Journal from Russia) 1-3, jährig; Juli 1793-Juni 1796 (St. Petersburg: Kaiserliche Buchdruckerei, 1794-96).

Heinrich Friedrich von Storch (1766-1835), *Historisch-statistisches Gemälde des russichen Reiches am Ende des 1800 Jahrhunderts* (Historical-statistical portrait of the Russian Empire at the end of the 18th century) (Riga: J. F. Hartknoch, 1797).

_______, *The Picture of Petersburg*, from the German of Henry Storch (London: Longman and Rees, 1801).

Adam Johann von Krusenstern (Russian: Ivan Fedorovich Kruzenshtern, 1770-1846), *Voyage round the world in the years 1803, 1804, 1805 and 1806 by order of His Imperial Majesty Alexander the First on board the ships* Nadeschda *and* Neva *under the command of Captain A. J. von Krusenstern*, translated from the original German by Richard Belgrave Hoppner (London: Printed by C. Roworth for J. Murray, 1813).

INTRODUCTION

Gawril Iwanowitsch Davidoff (Russian: Gavriil Ivanovich Davydov), *Two Voyages to Russian America, 1802-1807*, translated from Russian by Colin Bearne (Kingston, Ontario: Limestone Press, 1977).

Chapter 1

Departure from Kamtschatka. Voyage along the Aleutian Islands. The Islands of St. Paul and St. George. Description of St. Paul. Voyage to and Arrival in Unalaska.

On the evening of June 13, 1805 (old style), our belongings were taken on board the brig *Maria* and we sailed very early the next morning from Awatscha Bay.[1]

The *Maria*, built in Ochotsk, was a two-masted, heavy sailing vessel of about 150 tons. Navy Lieutenant Andre Wassilitsch Maschin was the commanding officer. Accompanying passengers were: Chamberlain von Resanoff together with his valet, the two officers mentioned above, Lieutenants Nicolai Alexandritsch Chwostoff and Gawril Iwanowitsch Davidoff, a hunter who was also to serve as taxidermist, and me.

When we left, the high mountains and headlands of Kamtschatka were still covered by snow. Alternately we had light winds and calms. We were enveloped in fog every day until June 24th when we were able to use the sun for observational purposes for the first time.

Instead of sailors we found sixty men on board who had worked as trappers or hunters (Russian promyshlenniks) for the Russian-American Company. Our crew was made up of adventurers, drunkards, bankrupt, depraved merchants and craftsmen and, in addition, several criminals who had been flogged and branded. All were in search of their fortunes. Most of them had sailed for the first time the previous year from Ochotsk to Kamtschatka. They even had to relearn the names of sails and ropes. They got in each other's way and, if the wind changed, fifty men could not do what ten ordinary sailors would have taken care of easily. Furthermore, the ship was so filled with cargo that most of the men had to take turns spending time on deck. Considering the fact that the Russian-American Company had fed the men very sparingly all winter in Kamtschatka — i.e., bread, dried and frozen fish, seal and whale blubber — but only in meager portions — no one should be surprised to hear that most of them had been suffering from scurvy, from which most had not yet recovered by eating wild Kamtschatkan garlic and fresh fish. Our situation was all the more questionable and risky because sailing in that part of the world presents peculiar difficulties, since the sun only rarely breaks through the almost continual heavy fogs. During the whole summer, there are only a few clear days. Nevertheless, the number of sick whom we had taken along from Kamtschatka did not increase as I had at first assumed would happen.

The crew was not only badly fed but also even more poorly and wretchedly clothed. Especially because of their lack of linens, the quantity of vermin on the men had to have increased mightily.

It was virtually impossible to go out on the small deck — the only place one could breathe some fresh air — because those disgustingly dirty men continually sat there picking vermin off of each other. There was no place to go. Day and night I could not go without being confronted by proof of those hunters' industrious love of the chase. The greatest caution and cleanliness of linens — since we were cooped up in a little cabin — still could not protect us from the vermin. Their discovery and the ensuing feeling of disgust and horror left me feverish.

After leaving Kamtschatka, hardly a day passed on which we did not see quantities of sea birds, especially *Alca cirrhata*, *Diomedea exulans*, various species of *Larus*, *Procellaria* and *Pelecanus*. On June 24th, the first clear day, toward evening we sighted the northeastern side of Attu to our south-southwest. It is the most westerly island in the Aleutian chain. The Russians call this island, together with Semitsch and Agattu, the Near Islands or Blishnie Ostrowa, because they are the closest islands to Kamtschatka. Attu has two harbors, one of which is on its southern coast at 52°56′ north latitude.

The following days were overcast and rainy, so that we could not see the Andreanoff Islands to the east.

On the 29th, the skies cleared and we could see through the fog, though indistinctly, Tschetiri Soposchnaia Ostrowi, or the Four Mountains, which are part of the Fox Islands. A brisk north wind had been driving us farther east and on the following morning we spotted land again. Upon closer inspection it turned out to be our first stop, the Island of Unalaska. The wind had almost ceased. At noon we were at the entrance to the harbor, but unable to sail in. We took advantage of a calm, lowered a boat and shot several stormy petrels (*Procellaria nigra*) which were swimming around in large flocks. They were so tame that we could come almost within a rudder-length of them. Those birds provided us with a quite good meal despite their fishy or oily taste. Toward evening a strong wind arose from the southeast that prevented us from approaching the island. Therefore, Mr. von Resanoff decided to visit the settlements of the Russian-American Company on the less known Islands of St. George and St. Paul, about 190 nautical miles northwest of Unalaska. At about 9 A.M. the ship was turned, thus changing that unfavorable wind into a favorable one. We sailed with full rig toward St. George at 6½ knots an hour. At noon we noticed large numbers of dolphins (*Delphinus*) with white bellies and horizontal tail fins around the ship.

On the morning of July 2nd, we saw an unusual flock of sea birds around our ship. Most of them were *Colymbus*, *Larus* and *Pelecanus*. Toward noon we took our bearings and had reached the location of St. George given on maps: 56°20′ N latitude and 169° W longitude.*

The innumerable quantities of sea birds, common seals and fur seals (*Phoca ursina*) and a sounding of the lead at 35 klafters all indicated the closeness of land. The wind had increased so much in the thick fog and rain that we had to exercise the utmost care to stay a proper distance from the land someplace nearby. Visibility was not quite a sea mile. Night fell without our sighting the island.

On the morning of the 3rd, we were in 40 to 45 klafters of water. Because the ship tacked so often and the wind and current were so strong, we had trouble keeping our bearings. The numbers of birds had decreased. The fog, rain and stormy, cold weather continued so that we held out little hope of finding the little island in such inclement weather without a midday reading of the sun.

Using a continuous strong southwest wind, we tacked first to the northwest, then to the east. On the 4th toward noon, we were again in 30 to 35 klafters of water and assumed we were in the vicinity of St. Paul. Thick fog, rain and wind, along with the unsuccessful attempts to sight land, made that day one of the most unpleasant since

---

*The calculations of longitude are seldom correct since they are only based on ship's reckonings.

our departure from Kamtschatka. We had minimal visibility and saw no land. In the afternoon we spotted a dead walrus (*Trichechus rosmarus*) near our ship.

Toward evening on the 5th, the wind finally ceased. After the horizon cleared some the following morning, we were delighted to see the Island of St. Paul not too far ahead of us. We sailed toward its northeastern tip and dropped anchor in 15 klafters of water. Boats were lowered into the calm sea. We were extremely anxious to see what we would find on the shore about two to three versts away.

There is a wide, open bay at the northeastern tip of the island whose water is so shallow that only smaller ships can seek shelter there. The terrain is flat with low hills. On one of them we saw a wooden cross like the ones the Russians erect at almost every new outpost.

Along the flat coast is found a black sand, shiny, heavy, most likely iron or titanium, which it seems to me was formed from powdered lava. Here and there heaps of seaweed had been washed ashore, in particular *Fucus laceratus*. Where the shore is steeper, the cliffs consist of horizontal strata of lava.

The hills and mountains were covered by a lovely carpet of grass that was a most welcome change for us, since the last land we had seen was the snow-covered mountains of Kamtschatka and the Aleutian Islands.

A little distance from the shore we found several abandoned earthen huts. Instead of beams they were supported by whale bones. Here and there we found tools, containers, rotten furs, sealskin, logs, etc., but not a trace of the inhabitants. We assumed that inhabitants of St. George had visited there a short time before and that no Russian hunters were there at the time. We left the desolate huts and went to the northeastern point of land to check out fur seals, Russian *kotja* or sea cats (*Phoca ursina Stelleri*), whose bellowing and bleating we could hear from a great distance. We armed ourselves with clubs lying around the huts and went into battle.

I find it almost impossible to describe this totally new sight for me. Thousands of these fur seals, old and young, grouped together into different herds, had collected there. As we approached they did not display any signs of fear. A great number of them hopped over the rough, coarse stones into the nearby sea and a still greater number of the old ones stayed on the beach to guard the pups. The largest and oldest of those defenseless creatures opened their mouths and hissed when we attacked them. Others tried to defend themselves by biting and trying to drive us, the enemy, away.

The babies that were still nursing bleated like sheep; the larger ones bawled like calves. Many sounded something like a person vomiting; others screamed like little children. Even though they tried to defend themselves with open mouths, it was easy to grab them by the tail and drag them away. Several — the victims of our excessive hunger — were skinned and cooked at once. In less than one-half hour we had slaughtered 40 to 50 large ones for the ship's crew. The sailors would have killed them by the hundreds if they had not been ordered to cease.

These animals are polygamous. The bulls often fight violently over the possession of cows. The stronger bulls carefully watch their cows and young. When danger threatens, he commands the herd to retreat and places himself defiantly in front of the enemy. If the bull sometimes appears enraged, the cows try to placate him and if they ignore his commands, he punishes their disobedience by biting them.*

After spending several hours on the field of slaughter and inspecting the surrounding area — all of which were so new to us — we hurried back to the hut, where a noon meal of tasty young seal awaited us. As long as they are nursing, their meat tastes almost like veal. The flippers taste especially good.

In the afternoon we climbed into our boats, better fed than we had been for a long time, and rowed to the ship with our rich booty of fresh provisions for our starved crew.

Here we found very unexpectedly a large leather baidara with several Russian fur hunters, who had seen our ship from their settlement on the southwestern tip of the island. The water was calm and the weather quite good. Therefore, we decided to stay at anchor and visit the settlement on the following morning.

At daybreak on the 7th, we went on land and found on the southwestern side of the island a spacious bay with several well built

---

*Since I do not intend to describe the history of these curious animals, I recommend to my readers the detailed description in G. M. Steller's work published in Halle, 1753.[2]

earthen huts about a verst from the shore. Fifteen Russians and a few Aleuts were living there. Some of them had been living there for several years collecting fur seals and fox for the Russian-American Company. They told us that at the beginning of the summer they were solely occupied with laying up stores for the winter, mainly dried seal meat, and during the summer into fall with the skinning and curing of skins. Those fifteen men had just slaughtered that year 30,000 seals for winter supplies and thrown the skins away because they had no time to stretch and dry them.

The islands of St. Paul and St. George were discovered by a navigator named Pribyloff sailing from Unalaska.[3] The former, according to our observations, lies 57°15′ N latitude and 170° W longitude from Greenwich and consists of several low mountains and hills whose valleys have ponds of fresh water formed from melting snow that can be used for drinking. The island, lying northeast to southwest, is about 30 to 40 versts long. It is covered with grass and low shrubs and is totally devoid of trees and bushes.

The northeastern point is a low-lying tongue of land. The cliffs to the southwest, formed of a brittle, porous, black lava, led us to believe that the island is of volcanic origin. If we had stayed longer, we might have discovered the crater. Given these circumstances, I found the fossils from the highest mountain about in the middle of the island, which one of the Russian hunters gave me after I had expressly asked him about unusual natural features, all the more remarkable because the whole stretch of mountains from Kamtschatka along the Aleutian Islands to the northwestern coast of America are composed entirely of primordial materials — granite, porphyry, coarse schist and volcanoes.

The climate is raw and it is almost incomprehensible that human beings would decide to live for years on this tiny island isolated from the rest of the world.

According to the inhabitants, there are terrible storms in spring and winter. The sea is filled with ice floes, sometimes carrying polar bears if brought by northwest winds. In summer the island is often covered by fog. Several of the Russian hunters who climbed the highest mountains on rare clear days maintain that an island lies to the north-northeast which has never been explored by anyone. According to several of these men, who had been living on St. Paul for twelve years, the island had been much barer, but during their stay the amount of earth and numbers of plants and shrubs had increased.

The main products of this little island are (1) stone or ice fox (arctic fox) which used to be snared in great numbers but now only minimally, and (2) fur seals (Russian *kottiki*) which arrive in the middle of April to come ashore and bear their young and then depart again in September. This species of seal is distinguished from the common seal (*Phoca vitulina*) by its beautiful fur pelt, which the Chinese and other Tartar peoples, especially the Yakuts, Tungus, Buriats, Bashkir and others, prize as trim for their clothing and headdresses. The English and Americans, I am told, hunt these animals on several South Sea Islands, especially the Island of Amsterdam, and sell their pelts under the English name fur seal at the markets in Canton. The Russian-American Company carries on a more than advantageous trade in them, for 15 men, whose maintenance costs almost nothing, can easily skin, prepare and cure upwards to 100,000 pelts in a summer. A pelt sells for 1 to 1½ Spanish dollars in Canton and 2 to 3 rubles in Kiachta. Several years ago, as a reliable informant assured me, they killed them in such numbers that the warehouses of the Company were filled with several million rubles' worth of rotting pelts, because they had only striven for quantities and had not paid attention to curing the pelts properly. The fat, an excellent oil when rendered, is always thrown away.

The seals are slaughtered by separating a group from the shore and driving them one or two versts inland where they are clubbed to death. This is done to avoid frightening away the ones left on the shore.

The valuable sea otter (*Lutra marina*) — in the first two years after discovery of the island nearly 3,000 were taken (with each pelt worth 100 to 150 rubles) — has almost totally disappeared. Only very rarely are individual animals sighted. *Phoca vitulina* and *Phoca jubata*, or seals and sea lions, are seen more frequently.

Walrus (*Trichechus rosmarus*) are taken from a rocky island called Morschowa Ostrowa lying several versts from the southwestern tip of St. Paul.

My greatest curiosity was for Steller's sea cow or *Trichechus manatus Stelleri*. This curious animal, described for us by that scientist, used to abound on the coasts of Kamtschatka and on islands in the Behring Sea not too long ago. It used to be the favorite food of the Russian fur hunters. It has not been found anywhere for many years now, not even near Tschuktschkoi-Noss, the most northern point of the Asiatic continent. Most probably this animal,* which still existed about 40 years ago, belongs to the list of extinct animals such as the dodo, the hairy mammoth, the carnivorous elephant in Ohio, etc.

There are very few fish near shore. The numbers of common seals, sea lions and fur seals frighten most of them away.

Despite the small and inconsiderable size of this island, it is still a collecting place for many millions of sea birds that come here to nest from the wide reaches of the ocean between America and Asia. The Russian fur hunters take advantage of them. In addition to fresh *kottiki* or fur seals in the summer and dried in the winter, bird eggs are a primary source of food during most of the year. For days and even several weeks in the spring, the entire hunting party undertakes the dangerous task of collecting eggs. One man lowers another with a basket on ropes down steep, 30- to 40-klafter-high cliff walls to collect eggs from nests. When they have collected a sufficient number, they wash them carefully, removing all dirt, dry them in the air and store them in casks full of clean, boiled oil. This way they can be kept not only for the entire summer but also for most of the winter. They are, indeed, as fresh as if they had just been removed from the nest.** The eggs of *Colymbus* or *Uria Troile* are preferred because they are the largest and best tasting.

During our short stay, I observed the following birds nesting there: *Alca cirrhata*, *Alca arctica*, *Alca pygmaea*, *Sterna hirundo*, several species of *Larus*, *Procellaria nigra*, *Procellaria grisea*, *Procellaria pelagica*, *Procellaria furcata*, *Uria Troile* and several others of the same genus. If we had stayed longer, I could have easily discovered other unusual subjects worth closer study.

The island is rich in vegetation. I saw the following edible plants: *Heracleum sibiricum*, *Epilobium*, wormwood, mugwort, sorrel, wild celery, *Pulmonaria maritima*, brooklime, cardamine and various types of watercress, several types of berries, *Rubus arcticus*, *Chamaemorus*, etc. Of new or unidentified plants, I found a species of *Androsace*, *Alopecu-*

---

*On page 185 of the German translation of Sauer's description of his voyage, he states that the last animal was killed in 1768 on an island in the Behring Sea, and no one has seen one in the area since then.

** This is most probably only possible in such a cold climate. I doubt if it could be done in a milder one. It is possible, however, using the same principle, i.e., the exclusion of air, to keep, for example, butter, fruit, etc., in wax fresh for long periods.

rus, *Achillea*, *Carex*, *Drabae*, *Ligusticum*, *Potentilla*, *Polemonium*, *Pedicularis*, *Saxifraga*, *Taraxacum*, etc.

Chamberlain von Resanoff, as official representative of the government, spent almost the whole day examining commercial aspects of the Russian-American Company. He had the stores of fox and fur seal pelts, walrus tusks, whalebone, sealskins, etc., brought to the ship. He decided there should be fewer fur hunters on the island in order to prevent a considerable reduction in the number of *kottiki* or fur seals taken in the future.

One would think that the hunters would have longed for such an opportunity to leave the place, but that was not the case. On the contrary, several of them fell to Mr. von Resanoff's feet and begged to be allowed to remain upon that desolate island: "Here we have everything in abundance. We make our clothes from fox and fur seal pelts. The fur seals which we treat like our herds are a plentiful source of food. We have no lack of all kinds of fruit, particularly berries, and of edible plants. The sea birds and their eggs are our delicacies. Even though the island is devoid of trees, this does not bother us as much as you might think. Our earthen huts are quite warm. Some driftwood, several ships of the Russian-American Company wrecked along the coast and oil-filled bones are adequate fuel for heat and for cooking our food."

After hearing this, one would assume that those fifteen men, three or four of whom had married Aleuts, lived in the greatest of harmony and friendship. Alas, we unfortunately saw nothing but discord and enmity among them. One of the fur hunters — a former merchant in Moscow, I was told — who had been sent to Siberia for fraud and finally had settled here and begun to carry on regular trade, acted as leader for the group. Displaying a true talent for oratory, he complained to Mr. von Resanoff of the injustices and hardships his decision meant for them. In view of the foregoing, most, if not all of them, were removed that same year. Even though our ship was full, we took a few of them with us.

During our two-day stay on the island, we feasted upon fur seal meat and eggs and were happy to be able to provide our large, hungry crew with fresh provisions for at least 10 to 14 days. It was striking to see how much weight those thin, consumptive men, who had been living on fish, gained in a few days on a diet of fur seal meat. Their scurvy disappeared. They all began to be unusually lively and cheerful. For five to six days the fur seal meat tasted quite good, but then it made all of us nauseous.

We left St. Paul on the 8th. On the same day we sighted St. George, a much smaller island lying to the southwest. Since we knew we would also find a hunting party there, von Resanoff decided to inspect conditions there too. On the following morning, we approached its southwestern tip. When we were about 1½ sea miles off shore, we fired a cannon to attract the attention of the inhabitants and invite them to the ship. At the very moment when the echo of the shot resounded off the cliffs, innumerable flocks of frightened sea birds rose suddenly along the coast. I am not one to exaggerate events or paint them in gaudy colors, but I can maintain that a thick cloud of birds rose from those rocky cliffs blanketing the sea with black as far as we could see. Almost simultaneously, a brisk wind arose, making the neighborhood of that rocky island of St. George dangerous and preventing its inhabitants from trying to visit us. We also were prevented from exploring the island and sailed straight southeast toward Unalaska. On the 14th we sighted land again. Because of a strong, contrary wind we could not reach the harbor of Illuluk on the northeastern side of the island. We were forced to sail through the rather narrow and dangerous passage between Akutan, Akun and Awatanok. The strength of the breakers indicated how close and dangerous the rocky reefs were. Several times the strong wind, the clumsiness of our ship and the rushing current made our situation dangerous. Messrs. von Chwostoff and von Davidoff guided the ship skillfully and well. By evening we were out of danger. On the afternoon of the 16th, we sailed into Sea Otter Bay, which Cook, Sarytscheff and others have popularized in the literature.[4] After establishing our location at noon at 53°41′ N latitude and 166° W longitude, we cast anchor in the little cove of Amagul, since the contrary wind had prevented us from sailing through the straits between Unalka and Unalaska or to the harbors along the northeastern coast.

Several Aleuts soon paddled out to the ship in their one-man leather boats or canoes, called baidarkas, and told us that it was possible to go over the mountains to the main settlement, a distance of about five to seven versts. An Aleut was sent immediately to inform the agent of the Russian-American Company, Lariwanoff, of our arrival.[5]

Von Resanoff, who was most interested in ascertaining the condition of the company outpost, decided to go there at once. Von Chwostoff, von Davidoff and I, along with several sailors and guides, accompanied him. Followed by several Aleuts in their baidarkas, our shallop was directed to the small cove Ugadachan north of our anchorage. We went overland from there. Several lovely little flowers were blooming along the shore — especially noteworthy were a new variety of *Mimulus* and a *Potentilla*, which has yet to be described. Incidentally, the low-lying areas of a nearby valley were covered by high grass. I had no time to dwell on the newness of everything as I would have wished: the jagged, rocky crags with conical, snow-covered mountains behind them, the steep slopes we had to climb up only to climb down again into the next valley. Soon night fell. Guided by several Aleuts, we made our way in the dark through that pathless terrain. Cliffs and boulders, fox holes, bushes, and piles of rocks made walking difficult. Near the end of our difficult hike, one of our companions, happily thinking he had discovered a footpath, ended up standing in a creek over his knees. Finally, toward midnight we arrived in Illuluk tired and exhausted.

Notes

1. In 46 B.C. the Julian Calendar was introduced in Rome. It established a 12-month year of 365 days with a 366-day leap year every four years. In 1582 the Gregorian Calendar was introduced to correct the Julian Calendar by suppressing 11 or, after 1700, 12 days from the year and declaring that only those centesimal years which could be divided by 400 should be leap years. The Gregorian Calendar was adopted in Russia in 1919.

2. Georg Wilhelm Steller (G. W. Stoeller) (1709-1746). *Steller's Journal of the Sea Voyage from Kamschatka to America and Return on the Second Expedition 1741-1742* is translated and in part annotated by Leonhard Stejneger (New York: American Geographic Society, Research Series 2, 1925). A more recent edition, edited with an introduction by O. W. Frost and translated by Margritt A. Engel and O. W. Frost, appears under the title *Journal of a Voyage with Bering, 1741-1742* (Stanford: Stanford University Press, 1988).

3. Pribüloff (Russian: Gavriil Loginovich Pribylov), d. 1796.

4. James Cook (1728-1779), *A compendious History of Captain Cook's First and Second Voyages* (London: Kearsley, 1784); *A compendious History of Captain Cook's Last Voyage* (London: Kearsley, 1784); Gavriil Andreevich Sarytschev (Russian: Sarychev) (1763-1833), *Account of a Voyage of Discovery to the North-East Part of Siberia, the Frozen Ocean, and in the North-East Sea* (London: Richard Phillips).

5. Lariwanoff (Russian: Emel'ian Grigor'evich Larionov, fl. 1806), an Irkutsk merchant, became Shelikhov's partner. In 1797 he was sent to manage the company's Unalaska district.

Chapter 2

Description of the Island of Unalaska. Its Inhabitants. Housing. Food. Clothing. Ornaments. Tattoos. Men's Activities, their Canoes, Harpoons. Whaling. Women's Activities. Religion. Marriage. Entertainment. Products of the Island.

The Island of Unalaska stretches from the northeast to the southwest. It is 70 to 80 versts long and very irregular in width. There are many bays and coves on the northern and northeastern sides, several of which could provide very good and safe anchorage. The southwestern coast has steep, inaccessible cliffs, as well as totally unexplored areas.

Here, as on most of the Aleutian Islands, one finds sizeable, high, conical mountains or peaks, including two volcanoes. From a distance the black, rugged, rocky coasts seem to be the clearest proof that the island is of volcanic origin. Therefore, it was all the more extraordinary to me that at every spot I visited I found mainly fine-grained granite and porphyry but no volcanic products.

The entire island consists of one rocky mass covered by a thin layer of earth. The mountains, which vary in height, are intersected by irregular valleys in which I found common clay and earth washed down from the mountainsides. Here and there, even at considerable elevations, I found ponds of fresh water formed by melted snow. The grass grows abundantly in the low valleys and could serve very well for raising cattle.

There are no trees on this island nor on the neighboring islands, only low shrubs and bushes, for example, dwarf birch, willow and alder and various berries, such as *Rubus*, *Vaccinium*, *Rhododendron*, etc.

The inhabitants collect driftwood along the coast for building their earthen huts and for the frames of their leather canoes, for paddles, arrows, etc. They sometimes find large logs of highly prized kinds of wood from America and the South Seas including camphor wood, most likely from Japan.

The inhabitants are evidently an intermediary race between the Mongolian and the American. They are of middle stature. Some have good, pleasing facial features. Their skin is dark, dirty-brown, undoubtedly the result of lack of cleanliness and their lifestyle. For the most part they are well-fed and have full, round faces, broad cheekbones, wide, flat noses, straight, thick, black hair, black eyes and eyebrows. The men have sparse, thin beards because they usually pluck the hairs out by the roots as soon as they appear. On other parts of their bodies, they have less hair naturally than other peoples.

They are generally pleasant and good-natured, servile and obedient, but if angered they are rash and irrational, even cruel and oblivious to all dangers, even of death.

Their dwellings are either yurts or pits covered by earthen roofs. If the hut has been standing for several years, high grass grows on its roof so that the village resembles a European churchyard with high burial mounds. One climbs down into a hut through the chimney or smoke hole. Several of the larger ones used by the Russians have low doors on the sides. Daylight comes in through small openings or windows covered by seal bladder or dried fish skin.

Inside along the walls, several compartments are created, usually from sealskins or straw mats, in order to mark the living areas and property of the various families living in one hut.

At present the population is very small. The Russians did not want to tell me the exact number, probably so that people would not learn to what a low level the population had gradually fallen.

Unalaska and the surrounding Fox and Andreanoff Islands now have barely 300 men on them. Between 1783 and 1787, in Schelechoff's time, there were several thousand. In 1790 Sarytschoff counted about 1,300.

The main cause of the rapid depopulation is probably that the agents at the headquarters of the Russian-American Company in Kodiak sent the best hunters to the islands of St. George and St. Paul, to Kodiak and even to the Northwest Coast of America on extensive hunting expeditions for sea otter, from which they usually never return to their families. In addition, the stress of their living conditions, the lack of proper care with ensuing results and the totally changed way of life which they are forced to lead undoubtedly have contributed greatly to rapid depopulation.

Fish, common seal and whale are their main sources of food. Among the fish are several well-known types of salmon, codfish, herring, and halibut (*Pleuronectes hippoglossus*). The most common and most highly desired fish is the halibut, which appears from time to time in huge numbers and weighs, to be sure only in rare cases, several hundred pfunds. If an Aleut is lucky enough to catch such a fish on the high seas, which is impossible to stow in his little leather boat, he kills it and either cuts it up into pieces or tows it home.

Aside from fishing, the primary occupation of the inhabitants is hunting seals (*Phoca vitulina*). Their importance is beyond belief, since I may correctly maintain that the Aleuts could hardly live without them. From the skins they make clothes, blankets, straps, shoes and other equipment. Indeed, even the canoes in which they go to sea every day consist of a wooden frame covered by the skins of these animals. The meat is eaten and the fat or oil used for food, fuel and light. They fashion watertight boots and leggings from the esophagus. Storage vessels for holding all kinds of liquids are made from the stomach. Rain wear is made from the intestines, as well as window coverings for letting light into their huts. Even the hairs of their beards are used, like ostrich feathers in Europe, as decoration. I can hardly name a part of the animal that is not put to some use.

Whale blubber is another favorite food of the Aleuts. Sometimes they kill whales, and sometimes they wash up from the sea. If they are old and rancid, they are then used for fuel and light in their huts.

The islanders either do not like to eat vegetables or do not want to take the time to collect or grow them. They eat small quantities of Siberian parsnip (*Heracleum sibiricum*), saranna or the bulbs of *Lilium Kamtschaticum*, which, by the way, I found tastes much more bitter than in Kamtschatka, mostly the fault of the soil. Edible berries of all kinds are available in quantity. I was able to identify the following: salmonberry (*Rubus idaeus*), *kneschenika* (*Rubus arcticus*), cloudberry (*Rubus chamaemorus*), mountain cranberry (*Vaccinium vitis idaea*) mountain bog bilberry (*Vaccinium uliginosum*), *klukva* (*Vaccinium Oxycoccos*), blueberries (*Vaccinium myrtillus*), high cranberry (*Viburnum Opulus*).[1] The women and girls collect these, as well as several kinds of roots when they are ripe, for use in the winter.

In recent years the Russians have begun to plant potatoes. They grow very well and the people enjoy eating them.

Great numbers of wild geese and ducks pass through in the fall and spring. They feast upon them and salt* and smoke them for the winter. The Aleuts, however, seem to prefer whale or seal blubber to salted or smoked goose.

Several neighboring rocky coasts serve as collecting places for many sea birds: *Colymbus*, *Larus*, *Pelecanus*, *Alca*, etc. Their eggs are collected in the spring, just as on St. Paul, and stored for the winter.

They have tried to raise pigs. Because they had no other feed, they gave them fish, thus causing their fat to be very thin and oily and their meat to taste disgustingly of fish.

The introduction of cattle would be very easy and advantageous for the Russians living there. A cow brought from Kodiak grazed for several years on the abundant grass until she disappeared in the mountains because she was simply left to run loose most of the year and not looked after.

Some hens belonging to Mr. Lariwanoff, the Russian-American Company's agent, for want of grain were fed mainly on chopped-up pieces of dried fish, which was not really especially suitable. Their meat was flabby, spongy, ill-tasting and unpleasant-looking, and their oily, thin fat was lemon yellow, as well as repulsive in appearance.

The agent told us that he had hardly eaten any bread in the previous five years on the island. Several years before our arrival, he had obtained six to eight puds of flour from Ochotsk. Only on very special occasions did he have bread or cakes baked from it.

The clothing worn by the men and women is almost the same in construction. It consists usually of a kind of carter's frock or shirt

---

*The inhabitants distill small amounts of salt from sea water by using seal bones saturated with oil instead of wood.

made without a placket but with a broad stand-up collar so that it can be comfortably slipped over the head.

The islanders make their clothes from sealskin as well as from various kinds of bird skins, especially of the sea parrot or auk or puffin (*Alca cirrhata* and *Alca arctica*) and cormorant (*Pelecanus urile*). They prepare them in their own manner and sew them together extremely skillfully. Although simple in design, this clothing is decorated in a variety of ways — either with glass beads or with the beaks of puffins or with long strips of fur seal or sea otter fur, sometimes also by sewing thin, artfully embroidered, brightly dyed strips of thin leather over the seams. Long, white goat's hair traded from Siberia or small red woodpecker feathers are also interwoven into the seams. These feather garments, that sometimes take at least a year to finish, are of such high artistic quality that the most accomplished European embroiderers would not be ashamed to claim the work. They are called parkas. They are worn first with one side out and then the other. When it is raining, the feathers are put on the outside. In cold and dry weather, they are turned inward instead of the fur.

While fishing, the men usually wear a kind of watertight leather leggings made from the esophagi of young seals. A few have begun in recent years to wear ordinary shirts of the coarsest Chinese cotton or of sailcloth imported by the Russian-American Company.

When on shore, the men wear boots whose soles are made of sealskin and uppers of the common seal's esophagus. They are so clever in making these boots that they can wade in swamps and creeks for days on end without getting their feet wet. The moment they climb in a boat they remove them. They use reindeer or whale sinew for sewing. Such fine, neatly turned threads resemble our catgut strings, because they swell when exposed to water, thus rendering a seam impenetrable.

To a nation so dependent upon the sea for its daily livelihood and food and located in such a damp, rainy climate, having waterproof clothing is undoubtedly of greatest importance. Most probably these islanders owe their rain wear (*kamleika*) to necessity, the greatest mother of invention.

A rain-shirt made from the bladder-like, barely three-zoll-wide intestines of the common seal is sewn together so ingeniously with sinew threads that no water can penetrate the seams, even though they have goat's hair, little feathers or other ornaments sewn into them. A small cap or hood that is attached to the back of the collar can be drawn over the head and tied tightly under the chin in heavy rain or a storm. At the wrists there are also strings that can be drawn tight. Thus dressed, one can spend days outside in the stormiest weather without getting soaked. The most elegant and expensive headdress is a pointed wooden hat with an umbrella-like projection over the eyes and is rounded cap-like in the back. If we remember, as mentioned earlier, that the Fox Islands are devoid of trees and that the inhabitants obtain the wood for the beams and supports of their houses and the frames of their baidarka and other utensils from driftwood driven by chance on shore, we can understand why even uncultivated people value objects for their rarity and how relative the concept of costliness is.

The Aleut, who only rarely comes into possession of a piece of good wood several zoll in diameter, frequently occupies himself for weeks in converting it into a board and then soaking it in water for a while to make it pliable so that it can easily be bent uniformly. If possible, he gradually tries to bring together the two back points of the board (which he has previously cut crosswise into an oval) and sew them together with sinew thread, thus creating a pyramid-shaped wooden cap. If he succeeds, which is not always the case because the board often warps unevenly or occasionally breaks, then he paints it with colored earth and ocher which he gets in the vicinity of the very distant volcanic craters. He ornaments it with ivory figures carved from walrus tusks,* with glass or amber beads obtained from the Russians and with beard bristles of sea lions, so to say, a substitute for the feathers used by Europeans. The Aleuts place high value on having a quantity of them — at the same time they are the trophies of a good hunter — since each sea lion only has four of them. I own such an Aleutian hat decorated with the beard bristles of at least 37 sea lions. It is worth almost 80 rubles in Unalaska according to European prices.

The women go mostly barefoot. They wear several strings of glass beads as bracelets and anklets and are very fond of rings on their fingers. The men's thick hair usually hangs wild and unkempt about their heads. The women comb the front half of their hair over their foreheads and cut it in a straight line over their eyes. They usually put the rest in back in a braid.

---

*The arduousness of carving ivory without tools does not need a special discussion.

There are several types of body ornamentation which are gradually falling into disuse and which we Europeans find very strange. Many islanders make a 1- to 1½-zoll-long incision parallel to their mouths just under the lips and insert in it, like we do with belt buckles, various ornaments made of glass beads. They also bore a hole through their nose cartilage and insert little pieces of wood or ornaments about the length and thickness of a quill. On festive occasions and for dances, they hang long strings of glass beads on these little pieces of wood over their mouths, which makes it very difficult for them to eat. Our European ladies only wear jewelry on their ear lobes. The Aleuts bore holes along their ears and fasten jewelry in them made of glass beads, enamel and other materials. From their ear lobes they hang long strings of glass beads and similar things. These sometimes fall down to their shoulders and breasts. Around their necks they often wear a stiff leather band with rows of colorful glass beads sewn on it.

The most highly prized of all the rarities used to decorate the ears, nose, lower lip, ankles or neck is an oblong mussel known as a sea tooth (*Dentalium entalis* Linn.). Formerly, when the inhabitants still lived in affluence, these tubular-shaped mussel shells were so prized that they gladly paid a sea otter pelt or the equivalent of 100 rubles or more for three or four of them. At present the inhabitants are happy if they have the most necessary of clothing to protect themselves from the cold and wet. Only a few dare think about luxuries.

In earlier times, tattooing, especially of the women, was very customary. They pricked their chins, necks and arms and then rubbed a mixture of coal dust and urine into the punctures. At present this kind of ornamentation is rare and mostly seen on old women, since the Russians have made it clear to the young Aleut girls that they do not approve of the custom. They, in turn, were accommodating and stopped doing that. It is, indeed, striking and strange to find among such uncivilized peoples totally opposite extremes. The men carefully pluck out their beard hairs and the women tattoo a kind of beard around their chins so that at a short distance it looks as if they really had blue beards.

The main occupations of the islanders are hunting and fishing and anything associated with them, for example, building canoes, paddles, harpoons, arrows, fishing equipment and line and throwing boards. The fashioning of tambourines, rattles of bird beaks, ornaments, wooden hats, dishes and bowls with carved figures, little models of their canoes, etc., are only of secondary importance.

Aleutian baidarkas resemble in the main those of the Greenlanders and Eskimos: they consist of a light, wooden frame bound together by whalebone and covered by stretched seal skins. They are small and long, usually for one, sometimes for two people and rarely for three. Each person sits in a round body-sized hole.

It requires a great deal of continual practice to paddle such a canoe. Experienced Aleuts venture out into the open sea even in stormy weather. Hardly has a boy turned six or eight but he learns to paddle one of these canoes, to build small models of them and to throw his harpoon at a target while on the water. An old chief on Unalaska, whose confidence I had gained, assured me that a kind of jealousy in the constructing of baidarkas existed among his people. Everyone was proud of being able to build a baidarka that could go to sea despite the high waves and move easily and agilely through the foaming breakers.

That chief called my attention to the best baidarka at the settlement and its special construction. I used the opportunity to measure it exactly and to note according to his information its mode of construction, a secret known to only a few of the islanders.*

Besides these one-, two- and three-man baidarkas, they also have large, open, leather boats or baidaras for 15, 20 and more men. They formerly were the common property of an entire village, but now they only belong to the Russian-American Company. They are used for ordinary business, e.g., for retrieving driftwood, at the arrival and departure of ships or for towing killed whales, etc.

The men fashion the wooden frame of the baidarkas. They also prepare the necessary sealskins and cut them. The women sew them together and know how to twist the thread or twine of whale or reindeer sinew very adroitly with their bare hands.

The arrows, or rather, harpoons, used by the islanders to kill whales, sea otters, seals, sea birds, etc., are of differing form and size according to their special uses. The most remarkable thing is that the harpoons are not shot from a bow but rather catapulted by means of a little board and have no feathers at the back.

This throwing board is about 18 zolls long and almost 3 zolls wide. It has a kind of handle at its lower end and an opening for the

---

*See explanation of the illustration.

forefinger so that it may be more firmly held. On the upper end is a little groove for the harpoon and a small point or knob of bone that serves to steady it. If one puts the harpoon on the back of the throwing board and places the middle finger and thumb on it while holding the wooden throwing board horizontally and pointing it approximately in the given direction, the harpoon can immediately be propelled forward with such skill and force that its target seldom escapes. Even whales are killed by this kind of harpoon.

The tips used for sea otters, seals, sea lions and birds are of bone, whereas those for whales are of lava glass or obsidian.

When an Aleut spots a whale, he pursues it, waiting for the moment when it raises its huge head out of the water to breathe, in order to wound it with a harpoon near the front fins. If this is done effectively, then the whale goes into a terrible rage and writhes around near that field of battle until it is exhausted and gradually bleeds to death.

The Aleut returns to the area daily and attempts to find the whale dead on the surface of the water, or, if that fails and a strong wind is blowing toward land, someplace on a neighboring island. He then informs his village so that they can bring it back and cut it up together. The tip of a harpoon, that is always found in the wound on the dead animal and is marked with an individual sign that belongs to each Aleut, serves as unquestionable proof in doubtful cases to determine which hunter should be given credit legally for the take. Formerly, when a whale was taken, it was divided up according to specific laws so that the village chief, the hunter who had harpooned it and all of the other villages received a certain portion. Now the Russian-American Company immediately takes half and leaves the other half for the Aleuts to divide however they wish. The fins, the blubber, the tongue, the baleen or whalebone, the intestines, the tendons or sinew and some bones are used; the actual meat is left to rot.

Many Aleuts spend their leisure time with hobbies, particularly with carving various figures of people, fish, sea otters, seals, walrus, birds, etc., on walrus ivory, which is harder than elephant ivory. These carvings display the progress they have already achieved in that type of fine art. Formerly, these objects were thought to be of religious nature, which they are not.

In summer the women and girls have to gut and clean fish and hang them up to dry, to collect berries and roots for the winter, to sew skins together for baidarkas, to make all types of clothing, boots and shoes and to draw thread from the sinew of reindeer and whale, which in turn is twisted to make loops needed for harpoons and fishing line, etc. They display admirable dexterity in sewing, embroidery and weaving. Each type of seam is different for each object; for example, the rain garments made of seal intestines are sewn together with a completely different stitch from the one used for bird skins and this is different from the one used for the sealskin covering on baidarkas and baidaras, and yet another one is used for sewing together boots. During their leisure hours, particularly on long winter nights, they weave little baskets and pocket books from straw. These are characterized by the regularity and symmetry of their decorative figures so that one might suspect they had been woven by the most skilled European hands. Therefore, we dare not deny these people, who otherwise are not very civilized, their sense of beauty. They dye the straw, leather and other materials used for ornaments many beautiful and gay colors. For want of better dyes, they mix urine very effectively with a variety of substances. They also do this for many other purposes, e.g., as a substitute for soap.

Their religion, as with all uncivilized peoples, consists of superstitions and witchcraft. Many of them are baptized and belong to the Russian Greek Church without knowing any more than how to make the sign of the cross. They have neither a priest nor a house of prayer, and the small number of Christians present have, on the whole, provided so few good moral examples that the natives cannot possibly understand how the benevolent Christian religion has manifested itself in human society.

They have no marriage ceremony. Marriage consists of a mutual agreement between a man and a woman to live together. The number of wives a man keeps depends upon his wealth. He usually has as many as he can comfortably feed. If he becomes poor as a result, he sends this or that wife back to her parents, and she then is free to find another husband. Occasionally, one and the same woman lives with two men, who share their common companion according to mutually agreed upon conditions. It is not uncommon for men to exchange wives. Certain handsome, young boys are often raised totally as girls and taught girls' work and functions. As soon as beard hairs begin to appear, they are carefully plucked. They are tattooed around the mouth like the women. They wear ornaments made of glass beads on their hands and feet and cut and bind their hair in the same manner as the women. They can act as substitutes in every way for concubines. Up to now no one has attempted to take measures to control, indeed, to end this immoral, unnatural inclination, which is a long-established practice from the remotest past. Such men are known as *schopan*.

The bodies of the dead, especially men, formerly were buried in a seated position during special ceremonies. Their best harpoons, clothes, train oil and other foods were put in the grave; indeed, even male or female slaves were slaughtered. Today they no longer hold any special ceremonies on these occasions.

Aleuts do not smoke but are so addicted to snuff that they will do the hardest labor for days if rewarded by a few leaves of tobacco. These are then pulverized to individual specifications together with ashes and a little water in a mortar made from whalebone.

Brandy is very scarce; therefore, the islanders very, very rarely misuse it, even though at the arrival of a ship from Ochotsk or Kamtschatka they try very hard to procure this foreign poison.

Dancing is one of their favorite amusements. During our stay, the agent of the Russian-American Company gave a dance. Dancers of both sexes in their best clothes and beautifully embroidered hats, which are only worn on festive occasions, assembled outside. The music came from a tambourine, struck rhythmically while accompanied by singing and the sound of a rattle made of a dried seal bladder filled with peas or little pebbles. The sole movement of the few people who danced at the same time was a kind of uniform hopping, which resulted in hardly anyone moving from their original places. If a dancer became tired, he withdrew and another took his place. If someone not wearing well embroidered clothes wanted to dance, he borrowed them as well as a hat from one of his tired comrades and threw them over his usual clothes in front of the spectators. The dancing was not especially strenuous or expressive, but rather simple in all its very slow and clumsy movements.

We did not see any of the masks previously used by these people at festivities, which earlier travelers observed and to some extent illustrated.

Our stay was too short to allow us to examine many aspects of that remarkable island in more detail. Fur, which attracted the Russians and caused them to found outposts there, is the primary source of wealth — especially black and silver-grey fox and river and marsh otter. The valuable sea otter (*Lutra*), once so common and taken by the thousands, has almost totally disappeared so that now barely two to three hundred are killed yearly.

Sea, marsh and migratory birds of all kinds are present in abundance. Had we stayed longer and studied them more closely, we undoubtedly would have discovered, besides the above-mentioned edible birds and fish, other, as well as other unidentified, products of the sea.

Just in the vicinity of Illuluk and on the way to and from Sea Otter Bay, I made the following list of identified and unidentified plants:

Achillea
Aira grandiflora
Andromeda, a new species
Anemone narcissiflora, Linnaeus
Arnica, a new species
Artemisia, a new species
Aster, a new species
Arbutus uva ursi
Bartsia, a new species
Campanula
Cornus canadensis
Cerastium
Claytonia, a new species
Carex, a new species
Empetrum (?) *nigrum*
Erysimum
Epilobium
Galium
Geranium
Geum rotundifolium, a new species
Holcus (?) *borealis*
Hieracium
Iris
Isopyrum, a new species
Lycopodium Alpinum
Linnaea borealis
Lilium Kamtschaticum
Lupinus nutkaiensis
Lathyrus
Mimulus, a new species
Polypodium vulgaris, affin.
Phleum an ruthenicum
Polygonum, a new species
Plantago
Primula saxifragaefolia, a new species
Pedicularis, a new species
Pulmonaria
Pinguicula
Pyrola, a new species
Pyrola an rotundifolia
Potentilla pulchra, a new species
Potentilla, a new species
Rhodedendron Kamtschaticum
Rubus
Salices, a new species
Solidago
Saxifraga, a new species
Sanguisorba
Vaccinium
Veronica
Viola, a new species
etc., etc., etc.*

---

*Sarytscheff's *Achtjäuhrige Reise* (Eight-year Journey), particularly Part 8, pp. 151-171, and other places of the Leipzig edition, contains several very interesting observations of this island.

NOTES

1. *Flora of the Aleutian Islands* by Eric Hultén (Stockholm: Bokförlags Aktiebolaget Thule, 1937) lists ***Rubus idaeus*** under ***Rubus spectabilis*** (p. 221fn) and states that "no trace of *R. articus* was found there" (p. 222) and that "it is questionable whether it (***Rubus chamaemorus***) is at Unalaska, Akutan and Unimak" (p. 221) and that ***Viburnum opulus*** "should be excluded from the flora of the Aleutian Islands" (p. 309).

Chapter 3

Departure from Unalaska. Voyage to Kodiak. Arrival. Description of the Island, its Inhabitants and their Customs. Religion. Conditions at the Russian Settlement at Kodiak. Products of the Island. Changes during our Stay. Departure from Kodiak and Arrival at Norfolk Sound.

After taking leave of the [Russian-American Company] agent Mr. Lariwanoff and his wife and daughter, who had showed us the greatest of hospitality, we set out from Illuluk on July 21. We again went overland to Sea Otter Bay. This time in daylight we could see its picturesque surroundings better than at our arrival. At many places along the little-used path, we came upon heaps of granite and porphyry rocks, which were intended to serve as guideposts in fog and stormy weather. We, however, had not been able to see them in the dark on the night of our arrival July 16th. Mrs. Lariwanoff gave us a small cask full of berries, several smoked, salted geese, fish paste and a lean, oily ham, the best she had, as provisions for the trip. Our Aleut guides and sailors carried these to Sea Otter Bay. On the way I saw hardly any land birds and, except for an unidentified *Carabus* that is also found in Siberia, not a single insect. Before evening we reached the ship.

Our miserable, half-starved crew from Kamtschatka underwent a change. The men most ill with scurvy and unfit for work were left behind and replaced by the youngest and healthiest men at the settlement.

In the meantime, our commander, Lieutenant Maschin, had procured supplies for the crew by ordering all the headmen in the surrounding area to bring as much fresh food on board as time and conditions permitted. Good water was to be had not far from our anchorage. Fortunately, we had brought along firewood from Kamtschatka since it was simply not available.

The following day we sailed out of Sea Otter Bay. We had just left it and were near the little islands of Ugalchan or Jaitschnoi, i.e., Egg Island (because sea birds nest there in numbers) when a strong sea wind sprang up making it impossible to reach the open sea. It forced us to return to the harbor of Illuluk, since we did not want to expose our ship, which sailed so poorly, to the wind and waves near so many rocky islands for several days. With the help of Sarytscheff's excellent map, we succeeded very easily in reaching the safety of the harbor in the night of the 22nd to 23rd. We remained there until the 25th, when we again put to sea by favorable wind.

The current or the influence of ebb and flood tide is very strong and irregular among the numerous islands and deserves the highest respect of all seamen. We left Unalaska on the 25th and sailed past the islands of Akutan, Awatanok, Tigalda, Ugamok and Botinski lying to the east. On the 27th the Schumachins Islands to the north came into view. They had been discovered by Captains Behring[1] and Tschirikoff[2] in 1741 and were named for a sailor of that name who was buried on one of them. This group, especially the islands of Unga, Nagai, Schumachins, Tankinak, Nunak and several others, about 13 or 14 in number, stretch from 55° north and 161° W longitude to the vicinity of the Alaksa Peninsula.

The following afternoon at 55°40′ N and 202° we sighted an isolated and very dangerous rock and soon afterwards the Island of Ukamok, the most southeasterly of the group of islands the Russians call Evdokijev, also including the more northwesterly Island of Semida, Achaiak, Gutchum and other smaller ones which stretch toward Alaksa. There had been a favorable southwesterly wind for several days, but suddenly the wind became so strong that by evening it and the waves put us in danger of shipwreck near Ukamok. During the night, we were barely able to sail at a very close distance past the dangerous, black, rocky southeastern tip of the island.

Most of the islands named above lying south of Alaksa are uninhabited but for many seals, sea lions and all kinds of sea birds. They are only occasionally visited by hunters from Unalaska, Unimak, Alaksa, Kodiak and other islands. Aleuts live continuously only on Sannach and Isannak. They, on the whole, as I was told repeatedly, still have the happiest living conditions of the Aleuts, because they are less directly subjected to the immediate influence of the Russian-American Company, or rather, much less often visited by the promyshlenniks. This island between 54° and 55° N latitude and 160°08′ W longitude is about twelve sea miles long and lies to the southeast of the passable straits of the same name (Isannaskoi Prolif) dividing the peninsula of Alaksa from Unimak. The entrance is marked by the little island of Ikatok or Ikatak lying south of it.

We were able to continue our voyage aided by almost constantly favorable winds and sighted early the 29th first Sitchinak and Tuchidok, two smaller islands separated from the southwest end of the Island of Kodiak by a narrow strait.* And then soon afterwards we saw the Island of Kodiak itself.

Towards noon we sailed past the Islands of Sadlidok or Schachlitak, lying to the southeast of the outpost founded by a merchant named Schelichoff,[3] which has been described by Billings, Sarytscheff and Sauer.

Recently, the outpost was moved to the northeastern coast of this island. Therefore, we headed toward the point called Cape Hermogenes when discovered by Behring (Cape Greville by Cook). This cape is bounded on the north by two small islands; in the native language one is called Giniak and the other Ugak.

On the 31st, north-northwest from the Cape, we arrived at a large spacious bay filled with a lot of islands. We anchored there surrounded by several rocks and low islands not very far from the main outpost of the Russian-American Company.

A Dane, Mr. Bander,[4] the present agent at the outpost, came on board as soon as he received word of our arrival in order to meet with Mr. von Resanoff. That is how we learned that Mr. von Baranoff, the head agent and director of all of the Russian-American Company's business interests on the Aleutian Islands as well as on the Northwest Coast of America, was not in Kodiak any more but had left a year before to found a new outpost at Sitcha on Norfolk Sound (as the English call it), where his presence was particularly required.[5] We also learned that the *Neva*, under the command of Captain von Lisiansky, had wintered in Kodiak and sailed for Sitcha in the spring to support Mr. von Baranoff's undertaking.

Then we all descended into a boat. As we were approaching a fort used to defend the settlement, von Resanoff, the agent of the Russian-American Company, was welcomed by repeated cannon salvos and a threefold Hurrah! from about twenty to thirty young boys

---

*I cannot guarantee the exact spelling and correct pronunciation of the names of these and other islands. Almost everyone hears differently. For example, Admiral Sarytscheff spells the names of the Islands Sitchinok and Tugudok. I found Tygijak and Sitkinak on the Russian map and Sauer in the description of his travels has Tugedak and Siktunak.

dressed in uniforms standing along the palisade of the fort. At the wharf three Russian priests and the boys met Mr. von Resanoff. They accompanied him to the church, whose bells were ringing, where a public prayer of thanksgiving was offered up for the safe arrival of such a distinguished man.

This unexpected scene made an unusually vivid impression upon my mind, since my daily surroundings had been so depressing. I felt a strange mixture of joy at my safe arrival, of hope and of regret. On the one hand, it had already become quite clear to me on several occasions during our short sea voyage and our stay on St. Paul and Unalaska that the promises made me orally and in writing in Kamtschatka to provide opportunities for scientific undertakings had met from the beginning with little willingness to let me carry them out. On the other hand, I felt here to the highest degree what one single individual might do for the well-being of humanity and for a totally lost people, if he carries out the position entrusted to him and applies the power vested in him appropriately — since our departure from Kamtschatka, my spirits had been very low upon seeing how the lives of the promyshlenniks were put at risk through the change in food and because of constraints and disappointed expectations and especially because I suspected that scenes of horror awaited me. I had decided to stay in my cabin so as not to become like the group around me. In contrast, on the *Nadeschda* I admired Captain von Krusenstern and my other companions, all upright friends, knowledgeable of human nature, who, with genuine integrity, had so prudently prepared me for the future. After the church service, we went to Mr. Bander's home. During a good meal accompanied by full glasses, we almost totally forgot that we were at the mouth of the so-called Cook River. A tasty soup, beef, vegetables, excellent fish, good baked goods, fruits canned in sugar and several European side-dishes, which we had not enjoyed in a long time, filled us with astonishment and made us more than ever before aware of the worth of an excellent housewife and cook like Madame Bander.

In the afternoon we took a look at the surroundings and the buildings and quarters which Mr. Bander had had prepared for us.

Mr. von Resanoff moved into a quite neat little house, which Captain von Lisiansky's sailors had built the preceding year.[6] Each of the rest of us was assigned an unimaginably small, miserable room.

Kodiak, Kadjak or Kuektak, i.e., Great Island, is the largest of all the northern islands lying between America and Asia. It stretches together with its surrounding islands from 56°45′ to 58°35′ N and from 151°30′ to 153°30′ W. The Russians have known about it since 1750.* Several speculative merchants from Ochotsk had individually visited the area to trade in furs, especially from 1760 to 1770,** until finally Gregori Schelichoff, a merchant from Irkutsk, founded a Russian outpost here.

Gradually, he subjected this island and then its neighboring islands, whose population he estimated at about 50,000,*** and laid the foundation of the present Imperial Russian-American Trading Company. Even if Schelichoff had bragged about the actual number of inhabitants and doubled the number, still there would have only been perhaps 20 to 25 thousand people.

The large population, the numbers of valuable furs, the location and nature of the country, a rather hospitable climate and several good harbors made this island the natural choice over others for the principal settlement.

The power of Russian firearms and powder prevented any resistance. That is why the Russians had quickly defeated and subdued the almost defenseless natives, who then were gradually robbed of their property and possessions. Since that time, their numbers have been decreasing from year to year.

According to Director Delaroff, in 1790 the total number of inhabitants on the Islands of Kodiak, Aphoknak, Sachlidok, Schujech, Tuchidok and Sichtunok was around 3,000.[7] According to the present business agent Mr. von Baranoff and his overseer in Kodiak, Mr. Bander, there are at present on the same islands only 450 men capable of labor. Marine Lieutenant von Hagemeister, who was in Kodiak in 1809 and claims to have seen the list of inhabitants in the Company's papers, asserts that the number of inhabitants on Kodiak was 7,000.[8] It appears to me strange that the Company's agents would give Mr. von Resanoff a smaller number, since they would not want to glorify the depopulation of the islands to this trustworthy and upright man

---

*See new information about newly discovered islands between Asia and America compiled by J. L. S. from reports and excerpts. Hamburg and Leipzig, 1776, Part 8.

**See Pallas, *Neue nordische Beyträge* [New Northern Contributions].

****Journal für Rußland* [Journal for Russia], Vol. 1, p. 64, and Pallas's *Neue nordische Beyträge* [New Northern Contributions], Vol. 6, p. 185.

who was supposed to inspect everything. For this reason, in my judgment of the number of inhabitants, I am inclined to believe the figure of at the most 500 men capable of working and hunting. The list shown Lieutenant von Hagemeister was perhaps deliberately exaggerated and forged by the office of the Russian-American Company. I support my contention by the following accurate copy of the list of the population at the main office in St. Petersburg.

Population List for Kodiak and Neighboring Islands

Names of Islands and Villages	1795		1804	
	Male	Female	Male	Female
Island of Ugak	50	55	48	51
Island of Agajachtalik	242	236	208	202
Island of Sitchinak				
Village of Ikuk	76	79	80	71
Village of Ubaguik	106	95	73	73
Island of Tuchidok	89	80	60	70
Island of Aphoknak				
Village of Igwik	52	46	30	26
Village of Naschkuchalik	46	47	29	32
Village of Nunatlak	61	45	35	26
Peninsula of Alaksa				
Village of Kukak	87	70	62	67
Total	809	753	625	618

Population List for the Island of Kodiak

Name of Village	1795		1804	
	Male	Female	Male	Female
Ugaschik	96	95	67	74
Igak	80	77	54	49
Ugatak	70	58	50	49
Scheschkak	103	98	74	80
Kilüda	283	233	177	173
Kijawik	95	91	63	75

Name of Village	1795		1804	
	Male	Female	Male	Female
Pai	90	83	54	65
Alitok	115	110	98	91
Askolick	116	98	71	67
Ischiok	89	90	48	64
Kaguik	95	108	76	90
Kaschkaek	84	84	68	77
Schettak	164	163	116	128
Itnak	149	138	83	100
Schanulik	65	66	44	56
Aduguak	64	58	62	53
Ak	30	29	28	15
Nukalik	109	132	76	104
Tschukak	122	110	93	87
Naschkukak	48	44	34	24
Kaschilok	26	27	23	20
Karluk	173	171	122	126
Teschiniak	86	87	56	55
Taüchtalik	15	11	16	8
Kischujok	36	28	22	18
Uganak	61	61	36	38
Schaschkachok	74	69	48	46
Population of Kodiak	2,538	2,419	1,759	1,832
Population of Neighboring Islands	809	753	625	618
Total	3,347	3,172	2,384	2,450

But even if Mr. von Hagemeister's numbers were correct, where, then, is the rest of the population of 50,000 claimed by von Schelichoff in 1784, or, if he had only doubled the number, the rest of the 25,000?

Changed living conditions, foreign customs and habits, lack of food and clothing, the spread of unusual and, in some cases, unfamiliar diseases, oppression and maltreatment of all types, especially compulsory, brutal hunting parties, cares and worries, mutiny and many similar causes, like the plague, have depopulated the regions and islands in an unbelievable manner. The same disruptive influences continue and threaten the rest of this people with total destruction.

The mountains, high in some areas and mostly made of granite, are covered with a thin layer of earth. The low ground and cliffs along the coast are of hardened schist. All around the island are bays, harbors and deep inlets, some of which run so far inland that only narrow necks of land lie between them. The island is only inhabited along the coast and rivers, not in the interior. Fish and products from the sea take care of most of the inhabitants' needs. The climate is better than one would expect at such a northern latitude. The main reason is undoubtedly the heavily snow- and glacier-covered mountain range on the mainland of America and Alaksa to the north, northeast and west, which protects the island from the rawest winds like high walls. In some years the winter is said to be so mild that in the lowest areas of Kodiak the snow does not stay long and the cold is rarely very severe.

The soil in the low areas is fertile, grassy and suited to the raising of cattle. They have 30 to 40 head of cattle and several pigs, which are fed fish just as in Unalaska, and several goats. Sheep would unquestionably thrive here.

The few attempts at growing grain have failed, because the plants bolted, thus producing very tall stalks without grain in their heads. This rankness of growth is ascribed to too rich soil. Potatoes and other kitchen garden plants grow very well. We saw, nonetheless, except for Mr. Bander's kitchen garden, no others of that type. All legumes, e.g., peas and beans, are said to bloom all summer without producing ripe pods.

The inhabitants differ only slightly from the ones on Unalaska. In general they are somewhat taller and more robust, although undeniably of the same race. Their language is different, but customs, habits, way of life, food and clothing are almost entirely the same. Even though their houses are essentially like those of other Aleuts, they differ in that they contain more wood and are more spacious. The entrance is not in the roof but in the side of the house and usually so small and low that they have to crawl into the house on their hands and knees. Instead of a door they mainly use sealskin stretched over a frame. The half-subterranean huts, also without stoves, are warm enough in winter to protect their inhabitants from the cold.

Their clothing, called *konägen* in their language, resembles that of other Aleuts and is made from the skins of sea birds, especially *Alca arctica*, *Alca cirrhata* and *Pelecanus urile*, and sealskin. Since

Kodiak produces a larger variety of food than the islands lying to the west of it, the inhabitants have richer and better sources for satisfying their needs more easily. They use, for example, bearskin for furs and covers and make their rain garments from seal as well as bear gut. One also sees clothing made of fishskin and winter clothing of marmot and squirrel.

The quality of the sewing, embroidery and basketry by far do not display the perfection of that on Unalaska. Formerly, they are supposed to have liked decorations of that kind and of glass beads, amber, etc. Now they hardly think about them and are happy if they can keep themselves covered. Instead of expensive wooden head coverings, they wear round, quite nicely woven hats of straw and tree bark, which are decorated with ocher in a variety of ways.

Now one seldom sees holes in their lower lips decorated with glass beads, mussels in the cartilage of their noses and in their ears, tattoos on their chins and necks or almost all other indigenous customs and habits. Slowly, these practices have almost totally died out under the yoke of despotism under which the Aleuts suffer. They do, however, often paint and smear their faces with soil, red clay or some other colored earth.

The baidarkas resemble those of Unalaska but are built neither with their artistry nor with their exactness and delicacy. They are wider, clumsier, heavier. They are seldom for one man, but mainly for two or three men. Their harpoons are also catapulted from a throwing board, but differ both in length and construction from those of the inhabitants of the western Aleutian Islands. Their games and dances are exactly like theirs, however. They also use the same kind of rattles made from a quantity of puffin bills (*Alca*) attached to a wooden hoop. The sound greatly resembles the sound of Spanish castanets.

They have become so accustomed to snuff that it has become an utmost necessity for them.

They know little more about the Russian Greek religion than the sign of the cross, even though the settlement has a church and a priest. They know no other law than the obedience and subservience which has been forced upon them. No one has given a thought to teaching them morality. Male concubines are more common than in Unalaska. I was informed that marriage between close relatives is not in the least prevented. Here, similar ties between siblings and, indeed, even between parents and their children occur. An Aleut I asked about the matter answered calmly that his people followed the example of the sea otters and seals in such matters.

Such moral degeneration does not seem to bother the management of the Russian-American Company in the least. Even some of the Russians are sometimes guilty of these kinds of unheard-of deeds. One day I inquired why Lieutenants Chwostoff and Davidoff fled from every opportunity to have any contact with a man serving as a naval officer who seemed very knowledgeable. I was told that this man had been sent to Siberia for defiling his mother and boys. Later, he had found a way to enter the service of the Russian-American Company. Why does the Company employ such men? Why does it not inquire about the conduct of people applying for employment? It is true that the man I was just describing was sent off after two or three years, but not solely for his previous despicable behavior. It was mainly because year by year he had made more and more debts than he could ever repay and his conduct was not lacking in any way when compared to his previous record.

The main occupation of Kodiak's inhabitants is exactly like that of Unalaska's: hunting and fishing. The men kill whales, sea otters, seals; they construct baidarkas, paddles, harpoons, throwing boards, etc. The women in the company of *schopan* clean the fish, gather berries and roots, sew the baidarkas and clothing, twist thread from sinew, plait loops, fishing line, etc.

The lack of wood for construction on the southwestern side of the island and the difficulty of hauling it there in order to build a warehouse and housing induced Mr. von Baranoff several years ago to move the post to the northeastern coast. There is rather good, tall timber nearby and a good harbor that offers protection from the wind and secure anchorage to the biggest ships.

High mountains, low hills, between them small creeks, charming valleys, green, partially wooded islands and neighboring bays full of fish provide the new location with advantages, liveliness and charm. The previous year the *Neva* had delivered a quantity of flour, sugar, brandy, cloth and other necessities and equipment needed there. Mrs. Bander's daily good meals — something we were unaccustomed to — gave us the best information about the plants and living standard of the whole community. In the beginning everything appeared to us very exemplary. The settlement has about thirty houses; especially noteworthy are a church, the men's quarters, business offices, the storehouse, the agent's and priest's quarters, the school, the craftsmen's workshops and, somewhat farther away, the Aleuts' homes.

Kodiak is a collection point for furs taken in the area, i.e., Alaksa, the Cook River, Prince William Sound, Behring Bay and other places where there are smaller posts. That is why the storehouse sometimes contains a stock of very valuable furs. In 1802 the number of sea otter pelts collected in the five preceding years came to 18,000.*

Among the Russians or promyshlenniks there were all kinds of craftsmen, some of whom worked in shops built especially for their use. One finds among them many men who were originally sent to Siberia because of their ingenious tricks. From there they decided to seek their salvation under the wing of the Russian-American Company in America. It should surprise no one that this human trash contains many very skilled craftsmen, e.g., watchmakers, shoemakers, tailors, gold-, silver- and blacksmiths.

The location, the climate and products of the area indicate that this settlement, if properly managed, could enjoy a high degree of prosperity. But, it seems to me, under present circumstances this is unfortunately not the case. This will remain impossible as long as the present organization of the Russian-American Company is maintained and almost all of the men in subordinate positions are dishonest and unprincipled.

Mr. von Baranoff is the head administrator of all of the outposts of the Russian-American Company on the Aleutian Islands and in America.** He has extensive knowledge of the local situation in the areas under him. Since the promyshlenniks and overseers are mainly the scum of Siberian criminals and adventurers of all kinds, we have to admire this man's ingenuity, effort and endurance in keeping these people at least partially under control. Incessantly, he visits first one and then another of the outposts and undertakes first this and then that project. Sometimes he has gone for several years in this miserable, god-forsaken part of the world without any news or support from the main headquarters of the Company

*In 1803 Messrs. Chwostoff and Davidoff brought this rich stock of sea otter pelts to Ochotsk. Their worth, together with fox, American sable, black bear and fur seal (*kottik*) amounted to almost two million rubles.

**Even though I first met this charming man in Sitcha, I believe this to be the most suitable moment to introduce my readers to him.

in Russia. Plagued by hunger and thirst, he and his companions have now and again lived like the Aleuts only from seal, fish and mussels. In the middle of this misery, he has built sailing vessels, established new outposts, hunted sea otters and continued to expand the territory and the rule of the Russian-American Company. Several times he has been helped out by the unexpected arrival of a ship from the United American States with whom he barters, thus preventing dire need from befalling him.

Mr. von Baranoff has already spent thirty years in the area. He was not a young man when he first arrived and can now request, as an honorable old man, peace and proper reward from the Russian-American Company. He has proved from the beginning that he is a just and honest man who continues to sacrifice his life and health for profit and in the service of the Company.

His long residence surrounded by crude rogues, his daily contact with sly and slippery criminals and the knowledge that only through perseverance and severity could he maintain his own and the Company's security and advantage have probably caused a dulling of his finer sensitivities and made him less compassionate. He knows how to maintain his dignity and reputation in every situation. He is hospitable and unselfish — often too impartial and generous toward people he has trusted or still seem important to him and toward people who have done him important service in carrying out some one of his plans. The result is that his generosity and leniency are often misused, although bringing profit for the Company or an individual at great expense and damage to the Aleuts or promyshlenniks.

The weakness of age, the shameless behavior of his subordinates and their management, the number of outposts and the distances between them and from the main offices in St. Petersburg, the lack of necessary supervision, of justice and of courts — in my opinion these constitute the main source of many of the misdeeds that this upright man alone cannot control.

The management of every single company outpost is completely despotic. The agents under the business office in Kodiak do exactly as they wish without being responsible to or supervised by anyone.

The Aleuts living on distant islands and areas are supervised by some kind of promyshlennik or, in other words, an ignorant, evil man, who suppresses and intimidates those placid and now defenseless natives in every way possible and, I am not saying too much, sucks them dry.

The unbridled rule of the office in Kodiak stretches from 55° to 61° N and from 135° to 190° W from Greenwich, an expanse that the present conditions of naval transportation will never let them keep track of.

I have often noticed and find it extraordinary that in a monarchy a free trading company exists which is not subject to any laws. It exercises its stern power over large expanses of land freely and unencumbered, indeed uncontrolled by any system of justice. The beleaguered Russian subject has no protection for his property, no safety of his person, no justice. The business agents and their subordinates act, according to their whims and interests, totally arbitrarily without responsibility to anyone. Of course, no one would think of reporting their shameful behavior and daily atrocities to the main office in St. Petersburg. Complaints and plaintiffs are there in quantities but no judges.* I have examples of how several Russian fur hunters or promyshlenniks rule over the lives of natives according to whim. They have tortured those defenseless creatures to death in the cruelest manner and gone unpunished. That is why the natives hate the Russians, including their wives and children, and kill them whenever an opportunity presents itself.

Three times already on the Northwest Coast of America, the Americans have overrun and wiped out this or that Russian settlement including all of the Aleuts, women and children.

The injustice and raw violence perpetuated by the assistant overseers and agents of the company go so far that the natives have lost all their possessions and own barely more than the clothing on their backs. One of the main reasons for their total suppression, as Sauer points out in the description of his travels, is the Company's having taken possession of their baidarkas or leather boats. If they steal the boats from people who have to get all of their food and clothing from the sea, they have then cut them off from all means of livelihood. At present the Aleuts are so enslaved to the Company that they get baidarkas, the bones for their arrows, and, indeed, even their clothing from the Company. The entire take of a hunt has to be turned over to the Company for disposition. The overseers and agents requisition as many persons of both sexes as are necessary to go hunting or to carry out other work, to prepare skins, to sew clothing, to build baidarkas, to catch and dry fish, etc. In other

*In no way do I want to imply that the honorable directors of the Company in St. Petersburg are guilty of anything. I am, however, convinced that not a one of them knows the true situation. I believe, therefore, I earn their appreciation by objectively calling their attention to some of the sky-high misdeeds being committed there.

words, the Aleuts have lost all powers to make decisions for themselves, even in the use of their time. It is disgraceful to see these people going hungry and almost naked and working as in a prison, while the Company's warehouses are full of provisions and clothing. Not only the Aleuts but also the Russian promyshlenniks who are not craftsmen or assistant overseers, but just work at construction, at cutting trees, or rowing, as sailors on the ships, etc., suffer in part no better fate. Their overseers force them to work and mistreat them until their strength gives out. If they become ill, they receive neither support nor medical care.

Just as little concern is being shown for the morality and spirit of these people, so also is little concern being shown for their bodily needs. Their food, consisting of fish, whale and seal meat, the damp, wet climate, the dirty living conditions in the barracks, the lack of sufficient linens and clothing — these are reasons enough to destroy the healthiest constitution. Usually, scurvy befalls these people a short time after their arrival. Not a year passes without several deaths from it. If it were known how many of the promyshlenniks have been sent to America from Ochotsk in the last 30 years or so, how few of them have returned to their fatherland or are still alive, and if the main offices were to publish a true list of the names of the former and present inhabitants of those islands, the validity of what I am saying here could easily be proved.

The mutual interaction of the Company and the promyshlenniks is governed by curious principles. They are supposed to receive a certain portion of the take but never know its exact size — as a result they never know how much the Company owes them. It takes the Company years to settle accounts. In the meantime, the promyshlenniks have to acquire goods on credit for their daily needs at extraordinarily expensive, often very arbitrary, prices. In this way, they usually end up in debt and can be kept as hostages against their will by the Company in order to work off their debts. They drown their sorrows in brandy. If they are strong enough of constitution to survive, they count themselves lucky, after many years and a sorrow-filled stay, to return to their families with destroyed health, poor and ragged. The number who receive a few hundred rubles from the Company at the end of their contract is probably very minimal.*

The following flora and fauna are by far more abundant on Kodiak than on the Aleutian Islands and are apparently the same as in America.

---

*For an accurate description and excellent discussion of the conditions and treatment of the promyshlenniks, see Mr. von Krusenstern's *Reise um die Welt* [Voyage around the World], Part 2, pp. 112-122.

There are large numbers of whale and seal, but fewer fur seals and sea lions.

Sea, river and marsh otter used to be caught by the thousands, but are now almost totally extinct except for a few hundred which are killed every year in the region. The Aleuts are excellent, adept marksmen. They usually set out in several baidarkas to hunt sea otter. As soon as they see an animal, they surround it and it seldom escapes, for, just like whales and seals, it has to surface from time to time to breathe fresh air.

The high price of pelts and the present interest in them has caused the Russians to pursue sea otters recklessly. They have killed so many young and old sea otters that they will soon be totally extinct. The very young ones have the trade name *medvedki*, the adults *koschloki*, and the old ones *matki*.

In the warehouses we had an opportunity to see pelts of the rarest varieties or species of fox. The very black fox (*Canis lycaon*) is called *tschernoburi*; other blackish, reddish and silver-grey varieties, that occur rather independently, are called *sevoduschki*, *krasnoduschki* and *beloduschki*.*

Brownish and reddish bears, whose skins are of no great value, are seen in abundance. The valuable skins of black bears stored in the warehouses come from the coast of the American continent, the Cook River, Prince William Sound, etc.

Arctomys Citilus, Russian *yevraska* or ground squirrel, are found on a small island north of Kodiak, Yevrascheschei Ostrova, in unbelievable numbers. They are used, especially by the Aleut women, for light, winter clothing.

The common squirrel, Russian *tarbogan*, is rather common. Beaver, *Castor Fiber*, reindeer, *Cervus Tarandus*, wolverine, *Ursus Gulo*, lynx, *Felis Lynx*, mostly of white-grey color with pale spots, and the tailless, hairy hedgehog, *Erinaceus ecaudatus*, are rarer on the islands, more common, however, on Alaksa and the American continent.[9]

Mr. Bander showed me the fine, whitish, very long wool of a wild American sheep, which the natives of the Northwest Coast weave into

---

*Stone Fox (*Canis lagopus*), Russian *peszi*, which are so common on St. George and St. Paul, are not found here.

blankets and clothes. I was unable to find out anything about the animal itself. It must be very different from the wild sheep, *Capra Ammon*, or the *Argali*, because they have smooth deer- or reindeer-like hair and not a trace of wool. As far as I know, no naturalist or seafarer has seen that American wool-bearing animal mentioned here.*

I saw hardly any land or song birds but instead marsh and water birds: swans, ducks, geese, cranes, herons, puffins, divers, sandpipers, etc., are present in the spring and autumn in countless swarms. The magpies, so shy and timid in Europe, are as tame as sparrows. They approach houses and land on the rooftops.

The most common fish, dried or fresh, mainly used for food are: herring, cod, halibut and several types of salmon, etc. Salmon appear at certain times and months in the bays and swim up the rivers. They are then caught in unbelievable quantities by nets and snares or dams.

The sea is rich in mollusk, medusa, shellfish, mussels and seaweed.

I saw only a very few insects. In the small apartment assigned to me there were so many bugs that I had no end of trouble. The inhabitants claimed that they had arrived a few years before by ship from Ochotsk and Kamtschatka.

There is another situation I find very much worth mentioning. Cockroaches or *tarokane*, *Blatta orientalis Linn.*, which multiplied to indescribable numbers on our ship and the *Neva*, were unknown in Kodiak. Soon after the *Neva*'s arrival, they immediately made their way into the houses. Their numbers were said to be so great that, while workers unloaded the ship and carried sacks of flour to the warehouses, they, like ants, built a living highway from the ship to the warehouses. This new plague fortunately did not last long, since they all died in a short time of their own accord. At our arrival there was not a single roach anywhere in the settlement. I find this situation all the more strange and worthy of mention, since that insect has gradually spread from European Russia through all of Siberia. In Kamtschatka it has come to plague the inhabitants in almost every house.

---

*G. Vancouver's *Voyage de decouvertes* [Voyage of Discovery], Paris, 8, Part II, p. 238.[10]

Kodiak's flora is different from that of the other Aleutian Islands. Here, for the first time, we saw tall forest trees: larch, fir, low birch, poplar, ash, alder and willow. The same tasty types of berries and roots, which I have already named for the most part in Unalaska, are also found here. The Saranna, frequently collected for use in the winter, does not taste as good by far as in Kamtschatka. It leaves a bitter aftertaste.

In addition to the plants listed in St. Paul and Unalaska, which I found here, I include the following:

Arenaria laterifolium
Aconitum
Angelica
Achillea
Arbutus uva ursi
Aspidium
Betula pumila
Comarum
Cacalia
Companulae
Epilobium spicato affin.
Galium an boreale(?)
Gentiana praetensi affin.
Heuchera, a new species
Lupinus
Parnassia
Rhinanthus an orista Galli(?)
Sanguisorba an officinalis
Spirea betulifolium
Solidago
Swertia perennis
Saxifraga, a new species
Veratrum album
Viburnum Opulus
etc.

Our short stay under the continual threat of departure, almost continuous rain, my lack of knowledge of the language and of support for scientific research made it impossible for me to use my time as I might have wished.

A detailed investigation of a region demands time to think, serenity of mind and comfort — all of which I had to do without. I had hardly gotten my bearings, hardly become interested in this or that object than I had to prepare myself to leave again, because Mr. von Resanoff considered it important to meet Mr. von Baranoff as soon as possible in order to ascertain exactly the condition of the Company. He was at Norfolk Sound on the Northwest Coast of America. We set sail for there on August 20th. Before leaving the Island of Kodiak, I dare not forget to mention several of the most excellent and important changes ordered by Mr. von Resanoff during our stay. These should lead to an improvement and advancement of the Company.

Mr. von Resanoff called upon all of the inhabitants, whether Russian or Aleut, to send their children to school. He explained to them its advantages: pupils distinguishing themselves through industrious learning could in the future work either as bookkeepers in the office of the Russian-American Company or as overseers and agents in its possessions, as pilots on ships, or even, if they acquired enough knowledge, as ships' commanders. Within a short period of time, most of the young people between the ages of 12 and 16½ were taken to the school. There they were instructed in reading, writing, arithmetic, geography, mathematics and French. They numbered before our departure between 60 and 70. They were to be fed and clothed at the Company's expense and taught by the priest and several naval officers.

Mr. von Resanoff had sent a library containing several thousand volumes from St Petersburg on the *Neva*. He himself had it placed in a house built by Mr. Lisiansky.

The hunter, who accompanied us from Kamtschatka and had been promised me in writing as help for me on the voyage with the practical aspects of hunting, skinning and taxidermy, now was ordered to take two young people as apprentices. They were to make a basic natural history collection, which would serve in the future for instructional examples in the school. This could be used to better acquaint the natives through visual means with the natural products of their island.

During our stay, all available objects were placed in the future museum. Mr. Bander was given a plan for a new building intended for the library and natural history collection, with orders to have it built the following spring. At the same time, he was to pay particular attention, while building this house and all future ones, to constructing the streets with a certain regularity so that in this respect Kodiak could be gradually compared with the most beautiful European cities. The electrical machine previously intended for Japan was installed there.

The well made meals placed before us daily by Mr. Bander's wife inspired the desire in Mr. von Resanoff to be able to provide future sea captains and every officer and official in the Company's service with the same advantages of such good food. He asked Mrs. Bander to supervise and teach several young 14- to 16-year-old girls housekeeping, cooking and gardening. His wish was taken as a command. During our stay, several promising children were taken in as boarders at the Company's expense. They were all dressed in the same kind of European clothing — Mr. von Resanoff often imagined the surprise of future seafarers arriving here and totally unexpectedly finding a well planned, magnificent city, a large school, a well stocked library, an electrical machine, a magnificent mineral collection, good cooks and a midday meal prepared in the European manner.

For the time being, no changes were made in the care of the ill or to provide better food and treatment of the promyshlenniks who were still reasonably healthy. They all groaned under the weight of their yokes and watched us, devoid of hope, as we sailed away. Being surrounded every day by so many unhappy human beings could not help but raise the most intense feelings of pity in anyone with a heart.

We needed a healthy crew for our voyage, especially to Sitcha, where ships were to be built. Once again, stronger and healthier men were selected and the ones suffering from scurvy or other diseases were cast to their fates and left in Kodiak.

Our ship, the brig *Maria*, had been supplied with wood, water and provisions. We sailed out of the harbor on August 20th full of fear and trepidation about our winter quarters. Accompanied by continually favorable winds, on the evening of August 25th we saw Mount Edgecumbe (57°2′ N and 135°55′ W), which marks the northwestern point of the entrance to Norfolk Sound. The following day we arrived happily at the outpost (57°5′ N and 135°8′ W), where Mr. von Baranoff greeted us most cordially.

NOTES

1. Vitus Be(h)ring (Russian: Ivan Ivanovich, 1680-1740) was a Dane who was invited to join the Russian service in 1703. In December 1724, Peter I appointed him to lead an expedition whose task was to determine if Asia and America were connected and to examine the coast of North America.

2. Tschirikoff (Russian: Aleksei Il'ich Chirikov, 1703-1748) was second in command under Vitus Bering on the First Kamchatka Expedition. He also assisted Bering in organizing the Great Northern Expedition from 1733-43. He has given us the first description of the northwestern coasts of North America and of the Aleuts in a report to the Admiralty College on 7 December 1741.

3. Schelichoff (Russian: Grigorii Ivanovich Shelikhov, 1748-1795) was the founder of the first permanent Russian settlement in Alaska (1784). He came from a family of small merchants in a small town in southern Russia. At the age of 25 in 1772 he went to Siberia, where he took part in the maritime fur trade in the Kurile and Aleutian islands and founded the forerunner of the Russian-American Company.

4. Johan Johansen Bander or Banner (Russian: Ivan Ivanovich, d. 1816) went to Siberia sometime before the 1780s. In 1797 he entered the employ of Shelikhov's company. In 1802 he was sent to Kodiak to gain experience in the administration of the Russian-American Company so that he might replace Baranov, who wanted to leave America. Archibald Campbell mentions him in *A Voyage Round the World from 1806 to 1812* (facsimile reproduction of the third American Edition of 1822; Honolulu: U. of Hawaii, 1967).

5. Baranoff (Russian: Aleksandr Andreevich Baranov, 1746-1819) was the head manager of Russian-American Company settlements in America from 1790-1818. He grew up in northern Russia, where he engaged in trade until 1780 when he went to Siberia.

6. Lisiansky (Russian: Iurii Fedorovich Lisianskii, 1773-1837) was the captain of the *Neva*. The house mentioned is believed to be the structure now occupied by the Kodiak museum.

7. Delaroff (Russian: Evstratii Ivanovich Delarov, ca. 1740-1806) was born in Greece but moved to the Ukraine with other Greek colonists early in the reign of Catherine II. As a young man, he went to the east coast of Siberia, where he participated in voyages for various fur trading companies.

8. Ludwig von Hagemeister (Russian: Leontii Andreianovich Gagemeister, 1780-1833) was born of a Baltic German family in Livonia. In 1795 he volunteered for the Baltic Fleet. In 1806 the Russian-American Company appointed him to take the *Neva* on its second voyage around the world to Sitcha with a cargo of supplies.

9. *Erinaceus ecaudatus*: Langsdorff identifies the animal in terms of the Old World hedgehog and not the New World porcupine, *Erethizon dorsatum*.

10. Langsdorff used a French translation of Vancouver's work, *A Voyage of Discovery to the North Pacific and Round the World* (London: Printed for G. G. & J. Robinson, etc., 1798), and not the German translation done in 1799. Captain George Vancouver (1758-1798), *Voyage de decouvertes, al l'ocean Pacifique du Nord, et autour du monde* (Paris: Impr. de la Republique an vii, 1799).

Chapter 4

The Capture of Sitcha. Conditions at the Outpost at the End of 1805 and the Beginning of 1806. Letter to Privy Councilor Blumenbach: Description of the Climate and Flora and Fauna of Norfolk Sound.

The decline in the numbers of sea otters, more apparent with each passing year, and the interest in trading in their valuable fur has caused the Russians to expand farther and farther eastward from Kamtschatka.* The number of sea otters on the Aleutian Islands diminished noticeably after they began being pursued and killed in ever greater numbers. This has caused the Russians to move farther and farther, first to Kodiak, from there to Cook's River, to Prince William Sound, and then to the bays and inlets farther south and then to the Northwest Coast of America. They have killed so many sea otters of every age that they are now either almost totally extinct or have moved farther south. It is now hardly worth financing hunting parties at the northern outposts.

The Company has decided to explore more and more country for sea otters in order not to lose a source of wealth and to maintain the reputation and patent of a respectable Imperial trading company. Norfolk Sound seemed like a good location for an outpost since large numbers of sea otters lived there. Therefore, Mr. von Baranoff laid claim to it several years ago. That courageous conqueror drove out the natives — the Russians usually call them Kalusch but they call themselves Schitchachan, i.e., inhabitants of Sitcha or Schitcha — and established a new outpost called Sitcha.

After spending some time there while living quarters and a storehouse were being built, Mr. von Baranoff returned to Kodiak in the belief that the Kalusch had been relatively placated by gifts. He entrusted that newly conquered area to about 30 promyshlenniks along

---

*Since most sea otters (Russian *bobr*) were taken originally only along the coast of Kamtschatka, they acquired the name Kamtschatkan beaver in Russia, a name still used even though sea otters are now a rarity along the coast of that peninsula.

with an overseer and several Aleuts. Several years later when most of these people were at scattered activities — fishing, felling trees, etc. — the Kalusch attacked and killed all of them except for a few Aleuts, who saved themselves by fleeing in their baidarkas along the coast to Kodiak. They spread the frightening news of the destruction of the outpost.

Because of the importance of the outpost and the numbers of sea otters in the vicinity, Mr. von Baranoff decided to reconquer the area and succeeded. It is strange how the reputation of a man can suffice in spreading panic and fear and can thus weaken the courage of even a superior force.

In the summer of 1804, Mr. von Baranoff set sail to hunt sea otters with the 100-ton *Alexander*, the 70- to 80-ton *Ekaterina*, and the 60- to 70-ton *Yermak* from Kodiak to Cross Sound, since he had received word of the arrival of the *Neva* in Kodiak. He left an order for the ship to sail immediately after arrival to Norfolk Sound. This happened. In August all four ships met: the *Alexander* and the *Ekaterina* with 58 men, the *Neva* with 54, and the *Yermak* with 15. They attacked the Kalusch village on August 11, 1804. When the Kalusch heard that the hero Nanok himself had arrived (all of the coastal inhabitants from the 48° to the 60° N know von Baranoff by this name), they did not dare attempt any resistance during the landing. Mr. von Baranoff immediately took possession of a small, isolated hill that forms a headland in the harbor. The Kalusch completely abandoned their large settlement at its foot.

The Kalusch had acquired firearms and gunpowder through barter with the American Free States and from the destruction of the Russian outpost. They retreated several versts from the hill into the woods to the mouth of a small river where they had constructed a very sturdy palisade on the long-held assumption that the Russians would be preparing an attack.

Several days later on August 19th, the Kalusch fortification was attacked. The *Neva* positioned herself at the mouth of the river and pointed part of her cannons toward shore opposite the headland or palisade and fired with another part at the headland itself. The hero, von Baranoff, did the same from land. Thus, a united force attacked the fortification with its 300 fighting men, not counting women and children.

The siege lasted four days and the battle was heated on both sides. Then the Kalusch, since a breach had been shot in the palisade, offered to make peace with the Russians. They gave the Russians nine sons of their most prominent chiefs as hostages and security. Even though they had been offered free access to the water, they fled by land at night. The Russians lost three sailors from the *Neva*, three promyshlenniks and several Aleuts. The number of wounded was considerable. Von Baranoff himself received a superficial wound to his right wrist. The Kalusch losses were unknown, but, according to information obtained from the hostages and several other captives, they were very high.

Once again Mr. von Baranoff was in possession of Sitcha. He immediately reinforced the natural fortifications of the hill and founded a new outpost which he named New Archangel. The *Neva* stayed there for a month and then returned to Kodiak for the winter. Mr. von Baranoff stayed with the above-named ships in New Archangel.

Since that conquest, an apparent truce has existed between both parties. From time to time the Kalusch visit the Russian outpost, their former residence, without displaying hostile intentions. They cannot, however, be trusted and the Russians have to keep a very watchful eye out for them in order not to become victims of their revenge.

That people's unchanged hate of the Russians is very natural because they have been driven from their paternal possessions and robbed of areas richest in fish, sea otters and other products of the sea and the source of their livelihood.

The natives of that area had formerly engaged in free trade with the ships of the American Free States, which came to the Northwest Coast of America every year and exchanged rice, cloth, knives, axes, hatchets, canvas, kettles, kitchen utensils and containers for liquids for sea otter pelts. Since the Russians do not engage in such trade with the natives and all the sea otters near and far are being killed by all the imported Aleuts, the ships of the United American Free States in the future will no longer derive any advantage from visiting the Kalusch. As a result, they have been robbed of sea otters and the means of acquiring clothing, food and other articles to which they had grown accustomed in the previous 15 to 20 years. Many of the ships coming from the United States now visit the Russians. They exchange necessities for sea otter pelts. Fortunately, the whole Kalusch tribe has no more than three to four thousand souls; a number, however, just large enough to keep the new settlers ill at ease and force them to be continually on guard against possible enemy attack.

It appears that the outpost New Archangel, formerly called Sitcha, will be the *non plus ultra* of the Russian border. Several trustworthy informants assured me that the peoples living to the south and southeast of there are much more numerous than the Kalusch. They are so bitter about the conqueror Nanok and his hunting parties that the Russians would probably meet with a sad fate if he decided he wanted to establish an outpost even farther south.

In addition, it is unlikely that the Russians can or want to lay claim to the islands, coasts and lands south of Norfolk Sound and Cape Tschirikoff.

As one can easily imagine, the settlement of New Archangel was in its infancy at our arrival. Because of the need for protection, the healthiest promyshlenniks and Aleuts had been brought there. The citadel hill had been fortified with cannon. Several Company ships armed with cannon lay at anchor and regular watch was kept day and night.

Under such circumstances normal human conveniences could not be expected. Quarters were, for the most part, unfinished and consisted of small rooms without stoves. Their roofs were so bad that the frequent rains continually penetrated them. All of the promyshlenniks had to work every day on the construction of the barracks, warehouse and other quarters that were so desperately needed.

As pleasant as it must have been for Mr. von Baranoff to meet such a high official of the Company in the person of his Excellency Chamberlain von Resanoff as well as so many other unexpected but interesting guests, he, the experienced good host, was still at the same time placed in an embarrassing situation by the arrival of such a large group of people. He did not know where he could obtain the additional provisions needed for the winter. His apprehension increased a week later when a lot more Russians and Aleuts returned from hunting sea otters in order to take up winter quarters in New Archangel.

Altogether there were almost two hundred people at the settlement, including overseers and assistant overseers, naval officers, master shipwrights, promyshlenniks and Aleuts. The following Company ships were lying at anchor in the harbor: the 120-ton brig *Maria*, the approximately 100-ton *Alexander* and *Elisabeth*, the 80-ton *Ekaterina*, the 22-ton *Rossislav* and the 40-ton *Yermak*.

In order to help alleviate the sad and distressing prospects for the coming winter, the *Alexander* was immediately readied to sail to the new harbor of Kodiak, where it was to take on as many dried fish, berries, train oil, saranna roots, whale blubber, etc., as possible. The brig *Maria* was also sent with the same orders to Schelichoff Harbor on the same island.

The 250-ton *Juno* from the United American Free States, from Bristol, Rhode Island, had been anchored there for several weeks. It had been trading for sea otter pelts with the natives in Noatka Sound at Queen Charlotte Island, in Chatham Strait and at other places along the Northwest Coast when its captain, J. D'Wolf II, had heard in May of this year about the settlement here.[1] He had used the information in order to take on wood and water at a secure harbor controlled by Europeans. He also wanted, if possible, to exchange high quality provisions, which he had in quantity on board, for sea otter pelts from the Russians. Similar reasons and the need for slight repairs to his ship had led him to return here for a second time several weeks ago.

Messrs. von Baranoff and von Resanoff entered into negotiations with Mr. D'Wolf and asked him if he wanted to sell his ship and everything on it to the Company? The bargain was readily closed. The *Juno* was bought for 65,000 piasters, or Spanish dollars, in a bill of exchange for St. Petersburg with the little ship *Yermak* included in the bargain. D'Wolf had to insist upon having the little ship, so that he could send his crew and the sea otter pelts obtained through the sale of the *Juno* immediately to the Sandwich Islands and Canton. He himself expressed the desire to winter in New Archangel and to sail to Ochotsk the following spring, if the Company would assure him that a ship would be ready for him by then. He had decided to travel from Ochotsk to St. Petersburg overland, since he suspected this would be quicker, in order to take care of the bill of exchange in person.

The *Juno* now belonged to the Russian-American Company. Mr. D'Wolf wintered in New Archangel. The little *Yermak* sailed in October for the Sandwich Islands and Canton under the command of Mr. Moorfields.

Through that purchase the Russian-American Company obtained an excellent, swift sailing ship and a rich store of goods originally intended for trade with the natives along the Northwest Coast — for example, quantities of English sheets, canvas, kitchen utensils, axes, knives, several muskets, etc. Above all, they obtained a considerable supply of excellent provisions which would alleviate the threat of famine. Actually, it could be said that the Company bought the ship on account of the provisions.

Except for a quantity of peas, beans, butter, tallow, etc., the provisions on board consisted mainly of the following items:

19 barrels of salted pork, each weighing 200 English pounds;
42 barrels of salted beef, each weighing 200 English pounds;
1,955 English gallons of sugar syrup (English molasses);
2,983 pounds of granulated sugar;
315 pounds of white sugar;
4,343 pounds of rice;
7,392 pounds of rusk;
11 barrels of fine white flour, each weighing 170 pounds

In addition, at the time of the *Juno*'s first visit in May, the following items had been purchased from Captain D'Wolf:

20 barrels of flour;
8 barrels of rice, each weighing 600 pounds;
6 barrels of rum, each containing 110 gallons;
6 barrels (hogsheads) tobacco leaves, each weighing between 1,600 and 1,800 pounds.

The *Maria* and the *Neva* had provided the outpost with many additional provisions, including, rye flour and brandy. By judicious distribution of these supplies, everyone could have received ample healthy food for the whole winter. Unfortunately, that was not the case!

Just as in Kamtschatka and elsewhere, the promyshlenniks were very scantily fed. And not the slightest attention was paid to the numbers of sick increasing with each passing day.

Immediately after the purchase of the large, swift-sailing *Juno*, she was put under the command of Messrs. Chwostoff and Davidoff and dispatched to Schelichoff Harbor on Kodiak instead of the sluggish little brig *Maria*.

These untiringly active officers sailed at the very advanced time of year, i.e., October 15th, from Norfolk Sound to Kodiak and returned again on November 7th, bringing with them around 70,000 dried fish (*yukola*) and a quantity of whale blubber, train oil, cooked berries, saranna roots and other gratifying Aleut delicacies. Because there was a scarcity of girls and women at the new settlement, something was done about this situation. These officers had brought a number of them along in compliance with an order which they had transmitted to the Governor of Kodiak, Mr. Bander.*

During Messrs. Chwostoff's and Davidoff's trip, one promyshlennik was blown from the mast by a strong wind and drowned.

The *Alexander* was expected back in vain. She did not arrive back at Norfolk Sound until the spring. This most likely also would have been the case with the *Maria*. The two above-named officers' quick trip with the *Juno* was immediate proof of the advantage the Company now had in buying the ship, since the settlement would have run short without the addition of considerable quantities of supplies from Kodiak.

After the *Juno*'s return, the shipwrights Messrs. Korükin and Popoff began to lay down the keel of a small ship which was being built under the supervision of Messrs. Chwostoff and Davidoff. The work went very slowly — the scantily clothed promyshlenniks, subject to the cold, rain and snow, with hardly a roof over their heads to keep them dry, were each given a daily ration of two or three dried fish or yukola, which had been boiled. Sometimes, for a change, they were given some old, rancid blubber from a whale found beached or perhaps already dead along the coast. Sundays, they got a thin soup made from salted meat with some rice in it and occasionally a little bowl of brandy and a bottle of molasses. All other provisions, such as rusk, flour, sugar, rice, salted meat, etc., were sold at high prices, and then only to favorites or as a special reward. Fresh fish, probably easily procured, were seldom caught because the promyshlenniks were needed for building quarters, fortifications, a ship and other projects.

At the beginning of 1806, happily, several sea lions and seals were killed. That was the only fresh meat which the workers had received in a long time. Many of the Aleuts, when not working, fished for themselves. When they had a good catch, they would sometimes barter several fish with the promyshlenniks for articles of clothing. The promyshlenniks, consumed by hunger, gladly exchanged

---

*From such and similar orders it is easy to see that the Aleuts are the total slaves of the Company. Absolutely no Aleut would voluntarily leave Kodiak or any other island to go to Sitcha. Only a very few of them ever return to their families.

their last shirt or another necessary article of clothing for a fresh fish, resulting in their going around almost naked, only clothed in dirty, stinking sheepskins teeming with vermin.

At the end of January when fresh fish had become rare, a Kalusch, a former resident of the present Russian settlement, arrived with his wife and a female relative and went fishing in places he knew about. He caught such a large quantity of the best quality halibut that he could supply almost all of the inhabitants with fish. He bartered them for shirts, canvas and other articles of clothing and became a rich man in his own eyes within a short period of time. After having satiated a quantity of hungry guests for fourteen days, he paddled his canoe loaded with all kinds of clothing back home to his people. His example, however, did not induce the management, even at least for a little while, to send the promyshlenniks and Aleuts out fishing. They were once again as poorly fed as before.

Many of these shabby, sick men, who worked hard every day, were unfortunately indebted to the Company. It did not give them credit to buy the food they needed. It did not even give them the food they requested for money. If they lay exhausted and ill in bed, they were often thrashed out to work. The result was soon very visible. All work began to stop. One after another, wholly exhausted, they became prey to scurvy. What shocked my sensitivities the most and made me feel ill under those circumstances was the fact that, while the majority of those poor wretches lay ill, the overseers and assistant overseers, the clerks and their friends, patrons and hangers-on, of their own accord, sent the Aleuts out fishing and hunting. They crammed themselves full of wild ducks, geese, fish and fish pastes. They had free access to flour, rusk, sugar, salted meat, rice, molasses, brandy — in short — to everything nature and the storehouse had to offer, and they fed lavishly upon them.

In February, eight of the 150 youngest and healthiest people chosen from all of the Russian-American Company's outposts and taken there had died. More than 60 were lying in the barracks exhausted. Several of them were covered with scurvy sores. The barracks had neither a fireplace nor a stove; the windows were nailed tightly shut. The only warmth came from the infected exhalation of the sick men, in whom not one thought of cleanliness existed. Every evening the workers returned home soaked and covered with snow. They went to bed in their wet clothes and sheepskins or hung them up to dry in the room without anyone protesting about the situation in the least.

The signs of scurvy are usually languor, ill-humor, depression, soon followed by larger as well as smaller gangrenous spots on the legs from the knees to the toes that finally turn into abscesses. The men thus afflicted did not have to work. Instead, they had to stand guard day and night in the cold and in the wet, to provide for general security and to die miserably for the love of their fatherland.

They had heard that exercise was very good for scurvy. Therefore, the weakest ones were dragged against their will around the barracks by their comrades and others who still had some strength left, or else they were forced to carry or drag heavy stones around the rooms.*

Christian love, sympathy and responsibility, which we should practice toward our fellow man, is unknown there. Mr. John D'Wolf, one of the gentlest and kindest men I know, with whom I shared common joys and sorrows, sighed one day about the frequent deaths and said: "It is, indeed, extraordinary that Christians practice so little charity towards each other! The promyshlenniks' bodies are hastily buried. The whole burial is left to the Aleuts. Seldom does a friend, a comrade or a fellow countryman accompany one of them to the grave site. Funeral or burial ceremonies, as practiced even by the most uncivilized of peoples, and, for the sake of an example, which would be especially appropriate and decent here, seem to be nonexistent here!"

Considering it my duty as a doctor, I had endeavored to do everything I could within my power to help. But my loud voice, as well as Mr. von Davidoff's, raised daily, was too weak. I demanded in vain a dry, warm, airy, clean space, and even pointed one out, where the sick could be properly treated. I offered all medical help possible under the circumstances — but — all for nothing! Finally,

---

*Messrs. von Chwostoff and Davidoff tried in every way possible to put a stop to these abuses. The latter, in particular, was a true father to the sick and ready to help each one with a degree of sympathy rarely found. But the harshness of the assistant overseers, who were in part carrying out the orders, was beyond belief. Mr. von Baranoff had transferred his command to Mr. von Resanoff and said, after frequent suggestions made in vain: "Lord, let thy will, not mine, be done!" Mr. von Resanoff, totally unacquainted with such administration, depended upon a certain assistant overseer K . . . , who trimmed his sails according to the wind. He is one of the most insensitive men on earth, exceeding any character ever created by Shakespeare. Humanity would be better off if such people never were entrusted with any kind of power.

when they were convinced that the growing number of sick came from the destructive atmosphere in the damp, dirty, barracks filled with poisonous, stuffy air, they took the most dangerously ill men to an almost open, low, damp, cold hut. They expended so little care and attention on these helpless creatures that they did not even give them wood for a fire.*

There was even less thought given to suitable food, and often, very often, they tried to make me look like a fool. When I sent those sick men, who were pleading with me for help, to the man in charge of stores, and openly maintained that sugar, rice, molasses and other good, fresh food was the best medicine and that we should brew a kind of beer from a fir tree found there and syrup, a wholesome, anti-scurvy drink for the healthy and sick alike: "Some doctor" they said, "who prescribes good food and drink for his patients instead of medicine!"

Conditions at the settlement became more critical with each passing day. All work came to a standstill and only a few of the promyshlenniks were really strong and healthy. Now, gradually, an attempt was made to stop the terrible devastation from scurvy. But it was too late. Most of the sick had used up any strength they had. The assistant overseers had been misusing the trust placed in them by Messrs. von Baranoff and von Resanoff for several months. Together with their favorites, they had consumed and squandered most of the best provisions so that even with the best of intentions the sick could no longer be well treated.

Those circumstances woke Mr. von Resanoff up. He developed a plan for a new expedition to be undertaken by the *Juno* in order to procure fresh supplies.

He chose the northern Spanish possession (San Francisco) on the coast of New Albion for political reasons, even though he probably should have preferred the Sandwich Islands for economic reasons.

---

*As soon as the sick were taken there, they looked upon it as a sign of the end, of impending death. They had the same foreboding feeling as if they were being taken alive to the graveyard. This all seems exaggerated and improbable, especially since it has to be to the Company's advantage to save the lives of these men. For exactly that reason I find the proceedings incomprehensible. What could or should cause me to invent such unpleasant descriptions? Truly nothing would give me more pleasure than to entertain my readers with charming scenes of flourishing human happiness.

As soon as the decision had been made, the *Elisabeth* was sent to Kodiak to pick up the priest there. He was to accompany the expedition because Mr. von Resanoff hoped to enter into a closer friendly relationship through him with the religious Spanish.

I would ramble unnecessarily if I were to relate any more such domestic scenes about the management. I am including here several more observations about the natural history of New Archangel, which I had intended to send to Europe. May my honorable friend and teacher Councilor Blumenbach now still find things of interest in this letter which was originally addressed to him!

New Archangel (Norfolk Sound),
Northwest Coast of America
February 1806

To Councilor and Professor Blumenbach in Göttingen

— The dreadful storms, which I mentioned in my last letter to you, are nothing in comparison to the terrible moral storms I have been subjected to since that time.

A blind zeal for natural history and repeated promises, both written and oral, of all possible support for scientific research led me to believe that my thirst for knowledge would be satisfied; perhaps also a special development of Gall's *Wanderorgan* [migratory organ],[2] led me to leave Captain von Krusenstern's expedition and accompany Mr. von Resanoff to the Northwest Coast of America. I left Kamtschatka last year on June 14th — and arrived here August 26th.

Since then I have found myself in this remote part of the New World with daily sighs and intense longing for the Old World my only consolation. We found upon our arrival at this new outpost of the Russian-American Company a lack of all the necessities of life.

My living quarters were a miserable little room without furniture. I could shove my bed wherever I wanted to but still the water leaked upon it in the frequent downpours. A hunter was assigned me for company in the same room. Light came mainly from an oil lamp. I ate lunch, as did all of Mr. von Resanoff's companions, at Mr. von Baranoff's. He is the general manager of the Russian-American Company. He showed a rare generosity toward us and fed us the whole winter gratis to the best of his ability under the circumstances, and that on the Northwest Coast of America is no trifle. When, however, I wanted to eat something aside from the noon meal, I at times had to shoot ravens, hunt mussels or beg a piece of blubber or seal fat to still my hunger. If I had bought several pfunds of rusk from the Company's storehouse to feed one of the hungry workers and then returned again after a few days, I was accused of wastefulness.* Among other things that were sold was old stale rye flour from Siberia. It had probably been lying around the storehouses in Ochotsk or Kodiak for many years. It produced black, bitter, dry, tasteless bread. The numerous crew of hunters or promyshlenniks and Aleuts were fed dried fish, berries, train oil, whale and seal meat.

As soon as I had somewhat got my bearings, my principal occupation was to hunt waterfowl. This had a two-fold purpose. The meat served me as food and I could use the skins for purposes of natural history. Fortunately for me, powder and shot were to be had from the storehouse. I sometimes only obtained it unwillingly after many objections and then for payment. In the beginning I did not understand well enough how the system worked. Shyly, modestly and discreetly, I requested a lot of things from the assistant overseers, to whom I had been sent, but received nothing. Finally, I simply took what I had been asking for and, thus, found myself often in possession of objects which had been refused me because they were not available. Among other things obtained in this fashion, I count, especially, a good leather boat (baidarka), without which I could not have undertaken my hunting trips and other excursions on the water.

The many abuses prevailing here, the outrages I had unfortunately to witness, the vexation and anger to which I was subjected daily and which dashed all of my spirits and activity — all of these, my most esteemed friend, do not offer you much entertainment, so I would prefer to relate some observations of natural history instead.

The climate is not as raw as you might suspect at such a northern latitude (57° N). The whole winter it was ten to twelve degrees Réaumur — the average on the thermometer. On January 11, 1806, the coldest day, we had 16° below the freezing point. Mr. John D'Wolf II, a free citizen of the United American States who wintered here, was surprised to find the cold on the Northwest Coast of America much milder than in Boston, Rhode Island and other provinces of the United States lying much further south. Shipping is possible here the whole year. Only

*Everything is sold on credit as a mater of course since no money is in circulation.

a few inlets totally surrounded by mountains and islands are sometimes covered with a thin coat of ice. Occasionally, violent storms come up or rather terrible gusts of wind of not very long duration. Heavy downpours are common throughout the year. Snow is of little importance and falls from December to March or April. Thunder storms occur rarely in the summer, more often, however, in December and January. In the winter months the atmosphere is often so highly charged with electricity that it is common place to see the bayonet on the muskets or the metal head of the flagstaff on the fortified hill emitting a blue-green electrical light (St. Helen's or St. Elmo's fire) for several hours in the darkness of the night.[3]

There is no level ground of any size in the neighborhood of the outpost. On every side are steep and almost inaccessible hills covered with thick, dark woods. If one can find level ground with a southern exposure anywhere in this area, perhaps at the foot of Mount Edgecumbe, and clear it, it would probably be possible to cultivate it. Barley, which Mr. von Baranoff had planted on a little island, ripened. Potatoes grow very well. There are supposed to be many hot days in summer, but the high mountains covered with woods continually attract clouds, making the area exceedingly wet. Mr. von Baranoff has often attempted to clear part of the woods near the outpost by fire but has never succeeded. In all of the low areas there are large, deep morasses.

Down the sea coast, the high mountains are made of solid, highly mixed, coarse and finely grained granite. Some are very pointed, rocky, broken and bare. Others are of middle height and covered up to the top with woods, especially spruce (*Pinus canadensis*) and balsam poplars. The woods and mountains are utterly impenetrable because of their rugged steep slopes and numbers of fallen trees. It is astonishing to see immense tree trunks hanging from rocks barely covered with earth, their roots encircling them in their search for stability and nourishment. Many of the trees here are over six fuss in diameter and 150 fuss tall. They provide good lumber for ships and masts. The natives make their canoes from a single tree trunk. I have seen them up to fifty fuss long, four and one-half fuss wide and almost three fuss high with room for up to thirty people.

One finds quantities of several types of tasty berries, especially the pricker-less American raspberry and black currant. The season was so far advanced that I could not collect any botanical treasures but for several flowering mosses.

Mammals found here include whales, seals, sea lions, sea, marsh and river otters, brown and black bears. The latter I have never had an opportunity to examine closely. On account of the size and the nature of the fur I have often seen, I have concluded that the American black bear must be a very different species from the brown bear.

I have observed the following birds on my frequent hunting trips:

Anas histrionica. This beautiful duck arrives at the end of September and winters here. It is shy, fast of flight and is always seen in groups of four to six.

Anas perspicillata. This duck, rarely seen in Europe, did not make its appearance before the end of September; after that it was common here. It is an exceedingly crafty duck, which lives in very large flocks. In the evening they fly out to open sea. In the morning they send one or several scouts to explore and inspect the area they want to visit during the day to see if ambushes are waiting. One or two ducks always stay on the surface of the water as guards while the majority of the flock dives for food.

Anas glacialis. Seldom seen at Norfolk Sound but common at Kodiak. It nests on that island and on the coast of the Alaksa Peninsula. The harmonious, trumpet-like call of this bird distinguishes it from the other ducks. It dives very deep and lives mainly from small mussels. When diving, it takes a large supply of air with it, which it releases in small quantities from time to time. In calm weather one can trace its path under the water by following the little bubbles rising to the surface. It swims very fast for long distances.

Anas bucephala. In my opinion, this duck, *Anas albeola* and *Anas rustica* in Gmelin's *Systema Naturae*, are one and the same.[4] It arrives at Norfolk Sound at the beginning of October.

Besides these, I frequently saw the following species: *Anas boschas*, *Anas marila*, *Anas crecca*, *Anas fusca* and several other less distinct types of ducks. In addition: *Colymbus auritus*, *Colymbus arcticus*, *Colymbus Grylle*, *Mergus Serrator*, *Mergus Merganser*, *Pelecanus Urile*, *Pelecanus Graculus*, *Larus glaucus*, *Larus marinus*, etc., *Alcedo Alcyon*, *Corvus Stelleri*, *Corvus an corax*, *Tetrao Lagopus* — the black stripe from the bill to the eyes is hardly distinguishable — *Ampelis Garrulus*, *Sylvia Troglodites*, *Strix nyctea*, *Strix passerina*, *Turdus naevius*.

Diomedea exulans or albatross — Of these birds I have only seen several black-brown ones and others that were almost completely white.

The former appeared to be younger, the latter older. Usually, they appear here in the north in March and April in large numbers. This is the time when shoals of herring appear that they eat with relish. The Aleuts call these birds *aglica*. No one living in these northern regions has seen their nests. Albatrosses have very strong bills and produce a call that sounds like the muffled, hoarse bleating of a goat or a sheep. That is probably the reason for the French calling them *mouton du Cap*.

In February, I was given one of these birds which did not appear to have the slightest injury. In answer to my question how it had been caught: by hand. After repeated, exact questioning, the Aleuts assured me that these birds are absolutely unable to fly in the calms that usually follow strong storms. If they pursued them, sometimes they would attempt to go faster by running on top of the water. They could, nevertheless, easily be overtaken by the Aleutian leather boats (baidarkas), caught by hand or killed with an oar or arrow. They are very thin when they arrive in the spring. But after a very short time of enjoying herring, they become very fat and are good to eat.

We, as well as many other seafarers, have observed this bird in the South Seas and between the Tropics of Cancer and Capricorn. I believe it most probable that these birds, which are only known to nest on Cape Horn, flourish from the most southern regions of the earth to the most northern.

Thus, I am saying that the albatross, which never touches the waves of the ocean during a storm but rather, even then, audaciously defies it by gliding quickly just above the surface of the water, which seems to enjoy the most terrible of winds, which has chosen the feared regions of Cape Horn as its favorite place to live, which can stand the temperatures in all climates, which flourishes from the South Pole through the hottest zones of the earth to the North Pole, is said to be unable to fly under certain circumstances and during an absolute calm, despite its gigantic wingspread of ten to twelve fuss!

Falco leucocephalus: Individual birds belonging to this species of beautiful, white-headed, white-tailed eagles can be seen here almost the entire year. In the fall they usually migrate south, only to return in the spring when the herring appear in great quantities along the coast. Even though fish are their favorite food, they do prey upon ducks, geese and young sea lions. Their meat is edible. The Russians, in the first year after their arrival, here killed and ate two hundred of them. I have often stilled my hunger with their meat and found it tasty. The intestines have to be carefully removed. The liver is said to be very harmful, indeed, even poisonous.

These birds nest in high trees at Norfolk Sound and on cliffs at Unalaska. They use the same nest made of twigs and lined with down for several years in a row. The eggs are said to be the size of chicken eggs.

The Kalusch or natives of this area use several parts of the birds for ornaments. For ceremonies and dances they cover their heads with their down, thus making themselves look as if they were powdered in the European fashion. They hold their tails and wings in their hands as fans. The wing bones, especially radius and ulna, are used as straws during illnesses, above all by young girls when entering upon an important period of their maturation. (See below.)

Haematopus ostralegus is rarer here than at Unalaska and on other Aleutian Islands. Its plumage is completely black at all ages and times of the year. I find no specific differences between this bird and the European one.

As you know, my esteemed friend, I spent a lot of time on ichthyology, especially in Lissabon and Japan. It must be all the more remarkable for you, then, to find no list of fish included here. The main reason is that the numbers of hungry people skulking around here try to eat them up immediately. Aside from the salmon, halibut, cod, and herring usually found off the Aleutian Islands, I have not seen any other species. The latter usually arrive in April to spawn in the area. The natives place a quantity of spruce twigs weighted down with stones in shallow water. These fish deposit their roe on them. Due to their natural glue they stick to them. These twigs have a beautiful red appearance when covered by roe and give the roe (which as a result is served as a delicacy) a not unpleasant aromatic taste.

The sea is rich in all kinds of products. There are usually large polyps, sea mice (*Aphrodita*). A new species of *Sepia*, mussels, especially *Lepas*, *Chiton*, *Pholas*, *Pinna*, *Mytilus* and quantities of worms, zoophytes and mollusks, medusas, *Echinus*, *Asterias*, *Spongia*, etc. My friend and traveling companion Councilor Tilesius, who has gained a lot of recognition in this branch of natural history, would probably like it better here than I do. I would have liked to have preserved this or that specimen for him, but I had to suppress the thought. Even if I had been given the necessary brandy and bottles — which I doubt very much would have happened — transporting them overland to St. Petersburg seems too costly and almost impossible.

With these admittedly short remarks from my miserable winter quarters I commend myself to your distant love and kindness and remain yours truly.

— Dr. L.

NOTES

1. John D'Wolf II (1779-1872) was a member of the very prosperous D'Wolf family of Bristol, Rhode Island. Probably using Langsdorff's book for a great deal of his information, he published *A Voyage to the North Pacific and a Journey through Siberia more than Half a Century Ago* (Cambridge: Welch, Bigelow, 1861).

2. Dr. Franz Joseph Gall (1758-1828) was the father of phrenology and an early researcher in the anatomy and physiology of the brain. Gall tried to localize feelings, activities, and instincts to specific parts of the brain. Langsdorff is probably referring to Gall's statement about hibernation or migration: "The homing organ every year preserves half of the animals from going to an unavoidable death. Man, driven by this organ, explores countries, the seas and the infinite space of our worlds. Without this organ how much less knowledge, how many fewer remedies, objects of admiration we would have. Eliminate for a moment the organs for painting, music, architecture, drawing, sculpture, and there would be no more masterpieces by Raffael, Mozart, Michelangelo, Canova, Homer, etc." (Franz Joseph Gall, *Naturforscher und Anthropologe*, ausgewählte Texte, übersetzt und kommentiert von Erna Lesky [Stuttgart: Huber, 1979], p. 91).

3. St. Elmo's (also St. Ulmo's) fire or light is named after the patron saint of sailors, St. Elmo (d. A.D. 303).

4. Johann Friedrich Gmelin (1748-1804) edited *Linné, Carl von (1707-1778) . . . Caroli a Kinne . . . Systema maturae per regna*, ed. 13, Lipsiae, impensis G. E. Beer, 1788-93. He was a professor of medicine and philosophy in Göttingen. His uncle, Johann Georg Gmelin (1709-1755), in Russian service, explored Siberia from 1733 to 1743.

Chapter 5

The Natives of Norfolk Sound (Kalusch) in the Russian settlement. Visits to them. Their Customs and Habits.

Immediately after the conquest of New Archangel and the conclusion of peace with the Russians, the Kalusch withdrew, choosing to live on a high rocky point of land at 57°46′ N and 134°40′ W on the northeastern part of the Island of Sitcha.[1] They have fortified it heavily against possible Russian attacks, even though they seem to be on very friendly terms and visit from time to time in New Archangel. Their friendly stance is undoubtedly caused mainly by the Russian victory over them as well as their fear and terror of the superior power of Russian firearms. Usually, parties consisting of several persons of both sexes arrive in large, artfully decorated canoes made from a single log. They always approach the Russian settlement singing and rowing rhythmically. Just before reaching the landing, they stop and one of them gives a long speech. They do not go on land until Nanok, i.e., Mr. von Baranoff or one of his representatives, comes down to the landing and gives them permission to land and assures them of a friendly reception. The interpreters told me that these speeches, of high rhetorical art and apparently of long connected phrases, always repeat one and the same thought, often using the same words, e.g., "We were your enemies, we did you harm, you were our enemies, you did us harm, we want to be good friends, we want to forget the past, we do not plan to do you any more harm, do not do anything more to us also, be our good friends, etc." This and similar kinds of speeches often last half an hour. Only after receiving assurances of friendship and a good reception do they go on land. Mr. von Baranoff, who has been studying their customs for years, usually has a tent erected immediately and a plentiful meal prepared. Only the chief or the highest ranking member of the party is permitted on the fortified hill, but none of the others. The quantity of food that one of these Kalusch can eat is incredible. They like rice, berries, seal meat, seal oil, fish, etc. They never eat whale blubber or whale oil, and ask each time not to be served such food. As much as they might perhaps like to drink brandy, they refuse to do so because they know its effect and are afraid of being robbed of their senses and then falling under the authority of the Russians.

The Kalusch are for the most part of medium build and strong body. They have black hair and dirty-colored skin (which they make worse by smearing themselves with earth, coal and bright ochers), usually large, fiery eyes without the characteristics of the Mongolian race, a small, flat, wide nose, wide cheek bones and very coarse facial features. The men usually have few or no beard hairs because they pluck them out immediately as soon as they begin to show. Several girls and women, most of whom lived with Russian promyshlenniks, whose skin had been cleaned of all dirt, were as white as Europeans and did not have unpleasant facial features.

Their clothing is very simple; aside from a loin cloth, it consists of a single rectangular piece of cloth, blanket, or fur about five fuss wide, whose two ends are fastened at the neck or with a button and button hole. In recent years the American Free States have traded a lot of European chenilles or overcoats made from woolen material, English boy, or frieze with the Kalusch. That is why one now sees a lot of Indians dressed in the European manner. They prefer red and blue.

This clothing is worn only for show or when the weather is coldest. When doing everyday activities, felling trees, fishing, building canoes, etc., they usually go naked. Small children still at their mothers' breasts were barely wrapped in old rags or mats even though it was 8 to 10 degrees outside. I often had to admire the physical stamina of these people, because it is difficult to find another people who have hardened their bodies so much against the effects of a raw climate.

Usually, the Kalusch came with the intention of doing a little barter. They brought along sea otter pelts, gave them to Mr. von Baranoff and then asked for items they needed equal in value to their gift. If they were not satisfied or asked for too much, they then took back the pelts they had presented as a gift.*

The usual entertainment during their visits, which lasted for several days, consisted of eating, drinking and dancing. Preparation for such entertainment required several hours. Only the men dance. Their toilet,

*I have already said above that the Russians did not really carry on any trade with the Kalusch. The few pelts traded during such encounters do not constitute trade in the true sense of the word.

which requires no less time than that of a European lady, consists of painting their faces and decorating their heads. They, as it were, powder their hair with eagle down (*Falco leucocephalus*) and adorn it with ermine fur. They paint many regular figures on their faces with coal dust, chalk, ochers and cinnabar. This, so to speak, is a substitute for tattooing, which I have not seen among these people. They have become dependent upon using little mirrors during their toilet. These are brought every year by the ships of the United American Free States.*

The women, who stand a few steps away from the dancers, substitute for musicians by singing a not unharmonious melody usually in three-eighths time.

The dance itself, in which the men hardly move from the position they take at the beginning, consists of frequent, very vigorous, intense leaps. They are all barefoot, covered only with a blanket, a wide woolen frock (chenille), as I have mentioned above. One of the dancers, as it were, leads the others. In his hand he has a thick staff decorated with the teeth of sea otters. With this he strongly marks the beat by hitting the ground. All of them without exception hold in their hands either the tail or the wing of a bald eagle or several ermine pelts, which they prize very highly as adornment and luxury articles. They not only braid them into their hair or hold them in their hands but also sew them on their clothes.

The women dress simply. Their bodies and breasts are always covered. Many of them wear long shirts. Their feet are bare. Aside from that, they have the strangest, most adventurous, and one may also say, most unnatural concept of beauty imaginable. I have already mentioned above that the Aleuts and inhabitants of Kodiak, of masculine sex, make a slit in their lower lips parallel to their mouths and insert ornaments made of glass beads, mussel shells or enamel into it. The Kalusch women have carried this concept of beauty much further. When a young girl reaches thirteen or fourteen or the period of becoming a woman, a small opening is made right under the middle of her lower lip. At first a thick wire is put in it and then a wooden double button or a small cylinder which is somewhat thicker at the ends. This opening, over the course of several months or years, is gradually enlarged. The lower lip is expanded wider and wider by inserting an

---

*Before acquiring mirrors they acted as hairdressers for each other since they could not paint their own faces and adorn their own heads.

oval or elliptical little board or plate into this opening. Thus, every woman looks as if a large, flat, wooden soup spoon had grown in the flesh of her lower lip. The outer edge of the little plate has a groove, so that the lower lip, which has been stretched considerably, adheres more firmly to it.

This kind of lip ornamentation, this very peculiar concept of beauty, which seems so abominable to us Europeans, is found along the coast of Northwest America from 50° to 60° N latitude. All of the women, no matter what rank, have such spoons under their mouths. Their size seems to be determined either by age or rank. It is two to three zolls long, about one and one-half to two zolls wide and at the most one-half zoll thick. The wives of the chiefs, however, wear ones that are generally much longer and thicker. I myself saw a lady of very high rank with a lip oval which was fully five zolls long and three zolls wide. Mr. D'Wolf II, who is one least likely to exaggerate and has sailed the *Juno* along the entire coast from 50° to 57° N while trading for sea otters, assured me that at Chatham Street [sic — Strait] he had seen an old woman, the wife of a chief, whose lip spoon was so large that, whenever she moved her lower lip, her entire face was almost covered by it.

In answer to the very natural question: what might be the possible purpose of this uncomfortable adornment? I can give my readers no answer — I could only list a lot of other tasteless and silly customs and habits of much more civilized peoples and compare them to this one and then ask in all honesty: why do Chinese ladies of rank consider it beautiful to render their feet useless in the name of art? Why do married Japanese women blacken their teeth? Why have people not yet thought of a cleaner method than carrying the dirt of their noses around in their pockets? Why do we, when appearing in gala dress, powder our hair with the finest flour? But let me return to the lip ornaments. Without knowing the purpose of this custom, the disadvantage of this artificial extension of the lip cannot be overlooked. Everyone has to recognize immediately that it makes it impossible to give the fair sex on the Northwest Coast of America a kiss.

Since my arrival at Norfolk Sound, I had been wanting to get to know the Kalusch better. This desire gradually became so strong that at the end of October I decided to visit these people, despite their natural hate and enmity toward the Russians, at their houses on the northeastern side of the island about 120 to 130 versts from the Russian outpost. Mr. von Baranoff thought that my excursion would probably not be dangerous because of the victory over them which was still fresh in their minds. Despite this, he advised me not to go because one can never know the character of these people exactly. Mr. von Resanoff thought the same thing. I, however, believed we would be well received, for Mr. D'Wolf, who had sailed during the summer to Chatham Strait, to Prince Frederik Sound and to other places and personally knew most of the chiefs through trade, wanted to accompany me. Mr. von Baranoff, to provide more security, permitted the only Kalusch woman (from Norfolk Sound) living among the Russians to go along and act as interpreter. She was the daughter of a chief who had been in the enemy fortification back then on the northeastern side of the archipelago. About five years before, at the time of the first conquest of Sitcha, she had been living with a Russian. At the time of the mutiny by her fellow countrymen, she had been spared and returned to her parents afterwards. During the last seizure of New Archangel after the conquest of the fortification, she voluntarily stayed there in order again to keep company with the Russians. She was very willing to accompany us to visit her parents and then return to the Russian settlement.

At this point, let me give a few geographical details before beginning with a description of the excursion.

We are indebted to the meritorious Vancouver for providing us with the exact location of the King George III's Archipelago (from 56°15′ to 58°28′ and from 134°18′ to 136°15′ W). He only explored and determined its coastline and assumed that the entire stretch of land was one island, since he could not carefully explore every single bay and inlet. Permit me to add the following supplemental information to his admirable work: Mount Edgecumbe is not joined to the mainland of the archipelago but is an island separated by a wide, navigable channel sprinkled with several small islands. It connects the Bay of Islands (baie des Iles) with Norfolk Sound.* King George III's Archipelago** is divided into two sizeable islands by this wide channel, which is several miles wide in a few places, and connected to the big Ocean by Chatham Strait.

The Kalusch, after the loss of their possessions on Norfolk Sound, had settled on the northeastern point of land at the mouth of

---

*This Bay of Islands (57°35′ N) leads to a spacious navigable strait, which runs from the northeastern coast (57°46′ and 134°40′ W) to Chatham Strait.

**See Vancouver's chart of King George III's Archipelago.

the above-mentioned strait. There they sought to protect themselves from further attacks, especially from the Russians, by building a kind of fort on a rocky elevation. Mr. D'Wolf and I were interested enough to want to visit their fort in the only area of the archipelago still inhabited by natives and also to get to know the strait discovered by the Russians and Aleuts. We were also forced, as it were, to think of interesting diversions, since our friends, our only companions and translators, Messrs. Chwostoff and Davidoff, had sailed on the *Juno* several weeks before for Kodiak, and as a result we were almost totally left to our own devices.

We, therefore, began preparations for carrying out our plan. We collected guns, pistols, powder and flint for hunting and protection; rusk, dried fish, rice, tea, sugar and brandy for food, some kitchen utensils, a small tent to live in, several axes for chopping wood and several *ells* of cloth, baize, and canvas, glass beads, sewing needles, tobacco, large fishing hooks, mirrors and other trifles as presents for the chiefs and other Indians. Thus outfitted, we were ready to depart at four o'clock on the morning of October 26th.

Thanks to Mr. von Baranoff's generosity, we had the use of three three-man baidarkas. Mr. D'Wolf sat in the one, the Kalusch woman, our translator, in the other, and I in the third. Each one of us had two Aleuts as rowers, whom we also helped since we had been going out on frequent hunting trips on the water for several months and had rowed quite often.

The weather was clear and beautiful. The very sharp cold fired us to row ever more quickly in order to warm up our bodies through motion. On that morning we rowed around Mount Edgecumbe. Toward noon we reached the mouth of the Bay of Islands (baie des Iles), where we could see the open ocean, and then headed toward the northeast. At first we found ourselves in a wide, roomy channel that large ships could use. The shores were steep. Here and there they were rocky and partially covered with dark fir trees up to the foot of the mountains. The influence of the ebb and flood tide, even though perceptible, was of little importance. After rowing about six versts, we found that the shores on both sides were growing closer and closer together until they formed a narrow passageway. The ebbing tide flowed so rapidly toward us that our diligent rowers could make no headway against its force. The sun was going down when the Aleuts suggested landing in the area, camping for the night and waiting for the tide to change. We, therefore, rowed as close as possible to the narrow passage and found about a verst southeast of it a comfortable landing place where we, stiff from cold and wearied by the day's exertion, looked first and foremost for dry wood in the nearby woods and fresh water. Then, warmed by a good fire with a teakettle on it, we pitched our tent and cooked a good soup from the catch of the day's hunt. I had shot a wild duck (*Anas histrionica*), several sea gulls and a large white-headed eagle. We readied the duck immediately for the kettle. It tasted, even though a bit oily and thin, quite good. I saved the eagle in order to skin it for purposes of natural history when an opportunity presented itself. While we were thus occupied, we saw a canoe in the distance with several Kalusch coming toward us. They turned out to be a chief and his wife and two other people, all acquaintances of our translator. They had seen our fire and said they had come looking for company. They asked for permission to stay and upon receiving it pitched their tent at once. It consisted of two forked poles that were rammed into the ground and used to hold a third. They leaned several branches from nearby trees up against it. They then covered this with thin, wide boards or tree bark which they had brought with them. This roof-like wall of the half open tent was placed towards the wind and a large fire was built in front of it. The fire, along with several rugs and fur blankets used as coverings, served to protect these people adequately from the cold, which dropped to two or three degrees below the freezing point in the night.

Soon, our Kalusch interpreter let us know that the chief had come mainly in the hope of receiving a gift. She suggested that we demonstrate our friendliness by giving him and his wife several leaves of tobacco, sewing needles and other trifles. We did this to his great satisfaction and proceeded to spend the night peacefully together. We parted the following morning as very good friends.

When we set out on the morning of the 27th, the tide was favorable. We had hardly reached the passage when we found ourselves unable to control our canoe because the current was so rapid that we felt like we were caught in a waterfall. The distance from one shore to the other at the narrowest point is 150 klafters at the most, the length of the passage probably 150 to 200 paces and the fall we guessed to be about five fuss. The middle of the passage is totally free of rocks. Along each side, however, there are individual rocks which would make it very difficult for a ship to pass through. Despite this danger, the Russians have already sailed through there successfully several times with ships of 150 tons or more. Mr. D'Wolf, a very experienced seaman, told me he had never experienced such a rapid tide anywhere and considered it a very risky undertaking by the Russians to put themselves and their ships in such danger. As soon as we were through the passage, we found ourselves in a wide, extensive bay. Inlets, islands and rocks alternated with each other. The distance between the shores at several points was about 15 to 20 versts. The wind blowing from the northeast slowed down our forward progress and prevented us from reaching our destination as planned. We rowed along the eastern shore and finally discovered toward evening, as we were looking around for a landing place and campsite, smoke several versts in the distance pinpointing a solitary Kalusch dwelling. We set out with renewed energy to reach the spot before nightfall. When we found no one there upon our arrival, I wanted to send one of our Aleuts, who understood some of the local tongue, up to the hut, but he and our interpreter said that the owner had to invite us. So we stayed in our baidarka until they noticed us and the chief or head of the family came toward us and asked us to come on land and spend the night at his place.

We found a little hut made of boards. It was somewhat longer than wide, covered with tree bark. It was warmed by a large fire burning in its middle. Several openings in the roof and the door acted as a chimney. That is why the inside resembled a smokehouse more than a home. This similarity was reinforced by the quantity of fish hanging in it and the lack of cleanliness. The chief's sleeping area was opposite the door. On all sides there were individual sleeping areas, separated by logs, for the rest of his family or servants, about twelve to fifteen people. We were directed to a place right in front of the chief's sleeping area just behind the fire. We were served freshly cooked fish and berries and then, tired, we let refreshing sleep overtake us.

The following morning we showed our gratitude by giving our host several apparently welcome, small gifts. He offered to sell us several sea otter pelts, but we did not accept his offer because we still had to hand out a lot of gifts on our trip and had to use our trade goods somewhat sparingly. I regretted not having prepared myself for more trading. In the hut I had spied a very large, completely black bearskin, the most beautiful and largest I had ever seen (it was about five or six fuss long and over four fuss wide). Our host offered to sell it to me for the extremely small sum of five ells of English cloth. Since, however, our future security perhaps depended upon our generously distributing gifts to the parents of our interpreter and other chiefs at the fortification, we did not dare to trade the most valuable article we had brought along.

We once again had all of our equipment carried to the baidarkas and were delighted to see that not a single one of these needy people had attempted to steal even one small item from us.

The channel once again narrowed. We had hardly left our night's lodgings when we saw to the east the mouth of the channel leading into Chatham Strait. It is only a few versts wide. On its north shore we saw another house which we did not want to leave unvisited. We soon reached the hut and found a chief named Schinchetäez, the only member of the entire Kalusch tribe who had become a hanger-on of the Russians from the beginning of their conquest and had thereby reaped the hate of all of his people, so that he, scorned by many, now lived separately only with his family. He received us very hospitably and readily offered us a meal of fresh fish (halibut) and a lodging place for the night. We, however, considered it more advisable to continue onto the fortification about ten to fifteen versts from there. The wind and waves were against us. The waves rolled so forcefully into the mouth of the channel that we could only row a few versts with the greatest effort. We were very worried to have night falling without having reached our destination. It was impossible to go back since our way was blanketed in darkness. Landing near the fortification would perhaps have aroused suspicion, since the fire we would have had to build to protect us from the cold would have betrayed us. We decided it was best to head to the fortification even in the dark. We had hardly made our decision when we were seen from land. There were repeated loud calls in a language I did not understand (probably: who is there?), but neither our interpreter nor one of the Aleuts replied: "Good friend!" This caprice embarrassed both Mr. D'Wolf and me. Just as I wanted to express my displeasure, a shot of alarm was fired from the nearby shore, thus causing them to acknowledge who we were. Almost at the same moment when the muffled shot was echoing through the woods and rebounding off of the nearby rocks, we saw a lot of movement on land. Several hundred naked men armed with guns and others carrying large firebrands and burning torches of fir thronged around the landing. The sight of them did not make a very happy impression upon us, since we did not yet know whether we were dealing with friends or enemies. As soon as we acknowledged who we were and our Aleuts had pulled our baidarkas up on the landing, boisterous Kalusch surrounded us immediately and carried us literally on their hands* across a small, shallow stretch

---

*Later I found out that this was their way of showing a guest the greatest respect and esteem.

of path and urged us toward the fortification. We did not even have enough time to tell our Aleuts to guard our belongings before numbers of ministering spirits took possession of them, we had no idea whether as plunder or not. Accompanied by a large number of torch-bearers, we moved toward the fortification standing on a high cliff whose access was protected by many felled trees, some of which we climbed over and some of which we had to go around, and this was not made less complicated by the darkness of the night.

We were immediately taken into the very spacious living quarters of the chief, Dlchătin, the father of our companion. He received us very graciously and directed us to a place opposite the entrance to the hut in front of his own sleeping area. Here we, while being gaped at by several hundred natives, spread out the blankets we had brought with us in the light of a large fire burning in the middle of a somewhat raised, free-standing hearth. What surprised us the most was that they brought us all of our belongings from the baidarkas and not even the smallest trifle had been stolen, even though undoubtedly there were things which the bearers would have liked to own and which they could very easily, unnoticed, have put to the side in the darkness of the night. In the haste of our reception, Mr. D'Wolf had even forgotten to take along his musket, pistols and powder horn when leaving the baidarka. They were all delivered to him untouched and undamaged.

We had hardly refreshed ourselves by drinking several cups of tea and a little glass of punch we had prepared when the oldest and most eminent chief or commander of the fortification invited us to him. He gave us a very friendly reception. He presented me with a sea otter pelt and Mr. D'Wolf with a beautiful sea otter tail. We then returned to our host's because we were tired from the day's trip and longed for quiet and sleep. While we ate a good tasting dish prepared from fresh fish and rice, we were entertained by cheerful, harmonious singing from a lot of people camped around the fire. I have never regretted so much knowing so little about music, otherwise I certainly would have immediately written down that lively, pleasing melody.

During the night it was cold and windy. Nonetheless, several people, probably members of the family, went out barefoot into the nearby woods and brought back blocks of wood on their bare shoulders. They gradually added them to the fire in the hut until it turned into a high funeral pyre. I still cannot comprehend why the roof covered with bark did not catch fire. The flames reached the ceiling which had only an opening instead of a chimney. The sparks flew through the air as if from a smith's forge so that we dared not fall asleep, despite our exhaustion, until the fire, which burned all night, burned less furiously and the apparent danger was past.

Early on the 29th, the first autumn snow surprised us. That morning we presented the commandant with the gifts which we owed him in return for his gifts the evening before. At the same time we also gave several gifts to our interpreter's parents, because she told us that such gifts, if presented later, would no longer be of any great value. We gave her father several ells of cloth, a large knife, fishing hooks and several pounds of tobacco and her mother a chemise, sewing needles, a small mirror, ribbon, glass beads, etc.

After we had carried out the usual ceremonies, we walked around all over the place without being bothered by escorts. I even shot several birds near the fort without capturing these people's attention. Perhaps this confidence was in great measure due to the fact that Mr. D'Wolf had traded with them the preceding summer when the *Juno* was in Chatham Strait and now met here many acquaintances who considered me his companion and also an American.

The Russians generally call the peoples along most of the Northwest Coast of America Kalusch or Kolosch. The ones I am describing call themselves G-tinkit, or G-chinket, or also G-chit-cha-chon, i.e., residents of Schitcha or Sitki. Formerly they lived at Norfolk Sound. Their only place of residence is the northeastern point of land at the mouth of the above-named strait, a cliff rising several hundred fuss perpendicularly from the water. The only possible access to it lies on a northwestern point of land. Easy access is blocked by a large quantity of enormous tree trunks or an entanglement. The cliff itself is secured against enemy attack by a double palisade twelve to fifteen fuss high and three to four fuss thick made of tree trunks placed closely together. In addition, on the side toward the sea, a high natural wall of earth protects the living quarters behind it so that they cannot be seen by any ships.

The houses within the fort are long rectangles of various sizes built in regular rows a few klafters apart from each other. The roof, made of wide pieces of bark placed on top of each other, rests on about ten to twelve thick posts sunk deep into the earth. The side walls of the hut are formed by setting wide, thick boards into these posts. The entrance is at the gable end, which is occasionally painted bright earthen colors.

The inside, like the people themselves, is extraordinarily dirty. The smoke, the stench of fish and train oil, their faces smeared with coal and earth and distorted by lip spoons are disgusting. Many of their unbelievable activities caused feelings of repugnance and loathing. For example, many of them hunted vermin in their stinking fur clothing and immediately put their living catch into their mouths.

Courage and natural intelligence, age, worldly goods obtained through successful sea otter hunts or through advantageous trade and the larger number of people belonging to a single family seemed to me to determine the rank and reputation of a Kalusch. When I say chief in reference to these people, I mean the head of a numerous family, who has the powers of an independent father of the family. He gives his subjects orders and punishes them when they disobey. It seems to me that a common interest in independence has forced these people to live together in one fort in order to provide security and resistance against enemy attacks. Every family, moreover, lives for itself and is often gone for weeks on end hunting and fishing. The family of Chief Dlchätin, our interpreter's father, had approximately thirty to forty members. They all lived together in his hut. The number of inhabitants at the fort was somewhere between thirteen and fourteen hundred people.

Individual families, just as with individual tribes, occasionally have disputes, for example the inhabitants of George III's Archipelago with the inhabitants on the large Admiralty Island lying to the east of them. But, as soon as a common enemy, for example the Russians, attack them, they unite to the common defense. All private quarrels are decided by the right of the strongest. When an enemy from a neighboring tribe is captured during a dispute, he must serve as a slave until a ransom is paid for him. This is usually a fixed price, such as a given number of sea otter pelts.

The principal food stuffs are: fresh and smoked fish, fish roe and seal. In the spring and summer various types of seaweed are added to their diet which, when cooked, produce a bitter soup. In addition, they eat mussels (*Pinna Mytilus* and *Mya*) mollusks (*Sepia*), fiber of spruce trees beaten into a square cake, and roots and berries mixed together with train oil. They love the rice and molasses which were introduced by the Americans. Instead of salt they use seawater. They never eat whale meat; perhaps some kind of prejudice is the reason. They abhor whale oil to the same degree that Jews abhor pork. Nevertheless, they do occasionally give large pieces of whales found beached along their coast to the starving Russian promyshlenniks and Aleuts to their delight. They even reject brandy, which the Russians offer them sometimes, as a destructive, stupor-inducing drink.

Along with hunting and fishing, their main occupation consists in skillfully building highly exact canoes from one single tree trunk. Some of these boats can carry thirty to forty people. In leisure hours they fashion wooden bowls, masks and fish hooks. Fishing line is mostly made from a kind of dried seaweed which is often ten klafters long. That people's weapons earlier consisted of bows and arrows. Since trade ships from the United American States have been visiting them every year, they have obtained so many guns and gunpowder that they only use arrows when hunting sea otter and seal. Captain D'Wolf assured me that one can now buy the best English arms on this part of the Northwest Coast of America more cheaply than in England. As soon as a screw is lost or a spring sprung, the weapon becomes useless. For this reason in recent years, the trade ships decided it was practical always to take along a skilled metal smith or gunsmith on board. Useless guns are bought at one place and sold again as new at another. The Kalusch, nevertheless, understand what constitutes a good gun so well that seldom or never do they buy a bad one. Even the women know how to use a gun very well. They often go hunting. Sometimes they make blankets of the delicate wool of a supposed wild sheep. As far as I know, the animal itself is not included in any natural history. They are expert basket weavers. They weave exceedingly delicate as well as thick baskets from tree fiber and grass capable of carrying water. The women's summer occupation consists especially of collecting stores for the winter, that is, in picking berries and cleaning fish.

The men place no great value on any kind of special decoration. They paint their faces and love European sailors' clothing, along with a round hat or a shirt, ermine fur and eagle tails. The women wear lip spoons and like to wear necklaces and earrings made of glass beads and mollusks (sea ear, *Haliotis* probably *Iris*). In recent years so many have been brought in that their value has fallen completely. Another mussel shell highly prized by the Aleuts, the tooth shell (*Dentalium entalis*), called *tache* or *heikva* here, is still highly prized. American seafarers, because of its value, have had this mussel shell produced in porcelain in England. The surface appearance of these artificial mussel shells resembled the real ones completely in color, size, luster. The Kalusch, despite this, detected the fraud and disdained them, thus bringing the speculation to naught. The women also like to wear many thick, steel iron wire bracelets. Children's clothing has rattling, ringing decorations hanging on them, especially sleigh bells, Chinese copper coins, which are easily sewn on because of the hole in them, and above all thimbles, in which they bore a hole in the top part and then sew them on the clothing in rows. At first the seafarers from the United American Free States trading along the Northwest Coast of America thought they had discovered the most industrious women on earth. They could not imagine what other than sewing would be the purpose of the many hundred thousand thimbles they had traded until they were taught otherwise.

Little chests for storing their valuables and other utensils are adorned with sea otter teeth and little pieces of polished sea ear (*Haliotis*).

When a young girl shows the first signs of the onset of sexual maturity, she has to live in a little hut away from her relatives and acquaintances. She is given nothing to eat for two days and then after that only very little to eat and a moderate amount. She has to suck liquid, that is water, through the wing bone of a bald eagle and dare not, even if she is thirsty, take more than three draws. It is generally believed by following this custom that the less a girl drinks during this period, the longer she adheres to strict temperance, and the more she spends her time with household tasks, the greater will be the resulting mutual dependence in marriage. In order to obtain a higher degree of happiness in her future marriage, a girl at this time in her life occasionally lives an entire year secluded, confined, cut off from all contact with her brothers and sisters and female playmates. In this way she earns, through habitual industriousness, temperance, modesty, etc., the love of a man and lays the groundwork for a happy home life.

It is too bad that such principles found here on the Northwest Coast of America cannot be introduced into our European education of women!

Usually a Kalusch has only one wife, but there are a very few, very rich and well-to-do chiefs, according to their standards, who have two — an old one and a young one. These people's women are characterized by morality, chastity, devotion, and conjugal fidelity, thus setting them fundamentally apart from all of the Aleut peoples living farther north.

As long as a woman is capable of bearing children, she is confined for several days each month in a special hut and is also considered unfit for all domestic activities.

Their method of catching fish is worthy of mention. A little bladder is fastened to every line at the surface of the water. This makes it possible for a single person to watch fourteen to fifteen lines at the same time.

I could not find out whether these people have any kind of concept of a godly being. They show particular respect for the dead. The body is put into a new coffin and buried in a remote part of the woods, usually in a square formed by four trees. All diseases are ascribed to their enemies' witchcraft. They, however, know that the root of the *Valeriana* is a very effective remedy. The climate is said to be rawer on the eastern side of the archipelago than on the western side. Aside from granite and a very fine talc soil, I found no special kinds of rocks.

On the 30th toward noon, we set out on our return trip. Our host Dlchätin gave us a considerable quantity of smoked salmon and other dried fish that we accepted all the more happily because we were so badly off for supplies in New Archangel. The first day we only went as far as the home of Chief Schinchetäez, where we had eaten our noon meal two days before. He was happy to see us again and gladly gave us a night's lodging and a good meal. It seemed to us as if we had known each other for a long time. We had hardly finished warming ourselves up and eating when we distributed gifts to our host and his family. They accepted them with a thousand pardons and regret that their poverty did not permit them to give gifts in return. Only his wife had a sea otter tail which she gave me as a gift, while at the same time, however, asking for another shirt in exchange.

We slept by a large fire that burned all night in the middle of the hut. At daybreak on the 31st, we again set out on our journey with our attention arrested by a new spectacle: this morning in 8° cold the Kalusch of the male sex were running totally naked across the ice on the nearby shore in order to bathe. We discovered that this is a common habit among these peoples. Small children are bathed in the ocean a few days after birth and at every season of the year. In this way their scantily clad bodies become hardened to the raw climate from childhood.

The wind and tide were favorable so that before evening we passed through the narrow, dangerous passage which had left such a great impression upon us on the 27th. Today the water appeared to be boiling and the rather brisk wind dispersed the sharp waves. The current carried our baidarkas so rapidly forward that we obtained a speed of at least ten to twelve knots and reached the spot on the other side where we had spent the night of the 28th. Here we pitched our tent. During the night it was 6° to 8° Réaumur. Our main activity consisted of going into the nearby woods and dragging out as much wood that we could keep ourselves warm in our open tent. On the first of November, we arrived back at the Russian settlement on Norfolk Sound, hale and hearty.

Notes

1. According to Richard and Nora Dauenhauer, of Juneau, Alaska, specialists on the oral literature of the Tlingit, the route taken by the Tlingit in their retreat from Sitka and the location of their new stronghold is now unknown. Presumably, they went by way of Olga and Neva straits to Salisbury Sound (named by Nathaniel Portlock in 1787 and called Bay of Islands by Cook in 1778), and then through Peril Strait (named after the death there in 1799 of over 130 Aleuts, in one of Baranov's hunting parties) to Chatham Strait. It is thought that the Tlingit settled on Rodman Bay.

Chapter 6

Departure for New Albion. Sea Voyage. Havre de Gray. Cape Disappointment. Columbia River. Attempt to enter it. Continuation of our Voyage. Arrival in the Bay of San Francisco.

Toward the end of February, after eight of the 192 Russians living in Sitcha had died and another sixty were suffering from scurvy, finally serious preparations were made to undertake the expedition to New Albion mentioned earlier.

The ship was soon ready to sail. Even though the priest had not yet arrived from Kodiak, its anchor was raised on February 25th old style (or March 9th, new style).

Every participant in this expedition left our miserable winter quarters with happy hearts. Using mild, favorable winds we lost sight of ugly Norfolk Sound by nightfall.

Before describing this new sea voyage I need to make some preliminary remarks.

The sailors of the Russian-American Company, as we know, are people whose former stations in life were totally different. Since our departure from Kamtschatka, we have been calling them promyshlenniks. These men had been working at various activities during the winter and living on scanty rations. Now, once again, they were supposed to become sailors on a ship. Only a very few of them were suited to the task and most of them were suffering so from illness and scurvy that Messrs. Chwostoff and Davidoff, therefore, expressed serious doubts and requested only twenty of the healthiest men at the settlement, despite the fact that the *Juno* required at least thirty trained and experienced sailors. All of the well-founded reasons and pleas did not help these two courageous officers at all. After many excuses and pretexts, they were refused the twenty workers they had requested (from among the strongest and healthiest) and given instead thirty-three men, eighteen of whom were capable of work and the rest so weak and wretched that they needed the help of others. They obstructed the others at work. Their rotten exhalations befouled the ship's air and they helped to eat the minimal three month's worth of provisions we had been given for the voyage. Thus manned, we set sail. The following day (February 26th) we had a brisk wind from the north and north-northeast. Most of the people on board, now long unaccustomed to being at sea, were lying seasick in bed.

The weather was cold and clear on the first day of our voyage. Soon, however, we found ourselves under the influence of a mild region, which cheered up our sick. On March 3rd, they could sun themselves in 14° weather at 51° N and 132° W. The sea was quite calm with an occasional stormy petrel, albatross or sea gull. On the 6th, to the north-northwest, we saw something resembling a waterspout or funnel. A black cloud approached the surface of the ocean, from which a perpendicular column rose that seemed to reach to the top of the cloud. We could not tell exactly from the distance of three to four sea miles whether it was really a column of water or a curious ray of light reflecting in this way by chance.

On the following day, we saw (at 48° N and 127° W) more birds than usual. We slowly continued sailing with alternating light winds and variable weather. On the 10th during an almost windless calm, we lowered an Aleutian leather boat brought along from Sitcha to give battle to a number of stormy petrels (*Procellaria grisea*) around us for several hours — and with very good results for us. On the evening of the 10th, with a south-southeasterly wind, we were enveloped in a penetrating, wet, drizzle-like fog that lasted for two days. It had an injurious effect on our sick. On the 13th the sky cleared again. Using a favorable wind from the north and northwest, we headed toward the Columbia River, which we wanted to enter if this could be done without loss of time. There we wanted to let our ailing crew rest for a few days and inspect the harbor, which could possibly become of great importance to the Russians living in the north.

At daybreak on the 14th, we had the pleasure of spotting the long-desired coast of New Albion. The horizon was extraordinarily clear. We saw a high range of mountains to the south and to the north low land. To the east the land spread out before us until it reached a high, round peak far in the background (Mount St. Helens — 46°9′ N and 238°4′ W*).

---

*Vancouver, Part II, p. 243).

Without an astronomical observation we could easily tell that we were in the neighborhood of a large river, because the ocean had a dirty, murky, reddish color and the water seemed to contain a lot of clay. We soon caught sight of Cape Disappointment (46°20′ N) and thought about anchoring if the favorable northwesterly wind continued. We were imagining eating wild ducks and geese from the numbers around us. Mr. von Resanoff had already moved the settlement at Sitcha to the Columbia River and was busy with plans for building ships when our hopes were shattered. The wind gradually shifted to the southeast and became so violent that we could not think of trying to enter an unknown harbor with a horizon covered in rain clouds. Aside from ducks and geese, the birds included many pelicans, stormy petrels, albatrosses and sea gulls. Toward evening the wind abated, and using little sail, we tried to spend the night at about 46° latitude. With approaching daybreak we again sailed toward the harbor or the mouth of the river we had seen the day before.

We had seen the chain of mountains the day before with one high mountain standing out in its midst that could have served as a guide, but now the entire landscape in the background lay enveloped in fog, as well as everything in the foreground, that is, the green cape partially covered with trees which we thought to be Cape Disappointment. The heavy surf on the northern and southern sides of the headland, the low, wooded coast to the south, the wide, expansive landscape or the prospective harbor — the day before all of this had so resembled the mouth of the Columbia River that no one on board had harbored any doubts about it. Possessed by this insanity, we tried to approach the northern foothills, where we soon spotted a wide, extensive sandbank just as described so exactly by Captain Vancouver. Toward noon, since we could not sail around the extensive breakers, we dropped anchor in seven fadens of water with a sandy bottom. We discovered with a complete noon observation that we were located at 46°58′. We were all the more surprised by our more northerly location, because it did not seem possible to us that the current and southern waves could have carried us so far north in the night.*

When in the afternoon it was decided to check our exact position by sending a sailor and two Aleuts in a three-seated baidarka to inspect the nearby harbor, I asked to be put in charge. Given permission, I took my seat in the leather boat in order to inspect the channel.

*Most likely one or another of the sleepy promyshlenniks had steered incorrectly during the night.

At our departure from the ship, I agreed to return at the latest by six in the evening. In case of darkness, a large lantern would be hung from the main mast.

I followed only a little distance away the foaming, pounding surf along the northern point of land and also soon saw the southern side of the entrance. It was about one sea mile wide. It was, as far as we could see, free of surf and seemingly navigable. We rowed between the violent waves breaking across sandbanks to the north and south of us toward the mouth of the harbor stretching out before us to the east. The sounding lead indicated five and one-half klafters of water at the narrowest part of the entrance. As we moved on into the bay, it increased in width and depth so that we gradually found six, seven and one-half to nine klafters of water.

Accompanied by high waves rolling into the bay, we finally reached the inner shore just before six o'clock in the evening. I had hardly looked around when I recognized the spot I was inspecting from Vancouver's book, where Mr. Whitbey described Havre de Gray (47° N, 123°53′ W).

The sandy beaches were littered with driftwood. A desolate region bordered by a green knoll stretched about half a German mile inland. To the northwest I saw in the neighborhood of a wood, smoke rising in several places, proof that the area was inhabited. Then I climbed to the top of a washed-up hill of sand and fired two shots with the intention of capturing the attention of any inhabitants in the area and inviting them over. Probably because of the distance involved, I was unsuccessful. I had, however, a quite good view of the area from this sand hill. The channel between the surf seemed wider to me than Mr. Whitbey had indicated and the inner half of the bay to the south was now freer. Probably, the location of the sandy shore had been somewhat changed by storms and tides since his stay there. There appeared to be a good, secure anchorage at the mouth of a little river on the southern part of the harbor. Due to the number of whales I saw, I concluded that the water was deep enough and fish were abundant. I saw countless flocks of water birds and sandpipers (*Tringae*). At low tide I found myself on land and concluded that the rise and fall of the tides at full moon is considerable. The northeastern inlet in the interior of the harbor described by Mr. Whitbey is almost totally choked by sandbanks. About twenty paces from the shore where I landed, the water is four and one-half to five klafters deep.

It was already evening, six o'clock, the day was almost at an end, and I had no time to linger any longer, especially since I wanted to work through the high, unfamiliar breakers before night fell and I had to find the ship in the dark where it lay anchored about thirty versts away at the open sea. How easy it would have been for a gust of wind or unfavorable weather to force the commander of the ship to weigh anchor. Then we would have been in a serious situation. We had barely passed the farthest breakers when night fell. The half moon I had counted on to help us was totally hidden by black clouds. At the same time a south-southeasterly wind arose making it impossible to see the *Juno*, partially because of the distance and the darkness of the night, partially because of the high waves and the baidarka rides so low in the water. Therefore, we rowed doubly hard in the approximate direction we assumed the ship was, when suddenly at about eight o'clock we spotted the flash of a cannon shot on the dark horizon without hearing its report due to the distance. For us that was indeed a shot of joy, serving all the more to aim us in the right direction since it was repeated every half hour. I answered the signal each time with a shot from the musket, which was not once seen by the ship. We were just as unable to see the lantern hanging from the main mast because of the high rolling waves when we were only a few versts from the ship. In the dark of the night toward nine-thirty, after a long detour undertaken to avoid any breakers, despite the swelling seas, foaming waves and rising wind, we climbed on board healthy and well, even though they had already thought we had fallen prey to savages or the tide.

As soon as we were on board, the anchor was lifted because the wind had become so brisk in the meantime that we sailed 66½ miles in seven hours. The wind blew from the south-southeast the whole night. The following morning (the 16th) it increased to storm proportions that only lessened toward evening. The ship's heavy rolling in the ensuing calm quite exhausted us. On the following days, this same unfavorable wind blew anew and prevented us from progressing south.

When we found ourselves on the 18th at 46°40′, we spied large flocks of many thousands of sea birds along with several whales, which were probably following migrating herring. The next morning the weather was rainy, dreary and foggy. Only toward evening did that unfavorable southeast wind that had been bothering us for several days let up. The horizon immediately cleared up somewhat so that we could finally see a large stretch of the nearby coast again. To the southeast were mountains we suspected were near the Columbia River.

To the northeast behind a long chain of mountains, towered up an exceedingly imposing high peak covered by snow. Its peak, probably because it was a former volcano, had an irregular shape. It was undoubtedly Mount Rainier, which Vancouver had also observed at a distance of one hundred geographical miles. We sailed slowly forward in light winds. Early on the morning of March 20th, we had the pleasure of a clear view of that pleasant region. To the east was the coast of Shoal Water, to the south-southeast high mountains which we assumed was Cape Lookout and between them the northern foothills at the mouth of the Columbia River, namely Cape Disappointment. Farther southeast from there stands a peak whose shape and form are so variable, depending upon the direction and distance one is from it, that if one were to use it as a landmark, one might on occasion be led astray. The walls of the crater I saw on its outer peak form four pyramids. One or another of them is often covered so that at times one can see two or three of them, seldom only one or all four at the same time.

To our sorrow, the favorable wind soon changed. A light southeast and south-southeast wind along with a strong southern ocean current carried us again to the north. Toward evening we were again becalmed. In order to prevent us from losing the distance gained during the day to a strong current in the night, Mr. von Chwostoff dropped anchor at about seven o'clock in 23 fadens. Several kinds of whales played around the ship. Some of them had dorsal fins larger than I had ever seen. During this calm the clouds spread in various directions and the waves grew high from the west, despite the fact that we had had a strong southeast wind for several days. We lay quietly at anchor for the night. Toward noon (on the 21st), we approached Cape Disappointment in a light wind rising in the west and northwest.

We were very much interested in landing because several of the sick men, due to the daily food and the few remedies on board for scurvy, were visibly using up their last strength from day to day. Some fresh vegetables and animal products,which we hoped to get on land and whose certain healing qualities could be counted upon, made it our duty to enter the next port we might see. Therefore, we were happy to sail eastward, knowing that we were in the vicinity of the mouth of the Columbia River. In order to avoid the heavy surf near the northern foothills, we kept more to the south, where our belief that we were in the channel was strengthened by the smooth surface of the water. Toward two o'clock we had sailed around the foothills rising up to the north of us. Toward five o'clock, to our greatest sorrow, we watched in an increasing northwesterly wind the eastern horizon fill with breakers. With greater and greater loss on the sounding lead, a strong current was carrying us too close to a southern headland, Cape Adams. The water would soon have been too shallow. Therefore, we immediately dropped anchor not far from the surf in three fadens of water. We were in the greatest danger of stranding on the nearby sandy beach. Since the wind almost at the same time picked up noticeably and came from a more northerly direction, Messrs. Von Chwostoff and von Davidoff thought it more advisable to leave these shallows by taking the greatest possible advantage of this favorable northwest wind which would probably continue. They presented their reasons to Mr. von Resanoff. They considered it more advisable not to lose any more time but rather to give up the idea of entering the Columbia River and by using this fresh, favorable wind to hurry straight to San Francisco. There we would be among civilized people, where, at any rate, supplies in abundance and more help for our sick should be available cheaply.

On the 22nd, one of the men ill with scurvy, who had been forced on us in Sitcha, died. Another fifteen of the promyshlenniks were in such deplorable condition that six to eight of them were facing unavoidable death if we did not reach a port soon. The continuation of a favorable northwest wind gave us comfort and courage and filled the spirits of everyone with renewed hope. The pleasant weather let us feel the lively transition to a southern climate at 42°.

The death had for the living the pleasant result that in the following days Mr. von Resanoff ordered a warm punch made from the brandy of the Russian-American Company, which was given to the entire crew gratis. I attempted to make it as pleasant as possible by adding molasses and oil of vitriol. This drink met with general approval. Those who were healthy found it as good tasting as the sick.

The following day, according to our noon observation, we were at 40°58′ N. Toward evening we could distinguish on a clear, southern horizon a high mountain spur which we took for Cape Mendocino. The ocean was extraordinarily dead and we only saw a bird once in a while. After nightfall we saw in the water near the ship a ribbon-like, brightly luminous object, totally in the form and shape of a fiery snake. It was probably a special kind of salpa or mollusk, which, as Peter Forskål has shown us, link up together in an admirable way.[1]

On the 25th, a southeasterly wind accompanied by fog and rain slowed down the progress of our trip at a distance of about three miles from Cape Mendocino. The mountains and slopes of that spur are high and steep. Only in the rugged, cracked, narrow valleys did I see any woods. The hills were mostly covered with grass. Nowhere did we see smoke or other signs indicating that the area was inhabited. Probably it is not, because the steep foreland, continually subjected to wind, undoubtedly offers little foodstuffs. At noon, for the first time we saw large flocks of wild geese flying from south to north. Toward evening the wind again turned to a more westerly direction so that we were able to continue our course.

The following day (the 26th), we found ourselves in the vicinity of a low point of land to the southeast that we thought was Cape Barro de Arena. Our noon reading was 39°18′. The weather was warm and dry. The eastern horizon was, however, mostly covered by fog. Later we could see from time to time a steep shore with mountains partially covered by snow in the background. In the afternoon, a woodpecker (*Picus auratus Linn.*) flew on board looking for a place of refuge but instead ended up dead, because its beauty and rarity was reason enough for me to kill it and preserve it for purposes of natural history.

In the night the wind was so brisk that we had to take the precaution of using less sail. Early the next morning, we caught sight of the rocky group, los Fallerones, to the south and to the east the cape Punto de los Reyes (37°59′), in whose vicinity the harbor of San Francisco lies. An ocean current was carrying us south at two miles an hour. We steered straight for the harbor. We had the pleasure of finding Vancouver's chart and information so exact that we could not have wished for anything better. Regular soundings can serve every seafarer as a secure guide when entering a harbor. Thus, with their help we would have been able to enter the harbor even in the dark, if we had considered it a politically advisable thing to do. During the night, we lay at anchor in four and one-half klafters of water about two to three miles from the mouth on the north coast of the Bay. At daybreak on the 28th, we approached the goal of our trip in a mild west wind. Toward nine o'clock, we reached the southeastern headland of the harbor, where we had already discovered a fort in the distance. As we approached, they called through a megaphone: "Who are you? Where do you come from?" and after receiving our answer, they instructed us to anchor near the fort.

NOTES

1. Peter Forskål (1736-1763) was a Swedish botanist and naturalist born in Kalmar. He studied at Göttingen. He returned to Sweden, which he, however, had to leave after publishing a pamphlet entitled *Pensees sur la liberte*

civile (Thoughts on Civil liberty) in 1759. Línnaeus recommended him to Frederick V of Denmark, who appointed him to accompany Carsten Niebuhr on an expedition to Arabia and Egypt in 1761. He died of the plague at Jerim in Arabia in 1763.

Chapter 7

Arrival in San Francisco. Reception there. Presidio and Mission of San Francisco. Description of them. The Indians at the Mission. Their Customs and Habits.

We had just reached our destination on the morning of March 28th after a thirty-two day voyage at sea when we saw fifteen horsemen from the Fort of San Francisco riding at full gallop along the nearby beach. Through calls and waves they demanded we send a boat. They waited very impatiently while the shallop was lowered that would carry Mr. von Davidoff and me to land.

We were received by a Franciscan monk and various military people. A young, well built man, disfigured only by his peculiar clothing, was introduced to us as the commander of the place. He was wearing a brightly striped wool wrap, similar to a bed coverlet, over his uniform. He had put his head through a hole in its middle so that the longer part covered his chest and back and the smaller parts his shoulders. He and the other military personnel were further distinguished by their very specially crafted boots and exceedingly long spurs. It struck us that most of them were wearing large coats.

Since none of us spoke Spanish, the priest and I used Latin, the only language we had for communication. He asked who we were and where we came from. We explained that our ship belonged to a Russian expedition, that its commander His Excellency Chamberlain von Resanoff was on board, and that it had been our intention to sail to Monterey, the seat of the government, but we had been held up by contrary winds. Due to lack of supplies, we had been forced to sail to the nearest harbor to seek help from its commander and fresh supplies.

We were then told that they had heard news of the expedition long since and had received imperial Spanish orders to greet us most cordially if we should put into port. Therefore, all of the refreshments the place and region had to offer were at our service. They wanted, however, to know why this expedition that had left Kronstadt under the command of Captain von Krusenstern and Captain von Lisiansky had suffered such a great change, so that now Chamberlain von Resanoff, whose name they seemed not to know, arrived in port with a different ship and different officers?

We explained that for various reasons these expedition ships had been forced to sail back to Europe from Kamtschatka. His Majesty, the Tsar of Russia, had given Mr. von Resanoff new orders, i.e., to use this ship, the *Juno*, under the command of Messrs. Chwostoff and Davidoff, to inspect Russian-American outposts on the Aleutian Islands and the Northwest Coast of America. He had just come from there. They were satisfied with this answer and promised us all services available and asked Mr. von Resanoff to come ashore. They waited on the shore in order to accompany him to the Presidio and the quarters of the commandant.

With this pleasant invitation we immediately returned to the ship. We picked up Messrs. von Resanoff and Chwostoff in order to go to the Presidio (as every military outpost is called in California). On the way there, we were told that the commander Don Arguello was absent but that his son, Alferez [Ensign] Don Luiz Arguello, with whom we were speaking, would be his representative. We reached the Presidio after half an hour, where we were cordially greeted by Madame Arguello, the wife of the commander, and her family.[1]

The entire settlement of San Francisco had the appearance of a German farmstead. Its low, single-storied houses surrounded a rather long, rectangular courtyard. The commander's quarters were small and unassuming. A room, painted white, one-half of which was covered by straw mats and contained a few pieces of bad furniture, served as a reception room. After a friendly welcome, we were offered refreshments and invited to a lunch as good as the kitchen and cellar could provide. Finally after such a long time, we once again thoroughly enjoyed ourselves. We were surprised, in view of the otherwise bad furnishings in the house, to be served on a table service of rich silver. This valuable Mexican metal is to be found in even the most distant of Spanish possessions. Friendship and harmony radiate from all the actions of these kind-hearted, good-natured people, who have almost no other diversion and amusement than family joys and domestic happiness.

We were so taken by their rustic natural sincerity that we immediately wanted to become acquainted with each individual, to know their names, and to share in the happiness of this charming family. Madame Arguello had had fifteen children, of whom thirteen were still alive. Several of the sons were in military service and absent. From among her grown daughters, several of whom were still unmarried, Donna Conception stood out especially because of her liveliness, gaiety, love-inspiring, fiery eyes, very beautiful teeth, expressive, pleasing, facial features, beautiful stature and a thousand other charms, and because of her unaffected, natural manner. Beauties of her kind, although rare, are to be found only in Italy, Portugal and Spain.

The son and representative of the commander, Don Luiz Arguello, informed us of the political news that England had declared war on Spain. He had at first thought we were a hostile English ship. He immediately showed his joy that this was a mistake. In the afternoon he sent a courier to the governor of Monterey to tell him of our arrival and ask for further orders. Mr. von Resanoff added several lines to the message. In addition to Padre José Uria, who had met us on the beach that day, we met Padre Martin.[2] The following day we received from both of them an invitation to visit the San Francisco Mission. This is a religious settlement one *legoa* or one short German mile east of the Presidio. That evening we happily returned to the ship and were given the joyful news that the commander had already sent more supplies than our starved promyshlenniks could eat in several days, among other things four large fat steers, two wethers, onions, garlic, lettuce, cabbage and many other kinds of vegetables and legumes.

On the 29th at eight o'clock, as agreed upon, saddled horses were standing waiting for us on the shore. Padre José Uria himself came to fetch us. Messrs. von Resanoff, Davidoff, Chwostoff and I were to take part in this pleasure trip. We had to ride past the Presidio, where we stopped for a moment in order to say good morning to the Arguello family and were served chocolate, before riding on to the Mission. It was hard going and riding, since the path consisted mainly of loose sand. The surrounding area is mostly bare. The hills, partially covered by low bushes, offer little of interest and variety. Only several birds I had never seen before, cranes, curlews, ducks, and eagles, now and then a rabbit or hare, drew our attention.

After three-quarters of an hour, we reached the religious settlement. Padre Martin, whose acquaintance we had made the day before at the Presidio, and a third padre, Reymundus, greeted us in the most friendly manner at the door to their living quarters. They immediately took us to the church for a short prayer and then to the chapel and sacristy to show us objects of interest, consisting mainly of church vestments. Our guide, Padre José Uria, by the way, a very enlightened man, who, as well as we knew him up to then and got to know him afterwards, could otherwise make very healthy and intelligent judgments about everything, took my hand in the chapel and pointed out to me, the natural scientist, as he said, a painting of a plant (*Agave Americana Linn.*). Instead of a flower stem, a sacred Madonna grew from its midst. She had subsequently performed a great many miracles; he assured me with such certainty that I modestly uttered my surprise at this striking situation and that I had to envy the good fortune of the painter to have witnessed such a great rarity with his own eyes!

We soon left the church and were taken to the building in which the priests lived. It contained a number of spacious rooms. They placed several kinds of refreshments before us and then acquainted us with the other accommodations and institutions of their place of residence, the Mission.

The word Mission designates a religious settlement established to promote the extension of the Roman Catholic Church. On the entire peninsula of Old and New California, each mission usually has two or three monks,* who are supported in their zealous service by the Presidio, i.e., by a standing military detachment.

Every member of these orders, who have gone there with the intention of converting the people wandering around in the area, have to pledge in their motherland Spain to stay in those parts of the world for ten years; after that, it is their decision whether they return to their fatherland or stay on there.[3] They are maintained during their sojourn at the cost of the Spanish king, They only have to provide themselves with a prayer book and Bible. Not a single one of those missionaries has personal wealth. It is impossible for them to think of obtaining wealth because everything that they lay by or spare ends up in the coffers of the mission. Thus, everyone of them has to leave as poor as when he arrived.

The number of priests transported from Europe to Vera Cruz every year is said to be about 300. Each one receives an allowance of four hundred piasters, which has to be used to pay for his necessities

*In New California they all belong to the Franciscan Order.

and to help his parish. They do not receive this sum in money but rather in the form of goods and utensils sent on government vessels from St. Blaz (a harbor on the northwestern coast of Mexico at 21°30′ N) by the Franciscan Collegium in Mexico, to which all of the missions in New California belong. These goods include canvas, cloth, wine, sugar, brandy, chocolate and cocoa, iron tools, church candles, kitchen utensils and agricultural tools, etc.

In the Province of New California, which stretches from San Francisco (37°55′ N) to San Diego (32°39′), there are 19 missions (and in the same province 600 to 1,000 or more newly converted Christians). If I am not wrong, they are protected by six presidios with a 200- to 300-man cavalry distributed among them.

The Santa Clara Mission between Monterey and San Francisco is supposed to be the most important and richest due to its beautiful location, the fertility of its soil, population, size and extent of its buildings and gardens, etc. All of these missions have a surplus of animals and other foodstuffs of various kinds. In general, the monks treat the neophytes with such forbearance, kindness, paternal solicitude and fairness that peace, unity and obedience inevitably result from their management. Disobedience is usually treated by corporal punishment.

The military command in the presidios is only used in extraordinary circumstances, especially when recruiting Christians, maintaining the mails, and, as a precautionary measure, for protection from attack. The number of soldiers is so small that it hardly seems worth maintaining them. There are forty men at the Presidio of San Francisco responsible for the security of three missions, i.e., the one of the same name, Santa Clara and San Jose, which was founded just a few years before. At any given time, there are only two or three soldiers always stationed at a mission. This apparently small number of soldiers has been up to now sufficient to keep the Indians within bounds. A reliable person assured me that the Spanish Court has to spend a million piasters a year for the pay and keep of the military and Church in the two Californias and derives no use from them except the reward of spreading the Christian religion to these lands.

Every monk has the use of several horses. Whenever he leaves the mission, he is always accompanied by one or more soldiers riding ahead. On these occasions, they usually wear a kind of leather cuirass or a short coat of buckskin over their shoulders. They do this as protection against hostile attack, i.e., when the missionaries ride into the interior to enlist recruits for the Roman Catholic Church as protection against the

Indians' arrows, which cannot pierce the leather. On other occasions, the cuirass serves as a dress uniform, which the soldiers put on when they are approaching a presidio or mission. By royal command, the monks may never leave their missions without this military escort, since their only personal weapons are the Cross and the Bible. They are supposed to be protected by the military at all times.

While listening to such and similar information, we enjoyed our breakfast and afterwards viewed the rest of the objects of interest at the mission.

Behind the monks' quarters was a large closed courtyard surrounded by houses. This is where the Indian women of the mission live and where, under the immediate supervision of the monks, they perform various useful tasks, e.g., cleaning, spinning and weaving wool. Weaving seems to be their main task and consists in manufacturing a kind of wool cloth and woolen blankets to be used by the Indians as clothing. The sheep's wool there is soft and of superior quality. Their tools and looms seemed to me to be very wanting. Since only the monks teach this handicraft and probably basically know little about it themselves, indeed do not even know to full, the woolen things produced here are far from the quality they could be.

All the girls and widows are guarded, as it were, kept under lock and key in various houses and encouraged to work. They may, with the permission of their superiors, leave the cloister by day, but absolutely never at night. As soon as a girl marries, she obtains her freedom and then lives with her husband in one of the Indian villages belonging to the mission called las Rancherias. Through such arrangements, the monks hope to bind the men more to the settlement and spread their religion with greater ease and safety.

The village, that is the quarters for the Indians, las Rancherias, is about one hundred paces opposite the main building of the mission. It has eight long rows of houses, which are divided so that each family lives separately. The number of converted Indians or neophytes living there is supposed to be about 1,200.

Meals made of a thick broth with vegetables, soup greens and legumes* are served three times a day, morning, noon and evening, when

---

*Because of a lack of fish or the means of obtaining them, these missions, with a special dispensation from the Pope, may also eat meat on holy days.

everyone is given a large spoonful (about the size of a German *maas* or two typical *bouteilles* [bottles]). At meal times a bell is rung and every family sends a container to the kitchen to get as many spoonsful of soup as there are members of the family. I was present when the food was distributed and it seemed to me impossible for a single person to eat such large portions of nourishing food three times a day. According to our guide, forty to fifty head of cattle are slaughtered every week to feed the community. In addition to this usual fare, flour, bread, maize, peas, beans and other legumes are distributed in abundance and without a predetermined quantity.

After satisfying our curiosity about the Indian village, we looked at other very useful means of providing for the needs and economy of the mission, for example a building used for rendering tallow, another for making soap, workshops for mechanics, smiths, carpenters and for sawing boards, etc., storehouses for tallow, butter, cattle hides,* salt and wool among other things, storerooms for grain, maize, peas, beans and several other kinds of legumes. When I consider the fact that two or three monks, in order to spread Christianity, go to the trouble of civilizing nomadic peoples, of teaching them farming, and at the same time of clothing, feeding and housing them as their own children while doing everything necessary to keep the whole thing in order — and this in the most altruistic manner — then I have to be more than a little happy about their activities and success in carrying out their undertaking.

In the meantime, we were called to the noon meal: a tasty soup spiced with herbs, salad, baked goods, preserved food and dairy products — all things which we had had to do without for so long that these dishes titillated our palates more than a little bit. The wine served us from the peninsula of California was certainly nothing special. Shortly after the meal, we were served tea (of bad quality) and especially good chocolate. We were then taken to the kitchen garden, which was by no means what we had expected. We found only a few fine vegetables and garden plants. Most of the beds were filled with weeds and several stunted fruit trees had, as they told us, only scanty and bad fruit. The northwesterly winds continually blowing from the coast and the dry sandy earth are insurmountable obstacles to the development of gardening, so that in that garden they only plant asparagus, cabbage, different kinds of lettuce, onions and potatoes. Outside the mission, in remote spots somewhat protected from the winds on

*These are articles of export.

extensive fields, peas, beans, Turkish corn, big beans and other legumes grow well. Grain crops grow less well there than in other places in New California. Despite this, the Spanish government considered it utterly necessary to maintain a mission in the neighborhood of the superior harbor at San Francisco and for its protection to build a presidio. Both settlements can flourish very well, especially because of the extensive stock-farming.

To give a more exact picture of the fertility of the soil that causes the monks of this mission to complain when comparing it with conditions on other missions, I am including a table showing the amount of seeds sown and the harvest for the last four years, which Padre Martin was kind enough to give me.

TYPE OF CEREALS[4]	1802		1803		1804*		1805	
	seed	crop	seed	crop	seed	crop	seed	crop
	fanegas		fanegas		fanegas		fanegas	
Wheat (trigo)	233	2,322	201	1,457	229	938	173	2,622
Barley (cevada)	108	1,289	122	1,720	143	826	195	2,414
Peas (chicharo)	12	525	11	509	9	344	8	330
Big beans (havas)	6	132	7	214	8	206	8	294
Beans (frigol)	2	10	1	60	2	30	3	40
Maize (maís) or Turkish corn	1	20	2	60	1	156	1½	100

Although we only got a fleeting acquaintance with the Indians that day, I would still like to include here a summary of what I was able to learn about them during our stay.

The neophytes at San Francisco are the original inhabitants of that and neighboring areas. Only a very few come from the north shore of the mouth of a large river which flows into the northeastern

*Because of a heavy drought almost all of the seeds sown withered.

part of the harbor. Still others come from the vicinity of Port de Bodega to the north of there. All these peoples of New California living along the coast are divided into various tribes, known to me by the names Estero, Tuiban and Tabin. There are others, their former enemies, living in bordering areas to the east, who call themselves Tscholban and Tamkan.

When free and independent, the original nomads live mainly from fish, seal, mussels and products from the ocean and partially from the hunt, seeds, herbs and roots. They consider these foods the highest delicacies. They have no permanent houses. Wherever they happen to be every family builds a little round, straw hut shaped something like a cone of sugar, and they then burn it down as soon as they leave. They do the same thing if someone dies in one. Both sexes, except for a careless covering over their genitals, go naked the whole year. In the winter they cover themselves with deer and sea otter skins. They make a kind of clothing from the feathers of many waterfowl, especially of ducks and geese. They tie them close together on a string and then put several of these stings together in such a way as to make a kind of feather pelt, which is completely alike on both the inside and the outside. It is so warm that it could be worn even in a northern climate. They also are said to work sea otter skins in a similar way by cutting them into very small strips and winding them around a string. Several of these fur strings are then fastened together until they form a pelt which is the same on both sides. These are worn especially by the women, seldom by the men.

These Indians are of medium, or rather of small stature, and have dark brown to almost black skin color, probably mostly caused by their dirty way of living, constant exposure to the sun, smearing their bodies with earth and charcoal and their careless clothing. They have large projecting lips, wide, flat, negroid-type noses. Indeed, many of their facial features, and almost their color, bear strong resemblances to Negroes. Their hair, however, is very different, since it is very black and straight. If left uncut, it grows to a considerable length, often hanging over their hips. Usually they cut it about four to five zolls from the roots. It does not, however, as with other races, hang wildly around their heads but stands up stiffly like the bristles of a brush, thus making an unfamiliar and unpleasant impression upon us Europeans. Their hair begins to grow not too far above their eyes so that their foreheads are very low. Their eyebrows do not have much hair and their beards are moderately thick. Many of them shave them off using mussel shells. All of the people we got to see were under five fuss, poorly built and had such a miserable, dumb, dark, foolish, slovenly appearance that we all had to agree that we had never seen a race of human beings on a lower level.

Their weapons consist of bows and arrows. Since they are mainly used to procure most of their food, they appear to concentrate all of their industry and skill into making them. The bow has a pleasing form. It is made of wood, about three to four and one-half fuss long, finely worked. One side of it is skillfully covered with deer sinew that adheres very tightly to the wood. This lends the wood such elasticity that it requires a great deal of power and skill to draw it. The arrows are just as finely and carefully worked. They have a point made of lava glass (obsidian) which is sunk in the shaft and then tightly bound to it with sinew. In early times the Spanish were often given enough reasons to complain about their skill at shooting arrows.

I saw among their household utensils very skillfully woven little baskets made from the bark and fiber of trees. They are so watertight that they can be used to hold drinking water and as soup bowls and even as frying pans. Because they have no other kitchen utensils, they roast grain and other legumes in these little baskets by turning them so quickly and skillfully over a low coal fire so that every little grain, as we do with coffee beans, roasts brown without the little basket suffering in the least from the heat. Many of these little baskets or bowls, which require a great deal of time and care to make, are decorated with the bright red feathers of *Oriolus phoeniceus* and the black crest feathers of the crested Californian partridge [quail] (*Tetraonis cristati**), as well as with mussels and coral.

However dumb and simple, dirty, ugly and repulsive these people may be, they do have a great fondness for adornments and games. They have all kinds of adornments which they make partially from feathers, partially from mussels, that is, from a species of sea ear (probably *Haliotis gigantea*) found frequently along the coast there and near Monterey. It is scarcely inferior in the magnificence of its iridescence to New Zealand's *Haliotis Iris*. They use a kind of mussel, which I did not get to see, for little rings that are of such admirable exactness that they are all the same size. Without the use of iron instruments, they bore a hole through the middle. These rings look something like our glass beads and are strung together to make necklaces.

*See *Atlas du voyage de la Pérouse*, No. 36.[5]

Their most beautiful head ornament is made from the two middle tail feathers of a woodpecker (*Picus auratus*), whose shaft is naturally a beautiful vermilion. They clean the feathers within a zoll of the end of their barbs. Then they are skillfully placed next to each other and bound together so that they form a kind of very attractive headband. Among other curiosities which I obtained from these people in trade for European glass beads, silk ribbons, knives and other objects was one of these headbands. It had 450 feathers in it, consequently 225 birds were needed to make it. I was unable to find out where and how these people obtained so many of these birds, since they prefer wooded areas and there are only a few wooded areas near San Francisco.

Another head ornament used by the Indians at dances is made from the feathers of a raptor (*Vultus Aura*), which is very common here. The tail and wing feathers of these birds are woven together into a kind of Turkish turban and worn at public festivities.

Tattooing is also practiced, principally by the women. Some of them have double or triple lines running from the corners of their mouths to the sides of their chins. Others only have several stripes below the middle of their chins converging concentrically. Most of them have simple, perpendicular and horizontal stripes on the front of their throats from their chins to their chests and on their shoulders.

Among all their pastimes they prefer dancing, which I will describe in particular. They have other social games. In one of them, which they call *tussi*, several Indians sit together in a circle. One of them has a little stick in his hand, which he stealthily passes back and forth from one hand to the other, while making all kinds of faces and singing, thus attempting to trick his fellow players and lead them astray. When he believes he has hidden the little stick in one or the other of his hands so that the others cannot easily guess in which one, he suddenly turns with a loud Ha! to one of the other players, stares at him while holding both fists toward him. If the other player finds the little stick, he takes it and does the same thing. If not, the rest of the players deride him for guessing incorrectly.

Considering the fact that two or three monks and four or five soldiers, with hardly a thought that the Indians might mutiny or rebel, control a community of 1,000 to 1,500 coarse, uncivilized people and attempt to make them live in a totally different way from their previous one, it must be to some extent due to the gentleness and forbearance, the love and friendship, with which the religious fathers care for their children. Furthermore, I think that the simplicity of these miserable creatures, who are only human in body but not in mind, contributes a great deal to their peace and satisfaction. I, at least, consider them absolutely incapable of planning any kind of common attempt to free themselves.

Even though there is hardly any doubt that human beings can live better in temperate climates and that mild zones of the earth were probably intended by nature to be the preferred areas of habitation, we think that, indeed, here we have found a remarkable and striking example of an exception to that almost generally held principle. Here on the west coast of North America at 38°, where the original inhabitants live in a temperate climate, where they have no lack of food and no problems finding housing and clothing, where they can easily feed themselves from the hunt, roots, seeds and fruit, from fish, mussels and all kinds of products from the ocean, they are, as we have just heard, ugly, small, ill-proportioned, simple and dumb. In contrast, several other peoples along the same coast, for example, the Kalusch at 58° and 59°, are strong, well built and such wily people that they have, by cunning, often been victorious against the English, as well as the Russians and other European nations. I truly have to confess that the appearance of these *Pescherähs* in a mild climate with so many sources of food around them has puzzled me to this very day.[6]

But let me return to the monks at the mission. They are actually only the managers under whose direction the neophytes produce comfort, homes, food and clothing. The jobs they are urged to do are mainly in farming and animal husbandry, in sheep shearing and skilled trades, in construction, in producing candles, soap and household utensils, and in accompanying goods being transported from one mission or presidio to another. The most laborious task, the grinding of flour, is done almost solely by the women. Grain is ground to flour between two rather long rectangular stones. The flour itself is very white, but when baked, it produces a very heavy, lumpy bread. La Pérouse, as an act of philanthropy (see his *Voyage*, Part II, p. 299), left a hand mill to rectify the situation, but it no longer exists. It also had not been used as a pattern to produce others. When one considers that windmills are used in no other land to the degree that they are in Spain, it would almost be impossible to understand why these useful machines have not yet been introduced there, and why they are satisfied with very poorly ground flour, if I had not found out that the monks have a political reason for not introducing windmills. They have more people than they can usefully employ for the whole year. Thus, they believe that building windmills would lead to a lot of idleness, which is now taken care of by having them grind flour in their off hours.

The cattle, horses and sheep do not require any special care. The herds are left to run free the whole year. Only as many animals as are needed for immediate wants are kept near the settlements. When the mission's kitchen needs beef, soldiers and neophytes ride out to the pasture. They use ropes with running nooses to catch as many animals as are needed.

The countless numbers of cattle originate from five animals brought to the mission in 1776. The Governor of Monterey,[7] whom we got to know afterwards, told us that in recent years their numbers at the three northern missions of San Francisco, Santa Clara and Santa Cruz had increased to the point that, a few months before, he had had to send out a commando of soldiers to kill 20,000 of them, wherever they found them, because he feared that they would multiply to the point that there would not be enough pasture to feed them.

Oxen are used for the field work. Mostly military and church personnel use horses. Along with mules they serve as pack animals to carry goods and supplies from one mission to the next. The carts and wagons are of very poor quality. As in Spain and Portugal, they have block wheels, which sometimes are not even round.

Neither the governor nor the monks have any other intentions than to spread Christianity. As a result, one might believe that the Indians, who only have to take care of their own personal needs, must be happier with this civilized way of life than they were previously. For, in addition to more food, they have retained all of their previous customs and habits which Christianity does not forbid, for example, their dances, pastimes, games, adornments, etc. They still enjoy many domestic privileges. They may keep their own chickens and pigeons. With permission they may go hunting and fishing. In general they can live by far more carefree lives than previously. Notwithstanding all of this, however, there smolders in one or another of them, probably a genius of his tribe, the feeling of freedom. The inclination to fish and hunt, to remissness and to a nomadic life free from bounds seems so very much to outweigh all of the advantages, as we judge them, of the mission that he secretly tries to escape. No sooner is he missed than they begin to search for him. Since they know which tribe he belongs to and because of the hostility among the various tribes, he cannot go to another one (a happenstance he probably had not considered before his escape), it is almost impossible for him to escape the search parties of soldiers and other neophytes sent out to find him. For this reason he is usually soon returned to the mission, where he bastinadoed. Then an iron rod of about one to one and one-half fuss in length and somewhat more than a zoll in diameter is fastened to one of his feet, thus preventing him from repeating his attempt to escape. It also serves as a deterrent to others with similar plans.

After becoming acquainted with the mission, its priests and inhabitants, we returned to the Presidio filled with gratefulness for their kind reception.

NOTES

1. José Dario Argüello (1753-1829) was the founder of the Argüello family, commandant of San Francisco when Langsdorff was there. Later (1814-15) he was acting governor of California and then governor of Baja California (1815-1822).

Ignacia Moraga was the wife of José Dario. She was the niece of Lieutenant José Joaquin Moraga, the founder of San Francisco. She died in Guadalajara in 1829.

Luis Antonio Argüello (1784-1830) was José Dario's son. He was an ensign when Langsdorff was there, but rose through the ranks to become a captain and then governor ad. int. of California from 1822-25.

Maria de la Conception (Concepcion) Marcela (1790-1857) was José Dario's daughter, who has become famous in history books and literature because of Resanoff's romantic interests in her.

For more complete biographical information, see Hubert Howe Bancroft, *History of California*, Vol. 2, 1800-1825.

2. See Maynard Geiger, *Franciscan Missionaries in Hispanic California, 1769-1848* (San Marino: Huntington Library, 1969).

Padre José Uria: José Antonio Uria served chiefly at San José and retired in 1808.

Padre Luiz: Luis Gil y Taboada (1773-1833) served at San Francisco and San José from 1801 to 1806.

Padre Martin: Martin de Landaeta (1760-1809) served at San Francisco from 1800 to 1806.

Padre Pedro: Pera de la Cueva (1776-?) served in San José from 1804 to 1806. Later he became a violent alcoholic.

Padre Reymundus: José Ramon Abella (1764-1842) served at Mission San Francisco from 1798 to 1819.

3. Langsdorff, indeed, does use *Mutterland* at the beginning of this long sentence and *Vaterland* toward the end. The reader may speculate if it is a reflection of the difference in usage between Spanish and German or subtle irony.

4. The spellings of the Spanish are Langsdorff's.

5. Jean François de Gallaup, Comte de la Pérouse (1741-ca. 1788), was a French navigator and explorer. In 1785 he set out to discover the Northwest Passage and explore large areas in the Pacific. On 7 September 1787, he put in at Petropavlovsk. He arrived at Botany Bay on 26 January 1788. After that nothing more was heard of him. In 1826 the wreckage of what must have been his ships was found on the reefs of Vanikoro, an island to the north of the New Hebrides.

6. Pescheräh: I wish to thank Professor Hermann Weiss of the University of Michigan for directing me by way of Heinrich von Kleist's "Brief eines politischen Pescherä über einen Nürnberger Zeitungsartikel" to Louis de Bougainville, *A Voyage round the World performed by order of His Most Christian Majesty in the years 1766, 1767, 1768 and 1769*, trans. by Johann Reinhold Forster (London: Printed for J. Noura, 1772). Bougainville says of the Indians on Terra de Fuego: "We called them 'Pecherais' because that was the first word which they pronounced when they came to us, and which they repeated to us incessantly, as the Patagonians did their 'shawa' . . . " (p. 164).

"These savages are short, ugly, meagre, and have an insupportable stench about them. They are almost naked; having no other dress than wretched sealskins, too little for them to wrap themselves in, these skins serve them equally as roofs to their huts and as sails to their periaguas . . . . Their women are hideous, and seemed little regarded by the men (p. 174) . . . . Upon the whole, they seem to be good people; but they are so weak, that one is almost tempted to think the worse of them on that account . . . . Of all the savages I ever saw, the Pecherais are those who are most deprived of every convenience; they are exactly in what may be called a state of nature . . . " (p. 176).

7. Governor of Monterey, Don Arrelaga: José Joaquin de Arrillaga (1750-1814). See Bancroft, *History of California*, Vol. 2, 205fn.

Chapter 8

Restraints upon Trade. Spanish Motives for Receiving us well. Trade Goods. Answer of the Governor. Further Negotiations. Arrival of the Governor at San Francisco. Attempt to Establish Trade between Russia and New California. Amusements. Hunting. Parties. Dance. Barrego. Bull and Cockfights. New Trade Plan. My personal View of Trade.

The Spanish government, as is well-known, is very suspicious. It essentially does not permit the vessels of another nation to enter any of its ports in North and South America. If, however, a foreign ship is forced to seek haven and help because it needs water, wood or food, or has been damaged in a storm, at any of the Spanish American settlements a guard is placed on board immediately, the ship is searched and often, depending upon the circumstances, assistance is refused. Foreign trade and barter in goods which have not passed through Spanish customs is forbidden by confiscation. They charge high duty, particularly on tobacco, which is a crown possession. American ships are guarded very strictly. The freedom of movement of non-Spanish seamen is so restricted that they scarcely may go on shore without permission and surveillance. Even Vancouver's* English expedition, which was most cordially received, had to accept these restrictions. We most likely would have had to set sail without accomplishing our goal had we had not made use of the royal Spanish mandates given Krusenstern's expedition.

We were so cordially received that we had no second thoughts about telling Padre José and Padre Martin, after we had got to know them, about our main purpose in coming and describing the famine in Sitcha and then asking them for grain in exchange for money, or rather goods. As much as they would have liked to help us, they dared not enter into any trade without the government's permission. They held out hope for us, since they had no doubts about our receiving it, and

*See his *Voyage*, Part IV, pp. 75 and 83.

already looked forward to obtaining permission in the near future. This would give them an opportunity to obtain some of the European goods needed by the Mission. They had heard that many of the articles on board were intended to meet their needs.* Accompanied by Don Luiz Arguello, they came to the ship the day after we arrived in order to inspect them. They liked the coarse linen, fine sail cloth, drill (Russian ticking) and English sheets very much. In addition, they inquired a great deal about iron, hardware, particularly about shop and farm tools, sheep shears, axes, large saws for sawing boards, large and small iron kettles (they did not like tin-coated copper ones, several of which we had along), kitchen crockery, containers, bottles, glasses and plates, fine handkerchiefs and scarfs, leather of all kinds, especially calf's leather and leather for shoe soles, etc. Among other things, we had a quantity of ready-made (Kasan) shoes and boots, round hats and other articles of clothing which they found very welcome.

The ladies of the Presidio had them ask if we had a kind of cotton or muslin shawl about three and one-half ells long and one ell wide, as well as fine, polished and embroidered muslin, fine printed calico, colorfully striped silk ribbons, etc.

We showed our intentions to be good, trustworthy, unselfish friends by giving Don Luiz Arguello a good English musket and each of the monks a piece of fine English cloth and the Mission church a piece of gold cloth. They thanked us very much for the gifts.

On April 2, Don Luiz Arguello came on board wearing his military dress uniform in order to greet Mr. von Resanoff in the name of the Governor of Monterey, to offer him all necessary services, to ask for official papers and proof that he really was the person he said he was and to ask him where the rest of the ships in the expedition and its leader were? And how long we planned to stay in San Francisco?

Mr. von Resanoff showed him various letters and letters of introduction from other countries. He excused himself for not having one from the Spanish Court, since it had not yet arrived upon his departure from St. Petersburg. Despite this, he had been cordially received at other Spanish settlements, for example, in Tenerife by Governor Marquis de la Casa Cahigal. Don Luiz Arguello was completely satisfied with this explanation and gave Mr. von Resanoff a polite

*Most of these things were purchased in Sitcha with the *Juno*.

answer in writing from the Governor in Monterey, Don Arrelaga. He promised to come in a few days and in his presence give us all the help we needed.

In the meantime, the news of our arrival and intentions had spread around the countryside. Among other places the news reached San José, the newest mission established about eight years before, south of San Francisco. That new settlement had a great need for many of the articles we had along and immediately delegated one of their monks, Padre Pedro, to negotiate with us. As soon as he had seen, in the company of the Commissioner of the Russian-American Company, some of our goods, he offered his and his mission's services and made a deal with us. For four pieces of blue English cloth and seven pieces of linen, which he had put aside until receiving permission from the Governor, he promised to deliver 104 fanegas* of the best wheat from his mission.

This priest acted very differently from Padre José Uria, who was always happy and pleasant company and did not appear to be trading for the first time. When we asked for a considerable supply of flour as well as the necessary sacks to stow it on board, he said that he had neither in the quantities we were asking for. Without much further thought, he offered, however, to have the Indians of his mission while we were there grind as much grain as possible, and if necessary, to work day and night. He hoped thus to be able to deliver about 42 arrobas** of flour and a sufficient number of sacks. For want of other materials, he would have the sacks made from horse, cow and steer hides.

On the 7th, we were told that the Governor, Don Arrelaga from Monterey, along with the Commandant of San Francisco, Don Arguello, and several other officers were expected at the Presidio. Toward evening we actually heard their arrival announced by a cannon shot from the fort. On this occasion we not only heard a nine-shot salvo in greeting from the fort we were acquainted with, which protects the entrance to the harbor, but also from a fort at the headland of an inlet stretching to the southeast in the interior of the bay. We were more than surprised to discover fortifications about which we had heard nothing up to then and also could not see from our

---

*A Spanish measure of grain, approximately 53½ of which equal a Hamburg *fass*.

**An arroba weighs about 25 pfunts.

A ship, entering the harbor with hostile intentions, could think it was far safer by perhaps keeping a great distance between it and the fort protecting the entrance to the harbor. It could then be more than embarrassed by the unexpected surprise of a cannon salvo; whereas every ship sailing along the north shore and in the northeast part of the spacious bay, which then anchors in the interior of the harbor, is out of all danger.*

As soon as the arrival of the governor was reported to us, Mr. von Davidoff was sent ashore to welcome him and to express the thanks we owed him for the especially cordial reception we had been given. The following morning, when we were expecting a return visit, two priests sent by the Governor arrived. Because of his age and infirmities, he asked to be pardoned for not coming and requested Mr. von Resanoff and all the officers to come to the Presidio. His invitation was accepted and we proceeded to go there. The Governor turned out to be an upright old man sixty years of age. He had ridden on horseback about 25 German miles in order to pay us his respects, energetically support us and make our stay as pleasant as possible.

The main purpose of Mr. von Resanoff's negotiations with the Governor of Monterey was the supplying of the Russian settlements with provisions. He also attempted to reach a mutual agreement which would help the needs of the settlements by establishing a regular maritime trade route between Russia and these Spanish provinces.

The Governor did not believe he had the authority to do either the one or the other, even though the advantages of such an agreement were çlear to him. For this reason, he relegated every suggestion to the Cabinet in Madrid and said that even the Viceroy of Mexico could not act in such matters on his own accord.

As far as supplies for our continued voyage were concerned, there would not be the slightest difficulty. On the contrary, the Governor immediately gave all of the surrounding missions orders to supply grain, flour, meat, salt and the other items we desired. He permitted us in lieu of money to pay with goods. In order to prevent dissatisfaction, jealousy or disorder, he had lists made of our needs

---

*Anyone wanting to know more about this and wanting to get a clearer picture of the above should look at map number 33 in the *Atlas* to la Pérouse's *Voyage*. Every enemy ship is safe from Spanish attack in the vicinity and to the north of Ile de los Angelos and Ponta de St. Antonio.

and of the stores at each of the missions. He himself then determined the quantity and kind of products which each should receive or deliver. Mr. von Resanoff's main intention was to buy a complete shipload of grain and other foodstuffs. In the beginning this demand met with a great many difficulties. Only after extended and long negotiations did the Governor allow the various missions to deliver the desired quantity of provisions. He, however, insisted that the Commandant of San Francisco, Don Arguello, in the name of the Governor, i.e., in the Crown's stead, take possession of the goods being traded and that the missions had to wait to receive them until permission for their delivery was obtained from Mexico.

This arrangement helped us. The missions expected a favorable answer and the Governor thought by this means to be protected from any unpleasantness on the part of the Court.

While horses, oxen and mules from the various missions were transporting the supplies we had obtained, the Governor, along with his staff and the Commandant's large family, made our stay pleasant in every way possible.

Almost every morning saddled horses stood waiting on the shore. We used them to ride around in the neighboring areas. We had permission to go everywhere except to the fortifications.

We often spent our time hunting the crested partridge [quail] and rabbits abounding in the sandy hills of the surrounding area.[1] One day, a party of twelve of us rode out together with thirty to forty Indians in order to undertake a kind of "hunting with hounds." Without using firearms, in less than three hours, we caught 75 rabbits and hares, mostly alive. Several times we tried in vain to find New World tigers and lions (*Felis Onca* and *Felis*, probably *Concolor*) and bears. Bears are abundant here, the other two less common. Along the north shore of the bay, deer hunting is very good. During various excursions on the water, I mostly found water birds I knew from Sitcha: *Pelecanus*, *Colymbus*, *Anas perspicillata*, etc., *A. nigra*, *Haematopus Ostralegus*, etc. Several kinds of seal and the much more valuable sea otter, almost unaccustomed to being waylaid, were swimming around in all parts of the expansive bay.

One or another of us was in the Presidio almost every noon. Evening parties were enlivened by dance and song.

Padre José came almost daily to the Presidio. His severity contrasted markedly with the happy disposition of Padre Pedro, who lived with the Arguello family. When he spoke, there was general silence and attentiveness. As soon as Padre Pedro opened his mouth, the whole party laughed. He seemed full of wit and lively thoughts and entertained the party in the most pleasant of manners.

The usual dance here is called the *barrego*. It is danced by two couples standing opposite each other. They begin singing a song in six-eight time while stamping rhythmically to the eighth beat. They make a figure of a *demi-chaine*. Then they slowly balance toward each other and begin the dance anew. We took some pains to teach the ladies English contra dances. They liked them so much that subsequently we usually danced them because more could take part, they being group dances. Several soldiers from the garrison who played violin and guitar were our musicians.

Don Arguello, who since our arrival had been telling us a great deal about animal baiting which they engaged in occasionally, ordered eight soldiers on horseback on April 10th to catch a live wild bear and bring it to the Presidio, where it was to fight wild bulls. That same evening these people actually brought in a large black-brown bear they had hunted up somewhere and caught with ropes and lassos. It was lying on an ox hide stretched over several logs which had been bound together. A pair of oxen had dragged it in from several miles away. Its paws and muzzle had been tightly bound together. The violence and constraint used on the bear had enraged it. As soon as it arrived at the Presidio, its bonds were removed for the most part. Its entire body was splashed with water. This seemed to refresh it very much. Finally, it was bound by only its hind feet to a stake driven in the ground for this purpose near a ditch filled with water. Soon it, of its own accord, began to drink and to enjoy cooling itself off in the little pool. No one dared to go near it because it gazed wildly enraged and vexed all around. The order was given to catch the wild bulls which were to fight with the bear. The baiting was set for the following day. The next day we waited impatiently for the horses at the appointed time, only to learn at their arrival, to our great regret, that our hopes and curiosity had come to naught. The bear had died in the night.*

In order to alleviate our disappointment to some degree, the Commandant promised to have a bull fight that afternoon. One after

---

*According to the Spaniards, the bear comes out on the short end in such battles.

another, several soldiers on foot and on horseback threw spears at a bull until it died after being wounded many times. Since such bull fights, a national pastime in Spain and Portugal, have already been described from time to time, I think it superfluous to repeat the same things here, especially since the fighters had displayed no extraordinary skills and adroitness. In the meantime, it has occurred to me that the priests, who seem to display tender, humane emotions in all of their behavior and try to awaken these in their neophytes, have not opposed these basically cruel, national amusements. Probably their concept of cruelty has been obliterated by these amusements, since they have been used to them from childhood and they are no more affected by the wanton, meaningless torture of animals than the people on Nukahiva when they are eating human flesh.

I have to include a similar kind of amusement enjoyed by the Spanish in New California in this category — cockfights. We saw none, only the penknife-like spurs bound to the fighting cocks' legs for such fights.

Our daily cordial meetings, the music, the songs, the games and dances had led Mr. von Resanoff's thought, aside from the important plans for trade he was developing, to yet other more important thoughts and speculations by far. Donna Conception had made a special impression upon him. The lightning of her fiery eyes had penetrated into the farthest reaches of his heart. His Excellency, Chevalier von Resanoff, therefore believed that by marrying the daughter of the Commandant of San Francisco (Captain Don Arguello) a lasting bond for future trade could be established between the Russian-American Company and New California. He, therefore, was firmly committed, for the well-being of the State and because of the importance of future trade, to sacrifice himself through marriage to Donna Conception, in order to unite both empires, the Russian and the Spanish, in most friendly of manners! The first difference to overcome, the difference of religion, was a trifle for a philosophically minded man like Mr. von Resanoff. When the Governor pointed out the questionable political situation in Europe, the well-known distrustful nature of the Spanish government and held out little hope for his gaining support for his trade speculations, Mr. von Resanoff answered that he himself, immediately after his arrival in St. Petersburg, would leave again, in the capacity of an imperial Russian ambassador extraordinary and authorized minister, for Madrid, where he would settle any differences between the Courts. He would then sail from one of the Spanish ports to Vera Cruz and Mexico and come from there to San Francisco to claim his bride and to pursue active trade! It can be seen from this that Mr. von Resanoff was bold as well as quick in carrying out his lofty plans to join peoples!

Mr. von Resanoff's main reason for wanting to trade with California was so that the northern Russian possessions from America to Kamtschatka and Ochotsk could be supplied with grain and flour in the future from there. As likely as it seemed, at first glance, that such a plan could be carried out and, as praiseworthy as such a deserving undertaking was, in my opinion, there were many obstacles in the way, even if the Spanish Court were to allow and support it. The settlements of the Russian-American Company lie so far apart from each other that support and communication among them can barely be maintained, given the present state of shipping. Furthermore, there is already a dearth of sailors and ships, which would have to become even more apparent if regular trade were established with California. Supposing they had the ships and crews, how would they pay for Californian products but with hard cash or such goods as they needed there? These are truly not to be had on the Aleutian Islands, in Sitcha or Kamtschatka. New California needs factory and manufactured goods, sugar, chocolate, brandy, wine, tobacco, iron and iron tools, etc. The Russian settlements from Ochotsk to the Northwest Coast of American have an even greater need for these than the Spanish settlements. If the Russians would use the most advantageous path and send ships from Europe to California to trade only for provisions, that is, flour, grain salted meat and possibly sea otters (for money and goods) and then take them from there to the Russian settlements, this, in my opinion, would be far more costly than if the Crown, or the Russian-American Company, sent a ship every year from Kronstadt directly to their outposts. Furthermore, grain in California is by far more expensive than in Kronstadt. In addition, if these ships wanted to go to California, they would have to make a considerable detour and suffer from a loss of time.

As far as sea otters are concerned — probably the only thing that would permit profitable trade — there is one big question: would the Spaniards agree to this kind of trade? I doubt it very much. Foreign seafarers are strictly forbidden by a royal Spanish decree, under threat of loss of ship, to kill sea otters within thirty legoas of the coast. Once the Governor complained a great deal about the behavior of the seafarers from the United American Free States, not only because they supply the inhabitants of the Northwest Coast of America with gunpowder and firearms, but also because they are so audacious as sometimes to have a large number of Aleuts with them and kill sea otters along the Californian coast. He related something we did not know. Several years before, a certain Captain Orean,[2] together with thirty men and four women from Unalaska, had secretly sailed to the coast of his province with this intention. Since then, the Spanish government has taken measures to stop this. Every year two ships from Acapulco sail the length of the coast to control the mischief. Indeed, during our stay, the news actually arrived that an American ship had been captured and seized in San Diego.[3]

If the Russians want to establish profitable trade with these regions and supply their northern possessions from there, it would only be possible by taking complete control of the area and founding their own colony. In a land like California with its mild climate, wood, water and excellent harbor and so many resources and natural products, an enterprising spirit could give such an outpost a very different appearance in a few years. With the help of the truly skilled workmen from Sitcha at Norfolk Sound, several kinds of water and windmills could soon be built, weaving looms constructed, and a distillery established. They would have to build large and small vessels and, with full granaries and large herds of cattle, hunt sea otter. Then, certainly, Kamtschatka and eastern Asia could be supplied sufficiently with all kinds of vegetables and animal products. Russia and the Russian-American Company already have enough sea otter and other sources of riches in their possessions and do not need to covet foreign possessions. Their possessions contain inexhaustible sources of wealth. Under good management they could even now be raised from their ruins if the management concentrated its energies and did not weaken itself too much through boundless expansion.

Notes

1. Here, as throughout the voyage, Langsdorff identifies birds and animals in terms of European ones with which he was familiar.

2. Langsdorff is probably referring to Joseph O'Cain, who captained the ship *O'Cain* and traded on the Northwest Coast in 1803-04.

3. This was probably the brig *Peacock*, Captain Oliver Kimball, of Boston, seized by the Spanish in February 1806, but soon released. F. W. Howay, *A List of Trading Vessels in the Maritime Fur Trade, 1785-1825* (Kingston, Ontario: The Limestone Press, 1973), p. 70.

Chapter 9

Need for Shipping and Communication by Water. Boat Excursion to San Jose. The Mission of San Jose. Description of it. Indians there. Their Dance. Pueblo of San Jose. The difficult Return to San Francisco.

Even though the three most northerly missions, San Francisco, Santa Clara and San Jose, lie not very far apart from each other in the vicinity of the southeastern part of the Bay of San Francisco and it would be most useful to maintain communications among them by water, it is almost incredible that not a one of them and not even the Presidio or the Port of San Francisco has any kind of boat or vessel available. Perhaps the missionaries are afraid that the introduction of boats would provide the Indians with an easier means to give in to their common inclination toward freedom and escape. Therefore, the only connection is overland by horse. The Spaniards, as well as their wards, the Indians, only very rarely have the need to entrust themselves to the waves. Undoubtedly, this is also the reason why navigation is still in its infancy. If an emergency arises, they bind together as many dry rushes, reeds and straw as they feel are necessary and set out with it. In front and behind it is tied together into a point with straw. It is called a *valtsa* and is used instead of a boat to get from one shore to the other. The paddle is a long, thin pole which is somewhat wider at each end. They paddle first on the one side and then on the other.

The total absence of a boat in the harbor, that is, as it were, the key to all of the southern and eastern settlements, is one of the greatest proofs of the government's negligence. This was the reason why the Spaniards, on the day of our arrival, had to stand on shore so long and could not take up contact with us until we sent our shallop to them.

Since the Mission of San Jose lies on the other side, on the southeastern shore of the Bay, a distance of about sixteen legoas straight across the Bay, it would be very advantageous for the missionaries to have a link by water. Despite this, they only use an overland route and have to cover at least twice to three times the distance around the Bay.

The difficulty of land transport, the small number of neophytes in San Jose and measles, a disease never before seen in New California, which had spread in that year from the peninsula of California to the northern settlements and had been causing great devastation among the Indians at nearby missions, thus preventing them from quickly providing us with needed supplies, caused Mr. von Resanoff to ask Governor Don Arrelaga for permission to send our launch and two shallops to San Jose to pick up a large part of the promised grain more quickly and easily. The advantage of going by water and thus saving men, horses and time was too obvious for Don Arrelaga to deny permission.

Accordingly, on the 12th several boats were readied. A courier was sent overland to tell the Mission of San Jose about our arrival and to give them the Governor's orders to mark our landing place by building a fire on the 14th, since the Governor and the Commandant had assured us that we would not be able to land anywhere without that precaution. Mr. von Davidoff commanded the expedition and permitted me to accompany him. Toward noon of the 14th, we left the ship and used the beginning tide to reach a large inlet stretching to the southeast. As soon as we had reached the headland lying to the northeast of the Presidio, we caught sight of the battery of five cannon defending the just-mentioned expansive, wide inlet to the southeast and southwest. The eastern shore to the left of us was a large, low plain several miles wide. Behind it rose a chain of mountains of moderate height, pierced by steep valleys and only covered by woods in some places. The western shore was bordered partially by desert and partially by hills covered by some brush. That shore has many headlands and small inlets, and the Mission of San Francisco is situated on one of them. Up to that point the water is deep enough for larger ships. Soon, however, it suddenly becomes very shallow, at the most, five feet of water of a totally different color. After we had gone several sea miles, while often dropping the sounding-lead, we caught sight of high land on the southern horizon rising like an island out of the surface of the water. At the same time, we saw rather clearly to the southeast the beautiful Mission of San Jose standing on high ground. At a great distance toward the south, on land we assumed to be an island, we noticed smoke. We could not imagine that this could be the predetermined signal. We assumed rather that it was another chance fire. We kept examining the eastern shore closer to us for the predetermined signal.

Only at sunset did we see our mistake, when we recognized that the land we assumed was an island was part of a point of land connected to a plain lying to the east. Because of our erroneous impression and a brisk southwest wind, we had already gone too close to the eastern shore. We could neither sail nor row to the signal fire. The darkness of the night forced us to drop anchor at a shallow spot in three fuss of water, thus, separating from the launch, which we had completely lost sight of. On the morning of the 15th, after another unsuccessful attempt to reach the high point of land, we had no other choice, because of a strong southwest wind, but to head back to the ship without having accomplished our task. The launch had fought the entire day with the wind and waves and considered itself lucky finally to reach the harbor of San Francisco undamaged on the 16th. The third boat had lost its mast and sailed into a small inlet.

This squally weather continued until the 19th, when the weather again cleared with north and northwest winds.

Because I really wanted to get to know the Mission of San Jose despite our unsuccessful expedition, I asked the Governor for permission to visit there. He gave me permission. Accompanied by a sailor and a hunter, I set out again on the 20th in the three-seated baidarka, which we had brought along from Sitcha. We left San Francisco in the morning and reached the flat land lying in front of San Jose toward noon. We looked for the main channel along its coast, which was supposed to be near several hills. These hills were the main landmark we were to use to find it. They stretch from the northwest to the southwest and are surrounded by muddy shallows, which extend for a considerable distance along the shore. To avoid them we had to steer to the west until the southern hill (which we thought was an island on the 14th) lies to the east. The channel one then has to follow winds between hills. One keeps the two lower ones to the north and the other higher ones to the south. The channel runs at first more to the northwest and then, after many bends, inland to the southeast. At flood tide it always has six to nine fuss of water. Small ships can navigate it even at low tide. Landing is almost totally impossible at low tide, because of the very loose mud, and even at high tide, difficult in most places. The many little channels running through the lowlands there form a true labyrinth, in which we got lost again and again when we missed the main channel and rowed into a side channel because we did not know the area.

Tired of going astray, I finally climbed up a nearby hill. From there, I found a landing place where we could go on land with dry feet and then reach the Mission lying about three and one-half legoas to the east-northeast. The countryside we had to walk through rises gradually from the low plain until it is bounded by a moderately high chain of mountains to the north-northwest and south-southeast. Numerous herds of horses and cattle roam free there like in a wilderness. The bulls occasionally are a danger to people traveling on foot. Besides these herds, we met a large wolf that timidly ran away and a large number of foxes. They seemed to live along with the calves in an incredible intimacy, also following the cows as if the cows were their mothers. Tired, we reached the Mission before sunset. It is run by only two priests, Padre Luiz and Padre Pedro. Padre Pedro welcomed us with open arms and immediately sent horses to the shore to bring our bags and the sailor whom we had left behind to guard the baidarka. It was now left in the care of several Indians. Padre Luiz had left a short time before our arrival and was in San Francisco. The morning of the 21st, the neophytes of the Mission gathered as usual in order to receive their orders for the day from Padre Pedro. He had promised me during his stay in San Francisco to have the Indians put on a dance. For this reason, he excused them all from work that day on the condition that they dress themselves for the dance as perfectly as possible. For this purpose, he distributed some finery among the best dancers. They left with it to prepare themselves for the coming festivities.

In the meantime, Padre Pedro showed me the buildings and grounds of the Mission. Since they had only existed for eight years, they were not yet very large and spacious. The grain stored in the granary exceeded all of my expectations — 2,000 fanegas of wheat, and a considerable quantity of maize, beans, barley, peas, etc. The kitchen garden had been planted for use and was growing well. The ground is very fertile and produces rich crops. The fruit trees are still small but look very good. A small creek flows through the garden and suffices to water it. Beginning several years ago, they have been planting vineyards which are thriving. The wine is said to be sweet, similar to the wine from Mallaga.

The whole location of the place has been exceedingly well chosen. It is generally thought that this Mission will be one of the richest and best in New California in a few years.

Its only disadvantage is that there are absolutely no tall trees. On occasion, the natives have thoughtlessly burned most of the woods, except for an occasional tree, simply for the joy of having a fire. For this reason, lumber has to be hauled from several miles away.

Despite this disadvantage, this Mission has a great many advantages over the others. There are hills of limestone and excellent clay, which have permitted them to start a brickyard and construct all of the main buildings of brick. The Mission has more grain than cattle. Therefore, fewer steers are slaughtered each week than at San Francisco. Here, however, the amount of vegetables, grain and legumes distributed is less by far.

Their furnishings and organization are exactly like at San Francisco. The Indian quarters (las Rancherias) are not yet quite finished; therefore, the neophytes live in family groups in cone-shaped straw huts.

Padre Pedro, after showing me all around for several hours, suggested that we watch the Indians' preparations for the dance. He took me to a creek where the Indians had gathered. They were occupied with smearing themselves with cinders, red clay and chalk. While one was thus busy beautifying his chest, stomach and thighs, another would be painting various regular figures on his back. Several were covering their totally naked bodies with down, thus giving themselves the appearance of ape-like animals rather than that of men. They decorated their heads, necks and ears with various kinds of adornments. Their entire bodies, except for coverings over their genitals, were naked. In the meantime, the women were getting ready in their huts. They, as is right and proper, are clothed. They only paint their faces and necks, which they also try to beautify in their fashion with adornments made from mussels, feathers, coral, etc.

The Indians at the Mission, who gathered in the courtyard toward noon, are totally different in size, appearance and culture from those in San Francisco. The men are well built, almost all are of above average stature, with only a few having small, thick-set bodies. Their color, to be sure, is dark but not negroid. Their physiognomy is to be sure not pleasant but also not revolting and has, in my opinion, a great similarity to that of the inhabitants of the Northwest Coast. Their black hair is very thick, and there are said to be individuals of rare muscular strength.

All of the women, in comparison to the men, are of more than normal stature. Many are more than five schuh high. Even though I did not see one single face that I could have called pretty, their appearance is, however, not as dumb and repulsive as that of the neophytes in San Francisco.

The Indians at San Jose are said to be the best looking in New California. This is why the Spanish soldiers, for the lack of Spanish women, often marry Indians from this Mission.

The dancers had divided themselves into two different groups. Each group was distinguished from the other by its adornments and special song. The one group consisted of coastal inhabitants, the other of neophytes from the interior. The first group is weaker, less well built and uglier than the other. From time immemorial, the greatest hostility had existed between these two groups. Here they are united by religion. The old hostilities are, however, so deeply rooted that they are still present, for example, in marriage. Despite all of the missionaries' efforts, the various tribes only marry among themselves. It is an exception if they mix socially with another tribe.

While dancing, they remain almost completely in one spot. While jumping rhythmically and making all kinds of body movements and grimaces, they portray scenes from war and domestic life with the help of bows and arrows and with feathers held in their hands and on their heads. Their music consists of singing and clicking produced by a little stick split on one end. The women have their own songs and special way of dancing. They hop near the men but never together with them. Their main movement or action consists in sliding their thumb and index finger rhythmically from one side to the other of their abdomens. As soon as the men begin to dance, the women also start to hop and stop as soon as they stop.

Toward two o'clock, we sat down to a good noonday meal. After eating, we again observed the Indians, who were still busy with their dance and were performing a battle. A large straw figure took the place of the enemy. While making frightening grimaces and threats, a number of Indians armed with bows and arrows jumped and danced around their adversary, who should have been doing likewise. Finally, an Indian in their midst gave a signal. At that moment, a quantity of arrows pierced the figure, which was then brought to the imaginary chief in triumph.

On this occasion, I observed that most of the Indians are very skilled marksmen. It seemed to me that if the enemy were brave and did less jumping and moving and used their weapons more, they certainly would almost always be victorious. Dead enemies are never eaten. During strife the greatest effort is expended on stealing young girls and women from the enemy.

Another party of Indians behind a large fire stood and hopped just like the others. From time to time several people took glowing embers about the size of a walnut, as though for pleasure, and stuck them into their mouths and then swallowed them. It was not a trick because I watched that pastime of theirs very carefully. I still do not understand why those people did not burn their mouths.

I was also entertained by a representation of a hunting party. The Indians, with antlers and some deerskin fastened to their heads, sneak up on deer in their grazing areas. They know how to sneak through the high grass toward the animals, that often suddenly raise their heads and look fearfully around, and to imitate their natural movements and shyness, so that they are able to get within a few steps of them with their bows and arrows and kill one or another of the animals. The animals suspect nothing of the deception and nearby danger.

Toward the east, about seven legoas from San Jose, is the branch of a large river that winds toward the north and then turns west, where it empties into the northeastern part of the Bay of San Francisco.[1] Near the river are numerous villages where Indians live, who are not yet baptized or living with the Spaniards. Shortly after the Mission was established, they caused trouble from time to time. The last time was a year and one-half ago, when five Spaniards were killed and a priest and a soldier dangerously wounded. After that incident, a well armed military expedition was sent out. It defeated the Indians handily and compelled them to be peaceful, which they have been ever since then.

The Spaniards and neophytes now go occasionally to these free Indians for two weeks or longer to recruit converts. Some of them also come to the Mission, where they are always given gifts of all kinds to take back to their villages.

Toward the southwest, three legoas from San Jose on an arm of the ocean, lies the Pueblo of San Jose. Pueblo means a village for invalid soldiers who have settled as peasants. These people cultivate the land and live from the plentiful harvest of their fields and cattle breeding. There are similar pueblos in several places in New as well as Old California. Their populations are growing from year to year. The Governor of Monterey told me that from one hundred this had grown to seven hundred in twenty years. In contrast, it is strange that the number of Indians at the missions, despite all of the good treatment, has been declining from year to year.

I took leave of Padre Pedro on the 23rd. I owe him public thanks for his kind reception and hospitality. He had the horses saddled. Accompanied by a soldier, we returned to the place we had left our baidarka. On the way a few wild bulls followed us, causing us to be more than a little afraid. A number of foxes we scared up fled timidly away. We rowed in the shallow water through the channel winding between the hills to the bay. We noted on both sides the wide muddy shores covered with sandpipers, snipes, wild ducks and sea gulls. We did not hunt them because we could not have retrieved them from the deep muck. We also saw a lot of sea otters. We wounded one but it sought refuge in a side channel and we did not want to pursue it.

We had just reached the bay when a very strong wind arose from the north that made it impossible for us to paddle forwards. Soaked by the high, tumbling waves, held back by the current of the tide and plagued by hunger and thirst, we had to give up any further attempts to go ahead at sundown. We had to look for a landing place in the vicinity and spend the night under the open heavens on a low, wet spot. Since we had not anticipated such an event and our provisions, some bread, cheese and a little bit of brandy left over from the trip there, were only enough for one day, we laid down with hungry stomachs. We were even less able to quench our thirst, since we were surrounded by puddles of sea water.

Using a wet sailcloth, we tried to protect ourselves somewhat against the strong wind and waited, almost frozen, for daybreak. Our clothing, totally soaked by the previous day's storm, dried out after the sun came up. Toward ten o'clock, we were once again ready to start out, but low tide and a muddy shore over a verst wide, which we could not cross, made it impossible for us to leave before high tide. It was toward noon before we climbed into our boat. Almost at the same time a strong wind arose from the north and northwest, leaving no possibility of reaching San Francisco that day. Therefore, we decided to row to the opposite shore, which appeared to lie considerably higher and boasted of woods and trees. We arrived there around three o'clock in the afternoon and found an expanse of low, swampy land covered only by salt water plants (*Salsola*) and intersected by many channels that made it impossible to walk to the woods several versts away.

We rowed our baidarka along the widest channel for about three-quarters of an hour around many curves until we finally were lucky enough to find a place where we could land. From there, with little difficulty, we could reach the nearby woods where we hoped to find fresh water. Carrying the last bit of our bread and cheese and an empty bottle, armed with musket and pistols, we wandered around, driven by thirst, looking for a spring or creek. Indeed, before nightfall we had reached the woods and had walked more than a German mile without finding a single drop of water. Finally, we discovered a large herd of wild bulls and cows grazing on one of the plains covered by high grass. After also crossing that plain while warding off the wild bulls with musket and pistol shots, we finally sank down to rest our spent limbs, exhausted from the burden of the day, tormented by hunger and thirst, longing for a drink of water. Without hope and depressed, we sank down when all at once we heard a frog croaking a little distance away. The song of a nightingale never sounded better to our ears. Like a flash, we pulled ourselves together and pursued the inviting call of that creature, whose voice led us in the dark of the night to a little creek with excellent water.

For two exhausting days, we had hardly been able to satisfy our hunger and even less still our thirst, so we fell greedily upon the water. Within less than two hours, the three of us emptied fourteen bottle-fulls of water.

The night was cool and wet. We tried to keep warm by a fire and rest until midnight. Then we set out again in the bright moonlight to find our baidarka. We frightened off several bears and wild bulls that crossed our path with shots. Toward three in the morning we again reached our boat. There was complete calm. We set out for San Francisco in the beautiful red of the sunrise. The channel we followed in order to reach the inlet was filled with sea otters and seals. Many of them were lying on the muddy shores and others stuck their heads up out of the water. The preceding two days were still fresh in our minds, and our stomachs longed so very much for food that we forwent all the joy and advantages of rich hunting, except for three sea otters which continued sleeping without a care in the world as our baidarka glided past them. We shot them one after another in passing and took them along.

Toward noon we were already rather close to Mission San Francisco. Once again a wind arising in the northwest held us up so much that we did not arrive at the ship until around three o'clock in the afternoon extremely tired, thirsty and exhausted.

To my sorrow, except for the sea otters, all of my other objects of natural history, mainly plants and bird skins, that I had collected on this excursion, fell prey to the stormy seas.

NOTES

1. This is evidently a garbled reference to the San Joaquin River, in the then little known interior valley of California. Langsdorff was never there, so he relied on information supplied by the Spanish, who except for a few punitive expeditions had not ventured east of the Coast Range. However, as Langsdorff reveals (pp. 122-123) plans were then being made for a more systematic investigation, perhaps with founding of a mission, but the decline of Spanish power prevented this.

Chapter 10

Geographical Description of the Harbor and River of San Francisco. Military Expedition to the Interior. Sierra Nevada. Communication by Land. Acapulco. San Blaz. Medical Remarks. Cowpox. Measles. Midwifery. Venereal Disease. Latido. Remarks about the Natural History.

The difficulty of obtaining geographical information from the Spanish had prevented us from getting more exact knowledge about the area. For this reason, I think that the little bit of information and remarks I collected during our stay in San Francisco may be of interest.

As incomplete and unsatisfactory as the copy of a Spanish original of the unlucky la Pérouse's map of the Harbor of San Francisco may be (see his *Atlas*, No. 33), at least it served to give us some idea of that archipelago.

Because of my excursion to San Jose, I have already had an opportunity to tell a bit about the arm of the sea stretching almost to Santa Clara to the east and southeast. To the north and northeast is another long, wide bay that is miles long. It has a quantity of larger and smaller islands strewn around it. From the east, four, others say five, very large rivers flow into it. It is very likely that they are the mouths of one and the same river, which comes from the south and southeast and flows into the northern part of the Bay of San Francisco. The Spaniards have ridden along the southern or left bank of this river far into the interior. Because they had no boats, they were unable to explore the right bank of the river more closely. It is said to run 80 to 90 legoas inland, be four to five klafters deep and so wide that a musket ball can hardly reach the opposite shore.

Every year military expeditions are sent out to collect more exact knowledge of the interior and, where possible, gradually establish overland communications between Santa Fe and the Northwest Coast of America.

While I was at Mission San Jose, one such expedition of thirteen soldiers together with one sergeant and a corporal returned. These people said they had gone 80 to 90 legoas into the interior and had reached the vicinity of a high, expansive chain of mountains always covered with snow, known to the Spaniards as the Sierra Nevada (snow-covered mountains). The river or rivers from San Francisco and another river, which flows into the ocean at 32° near San Miguel, are supposed to begin in these mountains.

Some inhabitants, or the Indians from the Sierra Nevada, claim they have seen men in blue and red clothing who looked completely like the Californian Spaniards a ride of three or four days away to the east of the above-named chain of mountains. They were probably soldiers from Santa Fe out on a similar expedition to explore the interior to the east and west. According to this information, the Spaniards had come rather close to each other between 35° and 38°, and it would soon be probable that they could establish a direct connection between Santa Fe and San Francisco.

According to these travelers, the interior has considerable woods, rivers and fertile land and is very populous. The Indians living near the coast are said to be generally ill-natured and warlike. Those living in numerous hordes farther to the east are said to be, for the most part, peaceful, shy and faint-hearted. The ones living along the shores of the large river are very good swimmers. When the Spaniards approach, they usually flee by swimming to the opposite bank of the river. Because of the lack of boats and the depth of the river, the Spaniards can never follow them.

The Indians have no other weapons than bows, arrows and stones. The Spanish soldiers, of course, are armed with muskets, two pistols and a long lance. They are superb riders and, thus, far superior to their weak, though numerous, opponents. The moment the Spanish suspect hostilities or danger, they throw a short coat made of thick deerskin over their shoulders that cannot be penetrated by arrows. They also have thick leather shields with which they very skillfully divert enemy arrows. If it is necessary to avenge hostile attacks, their lances are said to cause great destruction when they ride on their fast horses into the midst of the enemy and stab many of them to the ground.

During our stay at San Francisco, they were preparing a similar expedition to travel through the Sierra Nevada. The whole company, which would be leaving a few days after our departure, consisted of 25 men, Alferez (Ensign) Don Luiz Arguello and his brother, the Cadet San Iago Arguello, a corporal and our friend Padre Uria. He was going along with the intention, partially, to recruit neophytes, and especially to look for a place farther in the interior of the area that would be the most promising for the establishment of a new mission. This is how the Spanish attempt gradually to spread their sphere of influence in that part of the world and then to connect it without extraordinary expense to their various settlements to the east and west. The planning and establishment of a new mission is dependent upon the Padre Superior who resides in Monterey.

It would give the Spanish less trouble and cost the government less to send the expedition by water, to follow the course of the large river flowing into the Bay of San Francisco and to determine its course and source and navigability. The ships sailing there every year could conduct such an investigation with only the loss of a few weeks. The government could, in this way, collect more exact information about the province in one year than with their cumbersome overland military expeditions that are undertaken without the use of any astronomical instruments.

Due to a lack of small vessels and boats at the Harbor of San Francisco, the Spanish are completely cut off from the north shore, which is barely an Italian mile away. For this reason, they have absolutely no communication with the northern tribes in the neighborhood of Port de Bodega.

In contrast to this almost total lack of communication by water in Spanish American possessions, that by land exceeds all expectations. Regular mail goes out from Vera Cruz to all of the provinces in North and South America. A courier needs about two months to ride from Mexico to San Francisco, the most northerly outpost. News from Europe usually takes five to six months after being sent from Madrid. One can ride with the greatest of safety from San Francisco to Chile. All mail is carried by soldiers on horseback.

San Blaz is the unhealthiest place on the peninsula of California as well as a good seaport. Every year numbers of people die of virulent putrid fever, frequently accompanied by inflammation. For this reason, the Spanish Court has had to resort to offering high wages in order to entice people to live there. A sailor receives 30 or more piasters or Spanish dollars a month, a pilot 80 to 90, a lieutenant 200 to 300. A commander, because of his rank, receives instead of 400 to 500 piasters, 5,000 to 6,000. In August, most of the inhabitants leave the city because it is unhealthy to stay there during the frequent downpours at that period. Because of these circumstances, the government has often considered transferring the very important trade and shipping from San Blaz to another seaport. The merchants in Mexico and Guadalaxara, for whom the port is very convenient, have always opposed a change. Until now, no changes have been made.

Acapulco, a good port on the western coast of Mexico, was once a very unhealthy place to live and cost many lives every year. A Spanish surgeon put most of the blame on a large lake near the city and tried to get the government to drain it and let it dry out. This was then done. Since then, the place has not only very been healthy but also freed from indescribable swarms of mosquitoes.

In New California not enough is being done in the area of health care. Only the military has a doctor and a surgeon, who are usually stationed in Monterey. Neither the missionaries nor the Indians, their wards, have medical assistance. In the main, the climate is healthy and better than that of the peninsula of Old California. The Indians at the missions, however, are often taken ill with feverish diseases. They have such weak constitutions that they frequently die. Perhaps they were rarely ill in their former way of living. Perhaps the changes, the unaccustomed food, the exertion of unaccustomed labor and other conditions are the main causes of early death. The priests complain very much about the Indians' behavior. Whenever they become ill, they immediately become despondent and debilitated. They completely give into to their moods and feelings and neither follow the diet nor any other prescribed method that would lead to recovery. The missionaries have no medicines, except for a few emetics and cathartics which they keep for their own use.

Governor Don Arrelaga passed the important news on to me that cowpox had been brought to Mexico from Europe, and a surgeon there has already vaccinated numbers of people. He told me that recently, especially in the province south of Monterey, cowpox had been seen among the cattle and they had begun to immunize most successfully. But since true smallpox had not raged here for more than twenty years and its terrible devastation was unknown, most people considered it unnecessary to take the precaution of having themselves vaccinated. Cowpox is supposed to be a common disease among the cattle in California and is seen mainly in the spring. It disappears again as soon as the grass begins to dry out, i.e., in the warmer months of June, July, etc. As hard as I tried, I did not succeed in finding the disease.

For several months, measles have been causing a lot of devastation among the Indians. Several thousand natives in California have died of the disease. The Spanish, on the other hand, have survived them without any bad cases or further consequences. Apparently, the skin pores of the Indians are closed and eruptions could not occur easily. As a result, they suffer from a high fever which takes on a lingering, partially putrid character. Almost all of the Indian women who catch the measles when pregnant miscarry.

All over California, Spanish women are supposed to give birth very easily. Madame Arguello, who has born fifteen children, of whom 13 are still alive, said that she had no memory of a death in childbed. There are no midwives. One girlfriend helps another. Indian women are said, however, to die frequently in labor. This is due mainly, among other things, to their putting heavy pressure on the abdomen to quicken the birth. Miscarriages from the third to seventh month are supposed to occur frequently.

The most terrible of all diseases, known world wide as syphilis, is found here in all of its variations. It is common among the Spanish and the Indians and causes even greater devastation, because absolutely no medical measures are taken to prevent it. The usual results are spots on the skin, horrible rashes, persistently running sores, painful aches in the bones, throat infections, loss of the nose, deformities and death.

Among other complaints, I saw ophthalmia, rheumatism, virulent abscesses at the corners of the mouth and chronic diseases of various types, probably also thanks to Venus.

Padre Luiz in San Jose complained of a disease, which seems to afflict Spaniards as well as Indians in North and South America. I saw, however, too little of it to form a clear picture of the disease. The Spanish call it *latido* (pounding of the heart). It is characterized especially by pulsating sensations in the abdomen which gradually increase with age. The disease only occurs in adults of both sexes and never in children. Among other symptoms associated with the continual pulsation, the ill complain of pains beginning in the lower body and running toward the throat that make them feel as if a noose were being tightened around their throats, in the beginning an aversion to food, then the total loss of appetite, often nausea and heaviness in the abdomen as if it were knotted, frequent cramps, especially in the blood vessel system, and (also in men) all of the symptoms of hysteria. At this stage of the disease, the sufferers drag on in misery, more or less wasted away, until their deaths, which the disease, however, does not seem to accelerate. I saw old people who had had *latido* for years. Tape worms, aneurism and other known diseases, which doctors have said caused the disease, do not seem to play any kind of role here.

My research in natural history while in California met with more difficulties on the part of our expedition than are imaginable. Listing all of the details would cause me to ramble and seem petty. We lived continually on our ship. Loading and unloading was constantly going on. Seal and bird skins I had put on the deck to dry were thrown overboard. One day, when I was on land, the paper I was using for drying plants was carried out of the way, and I was told put by mistake into the lowest hold of the ship. The whole ship would have to be unloaded to retrieve it and that would not be possible before Sitcha. Live birds I had bought and brought on board were turned loose as soon as I turned my back. Whenever I required the help of a sailor on a water excursion, the request was denied under the pretense that the men had more important business and our expedition had not been undertaken for purposes of natural history. Evenings, tired from the hunt, I would bring various ducks and sea birds on board the ship intending to skin them. During the night, someone would petulantly cut off their heads. As a result of these incidents and hundreds of similar ones, discouraged and depressed, I was forced to give up any thoughts of doing research and had to acquiesce to Mr. von Resanoff's wish that I act as an interpreter with the priest in the trade and purchase of grain and other goods we needed.[1]

I saw among others the following mammals: large numbers of whales stranded on the beaches, especially in the Bay of Monterey. Seals and sea otters were caught in nets, though in small numbers. American lions, *Felis concolor*, American tigers, *Felis Onca*, stags, deer, wolves, fox, bears and skunks, *Viverra Putorius*, known here as *sorrillo* [*zorrillo*]. The urine that these animals can spray for protection against their enemies is said to have a terrible stench that surpasses all others imaginable. The priests told me it glows in the dark and, if it is stored in a little glass, it will continue to glow for a long time.[2]

Among the birds I saw was *Vultus Aura*. Their feet are very different from those of other birds. Claws and nails on the toes are thin and small. The three front toes are half-webbed so that the bird, judging by its feet, should be classified with marsh birds, but judging by its bill with the birds of prey. I was told that a soup prepared from their meat is very healthy and, after eating it, all bodily diseases can be determined by looking at the skin. The meat perhaps causes an allergic reaction in the same way that strawberries do in some people. These birds live in groups, fly sluggishly and feed on carrion, very often in the company of ravens with whom they seem to be on good terms. *Oriolus phoeniceus*, like our sparrows, fly in flocks over the buildings of the settlement. *Oriolus icterus*, *Alauda Calandra*, *Picus auratus*, *Tetrix cristatus*, *Trochilus mosquitus* and others of these species are common. There are lots of hummingbirds in the summer, but none at all in the winter. They say, in general, that they hibernate in this area in the winter. That is why the Spanish call them *paxaro resuscitado* (the resurrection bird).[3]

There are all kinds of marsh and water birds: *Ardea*, *Tringa*, *Scolopax*, *Pelecanus*, *Larus*, *Colymbus*, *Mergus*, *Anas*, etc. In the winter the number of wild geese is said to be so large in the swampy, southeastern inlet that their visit is considered a virtual plague. They often destroy a lot of the seeds sown in autumn. They are said to be so fresh that they can barely be frightened off by shooting muskets at them repeatedly.

Raya aquila and a kind of *Acipenser* were the only fish that I saw.

Notes

1. Langsdorff voiced the same complaints in *Plantes recuiellies pendant le voyage des Russes autor du monde*, with F. Fischer, v. 1, Premiere partie, Tübingen, 1810, in which he writes "I regard the year and a half that I spent on this expedition as a time virtually lost for me. For on these sterile, almost uninhabited coasts I obtained nothing at all that I had hoped for."

2. This alleged property of skunk urine appears not to have been tested in modern times by any known researcher.

3. Hummingbirds do not hibernate but the Californians may have got the idea from seeing examples of "night torpor," a state of inactivity brought on by cold nights.

Chapter 11

Departure from San Francisco. Condition of the Promyshlenniks. Sea Voyage. Arrival at Sitcha. News there. Parties Forced to Hunt Sea Otter. Departure from Sitcha. Visit in Kodiak. General Remarks about the Settlement.

Mr. von Resanoff finally was able to obtain a cargo of 4,294 fanegas of wheat and quantities of flour, beans, peas, Turkish maize, big beans, several tons of salted meat and a small supply of salt, soap, tallow, etc., in exchange for goods worth 24,000 piasters or Spanish dollars. It certainly seemed to me that, in proportion to such a supply of grain, he had taken so little meat, which was indeed excellent salted, since it would have been obviously cheaper and more practical. But Russians are known to prefer, in general, a piece of bread to a commensurate piece of meat. That is probably why Mr. von Resanoff thought purchasing grain would take care of all their needs.

The promyshlenniks, who in Sitcha had been living only on a meager diet of fish, seal and whale train, berries, saranna and a little rice, found themselves from the beginning eating a rich diet of meat and vegetables in New California. They had soon recovered from scurvy. A fat bull was enough to feed the crew for three days and only cost four Spanish dollars. It was soon apparent that it was cheaper to feed the sailors more meat than vegetables. They were even given bread so seldom and sparingly that they became tired of the tasty beef and longed for peas, beans and other kinds of vegetables.

Among other things, I found it remarkable to observe the various and sudden changes that the influence of food had on these men. In Sitcha almost all of them suffered from scurvy which developed to its highest degree. Soon after our arrival in San Francisco, most of them got well very quickly after eating fresh food. After two to three weeks, all had regained a lot of their color and strength. Everyone praised the beneficial influence of the climate and food. Shortly before our departure from San Francisco, however, one sailor after another suddenly had been struck down by an inflammatory, rheumatic fever, which meant that we had to set sail with fifteen of the best sailors ill; but they soon recovered.

Given these circumstances, we left San Francisco on May 10th (old style). We felt very grateful for the kindness and friendship of the Arguello family, who had treated us with such hospitality. Our long stay must have made it really difficult for them in the end. We are equally indebted to Governor Don Arrelaga, that dignified elderly man, who supported our business in every way he could, and to the missionaries who displayed multitudinous proof of their friendship. Above all, Padre José Uria deserves special mention for his friendliness, sincerity and generosity. Occasionally, he appeared to be seeking his own advantage. But since anything he could obtain from us would be expended upon his wards, this character trait also speaks favorably for him.

Toward four o'clock in the afternoon, we sailed with a favorable tide out of the harbor. When sailing past, we saluted the fort with a seven-cannon salvo which was answered by nine cannon shots.

The Governor, the Arguello family and other friends and acquaintances had gathered on the fortifications and waved farewell with hats and handkerchiefs.

We were not only setting out on our return trip to Sitcha but also to Europe, and the thought of this cheered and brightened all of our spirits. A continual northwest wind after our departure forced us to steer toward the west. The weather was variable, first clear, then cloudy and foggy. The water was rather calm. During the first few days of our voyage, we saw hardly a bird or other live creature.

After leaving San Francisco, it was not until the 18th that the first favorable wind came up. Our noonday position read 37°49′ N and 132° W. The following day we saw a lot of whales and several turtles. The water was alive with a quantity of salpa, beroe and other kinds of mollusks. Toward evening a lot of stormy petrels appeared without, as is generally incorrectly believed, a strong wind coming up.

Very early on the morning of the 21st, I was awakened to a new spectacle. About two miles away the sea was choppy. It looked as if we were in the vicinity of a rocky reef with the waves breaking over it. Closer observation showed thousands of seals or (judging by the way they swam and that they often leaped from the water) fur seals (*Phoca ursina*). They came from the northwest and swam toward the southeast. The pod was so large that they stretched out for at least two sea miles. Their appearance struck me as extraordinary because, with the approach of summer, they should have been swimming toward the north and to the south in winter. I had no idea where the animals had come from and where they were going. Perhaps they had been scared by Russian promyshlenniks in the north and were fleeing to the south seeking protection and safety? Or maybe there was an unknown island here in the neighborhood?

That same morning I observed another unusual phenomenon. The upper and lower layers of air were in strange disagreement. The sea was very quiet, almost flat as a mirror. The large lower sail hung loose as in a calm. The upper sails, however, were so full in a regular continuous wind that we sailed six miles an hour for a short time. The wind was from the southeast and the thermometer read plus 13°. The latitude was 39°49′ N and 133° W.

For several days after the 22nd, we sailed northward with a favorable southwesterly wind in variable weather, with gusts of wind, rain showers, fog and sunshine. In a temperature of six and one-half degrees, we felt we were near a rawer climate, which was confirmed at 44° by the appearance of puffins every day.

On the 26th, we again had mostly contrary north and northwest winds. On the 28th, we unexpectedly sighted Cape James, the southern tip of Queen Charlotte's Island. A current must have carried us farther to the northeast than we had expected. At the same time, we did not have the slightest sign of any land nearby. We saw neither seaweed nor birds. Thus, it is now and then possible to be near a coast without spotting any signs of land, and undoubtedly the opposite is just as true, that now and then supposed signs of land are spotted without its existence being confirmed.

On the 29th during a complete calm, the water was covered with oil caused by the presence of a lot of whales. There were quantities of seaweed and mollusks swimming around the ship. We were at 50°. The calm held for several days. Only on July 5th did a steady brisk southeasterly wind continue for several days. The following afternoon we discovered land. Probably, it was the southern tip of King George III's Archipelago known as Cape Ommaney or Cape Tschirikoff. Our noon observation read 55°3′ and 137° W. On the 7th on the clear, distant horizon, we saw a high chain of mountains. Our noon reading of 56°49′ convinced us that the high, round mountain that had been visible the entire morning (which we had first thought was a separate island) had to be Mount Edgecumbe at the entrance to Norfolk Sound. We approached it on the afternoon of the 8th. When we were only about twenty to twenty-five sea miles from the Russian outpost, we were becalmed. After firing several cannon shots, we spotted a baidarka coming our way toward evening. The rowers were emaciated, living skeletons, a striking contrast to the well-fed, healthy sailors we had brought back from San Francisco.

We were extremely anxious to hear about everything that had happened since out departure. We were met by the following:

About ten people had died in the most wretched way of scurvy caused by lack of food, clothing and cleanliness.

The ship *Elisabeth*, which had been sent to Kodiak, had run aground in the winter when trying to leave the harbor. The ship and many of the supplies had been lost, only the crew had been saved.[1]

The Kalusch had surprised all of the Russians and Aleuts at the outpost of Yakutat or Behring's Bay and killed them. Due to lack of boats and crews, the outpost had not been visited or supported for more than two years.

During our absence, a ship from Boston, Captain Winship, had arrived at Norfolk Sound.[2] The Russian-American Company had contracted to deliver 52 baidarkas and over 100 Aleuts for a voyage to the coast of New Albion north of the Spanish settlements in order to hunt sea otters for half the price. That is how the Russians, because of a dearth of ships and sea otters, are trying to expand their sphere of influence in other ways to the south.

The little 60-ton ship, whose keel had been laid several months before and on which more than 30 to 40 men had worked the whole winter, was not yet finished.[3]

Nothing had been heard from a large party of 140 baidarkas and 300 Aleuts sent out in November 1805 from Sitcha to Kodiak to hunt sea otter.[4] According to the latest report, they had not arrived in Kodiak. It was suspected that they had fallen victim to Kalusch hate and vengeance.

At the time of Vancouver's expedition, several similar, and by far, larger hunting parties were sent out. He met, among others, a flotilla, which according to its commander, the Russian Portoff, had

700 baidarkas and 1,400 Aleuts.* This example serves well to illustrate to what extent that area has been depopulated in the last twenty years, since now the Russian-American Company would have trouble even finding 400 baidarkas at all of its outposts put together.

The aforementioned hunting party of 140 baidarkas lost last year had been the largest of all the ones sent out. After spending the summer killing sea otters in Chatham Strait and Cross Strait, they were sent in October to Kodiak, that is, the Aleuts were supposed to paddle their baidarkas from 57° along the coast of Prince William Sound and Cook's River and then head south again to Kodiak. They thus had to undertake a sea voyage in their fragile boats of 16 longitudes, namely from the 135° to 151° W, and at the same time also three latitudes to the north and just as many again to the south. Winter was, however, already so far advanced that most of the people, given the storms at that time of year (November), were driven off course, and numbed by cold, most of them froze to death at sea.

I later heard that of the whole hunting party about thirty baidarkas and about sixty people were saved.

The practice of forcing Aleuts to go out on such hunting parties has cost many a person his life and is the main reason for the depopulation of the Aleutian Islands. Even if they survive the trip, most of them arrive in Kodiak, as a result of the exertion of continually rowing, usually suffering from pneumonia, which causes their deaths sooner or later.

Together with all of this really not very happy news, we arrived at the settlement of New Archangel in Norfolk Sound very early on the morning of the 9th.

After our departure from Sitcha for New Albion, Lieutenant Maschin, commander of the *Maria*, had been ordered to ready his ship to sail to Ochotsk at the beginning of May. Captain D'Wolf, from whom the Russians had bought the *Juno*, had been promised transportation there in the spring. To our great surprise upon our return from San Francisco, we found the *Maria* and our American friend still there. The latter seemed very unhappy with losing so much time to no purpose. Lieutenant Maschin complained that they had not wanted to

---

*G. Vancouver, *Voyage de decouvertes au tour du monde*, Paris an X. 8. T. V., pp. 125-126.

give him any men. Therefore, he had not been able to set sail even though his ship had been ready for a long time.

We had barely landed in Sitcha when Mr. D'Wolf urged Mr. von Resanoff, the plenipotentiary of the Russian-American Company, to fulfill his guarantee made the preceding September and provide for his early departure. After making and changing plans many times, it was finally decided that Mr. D'Wolf would have the little ship *Rossislav* of 22 tons put at his disposal. He would sail to Kodiak where he would pick up a coxswain, since there was none available in Sitcha. In case Captain D'Wolf deemed the ship unsuitable to continue the voyage, he should wait for the *Maria*, which was scheduled to sail at the latest eight days later for Kodiak and sail her to Ochotsk, his first choice. All necessary orders were given. The *Rossislav* was turned over to the command of the American free citizen D'Wolf. He set about supplying the ship with wood, water and provisions as quickly as possible. It was ready to sail in three days.

Sitcha was now filled with bustle and activity. The *Juno* was unloaded. Mr. von Baranoff, the manager of the Russian-American Company, was incredibly delighted to receive so much grain provided by Mr. von Resanoff. He regretted, however, very much that he had no mill to grind the quantity of wheat brought along, something Mr. von Resanoff had totally forgotten when purchasing it. Thus, part of the grain had to be roasted in the manner used by the Indians in New California and another part cooked in soups instead of groats or rice.

Now so much work was being done on the new little ship, whose keel had been built the preceding autumn and had been named the *Awos* [*Vielleicht*, "Maybe"], that it most probably would be ready to sail in a few weeks. Mr. von Resanoff decided to remain in Sitcha until it was finished and then to sail to Ochotsk aboard the *Juno* under the command of Lieutenant von Chwostoff accompanied by the *Awos*, whose command would be given Mr. von Davidoff.

The political situation in New Archangel was at that time was very questionable. Trustworthy intelligence had come in that the Kalusch had gathered in large numbers at their fort a few days before the *Juno* had arrived and they planned to storm the Russian settlement and kill all of the Russians. The unexpected arrival of the *Juno* had frightened them off, and they only made threats for the future. In the meantime, they themselves made known that they had attacked four baidarkas recently sent from Sitcha to Behring's Bay to find out about the fate of the missing hunting party. Two of them, along with six men, had fallen victim to their revenge. The Russian promyshlenniks were also dissatisfied. Most of them, as a result of the dry weather and frequently eating fresh fish, seal and spring herbs, had recovered again somewhat from scurvy, but they were grumbling about the meager portions they received despite the hard work and the surplus of fish available. When they formally complained to Mr. von Resanoff, he immediately gave an order for them to be freed from all work the following day and to do nothing but eat fresh fish the entire day!

For my part I had been in Sitcha long enough, was tired of fish, seal and mussels. I had firmly decided, and had long ago made my intentions known to Mr. von Resanoff, that I wanted to sail with the first ship returning to Europe. As uninviting as the thought was to undertake the long voyage to Ochotsk (the trip covered 80 longitudes and about 16 latitudes) in that 20- to 22-ton vessel built by promyshlenniks in America and turned over to Mr. D'Wolf, I still explained, despite the well-intentioned remonstrations, that I was sticking by my decision. I would rather accompany Mr. D'Wolf on such a ship to Ochotsk than stay an hour longer than was necessary in Sitcha. Mr. von Resanoff could not and did not want to force me to stay. He provided me with the necessary papers and references I requested for Ochotsk, Jakutsk, Irkutsk, etc.; and, thus, I left Sitcha on June 19th in cheerful spirits in the company of my friend, Mr. D'Wolf, and ten sailors, including three natives from the Peninsula of Alaska or Alaksa. Seldom has a *Te Deum* been sung with warmer feelings of thanks and gratitude than that one. I felt as if I were breathing freer as soon as Mount Edgecumbe was lost from my sight.

In the beginning, wind and weather were not very favorable. The almost continual northwest and southwesterly winds, as well as calms, and the poor navigability of our little ship would have made our voyage very boring if we had not undertaken occasional little hunting trips in one of the baidarkas we had brought along. Almost every day, we saw seaweed and numbers of whales. The sea was usually very rough; the short, choppy waves were probably caused by contrary winds and a strong current. This current carried us into the vicinity of Kodiak at least 15 to 20 sea miles to the south in 24 hours. Along the coast of America up to the Cook's River, however, the current is supposed to be to the north.

On this voyage on the high seas I saw the following birds: *Alca arctica*, *Alca cirrhata*, *Procellaria furcata*, *Procellaria glacialis*,

Procellaria aequinoctialis and *Diomedea exulans*. At the distance of 20 to 30 sea miles from land, *Pelecanus violaceus*, *Colymbus Grylle*, *Colymbus Troile*, *Larus fuscus*, *Sterna Hirundo* and many other birds began appearing.

We finally saw land on the evening of July 16th. On the 17th toward noon, we dropped anchor in the new harbor at Kodiak. Mr. Bander, my old acquaintance, came out and greeted us most cordially. We heard to our sorrow about the sudden death of his dearly beloved wife, who had understood so much about cooking and gardening. Her by no means weak constitution, after so many years of abstinence, must have no longer been used to the strength of the spirits brought by the *Neva* and she had succumbed suddenly. She had died several months before.

Even though this loss had brought Mr. von Resanoff's well thought out plan in many ways to a standstill, it had also helped very much to comfort Mr. Bander and alleviate the pain of his loss; for one of the young girls entrusted to his dearly departed wife in the preceding year had already learned enough about running a household to do almost everything in Mrs. Bander's place.

The outpost at Kodiak has already been described in enough detail in the third chapter. Grigori Schelichoff founded it. The island is large and was formerly very populous. Around it are numbers of larger and smaller rocks, bays, inlets and harbors. Here and there gentle hills rise from the sea's surface, just as in other places steep, inaccessible cliffs. The interior is alternately covered with mountains and valleys, plains and hills. The climate is unexpectedly mild. The high, eternally snow-clad mountains and glaciers of the Alaksa Peninsula seem to hold back all of the cold. Cattle raising, as a result of Mr. von Baranoff's concern, has already made great progress here, although only the Russians and not the Aleuts benefit from it. If there were more workers and experts, agriculture could be productive. Potatoes thrive. They should, however, go to the trouble of obtaining better seed potatoes. Several promyshlenniks have begun to take up farming. To my sorrow, I had to observe a very clumsy plow being pulled by Aleuts, that, indeed, these helpless human beings and not the cattle were being hitched to the plow. No member of the management here has reported this and similar things to the Directors in St. Petersburg.

In other countries, where I have seen Negro slaves, care is taken to maintain their health and lives because they are expensive to buy. This does not seem to be the case here. The conquered and suppressed Aleuts are badly fed, badly clothed and subjected daily to danger. They have had all of their possessions confiscated. They are mostly ruled by promyshlenniks, some of whom are Siberian criminals. Under these conditions, depopulation becomes more noticeable with each passing year. I saw only used-up old people, women and children. Aleuts capable of working are almost all out on forced sea otter hunts, a long way from their parents, women and children.

The settlement at Kodiak has gradually taken on the appearance of a European town. It has over thirty houses, one church, storehouses, barracks, workshops for craftsmen, etc. In recent years a school has been opened. It certainly does the Russian-American Company honor to have established institutions to teach the young people religion, counting, writing, reading, mathematics, etc. Often, however, the best intentions can be brought to naught by unfortunate success. And this seems to be the case. Mr. von Resanoff had forgotten before his departure the previous year to leave orders for the food for the schoolboys, whose numbers had grown to almost seventy. These young people, who, as long as they were with their parents, had been occupied with hunting seals and catching fish and, thus, increasing the amount of their parents' and the Company's winter provisions, were now studying. For this reason, in many places in the summer, not as many fish as usual will be caught. Furthermore, the supplies taken by the *Juno* to Sitcha and the loss of the *Elisabeth* had depleted the store of provisions at Kodiak to the point that there was a lack of provisions. The school boys, especially in the winter, had almost nothing to eat.

As praiseworthy as a school for Aleuts might seem and as necessary as it might be to teach them religion and basic moral principles, I, nevertheless, have a totally different view of the matter. Why do they want to teach the Aleuts to write, read, count? At present Kodiak is depopulated. Instead of educating the few remaining young people to be good citizens and occupying their time with fishing and hunting seals and whales, instead of having them practice rowing and shooting arrows, they are all, without exception, being taught reading, writing, counting, mathematics, geography and the French language!! They are being raised and coddled using European methods. In a few years there will be no young Aleut who can go barefoot in the winter and summer despite the wet and the cold, who understands how to catch fish or hunt whales, seals, sea lions or sea otters. What does the Company plan to do with its educated Aleuts? Or where will they find people to fish, to hunt sea otters, fox and other animals, which clearly provide them with food and articles of trade.

These arrangements have already put down deep roots before the main office in St. Petersburg has even become aware of the seeds beginning to germinate!

NOTES

1. The vessel *Zakhariia i Elizaveta*, under Midshipman Karpinskii, was wrecked at the outset of her return voyage from Kodiak to Sitka.

2. Captain John D'Wolf, in his *Voyage to the North Pacific and a Journey through Siberia*, relates that on about May 10th the ship *Okain* [*O'Cain*] under Captain Jonathan Winship arrived, straight from the United States, without any cargo, to pick up "Kodiak Indians" and baidarkas for a voyage to California to hunt sea otters. He sailed about the middle of the month.

3. The "little 60-ton ship" was the *Avos*, soon to take part in the notorious raid on northern Japanese trading posts.

4. The hunting party was en route back to Kodiak when the leaders heard of the destruction of the Yakutat colony. They went there and saw the ruins. Fearing attack, the majority, under the Russian T. S. Dem'ianenkov, put to sea, where they were caught by a storm and all drowned. Only about 60 Aleuts, with 31 baidarkas, too exhausted to go on, sought shelter on the shore regardless of the risk, and survived.

Chapter 12

Departure from Kodiak. Schelechoff Strait. Coast of Alaksa. Bay of Kukak. Description of the Inhabitants and their Dwellings. Departure from Kukak. Voyage. Arrival in Unalaska. Events of our Stay. Description of the Formation of a new Island. Departure from Unalaska. Voyage and the Necessity for Wintering in Kamtschatka. Arrival in the Harbor of St. Peter and St. Paul.

On July 24th, after Mr. Bander had richly provided us with fresh fish and meat, wood and water and the coxswain promised Mr. D'Wolf had come on board, we took up our distant voyage in our miserable vessel. A strong southeasterly wind prevented us from sailing around Cape Greville, so our pilot decided to sail to the north through Schelechoff Strait between the Peninsula of Alaksa and the Island of Kodiak. Three of our sailors were natives of Alaksa. They knew the area and assured us that the strait was navigable and safe. Thus, we set sail from the Island of Kodiak heading to the west and southwest and sailed between it and the smaller island of Yellova (Spruce Island) and Aphoknak to the north. The passage is about one sea mile wide and so deep that the largest of ships can sail through it. Opposite the middle of the entrance, a few sea miles away, are several rocks which can easily be avoided in moderate winds. Ebb and flood tide are of little importance. A calm forced us in the evening to anchor in a little inlet on the northeastern side of the strait in eight klafters of water. Early on the morning of the 25th, we followed the strait, which runs straight from the east to the west and is bordered to the north by Spruce Island (Yellova) and to the south by Kodiak and on the northwestern horizon by Aphoknak. After we had sailed three to four sea miles straight west, a big bay opened before us. The coast of Kodiak, which we were following, has alternately inlets and harbors. Farther to the northeast, we saw several islands, whose names we did not know, and between them and Kodiak the mouth of a passage leading to Schelechoff Strait. Despite the width of two sea miles, the current of ebb and flood tides here is far stronger than at other much narrower places. The whole night and following day, held up by contrary winds, we tacked about a large bay near the mouth. Everywhere along its shore there are safe anchorages. We were more than a little surprised that, since leaving the harbor of the settlement, we had not seen a village or an Aleut anywhere on the nearby shores and islands.

Finally, in the night a favorable wind came up so that we reached Schelechoff Strait at daybreak. At its narrowest point it is about forty versts wide. The joy over the favorable wind did not last long, because a few hours later a strong southwesterly wind came up that grew into a terrible storm and forced us to seek protection in a nearby inlet. The natives from Alaksa, whom we had as sailors on board, assured us that there were several good harbors along the south coast of the peninsula. The ones at Karluk to the northwest and Kukak to the northeast of the mouth of the passage were excellent. Therefore, we raised our storm sail and headed for the spacious Kukak Bay north [sic, west] of the Island of Aphoknak.

We had barely reached those more quiet waters in the afternoon when several baidarkas came toward our ship. It was the first ship that had ever sailed in there and had very soon attracted the attention of the inhabitants of that area. The Alaksans differ little in appearance from the Konäg on Kodiak, except that the men, unlike the islanders who mostly pluck out their beard hairs, have little mustachios on both sides under their noses in the old Spanish fashion.

Those people radiate friendly trust and unusual good-heartedness. They accompanied us into the inner bay, where in the evening around eight o'clock, we dropped our anchor on the rocky bottom in six klafters of water. We were completely protected for the night from the stormy southwesterly winds, but the severe, raging gusts of wind coming off of the nearby mountains alarmed Captain D'Wolf so much, especially because of the poor anchoring bottom, that he had another anchor dropped.

Very early the next morning several of the previous days' acquaintances visited us. Each brought his wife along in order to show her the unusual guests and their European vessel. Two young girls had climbed inside one of the two-seated leather boats and, when we thought they were all quite empty, they stuck their inquisitive heads up out of the holes to observe us. Together with the men and their wives, these two, at our invitation, climbed on board without showing any shyness whatsoever. They brought us fresh fish and a lot of little trifles, i.e., little purses made of bird and seal esophagus, some also made of fishskin, string and loops for arrows skillfully worked using twisted sinew from whales and reindeer, beautifully woven little baskets, caps made of ground squirrel skins, lip and ear ornaments and other adornments and tools, which they offered us in trade especially for tobacco, glass beads and very fine sewing needles. Trading took place without the slightest of difficulty to the satisfaction of both sides.

Since the wind was still raging outside the bay and we did not dare to leave our quiet anchorage, Mr. D'Wolf and I took advantage of our stay to climb up a nearby hill on the little island of Ilak with a compass. We examined our surroundings and made a sketch of the bay. In the west and northwest lie very high mountains covered with eternal snow and glaciers, to the north lower mountains, to the east the mouth of the harbor, to the southwest the bay of Ichock, which runs so far into the interior behind a tongue of land to the southwest that we could not see its end several miles away.

Upon our return we decided to use our three-seated baidarka to visit the natives' summer huts on the northeastern shore of the bay, about one sea mile away, near the promontory of Amavack. The inhabitants gave us a very friendly reception in their small earthen-covered hut with grass growing all over the outside and an entrance that was so low and narrow that we could only crawl in hunched over. Everyone sat around a fire burning in the middle of the hut. A kettle of fish was hanging over it. Several small salmon, spitted upon sticks stuck in the earth around the fire, were being roasted. They were offered us together with saranna root. The latter had a bitter-sweet, unpleasant taste. Opposite the door, the floor was covered with fine, dry wood shavings and several clean seal skins, where we were asked to sit. Upon a whole, the place was cleaner than those of the inhabitants in Kodiak. During our conversation, we learned that the population in the last ten years had declined considerably. Most of the young people had been forced to go to Sitcha to hunt sea otter. Therefore, we also saw here, as in Kodiak, mainly old men, widows and orphans. Of the thousand people who used to live here, hardly more than forty remained. The whole Peninsula of Alaksa is said to have been depopulated in the same proportions. The village of Tonjajak owned only four two-seated baidarkas and one communal baidara. We were especially interested in the latter. Its form and delicate construction, its complete artistry and harmony were so perfect and beautiful that we had up to then seen nothing similar. We were surprised that the Russians in Kodiak did not build their big leather boats using one like it as a model.

The customs, habits and, in part, the clothing, even the language of the inhabitants of Alaksa, are the same as in Kodiak. Only in food is there a noticeable difference, since the peninsula is connected to America where there are quantities of reindeer and wild sheep. The inhabitants usually hunt them in the fall for use as food and clothing.

The men seem as little jealous of their wives as the young girls are miserly in distributing their favors. A handful of beads, several leaves of tobacco and a half dozen fine sewing needles or other European trifles take care of all difficulties. The features of several of the girls were not at all unattractive, but for very disfiguring chin tattoos and lip ornaments.

The winter is supposed to be very cold and long. The morning of the 29th, since the weather had cleared, we weighed anchor in moderate winds in order to leave the bay. A calm soon followed and we could not leave. With a very good noonday observation, we determined the middle of the bay to be 58°32′. Alaksans of both sexes, delighted by the calm, came out again in their boats to see us. They brought fresh fish and many other kinds of utensils and tools to arouse our curiosity and to try to get presents in return. Toward evening a light, south-southwest wind carried us out of the bay into Schelechoff Strait, where we could only progress forward slowly in changeable winds and weather. Finally, on August 1st, we lost sight of Kodiak.

After leaving the harbor at Kodiak, we had discovered that not one of the Russian maps charted the area correctly. Therefore, we had to sail exercising the greatest caution in the almost daily contrary west wind. On the 4th we discovered several islands. We thought the most northerly one was Sutchum. Toward noon we saw a single dangerous rock, about 15 to 20 sea miles south of the Alaksa Peninsula, according to our calculations at 56°2′, according to Sarytscheff's map, however, 11′ farther south. Near it were extremely large pods of seals and sea lions. Accompanied by variable weather, we followed the stretched-out Alaksa Peninsula, whose high, eternally snow-clad chain of mountains and round peaks we could see very clearly from time to time. On the 7th, we found ourselves in a wide bay not far from the Isannach Strait, which separates the Island of Unimak from Alaksa. Its mouth can be recognized by the little Island of Ikatok lying south of it. The following day we were at 54°38′ near the southwestern tip of Unimak, where we were held up for several days by southwesterly winds.

Finally, on the 10th a strong current from the northwest carried us through the strait between Unimak and the Island of Akutan, thus shortening our trip to the sea north of the Aleutian Islands. Around two o'clock in the afternoon, several inhabitants of the west coast of Unimak visited us. They brought us a very pleasant supply of halibut, for which they were given tobacco leaves. We were doubly grateful for these provisions, because we were making so little forward progress that we had hardly covered a third of the voyage after so many weeks. Our provisions had been shrinking noticeably with each passing day. Because of this, our leader D'Wolf had already decided to go to Unalaska in order possibly to replenish our low supply of food.

On the 11th, we sighted the Island of Unalaska and on the following day we sailed into the harbor of Iljuljuk.

High, steeply sloping mountains with large clefts form an open, deep bay facing to the north that leads straight to the harbor. It can be recognized at a distance by a table mountain. It is protected on all sides and offers an excellent anchorage with a sandy clay bottom that drops off gradually, so that a boat can anchor very close to the shore in two to three klafters of water.

The Company's agent Jemilian Grigoritsch Lariwanoff, an honorable old man whom I had met the preceding year, had died at the beginning of the year. His integrity and humaneness had won him the affection of all of the islanders during his ten-year stay. No one questioned the fact that he was the best manager at any of the Russian-American outposts. His integrity and paternal concern had produced unparalleled harmony and satisfaction, which had made less of an impression upon me during my first visit, because I had not yet become acquainted with the other outposts and settlements of the Company.

After Mr. Lariwanoff's death, the control of the business was turned over to his former clerk (prikashchik). Within six months after this change, instead of peace, unity and order, everything had turned into chaos. The new manager wanted to make changes whose damaging results he could not perceive and consider. Even though this man had to have known that neither Unalaska nor any neighboring island had tall trees, it did not stop him from building a big Russian-style house immediately after taking over the administration. He took all of the wood which had arrived from Sitcha, Kodiak and other places for the past several years. Due to the lack of driftwood, it had been distributed and used most sparingly for the islanders' most necessary needs — for the main beams in their earthen huts, for canoes, arrows, throwing boards and other household utensils. Since Aleuts know little or nothing about carpentry, he had all of the Russians from near-by and distant islands come to Unalaska in order to help with the building of the house. The wood was wasted in the most childish of ways and all other business was thrown into confusion.

For six years, Mr. Lariwanoff had been requesting permission of the main agent in Kodiak to return to Russia. He always made many excuses and difficulties, which Mr. von Resanoff during his stay took care of, by issuing orders that a ship of the Russian-American Company should take that worthy man and his family to Ochotsk. After her husband's death, the widow, and her daughter, believed that she was justified in expecting those orders to be carried out. The new agent, however, frustrated her hopes of returning to her fatherland that year by sending the ship intended for her husband to St. Paul and St. Matthew and telling her that the Russian-American Company had no ships to serve women.

When, during our visit, Madame Lariwanoff heard that Mr. D'Wolf planned to sail to Ochotsk, she beseeched him to take pity on her; something he did out of a feeling of humaneness, even though the 22-ton vessel was not suited to carry many passengers, especially women. As soon as the agent heard about it, he tried to cause difficulties by using many pretenses. Captain D'Wolf, however, put an end to them by simply taking Madame Lariwanoff and her daughter on board.

During our stay in Unalaska, we were mainly occupied with obtaining provisions for our long voyage. Madame Lariwanoff helped us the most. She brought aboard considerable quantities of salted fish and geese, several hams, granted lean and oily, several barrels full of birds' eggs, several chickens, and roots and other products which she had put up for the winter. Only with a good deal of trouble did we obtain from the agent several things needed for repairing the ship and a small supply of fresh fish, because he had so fallen in love with a little barrel of brandy which Mr. Bander had sent him that he was unable to tear himself away from it. During our five-day stay we only saw him half sober for a few hours.

Here I will not say anything about the particular customs, habits and way of life of the islanders because I have already done this extensively in Chapter 2. In my opinion, it is more important to mention that I had an opportunity to make remarkable, physical-natural historical observations about a new island in the vicinity of Unalaska.

On the one hand, the creation or destruction of a large section of land or an island is not a totally unknown phenomenon in the history of the evolution of our planet. On the other hand, it is, indeed, very rare that someone has an opportunity to observe such an event exactly. Therefore, the following example is especially worth mentioning.*

At 54° N and 268° W longitude from Greenwich, about 45 versts straight west of the most northerly point of land on Unalaska, there is an isolated, rocky protrusion in the ocean. The Aleuts say that their ancestors knew it as a main collecting ground for seals and sea lions. They visited it at least once, or several times, a year in the hope of safe, rich hunting.

In 1795, near that rocky protrusion the islanders saw fog, which did not disperse even though the rest of the sky was completely clear. It was even more disastrous for the inhabitants of Unalaska and the neighboring island of Umnak, because they lost one of their main sources of food. After waiting in vain for several years, finally a hale and hearty Aleut set out on his own to visit the rocky protrusion in the fog in order to kill several sea lions. He soon returned in utter confusion, bringing the news that the water near that place was boiling and that the fog was really smoke (steam). As a result, no one wanted to visit that place inhabited by evil spirits until 1800, when the sky suddenly cleared again and the Aleuts, to their greatest surprise, instead of the rocky protrusion they had known, saw a peak-shaped island burning and smoking like a chimney.

Since nature's great workshop was totally busy at the bottom of the sea, Unalaska had heavy earthquakes almost every month until 1802, when finally there was an extraordinary earthquake, one never experienced there before, that destroyed several huts. In 1806, they could no longer remember exactly in which month it had happened, so

---

*A very interesting compilation of such events can be found in Johann Carl Voigt's *Praktische Gebirgskunde* (Practical Science of Mountains), second edition, Weimar, 1797, 8, p. 215, as well as in the chapter: "Beytrag zu einem Verzeichniß der durch innere Kraft hervorgehobenen Berge, Inseln und Erdstriche" (Contributions to a catalogue of mountains, islands and parts of the earth elevated by an inner force), where several remarkable examples are described.

unremarkable is such an exceptional natural event for the inhabitants of that area.

Since then, the peak of the new island has ceased to burn brightly. The volcano on Unalaska, however, suddenly roared again mightily for the first time in many years. It, as well as the volcano on Unimak and the new island, reciprocally burned and smoked. The active volcano on Umnak (a little island west of Unalaska) has been totally still for a fairly long time.

That year in April, that is a short time before my arrival, several inhabitants of Unalaska visited the new island and related the following:

It took them about six hours to row around the whole island. According to their way of calculating, that would be about 30 versts. They could not determine the exact height of the peak, although they believed, if it were possible to climb straight up it, they would need probably 5 to 6 hours to reach its highest point. A volcano was active on its north side. Lava (they said it was of soft material) ran from the peak to the sea. Because of the heat it was impossible for them to land there. Only in the south, where the shore was not so steep and it was cold, could they land their three baidarkas. They tried to climb to the peak but found climbing extremely difficult because of clefts, steep slopes and sharp stones. They did, however, succeed after many detours to climb about half way up to the peak. There, however, it seemed too dangerous for them to continue because the earth was gradually becoming hotter, and the farther they went the more clefts and holes they saw throwing up steam and intense heat. They stopped to rest and hung some sea lion meat they had brought along for food in one of the holes. They were beside themselves with joy when they saw that the meat was cooked in a short time without their having to build a fire. They were forced to turn around by thirst and lack of any drinking water, which they searched for in vain. It would not have occurred to a single one of those people to pick up a little stone of some kind from the island and take it along, if they had not smelled natural sulfur which is useful in building fires. They said the other stones looked like those on Unalaska. According to the Aleuts, the shape and size of the island's peak changes from time to time. Sometimes it is column-shaped, high and pointed, sometimes rounded and low, sometimes it burns brightly, sometimes it smokes more or less. From year to year the island grows in circumference and the peak in height.

On the afternoon of August 17th, we left Unalaska. On the following day, we saw the new island that lies straight to the west of the northern tip of Unalaska. It is of medium height and has a complete peak.

On its northwest side there are four cones rising step-like one over the other. The highest peak and the one in the middle appear column-shaped and to rise up perpendicularly. We were about 12 to 15 sea miles away from that remarkable island. We only became aware of it when sailing past because of a thick fog on it. Because of a light, favorable wind that had come up that morning, Captain D'Wolf did not think it advisable to stop to inspect the island, though it cost him a great deal of effort to suppress his scientific curiosity.

On the 19th, we lost sight of the new island and Unalaska. The latter's west side has a very singular appearance. At intervals on its high mountain ridges, there are enormous, perpendicular masses of rocks, which seen from the northeast to southwest, appear to be a row of vertical columns planted on the mountains. On our continued voyage we saw indescribable numbers of whales. At night the sea was extraordinarily luminous. Even though I had completely convinced myself in the southern seas, through frequent and careful research, that the sea's luminosity was caused by various kinds of living creatures, I could not help but think of the opinions of other researchers who attribute it to the quantity of rotting, fatty tissue from whales, which obviously had saturated the sea, causing there in those northern waters a great deal of the luminosity, or rather, the quantities of train produced and fed on by numbers of little creatures of all kinds. Thus, they contributed their part to that remarkable phenomenon. Using a light southeasterly wind, we sailed in fog and rain extremely slowly. Here and there we saw large stretches of the sea covered with feathers. I suspect that innumerable flocks of wild ducks, perhaps also other kinds of sea birds, were molting and causing it.

Colymbus Troile, *Procellaria surcata* and *Procellaria glacialis*, *Procellaria nigra* and *grisea*, along with several kinds of *Larus*, flew round us every day in large numbers. Auks, or *Alcae*, usually so common in that part of the world, seldom appeared; perhaps they stay more on the south side of the island. Instead of them, we saw more than the usual number of another kind of sea gull (*Larus parasiticus*, Linn.). They never catch their fish or food themselves but watch other sea gulls. As soon as they catch a fish, they pursue them and take it away. Every day we had opportunities to watch the combat in the air. We were most surprised that the common sea gull, despite constant pursuit, does not flee the vicinity of the parasitic gulls but always stays near them.

Up to then the wind had been so weak that we had traveled hardly 8 degrees of longitude by the 23rd. On the 26th toward noon, four wild geese (*Anas canadensis*) appeared in a moderate wind nearby. I lay in wait at the front of the ship until we had come within 30 strides of them. I shot all four of the geese with one shot to my great joy and that of my companions. I got for us several days' worth of excellent fresh meat. Such luck hunting is most unusual on a voyage and brings double the pleasure.

On the 27th, we had our first brisk, favorable wind since leaving Unalaska. It carried us forward at a speed of five to six miles an hour, bringing us in 24 hours to about 15 miles east of an island, which we took for Buldir, that is, Round Island. Our noon observation read 52°37′. To the southeast, we saw the Island of Kiska and farther to the west a larger island, probably Agattu. On the following day, we were again becalmed. In the clear weather we could see the surrounding islands very clearly. On the 30th, the water at 52°14′ and 185° W appeared colored to us. The weather was very variable and changeable. We mostly had fog and rain, light, usually unfavorable winds and calms. A new, stormy month arrived and we still had not gotten very far on our voyage.

On September 3rd at 51°51′ N and 185° W, more than a degree south of the most westerly Aleutian Island of Attu, we saw that the sea was colored very strongly. The continual, constant westerly wind blew so unyieldingly that with each passing day, given the advanced season of the year, we thought it unlikely that we would be able to reach Ochotsk. Therefore, we were already half prepared to winter in Kamtschatka. Finally, on the 5th a long desired favorable northeasterly wind came up, which for the first time since leaving Sitcha continued for two twenty-four hour periods, thus bringing us into the neighborhood of the Kuril Islands. We just had regained our hope of reaching Ochotsk that year when a terrible storm arose, coming first from the northwest and then from the west. We were barely able to use the storm sail. Finally, Captain D'Wolf had to decide that it would be better to winter in Kamtschatka than sail in such a miserably built vessel into the threatening equinoctial gales. On the 8th, the ship was turned and directed toward the Harbor of St. Peter and St. Paul.

The following day in quiet, mild weather at 51°32′, upon seeing an albatross swimming near the ship, I asked Captain D'Wolf to permit me to go out in a baidarka. I rowed out with my gun in the company of one of our Aleuts, approached the albatross to within about 10 to 12 strides and shot it to my joy. But how great was my surprise and fright when I looked around for the ship and could no longer see it. A thick fog covered it. Neither my companion nor I knew which way to paddle to reach the ship, which we thought should be about a sea mile away. Therefore, we decided to paddle quickly toward the place we thought the ship would be. To our great joy about five minutes later we saw a black column shimmering through the fog bank, where we recognized our ship. We paddled toward it with united, doubled power.

Manifold are the dangers! Had we not found that ship, what might have been our fate?*

As I have already said, the season was so far advanced that it seemed advisable in the continuing westerly and northwesterly winds to stay at sea. As unpleasant as the prospects were, we saw ourselves in the position of having to spend a winter in that destitute land devoid of all amenities of life. We comforted ourselves with the thought that we were going to a harbor that probably had all kinds of provisions, that we would find several sensitive, civilized human beings. Thus filled with all kinds of apprehensions and the saddest memories of the preceding winter in Sitcha, thus filled with fear and hope, we sailed into the Harbor of St. Peter and St. Paul on September 13th (25th).

The weather was exceedingly pleasant and dry. Since leaving Sitcha, we had not had such clear, warm days as during the first ones after our arrival in the harbor.

The high table mountains and ridges were covered with snow. The lower elevations offered an all the more happy view, since in Sitcha and Kodiak we had seen only conifers and no deciduous trees.

We had just anchored when the commissioner of the Russian-American Company greeted us with the pleasant news that he had at the present time about 600 puds of rye flour and a considerable supply of tea, sugar, butter, brandy, etc., in the warehouse. His obliging manner of offering service, the listing of provisions there and the assurance that we could still catch a lot of fish in order to supply the crew with sufficient food sounded like the most beautiful melody to our ears. We thanked Providence for guiding us with his paternal hand.

Considerable changes had been made in the management of the Russian-American Company during my absence (since June 13, 1805).

---

*During that experience, I could feel how the honorable G. G. Forster must have felt under similar circumstances. G. G. Forster, *Reise um die Welt* [Trip around the World], Berlin, 1778, Vol. 4, 1, pp. 74-75.[1]

Commissioner Wichezoff, who had been in charge of business for several years, had finally been arrested for fraud and embezzlement and turned over to the courts. His place had been given to Mr. Mjasnikoff. All of the inhabitants characterized him as a very fair-minded, honorable man. He treated us the whole winter in the most cordial of manner. I considered it my duty to notify Major General Paul Iwanowitsch von Koscheleff, the Commandant of Kamtschatka, with the next mail of my arrival and to ask him for permission to take the first sledge run to his residence at Nischna-Kamtschatka by providing me with the necessary assistance to make the journey.

In the meantime Mr. D'Wolf and I rented private lodgings and prepared to winter in Kamtschatka. Mr. Mjasnikoff, as commissioner of the Russian-American Company, provided for Madame Lariwanoff and her daughter, as well as for the ship and its crew.

Notes

1. Johann Reinhold Forster (1729-1798) is the father of Georg Forster, i.e., Johann Georg Adam (1754-1794).

George Forster, *A Voyage round the World in His Britannic Majesty's Sloop, Resolution, commanded by Captain James Cook, during the years 1772, 3, 4, & 5* (London: B. White, 1777). He based the work on his father's journal and later translated it into German.

Chapter 13

Kamtschatka. Climate. Agriculture. Cattle Raising. Products. Mammals. Birds. Fish. Berries. Roots. Timber.

All of the scientists who have examined Kamtschatka, all of the commanders who have lived there for several years and all of the seamen who know the country more closely have commented upon its climate and abundance of products, upon the great advantages which the peninsula has over so many of the other provinces in Russia. Despite of all this, undeservedly and incomprehensibly, the country has acquired a bad reputation, so that people, in general, automatically associate the worst climate and incredible cold with Kamtschatka without any basis.

I suspect that the thought of the cold in Siberia causes many to make the mistake of thinking that Kamtschatka has to be even colder because it is much farther away than Siberia. They do not take into consideration either its geographical location farther south or descriptions of it.

I could perhaps be reproached for having an especially good opinion of Kamtschatka, or it might be assumed that I experienced an unusually mild year there, since I am beginning by describing the advantages of the peninsula. For this reason, I will begin with several men's observations whose knowledge and objective opinions certainly deserve to be believed.

Krascheninnikoff and Steller are at the head of the list among all of the older and more recent travelers who have written descriptions of the country. In addition, in Cook's *Third Voyage*, in La Pérouse, Lesseps, Pallas, Sarytschew, Sauer, Zimmermann, von Krusenstern* and others are found very interesting remarks about conditions and circumstances there. The results of their observations

---

**Beschreibung des Landes Kamtschatka* (Description of Kamtschatka) by Stephan Krascheninnikoff,[1] Lemgo, 1766, with maps and engravings.

show that the climate is not by far so forbidding as generally believed, that the country can support a higher degree of cultivation and that there is a superabundance of natural products of many kinds.

Here in their own words:* "Concerning the cold it is never so severe even around Bolschaia Reka and Awatsch, even though they are the coldest places in Kamtschatka. In Lower Kamtschatka Ostrog it is far warmer than in other places in Siberia lying south of the same latitude."

"The winter is moderate but constant. There are not such heavy cold spells nor such sudden thaws as around Jakutsk in Siberia. There are, however, occasional thaws in December. The temperature usually ranges between -5° and -15° Réaumur. During extremely heavy colds it falls to -27°. In January, the coldest month, it usually ranges between 10° and -22°. During the other seasons of the year it ranges from +2° to +10°. In two different years the highest temperature was +21°5 Réaumur."**

Sauer writes:*** "After the arrival of Billings's expedition in the Harbor of St. Peter and St. Paul, the weather was very beautiful. This good weather lasted until November 26th when winter began to set in. We had temperatures between 2 and 4 degrees Réaumur. Several times it was between 5° and 8° and the coldest time was not

---

George Wilhelm Steller, *Beschreibung von dem Lande Kamtschatka* [Description of Kamtschatka], Frankfurt and Leipzig, 1774, with engravings.

De Lesseps, *Voyage de Kamtschatka en France* [Voyage to Kamtschatka], Paris.

Peter Pallas, *Neue nordische Beyträge* [New Northern Contributions].

Gawrila Sarytschew, *Achtjährige Reise in nordöstlichen Siberien* [Eight-year Voyage in northeastern Siberia], translated from the Russian [into German] by J. H. Busse, 2 vols., Leipzig, 1806.

Martin Sauer, *Reise nach den nördlichen Gegenden von russischen Asien und Amerika in den Jahren 1785 bis 1794* [Journey to the northern areas of Russian Asia and America in the years 1785 to 1794], Weimar, 1803.

Zimmermann,[2] *Geographisches Taschenbuch für das Jahr 1809* [Geographic Pocketbook for the Year 1809].

Von Krusenstern, *Reise um die Welt* [Voyage around the World], St. Petersburg, 1810, Part 4.2.

*G. Steller, pp. 65 and 66; and Krascheninnikoff, pp. 82 and 76.

**Sarytscheff, p. 66.

***Pp. 154, 155 and 267.

more than 18° to 21°. The climate in the middle of the peninsula is far milder than on the coasts. Along the Kamtschatka River there is a valley about 180 English miles long that is protected from ocean winds by a chain of mountains to the east and west. The vegetation is far more active here and begins to grow already in March."

Given the not very raw climate of this peninsula between 51° N latitude and 61° it is easy to understand that the fertile soil is suitable all over for agriculture and cattle raising. As proof for this assertion I prefer to let others speak for me again:

"There is no doubt that around Verschnoi Ostrog and Kosirefsky areas winter and summer crops can grow as well as in other places of the same latitude.* By judiciously choosing the places suitable for crops, not only enough grain can be raised for the inhabitants but in time also as much as is needed to supply Ochotsk and other towns. Even though the country is not suitable everywhere for agriculture, there still are enough spots that are sufficient to supply grain not only for the whole country but also for its neighbors"

"The ground," Cook writes on page 354 of his third voyage, "appears to be very suitable for growing all kinds of common vegetables, even though to my amazement I did not see even the smallest spot being used."

Recently, especially under Reineken, the successor to the worthy Major Behm, they have finally become convinced that Kamtschatka can be cultivated.[3]

Pallas says:** "Agriculture is, by a judicious choice of land, at present as promising in Kamtschatka as in the most northerly parts of Europe. Barley and summer rye produce a rather good harvest and the villages of Klutschewskaia and Milkova, which have taken to agriculture, are the most flourishing villages in the whole country."

Baron Steinheil, Reineken's successor who spent several years in Kamtschatka, says in a plan he proposed to the government for improving the country: "A series of observations made during my stay

---

*Steller, p. 52, and Krascheninnikoff, p. 74.

**See his *Nordische Beyträge* [Northern Contributions], Vol. 4, pp. 148-150.

has convinced me that Kamtschatka's climate is suitable enough for agriculture."

Sauer, who wintered there in 1790 and 1791, gives the following description (page 153): "The Cossacks' gardens are filled with cabbage and other vegetables. Seeing them delighted me more than anything else I have ever seen. We had a superabundance of fish and wild fowl as well as potatoes, carrots, turnips, cabbage, and various wild, good-tasting roots, herbs and berries. We brewed spruce beer: There is a village twelve versts below Verchnoi Kamtschatka named Milkovoi.[4] Siberian peasants live there. They have gardens of beautiful potatoes, cabbage, carrots, turnips, cucumbers, etc. For their own use they raise buckwheat and rye, that grows very well. If they had proper supervision, they could produce enough grain to feed not only the peninsula but also the entire surrounding area."

There is not the slightest doubt that the raising of cattle could reach a high degree of perfection in Kamtschatka because "the grass grows so high and juicy that it is hard to find anything equal to it anywhere in the Russian Empire.* It grows naturally to over four fuss high. It could provide incredible quantities of hay for the winter.** In some places it shoots up so fast that it could be mowed more than three times in a summer. In addition, there are several places where cattle graze outside the whole winter."

These remarks should say enough about Kamtschatka's climate. I wish, however, to include several of my own observations:

Snow first fell on September 28th old style and October 10th new style. Up until then the weather had been very beautiful and mild every day. According to Kamtschadals, the winter of 1806-07, when I was there, was worse than usual because Awatscha Bay froze almost completely, something that very seldom happens. The coldest temperature was -22° Réaumur.

When I took a trip from Tigil to Bolscheretsk from March 12th to 23rd, I found that the snow had already melted in several places and that the rivers were free of ice. Upon my arrival at the Harbor of St. Peter and Paul on March 25th, I still found deep snow. At the begin-

---

*Krascheninnikoff, p. 72, and Steller, p. 54.

**La Pérouse, Vol. 3, p. 177.

ning of April, I traveled from there again to Verchnoi Kamtschatka. On April 8th, I found all of the rivers and creeks breaking up and the snow near Malka and Ganal almost completely melted. Upon my arrival at the Harbor on April 22nd, everything was green and the first spring herbs, among others wild garlic, had already shot up. It was collected for the ones sick with scurvy. By the beginning of April, cows grazed on new grass next to the half-melted snow.

The nights were usually cold, but by day the benign influence of the sun's rays could be felt in all their strength.

I am completely convinced that Kamtschatka's climate is the same as that of northern Europe at the same latitude. The inhabitants of the peninsula, under appropriate management, could provide very well for their needs with the richness of the products available in the country.

The efforts and zeal of His Excellency Mr. von Pestel, the present Governor General of Siberia, to improve that good-natured people's lot give hope for the happiest results. How rewarding it must be to be the benefactor of an entire people?!

The present political climate and administration of the Peninsula is treated by Mr. von Krusenstern in the eighth chapter of the second volume of the description of his voyage. Therefore, I rather confine my discussion to the natural character of the country and its products in order to call attention to less known treasures found in other older writings.

Kamtschatka has a superabundance of mammals, birds, fish, fruit or rather berries of all kinds, nutritious herbs and roots along with stately tall trees. To prove this I will list several of the most notable examples.

Bears, *Ursus Arctos*, are found in large numbers. Their hides are usually used for sledge blankets or beds under blankets, seldom for clothing. Stripped of hair, they are frequently used for boot soles, because they keep one's feet very warm and do not freeze in the severest cold like other kinds of leather. Their meat is considered a delicacy and their fat is eaten instead of oil. The latter is also used for light. Well cleaned and dried, the guts are sewed together and spread over a frame instead of window glass. The animals feed mainly on fish.

Wild sheep, *Ovis Annom*, live primarily on the highest parts of the mountain chains to the east and west. The Kamtschadals make very warm clothing from their hides. Their meat is unusually tasty. A large number of them are killed in the fall as winter provisions.

Reindeer, *Cervus Caribou*. This unusual species is found frequently, both wild and tame. The entire riches of the Koriaks (the next neighbors of the Kamtschadals) consists of the possession of larger or smaller herds of those animals, which provide all of their needs, i.e., clothing, food and housing. There used to be numerous herds of tame reindeer on the western and northern coasts of the peninsula. The greedy commander either bought or misappropriated them. The present commander, Major General von Koscheleff, convinced of their usefulness, has begun to buy new herds for the Crown from the neighboring nomads. By continuing this well considered measure, in a few years reindeer alone can provide the peninsula with enough healthy, good-tasting meat, and, thus, with good nutrition to keep the inhabitants healthy. This measure is all the easier to carry out because the Koriaks drive their herds through the country every year and sell hundreds of reindeer, either dead or alive as desired, to the Kamtschadals.

Even though there are an abundance of hares, *Lepus Lagopus*, marmots, *Arctomys Bobac*, and ermine, *Mustela Erminca*, they use neither their fur nor their meat and do not think it really worth the effort to kill them. In 1805, a Kamtschadal presented General von Koscheleff a very black ermine, a highly unusual rarity.

They do hunt the black, red and stone foxes, *Canis Lycaon*, *Canis Vulpes* and *Canis Lagopus*, a little, but they are little valued; whereas the fur of wolves, *Canis Lupus*, is considered more valuable and frequently sent to Ochotsk. Occasionally, wolves gather in large packs and become aggressive and cause a great deal of damage.

Sables, *Mustela Zibellina*, have the most valuable fur. The fur of the Kamtschatkan species has very thick fur, but it is by far not as good as the ones trapped along the Lena River in Siberia, which have a glossy dark color. In former times the quantities of sables taken were so great that pelts worth 80,000 rubles were sent to Ochotsk in some years. Now the government exacts so much service from the Kamtschadals that they can rarely go hunting and can barely pay the tribute demanded of them. The worth of the sables exported in recent years has been hardly more than 3 to 4 thousand rubles. Only very rarely are white sables found.

Wolverines, *Ursus Gulo*, are rare. Their fur is highly prized and used to trim or face other fur clothing.

Seals, *Phoca jubata, Phoca vitulina* and other species, are frequently killed or taken in nets. They are incredibly useful. Their skin can be used for straps and sledge harnesses, for blankets, boots and shoe soles, the fat and train oil for food and lighting the huts. They eat the meat although it is black and tasteless. The innards of some species, just like those of the bears, are used instead of window glass.

Sea otters, *Lutra Marina*, are seldom seen. Their highly prized fur is now imported from the Aleutian Islands and America. Fish otters, *Lutra vulgaris*, can frequently be seen near lakes and are used for trimming winter clothing.

Various species of whales (*Cetaceae*) are plentiful. They do not hunt them specifically but rather use those that strand every year on the beaches for train. Especially during the herring run, they come right into the Harbor of St. Peter and St. Paul. By whaling the Kamtschadals, if they wanted to, could have a rich source of trade and business.

Cattle, horses, reindeer and dogs are the domesticated animals worth mentioning.

Cattle raising has increased in recent years. In certain villages, for example, Milkova, Klutschefskaia, Malka and other places, herds are as large as 70 to 80 animals. At several places along the Kamtschatka River, i.e., the village of Kosirefsky, I have seen cows grazing in the open in the middle of winter. With a little prudent attention in a few years cattle raising could be very profitable. Milk, butter and cheese would be superabundant in Kamtschatka.

They have, indeed, over one hundred horses, some of which they have bred themselves. They, however, can only be used in a few areas of the peninsula, because of the deep snow in some areas and the difficulty in making hay. Therefore, dogs always have an advantage, because they can easily run over the deepest snow and eat fish, which can be caught by the thousands without any trouble. In summer dogs are not necessary because almost all communication goes by water, since the Kamtschadals live along the rivers. Horses can only be used in a few areas in which the villages are separated from each other by mountains, and without horses they would have to travel on foot. The use of horses will always remain very limited.

Dogs are without a doubt the most useful domesticated animals on the peninsula. Even with a superabundance of horses, dogs would still be preferred as draft animals.* Their importance is my reason for describing them more completely.**

I have already expressed my opinion about the necessity and usefulness of introducing reindeer.

The quantities of the tastiest of fish on the peninsula are unbelievable, beyond all imagination. The Kamtschadals hardly know any other food. They eat them fresh, salted, frozen, dried and smoked, raw, cooked and fried. Bears and dogs, foxes and wolves, river otters and seals, marsh birds and birds of prey of all kinds — all of them live from fish.

When the salmon run begins up the rivers in spring and summer, their numbers increase so much that they inhibit each other's progress. The nets caste out to catch them often tear from the quantity of fish. Sometimes they haul them out of the rivers with hooks. The usual method of catching fish is to build weirs of chests, baskets and dams which trap the fish so that they can be taken out. One night I witnessed them making a catch of 10 to 12 thousand salmon. Smaller fish, for example, herring, sticklebacks and similar fish are caught in flat nets or with round fishing nets or dip nets.

The best kinds of salmon are: *Tschawitscha*, *Kunscha*, *Mikischa*, *Crassna riba*, *Korbussa*, *Kisutsch*, *Golzi*, *Galtschik*, *Korucha* and *Chaiko*. Along with these there are numbers of other ocean fish which arrive in large numbers at certain times of year, for example, *Wachna*, *Ramscha*, *Kambala*, *Uiki* and extremely excellent herring and cod.

It is sad and inexcusable of the short-sighted Commandant at the Harbor of St. Peter and St. Paul that the inhabitants and their dogs are

---

*G. Steller, p. 136.

**See the next chapter.

sometimes without food even though, for example, herring swim into the inner harbor right up to the inhabitants' doors in such quantities that they could and should make considerable catches of herring. The same thing can be said about cod. These fish are superabundant in the vicinity of the Harbor of St. Peter and St. Paul and on the western coast of the peninsula (I myself caught over thirty of them in a half hour). You only have to be as ignorant as the officers and their soldiers in Kamtschatka not to be reminded immediately of the important and lucrative harvest of stock fish and cod around Labrador, New Foundland, Iceland and on the northern coast of Great Britain. It could be just as good here. Seventy years ago, the admirable Steller expressed this thought and still nothing has been done. On page 384 he says: "From Japalla to Kampakova on the Penzhinskaya Bay there could be as large harvest of stock fish and cod as in Iceland or New England in America."

The superabundance of edible birds is equally extraordinary. Auks (*Alca cirrhata* and *Alca arctica*) gather in innumerable flocks along the coast in the spring. While nesting, they can be caught by hand in their holes and salted for winter provisions. Eggs of various sea birds — *Alca*, *Larus*, *Colymbus*, etc. — are present in such myriads that whole boat fulls could be collected and stored in oil just like on the islands of St. George and St. Paul.

In the spring and fall (April and September), along most of the Kamtschatka River, migrating wild geese and ducks settle in large flocks so that they could be killed or netted by the thousands. Despite this, they are rarely seen on Kamtschatkan tables, because they have no time, no nets and no gunpowder for hunting.* On the Awatscha River wild ducklings are spiked with three pronged wooden forks by the hundreds or taken by the thousands in nets. Kamtschadals could, if other activities permitted, live well both in winter and summer from hunting reindeer, wild sheep, bears, seals and various birds.

The following is a list of birds I observed:

Anas Cygnus
Anas Segetum
Anas Clangula
Anas dispar
Anas glacialis
Anas Boschas
Anas acuta
Anas Crecca
Colymbus septentrionalis
Colymbus Troile
Mergus
Pelecanus Graculus

---

*Mr. von Pestel, Governor General of Siberia, has remedied this situation.

Pelecanus Urile
Alca arctica
Alca cirrhata
several kinds of *Larus*
Tetrao Lagopus
Tetrao Tetrix
Tetrao Urogallus and numbers of marsh, song birds and birds of prey, whose natural history deserves to be known more exactly

One finds little domesticated poultry — chickens, ducks, geese, etc. They can scarcely be kept because of the thieving dogs.

The richness of plant life is equal to animal life. In the woods, on the mountains and in the valleys there is a superabundance of excellent berries which can be collected by the barrel to produce vinegar, brandy and other useful products, if the Kamtschadals were not so incomprehensibly ignorant, apathetic and frivolous. They only think of the present. They almost never prepare for the future and have during berry picking season an imposing supply but in the winter only a very moderate store. The variety and quality of these berries make them a complete substitute for the total lack of garden plants and orchard fruits, which, with care, could be raised there in the same way as the many foreign kinds of fruit that we have gradually acclimatized and homebred in Europe.

Among the wild berries the following are excellent:

Yellow raspberries [cloudberry] .... *Rubus Chamaemorus*
Mountain cranberry .... *Vaccinium Vitis idaea*
Mossberry [cranberry] .... *Vaccinium Oxycoccos*
Bilberry .... *Vaccinium uliginosum*
Woodsour .... *Berberis vulgaris*
Red currants .... *Ribes rubrum*
Crowberry .... *Empetrum nigrum*

In addition:

Lonicera coerulea
Prunus Padus
Sorbus aucuparia
Rubus arcticus
Arbutus uva ursi
etc.

Nor is Kamtschatka poor in edible roots; the saranna, wild garlic, wild carrots and others are nourishing. Turnips and radishes grow very well, are tasty, and some grow to unusual sizes. Horseradish is still unknown. Potatoes grow as well there as anywhere in Europe. With proper cultivation they could replace bread, and together with berries, fish, reindeer, bears, seals, wild sheep, wild ducks and geese, etc., furnish abundant food for the Kamtschadals.

In addition to this abundance of foodstuffs, there are almost impenetrable forests with wood not only good enough for fires but also for building homes. In some areas, i.e., Tolbatsch and Tschabina, I was astonished by the sumptuous growth of larch. Some of them were 80 to 100 fuss or more tall. The grain of the wood is, furthermore, better and harder than in Ochotsk, where the wood is used for building ships. At various times sturdy ships have actually been built on the Kamtschatka River and at Bolscheretsk. Captain Hall of the Billings expedition built the *Black Eagle* there (in the winter of 1790). In 1806, before it went aground in the Bay of Yamsk, it was still in very useful condition.

The following are the most common kinds of trees in Kamtschatka:

Various kinds of birch: *Betula alba*, *Betula nana*, etc. They are the most common kind of tree found all over the peninsula. The natives use them in many ways, especially for firewood and building sledges. The bark, as almost all over Russia, is used to make various types of barrels. The sap is not used.

Larch, *Pinus larix*, is very useful for building houses and ships.

Poplars, *Populus alba*, are mainly used for canoes hollowed out of a single log.

Firs, *Pinus abies*, only grow in some areas of the peninsula, especially between Tigil and Nischna-Kamtschatka. Cedar pines, *Pinus zembla*, are found almost all over. Even though the Englishmen King and Gore* brewed a very healthy anti-scurvy beer from them during their stay, it was not sufficient enough to convince the inhabitants of the usefulness of that beverage. The tree has small berries. For this reason they are only gathered and eaten to pass the time.

Maple, *Plantanus orientalis*, as far as I know, is not put to any special use.

Alder bark, *Betula alnus*, is used for tanning reindeer and other hides and dying them red.

---

*See Cook's *Dritte Reise um die Welt* [Third Voyage Around the World].

Willows, *Salix arenaria*, *Salix pentandra*, etc., are used for firewood.

Junipers, *Juniperus communis*, and several other bushes, *Crataegus oxyacantha*, *Rosa canina* and *Rosa spinosissima*, *Lonicera coerulea*, etc., grow in profusion.

I dare not leave unmentioned the advantages which might be derived from minerals.

It would be very advantageous for the country if earthen plates, bowls, mugs and glasses and cooking utensils were made on the spot. Very good white clay can be found near the Harbor of St. Peter and St. Paul and Daria Buchta and the hot springs of Paratunka; at the latter, it is especially fine. A skilled craftsman could make such wares with the utmost success.

Ignorance of how to work with and bake clay and the negligence and bad management of the commander at the harbor have caused them to have barely enough bricks to build and repair the stoves, despite the superabundance of excellent clay.

Salt could and should be procured from the ocean. It is generally so scarce that a pud costs 10 to 12 or more rubles.

Numerous volcanos produce quantities of solid sulfur which could be used for export. On the western side of the peninsula at Itscha, there is good quality sandstone. Near Tigil many traces of iron ore are supposed to have been found. Yet, no matter how rich the country may be in metals, it would be imprudent to open mines in a country that does not have enough hands to work them.

All of these facts are the basis of my conviction that Kamtschatka is capable of being cultivated. The peninsula's climate is by far not as terrible as is generally believed. On the contrary, I am very inclined to maintain that few Russian provinces have a similar superabundance of all the necessities for life and that the Kamtschadals with their abundance of products could have far easier lives than many European peoples with far milder climates.

Regulations recently issued by Our Most Gracious Monarch and the appointment of a special committee to examine abuses and to suggest improvements are important steps to improving conditions on the peninsula. The means are there to alleviate the scarcities and needs of that country and to increase trade and industry.

Notes

1. Stepan Petrovich Kras(c)heninnikoff (1713-1755), *The History of Kamtschatka and the Kurilski Islands with the Countries adjacent*, translated from Russian by James Grieve (London: T. Jefferys, 1764). Note the variations in the spelling here of Gawrila Sarytschew, Gavrila Sarytschef(f).

2. Eberhard August Wilhelm von Zimmermann (1743-1815) was a prodigious author of geography and travel books.

3. Magnus Karl von Behm (Böhme) (1727-1806). Franz von Reinken (Reineke).

4. Milkowa — Milkowoi: In searching for the modern names of villages in Kamtschatka and Siberia, if they still exist, I quickly became aware of the fact that Langsdorff's transliterations of their names from Russian reflect Russian case endings.

Chapter 14

Kamtschatkan Dogs as Draft Animals. Kind of Dog: Its Way of Life. Castration. Docking. Former Breeding. Names. Food. Feeding. Post Stations. Number in a Team. Speed. Control. Price. Advantage over Horses. Diseases. Harness. Sledges. Ostoll. Snowshoes. Ice-Shoes (Posluki). Travel by Sledge.

Europeans know about the manifold uses of dogs. They are indispensable hunting companions. Shepherds entrust their flocks and landowners and travelers the safety of their property to their care.

Many South Sea Islanders fatten them as we do pigs. All along the northern polar sea from Ob through all of Northern Siberia, in Kamtschatka, on the Kuril Islands to the most northerly Japanese possessions, all of the peoples living a distance of over one hundred degrees of longitude, i.e., the Ostiaks, the Samoyeds, most of the Tungus, the Koriaks, Tschutski,* Kamtschadals, the Kuriks and the Ainus on Jesso and Tschoka use dogs as draft animals in the winter.

Since, of all these peoples, the Kamtschadals exercise the greatest care in raising and training their dogs and mentioning the name of the peninsula usually calls to mind their use for the mails and since we, as far as I know, except for the few facts that Steller and Krascheninnikoff have given us, know little about them, I will devote a whole chapter, because of the general interest expressed in the subject, to the observations of dogs as draft animals I collected during my stay in Kamtschatka.

Kamtschatkan dogs have long, sharp snouts, pointed, erect ears, long, thickly haired, shaggy tails. In appearance, form, size, and even behavior, they resemble wolves very much. They look the most like our Pomeranian and European shepherd.

---

*Certain groups of this people use reindeer more, others dogs. The former are nomadic, the latter settled in one place.

Their coats in some spots are smooth and short and in others long and shaggy. Their skin is covered by a true blanket of wool, long, fine and soft. If it is carefully collected, washed and prepared, it can be spun just like sheep's wool. The dogs with such long, shaggy, wool-like hair are generally called *magnate* or hairy. Their hides are highly prized for warm furs and trim for clothing. That kind of dog is mostly too clumsy to hitch to sledges. They often can hardly be used in fresh-fallen or deep snow, since the snow easily forms balls in their hair, freezes and prevents the dogs from running fast. Long-legged, thin-haired dogs are especially preferred for light sledges. There are certain dogs that, like ours, bark, but most of them only howl and bark only rarely. The color of their coats varies greatly — black, white, grey, red and all possible mixtures of these colors.

They live outside year round without ever going into the house or stable. In the summer they dig holes in the earth to make a somewhat cooler place to rest. In the winter they do they same thing in the snow to protect themselves against the cold. I saw them often in winter in stormy weather covered all over with snow. They would lie under the deep snow without moving and had to be called out when wanted. Those dogs can bear cold better than heat. In the spring and somewhat warmer weather, they pant as if they had been on a long trip.

A few weeks after the puppies have been weaned their training begins. They are tied to a post by means of long, narrow sticks or chains fastened to their collars. This prevents them from chewing up the leather straps that are used for harnesses and also forces them to get used to lying quietly.

As long as they are still young, they are fed well cooked fish soup that they like to eat. They eat so much that they sometimes can hardly move and you might think their bellies would burst. The soup is fed lukewarm and never hot. When fed such food, the dogs very quickly become large and strong. The ones that eat quite large quantities are thought to be the ones that will prove to be very useful, strong sledge dogs. The dogs with strong bone structures, high wide feet, long, pointed, erect ears, wide, pointed, protruding snouts joined to thick heads and wide chests are considered the best.

At five months or between the fifth and sixth month, all of the dogs intended for use as sledge dogs have to be castrated (the first operation in preparation for their future use). As with our horses, this makes them better able to bear stress and also keeps them from many distracting thoughts. The operation is preferably done in the spring or summer, or at least as long as it is warm, because in the fall or winter it usually takes a long time for the wound to heal.

Neither the few un-castrated dogs intended only for stud service nor the bitches (at the most in time of emergency) are used on sledges.

It is a curious fact that castrated common sledge dogs act like sworn enemies of the others and roughly bite around on them at every opportunity.

The second operation the sledge dogs are subjected to is docking. Since they normally have very long, thickly haired tails that hinder them from running fast, one seldom sees ones that are un-docked.

This operation is only carried out when it is thought that the dogs are full grown, usually when they are two or three years old. The Kamtschadals believe that their growth will be damaged and their strength lessened if it is done earlier.

It is very remarkable that by constant docking and repetition of this operation in every generation that nature now and then, to a certain degree, is put under pressure and dogs without tails are born. I myself saw such a case in Malka, a quite large village in the interior of Kamtschatka. I am also aware of the fact that now and again in England (especially among the large cart horses) foals are born without tails.

As long as the puppies are growing, they dare not be harnessed if they are to attain full strength. Formerly this rule was strictly adhered to. In recent years the Kamtschadals, due to lack of time, having to provide for the winter and for frequent services required by the Crown, have lost a great many sledge dogs. This has forced them to harness young animals that are only seven or eight months old. Their quality and usefulness are so greatly reduced that instead of the three or four formerly needed for a light team now five or six are necessary.

The Kamtschadals looked back with sorrow to the time of their ancestors when they had time to train their dogs very carefully. In earlier times, they were confined to pits and fed every day by the same person. After the first operation, they would occasionally be harnessed up with trained dogs in order to learn to pull. Afterwards, they would be returned to the pit until their training was completed. Dogs trained in this fashion were afraid of light and humans. They would become alarmed at the slightest sound or flight of a bird and pull with all their strength. Three dogs trained in this way, which were first put into service when they were three years old, were stronger than six of the kind now used. Young dogs, which are naturally more eager than old ones, very easily overexert themselves. For this reason, they are usually not used for long trips but rather for shorter ones and light work in their first few years. Five- to six-year-old dogs are the best for long trips and loads.

Every dog is given a name when it is young. It usually is derived from its color or some special characteristic, for example, black ear, long ear, hanging ear, pointed nose, red spots, grey or black head, tiger, white foot, stump tail, etc. This is an advantage. If a driver has a number of dogs in harness and one or the other is not working well, he only has to threaten it by name. This is sufficient to spur it on. This is all the more necessary since the entire team, as I talk about later, is not controlled by reins and whip but only by words.

The dogs are fed mainly on fresh, frozen, cooked, dried and rotten fish. They have to be very carefully fed. Every Kamtschadal, who is a good peasant, and, as a result has dogs, follows these rules which are most advantageous for breeding and training dogs. In the summer most of the dogs fend for themselves. They spend their time near the seashore or along the rivers watching for fish. They stand in the water up to their bellies and wait until they see a fish. Their aim is so good that when they snap at it they seldom miss. Often they stick their whole head under water. Given the superabundance of this food, for example, when the salmon come up the rivers in droves, the dogs only eat their heads and leave the less tasty rest of the fish to rot.

In the fall, the dogs that have run free all summer and have fended for themselves are driven by hunger to return to the villages. Their owners catch them and tie them up so that they cannot run away when it is time to be harnessed to a sledge. They are very fat and only receive a little piece of dried or frozen fish every day, now and then for several days nothing at all, so that they gradually become thinner again. A fat sled dog is clumsy and does not pull well. Day and night they express their hunger and lament over their lost freedom by howling plaintively. Since every Kamtschadal has at least six dogs, i.e., as many as he needs for a team, this means that in a village with fifteen to twenty inhabitants there are at least 120 to 140 dogs. As soon as one begins to howl, all of the others suddenly begin to howl dreadfully. With the incredible superabundance of fish in the summer and lack of time to clean and dry them, they dig large pits and throw the fish into them by the thousands. They are then covered with straw, boards and earth. When such a pit is opened, the whole neighborhood is filled with the most horrible pestilential odor imaginable. This odor seems to make no impression whatsoever upon the olfactory nerves of the Kamtschadals. These stinking fish along with other carrion are delicacies for the dogs and are only given to them occasionally in small quantities. With more contact between the Russians and the Kamtschadals, this kind of food has rather gone out of style. In winter the main food for dogs consists of frozen or dried fish, the latter are called yukola. These are measured out sometimes in larger, sometimes in smaller portions, according the size of the fish or the fatness or leanness of the dogs' bodies. I was especially struck by the fact that the parts of the fish that the dogs prefer in summer, that is, the head, is the one that they totally look down upon in winter. This, by the way, is quite natural, because the bones and the sharp, hard teeth of the dried salmon heads give the ravenously hungry dogs bloody mouths almost every noon when they are fed.

As long as the rivers are frozen in winter and water is not readily available, the dogs quench their thirst by eating snow or ice.

A horse, if it is to be of any use, has to be well-fed. The situation is totally different with dogs. They cannot run on full stomachs. If one, perhaps in well-meaning ignorance, feeds them well before harnessing them up, they vomit and get diarrhea underway and plainly lose their strength and health. For this reason, they are always harnessed with empty stomachs and only fed in the evening after having worked. If one wants to give them something in the morning before setting out for a ride or going on a trip, then one does it just as one is leaving by throwing them about half of a dried fish. Then they will run and pull the whole day and are capable of traveling on empty stomachs from 60 to 80, indeed, even 100 versts.

When one reaches one's destination, one does not immediately feed the overheated dogs but lets them wait at least one hour if they have traveled 30 to 40 versts and two hours if they have traveled 60 to 70 versts, so that they are completely cooled off. Only then should they be fed and left to rest for the night so that they are rested the following morning and ready to go again.

If one wants to treat one's dogs especially well, then one lets them rest some after they have gone about half way and throws them a little piece of dried fish. This fortifies them and makes them so eager that they travel the second half of the trip far more rapidly and easily. On long trips the dogs run better on a somewhat reduced diet than on a full one. The first days of a trip have to be made shorter then the last ones. If one has dogs travel 40 to 50 versts a day five to six days in a row, it is advisable to let them rest for a day and to feed them very well, which then picks them up again for several days.

The dogs, because of mischievousness, lack of good training and bad habits or also because of hunger, often gnaw on the harnesses and straps which are made of sealskin. This can often cause a traveler the greatest embarrassment, since he then has to walk the rest of the way because he has no leather straps. A good dog should not gnaw on the straps even when suffering from the greatest hunger.

A propensity for thieving seems to be such an innate quality of Kamtschatkan dogs that even the coarsest of punishment does not prevent them from stealing anything and everything they can find. This part of their nature corresponds to that of wolves and fox.

When I was with the Koriaks, my dogs got lost one night and chewed up my host's sack of train and ate it all, thus giving them a very bad case of diarrhea the following morning.

Smelly carrion is very welcome food for them. They often even fight violently over human excrement. In the spring when dried fish stores have been used up, they are fed bear fat or seal blubber. They are only given as much as is necessary to keep them alive until fresh fish begin to run in the rivers. Feeding a lot of meat ruins the dogs and makes them sluggish.

In the spring when there is still a lack of food and the sledging season is past, they gather in packs, attack cattle and tear them up and eat them. I was told that they have even raged among themselves and the stronger dogs have eaten the young and weak ones. For this reason it would almost be impossible to keep sheep or pigs in Kamtschatka. They would have to be kept inside.

After the dogs have been scantily fed the whole winter on dried and frozen fish and the fish begin to run again in the spring, the Kamtschadals do not permit the dogs immediately to eat to their hearts content but maintain that they have to become accustomed to the food gradually, that a quick change in diet is damaging to the strength and health of the dogs. Perhaps they will overeat and get diarrhea. This is the reason why all of the owners of good dogs have fresh fish soup made in the spring. They feed the dogs with it until they have gradually become accustomed to their summer diet of fresh fish.

The Kamtschatkan dogs possess almost none of the natural watchfulness of the canine race. Their aptitude consists solely of pulling. They seek to show their loyalty and dependence by exerting their strength especially for the one who feeds them and they recognize as their master. This is the reason why every dog lover feeds his dogs himself and stays with them until they have eaten. This is mostly necessary because otherwise one dog will always try to steal the food away from another dog.

In winter there are regular post stations all over Kamtschatka where the traveler may be furnished with dogs just like in Europe with horses. The stations are 30 to 40 or 50, and a very few up to 70 versts apart. Every traveler is given a sledge with a six-dog team for himself and his baggage and a companion, i.e., a Kamtschadal with another six-dog team and sledge for the rest of his baggage and to take the dogs and sledge back to his post station. There are as many individual sledges as there are travelers, since usually each person has to be his own postilion and drive himself. The post dogs are less accustomed to belonging to one person than others. Therefore, they are happy to pull anyone. In addition, a Kamtschadal, who usually also owns the dogs, goes ahead of the traveler. As a result, the dogs always have their owner ahead of them and are happy to follow his sledge.

If one begged the chief of a village or any other lover of dogs to harness up his best dogs that are only used to him, one would, at least not alone, get as far as with the poorest of post dogs, for as soon as they hear a strange voice not belonging to their master, they become indifferent and hardly move. One can threaten them or punish them anyway one wants. In a small village I once bought a dog that had been recommended to me as very good. He, however, had never known any other master than the one who had raised and fed him every day. After purchasing this dog and harnessing him together with others so he would get used to me, we left his birthplace. He kept looking back, did not want to go forwards, and despite all punishment, pulled badly. At the next post station he did not even want to eat the food that I threw to him. He was restless and looked continually down the path where we had come. He howled for several days until he finally got used to me and showed that he was worthy of the recommendation he had received.

The number of dogs harnessed to a sledge depends partially upon on the load being carried from one place to another, and partially upon the quality of the dogs and the path or sledge run to be used. For a light sledge with one person and little baggage, four or five dogs are necessary into order to move fast. Six dogs can easily pull a sledge loaded with 14 to 16 Russian puds or 640 pfunds on a good path. If the load is heavier, more dogs have to be used.

Young dogs are spoiled if they are forced to pull heavy loads. They get used to going slowly and as a result can no longer be used together with fast running dogs.

Typical post dogs will cover ten to twelve versts in an hour, and the best dogs fifteen to twenty versts. This is only possible on a good sledge path and for a short period of time. It means with the same dogs one can travel 40 to 50 versts in two and one-half to three hours but never 80 versts in six hours. With very good dogs one can travel, at the most, without changing dogs, 200 hundred versts in two days and 300 in three days. But then a day of rest is necessary.

The dogs usually trot at a steady pace. This means that, once they have begun moving on a path that is uniformly good, they can run almost the same distance every hour.

With post dogs used to running and hard work, and these are always the best of dogs, one can travel very fast if one goes day and night. In Tigil, a village on the northwestern coast of Kamtschatka, I met a non-commissioned officer who had been sent as courier. In nine and one-half days he had traveled 1,500 versts, that is, over 150 versts a day by changing dogs at every station. Steller says (p. 374): "In good weather and over good paths one can travel nonstop one hundred to one hundred and forty versts in fifteen hours."

If the dogs do not pull well and are sluggish and they do not react to threats, they are punished along the way. Punishment is usually carried out by using a switch, only rarely a rod, because one can easily break a leg or rib and make the dog unable to pull.

The whole post team is not controlled by bridle and reins but only with words. That is the reason why there is a big difference between the other dogs and the leader dogs, which are always placed up front and always obey, if they are good, the commands of the driver calling to the right or left, fast or slow in Kamtschatkan.* (See *ostoll*, below.)

The price of a dog in Kamtschatka varies just as much as the price of a horse in Europe. A typical draft dog costs thirty to forty rubles and a very good racing or lead dog often as much as 100 to 150 rubles. A newly weaned puppy whose potential is unknown usually costs ten rubles.

The best dogs are now found along the western side of the peninsula between Tigil and Bolscheretsk because the inhabitants are subject to less tribute [*Frohndienst*] and the dogs to less wear and tear.

Many experts maintain that when buying a dog, if the hair has been rubbed off on the top half of the hind leg, this is the best proof that the dog works very hard since the harness leathers bear down there when the dog is pulling hard. With lazy dogs one never sees a trace of rubbed-off hair. Others deny that this is proof of the quality of a dog.

A good team simply has to have an intelligent lead dog. The comfort of a trip is totally dependent upon him because the rest of the team follows him. For this reason if the lead dog is bad and runs along with all of the other dogs to the left when the driver wants to go right, it becomes dogged drudgery to get anywhere.

If one happens to have bad dogs and perhaps no lead dog at all, then one has to let a good team go ahead so that one can comfortably get from one place to the next because even the worst dogs will follow the trail without causing any trouble. If one owns a very well trained lead dog, in the winter one has to go out on runs as often as possible to keep him in form. If one does not use him enough and he runs most of the winter behind other sledges, he forgets his skills and is far less valuable.

In Kamtschatka and many other northern lands, dogs are preferred as draft animals to horses for many reasons.** The dogs can

*In Kamtschatkan, right is *kachkach*, left *huchahucha*, fast or forward *has* and slow or stop *ayng*, spoken through the nose, approximately like a long French *en*.

**See Steller, p. 136.

pull a sledge over the deepest snow, over lightly frozen swamps and morasses, over rivers and steep hills, where horses cannot go at all.

The winter's supply of fish needed to feed the dogs, given the incredible quantities of fish available, is far easier to put up than hay for horses.

Dogs can stand more than horses. Often for two or three days on long trips, they have to eat a few dried fish brought along as provisions for man and dog alike; indeed, they have a liking for them and work too, hardships horses could not endure without proper fodder. In the coldest of winter weather they do not need any special care in a stable like horses. The entire summer they also find their own food without the slightest help from their master.

The skins of old, worn out dogs or ones no longer good for pulling are most advantageously used to make very warm fur clothing. In general raising dogs is much less difficult than raising horses.

Dogs used in harness have to be kept chained the whole winter. That is the way, according to Kamtschadals, they keep their strength.

It is extremely necessary to keep dogs tied or chained because one has to have dogs readily available at any time. If they are left to run free, then many of them, when they see that they are going to be put in harness, cleverly run away and do not return until hunger forces them to.

In addition, they dare not run free because they fight easily among themselves. Sometimes the best lead or draft dog can be disabled by an unlucky bite for shorter or longer periods of time.

If the dogs are very fat and, as a result, less suitable for harness, then they are let run free for a time. Experience has shown that frequent, instinctive exercise slims them down more quickly.

Finally, I wish to mention here several diseases I observed that are characteristic of draft dogs. Good draft dogs, especially those used to pull sledges, are often subject to dislocated shoulder joints. If on very uneven paths the sledge often suddenly falls into a hole, this throws the weight of the loaded sledge upon the harness around the shoulders and chest with such a sudden force that the straining dog is thrown on his side, thus ripping his shoulder joint out of place. Almost every Kamtschadal has had this happen, so when this happens, he immediately puts the bone in place again without any further harm. If, however, he does not see it and does nothing, then even the best of dogs is no longer worth very much.

If a dog in continued cold (in December and January) gets wet in a stream, it easily can happen that his feet freeze, disabling him for the sledge for the whole winter.

In the spring when the water from the melting snow by day is covered by a thin sheet of ice in the cold nights, which will barely carry the weight of a sledge and dogs, one has to try to protect the dogs' feet. They can run their feet raw on the sharp, roughly frozen snow and injure their leg joints on the sharp edges of the ice during breakup. In order to prevent this, they usually wear leather socks that are fastened above the front and hind knee joints. Many of the dogs cannot bear the feeling of being encumbered and tear them off.

On hard, slippery paths, when the dogs are spurred on to pull a heavily loaded sledge up a steep slope, they strain so much to keep their foothold that they rip out their toenails and thus damage their feet for a long time.

Sometimes dogs suddenly do not want to eat and become very thin. The Kamtschadals then cut out the ligament under their tongues, commonly called the worm. They claim that this causes the disease (perhaps increases it) and soon after its removal the dogs get well again.

Other more general problems are: tapeworm, vomiting blood, dysenteries, and according to the Kamtschadals, all kinds of illnesses to which man is also subject. It is striking that, despite repeated and exact research, I could not find a single example of rabies among the dogs all over Kamtschatka.

I think an exact picture of dogs in harness can give a clearer view than an extensive description.

The sledges are built only from birch wood and leather straps in a simple and very ingenious manner without the use of nails. They are built higher and stronger, or lower and lighter depending upon whether they are to be used to transport goods or only for hunting or for transportation. Certain rules have to be followed to ensure their quality.

It is striking that sledges all over Kamtschatka are of the same width. Thus, all good sledge paths consist of two tracks equidistant from each other into which all sledge runners fit.

A good, light sledge seldom weighs more than 20 to 22 pfunds. Despite this, it can be thrown violently into a tree without breaking. All of the parts of a freight sledge are stronger and, thus, heavier.

At the front of the sledge the runners have to be about one-half zoll farther apart than at the back, so that the sledge glides much more smoothly over the path. Its actual seat rests on four legs, of which the front ones have to be one-half zoll higher than the back ones. The seat, in addition, dares not be too high or else the sledge will turn over easily. Even though most of them are only intended for one person, in case of emergency two people can ride comfortably on them if they sit sideways, that is, if the one sits on the right side and the other on the left side like on a bench.

The driver always sits to the side and has to be ready at any time to jump off and keep the sledge upright while running along beside it and then jumping back on. The skill of the driver consists of his way of maintaining balance and always keeping the sledge under control.

Besides the usual sledges, there is another kind used only for loads and called a *narden*. It resembles a long bench with railings on each side sitting on small feet. The runners underneath have the same width or gauge as other sledges.

On a sledge trip the most important tool to have along is an *ostoll*, a knee-shaped, strong rod bent at an angle. On the bottom end it has a iron point and at the top delicately braided straps with bells or clattering rings. This rod almost takes the place of lead reins and whip. If the dogs are to be spurred on, it is rattled; if they are to go slow or stop, the ostoll is thrust into the snow or ice with the necessary force in front of the runners into the snow, thus checking the dogs. In a similar way, it is used to keep the sledge under control when going down a steep slope. Otherwise, if the sledge is heavily loaded, it will go faster than the dogs and run over them, thus reaching the foot of the mountain first, while dragging the whole team of dogs behind it. Usually, in such cases, the driver is thrown off along the way and comes down on foot.

The ostoll is a true commanding rod. When, for example, one is hunting in the woods, the continual cry of *kachkach* (right) and *huchahu-*

cha (left) would very soon chase the game away. A good leader dog has to pay attention to the ostoll. If he wants to go left, the driver strikes the snow on the right with it or knocks lightly on the right front runner, or the other way around, he knocks on the left side of the sledge if he wants to go right. It is an absolute pleasure behind a good lead dog without opening one's mouth to approach game, to be able to go up to the exact tree or bush from which one wants to shoot.

A Kamtschadal seldom goes out on a sledge without taking along a pair of snowshoes, which he considers are of utmost importance. He uses them in the deep snows of the woods and mountains when looking for sable tracks. He can travel through deep, freshly fallen snow, in which dogs can only work their way with the greatest exertion and difficulty, by going ahead of the sledge and tramping the snow down, making it easier for the dogs to follow. Finally, snowshoes are especially important for keeping the sledge paths in good condition. If a driver wants to get off of the sledge, he often sinks up to his knees or his body in snow and makes a big hole or depression which makes traveling for sledges behind him very difficult.

Snowshoes are pointed in front and back and made of long, thin slats. In front they are curved upward, in the middle arched, thus giving them a very high degree of elasticity. To make walking easier, especially when going uphill, the side of the shoe to the snow is covered with seal or fur seal skin so that the nap of the hair runs from front to back. The smoothness helps when going forwards but prevents sliding backward, because the hair rubs so much against the snow.

Straps are fastened to the front half of the slats, which makes it very easy to tie the snowshoe to your foot. These straps are put in the front of the snowshoe, since the back half then tips down of its own accord. This facilitates walking very much because the front part then goes up of its own accord.

An average size snowshoe is about four and one-half fuss long and seven zoll wide. In general, length and breadth are determined by the weight and size of the person who will use them. Twelve- to fourteen-year-old boys have much smaller ones than grown men.

There are people who can travel up and down hills on such snowshoes with extraordinary agility. I was told that certain well trained men on snowshoes, that is, with good elastic ones arched in the middle upwards, can stride the distance of five normal steps or fifteen fuss at one time. In this case, going on snowshoes would resemble ice skating.

Kamtschadals, who seem to be born to hunt, occasionally climb up to the high mountain glaciers in order to shoot argali or wild sheep. For this purpose they use ice-shoes. They look approximately like snowshoes. They are made of slats, about two and one-half to three schuh-lengths long and seven to eight zoll wide. They are placed almost parallel to each other and fastened together in front and in back. Little pointed bits of bone are embedded on each side of their lower surface which cut into the ice and prevent slipping. Ice-shoes are fastened to the feet in the same way as snowshoes. They are used on hills in place of snowshoes and in places where the snow is deeper and on frozen, slippery snow. The space between the slats is filled in with struts and straps.

In several areas of Kamtschatka, where the inhabitants have to climb high mountains and glaciers, they use sharply pointed irons to make it easier to climb. These are fastened under their feet (usually tied). They are called *posluki* and with them they can climb the steepest of ice-covered slopes and mountains with them.

As fast as traveling by dog sledge is, it still has its great drawbacks; for each person has to be his own driver; and, in thick woods and especially going downhill, it is almost impossible to stop the dogs. As a result, even the most skillful of drivers sometimes runs into a tree and probably ends up going home on foot with a bloody head or other injuries. In general, a fast, happy trip is very dependent upon the weather, so that such a trip overland can be compared with a voyage at sea.

One anxiously watches for good weather and departs when the wind is favorable. There is much talk of present, future or past storms or of fast trips when the wind and weather were good. A trip can be held up by snow flurries, storms and contrary winds, forcing a driver to seek haven in nearby woods or in a hut or to return to the last station he was at, like returning to a harbor to wait several days for good weather. Then he often finds himself facing a wide expanse of snow, in which he seeks to spot a recognizable tip of woods, a hill, a mountain or an island-like stand of trees to use as a landmark, like the seafarer orienting himself from a promontory or an island.

Chapter 15

Noteworthy Events. Arrival of Messrs. von Chwostoff and von Davidoff in the Harbor of St. Peter and St. Paul. Secret Expedition. Death of Mr. von Resanoff. Continuation of the Secret Expedition. Deaths of Messrs. von Chwostoff and von Davidoff. Winter Stay in Kamtschatka. Balls, Music. Hot Springs in Malka. Trip to Nischna-Kamtschatka. Werchnoi-Kamtschatka. Milkowa. Klutschi. Capital City of Nischna-Kamtschatka.

It would be long-winded of me if I were to relate everything I did and said during my nine-month stay in Kamtschatka. Therefore, I will restrict myself to the most noteworthy occurrences and hope at another time to find an opportunity to describe the peninsula in more detail.

During a period of good weather at the end of September, Mr. D'Wolf and I visited a neighboring area including the hot springs of Paratunka. Upon our return I was delighted to find at the harbor, unexpectedly, my old traveling companion and friend von Davidoff, who had arrived aboard the *Awos* on October 2nd.

Here is a summary of his story:

Several weeks after our departure from Sitcha the ship *Awos* was ready to sail and was turned over with its crew to Mr. Davidoff. Mr. von Resanoff went on board the *Juno*, which was under the command of Mr. von Chwostoff. In August both ships left Norfolk Sound.

Mr. von Resanoff, who had been carrying a grudge in his heart against the Japanese since his unsuccessful mission there, planned a secret expedition on which Mr. von Davidoff was to head straight to the southern Kuril Islands to see if there were really Japanese outposts as was being claimed, since, as we know from Pallas's *New Northern Contributions*, they are considered Russian possessions. As a result of this order, Mr. von Davidoff took leave of the *Juno* in the vicinity of Unalaska and headed toward the Island of Urup, where Schelichoff had built a Russian outpost twenty years before. It had been abandoned soon after his death. Contrary winds and terrible storms made Mr. von Davidoff decide that it was not advisable to try to land and inspect the islands that year, so at the end of September he returned to the Harbor of St. Peter and St. Paul to winter and rendezvous with the *Juno*.

In September, Mr. von Chwostoff reached Ochotsk. In October, as a result of the orders he had received to join Mr. von Resanoff's secret expedition, he left and arrived in Kamtschatka on November 6th.

It is easy to imagine Mr. D'Wolf's and my joy at unexpectedly finding friends in Kamtschatka with whom we had been most friendly the preceding winter on the Northwest Coast of America. Mr. von Chwostoff told us that Mr. von Resanoff had arrived in Ochotsk at the end of September and had immediately set out for Irkutsk and that an Imperial Russian mission under Count Goloffin recently sent to Pekin had suffered a similar end as ours to Japan and that the mission had dispersed. One of the natural scientists, Collegiate Assessor Dr. Redowski, was in Ochotsk. For scientific reasons he wanted to visit Kamtschatka and the Aleutian Islands and in the winter to travel around the Penschinskaya Gulf by post dog sledges.

Before his departure from Ochotsk, Mr. von Chwostoff received additional orders for the planned secret expedition. In October he sailed for a southern (Russian) island, where he found a Japanese outpost and sizeable storehouse. He overpowered it without any resistance and asserted earlier rights to the island. He took upwards to one thousand puds of rice, a quantity of smoking tobacco, fish nets, many lacquered wooden bowls and containers, pipes, a rather large supply of salt and an insignificant quantity of salted fish, things made of cotton and silk, paper, ink, pictures, etc. He gave the natives (Ainu) a much larger supply of all these articles than he could take along. He took along on his ship to Kamtschatka four Japanese who had been in charge of the storehouse.

Thus, for the first time, the Japanese felt the Russian superiority because they had frustrated the ambitions of an ex-ambassador. The whole undertaking had the appearance of legality. Mr. von Resanoff escaped further responsibility in the matter and having to justify his actions because the following year, during his return trip to St. Petersburg (as a result of his horse falling on the Ochotsk Road), his glorious life came to an end in Krasnojarsk.

Since later I will have little opportunity to talk about Messrs. von Chwostoff and von Davidoff's undertaking against the Japanese, I am going to relate events somewhat out of chronological order and tell about the course of their secret expedition and their later fate.

After having spent the winter in our huts in the Harbor of St. Peter and St. Paul enjoying fish, reindeer meat and other products of the countryside, and most especially the excellent Japanese rice brought by the *Juno*, and having undertaken several pleasure trips together in the greatest of harmony, those friends prepared to continue their secret military mission in the spring of 1807 in accordance with their instructions. They were to free all of the southern Kuril Islands previously claimed by Russia of their recent new Japanese inhabitants and outposts.

On May 2, 1807 the *Juno* and *Awos* sailed with this intention straight to the Islands of Urup and Iturup. On the latter they found several armed Japanese, who at first tried to defend themselves using bows and arrows but fled very quickly leaving all of their housing and storehouse to the Russians. Here they found beautifully lacquered utensils, books, maps, a large supply of rice and salt, tobacco, clothing, tools of various types, in short, everything necessary for maintaining life. In addition, the most remarkable things confiscated were several cannons, many guns and pistols, sabers, armor, helmets, bows, arrows, etc. We have these brave men to thank for information which we could not obtain during our six-month stay in Nangasaki. I am grateful to Mr. Korukin, a master shipwright, for providing me with an exact plan of the Japanese cannons. I was very inclined to think they were originally old Spanish ones. Meanwhile, my informants found other cannons similar to these that, according to the letters forged on them, were Japanese work.

The four Japanese brought to Kamtschatka the previous fall had learned some Russian during the winter. They were returned to their mother country and asked to inform their fellow countrymen of Russia's more legitimate and older claim to the islands than the Japanese, who had not been living on them very long. For this reason, [the Russians] had legally taken possession of them once again. The Japanese were given a Russian paper containing this information, on which a Russian flag had been painted.

The majority of the most interesting of the objects listed above were taken by our seamen to Ochotsk. There the commander, Captain Bucharin, illegally confiscated them and sold them cheaply, to the great detriment of the Crown and the Russian-American Company.

The two naval officers, von Chwostoff and von Davidoff, suffered a lot of hardship and trouble on their trip to Irkutsk in the fall of the same year. They reached St. Petersburg in the spring of 1808.

They were known for their courage, determination and talent. Therefore, they were sent to fight in the war against the Swedes. They distinguished themselves in the command of gunboats. Crowned with laurels they spent some time in the Imperial capital. In September 1809, our common friend Captain D'Wolf appeared in Kronstadt with a cargo of goods from the United American Free States. We were overjoyed when he surprised us with his visit in St. Petersburg. The four of us, who had spent one miserable and wretched winter together on the Northwest Coast of America and another one in Kamtschatka, were delighted to find ourselves happily united once again in the capital.

We happily sat together and recalled with pleasure all of the dangers we had suffered on land and on water and all of the adventures we had survived. We took turns telling each other of our further adventures and reminded each other first of this and then of that happening during the years spent on the other side of the earth. We conversed with the warmest of mutual feelings until late in the night. It was after two in the morning when our friends von Chwostoff and von Davidoff left my apartment (in Wassili Ostrow) to hurry home (they lived on the other side of the river). Captain D'Wolf and I accompanied them to the ship's bridge across the Neva that was just to be raised for the night so that ships could pass. Therefore, our friends walked along a plank from one bridge support to the other and called good night to us when they safely reached the other side. Mr. D'Wolf (in St. Petersburg on a visit from Kronstadt) returned home with me.

The following morning we were informed that two naval officers had been devoured by the Neva — oh, what horror! — oh, what a terrible fate! — our friends, who — for God knows what reason — after we had left, had decided to return to us in Wassili Ostrow. In order to get across the river more quickly, they had tried to jump onto a barque just passing between the bridge supports; instead, they hit a sail projecting over it, which tipped and let them fall into the rapacious current of the Neva.

The night was very dark and all rescue attempts — alas! — were in vain.[1]

Thus was terminated the careers of those two brave, talented men without their suspecting the least of danger. That, after they had twice traveled from St. Petersburg to Ochotsk, from there had commanded ships to the Northwest Coast of America, California, and the Aleutian and Kuril islands and happily returned from all of their expeditions — after distinguishing themselves in the last Finnish war and despite manifold dangers had been victorious. Thus, these two friends, who had been almost inseparable for years, were united in an unusual manner even in death. Thus, the state also lost two of her most promising men. In service and sentiment my two bosom friends whose memory will always merit the greatest regard and respect:

Like two eagles in proud flight
Espying the power of youthful wing,
Piercing ether's high regions —
Thus they pressed forward — in bold daring
  flight
With heroic power in their youthful blood
To distant goals through unchartered seas,
Revenging their country's honor,
Punishing islanders' vain arrogance.
The savage on distant shores
Amazed by Russian courage and Japanese shame
They escaped from enemy wrath,
From poison arrows unscathed,
To arrive back at the hearth of home,
Where those seafarers could rest after so much
  danger.
Caution drew back her hand,
Devastation and stormy waves,
Foreboding fate's circling power.
Two friends standing on Neva's shore
She carried inseparably bound
With one step to a watery grave.
And numbed, waits a friend on shore
Quietly mourning the eternally departed.

Noble actions are a reward in themselves. Heaven will certainly reward them for the many good, selfless deeds done for the Aleuts in Unalaska, Kodiak and Sitcha.

May I be excused for this digression, but the eulogy is for two unforgettable friends who spent the last evening of their lives with me.

I now return to my winter stay in Kamtschatka. We began training in dog sledding at the end of October. By the 9th of November, winter had permanently established itself. With typical temperatures of 12°

to 18° Messrs. von Chwostoff, von Davidoff, Captain D'Wolf, I and others often took trips to the neighboring areas and villages of Paratunka, Awatscha, Korak, Natschika, Malka and others. When we all happened to be at the harbor, we would sometimes put on little dances. Several officers' wives and the wife of the Russian-American Company agent, Miss Lariwanoff, several petty officers, their women and daughters — as the rules of etiquette were not strictly followed — were invited to the balls, where we usually danced English contra dances. Several soldiers playing a pandora (bandura), balalaika* and violin were our musicians.

For a change of pace, sometimes Kamtschadal women were invited to present a national dance. The male and female dancers imitated the movements and manners of seals and bears. They would begin with the gentlest of head and shoulder movements and end with the wildest of hip and knee movements. They sing their own music. At the same time they stamp the rhythm on the ground, while moaning repeatedly short ha! or ach!

The main national song is called the *bachia*, a word whose continual repetition constitutes the text of the song. It is said to have no special meaning. The melody of the song is not without expression. I include it here and am grateful to Councilor von Tilesius, who wrote it down during an earlier stay at the Harbor of St. Peter and St. Paul, for music to a Kamtschadal national dance.

After having practiced dog sledding some and daring to go out on a long excursion, I traveled the 138 versts from the Harbor of St. Peter and St. Paul to the rather distant village of Malka in order to inspect nearby hot springs.

Boiling water flows from the earth at the foot of several hills in a charming valley. The surrounding area is enchantingly beautiful. In summer, when the bare woods are green and the surrounding plain is covered with a flower-filled carpet of grass, I can imagine the area exceedingly lovely and full of variety. On the stones of the main spring, a white, either kidney-shaped or leafy calcsinter builds up. The water tastes and smells of weak saltpeter. In an area about one-half verst in size, there are three to four of these hot springs which unite into a small stream. Even though in several places it is more than lukewarm, small fish live in it. I thought they were sticklebacks

*A two- to three-stringed Russian folk instrument.

Bachia,

oder Musik zu einem kamtschadalischen National-Tanze.

(*Gasterosteus*) and exactly like ours. Close to the stream is a small container in which the water cools down. It is used by the people who go there for bathing. Several huts have been built near the springs in which, if needed, people suffering from gout or arthritis or other diseases can live. The inhabitants of Malka use the warm water for bathing as well as laundry. Meat and fish left for awhile in the springs are soon cooked.

I returned from there to the harbor, which I had left on January 15th, in order to go to Nischna-Kamtschatka. After reaching Malka on the 19th and resting there, I set out again the following day for Ganal, forty-one versts away, where I stayed overnight and continued my trip on the 21st for Puschtschina. This is one of the longest stretches between post stations on the western side. It counts as 64 versts, but the Kamtschadals say it is 76. To help out dogs and travelers, a hut has been built about 25 versts from Ganal. During the winter, a Kamtschadal is stationed there, so that travelers can stop and rest some, and their dogs can be thrown a little piece of dried fish (*yukola*).

Several versts from there the two chains of mountains running from the north to the south of the peninsula approach each other and are connected by several hills which, in my opinion, form the natural division between the southern and central parts of Kamtschatka. The area is remarkable and probably of very high elevation because the neighborhood is the source of the Büstra River, which flows near Bolscheretsk to the southwest, the Awatscha River, which flows to the southeast into the Bay of the same name, and the Kamtschatka River, which flows to the northeast and after more than 400 versts empties into the sea near Nischna-Kamtschatka. On the 22nd I reached Werchnoi-Kamtschatka, one of the most important towns on the peninsula. It once was right on the Kamtschatka River. In the summer of 1805, the river swelled so much as a result of unusually heavy snowfalls during the preceding winter that the inhabitants were threatened by flooding. That happily did not occur because the river — at the height of danger — broke through a new bed a few versts from the village. This has made fishing very difficult, since the old branch of the river has become a very quietly flowing stream with only a few fish.

Two priests live there. The church has few visitors. It is old and tumbledown. The military hospital, which was of special interest for me, I found had been terribly neglected. It is much too small for even the few patients confined there. The windows were closed so that there was no way whatsoever to let in any fresh air. The latrines are far over the courtyard and there is not even a kitchen. Cooking has to be done on the same stoves used to heat the rooms.

The only medicines were the rest of the supplies left by Captain von Krusenstern. The generosity of that expedition was still visible two years later.

Werchnoi-Kamtschatka has about 60 soldiers and 30 cossacks, who are mainly employed in agriculture or are supposed to be. There are over one hundred head of cattle and a number of horses belonging mainly to the Crown, without being of use to anyone. Due to negligence, the inhabitants often have hardly anything to eat in the spring, since they provide very poorly for winter provisions and the fish only begin to run very late.

Neighboring areas are quite populated. Along the first thirteen versts, there are three villages whose inhabitants live mostly from raising cattle and farming. The largest of these villages is Milkowa Derewna. Russian peasants live there whose ancestors, seven in number, were sent there from Russia about seventy years ago in order to introduce farming. In the meantime their number has increased to eighty souls. The mayor of the village told me that he had harvested five to eight times the amount of his seed nine years in a row.

The mayor, upon the recommendation of His Excellency Major General von Koscheleff, was awarded a medallion by His Imperial Majesty for his promotion of farming.

All of the peasants in his village live from the rich harvest of their fields. They have bread from their own grain, potatoes, cabbage, carrots, radishes, cucumbers, fish, meat, milk and game in abundance. There are 85 cows and 22 horses, which can be used the whole year since the area is flat. Is then farming still impossible in Kamtschatka?

On the continuation of my trip, the areas around Kosirefsky and Tolpatsch especially caught my attention, since the snow never falls heavily but always so lightly that the cows can graze all winter.

On the evening of the 30th, I reached the village of Klutschi or Klutschefskaia Derewna. Like Milkowa, mostly Russian peasants and several cossacks live there and are quite well-off. Farming, cattle raising, hunting and fishing supply the inhabitants with an abundance of food. The climate and the earth are not as good as in the neighborhood of Werchnoi-Kamtschatka. Klutschi is almost at the foot of a very high volcano, which smokes continuously or burns brightly, and then can be seen at night at a distance of 300 versts or even farther.*

The village has over twenty houses, a church and the only school on the peninsula, where only the sons of soldiers, not of the Kamtschadals, are taught reading, writing, arithmetic and music. The whole organization of that school is in need of many improvements, as are the much too small living arrangements for the seventy boys living there. The rooms are small and dark. The window panes are made of fishskin instead of glass. There is no kitchen. For this reason, cooking is done in the schoolroom. The pupils have to catch for themselves the fish that are their main source of nourishment. They often do not have enough to eat and suffer from hunger and, as a result, from scurvy. The teacher is an old, retired petty officer who discharges his duties to the best of his ability and strength.

In the hospital, which was in a similar wretched condition, I found mostly schoolboys suffering from scorbutic sores on their feet due to lack of cleanliness, good air and proper food.

---

*A, granted, very incomplete, description of this mountain can be found in the excellent *Mémoires de la societé impériale des naturalistes de Moscou* (Memoirs of the Royal Society of Naturalists in Moscow), 1809, Vol. 4, II, pg. 189, etc. As believable as this description appears to be, I completely doubt the possibility of being able to climb that extraordinarily steep mountain cone. In the summer of 1804, Major von Friederici, full of the zeal necessary for such an undertaking, attempted to climb the mountain but had to give up after becoming convinced of the impossibility of climbing it.

After enjoying the hospitality of the head of the village, Vassili Ivanovitsch, I set out on the last day of my journey. On February 2nd I reached the present capital of the peninsula, Nischna-Kamtschatka.

The commander, Major General von Koscheleff, greeted me with all possible testimonies of friendship. He did everything possible to ensure me as pleasant a stay — it was carnival season — as possible.

The city lies on a point of land at the mouth of the Raduga River, which flows into the Kamtschatka River. It has two churches (a cold and a warm one) and over one hundred houses. The general staff, officers of the Crown, priest, that is, a chief priest (*protopop*), and two assistant priests, the battalion's surgeon, merchants, citizens, soldiers and cossacks live there.

During the night of the 13th to the 14th, a strong earthquake awakened me. That is not an uncommon occurrence in that country. Its main source is probably the volcano near Klutschi. Despite the mostly very stormy weather, the carnival was, indeed, merrier than I would have imagined in Kamtschatka. General von Koscheleff had two hills of ice, that national pastime of the Russians, constructed. He put on several balls and, on the last day, a masquerade attended by more than 60 persons of both sexes. The General keeps a public table for his officers every day throughout the year. That is no trifle in Kamtschatka. He let me partake of the same hospitality and generosity and treated me to the best of dishes. Fish, salted and smoked duck, fresh and smoked reindeer and argali (wild sheep) tongue, the most excellent salmon and several other tasty dishes would have chased away the thought that I was in Kamtschatka, if, unfortunately, many other circumstances had not reminded me often where I was. It is sad helplessly to stand by and see the suffering of the many ill Russians and Kamtschadals, who have almost no medical help. The battalion's surgeon complained more than a little about his situation and the lack of even the most essential means of help for the ill.

The small supply of medicine in the country is sent from Russia to the battalion stationed there. Since the supply is by far too small, the staff surgeon very often finds himself, despite all his knowledge of medicine, which no one can deny him, unable to offer necessary help. Given the conditions there, I was struck by the fact that, on the one hand, among the medical supplies, which had been sent several thousand versts at great expense from Russia, were, among other things, iron filings, juniper berries, essence of spruce (many puds' worth), calcareous powders and several similar items. On the other hand, except for the remains of supplies left by the Krusenstern expedition in Kamtschatka, there was hardly

1. *Northern Lights observed along the Norwegian Coast, September 19, 1803.*

2. *Clothing of the poorer inhabitants on Teneriffe.*

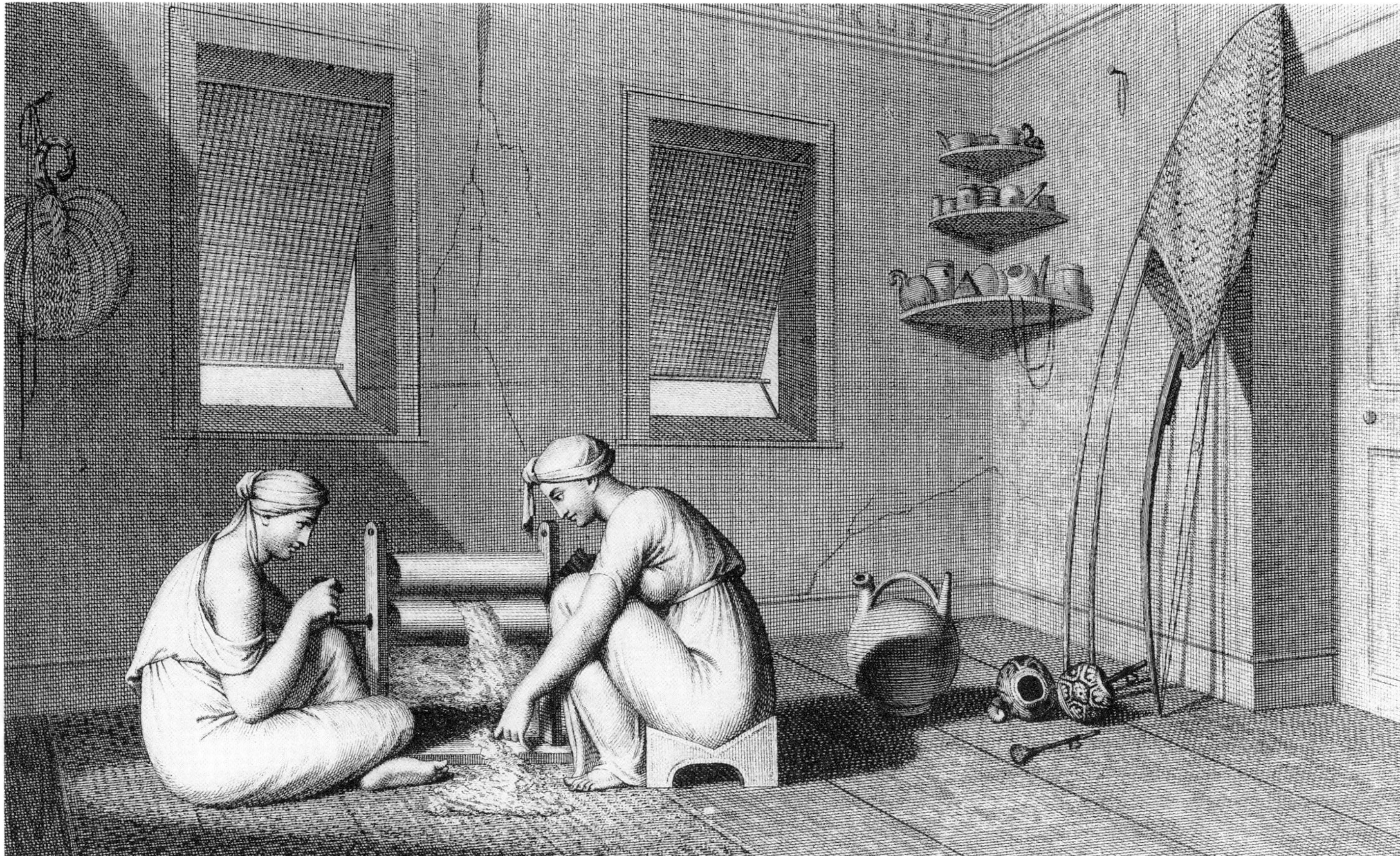

3. *The Interior of a Brazilian Dwelling.*

4. *A View of the Island of Nukahiva.*

5. *A second view of the Island of Nukahiva.*

6. *Jean Bapiste Cabri.*

7. *An inhabitant of the Island of Nukahiva.*

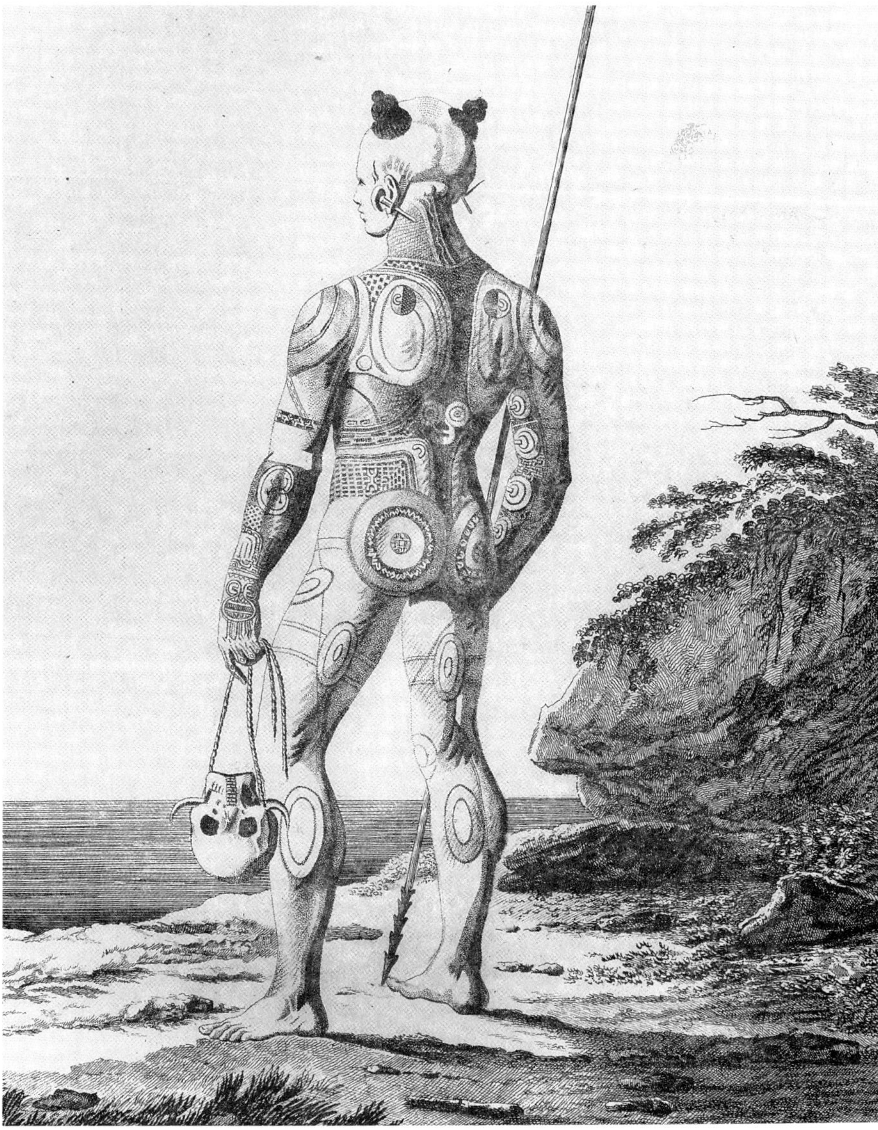

8. *View of a young Nukahivan's back, which is completely tattooed.*

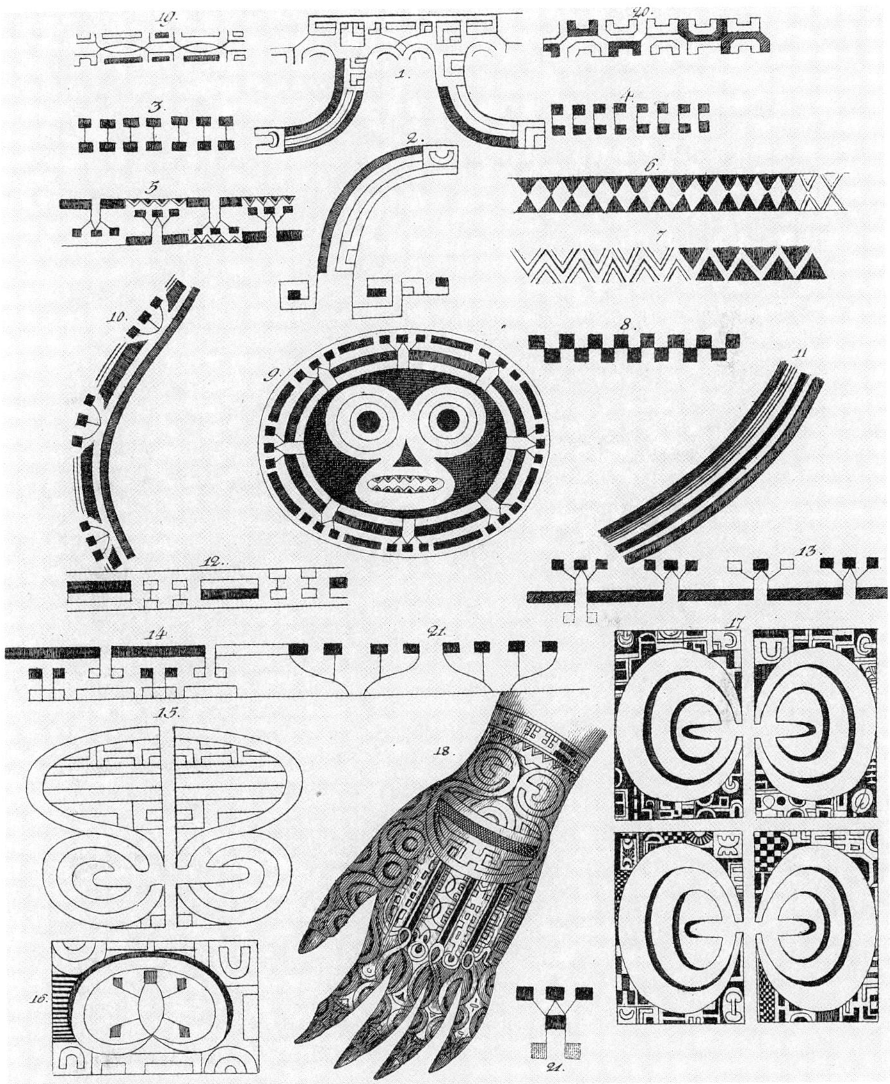

9. *Representation of various main figures, several in actual size.*

10. *A view of an inhabited valley on Nukahiva.*

11. *Interior of a Nukahivan hut where a tattoo artist is sitting and practicing his art.*

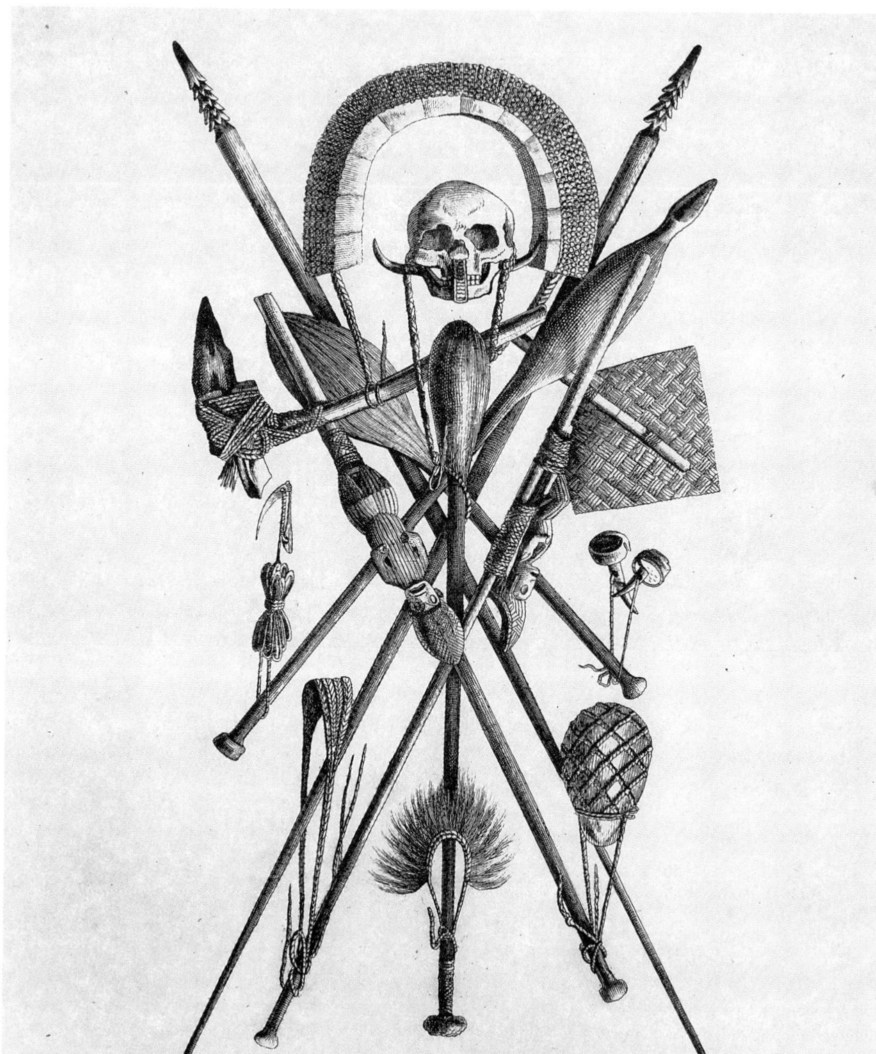

12. *Nukahivan weapons and utensils.*

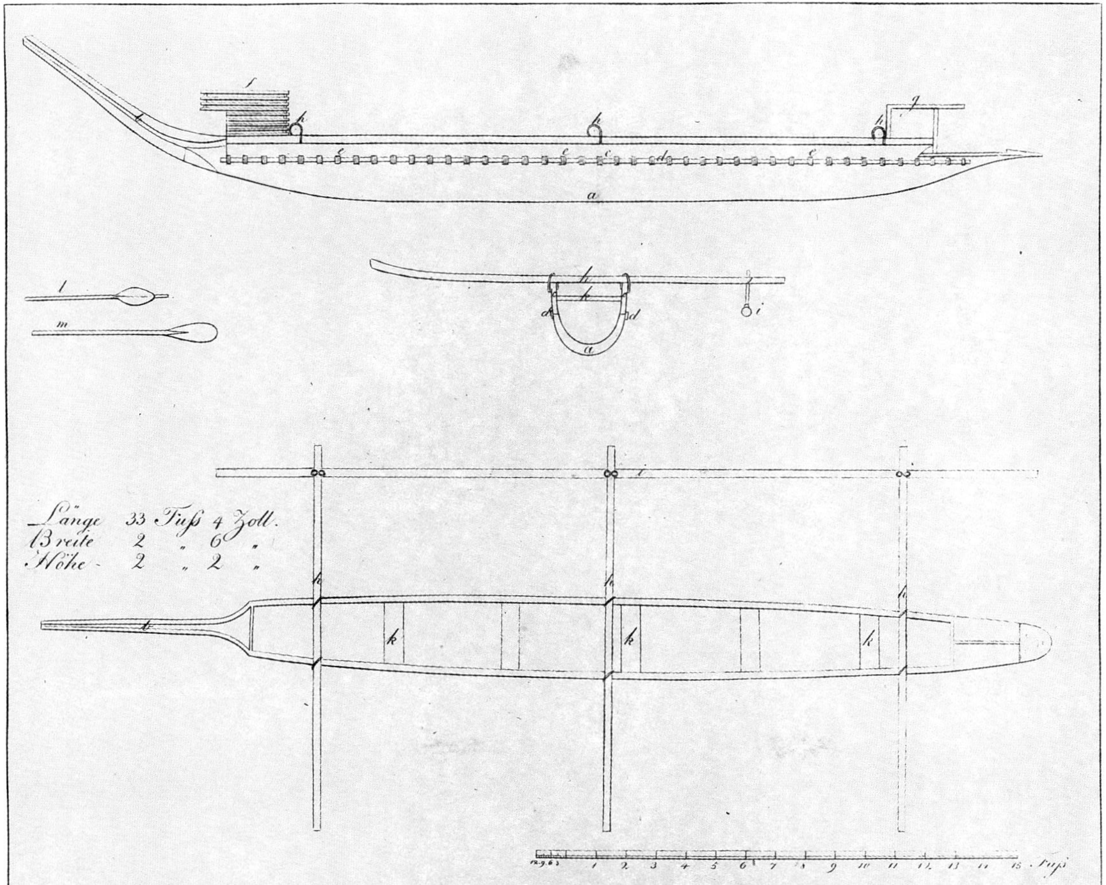

13. *Plan and measurements of a Nukahivan canoe.*

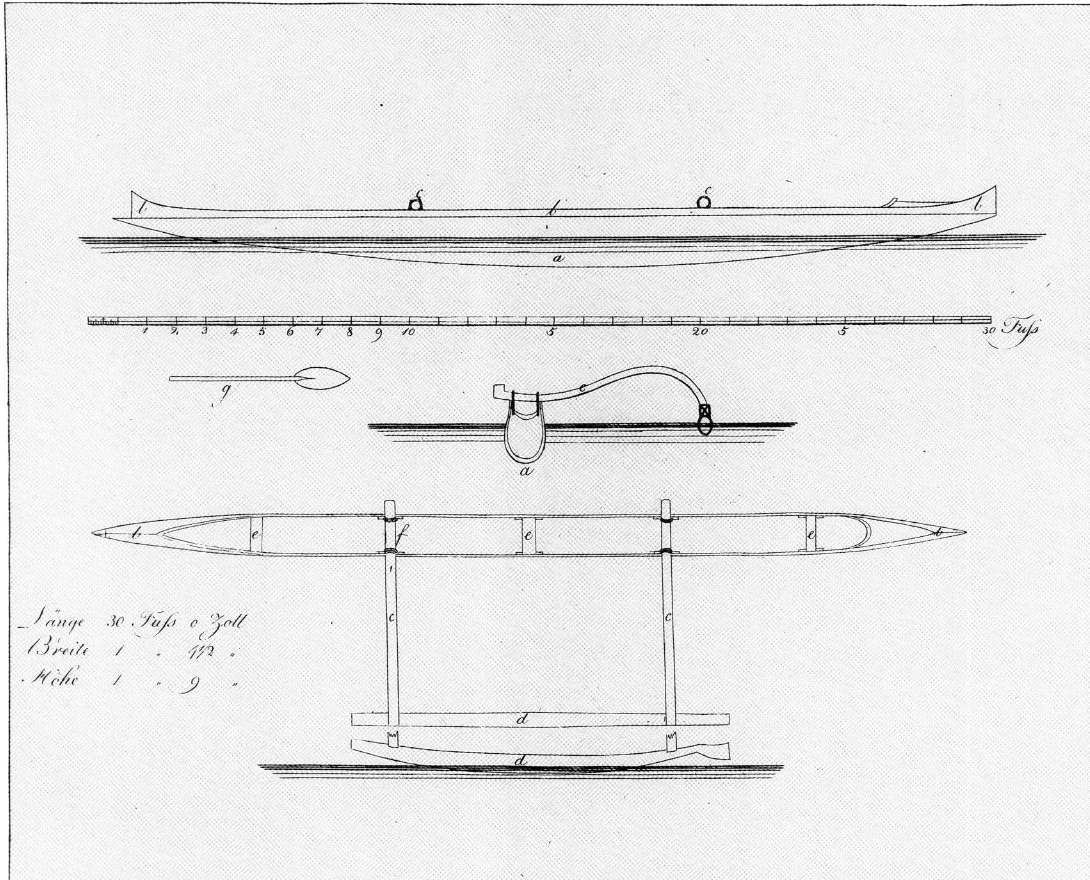

14. *A Canoe of the Sandwich Islanders.*

15. *View of Kaminosim, a landscape in the Harbor of Nangasaki.*

16. *A Japanese Fort.*

17. *Ambassador von Resanoff's Dwelling at Megasaki.*

18. *One of the Prince of Omura's military officers taking up guard duty.*

19. *A Japanese Doctor.*

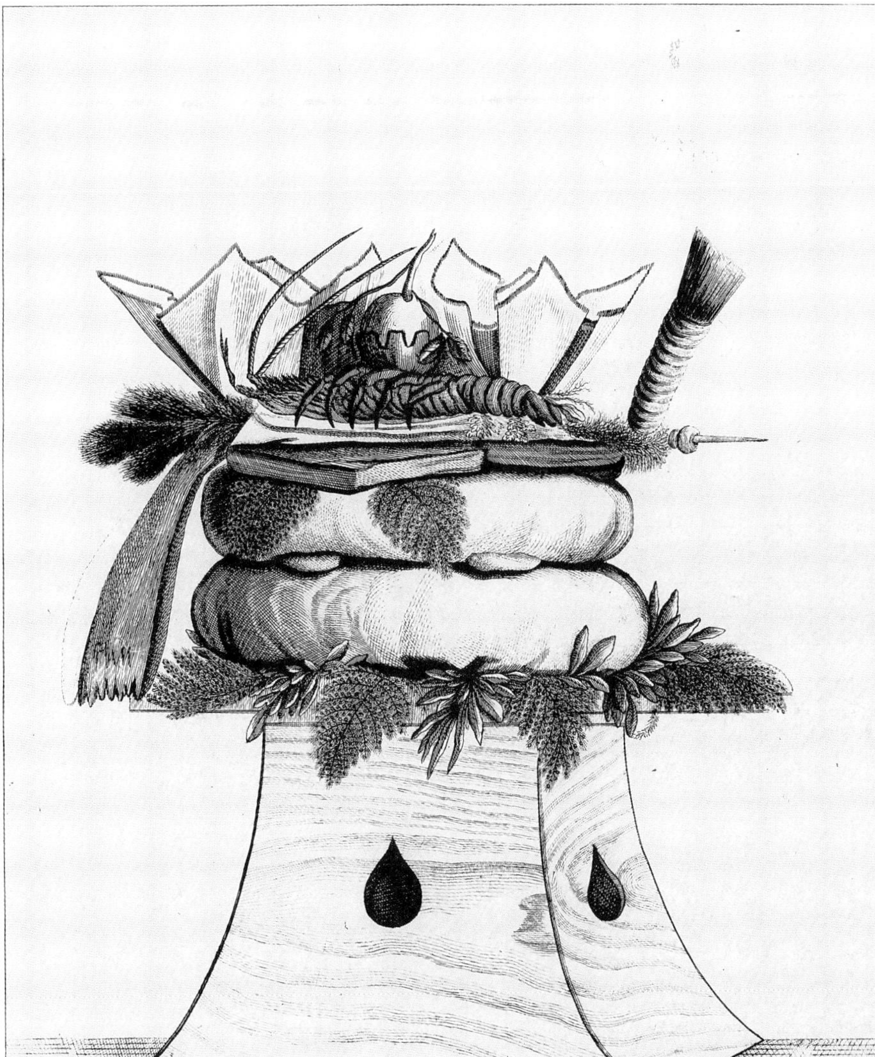

20. Kakaminotschi *or New Year's gift given the Russian Ambassador von Resanoff by the governor of Nangasaki.*

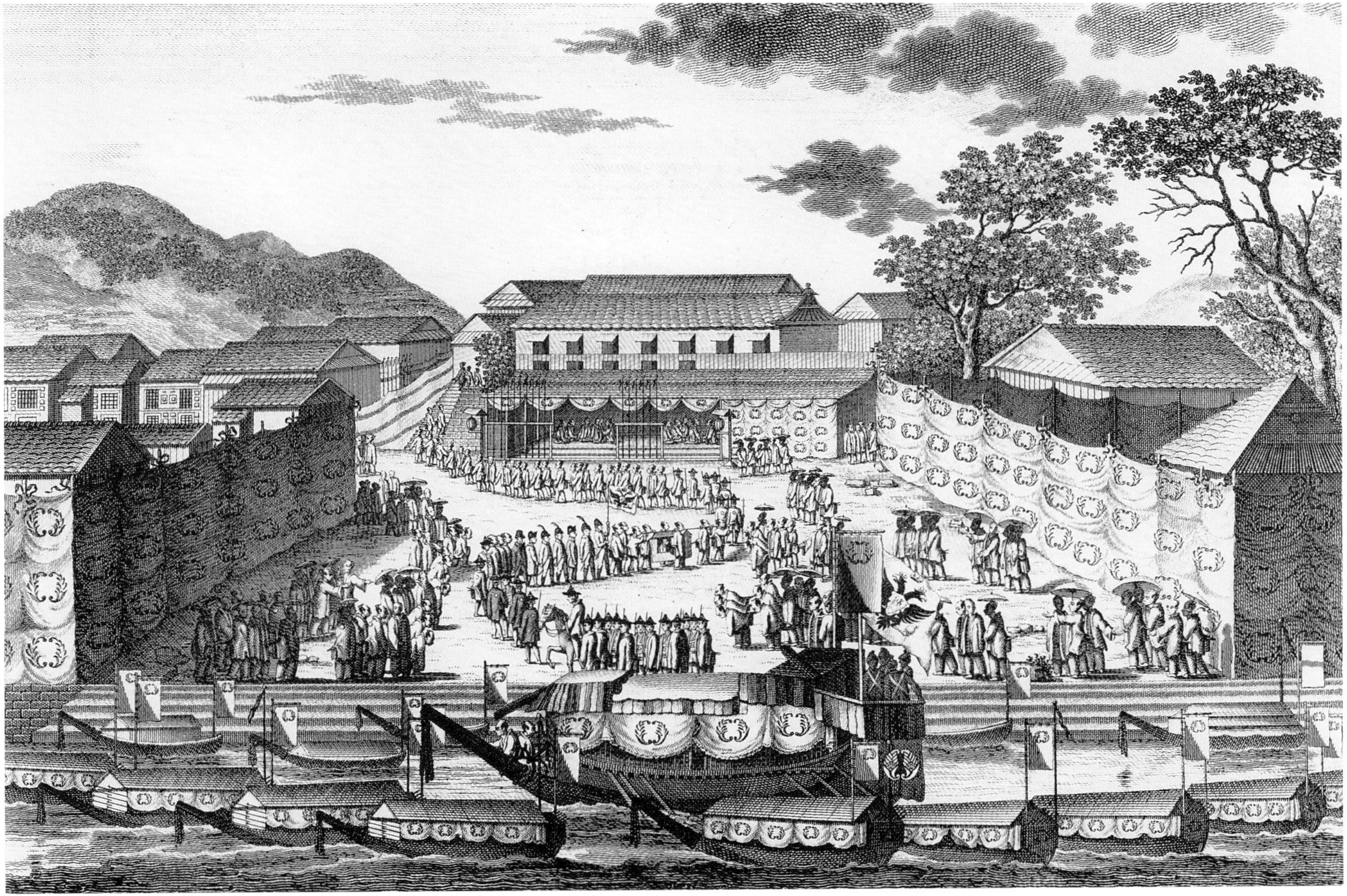

21. *Landing in Nangasaki on the day of the audience.*

22. *Japanese in various costumes.*

23. *Japanese in various costumes.*

24. *Japanese in various costumes.*

25. *Japanese in various costumes.*

26. *Japanese in various costumes.*

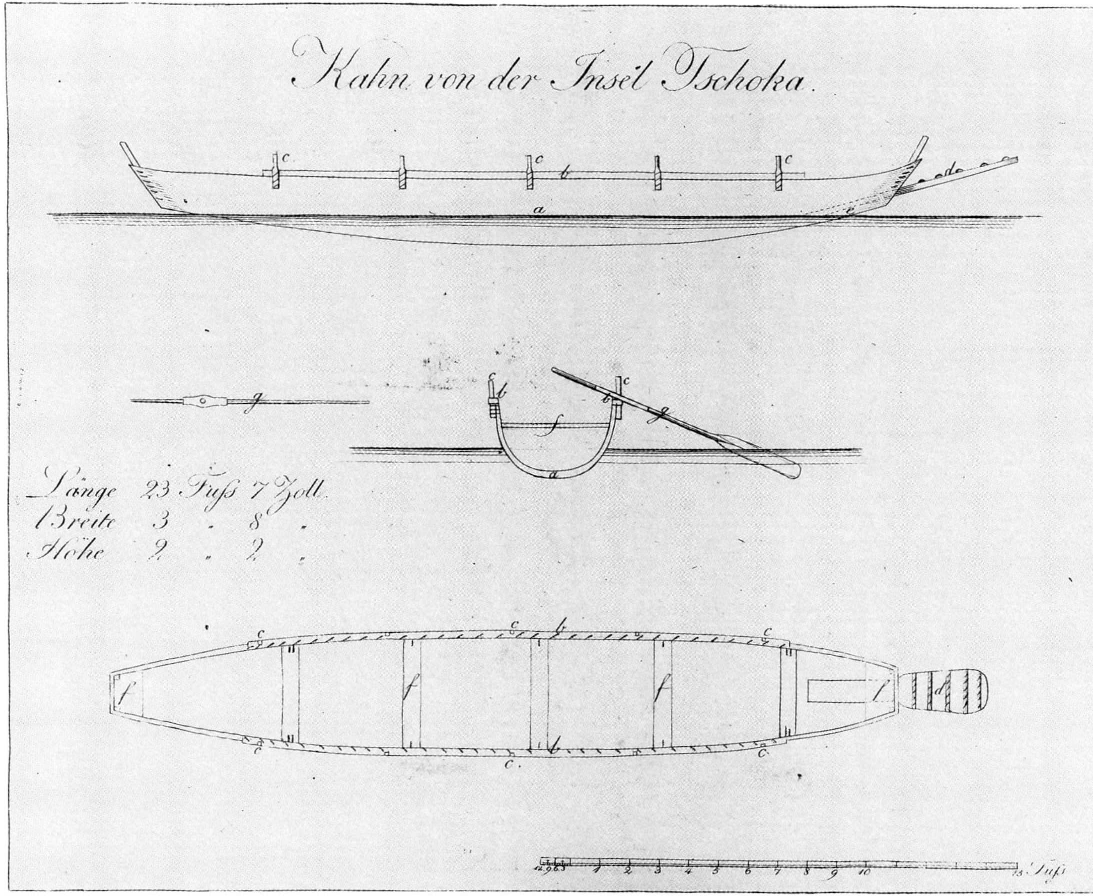

27. *A Boat from the Island of Tschoka.*

28. *View of St. George Island.*

29. *View of the Russian Settlement at Unalaska.*

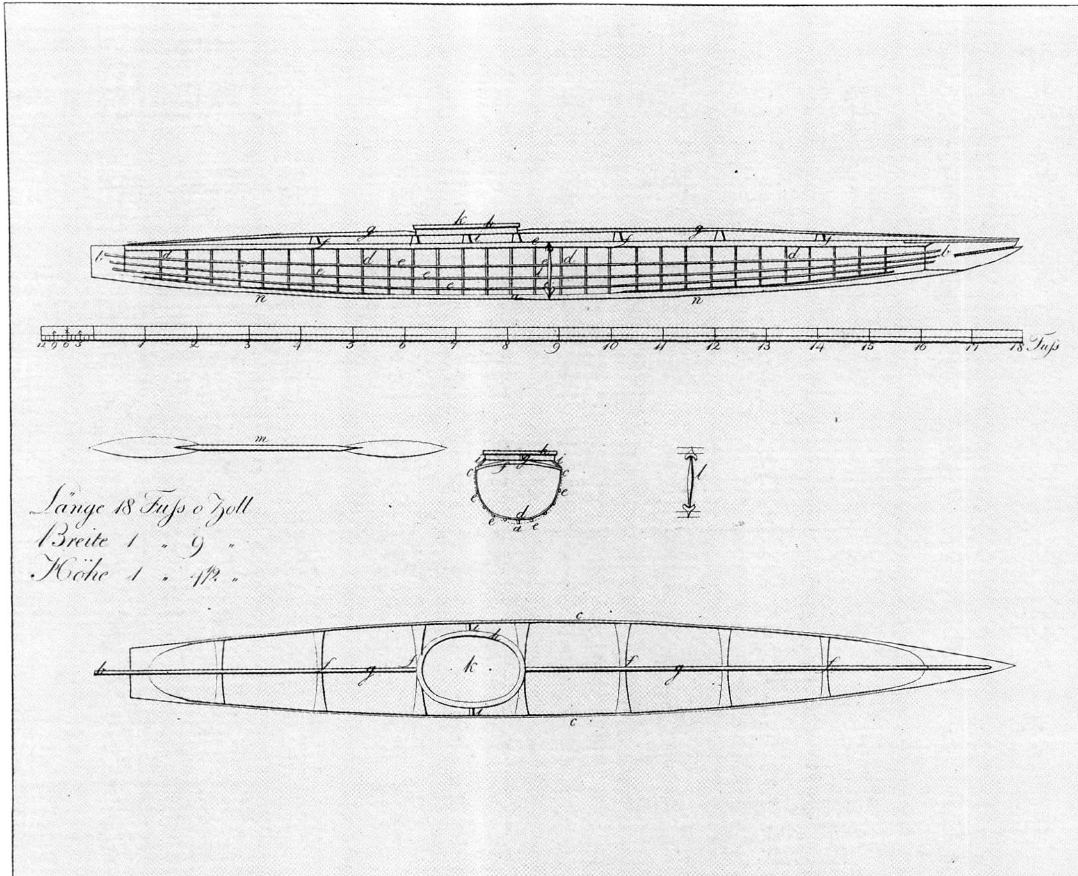

30. *A single-seated baidarka from the Island of Unalaska.*

31. *The main Russian Settlement on the Island of Kodiak.*

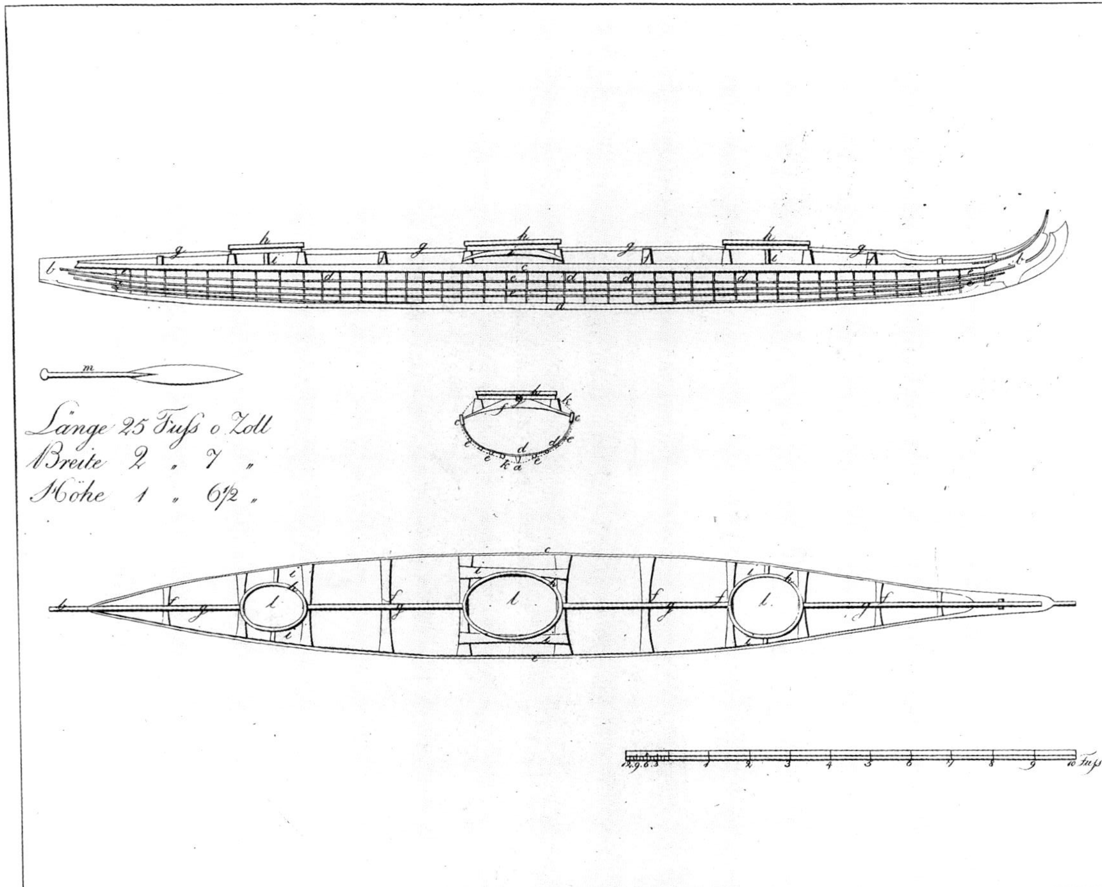

32. *Three-seated baidarka from the Island of Kodiak.*

33. *View of the Russian-American Company's Outpost at Norfolk Sound or Sitcha.*

34. *The Kalusch in Sitcha dancing.*

35. *View of the Spanish settlement at San Francisco in New California.*

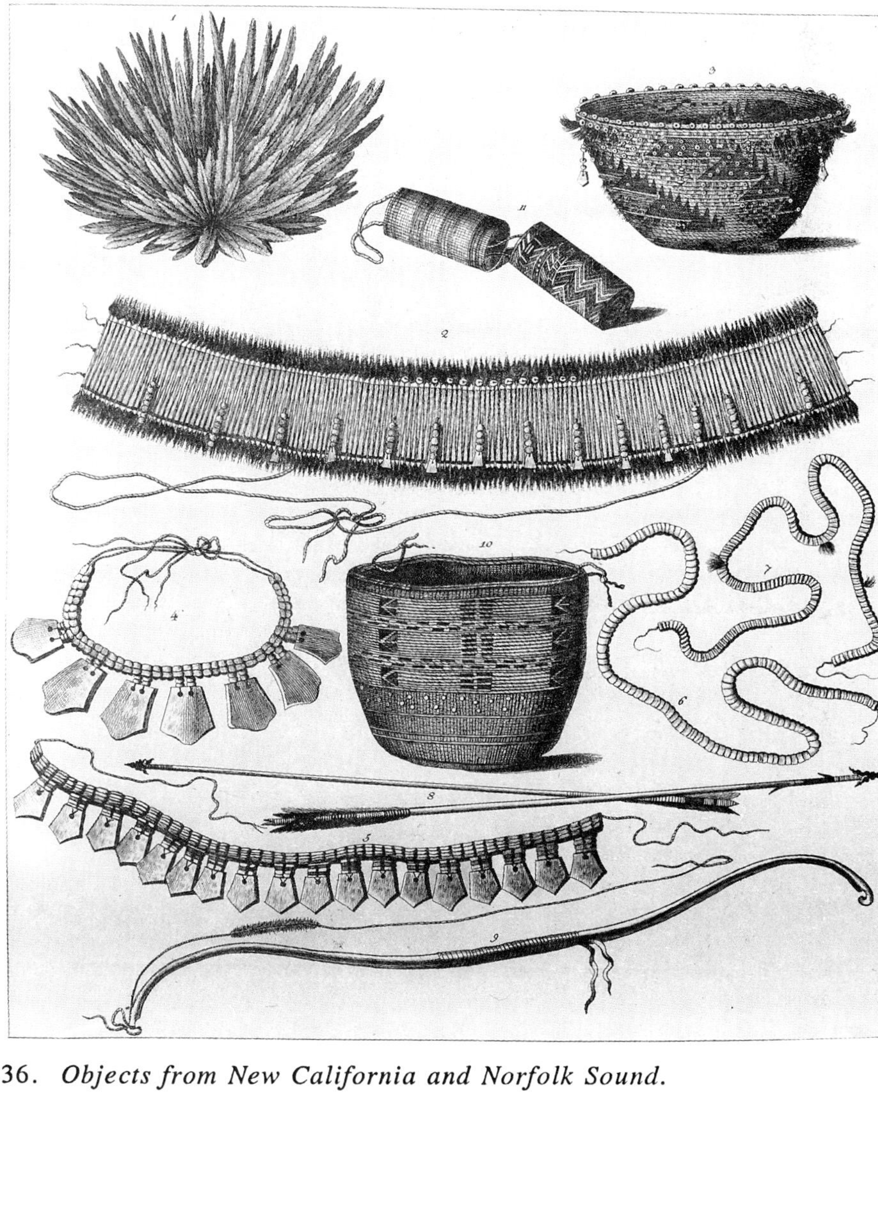

36. *Objects from New California and Norfolk Sound.*

37. *An Indian Dance at the Mission of San Jose in New California.*

38. *Objects from Alaksa and Unalaska.*

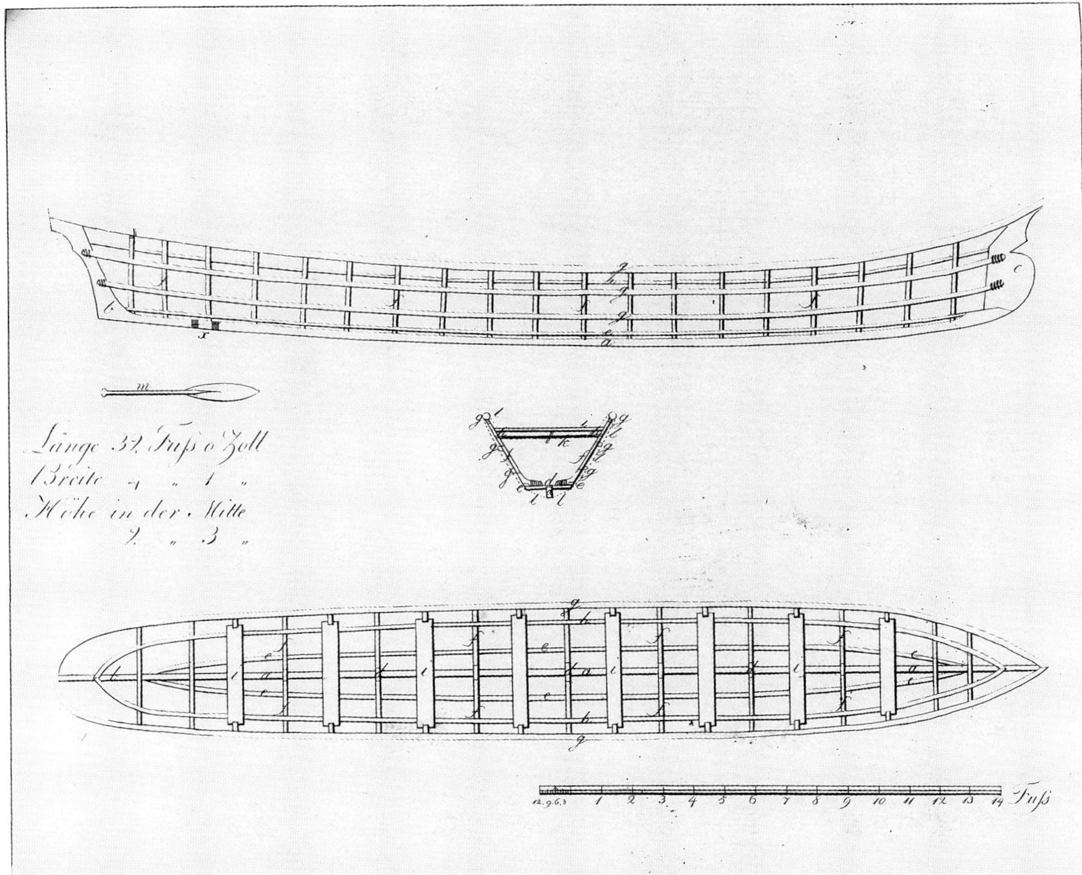

39. *Baidara from the Peninsula of Alaksa.*

40. *A view of St. Peter and St. Paul in Kamtschatka.*

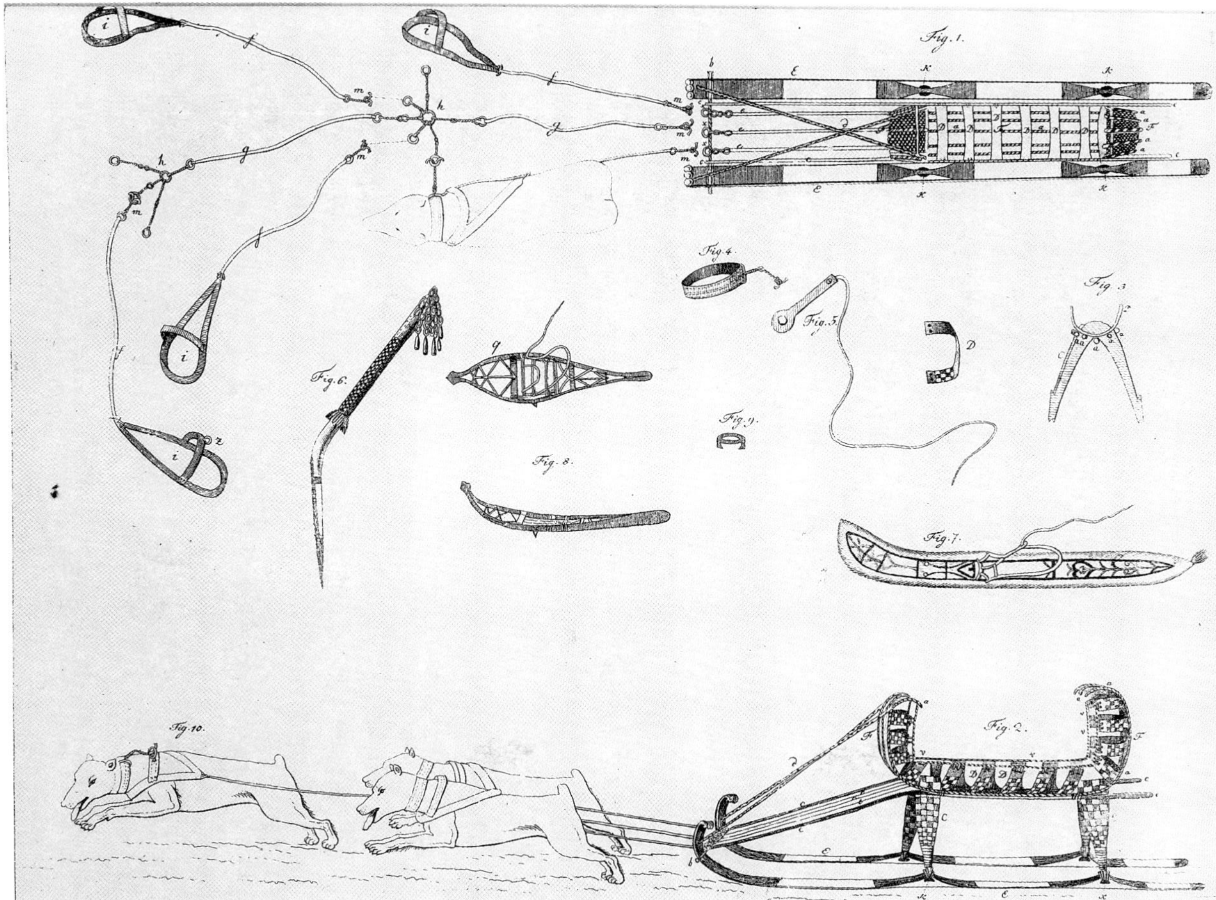

41. *Sketch and description of a Kamtschatkan sledge and dog harness with accessories.*

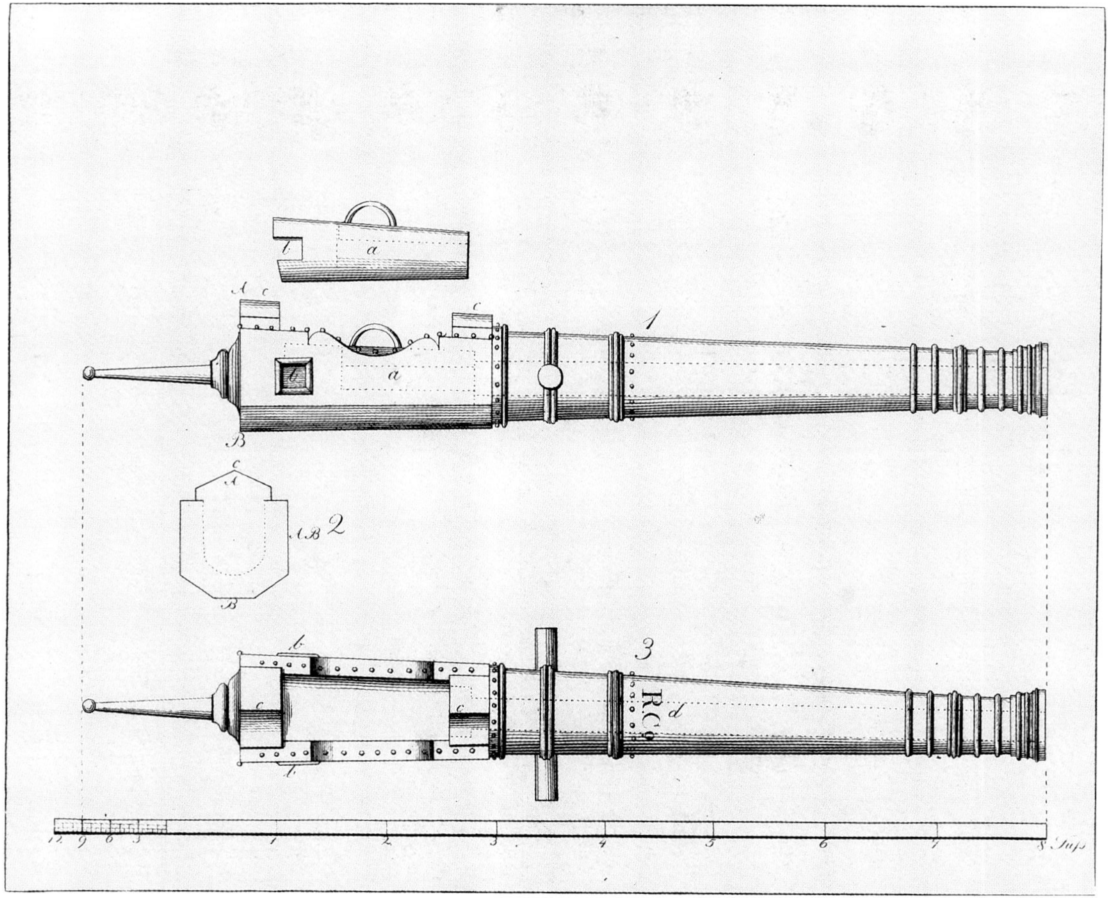

42. *Sketch of a copper cannon, 1/12 of its actual size.*

43. *View of an area along the Aldan River on the way to Irkutsk from Ochotsk.*

Brasilian Air.

1	2
Quando o mal acaba O bem principia Meu mal acabou O bem se seguia Pois sim, meu senhor, Meu mal acabou Mas penso que vou De mal a peor.	Vem a noite escura Succedes o dia Depois da tormenta Vem a calmeria Pois sim, meu senhor, Meu mal acabou Mas penso que vou De mal a peor.

44. *Brazilian Air.*

Song of the Natives of Nukahiwa.

45. *Song of the Natives of Nukahiva.*

an emetic or purgative medicine, no opium, no china[2] and not one single preparation of mercury. The most necessary of remedies were missing.

How advantageous would it be for Kamtschatka if well organized shipping could bring that country medicine, clothing and many other things which are needed cheaper, better and in larger quantities? Would it not be advantageous for the state and that distant, forgotten peninsula if upright, well-meaning, knowledgeable men would decide to visit that undeservedly ill-famed land, study its natural products more closely and would develop suggestions for improvements based on general knowledge and knowledge of the local situation? This seems to me to be all the more necessary, since, as far as I know, during the entire period of the military rule, not one single officer of the many who have been stationed in Kamtschatka has come forward with a philosophical overview of the whole situation to make suggestions based on general knowledge and knowledge of the local situation, which would have promoted the general welfare of the peninsula.

NOTES

1. Langsdorff's description of the events is rather unclear. John D'Wolf describes the events as follows: " . . . While I was visiting the Doctor, they came over to pass an evening with us, and we sat talking of old times until two in the morning. They then started for their own lodgings, which were on the other side of the river. Langsdorff and myself accompanied them to the drawbridge, which was open for ships to pass in the night. Our friends, therefore, passed over a plank which lay from the bridge to a vessel in the river and regained the other side of the bridge by another plank, calling to us and wishing us goodnight, when they were safe over, and we then went back to our quarters. The next morning we received the melancholy intelligence that two naval officers had been drowned in the Neva during the night, and, upon further inquiry, we learned that they were our friends. After we had parted from them, they became desirous, God knows for what purpose, to return to us again, and, in order to get over quicker, they attempted to spring from the bridge upon a bark that was going through. They mistook a sail for the deck of the vessel, and both fell into the water. The people in the bark endeavored to rescue them, but the night was so dark, and the current so strong, that they went under before they received an assistance. Though fifty years have gone by since the death of these young men, I cannot forbear to recall their many virtues and lament their untimely end" (John D'Wolf, *A Voyage to the North Pacific*, [Fairfield, Washington: Ye Galleon Press], pp. 146-147).

2. China is also called Peruvian bark, Jesuit's bark or chinchona after Francisca Enriques de Ribera, Countess of Chinchon (d. 1641), who was supposed to be associated with its introduction into Europe.

Chapter 16

Departure from Nischna-Kamtschatka. Redowski's death. High Chain of Mountains. Tigil. Excursion to the Koriaks. Their Reindeer. Customs and Habits. Western Side of the Kamtschatka Peninsula. The largest Villages: Chariusoff, Moroscheschna, Soposchnowa, Itschi, Worofskaia, Bolscheretsk. Return to the Harbor of St. Peter and St. Paul. Overview of the Names, Distances and Population of Kamtschatkan Villages.

Toward the end of February, I prepared for my return to the Harbor of St. Peter and St. Paul. I intended to take the longer, new way along the western side of the peninsula by way of Tigil and Bolscheretsk in order to get to know more closely a larger part of that remarkable land. On March 2nd everything was ready for departure. It would be most ungrateful of me if I did not publicly thank His Excellency Mr. von Koscheleff and his brother for their most cordial reception and their many acts of friendship, love and respect. With their warmest wishes for my distant well-being, I left Nischna-Kamtschatka on March 2nd after breakfast at Mr. von Koscheleff's.

After going little more than 16 versts, I met the post team from Europe, for which I had been longing for quite some time because the natural scientist Dr. Redowski was supposed to be on it. For several months I had been wanting to make his acquaintance very much. Thus, my first question was: Where is Redowski? You can imagine my shock when I was told he was dead! According to the cossacks who brought the mail, he had died a short time before in Ischiga. For this reason, I immediately returned to Nischna-Kamtschatka, where I found out in a letter that had arrived — in reality, in a melancholy moment, which he had given in to, he had ended his meritorious life after having withstood the greatest of difficulties on his journey and having reached his destination.

At daybreak on the following day, I resumed my trip. By one o'clock I had already reached Kamina, 65 versts from Nischna-Kamtschatka, where the two roads forked, one branch going to

Werchnoi-Kamtschatka and the other to Tigil. The first station along the latter road is the village of Chartschina, famous in the whole country for its very tasty fish *golzi* (a kind of salmon). I stayed overnight in Chartschina. The following day I reached the station of Jellofka, 57 versts farther, whose surroundings are agreeably very varied by groves of birch, fir and alder trees, mountains and charming valleys. In order to go from there to Tigil, I had to cross a quite high chain of mountains stretching from north to south. They divide Kamtschatka into its eastern and western parts. Many fear this road. The continual stormy winds, snow flurries and partially unbeaten tracks often force travelers to wait up to two weeks for good weather to undertake the 160-verst stretch. Now and again they also have to give up their intentions for lack of provisions. Since there are no villages along this stretch over the mountains, two huts have been built for the comfort of travelers. The first one is 46 versts from Jellofka and the second 39 versts beyond that. In stormy weather both offer a roof and shelter.

Around seven o'clock on the morning of the 6th, I set out on the notorious trip in the company of several soldiers and cossacks who had collected in Jellofka. The roads were in excellent condition, the weather of a rare serenity and clearness. We had to travel over several larger and smaller hills and mountains, including two particularly high mountain ridges. On one of them we experienced one of those happy days on which we had an extraordinarily picturesque view. The active peak of Klutschi seemed to be in our vicinity. We saw the scattered mountains, some of them of considerable height, at our feet like hills disappearing into the distant plain. The snow on the summits is never very deep because of the continual winds, which disperse it, and the constant cold of the upper atmosphere. It is always hard and firm, making it possible for us to travel about all over freely and safely without any difficulty and worrying about taking a specific road. There was no vegetation, only here and there a dwarf cedar crept up a slope.

The other high ridge facing the northwestern side is extremely steep. A driver is a master at dog sledding if he can balance a sledge with dogs in harness down its quite steep slope without being thrown over. Normally, for this reason, the dogs are unharnessed on that slope and tied tightly to the back of the sledge, while the driver tries to guide and slow the sledge down with his ostoll. Most of my traveling companions (soldiers and cossacks) and even my Kamtschatkan guide fell along the way and came sliding on foot behind. In reality, the prospect was worse than the event itself. There are no trees, rocks or precipices in the area, so that we did not have to be afraid of an accident. That is why it was at times funny to watch how one after the other, first in this way and then in that, we rolled and tumbled down the slope.

At the foot of the mountain not far from a woods, we reached the first hut with still a lot of daylight left. There we found a lot less snow than on the other side of the mountains. The clear, calm weather, along with the expected moonlight, caused us unanimously to decide to try to continue on over the rest of the difficult road to the second hut. After resting, drinking tea and eating dried fish and bread and refreshing our dogs with some yukola, we set out again around three o'clock. Nature has, as it were, broken a road through the mountains, because between the high mountains and the partially perpendicular cliffs, a trail ascends gradually, winding first to the right and then to the left through the mass of rocks. After several hours, almost unnoticed, one has reached a considerable height.

Occasionally we went through small, narrow passes and then over wide, open areas where the gusts of wind and snow are supposed to be terrible. In the level places, posts have been rammed into the ground quite close together. During storms when the mountain tops and cliffs are shrouded in clouds of snow and fog, they serve as guide posts. Despite the posts, travelers have often lost their way in snowstorms, which sometimes raged so furiously that they could barely see the lead dog ahead of the sledge.

After laboriously traveling about 20 versts, we reached the last rise. We were suddenly surprised by the sight of the western plains of the peninsula lying at our feet in the sunset. From there the road descended. The dogs could barely be held back. They were fired up by the scent of the many wild reindeer we had seen. In several places there was so little snow that some rocks, earth, dry grass and moss stuck out. It was already so dark that I could not examine any of these objects exactly. Since I could not get my dogs to stop, I called to my Kamtschatkan guide and asked him to pick up several of the stones and keep them until we arrived at the hut. He absolutely refused, telling me that if I dared take a stone from that area or even to touch one, a violent storm would come up immediately.

About eleven o'clock in the evening, tired, we reached the second hut. In many places when approaching it, we had had to travel over dry dirt and grass for lack of snow. Upon our arrival we found several travelers coming from Tigil, who were very fearful of the coming trip and envious of our having had an extremely happy crossing. The night of the 7th I stayed in Sedanki, whose inhabitants were originally Koriaks. They speak a dialect that is different from dialects spoken by the Kamtschadals and Koriaks. It is used from Palan in the north to Itschi in the south. The next day I reached Tigil, where I stayed for a day in order to give my dogs rest and recuperation.

Tigil, usually called Tigilskoi Krepost, that is the fort of Tigil, lies on the right bank of a river of the same name, which small ships can navigate. The anchorage for ships coming from Ochotsk is about 15 versts up the river from its mouth and 30 versts from the fort. Tigil has an interesting place in the history of Kamtschatka. It is the place where the Russians first established themselves and from where they began their distant conquests. Aside from several buildings belonging to the Crown, there are about 30 houses and a church. Even though the place is poor in fish and the river is so fast that they can hardly be caught by using either weirs or nets, still Providence has provided for the place in other ways. There are large quantities of reindeer in the vicinity. The Koriaks, the neighbors bordering to the north, migrate year round with their innumerable herds of reindeer and sell them to the Russians and Kamtschadals in such quantities for trifles, especially tobacco, brandy, mushrooms, kettles, axes and other utensils, that they obtain enough meat for food and hides for clothing.

I learned that those nomadic people were camped a short distance to the north and decided to visit them the following day. The commander at Tigil, a non-commissioned officer, provided me with dogs and an interpreter. On the 10th, I set out with them to meet an unknown people.

We crossed many valleys. After traveling about 30 versts, we reached the Omanina River, which flows into the Ochotsk Sea about seven or eight versts from Tigil. A little village of the same name is found on that river. At that time, it had almost died out and had only three inhabited houses. Not far from this river I found the first signs of the Koriaks or rather of their reindeer. It looked as if an army had just broken camp. Many thousands of reindeer had trampled the snow into paths every which direction, thus making the area very rough and uneven for our dog sledges. I followed my guide through the valleys, recently so alive and now so desolate, until toward evening I had the pleasure of sighting the Koriaks with their herds of reindeer.

I turned into the largest hut of the most prominent Koriak named Prolok. He owns at least 2,000 reindeer which were grazing around his hut. He immediately had two slaughtered for me, my guide and our dogs. The marrow from the bones, still warm with blood, was brought to me as a delicacy, a sign of welcome. The tongues, the most prized part, were immediately cooked.

The Koriaks speak a different language from the Kamtschadals but, otherwise, they have basically the same facial features and build. Their clothing is almost the same, except that they have a hood on their garments instead of a collar. Under their chins, instead of a slit, they have a piece hanging down over their chests. Men and women wear the same style clothing. They can only be told apart by the fact that the women do not cut their hair. I did not see any men with beards. I was told that they pluck them out with small tweezers. Their hair seemed to me to be not quite as dark black as the Kamtschadals. The Koriaks live in conical huts with pole frames. These have untanned reindeer hides with the hair still on stretched over them. Sixty to seventy sledges were standing around the hut. During their nomadic migrations, they are used to transport poles, skins and other utensils. They need such a large number of sledges because reindeer are very weak and can only pull a small load. Daylight enters the hut through the same hole as is used for smoke.

All around the inside, there are little compartments made from reindeer skins which are open toward the fire. They can be closed off by a tanned skin that acts as a curtain. If this happens, then the little chamber is robbed of daylight but is protected against smoke and cold. The chief lives in a somewhat roomier compartment opposite the entrance. The rest of his relatives and dependents live in the side compartments. The inside of the hut looks like a smokehouse. The most disgusting filth reigns everywhere. A number of large dogs, mostly used for hunting and whose skins are used for trimming clothing, have free run of the hut, even in the small sleeping compartments.

The undigested moss taken from reindeer stomachs, mixed with train oil and cooked, is mostly fed to the dogs, although sometimes human beings eat it.

It was remarkable for me again to get to know a people whose livelihood and wealth, whose way of life and well-being, whose food and clothing, almost completely and totally depend upon reindeer alone, just as the existence of the Aleuts is dependent upon the seal. Huts and all kinds of clothing are made from reindeer skins. Their stomachs are used for storage of various liquids, and their meat for daily food.

Since they have a superabundance of animals, they trade with the neighboring Russians and Kamtschadals. In exchange for reindeer, they buy iron and copper kettles and other kitchen utensils, knives, axes, tobacco leaves, brandy, fly fungus,* powder and lead, straps from sealskin, train oil and other articles.

When trading, offering them a glass of brandy brimming over, however small the glass might be, has more value in their eyes than a large beer glass only half full. My host loaned me a little glass, barely a half *unze* in size, that he prized very highly to take along on that day's excursion.

Instead of bowls, they eat out of wooden troughs, men and dogs together. For most of the year, they drink water obtained from ice and snow. A kettle hangs continually over the fire for that purpose. Several doctors who maintain that the common occurrence of king's evil in many of the Swiss Cantons and in Tyrol comes from drinking snow water should become somewhat insecure in their assertion, since there is no king's evil among the Koriaks. Even at the height of summer, they trek with their reindeer into the mountains, where they use snow and ice water.

The men occupy themselves with hunting sable, wild reindeer and argali. In addition they care for their large herds of reindeer, grazing like cattle near their huts, which are caught by the use of a leather loop when wanted for slaughter.** As soon as the animal has been caught and killed by a thrust of the knife into its heart, it is turned over to the women. They skin it, dress it and prepare the meat for the kitchen. Then they prepare the hide for making clothing. It is solely and completely the duty of women to dismantle the huts, to transport them on the sledges when migrating and to reassemble them at the new location. As soon as the moss around the huts has been grazed bare, which, depending on the size of the herd, varies in length of time needed, the horde moves several versts farther with their reindeer. In this manner, they migrate during the course of the year from a stretch of land beginning in the north, that is, near Ischiga, to the south in the middle of Kamtschatka, that is, near Itschi. Thus, along

---

*The Koriaks prefer fly fungus for use as a narcotic or intoxicant even to brandy. My special remarks about this are found in the *Annalen der wetterauischen Gesellschaft für die gesammte Naturkunde* (Annals of the Wetterau Society for Biology), Vol. I, p. 249.

**This is done exactly like in Brazil and California with cattle.

the way, they provide reindeer meat for almost the whole west side of the peninsula.

The Koriaks live in a state of constant dispute with their northern neighbors, the Tschuktsch. For this reason, they prefer to align themselves with the Russians, from whom they can obtain necessities without fear of reprisal.

Their weapons consist mainly of bows and arrows, though some individuals know how to use powder and firearms. They know that they are far superior to arrows for hunting.

I saw no other musical instrument but for a tambour with iron rings that is struck with a stuffed dog foot. Their singing resembles that of the inhabitants of the Aleutian Islands and western America. Their dancing consists of a simple movement of the body performed all at the same spot.

Late on the evening of the 11th I arrived in Tigil. The following day I set out on my trip to Bolscheretsk. For the novelty of it, I used reindeer to travel the 20 versts to the first station at Napani. Despite the interesting novelty of it all, I have to prefer dogs by far as draft animals. Reindeer, to be sure, are much faster for a short time, but they have little stamina. After ten or, at the most, twelve versts, they have to be fed. This causes a break of a length that makes it possible, even with only mediocre dogs running at an even, steady pace, to reach a distant place sooner or, at least, just as fast as with reindeer, which, as I have already said, tire very quickly and are only capable of pulling a small load. A traveler is also very bothered by the snow which their hooves continually throw up into his face. I was, therefore, glad on the 13th to be in charge of dogs once again. I flew along the west coast of Kamtschatka, where there is never as much snow as on the east side. On the whole, partially because of the higher elevation, partially also because of the more frequent and severe northwest winds and fog, it is colder, desolate, less inviting and grown over with reindeer moss in many areas. In general the rivers are not as rich in fish and farming is only possible in isolated villages. It is exactly the lack of fertility which accords the inhabitants of the coast the advantages of herding reindeer. Before the arrival of the peninsula's present commander, it had been very neglected and only recently taken up again. General von Koscheleff began once again to purchase some reindeer from the Koriaks for the Crown. Their number has already grown to over 300. If his successor continues to pursue his plan to increase the herd just as diligently, this alone in a few years will help very much to alleviate the present great lack of meat there.

The largest villages along the distant road from Tigil to Bolscheretsk are:

Chariusoff on the river of the same name, where here and there is found a schistous-jasper mixed with petrified wood that the inhabitants use as whetstones. Thirty versts from the coast are several rocky islands the inhabitants visit every spring in order to collect the eggs of sea birds and to kill seals. I cannot understand why these people expose themselves to such apparent danger in their very bad canoes just for a few eggs. Why have they not been taught to build better, more practical vessels?

The snow had already melted so much from Chariusoff to the next station, Brellagolowa, that I had to go on foot in places.

Moroscheschna, on the right bank of the river of the same name, is a rather large, pleasantly situated village on the slope of a low hill. In the valley below it, the river flows toward the sea. Particularly at its mouth, many seals are taken, captured with nets. Their skins and train oil are important trade items with the nomadic Koriaks.

Soposchnowa. Sometimes from here the Kamtschadals cross the mountains with their dogs to Werchnoi-Kamtschatka. The road is supposed to be good because the chain of mountains is very low. But the many creeks that do not freeze over made traveling laborious, indeed, even dangerous. Thus, only in the coldest month, in February, is travel possible.

On the 17th I reached Itschi, a not very small village with a church served by two priests. There, as almost all over on the whole western coast, the snow for the most part was melted. Potatoes, cabbage, carrots and radishes grow well here. Grains, among others buckwheat, grow less well there than along the Kamtschatka River because of the many cold northwesterly winds and long periods of night frost. Cattle are raised. In addition to a large number of cows, I found 26 horses.

Near this village is the most southerly border to which the Koriaks bring their reindeer and from where they again migrate northwards. Fifty versts from there is found a fine-grained sandstone which the inhabitants send all over the peninsula to be used as grindstones.

After letting my dogs rest for a day, I set out again on the 19th. Several rivers I had to cross were already free of ice, a circumstance that slowed down my progress since I had to cross them. On the 21st I reached Worofskaia on a rather large river of the same name whose mouth flows into a wide bay that is deep enough for little ships coming from Ochotsk. They have, indeed, wintered there several times.

Since fog from the sea is perhaps thicker and more common there than in other places, fish are not as easily dried; indeed, they often even rot. For this reason, the fish intended for use as yukola are first smoked for a day, something done less often at other places. A Russian who has settled there as a peasant is the richest man in the village. He hosted me with large, tasty potatoes, beef, fish, berries and game. He told me, among other things, that the buckwheat in the last five years had produced a small harvest four times and once six to seven times the amount of the seed grain. He has 22 cows, two horses, a number of dogs and lives from the rich fruits of his industry which he puts into farming.

The following day I came to Bolscheretsk, formerly very populous but now the very lonely capital of Kamtschatka. It is situated on a large plain stretching from Itschi the length of the sea coast. There are open heaths covered with reindeer moss all over it. In earlier times those lonely steppes were enlivened by numerous two- to three-thousand-head herds of reindeer belonging to the Crown. The commander at the time sold all of them out of avarice. The present commander, General von Koscheleff, as I have already said above, by being stubborn and persistent, has reintroduced the herding of reindeer. At the mouth of a large river, 30 versts from the city, is a bay. The river itself admittedly does not form a very good harbor. It is not deep enough and can only be used by small ships. By the way, that river is the richest in fish of the whole peninsula. For this reason, in spring and summer its shores are the collecting point for numbers of bears.

On the evening of the 23rd, I left Bolscheretsk. On the 25th I reached the Harbor of St. Peter and St. Paul, where, to my surprise, I found it was still winter. The sledge trails were still good. A large part of the bay and harbor was covered with ice. Messrs. von Chwostoff and von Davidoff were trying to get their ship ready to sail. They were expecting the ice to go out at the end of April and then to go to sea. The snow was, at the time, mostly melted. Wild garlic was being collected frequently for the scorbutic promyshlenniks.

On the 1st of May, my friends went on board ship. They weighed anchor the following day and left us with the best of wishes for a quick reunion in St. Petersburg. They were heading for the Kuril Islands in order to carry out Mr. von Resanoff's plan for a secret expedition.

Captain D'Wolf set about getting our little ship ready to sail again so that we could leave the Harbor of St. Peter and St. Paul as soon as possible.

Perhaps some of my readers would like to have an overview of the length of my trip around the peninsula, the names of places and the distances between them, along with the number of inhabitants. For this reason, I am including the following table as supplemental information to my description.

Place Name	Distance in Versts	Population
From Harbor of St. Peter and St. Paul		200
to Awatscha	12	32
From Awatscha to Koräk	45	27
From there to Natschika	41	14
From there to Malka	40	76
From there to Garal	41	36
From there to Puschtschina	45	20
From there to Scharom	32	50
From there to Werchnoi-Kamtschatka	35	200
From there to Warlatomskoi Selenie	6½	10
From there to Schikatschi	4	10
From there to Milkowa	2½	80
From there to Gerganika	14	40
From there to Maschuri	35	40
From there to Tschapina	51	65
From there to Tolpatsch	38	40
From there to Kosirewski	52	20
From there to Uskoff	51	27
From there to Krestoffski	39	18
From there to Klutschi	31	200
From there to Kamina	18	36
From there to Kamak	22	16
From there to Tschakoff	25	12

Place Name	Distance in Versts	Population
From Tschakoff to Nischna-Kamtschatka*	18	300
From Klutschi to Chartschina	25	17
From Kamina to Chartschina	33	
From there to Jelloski	57	52
From there to the first hut	46	
From there to the second hut	39	
From there to Sedanki	75	50
From there to Tigil	45	90
From there to Nabani	20	38
From there to Utcholoka	80	31
From there to Gabran	50	47
From there to Chariusoff	40	71
From there to Bellagolofka	27	54
From there to Moroscheschna	35	77
From there to Soposchnowa	50	77
From there to Itschi	52	80
From there to Oblukominski	40	26
From there to Krutogorofski	24	21
From there to Kolbakowa	32	46
From there to Worofskaia	34	38
From there to Golofski	50	17
From there to Kichtschinski	46	18
From there to Utka	35	24
From there to Bolscheretsk	25	130
From there to Obatsch	44	30
From there to Natschika	60	See above
From Obatsch to Malka	62	See above

The distance from Bolscheretsk to Lopatka, the southern tip of the peninsula, is about 200 versts. The various stations and villages, whose population size I do not know are: from Bolscheretsk to Tschekafka, from there to Gollikin, from there to Jawinnoi and then to Lopatka. Aside from these places, there are several north of Tigil on the way to Tschiga. That fort is also counted as part of Kamtschatka. At least three to four hundred people live there.

---

*From here, one has to go back by way of Tschakoff, Kamak and Kamina. From Kamina one road goes to Klutschi and the other to Chartschina and Tigil.

Chapter 17

Departure from Kamtschatka. Voyage to Ochotsk. Arrival there. Short Description of the Place. Preparation for the long Journey Overland. Departure from Ochotsk for Jakutsk. Notable Events and geographic Remarks: Medwescha Golowa, Torotolom, Borokskei and Magilnoi Brod, Urakskoe Plotbischtscha, Judomskoi Krest, Okatschan, Lanku, Mosootlo, Capitanskaia Saseka, Tastelon, Kurtat Urach, Kamenoe Pole Saseka, Antscha, Allach Juni, Werblud, Dulchaaschlick, New Road. Allach Junsky Jaellan, Kinkwich, Valley of Achara, Elkakan Bacha, Loochlohr, Junikan, Aldan, Notara, Padjesebut, Massapinskoe Periwos. Post Stations from Massapinskoe Periwos to Jakutsk, Jahrmonka. Arrival in Jakutsk. List of the Plants collected on the Journey.

Our little ship was completely ready to sail on the 13th. The following day we headed to sea to begin our trip to Ochotsk. The weather was clear, though so intolerably cold that we had to put on our fur clothing. For the first days we had very light wind. Only on the 29th did a somewhat brisk wind arise from the northwest. An uncommonly large whale, its body larger than our ship, was lying on the surface of the water. No one on board noticed it until it was too late to sail around it. We ran into it at full sail. We were thereby placed in the greatest of danger, since that giant creature hardly moved from its position but instead raised its colossal, massive back, throwing our ship more than three fuss out of the water. The masts waved. The sails collapsed all at once. Frightened, we all jumped on deck. We all had been thinking we were in danger because of nearby rocks, but, instead of that, we saw a whale swimming very ceremoniously past us. If it, at the moment of that violent impact, had immediately dived energetically, most likely its tail would have destroyed the front of the ship and sunk us. Captain D'Wolf had the pumps started at once. He found that, luckily, the ship had no leaks or considerable other damage.

On May 22nd we sighted the second and third of the Kuril Islands. The following day, using a brisk east wind, we sailed through the about thirty-mile-wide strait between the third and fourth island. In the afternoon we happily found ourselves on the Ochotsk Sea in very heavy seas caused by the wind and current. To the northeast, we saw a very high, isolated peak, the Alaid, which lies not far from the strait between the promontory of Lopatka and the first Kuril Island. It is a steep, conical mountain rising up from the surface of the water to which the Kamtschadals attach various wonderful stories. It is supposed formerly to have been next to Opalskaia Sopka (a peak near Bolscheretsk). The two mountains are supposed to have fought continually about their size. Finally, Alaid, the more clever one of the two, tired of the continual strife, decided to live at the sea away from all of the other mountains.

We sailed slowly forward in variable weather. Toward noon on June 2nd, we were still about 70 sea miles from Ochotsk, so that with an even somewhat favorable wind we hoped to reach the harbor the following day.

Seamen do not like it if someone predicts ahead of time the day of arrival in a port or counts on having continual, favorable winds. They all probably know from experience how often their hopes have been dashed. That time we also experienced a striking example of that kind of thing. In the afternoon an extensive and dangerous field of ice floes to our northwest held us up. During the night, we were forced to seek safety by sailing into the open sea to the east.

If I were to continue to describe the rest of the voyage, I would tire out my readers. Therefore, I will only remind them cursorily that, until June 14th, we stayed at a distance of about 30 to 40 sea miles from the entrance of the harbor at Ochotsk. Because of the passing fields of ice floes, and, indeed, in part very large blocks of ice, we dared not sail ahead. Most days of the voyage were very foggy. Sometimes the weather was so cold that the ship's riggings were crusted with ice. We finally approached the harbor under such conditions on the 15th and took a pilot on board. Without him we would probably not have dared enter the harbor. Because the channels shift considerably every year, ships are always in danger of stranding on sandbars. The following day at about noon, we reached the harbor which had only become free of ice three days before. Of all the news we heard, the most unexpected was of the death of Mr. von Resanoff, who had died in March of that year in Krasnojarsk. He died on his way to St. Petersburg, too early to carry out the many plans he had formulated in the preceding years.

Ochotsk is situated on a flat, small, sandy point of land about two to three versts long. It is bordered on the one side by the Ochota River and washed on the other side by the sea. Opposite the extreme point of that tongue of land, another river, the Kuchtui, flows into the Ochota. Together they build the mouth of a harbor that is so shallow that only small ships, at the most with eight fuss of draft, can use it. Due to the rugged climate, it is only open to vessels for three months of the year from June 15th to September 15th.

Despite the fact that the government has often had the coast from south of Ochotsk to Udskoi Ostrog carefully examined, hoping possibly to find a better harbor, they still have not found one that is better than Ochotsk. Near that harbor there is rather good wood which can be used for building ships. The rivers are full of fish. Communication with Jakutsk, although difficult, is easier than with other places along that coast.

The location of the buildings is unhealthy and was only chosen because it is convenient for loading and unloading ships from the nearby point of land. The water of the Ochota River can only be drunk at low tide. The rest of the time the sea water flowing in makes it too salty. Despite this, the inhabitants use it all the time, so that I could only get a good glass of water or an unsalted cup of tea in a few of the houses. Almost daily the coast is covered by a thick, wet fog. That, together with the bad water and the fact that fish are the prime source of food, can be seen as the main source of the many diseases prevalent there, especially scurvy. Because of the low elevation of the land on which the houses are built — only a few fuss above sea level — they are often in danger of flooding from the periodic high tides. That was the case in 1801. A part of the place was swallowed up by the waves and only saved from total destruction by a sudden change in the direction of the sea winds accompanying the high tide and causing it to be even higher in the beginning.

Living quarters consist of little wooden houses. In size and architecture they are little different from those in Kamtschatka. They are supposed to contain about 2,000 souls.

When I went on land, I heard in all of the streets the rattling chains of the many criminals and exiles. They are forced to perform various kinds of jobs while guarded by soldiers. The horrible looks of those long-bearded, formerly dangerous scoundrels with their uncommonly expressive physiognomies were less pleasant to me than interesting. Dregs formed from the most ruthless and terrible of men who had already earned the wheel many times over, murderers, arsonists who had caused the death of others, committers of incest and highway robbers, branded and with slit noses — their horrible deeds stir up fear and horror. Their baseness, at the same time, gleamed from their eyes and could be seen in the most active of features upon their foreheads. Such men rattled through the streets in their chains.

The important buildings and installations in Ochotsk are: The admiralty building and the docks which cost about 400,000 rubles a year to maintain, a sum that could be saved for the most part if ships needed in those waters and other necessities were shipped by water from Europe.* A small ship of about 200 tons, built of good wood and easily outfitted with anchor, riggings, anchor cables, etc., in Kronstadt or in Archangel for 15,000 to 20,000 rubles, costs from 70,000 to 80,000 rubles in Ochotsk and is made of bad wood and outfitted with bad riggings. Larch trees for building ships are felled along the River Urak 30 versts from Ochotsk. The transport costs for one anchor used to be many thousand rubles. For that reason, in the preceding years, an anchor smithy had been established and numbers of skilled craftsmen, locksmiths, smiths, carpenters, etc., sent out there. Bar iron is pulled by horse from Jakutsk and processed upon the spot, thereby, at the most, reducing the former costs only in part.

The warehouses for storing flour and ammunition intended for the command there and the troops in Kamtschatka are new, roomy and well kept.

The church is old and tumbledown. Halfway between Ochotsk and the River Urak are salt-works. During the winter, about 2,000 puds of salt are produced. Part of it is sent to the Kamtschatkan battalion.

Bulgin lies on the left back of the Ochota five versts away. Its surroundings are rather pleasant and fertile, as fertile as the very cold climate permits. It has a well equipped hospital with several gardens nearby, in which cabbage, carrots and potatoes are grown, granted only moderately well. Its geographic location is by far healthier than on the right bank of the Ochota. That is why plans have been drawn up several times to move the town to that area. Several merchants and employees of the Crown live there even in the winter, because Ochotsk

---

*See von Krusenstern's *Reise um die Welt* [Voyage around the World], Vol. 4, "Introduction," p. xiii.

is only inhabited in the summer for purposes of trade and shipping. That point of land is then a collecting place for wares and supplies from and to Kamtschatka, the Aleutian Islands and America. In some ways it resembles a fair enlivened by the building of ships and the comings and goings of ships, sailors, soldiers and caravans of Yakuts. They come in numbers at the beginning of June, bringing up to 6 to 8 thousand horses, provisions, ammunition, brandy and all of the goods and wares needed there and on the other side of the Gulf of Ochotsk. Each horse is usually loaded with five, at the most six, puds of pack. The Crown, on an average, pays the owner thirty rubles for transport, the Kamtschadals, however, forty. As much as it appears that this kind of transit trade gives the Yakuts several advantages, the opposite is nonetheless true. That people, whose sole wealth consists of horses, has suffered in recent years irreplaceable damage from a cattle murrain that has killed many thousands of horses.

The Russian-American Company plays a large role in Ochotsk. It builds ships there from time to time for use in the trade between Kamtschatka and America. It would undeniably be more advantageous if they sent necessary ships and goods from Kronstadt to their outposts.

In the areas around Ochotsk, especially in the Mariaka Mountains, mineralogists and geologists would find a great many opportunities for remarkable observations.*

As much as I would have liked to have extended my stay and explored my surroundings, since they were once again coming to life, I could not, since I had to give priority to preparing for the continuation of my journey. I had to pack the objects I had brought with me from America for the ten-thousand-verst trip across land to St. Petersburg. I had to arrange to have the boxes sewn in leather and to provide for an appropriate number of horses and provisions, etc.

The journey from Ochotsk to Yakutsk has many of its own peculiar difficulties. Along wide stretches of land of about 900 to 1,000 versts, there are deep swamps and morasses, swift forest streams, large rivers without ferries, thick, almost impenetrable woods and in some places, only after several days' travel, a hut. Therefore, one has to do without all of the amenities of life and travel. The road

---

*See Pallas, *Neue nordische Beyträge* [New Northern Contributions], Vol. 4 and Vol. 5.

can only be traveled in summer on horseback and in winter with dogs or reindeer. Since one mostly travels through desolate terrain, one has to take along a tent, a bed, which usually consists of one or two bear skins, provisions for several weeks, kitchen utensils, axes for felling trees, guns for protection, a tinder box, tobacco leaves to be used to reward the Yakuts and many other objects needed for daily use.

Through the kind recommendation of Mr. von Resanoff, the business manager of the Russian-American Company, Mr. Petroff, had received Mr. D'Wolf and me in a most kind and hospitable manner. He tried, in accordance with my friend's wishes, to speed up our departure. He immediately commandeered the few rested horses that had arrived that spring with the first caravans, because Mr. D'Wolf wanted to arrive in St. Petersburg by autumn of that year and, after completing his business, return to America on one of the ships sailing from there. He was ready to leave in a few days. We parted on June 21st with the warmest assurances of friendship and esteem on both sides.

I cannot remain silent about a short, touching scene which occurred before his departure. Three Aleuts, who, as I remember, served as sailors on our ship, went to Captain D'Wolf and threw themselves to his feet weeping, with the request that he take them to his fatherland. "We will not cost you anything," they said, "only some bread or fish. We will follow your horse, even if we have to walk our feet off up to our bellies. We would rather go with you than return to our fatherland." Mr. D'Wolf regretted very much having to deny their request.

While Mr. Petroff was making arrangements for my departure, the unpleasant news arrived that seven of the craftiest rogues, who had been sent under guard with many others to fell trees, had found an opportunity to escape. The harbor commandant, Mr. Bucharin, sent out at once a strong commando of Cossacks in to order capture the criminals wherever possible and to protect the many caravans arriving and departing from those men, who could become dangerous highwaymen. Mr. Petroff had, in the meantime, signed a written agreement with several Yakuts, whom he knew, to take me within 20 to 22 days to Yakutsk. Mr. Bucharin was so generous to me that he sent along a cossack to insure my safety. I needed thirteen horses to carry my boxes and chests, tent and provisions, companions and guides. So that I might travel with greater ease and occasionally change part of the horses if they tired and so that I might not be embarrassed by the loss or sickness of a horse, I followed the advice of experienced people, who generally advise hiring twice as many horses as are needed. I paid twelve rubles per horse.*

On June 25th, everything was ready for my departure. Impatiently, I waited for my horses which were grazing on the left bank of the Ochota. They could not swim across because of high tide. Only toward five o'clock in the evening with the coming of ebb tide did they arrive. It was already dark by the time they were packed and I could set out on my journey.

After traveling 20 versts, I stopped near several huts named Uglia Sawoda (the charcoal manufacture), my first camp. The night was foggy, wet and cold. I had a bright fire started. While my tent was being pitched, I wanted to warm myself up with a cup of tea and a little glass of punch. To my regret, I discovered that, while packing everything in Ochotsk, the little supply of brandy intended for the journey had been forgotten. Rather than causing a delay by sending back for it, I decided to continue my journey without that comfort.

We set out again on the following morning at ten o'clock. The area was flat, intersected by many small creeks and stands of fir, larch and birch. Now and again we saw little huts of several Yakuts and invalid soldiers who had been settled there. Unlike the Kamtschadals, the former were not required to do daily compulsory work but lived free, although in part poorly, from cattle raising, hunting and fishing. The only tribute each one has to pay to the Crown consists of sixty squirrel skins, known as Siberian grey squirrels on the market. They are of excellent quality in that area. A single squirrel skin usually costs 20 to 23 kopeks. Toward noon we reached several houses, Medwescha Golowa (Bear Head). That is the usual length of the journey on the first day from Ochotsk. There are several huts from whose inhabitants one can always get good milk. That evening, after traveling about forty versts, we arrived at a picturesque area called Jakuten Meta. It lies in the middle of a woods where an invalid soldier has settled. We decided to spend the night there and refresh ourselves with the excellent milk which we acquired from the nearby house.

Early the next morning two Yakuts, our caravan leaders, left in order to look for the horses. They left me with the cossack and

---

*Since the horses have to be returned and the caravans mostly have to return from Ochotsk to Yakutsk without a load, occasionally, it is possible to hire a horse for six to eight rubles.

baggage in an embarrassing position for over an hour and one-half, for they did not return. A day's journey is determined by the grazing areas which also serve as post stations. When one arrives at one of them in the evening, the horses are immediately unpacked. The baggage is put in a heap and the horses are turned out to graze at will. The Yakuts watch the horses in turn one after the other for the whole night, that is, the one on watch takes a look around every hour to see where, in the often very wide valley, they are grazing. If, however, he is tired and falls asleep, which sometimes is the case, it can happen that not only the whole horse herd but also the Yakuts, who go looking for them off of the known trails, get totally lost. As soon as they have been lucky enough to find the horses, they drive them into a small pen or fold, usually left by caravans near the grazing area, and catch them. They could, to be sure, as in Europe hobble their front feet to prevent them from going very far, but the Yakuts do not do that, or only very rarely. Every night, they have to be afraid of attacks by highway robbers and riffraff who could easily sneak up unnoticed and steal the horses. That is impossible if they graze at will. After a long wait, the horses finally arrived. After they were loaded, we continued our journey. After traveling fifteen versts on that foggy morning, we arrived at the first swift woodland stream, Torotolom, which we had to cross. The dry weather up to then meant that it was not as deep as usual. It only came up to the horses' bellies. During rainy weather, it sometimes happens that caravans have to wait for weeks until the water goes down so that crossing is possible. The woods were beautiful and very pleasant with their varied stands of fir, larch, maple, birch, alder and hazelnut bushes. We were very happy to find the many swampy spots, that at other times are barely passable, dried out. The area was less dead than the area we had passed through the previous day. We saw two bears. I killed a snow partridge in summer dress and a gull (*Larus*).[1] Toward evening we heard from a passing caravan that one of the criminals who had recently escaped from Ochotsk had been caught by the commando sent out. The rest had scattered and fled. In the evening, after completing a day's journey of 50 versts, we camped in a narrow valley, abutting naked cliffs, which was an excellent grazing area. A nearby valley was covered with ice and snow. It made the surrounding area so cold that we — to our greatest pleasure — were almost totally saved for most of the night from mosquitoes. That evening I was able to enjoy my soup of snow partridge and gull without having those restless guests around.

The next morning, after taking the tent down, capturing the horses, packing them, and eating a good breakfast, we again set out along a winding way through the dark woods between mountains of moderate height. After we had traveled about ten versts, we ascended a low spot in the mountain chain called Plutnei Chrebta (Rogue Mountain). It is the usual collecting place and whereabouts of the rascals fleeing from Ochotsk every year. The day before our arrival, one had been caught in the area and the rest had fled. That meant that we could happily pass through there without fear of being harmed. Of the several larger streams, which are sometimes dangerous, we crossed the Borokskoi once and the Magilnoibrod twice (the Brodski and Magilnoi ford). We rode until late at night, because we found numerous caravans heading for Ochotsk camping on all of the grazing spots. My caravan leader felt it was better to continue on than to chose one of the large number of common camps. For this reason, we pitched our tent near a smaller caravan late at night after traveling at least 70 versts.

Even though the continued hot weather was tiring, it did, indeed, give us the advantage of finding the streams almost dried out. We could cross them without difficulty or danger.

According to my guide, our camp was ten versts from several storehouses and buildings: Uraskoe Plotbishtscha, where several cossacks lived. It was their business to transport to that place and guard flour, ammunition and other goods intended for Ochotsk and Kamtschatka, in case they could no longer be transported to Ochotsk because of the loss of horses or lateness of the season. Without that provision they would be subjected to the influence of the winter weather in that desolate area and spoiled.

On the 29th, one of the Yakuts set out early to find the horses which had wandered farther than usual. He returned more than two and one-half hours later, crossed himself and said: "God has given us horses!" We set out later than usual and were bothered very much by the heat of the sun. In the beginning, we wandered through flat, low land. Here and there we saw very beautiful stands of birch and larch, along with a number of little creeks, springs, ponds and morasses formed by recently melted snow and ice which was still lying around for long stretches.

We rode by Plotbischtscha without stopping. Toward evening we met the post coming from Yakutsk. They had been on the road for sixteen days and said that fifteen versts from there one of the highway robbers had jumped out of the bushes. As soon as he knew it was the post, he called out: "Comrades, there is nothing to be had here. Let the post pass without trouble!" Upon hearing that news, we (the cossack and I) put our hands on our weapons and continued on our way untroubled. We knew that the escapees were still without weapons. At sunset, after a day's journey of 45 versts, we had just reached the area where the post had met the highway robbers. We pitched our tent about two to three versts away from the large caravan trail in an area with meager grass for our horses. Since we had to be afraid of attack, we stacked all of our baggage in front of the tent. We then agreed that the four of us would alternately stand guard through the night and take to our weapons at the slightest sign of danger.

Because of several small clouds that collected toward evening, the Yakuts predicted it would soon rain, which it really did during the night.

The following day we approached the Urak Mountains. A river of the same name originates there and flows into the Sea of Ochotsk. The mountains, which we had to ascend, are not very steep. They offered, however, a greater variety and change of scenery than all of the preceding areas on our journey. From a caravan coming toward us, we heard the comforting news that the cossacks had captured one of the escapees in the night. A few hours later we reached a friendly, charming valley on the other side of the Urak Mountains. We found a pond, at least three to four versts in circumference, where part of the cossacks mentioned above were camping on the shore. In order to satisfy my curiosity, I approached the captured escapee. His look and appearance caused repulsion and horror. He had deep-set, crafty eyes, a large protruding forehead, high cheek bones, long, coal-black hair hanging wildly about his head, a very long beard and completely ragged clothing. Toward evening, making good time on our march of 45 versts, we reached the first large station after Ochotsk, Judomskoi Krest. That place consists of several houses and a small chapel. It lies on the River Judoma, which in places is a verst wide and very deep. In the dry season it is, however, often so small that it can be waded on horseback. It flows into the Maya and that into the Aldan River, which in turn flows into the Lena River.

Four workers and an overseer do the ferrying by using three boats. Crown goods are transported free. Merchants pay ten kopeks for every horse-load of goods (five puds) ferried across.* The people who have been sent there live in the greatest of poverty. Because of bad pastures, they have no cows or horses. Gardening is impossible.

*Generally, one Yakut is always assigned to ten horses.

The river also produces very few fish. They live mainly from bread and water.

Since pastures on the other side of the river are not much better, we stayed overnight on that side of the river. Some of the cossacks had posted themselves along the river bank, so that the robber band would not be able to steal the boats unpunished in the night and cross the river.

Early the following morning, everything was packed and transported across. The horses had to swim. Because of the strength of the current, they were torn away and reached the bank about two versts farther downriver. As on several other occasions on the journey, I had to admire the talent for swimming of the Yakut horses.

After traveling twenty versts through a flat, very swampy and rather free, that is, less wooded area, the Yakuts asked me for permission to rest for a day because the horses had had meager grazing for the preceding two days. We were in a very grass-rich lowland. I was happy to agree and used the time to collect several beautiful little plants. We spent the night in a swampy place with excellent forage for the horses, but, because of the indescribable quantity of insects, was a very unpleasant place for us. Indeed, the horses came back to us after a short time, because they knew from experience that the fire and smoke usually put around the tent in such areas decreased the numbers of insects.

The horses were saddled again after sunrise and we continued our journey. On that day, we approached a chain of high, bald mountains forming a large valley that we followed. The River Okatschan winds through it. At certain times of the year, it appears to rise considerably because the valley is filled with detritus, making progress over the path very difficult and unpleasant. We had not gone very far into it when another valley opened into it with the River Lanku flowing through it. That river flows at that point into the Okatschan. I remember the area for its surprising display. The part of the valley Okatschan, in which we were, as well as the part of the Valley Lanku we could see, was covered for several versts with at least three-fuss-thick ice. The unique appearance of that winter scene was heightened by the tall willow trees with leaves and blooms shining in the middle of the ice fields.

On that and preceding days, I had seen along the road several dead horses. Upon asking, I was told that they had died of a murrain.

Suddenly, on some part of the animal's body, especially its head, a boil or swelling appears. It begins to tremble and dies within an hour or half a day at the most. The murrain appears only in the hottest months, July and August, and is reported to have first broken out in 1804. At that time, it is reported to have wreaked such havoc that, from a caravan of eighty horses, only ten remained healthy.*

Since the Yakuts did not at first know the disease and they like to eat horse meat, they thought it was a shame to let a good fat steak go to waste and ate the meat. As a result, most of those who ate it died in one or two days and some lingered on for fourteen days. Among the few survivors, nasty boils erupted on their upper lips and checks, distorting the greater part of their faces. The following year, 1805, not a single horse died. In 1806, however, again a great many did. In 1807 that destructive disease reappeared. Probably, they were not yet aware of it either in Ochotsk or Yakutsk, since the Yakuts said that, as soon as the government knew of its presence, they sent men out to burn the dead horses.

After riding about forty versts, we pitched our tent on the shore of the Okatschan River near a good grazing area. The next day we continued to follow the river, crossing its windings three times. The valley gradually became narrower. After thirty versts, we found ourselves at the foot of several very steep, high mountains called Mosockotlo or Mosootlo by the Yakuts. I have no memory of ever seeing mountains of that height so totally devoid of all plants and trees from their peaks to their feet. If I may say so, they resembled heaps of rubble covered with detritus. The stony valley had extraordinarily meager, miserable soil. I saw schist, granite, porphyry and several other kinds of mixed mountain rocks, which indicated the present of primeval mountains. Nearer to Ochotsk are found limestone seams and, instead of the desert as here, beautiful, charming stands of trees. The naked rocks are barely covered with earth to a height of two fuss. The roots of the mainly stunted trees grow horizontally in thin stands over the rocks. They offer so little hold that the trees can easily be uprooted by a strong wind. All over I saw similar trees, seldom with a diameter of more than a fuss, with roots spread out star-like in every direction.

---

*The Yakuts maintain that cows, reindeer, bears, etc., as well as horses, have died of it and not without reason. The same murrain is known in Europe, where it is called spleen disease or carbuncle disease and befalls the most varied of animals.

After we had moved away from Okatschan and had left the Mosootlo about eight versts behind us, we crossed various kinds of hills and came to a lake about two versts in size, where, for the first time since leaving Ochotsk, we saw several wild ducks. Right next to the lake, we found two hills with a natural gate or opening between them through which we suddenly left summer and entered winter. As soon as we rode through that gate, we came upon extensive fields of ice, five to six versts long and at least four wide, called Capitanskaia Saseka. There in that valley, surrounded by high mountains, the ice never thaws — thus, those are eternal glaciers. In many places the ice was still four to five fuss thick. Streams flowed through several fissures making the area impassable. The area was so cold that we had to put on our furs to warm ourselves.

On the previous day's journey, I noticed little bunches of horsehair on the branches of trees. At first, I ascribed them to chance, until I saw them so often and asked questions. The Yakuts, as a matter of precaution, tie the hair to the trees because they want to trick the devil and rob him of any power he might have over their horses.

The prevailing weather was dry, letting us cross without difficulty the many swamps and morasses that are almost impassable in the rainy season. After sunset we rode over fifty versts. We camped near a place called Tastolon by the Yakuts and Kamenoe Pole, that is, stony field, by the Russians. That station, as the name implies, offered very poor, meager fodder. The following morning, my Yakuts suggested that we take a somewhat shorter trail, richer in grass, which, because it is more difficult and goes over a high, steep mountain, is little used by the caravans. I accepted the suggestion. They conducted me over the Bremoi Retschka Ehreböt or, as the Yakuts call it, Kurtat Urach. The road went up and down steep slopes, but offered, however, varied scenery and here and there good grazing and stands of trees. After going over the mountain and traveling ten versts, we arrived at the normal caravan route. We entered a cold, icy valley, Kamennoe Pole Saseka. A small creek flows through it that connects with the Antscha and near Allach Juni (an inhabited village with a Crown ferry) flows into a river of the same name.

After traveling about forty versts, one of my Yakuts took me to a place near the road with a big cross made of round stones. He continually repeated the word *Dimänn*, but I could not understand him. My cossack explained that a giant animal was buried there the exact length of the stones. According to my measurements, it was 35 fuss long. Two of those animals are supposed to have existed twenty years before. One of them disappeared while grazing, and the other died at that spot on the journey from Yakutsk to Ochotsk. They were very large, grass-eating animals with a long trunk used to put food in their mouths. They said such an animal could easily carry 30 puds. They could only be loaded when on their knees, something they did as soon as they were hit on the front feet with an iron rod. I had already begun to suspect a tradition about the existence of mammoths when I heard the name *verblud*. The miraculous animal being talked about was a camel; poetic license had given it a trunk and more than doubled its size.

In the afternoon we rode past high wooded hills, one of which was completely on fire. The Yakuts had probably built a fire at its foot or set fire to an old tree which had then spread out terribly. In the preceding days we had seen many bare, burned mountains, devoid of trees, caused by the negligence of the Yakuts.

That was the first day since leaving Ochotsk on which we met not one single caravan. After a day's journey we pitched our tent at Dulchaaschlick (Koschka Kormanwischa), that is, near a hill with good grazing. Our horses really enjoyed the best of grass.

The morning of the 5th, we rode through the stony valley of the River Antscha, which we had to cross several times. Some hills lying in our way were steep and arduous to climb. The most unpleasant event of the day was having to ride through a burning woods. We were afraid that we would either suffocate from the smoke or be roasted by the flames. We met many caravans and, among other things, large herds of cattle being driven to market in Ochotsk.

The leaders of the caravans passed on the highly sad news that smallpox, which had not been seen in many years, had broken out in Ullach Juni and several other areas along the Aldan River and was causing great devastation. My companions, who had never had the pox, became very anxious and asked me to permit them to use another trail, the so-called new road (that is a newly projected one), so that they could avoid the places which would be dangerous for their lives. I found their request so reasonable that I immediately gave permission, even though I would have to make a detour of 120 versts.

For this reason, toward evening we left the usual caravan trail and turned toward the River Allach Juni, which, about thirty versts downstream from where we left the caravan trail, has a Crown ferry.

For want of a ferry boat, we had to swim across the river on our horses. The water reached half way up the horses' bellies and was so strong and rapid that we were in danger of losing several horses with packs.

After a day's journey of forty versts, we stayed overnight in a wide, open and very wet valley: Allach Junsky Jällan. In wet weather it is probably barely passable. The next day we continued our way through it and then, after crossing several insignificant hills, we arrived at the stream Kinkuich (Kinkwich) rushing through a narrow valley. On the river bed I found slate and quartz, part of which was in the form of small crystal clumps. We rode fifteen to twenty versts along the stony bed of that woodland stream, which served as a trail for crossing the mountains. The banks are, in part, flat and shaded by beautiful trees. Now and again, they are so very close together that the very narrow valley with its slate mountains overhanging both sides presents many a picturesque view. Farther on, we ascended a gently rising hill from which we entered the Achara Valley, watered by a river of the same name that flows into the Aldan. The mountains, of moderate height, have been denuded of trees by fire in spots. In other spots they are charming and covered with woods up to their peaks. Instead of larch we again saw fir trees for the first time in a long while. We camped after a march of about sixty versts in a swampy woods with intolerable numbers of bugs and insects.

On the 7th, in that valley (Achara) I found a totally different kind of landscape: fir and pine trees, juniper bushes and many a plant I had never seen before offered a very pleasant change for me. In addition, there were several caravans on the trail, which, like my Yakuts, wanted to avoid smallpox. Since my guide told me that on the following day the trail would be very bad with hardly any grazing areas, we stopped after traveling forty versts to rest the horses and let them have a good graze for the day.

At dawn we set out again. Contrary to my expectations, I found a good trail and excellent grazing. I realized that my Yakuts the day before had wanted to spare their horses by traveling less. After thirty versts, we left that beautiful, fertile valley along the Achara River and ascended a high, morassy, thickly wooded mountainous area, Acharinskaia chrebta. We had to chop our way through with an ax. That was indeed a new trail! As darkness fell, we were forced to spend the night in a desolate, sad spot with neither water nor grass.

Early the next morning, July 9th, we set out with empty stomachs in rainy weather. Several hours later we reached a small stream, Elkaka bacha, or the source of the Elkakan. We stopped by it for awhile, fortified ourselves with tea and rusk and left our horses to graze, since they had had nothing to eat since the day before. We spent the rest of the day working through morasses and thick woods, over mountains and through valleys. The new trail was even more unpleasant than the old one, on which we had climbed through fields of ice, waded rivers and stumbled over detritus. Toward evening we saw ahead of us a high mountain ridge, Loochlohr. My Yakuts said we would reach the River Junikan at its foot that day. After an arduous day's ride of about fifty versts, we, indeed, did reach it well after sunset.

We spent the night on that side of the river (Junikan). With the least amount of rain, it rises so much that it often cannot be crossed for a week. Even though there had been almost no rain for three weeks, it was still so deep that the horses the next morning had to wade through water up to their bellies. We did not set out as early as usual, since our goal for the day was the Aldan River about thirty versts away. The area from Loochlohr to the Aldan is mostly flat and swampy. Its very fertile earth produces very excellent grasses for fodder.

In the afternoon we reached the right bank of the Aldan, a large river that, at that point, is probably more than a verst wide. I had reason to believe there would be a regular ferry as in Judomskoe Krest. The Yakuts had been talking often a short time before of a ferry in Notara, a village that was supposed to be here on the left bank of the river. Immediately upon our arrival, we began to try to announce our presence by shouting, shooting off our guns and building a large fire. All to no avail. The leader of the caravan had already had our horses swim across in order to let the inhabitants of Notara know we were there.

My cossack, a very clever man, got the Yakuts to build a raft immediately in order to cross the river and fetch us a boat. He helped them. After we had found several dry logs, tied them together and made two oar-like pieces of wood, the Yakuts entrusted themselves to that flimsy, clumsy emergency vessel in order to cross that very large, fast-flowing river. We (the cossack and I), in the meantime, pitched our tent and awaited their return. They arrived back before sunset on the 11th with a boat which we used to transport our baggage to the left bank. They also brought the information that the boats were usually there, because it was a better crossing, but that the Yakuts lived about ten versts farther up the river. I left my Yakuts with the baggage and horses and set out with the cossack to get to know the Yakuts living there better. I found a 75-year-old man named Kapitohn in a little hut. He and his not very numerous family proved to be very kind and ready to serve. His wealth, as with all Yakuts, consisted of large herds of cattle and horses whose meat and milk, along with the arrival of numerous fish in the spring and fall, are those people's main source of food.

Even though the Yakuts have had contact with the Russians for a long time, they are less acquainted with the language, customs and habits of the Russians than the more distant Kamtschadals and Aleuts. They pay the Crown a small tribute and live undisturbed with their families. Their weapons, as in former times, still consist of bows and arrows. Hunting and raising horses are their favorite activities. They drink horse milk and consider horse meat a delicacy. Some well-to-do Yakuts own 100 to 150 or more horses.

I learned from my elderly host that in 24 hours by boat I could reach the Aldan ferry or Massapinskoe Periwos, that is the usual old Ochotsk Trail, about 120 versts downstream. From there I could travel with the post horses very comfortably in three or four days to Jakutsk. Tired of the caravan and convinced that I would be able to travel far more comfortably, I accepted the offer of the good Kapitohn to have some of his people take me by boat. I ordered my caravan guide to take my baggage straight to Yakutsk, where I would be expecting it at the business agent's of the Russian-American Company.*

In the afternoon my bed, a bearskin, some provisions, (linens), a tea kettle and similar things were brought to the canoe in which I, along with my cossack and two Yakuts, embarked.

The Yakuts' canoes are very flat, with pointed backs and fronts. They consist of a frame that is almost similar to the Aleutian baidarkas, but too open on top. The body is covered with pieces of boiled birch bark that have been sewn together. The seams of each individual piece are smeared with tar so that they are completely water tight. These canoes are very light and can travel very rapidly. But most, however, lack balance because the birch bark often buckles, first one way and then another. The oars are extremely similar to those found in Unalaska.

---

*I could more readily entrust by baggage to them because I, as mentioned above, had signed a written contract with them in Ochotsk. They, indeed, delivered them to me three days after my arrival in Yakutsk all in one piece.

After all of the difficulties of traveling by caravan, I found traveling on water very pleasant. The shores of the Aldan are varied, mostly moderately high and pleasing with their meadows and shade of birch and larch. In that area the banks are of a loose, clay sandstone. Among the gravel I found fine, finely mixed granite and schist. Now and again, one sees beautifully wooded islands. It is a pity that this majestic river flows through such a desolate, little-inhabited and cold stretch of the earth. Thirty-five versts from Notara, a stream of the same name flows into the left side of the Aldan. Ten versts farther is Berry Island (Jagodowa Ostrow), which has quantities of strawberries, currants, cranberries, etc. Soon afterwards, on the right bank, rises the towering rock Nosowoe Kamen and the neighboring mountain Nosowai Gora and on the opposite shore Salanginski bereg.

After sunset we stopped at Ochojanskaia Ostrow, where we drank tea and ate something. The Yakuts had brought along several fish nets, which they put out in order to use them as much as possible during our stay. The nets are about three fuss wide and 150 or more fuss long. The string is made of horsehair and is very strong, despite the fact that a thread is only made up of five horse hairs. Those long, narrow nets are spread out in the water by means of several willow sticks. The fish fins get so caught in them that it is impossible for them to escape. After we had eaten our food and drank our tea, to our pleasure several sturgeons (*Acipenser ruthenus*) and a pike were pulled out of the river in the net.

Early on the morning of the 12th, we reached Kerbin, another small Yakut village, where I changed boat and crew. I gave my previous rowers several tobacco leaves as reward, with which they left for home highly pleased. The banks of the Aldan River, consisting partly of steep towering rocks, partly of gently rising slopes and a number of shaded islands, offered variety and excellent scenery only in need of houses and living beings. At the place where I breakfasted, I drew a little sketch. My guide called a steep rock on the opposite left bank Padjesobut, in Russian Palmupotiral. Two or three versts farther downriver, I was delighted by a picturesque area: Tschelobscha (Dwerpad). There is a gate-like opening in the high rock wall leading to a cavern that is supposed to run far into the slope. The river divides into several branches, forming a number of islands, some of which are inhabited. On many of them there are ponds and streams full of fish which swim in from the river. The large herds of the Yakuts living there feed on the rich grasses. On the right shore are usable sandstone deposits.

In the afternoon I visited a rich Yakut's summer home. He lived together with his family in a roomy, round, flattened, conical hut. It was about eighteen fuss in diameter and consisted of a frame covered with birch bark. None of them could have expected the arrival of a stranger. That is why I was surprised to find a very special cleanliness, which I had looked for in vain in the poor homes in Kerbin.

I was especially impressed by the great variety of uses those people have for birch bark. Little canoes and big boats, drinking vessels, milk containers, water containers, the outside covering of huts and the various dividing walls within — everything is made of birch bark. Even screens and curtains for the beds are made of it and embroidered in various ways. They showed me some birch bark embroidered with horse hair that a Yakut woman had worked on for over a year. In order to make the birch bark durable and pliable, it is boiled for a whole day in water (perhaps it is also prepared in another manner), thus making it, according to the Yakuts, last for sixty to seventy years. A carpet or wall or bed screen made from it can be handed down as an heirloom from parents to children.

It is, indeed, admirable to observe how various, still uncivilized peoples are able to satisfy their needs by using simple materials present in nature.

For many South Sea Islanders bamboo is the answer. Aleuts, Eskimos and some other groups would hardly be able to exist without whales and seals. The Tschuktschi and Koriaks, the Lapps, Samoyeds and other inhabitants of the northern part of the earth live almost exclusively from reindeer. They even know how to use the moss found in their intestines. Sheep are indispensable for the Buriats, Kirgese and several other steppe peoples. They provide clothing, food, housing, etc. The Yakuts satisfy the greatest part of their needs from horses and birch bark.

Toward evening I reached the large, usual caravan trail from Ochotsk to Yakutsk and the Crown ferry over the Aldan, named Massapchinskoe Perewos.

The father of the cossack assigned to accompany me from Ochotsk was in charge of the ferry. He was very happy at the unexpected arrival of his son. They immediately set about entertaining me in the most hospitable manner with excellent milk, cream, fresh butter and strawberries. They prepared a wild duck (*Anas fusca*) for the evening meal. This year they had appeared in unusually large numbers on the river. In contrast, the inhabitants of Ochotsk had complained a great deal, saying that the ducks they had formerly caught by the thousands in nets and beat to death with sticks were becoming fewer year by year.

Tired from the difficult journey and met with the best of hospitality in a place that consisted of several houses built in the Russian manner, I decided to take a day of rest on the 13th, to the joy of my cossack, his parents and relatives. A small party of soldiers from Yakutsk contributed a great deal to the liveliness of the place. They had been sent there because occasionally escapees and criminals collected in the area and endangered the ferry operation.

The Yakuts living in the area were occupied with making hay. For the most part, they seemed to live in poverty. They sold me their bows and arrows and other small items for tobacco leaves, which they accepted with such great pleasure that I could easily see how scarce the item was that they considered a necessity. A cow usually costs 10, a good horse with saddle and bridle 70 to 80 rubles. Since the provisions I had brought from Ochotsk were almost used up, I bought a year old calf for six rubles.

Their winter housing consists of an earthen wall covered by upright wooden planks on the inside. Usually, only one family lives in a dwelling. In contrast, summer housing is intended for the common use of several families. The living room usually has a wooden floor. In its middle is a fireplace which is open on two sides. At the back it has a somewhat slanted fire wall on which a rather free-hanging chimney has been built. In a country that does not need to worry about saving wood, that arrangement offers the advantage that a traveler can build a good fire any time for warmth and for drying his clothes. The cowshed is right next to the living room and only separated from it by a door. All of the horses live outside the whole winter. They assured me that it is better for them the colder it is, that they would become thin in a warm stall — and this in a part of the earth where 30° cold is nothing unusual.

Even though I found myself deep in Asia, signs of European civilization were noticeable. Beginning here, there are regular post stations at about 30- to 50-verst intervals all the way to St. Petersburg.*

*From here to Yakutsk only horses are used and no carriages.

Even though I had ordered post horses for early the following day, they only arrived in the afternoon and were immediately ferried across the river with my little bit of baggage on a large flat boat. Caravan horses always have to swim the one and one-half verst wide river. Carried by the current, they travel four to five versts by the time they reach the other side. If the river is swollen and, as a result, much wider, often several horses drown in the procedure.

The post stations from Massapchinskoe Perewos to Yakutsk, along with the distances between them, are:

From Massapchinskoe Perewos to Nagunskaia Stanzija	33 versts
From there to Amkinskaia Stanzija	47 versts
From there to Melschinskaia	25 versts
From there to Arelatskaia	37 versts
From there to Schirapschinskaia	34 versts
From there to Borotofskaia	32 versts
From there to Tonkolinskaia	30 versts
From there to Tubijachtaskaia	17 versts
From there to Jahrmonka	23 versts
From there to Jakutsk	7 versts

The road between the first three stations is as bad as the one to Ochotsk. Swamps, morasses, thick woods, mountain and woodland streams are unavoidable obstacles preventing faster progress. Then, however, come dry plains where even the villages with post stations are more prosperous. In almost all of them, one can obtain milk and cream as well as fish from the frequent ponds. The daytime heat was oppressive and the quantities of insects intolerable. Therefore, I traveled in the clear, cool nights and rested during the noonday heat.

Between the stations of Arelatskaia and Schirapschinskaia, the terrible racket of thousands of ravens filling the surrounding area for long stretches caught my attention. I could not find out why they were probably there. My guide told me that the parents were instructing their children in eating and singing.

At the station of Schirapschinskaia is a salt storehouse which supplies the Yakuts with salt. Brandy is also sold there. Between Tonkolinski and Tubijachtaski I saw a tree with something hanging in it that looked not unlike a pig trough. By asking, I found out that it was the coffin of a Yakut child and that the Yakuts never bury their dead but always hang them in trees in the woods.

I never stopped at a station longer than was necessary to change horses. On the 18th toward noon, I reached Jahrmonka, the last station before Yakutsk that lies about one and one-half versts from the right bank of the Lena. My baggage was taken to a small boat used to carry me across the river, which is one of the most imposing in the Russian empire. Its breadth with the inclusion of many islands is seven versts at this point.

Toward four in the afternoon, I approached the city of Yakutsk (62° N) on the left bank of the river. The lofty towers and cupolas of the churches make it beautiful in the distance. On the bank there were numbers of one-masted, flat boats, called ships there, as well as large, covered rafts, which are made from tall trees found on the upper Lena near Wercholensk. Here they are taken apart and used for building houses. The city, inhabited by Yakuts and Russians, has about 500 to 600 buildings, all made of wood and in part very roomy. Almost every one of them has a roomy courtyard and garden, thus making the circumference of the city much larger. The streets are wide, irregular and unpaved. Some well built houses only make the many miserable huts standing near them unpleasant in contrast. There are five churches and a monastery. Very close to the edge of the city are old wooden towers, the remains of the first fort used for protection against the Yakuts during the conquest of the area. When the Lena breaks up in spring, the city and islands are sometimes subjected to terrible flooding. That happened in 1807 and about thirty years ago. Many Yakuts and over a thousand head of cattle were washed away and drowned.

I was told that the cold in winter often goes to 30° to 40° Réaumur. During the hottest of summers, the earth never thaws more than two fuss deep. The meat in the shallow cellars froze during my stay. During the whole summer, ice is found in the wells. Grass grows extraordinarily well. Cattle raising and fur trading are the most common source of livelihood for the inhabitants.

On the way from Ochotsk to Yakutsk I found the following plants:

Aconitum ochroleus affin.
Achillea alpina
Anemone narcissiflorus
Anemone sylvestris affin.
Andromeda polyfolia
Artirrhinum Linaria
Atragene alpina
Aquilegia
Aster alpinus sibiricus
Androsace filiformia
Artemisia laciniatae affin.
Aspidium

Alnus
Astragalus uliginoso affin. aliæq. species hujus generis
Arbutus alpina
Arbutus uva ursi
Anthericum calyculatum
Bartsia pallida
Betula nana fruticans
Betula fruticos affin.
Betula alnus
Beckmannia crucaeformis
Blechnum calophyllum
Carum simplex
Campanulae
Cacalia hastata
Carices
Cinerariae
Chrysanthemum arcticum
Carduus crispus
Cornus sanguinea
Chelidonium majus
Dianthus
Drabae
Delphinium grandiflor.
Epilobium
Erigeron acre
Euphrasia officin.
Festuca
Fragaria vesca
Gnaphalium dioicum
GnaphaliumLeontopodioides
Geum intermedium
Galium rubioïdes
Galium boreale
Gentiana macrophylla
Gentiana triflora
Holcus borealis
Hypericum Ascyron
Hedysarum flor. rubr.
Hedysarum alpinum
Inula brittanica
Inula Hirta
Juniperus Sabina
Juniperus communis
Linum boreale
Linum perenne
Ledum palustre
Linaria, n. sp.
Lysimachia thyrsiflora
Lycopodium annotinum
Melanthium sibiricum
Marchantia conica
Mentha aquatica
Potentilla anserina
Potentill. fruticosa
Potentilla hirta
Phlox, sibiric.
Prenanthes, n. sp.
Pyrola rotundifol.
Pyrol. secunda
Pedicularis verticillata
Pedicularis euphrasioides
Pedic. resupinata
Pedicularis sceptrum
Polygonum viviparum
Populus alba
Populus balsamifer.
Pinus Cembra
Pinus Larix
Pinus Abies
Platanus orientalis
Polytrichum
Phaca astragalin. affin.
Primula sibirica
Primula, n. sp.
Phlomis tuberosa
Plantago
Paris quadrifol.
Ranunculus aquatilis Multifidus
Ranunculus pulchellus in udis
Rubus arcticus
Rubus chamaemorus
Ribes rubrium
Rhododendron tauricum

Rhododendron chrysanthum
Rheum
Salices
Spirea lobata
Spirea sorbifol.
Stachys palustris
Stachys sylvatica
Senecio saracenicus
Selinum
Scutellaria galericulata
Swertia perennis
Sanguisorba officin.
Sedum
Stellaria
Saxifraga oppositifol.
Serratula alpina sibirica
Scorzonerae
Sonchus sibiricus
Sphagnum capillifol.
Trifolium lupinaster rubrum
Tanacetum vulgare
Taraxacum
Thymus latifolius sibiricus
Trientalis europaea
Trollius asiaticus
Valeriana officin.
Veronica incana
Veronica maritima
Vaccinium Vitis idaea
Vaccinium uliginosum

NOTES

1. "Curiously enough, there are no ptarmigan on the high mountains of South Central Asia, where one finds instead the snow partridge *Lerwa lerwa* and the snow cocks" (Sir A. Landesborough Thomson, ed., *A New Dictionary of Birds*, New York, McGraw-Hill, 1964, p. 343.)

Chapter 18

Journey from Yakutsk to Irkutsk. Departure from Yakutsk. Difficulties along the Way. Names and Descriptions of the Principal Places: Olekma, Vitim, Kirenki, Vercholensk and the Distance from one to the next. Noteworthy Events. Plants, Minerals, etc. Arrival in Katschuk. The Bratsks or Buriats. Arrival in Irkutsk and its Description. Visit in Kiachta. Journey by Way of Tobolsk, Kasan, Moscow to St. Petersburg.

On the advice of the general manager of the Russian-American Company in Yakutsk, I turned all of my chests and large baggage over to him to be transported by merchant vessel to Irkutsk at the usual price of four rubles a pud (forty Russian pounds). I only took my papers, drawings and a portmanteau of linen with me. Thus, I was able to travel in the fastest and easiest way.

The distance from Yakutsk to Irkutsk is 2,599 versts.* Except for the last 270 versts, the whole way is on the beautiful Lena River. At regular intervals along the way are post stations, mostly on the left bank of the river and usually 25, 30 and 40 versts apart. Each one has a small boat that is drawn upstream by horses, as well as the necessary guides who could row if need be.

If the traveler has time to travel leisurely and wants to travel most comfortably, then he can rent a boat in Yakutsk** and take all necessities with him, i.e., food, kitchen equipment, bedding, servants, etc. If, however, he is in a hurry and not burdened by a great deal of baggage, then he can travel comfortably like a post traveler or courier, using the mostly small, open boats standing ready at every station, which he exchanges for

---

*According to others, only 2,486. Since no exact geographical measurements have ever been taken in that area, an error of one hundred versts on such a distance can easily be made.

**If he begins his trip in Irkutsk, then this has to be done in Wercholensk, where the Lena becomes navigable.

another one at the next. In the locations where the river has a big bend or where a big detour has to be made because the water is shallow, he can ride straight across country and shorten his way considerably.

If I were to relate my journey as recorded in my journal, as I have been doing, then I would have to be afraid of wearing out my readers' patience. Therefore, I will only relate the principal events and observations. In respect to natural history, geography and geology, the journey offered many objects worthy of reflection and more exact study. That is why I regret unendingly, for reasons that would be too diffuse to relate, that I had to travel as fast as possible. Day and night, I simply flew through those areas, where daily I found unexpected difficulties and unpleasantness of all kinds coming my way. At many stations everyone was busy making hay, so that upon my arrival I did not find a living soul in the houses. To my sorrow, I had to wait for hours, indeed, half or the whole night, before I could continue on. At others, the post boat was in the most miserable condition and leaky. Once in the night, due to the sleepy rower's inattention, the boat capsized so that it was half full of water. At the next station, I had to dry out my papers, drawings, packages of plants, clothing, etc., and separate the still good objects from the damaged and destroyed ones. Another time, when sleep had overpowered me in the night, my rowers secretly got into my brandy and had become, before I was aware of it, so very drunk that we could not continue and had to wait until they sobered up. In some areas, a layover consisted of the mouths of the rivers flowing into the Lena and the time needed to unharness and harness the horses. At other stations, the horses, upon my arrival, were grazing on an island 8 to 10 versts away. At others, I had to use covered boats in fine weather and an open one in a terrible, stormy rain shower. Only at a very few stations did I find everything ready for a speedy continuation of my journey. In rare cases, I could travel 140 to 170 versts in 24 hours; usually I could only travel 50 to 60 versts in the same period.

The Commandant in Yakutsk was kind enough to assign a cossack to accompany me. He, however, was so stupid and useless that I sent him back after eight days. I preferred to be alone than in the company of a man who was a burden to me. Along the route ahead of me were several small market and rural towns, which I assumed would offer the best places to stop and rest because I could procure in one or the other fresh provisions.

The names and distances from one to the next:

From Yakutsk to Olekma	588 versts

From Olekma to Vitim	632
From Vitim to Kirenki	416
From Kirenki to Wercholensk	693
From Vercholensk to Irkutsk	270
	2,599 versts

On July 23rd, everything was ready for my trip to Yakutsk. I traveled to the first station overland in a low, miserable wagon, in Russian called *rospuski*. Traveling on the river with its many islands, sandbanks and bends was said to be extremely fatiguing and slow. A high, prominent sandstone rock jutting up at about the halfway point on the left bank of the Lena is called Chalanski Kamen. I found several *astragali*, which had already bloomed, that I had never seen before. The following day, I arrived at Potrofsky Monastyr or monastery, where two priests lived. The surrounding area was very picturesque. The river is covered with islands and the herds grazing on them and the huts with smoke rising from them enliven the landscape.

Between the fourth and fifth stations, Tõnari and Titori, along the river there are rugged cliffs made of horizontal, crumbling strata of limestone. Without having to use one's imagination, these cliffs have the appearance of old walls or ruins. Near the next station, Batamai, are also steep, in part isolated, cliffs (*stolbi*). The little river Stolbawoia has forced its course through them and rushes between the cliff walls as if through a gate.

The area around the station Schura I found more pleasant than many of the others. The hills rise gently and stands of trees alternate charmingly with plains. The Lena becomes considerably narrower here. It is hardly more than three versts wide and totally without islands. The opposite shore is rocky and bordered by woods. I went from the station at Malikan to Sanajachtak by horse because I was told that the boat, due to the steep shores, could not be pulled by horses and rowing was slow. The road leads over a rather high hill, from whose top one has an excellent view. I found among others the following plants:

Pediculareae
Viola, a new species
Saxifraga geifolia
Cortusa
Fumaria paeonifolia
Salicum, sp. *complures*
Polypodium fragrans
Spondylus ceramboides
Ophyrs
Caryophylacea
Spirea crenata
etc.

About seven and one-half versts below the third station from Olekma, near Charabalick, there is a rather high hill made of sandstone detritus. From a mineralogical point of view, it contains many an interesting object — among others, dark colored chalcedony, flint and petrified wood in chalcedony. On a little river, Taeba, seventy versts from the station, according to the Tungus, there is supposed to be beautiful red flint (probably carnelian).

The closer I came to the commissariat town of Olekma, the worse the post stations were. The last, Soljanka, whose name is derived from salt wells in the neighborhood, lies 25 versts from Olekma. It is known for the fact that the postilions usually run away as soon as a traveler arrives. That was also the case upon my arrival. To my greatest regret, despite all attempts and efforts, I was only able to travel 155 versts in the last four days.

On July 31st, I arrived on board a rotten boat, totally soaked, in Olekma. I was forced to spend the day there in order to dry out my clothing and papers. The commissioner, the head person in the place, gave me quarters and invited me for the evening meal. Since my departure from Yakutsk, I had hardly had a regular meal; I found that one very tasty.

Formerly, Olekma had city rights. In recent years, however, it has been turned into a commissary post and is inhabited mainly by some merchants and peasants. Hunting, fishing, raising cattle and some grain are the main sources of food. The sable from here and the Vitim sable are considered the best in all of Siberia because of their dark color and very shiny coat. They are preferred to ones from Kamtschatka even though they have a far thicker fur.

Their houses are situated on the slope of a wooded hill right next to the Lena River that is here again filled with islands covered with rich grass. The lower part of the town next to the river is often subjected to flooding and is wet the entire year. I am inclined to ascribe the intermittent fevers in the fall to this fact.

The following day I left Olekma again. Right by the town I found limestone and gypsum. I rode on horseback to the first station because the road overland is good, whereas the one by water, due to many shallow spots, is supposed to be very difficult. I found several new plants, among others a *Moraea* and *Dryas*, between the second and third station, Tscherindei and Bertimskoe. On the opposite right bank, I saw the Tolokowenoi Mountains, whose brilliant white sandstone catches the eye from afar. In Tscherindei, I sent my cossack, who had become more of a burden than a help, back to Yakutsk and continued my trip totally alone.

Upriver from Olekma, the climate seemed rawer to me than toward Yakutsk, at least the vegetation was appearing much later. The area was more mountainous and less useful for farming. The Lena River gradually becomes smaller. At a distance of 100 versts from Olekma, it is only one verst wide. Between the stations of Charatiba and Matscha, which I traveled at night, are found on the right bank of the Lena the Harp Mountains (Guslinaia Gora). These naked, bare mountains, whose side toward the river is a flat triangular surface, are made of red and green stratified marl.

On the way from Schadai to Uschagan and Schoerba, the cliff formations are very remarkable. Their picturesque appearance changes continually. Here and there cliffs in the form of pillars and towers rise up. They look exactly like old gothic ruins and seem to provide the clearest proof of their having been produced by a terrible natural convulsion or powerful explosion.

Near Nuja, about halfway from Olekma to Vitim, there begin to be fewer and fewer Yakut dwellings but more and more Russians who live from farming and cattle raising. The posts also begin to be better, so that I could travel fast farther without strife and layovers. I could only call certain individual stations bad.

Between Chamra and Jellofka, excellent, beautiful timber grows. It is used for building boats, vessels and rafts. I rode in a canoe hollowed from the trunk of a single poplar. It could carry a weight of more than 120 Russian puds. The quantities of insects that had not plagued me for a long time were intolerably irksome. From Chamra to Vitim, the land is mountainous and offers a botanist a rich harvest, for example:

Arbutus uva ursi
Arenaria
Carex
Convallaria trifolia, which is known by the name of Yakut tea
Empetrum nigrum
Fumaria paeonifolia
Hedysarum, a new species
Rubus arcticus
Salices
Saxifraga geifolia, etc.

In Peledui, the last station before Vitim, everyone was busy making hay. That notwithstanding, I obtained people, boat and horses.

The postmaster was one of the wealthiest men I met on my journey. He understood how to win the love of his fellow countrymen and affluence by good behavior and orderliness.

From Peledui to Vitim, traveling by water is difficult, by land almost impossible. At sundown I reached the spot (*sloboda*) that is usually called a town without, however, having the right to be called one. It lies straight across from the mouth of a river of the same name (Vitim) on a flat point of land right on the Lena River. That is the reason that it is subject to floods almost every year. Sloboda Vitim has one hundred houses, a wooden church and somewhat more than six hundred inhabitants. They live partially from farming, partially from cattle raising, but mostly from hunting sable. The sable hunters usually go out at the end of August, taking a year's provisions with them. They row up the Vitim River to the area of the large lake Aron or Oronne. It is 25 versts long and eight versts wide, lies on the left bank of the river and is said to be 800 versts from Vitim.

Sable prices vary greatly. A couple of the worst pelts can sometimes be bought for fifteen to twenty rubles; pelts, however, that are completely black and have a truly shiny, satin coat cost seventy to eighty rubles.*

The place seemed to me to be very poor, because I looked all over the place and was not able to obtain coppers for 5 rubles Banco Assignation.[1]

Near Vitim, there are supposed to be saline springs and alabaster of excellent quality is quarried.

In addition to the plants already listed on the way to Olekma, I found:

Pulmonaria sibirica	*Thalictrum alpinum*
Hedysarum flore rubro	*Anemone narcissiflora*
Potentilla fruticosa	*Cypripedium macranthos*
Lycopodium	*Cypripedium guttatum*
Lychnis	*Pedicularis*

---

*For more information about Vitim sable and the way they are caught, see Krascheninnikoff's *Beschreibung des Landes Kamtschatka* [Description of Kamtschatka], page 132, the 7th main section.

Aquilegia alpina
Astragali
Polemonium lanatum
Actaea spicata
Carices
etc.

Late on the evening of August 8th, I left Vitim and arrived that night in Schuja, the first station on the right bank of the Lena where only Russians live and no Yakuts. Along the shore of the Lena from Vitim, several villages are situated not far from each other. Fishing is more productive than on the lower Lena, where the river bed spreads out for miles and makes fishing difficult. Cattle raising and farming flourish. The hilly country found along the first fifty versts consists, in part, of red and black schist with quartz and, in part, of hard sandstone with layers of limestone, which have been displaced sometimes horizontally, sometimes at various angles. The plants that especially caught my eye along the way are:

Cheiranthus, a new species
Spirea lobata
Euphorbia
Alyssum montanum
Anemone
etc.

Parschinskoe, the third station 69 versts from Vitim, is notable for its location near stinking springs. Several springs containing rotten egg gas bubble quite noisily from the rocks. The water itself foams a great deal, gives off sulfur sinter and tastes salty. The inhabitants heal rashes with it and even send the water to Irkutsk.

Between the stations of Dubrowa and Tschestue, the valley of the Lena becomes narrower and narrower and the cliffs on both sides become steeper and higher. About ten versts from the latter is a truly narrow pass that the Lena River seems to have carved between the cliffs. The steep cliffs or walls along the shore are called Schtschoki, especially three of them, two on the right bank and one on the left bank of the river. The river is very narrow and, therefore, at several places rapid. Navigation is dangerous. That part is never traveled at night. Those *schtschoki*, whose rock consists mainly of a fine limestone mixed with sandstone and are enlivened by a quantity of swallows, are living proof for a violent natural convulsion sometime in the past. Here, shapeless columns loom up; there, one catches sight of fearful, collapsed, rocky ruins or widely overhanging cliffs threatening soon to fall. Here are steeply rising walls; there grottos and caves resounding muffled echoes — objects suitable for a picturesque trip, the most beautiful picture of wild and rugged nature. A botanist wishing to hike leisurely through these varied mountains would certainly find rich rewards worth his effort between the above-named station and the next two stations, Gartschanowa and Mudinsk. Among the most noteworthy flowers of the area, although I found some had already bloomed, I count:

a *Liliacea* previously unknown to me
Androsace villosa
Phlox sibirica
Valeriana rupestrum
Cheiranthus
Geranii, two species
Rhododendron ferrugineum
Dryas octopetala
Anemone narcissiflorus
Lichenes
Betula nana
Salices
etc.

Grotschanowa has a pleasant and advantageous location. The inhabitants raise cattle and plant grain. They own, among other animals, sheep from whose wool they knit socks, and pigs, which I had not seen anywhere along the way from Yakutsk. Many Reindeer Tungus camp in the neighboring highlands. I was struck by the large number of inhabitants with scrofula. Future observers during a longer stay can perhaps find the particular cause of that disease.

One of the largest and most populous spots is Sploschnoi (84 versts from Kirengi).[2] It lies on the right bank of the Lena, has over fifty houses, a Crown storehouse for salt, a church with two priests. On the continuation of my journey from there, it seemed to me that the shores of the river were more populated by far. Almost every five to ten versts there are houses, mills, large and small villages and church parishes, some with very pleasant and advantageous locations. One beautiful landscape after another appeared and disappeared, so that it seemed to me that I was seeing that picturesque scenery in a phantasmagoria.

In that area, the highlands along the shores look totally like primeval hills and consist mostly of limestone deposits with hornstone. Early on the morning of August 12th, I reached the little town of Kirenka after having discovered the following plants at the previous two stations:

Atragene alpina
Potentilla nive
Saxifraga bronchialis
Mitella nuda
Marchantia conica
Sambucus racemosa
Astragalus frutescens
Arbutus alpina and
Arbutus uva ursi
Geranium
Draba
Asplenium
Lichenes
etc.

In vain did I try all over the place to have a 25-ruble Banco Assignation changed into copper money — clear proof of the poverty of the place.

The little town lies on the right bank of the Lena, where it unites with the Kirenka. Nearby, I found striped jasper, sandstone and limestone moraine. The town has several churches and a small, unsightly wooden shop. The town of Kirenka is only distinguished from a village by the presence of a not very large commando of soldiers stationed there. Because of bad horses and even worse post servants, who forced me to lay over and wait a long time, I only could set out again late in the afternoon.

The trip from Kirensk to Wercholensk, 693 versts, went so smoothly that I hardly found time to make any observations or write anything down. Because of the well equipped post stations, I found to my greatest joy that it took me five days to make the trip.

The shores of the Lena are very cultivated and enlivened by a number of villages and houses. In Markofski, 125 versts from Kirenka, a governmental agency (*pravlenie*) was established not very long ago that reports to the Governor in Yakutsk. The inhabitants are very dissatisfied with it. The place is quite large, has one church and a Crown storehouse for grain, whose special purpose is to support newly settled peasants with seed and food grain in case of need, because it is very common for them almost yearly to lose larger or smaller parts of the one or the other in the floods that occur almost yearly. The grain fields were just full of grain and ready for cutting. Rye, wheat and barley grow very well. It is too bad that the lower meadows and fields are often flooded with earth and sand and made unusable for several years. It is strange enough that the inhabitants, despite the damage they suffer so often, nevertheless, begin every time anew to work the low-lying shore areas.

Early on the morning of the 14th, I arrived in Ustkuta. From there, the Lena is navigable by large merchant vessels which draw a Russian ell (*arschin*) of water. That is why all goods coming from Wercholensk are loaded into smaller boats and the goods coming from Yakutsk are loaded onto transport boats. Part of the goods are transported on the Lena to Wercholensk and part over a small stretch of land of about one hundred versts to Ilimsk and then on the Angara and other rivers to Jenissei and other places. The location of Omoloi, the next station after Ustkuta, is less advantageous for growing grain than many of the previous ones and the ones after it. Not even barley ripens there. The hills are high, stony and wooded. One sees little land that can be cultivated. The inhabitants are forced to do more hunting and trade the many good gray squirrels they catch to their neighbors for grain.

In the following days, I continued by journey, sometimes on the water and sometimes on land. Late on the evening of the 16th, I reached Wercholensk, the site of a rather large garrison. It has about 200 to 300 houses and lies on the right bank of the Lena River. Up-river, there is hardly a station, that is until Katschuck, that can be reached by boat.

Even though I had firmly intended to continue my journey late in the evening, I stayed the night upon the advice of the Commissioner Mr. Scheweleff, who had welcomed me most politely. He told me the road overland was horrible and at night almost impossible to travel on. He said that traveling on the water was only possible in little, very flat boats. Because of the many bends in the river, going by water would mean the loss of a great deal of time.

Very early on the 17th, I set out on horseback over the land route. I found extraordinarily steep, barely climbable mountains. Tired, I reached the next station, Katschuck, 30 versts away. There, for the last time, I was ferried across the Lena, now a very insignificant stream.

From Katschuck to Irkutsk, a distance of 196 versts, there is a post carriage with which one can reach the capital of Siberia in 24 hours.

The Bratski or Buriats, a people of Mongolian origin, live in that area. In general, they are more robust than the Yakuts. The Bratski wear long, wide, nightgown-like clothes trimmed with fur with a sash around their waists. Part of them are nomadic and live in felt yurts; others that have settled along the road speak Russian and live in small wooden houses built in the Russian manner. Their main source of food is cattle raising. Only a few of them raise crops.

The closer I got to the capital, the greater the number and size of the Russian villages, some of which had 200 to 300 houses. The fields were sowed with rye, barley, oats and hemp.

About eight versts from Irkutsk, I found myself on a little hill, which gave me an excellent view. The valley of the Angara and the governmental town of Irkutsk lay before me. The latter, with its many stone churches with shining cupolas and towers, gave me the impression that I would find splendor and wealth there. The quantities of miserable wooden huts upon my approach erased that impression for the most part.

On August 18th, I arrived in Irkutsk and was given quarters in the home of the agent for the Russian-American Company. I had gone to him with a letter of recommendation. Even though in all of Siberia there are, properly speaking, no inns or hotels, it is never difficult for a traveler to find quarters with someone, even a slight acquaintance, that is, if the traveler has his own bed along.

Irkutsk lies on the right bank of fast flowing, crystal clear Angara River. Its streets are wide, for the most part, regular, but unpaved. The houses are mainly of wood, but there are some, especially the government buildings and churches, made of stone. It is supposed to have about 30,000 inhabitants, over 30 churches and two cloisters. Since it is the seat of government, the Governor General,* the Civil Governor, Vice Governor, the City Commander, a City Captain and an archbishop are stationed there, as well as a number of high servants of the Crown.

Among the public buildings the following are noteworthy: the bazaar or market shops (*gostinnoi dvor*), whose buildings are roomy and made of stone. The secondary school has a library containing several thousand volumes and a mineral and shell collection. Curious it is, that, on the order of Her late Highness Empress Catherine II, Japanese is taught there with a native of Japan as teacher. As small as the theater is, its existence deems it worthy of mention. It presents little national Russian plays not all that badly. There is a large workhouse or prison outside the city. And not very far from it, an admiralty which ships a number of things needed for Crown ships to Ochotsk and which are also intended for navigation on Lake Baikal. The construction of a large public hospital was almost finished. The Crown apothecary shop is large and in very good condition. The present apothecary has been given garden land for growing authorized plants. It is too bad that he derives little or no advantage from it due to lack of time and people. A medical police station (*uprava*) exists, at least in name. It employs an inspector, surgeon and accoucheur. Perhaps someone else knows what they do more than I. Oh, how many useful things could be done by a man with head and heart in such a place? As long as the higher powers do not try to appoint scientif-

---

*The present Governor General is Privy Councilor and Senator von Pestel. He had left on the morning of my arrival to go to Tomsk and Tobolsk.

ic men, who work industriously in their field out there, that area will know nothing of the many advantages and the sciences of many a worth-while observation.

The city of Irkutsk carries on considerable trade. It is the collection point for all of the furs from America and the eastern part of Asia. At the same time, it is the depot for all the goods going from Russia by way of Kiachta to China and by way of Ochotsk to Kamtschatka and America or coming from there. For this reason, a European can find for money almost anything he would consider a necessity in his fatherland, indeed, that most excellent foreign wines were available during my stay at a very cheap price.*

The inhabitants' way of living has many a peculiarity. One finds many Oriental customs and little sociability. In general, inhabitants of all ranks mistrust each other. A foreigner seldom gets to see wives and daughters of the leading citizens, except at feasts, balls, weddings and christenings or in the churches. There are numbers of exiles or unhappy ones who enjoy complete freedom here. Among them are several who have acquired considerable fortunes through their industry. Among those men, I met the most skillful artists and craftsmen of all kinds.

Irkutsk lies below 52° N latitude; therefore, it is not in a very rugged climate. The summer is pleasant, and a stay in that part of Siberia is by far not so terrible as many people imagine. The surrounding areas produce grain in abundance. And, if one can do without luxury goods, one can live cheaply.

The format and length of this book does not allow for me to relate the rest of my journey as it stands in my journal. Furthermore, on a quick trip in winter like mine, I could note down only a few things which have not already been described in more detail by other more careful travelers. After spending a few days in Irkutsk, I set out on August 28, 1807, for the Russian-Chinese border town of Kiachta.** I returned from

---

*That a lot of things have changed since then is without doubt true, since, at present in St. Petersburg, far poorer wines than the ones sold at that time in Irkutsk are twice as expensive.

**The latest and most exact news about the Chinese-Russian border and Kiachta can be found in a very interesting work: *Archiv für Litteraturgeschichte und Sprachkunde* [Archive for the History of Literature and Philology] by Julius von Klaproth, St. Petersburg, 1810, 4.1 Bd., page 159.

there to Irkutsk again on September 12th. My eye was now set on reaching St. Petersburg. Since I had so much baggage, I was advised to wait until I could use sledges. In autumn with wet weather and bad roads, I would not be able to travel fast anyway. I had to listen to reason and, therefore, did not leave Irkutsk until November 22nd with the first train of sledges. All travelers found the post stations all over Siberia equipped to their satisfaction.

On November 27th, I reached Crasnojarsk, a rather regularly built city, on the Jenissei River in a fertile and charming area. It has about 500 houses and four churches. It is noteworthy for me for several reasons, especially since it was here that Chamberlain von Resanoff died in March 1807. I had just arrived at the quarters assigned me by the police when I was honored by a visit from the captain of the town soldiery, Councilor Keller. He made me all the happier when I heard that he came from Frankfurt. I stayed the night in Crasnojarsk and ate in the evening with my fellow countryman. Early on the 28th, I visited the grave of Mr. von Resanoff. It is marked by a large, altar-shaped stone without inscription.

On December 1st, I found myself in the government town of Tomsk. A few days later I traveled across the Barabinski Steppes, where almost every summer a terrible cattle disease raises havoc. My friend Bojanus, professor of veterinary medicine in Vilna, has just determined it to be anthrax.

On December 11th, I arrived in Tobolsk, the former capital of Siberia, where I made the interesting acquaintance of Mr. von Pestel, the former Governor General of the three provinces, Irkutsk, Tomsk and Tobolsk. He received me most cordially. I was honored by the true empathy and attention he gave to my observations about the remotest parts of his administrative territory, especially Kamtschatka. I accepted his friendly invitation and stayed longer in Tobolsk than I had planned. The days I spent with his amiable family are among the most pleasant I have had in a long time. For a traveler who had spent several years among savages, the acquaintance with such an excellent and educated woman as the wife of the Governor General had to have a very beneficial effect — this all will gladly accept as the truth. Not without feelings of regret and gratitude, I departed on February 22, 1808, from that honorable couple and continued my journey.[3]

On March 1st, I arrived in the beautiful city of Kasan, on the 8th in the noteworthy city of Moscow and finally on the 16th of the month in St. Petersburg. Here, for the first time, I got to know this magnificent Imperial city after having traveled through the vast Russian Empire from east to west.

Notes

1. Banco Assignation refers to the assignats or paper money used by various European countries in this period. In Langsdorff's time Russian assignats had fallen to about one-fifth of their face value.

2. Note Langsdorff's variations in spellings: Kirengi, Kirenka, Kirensk, a reflection of the Russian case endings he was hearing.

3. Ivan Borisovich Pestel (1765-1843) was governor-general of Siberia from 1806 to 1818.

APPENDIX

Weights and Measures

Langsdorff's *Remarks and Observations* attest well to the fact that before the introduction of the metric system there was no unified international system for weights and measures. Langsdorff changes his as he moves around the world. The retention of German words (*fuss*, *unze*, *zoll*) in the translation are to make the reader aware of the variations, i.e., that *zoll* is not always an inch or a *pfund* a pound as we know them today, that dictionaries and other sources do not always agree upon equivalents. Pity the merchants, scientists and ordinary travelers of that day: 100 English yards equaled 137.102 Prussian ells but at Prussian fairs 8 yards were reckoned equal to 11 Prussian ells, but one French ell equaled 1½ English ells or 1½ yards or two Brabant ells. Most of the information given here is found in *A Dictionary of English and German Language* by Chr. Fr. Grieb (Philadelphia: Schaeffer & Koradi, 1866) and in *The Shipmaster's Assistant and Owner's Manual* (London: David Steele, 1796).

ACKER (acre): 1 U.S. or English acre equals 160 square rods or 25.293 square meters. The German *acker* varied from place to place. In Saxony 300 square *ruten* equaled 55.34 *acker*; in Hesse 150 *ruten* equaled 23.87 *acker*. *Ruten* varied in length from 10 to 14 *fuss* or more, or approximately 3.6 meters.

ARROBA: A Spanish measure Langsdorff says equals 25 *pfund*, approximately 24 U.S. or English pounds or 11.52 kilograms.

ARSHIN: A Russian measure of length varying from 28 to 39 inches or 71.1 centimeters to approximately 1 meter.

ELL: At one time German lands had 132 different ones. A Prussian *ell* equals 25.5 *zoll* or .6669 meters. A Russian *ell* equals one *arshin*.

FADEN: Seven *fuss* equal 3 *arshin* or 6.99 U.S. feet or 2.131 meters. An English fathom equals 6 feet or 1.83 meters.

FANEGA: A Castilian *fanega* equals 1.56 U.S. bushels.

FASS: One Hamburg *fass* equals 1.56 U.S. bushels.

FUSS (foot): A Dutch foot equals 11 U.S. inches or 27.94 centimeters. A Parisian (*pied de roi*) equals 12 *pouces* or 1.07 U.S. feet. A Prussian *fuss* equals 12 *zoll* or 144 lines or 1.13 U.S. feet or 34.44 centimeters.

GALLON: The English imperial gallon equals 4.546 liters; the U.S. standard equals 3.785 liters.

KLAFTER: The Prussian *klafter* equals 6.18 U.S. feet or 1.88 meters. See *FADEN*, English fathom.

KNOT: This is a unit of speed equal to one nautical mile or about 1.15 statute miles per hour. A knot equals 47 feet 3 inches U.S. on a log line marked off by knots. See mile.

LEGOA: In Rio de Janeiro 1 *legoa* equals 6.6 kilometers or 4.1 U.S. miles.

MASS: It varies in size, but is approximately 1.5 liters. A Bremen *mass* equals .42 gallons U.S.

MILE:

a) An English statute mile equals 1,609.315 meters. There are 69.042 of these miles to 1 degree of the equator.

b) A Prussian mile equals 4.68 U.S. miles or 7.53 kilometers.

c) An Italian mile (*miglia*) equals .92 U.S. miles.

d) A sea mile equals a nautical or geographical mile or 6,080 feet U.S. It is now standardized to equal 6,076.1033 feet U.S. or 1.852 kilometers. It is the 60th part of a degree of the equator.

PFUND (pound):

a) An English or U.S. pound equals 16 ounces or 454 grams.

b) A Prussian *pfund* equals 1.03 pounds U.S.

c) A Russian pound equals 9.03 pounds U.S.

PUD (pl. *PUDY*): A *pud* is 40 Russian pounds or 36.07 pounds U.S. or about 16.5 kilograms.

RI: A Japanese *ri* equals 2.43 to 2.56 U.S. miles or about 3.91 kilometers. 26.95 *ri* measure a mean degree of the meridian.

SCHUH (shoe): At Frankfurt am Main a shoe equals 12 *zoll* or 144 lines or .28 meters or .92 feet U.S. See *FUSS*.

TOISE: A French *toise* equals 6 *pieds* (see *FUSS*) or 1.949 meters.

UNZE (ounce): See *PFUND*.

VERST: A Russian *verst* equals .663 miles U.S. or 1.067 kilometers.

ZOLL: See *FUSS*.

ALPHABETICAL LIST OF SUBSCRIBERS[1]

	German Type	Latin
His Royal Majesty the Reigning Grand Duke of Baden	3	
His Royal Highness Friedrich, Margrave of Baden	1	
Her Royal Highness the Margravine of Baden	1	
His Noble Lordship Franz, Count to Erbach-Erbach	1	
His Royal Majesty the Reigning Grand Duke of Hesse	1	
Her Royal Majesty of the Reigning Grand Duchess of Hesse	1	2
His Royal Highness the Grand Crown Prince of Hesse	1	
Her Royal Highness the Grand Crown Princess of Hesse	1	
His Royal Highness Georg, Prince to Hesse	1	
His Serene Highness Wilhelm, Prince Elector of Hesse	1	
Her Serene Highness the Princess Elector of Hesse, née Princess of Prussia	1	
His Grace Friedrich, Landgrave to Hesse	1	
His Grace Christian, Landgrave of Hesse	1	
His Grace the Landgrave of Hesse-Homburg	1	
His Serene Highness Louis, Prince of Hesse-Homburg, Imperial Prussian General Major	1	
His Grace the Count of Hesse-Rheinfels-Rothenburg	1	
His Serene Highness Carl, Prince to Hohenlohe-Langenburg	1	
His Serene Highness the Reigning Prince to Isenburg	1	
His Highness Heinrich Ferdinand, Count to Isenburg-Philippseich	1	
Her Serene Highness Dowager Princess Kinsky, née Countess of Harrach		1
His Serene Highness Emich Carl, Prince to Leiningen	1	
His Serene Highness the Prince to Löwenstein	1	
His Noble Highness Friedrich Carl, Count to Löwenstein	1	
His Noble Grace the Reigning Duke of Mecklenburg-Strelitz	1	
His Grace the Reigning Duke of Nassau	1	
Her Grace the Reigning Duchess of Nassau	1	

	German	Latin
His Serene Highness the Reigning Prince of Nassau	1	
His Serene Highness the Crown Prince of Nassau	1	
His Royal Highness Max, Prince to Wied-Neuwied	1	
His Imperial Highness Anton, Archduke of Austria	1	
His Imperial Highness Johann, Archduke of Austria	1	
His Royal Highness Ludwig, Crown Prince of Oettingen-Wallerstein, Royal Bavarian Crown Tutor to the Court		1
Her Royal Highness the Princess of Orange-Nassau	1	
Her Royal Highness the Dowager Princess of Orange-Nassau	1	
His Royal Majesty Friedrich Wilhelm III, King of Prussia	6	
His Royal Highness Friedrich Wilhelm, Crown Prince of Prussia	1	
His Royal Highness Wilhelm, Prince of Prussia (Son of His Royal Majesty)	1	
His Royal Highness Carl, Prince of Prussia (Son of His Royal Majesty)		1
His Royal Highness Wilhelm, Prince of Prussia (Brother of His Royal Majesty)	1	
His Royal Highness Friedrich, Prince of Prussia (Son of the deceased Prince Louis)	1	
His Royal Highness August, Prince of Prussia	1	
Her Royal Highness Ferdinand, Princess of Prussia		1
His Grace August, Reigning Duke to Saxe-Gotha and Altenburg	1	
His Serene Highness Friedrich, Prince to Saxe-Gotha and Altenburg	1	
His Royal Highness Albert, Duke to Saxe-Teschen	1	
His Grace Carl August, Reigning Duke of Saxe-Weimar, Eisenach, etc.		1
Her Grace Louise, Reigning Duchess of Saxe-Weimar, Eisenach, etc.	1	
Her Imperial Majesty Maria Pavlovna, Grand Duchess of Russia, Crown Princess of Saxe-Weimar, Eisenach, etc.	1	
His Serene Highness the Prince of Schaumberg	1	
Her Royal Majesty the Queen of Sweden, née Princess of Baden	1	
His Serene Highness Prosper, Prince of Sinzendorf	1	
His Grace Friedrich, Count to Solms-Laubach		1
His Grace the Count of Solms-Rödelheim	1	
Her Grace Countess Tascher, née Princess of Leiningen	1	
His Royal Majesty Friedrich I, King of Würtemberg	1	

	German	Latin
Aachen[2]		
Doctor of Medicine Lesoinne	1	
Altenburg		
Commercial Councilor A. Reichenbach	1	
Privy Councilor Geutebrück		1
Amsterdam		
Mr. Müller and Co., Booksellers	2	
Mr. Jean Calkoen		1
Aschaffenburg		
His Excellency the President Count zu Elz	1	
Mr. C. C. Ettlinger, Bookseller	1	
Mr. August Fischer, Court Chaplain	1	
Ballenstadt		
The Ducal Library	1	
Berlin		
Privy Councilor l'Abaye	1	
Privy Secretary Bratring	1	
General Lieutenant von l'Estocq	1	
Mr. Joh. Carl Fisher	2	
His Excellency Count von der Goltz, State and Cabinet Minister	1	
His Excellency State Councilor Baron von Hardenberg	1	
Baron von Hertefeld, District Magistrate	1	
Privy Councilor von Heydeboeck	1	
Mr. F. C. Hitzig, Bookseller	2	
His Excellency Count von Kalkreuth, General Field Marshall and Governor	1	1
Privy Councilor von Klewitz	1	
His Excellency Count von Lieven, Imperial Russian Ambassador	1	
General Major Count von Lottum	1	
Mr. August Mylius, Bookseller	1	
Imperial Russian Privy Councilor von Oubriel	1	
Professor and Doctor of Medicine Reich	1	
His Excellency the 44th Count Reuß	1	
Privy Councilor Sack	1	
Privy Councilor von Schuckmann	1	
Privy Councilor von Stägemann	1	
Imperial Russian Collegiate Assessor von Strandmann	1	
His Excellency General Lieutenant von Tauentzin	1	

	German	Latin
Biebrich		
Mr. L. Langsdorff, Head of the Office for General Ducal Military Administration	1	
Braunschweig		
Mr. J. W. Huyssen van Kattendyke, former Privy Councilor of His deceased Grace, Duke of Braunschweig	1	
The School Bookstore	2	
His Excellency Count von Schulenburg, President of the Estate for the Kingdom of Westphalia, Knight of the Westphalian Crown	1	
Mr. W. A. von Spiegel, Baron zum Diesenberg auf Seggerde, Maltese Knight of the Order of St. John and Cathedral Canon in Halberstadt	1	
Count von Veltheim	1	
Bremen		
Mr. Eberh. Delius	1	
Doctor Focke	1	
Mr. Conrad Hagedorn	1	
Mr. J. M. Lameyer	1	
Professor Mertens	1	
Mr. J. E. Pavenstedt	1	
Mr. J. D. Shepeler	1	
Mr. Tatjenhorst	1	
Dr. C. L. Treviranus	1	
Breslau		
Mr. Wilh. Gottl. Korn, Bookseller	2	
Mr. Joh. Friedr. Korn, Bookseller	2	
Brody		
Mayor Gruber	1	
Burtscheidt		
Mr. Abraham Königs		1
Carlsruhe (Karlsruhe)		
His Excellency Baron von Andlaw, the Minister of the Interior for Baden	1	
His Excellency Baron von Gayling, the Minister of Finance for Baden	1	
Her Grace Countess von Hochberg	2	
The Worthy Museum	1	
Cassel (Kassel)		
Councilor Grandidier	1	
Tourneisen & Son, Booksellers	1	

	German	Latin
Chemnitz		
Mr. Christ. Gottfr. Becker		1
The Brothers Hübner & Sons		1
The Brothers Krause	1	
Superintendent Unger	1	
Coburg		
The Ducal Library		1
Mr. Joh. Daniel Meusel, Bookseller	1	
Cologne		
Mr. Esser, Judge in Canton Weiden		1
Mr. Conrad Jacob Moll		1
The Keil Bookstore		1
Dessau		
Mr. C. R. Illing	1	
Dorpat		
Otto, Count van Stackelberg, Lieutenant and Knight of the Order of St. George		1
Dresden		
Councilor Dr. Althof		1
The Royal Saxon Library	1	
Baron von Block, Royal Saxon Privy Councilor	1	
Privy Councilor Böttiger	1	
General von Emmerich auf Kreischa	1	
The Hilscher Bookstore	1	
His Excellency Royal Saxon Conference Minister, Count Hohenthal Königsbrück	1	
Major von Olsuffief auf Niederpoyritz	1	
First Chaplain to the Court Dr. Reinhardt	1	
Eibigheim		
Pastor Franz Mohrenhofen	1	
Erfurt		
Mr. Georg Adam Keyser, Bookseller	1	
Eupen		
Mr. Adam Römer, Arnold's Son	1	
Frankfurt am Main		
Mr. Daniel Andreae		1
Mr. J. C. Andreae	1	
The Andreae Bookstore	2	
Mr. Aubin Claus	1	
Mr. C. W. Bansa	1	
Mr. Remmy Bansa	1	

	German	Latin
His Excellency Minister Baron von Barkhaus	1	
Mr. Carl Beck	1	
Mr. Dominicus Behrends	1	
Mr. J. D. Bernard	1	
Mr. Moritz von Bethmann, Imperial Russian Privy Councilor		1
Mr. Joh. Anton Bolongaro Crevenna	1	
Mr. Bernh. Brentano	1	
Mr. Brentano Walz	1	
Mr. Wilh. Busch	1	
Mr. J. H. Catoir, Father	1	
Mr. Anton Christ	1	
Mr. Joh. Noe du Fay	1	
His Excellency Baron von Eberstein, the Minister and State Secretary	1	
His excellency Baron von Ende, the Ambassador for Saxe-Gotha		1
Mr. Joh. Jac. Ettling	1	
Mr. Constantin Fellner	1	
Mr. Max Fingerlin	1	
Mr. Joh. Noe Gogel	1	
Mr. Alexander Gontard, Senior		1
Mr. Franz Gontard	1	
Mr. A. Goullet	1	
Doctor Grambs	1	
Mr. Andr. Grunelius	1	
Mr. Ph. Heir. Guilhaumann, Bookseller	1	
Prefect F. M. von Günderode	1	
Mr. J. L. Günther	1	
Mr. von Haack	1	
His Excellency the Royal Prussian Ambassador von Hänlein		1
His Excellency General Lieutenant von Hahn	1	
Mr. R. Hebenstreit		1
The Hermann Bookstore	2	
Mr. F. C. Hess		1
Mr. G. Heyder	1	
Doctor Hiepe		1
Mr. George von Holzhausen		1
Privy Councilor von Itzstein, the Director of Police	1	
Doctor Kappes	1	
Mr. C. F. Kellner	1	
Mr. J. Ph. Kessler	1	
Mr. Bernh. Körner, Bookseller	1	
Mr. Daniel Köster	1	

	German	Latin
Madame Kraus	1	
Mr. J. A. Kuntz	1	
Mr. J. Ph. Leerse, Sarasin	1	
Mr. Carl von Leonhardi	1	
Baron von Leykam	1	
Mr. G. W. Lindheimer	1	
Mr. Joh. Dav. Mack	1	
Mr. F. A. Mainoni de Peter	1	
Mr. C. B. Metzler	1	
Mr. J. Fr. Metzler		1
Mr. Anton Meyer	1	
Mr. J. G. Meyer	1	
Major E. von Meyer	1	
Mr. Mühl	1	
Mr. Heinrich Mülhens	1	
Mr. J. Theodor Mülhens	1	
Mr. J. C. Müller	1	
Mr. Wilh. Mumm Rübel	1	
Mr. Mumm Scheibler	1	
Mr. J. Nestle	1	
Mr. Fr. Osterrieth	1	
Pastor Passavant	1	
Mr. Berhh. Pensa	1	
Privy Councilor von Plitt		1
Mr. M von Riese	1	
Mr. J. M. Sarasin	1	
Mr. Georg Schepeler	1	
Mr. Joh. Schmidt	1	
Mr. J. D. Schmid	1	
Mr. J. F. Schmidt	1	
Mr. Joh. Dietr. Schmöle	1	
Mr. J. C. Schnerr	1	
Mr. Friedr. Schönemann		1
Baron von Seckendorff	1	
Mr. Sintzheim, Director of the Lottery	1	
Mr. C. C. Souchay	1	
Mr. Joh. Stern	1	
Mr. Carl Sues	1	
Narrentrapp & Son, Booksellers	2	
Baron von Vrints Berberich, State Councilor and the Director of the Central Post Office	1	
His Excellency Count of Westphalia	1	
Baron von Wiesenhütten	1	
Colonel Baron von Wiesenhütten	1	
Mr. Ph. Chr. Zickwolff	1	

	German	Latin
His Excellency General Lieutenant von Zweyer	1	
Freiburg im Breisgau		
Count von Henning, Grand Ducal Court Councilor		3
Baden-Freiburg in Saxony		
Craz & Gerlach, Booksellers	1	
Mr. Hoffman	1	
Mr. Meuder, Assessor for the Board of Mines	1	
Mining Superintendent Werner	1	
Fürstenau		
The Count's Erbach Library		1
Görlitz		
Doctor von Anton	1	
Gotha		
The Ducal Library	1	
His Excellency Count von Hardenberg, Privy Councilor and Marshall in Altenburg	1	
Doctor of Medicine Heydenrich		1
Mr. B. A. von Lindenau, Chamberlain and Councilor of the Exchequer	1	
Göttingen		
Mr. Carl Becker, Student of Cameralistics	1	
Mr. J. F. Dankwerts, Bookseller	1	
Mr. Heinr. Dietrich, Bookseller	1	
Count von Plessen auf Ivenack	1	
Greifswalde		
Mr. C. Mauritius, Bookseller	1	
Halle		
Messrs. Hemmerde and Schwetschke, Booksellers	1	
The Renger Bookstore	2	
Hamburg		
Mr. Carl Ernst Bohn, Bookseller	3	
Mr. J. F. Edlefse	1	
The Worthy Hamburg Society for the Advancement of Useful Arts and Trade	1	
Mr. J. G. Hanff, Bookseller	17	
Licentiate Heise	1	
Mr. R. Carl Janssen	1	
Mr. Joh. Heinr. Nagant	1	
Doctor Math. Paulsen	1	
Mr. Fr. Perthes, Bookseller	12	
Doctor Jac. Schleiden	1	

	German	Latin
Mr. Georg Schuback	1	
Mr. G. H. Schünemann	1	
Mr. J. C. Sievers	1	
Mr. Georg Wolbrecht	1	
Hanau		
Mr. von Motz, Privy Councilor and the Chamber President, Knight of the Hessian Order of the Lion	1	
Hanover		
The Brothers Hahn, Booksellers	4	
Heidelberg		
Mr. Kessler, Major of the Grand Duchy of Baden	1	
Mohr & Zimmer, Booksellers	4	
Hildburgshausen		
Government Assessor Döhner	1	
Privy Registrar G. Fr. Kesselring	1	
Hirschberg		
District Administrator Klotz	1	
Hof		
Mr. G. A. Grau, Bookseller	1	
Kiel		
The University Library	1	
Privy Councilor David Reinh. von Sievers from Livonia, Knight of the Imperial Russian Order of St. Anne, First Class	1	
Königsberg		
Mr. A. W. Unzer, Bookseller	1	
Lahr		
Vice Chancellor Langsdorff	4	
The Worthy Theological Diocesan Reading Society	1	
Mr. Conrad Schmidt	1	
Landshut		
The Royal Bavarian University Library		1
Mr. Ph. Krüll, University Bookseller		1
Leipzig		
Mr. Chr. W. Vegel, Bookseller	1	
Lüneburg		
Herold & Wahlstab, Booksellers	1	

	German	Latin
Magdeburg		
The Creutz Bookstore	2	
Fr. Wilh., Count von der Schulenburg	1	
His Excellency Former Prussian State and Cabinet Minister Kehnert	1	
Mannheim		
Mr. Dom. Artaria	3	
Count von Clam-Gallus, Chamberlain and Knight of the Order of St. Leopold	1	
Marburg		
The Worthy Library		1
Meinungen		
The Ducal Library		1
Münster		
Privy Councilor Kottmeyer	1	
Neustadt an der Hardt		
The Worthy Reading Society	1	
Nordhausen		
Mr. J. Ad. Nitzsche, Bookseller	4	
Offenbach		
Mr. Joh. Friedr. Boehm		1
Mr. Heinrich Kirschten	1	
Privy Councilor Dr. Meyer	1	
Mr. Simon Reininger		1
Mr. Heinr. Wilh. Schwaner	1	
Mr. Joseph Speier		1
Mr. Wilh. Speier	1	
Mr. Bernh. Walter	1	
Paris		
Mr. G. F. Pannifex	3	
Planitz		
Mr. C. von Arnim		1
Prague		
The Calv Bookstore	1	
Rödelheim		
Mr. Kugler	1	
Justice Councilor Doctor Hoffmann	1	

	German	Latin
Rudolstadt		
Privy Councilor von Ketelhodt	1	
Schafhausen		
His Excellency Mr. von Arand, the Royal Ambassador for Würtemberg Switzerland, Commander of the Order of the Civil Service and Vice Director of the High Tribunal in Tübingen	1	
The Royal Reading Society at the Kaufleutstube	1	
The Worthy Reading Society at the Sternen	1	
Schneeberg		
Chamberlain and Head Forester von Lindenau	1	
Sondershausen		
The Princely Library		1
Strasbourg		
Mr. Friedr. Dournay		1
Mr. J. R. Frank		1
Mr. G. Fr. Klose		1
Mr. G. L. Müntz		2
Mr. Schmalzigang		1
Mr. Steinheil		1
Treuttel & Würtz, Booksellers		2
Mr. G. L. Wagner		1
Mr. F. Wagner		1
Stuttgart		
The Royal Würtemberg Library		1
Court Physician Dr. Klein		1
Mr. Franz Chr. Loeflund, Bookseller	1	
Mr. J. B. Metzler, Bookseller	1	
Sülz		
Councilor Koch	1	
Ulm		
The Stettin Bookstore	3	
Usingen		
Forester von Fürstenrecht	1	
Warsaw		
Mr. J. A. Willink	1	
Weilburg		
The Worthy Government	1	
Weimar		
Privy Councilor Wieland	1	

	German	Latin
Countess Henkel von Donnersmark, née Countess Lepel		1
Vienna		
His Excellency Anton, Count von Appony, Imperial Royal Austrian Chamberlain, Privy Councilor and Commander of the Imperial Royal Order of Leopold		1
Moritz, Count von Fries, Imperial Royal Knight of the Order of Leopold	1	1
His Excellency Carl, Count von Harrach, Imperial Royal Austrian Chamberlain, German Heraldic Consultant and Doctor of Medical Science		1
His Excellency Count von Metternich Winneburg, the Imperial Royal Austrian State and Conference Minister and Minister for Foreign Affairs		1
Andreas, Count von Rasumoffsky		1
Carl Schaumburg & Co., Booksellers		4
His Excellency Franz, Count von Schönborn, Imperial Royal Austrian Privy Councilor and Chamberlain		1
Wiesbaden		
Government Assessor Lange		1
His Excellency State Minister Baron von Marschall	1	
Wollershausen am Harz		
Mr. L. von Minnigerode	1	
Würzburg		
Cathedral Prior Damian von der Leyen	1	
Mr. Joseph Stahel, Bookseller	5	
His Excellency Baron von Reding, the Royal Bavarian Ambassador	1	
Zeitz		
The Worthy Resource Library		1
Zerbst		
Mr. Andr. Füchsel, Bookseller	1	
Zürich		
Ziegler & Sons, Booksellers	2	

LIST OF SUBSCRIBERS SUBMITTED BY THE AUTHOR

	No. of Copies
Her Majesty Maria Feodorovna, Dowager Empress of Russia	3
Her Imperial Majesty Catharina Paulovna, Grand Duchess of Russia	1
His Imperial Majesty Michael Pavlovich, Grand Duke of Russia	1
Her Imperial Majesty Anna Paulovna, Grand Duchess of Russia	2
His Imperial Majesty Nicolai Pavlovich, Grand Duke of Russia	1
His Grace the Duke of Holstein-Oldenburg	1
His Grace the Crown Prince of Holstein-Oldenburg	1
His Imperial Majesty Georg, Prince of Holstein	1
Abo	
The University Library	1
Barbarova	
Mr. Heinr. von Holst	1
Bristol, Rhode Island, in North America	
Mr. John Dwolf, I	1
Cassel (Kassel)	
Mr. von Struve, Privy and Legation Councilor of the Imperial Russian Embassy	1
Friedrichshamm	
Mr. von Clayhills, Privy Councilor and Knight	1
Hamburg	
Mr. O. C. Gaedechens	1
Mr. J. Ossy	1
Humann in the Province of Kiev	
Mr. Hansen von Dittmar, the Brothers Ferdinand and Wilhelm	1
Josephathal in the Province of Ekatherinoslav	
Mr. C. Fr. Chr. Biller	1
Irkutsk	
Mr. Joh. von Müller, Privy Councilor and School Inspector	1
Korczec in the Province of Volhynia	
Mr. Carl Herlit, Apothecary	1

No. of Copies

Kronstadt

Mr. von Essen, Doctor of Medicine 1
Mr. O. Fr. Niemann 2

Leipzig

Mr. Chr. von Kleist, Royal Prussian Captain and Member of the Economic Society 1

Lisbon

Mr. A. T. Lindenberg 1

London

Mr. Joh. Friedr. Beland 1
Mr. Ludw. Engelbach, Esq. 1

Lupna

Apothecary Winding 1

Luvar in the Province of Volhynia

Mr. Samuel Wittke 1

Minkovcach in the Province of Podolia

Mr. Math. von Lauterborn, Textile Manufacturer 1

Mitau

The Library at the Gymnasium illustre 1
Professor and Doctor G. S. Bilterling, Master Teacher at the Gymnasium illustre 1

Moscow

The Imperial University Library 1
The Library of the Imperial Society of Natural Scientists 1
Privy Councilor and Professor von Buhle 1
Dr. Goth. von Fischer, Privy Councilor, Knight and Professor 1
Mr. Henning, Apothecary 1
Mr. Ph. von Pfahler, Doctor of Medicine and Collegiate Councilor 1
Anonymous 12

Mühlhausen

Mr. L. A. W. Lutteroth 1

Narva

Mr. J. Wibbelmann 1

Niemerow

Mr. Gottlieb Jokisch, owner of the textile mill in Niemerow, as well as the cloth canvas and linen mill in Darschou 1
Mr. J. Chr. Rössner, Imperial Russian Crown Chaplain for the Lutheran Church 1

	No. of Copies
Pedrosovodsk	
Mr. M. von Otseliq, Collegiate Assessor and Inspector of the Otonitz Medical Public Assistance Office	1
St. Petersburg	
Mr. John Quincy Adams, the Minister of the United American Free States	1
Fiscal Councilor and Knight von Adelung	1
His Excellency Mr. D. von Alopeus, Privy Councilor and Ambassador at the Royal Court of Würtemberg	1
Mrs. von Bakunin, née von Kutusoff	1
His Excellency Mr. von Balaschoff, the Minister of Police	1
Mr. Andreas Bardewieck	1
Mr. Heinr. Bardewieck, Privy Councilor	1
His Excellency Mr. von Bauer, General Lieutenant and Knight	1
Mr. C. L. Baum	1
His Excellency Burchard von Berg, General and Knight	1
The Library in the Marble Palace	1
Mr. J. W. J. Biller	1
Mr. J. J. Blanckenhagen	1
Mr. Thomas von Böhm	1
Mr. Brieff	3
Mr. Hans Bruun	1
Baron von Buddenbrock, District Magistrate and Knight	1
His Excellency Mr. von Bühler, Privy Councilor, Senator and Knight	1
His Excellency Count von Busch, the Royal Westphalian Ambassador	1
Mr. Franz Chameau	1
Mr. Bened. Cramer, Commercial Councilor	1
His Excellency, Doctor von Crighten, Fiscal Councilor, Knight and Physician in Ordinary	1
His Excellency Mr. von Derebine, the Head of Mining	1
Mr. von Derschau, Fiscal Councilor, the Imperial Russian Head Forester in Courland	1
Mr. von Essen, Knight	1
His Excellency, Mr. von Friederici, General Major and Knight	1
Mr. W. Friel	1
Mr. von Gebhardt, Collegiate Assessor	1
Mr. Fr. Geiger	1
His Excellency Fiscal Councilor and Knight Mr. von Grater	1
Mr. Harbauer, Doctor of Medicine	1
Mr. Anton Heindsker, Staff Surgeon and Collegiate Assessor	1
Mr. Hielbig	1
Mr. K. Holm	1

	No. of Copies
Mr. J. Janssen, Titular Councilor, Teacher for the First Imperial Cadet Corps	1
Mr. Joh. Joers	1
Mr. Fr. Kirchenpauer	1
Mr. von Korff, Privy Councilor, Knight and Hereditary Land Owner in Courland	1
Mr. Kron	1
Mr. J. von Kruse, Collegiate Assessor	1
Mr. A. J. von Krusenstern, Captain of the First Order and Knight	1
The District School for Lemhal	1
Mr. Friedr. Leopold	1
Mr. Harris-Levett, Consul General of the United American Free States	1
Mr. von Librecht, Collegiate Councilor	1
Her Highness the Countess von Lieven	4
Mr. Livia, Court Banker	1
Mr. Lohmann	2
Mr. Joach. Chr. Meyer, retired	1
Mr. J. L. Meyer, the Danish Consul	1
Mr. Jac. Mollow, Commercial Councilor	1
Mr. Ludw. Müller	1
Ludw. Heinr., Baron von Nicolai	1
His Highness Count von der Pahlen, Cavalry General, Knight of Several Orders and Hereditary Owner of several Estates in Courland	1
Mr. Wilh. Parker	1
Mr. von Peche, Marechal de Camp, Chevalier, etc.	1
His Excellency Joh. von Pestel, the General Governor of Siberia, Privy Councilor, Senator and Knight of several Orders	1
Mrs. Elizabetha von Pestel, née von Kroock	1
Mr. Platzmann	1
Mr. C. L. Prehn	1
Baron R. von Rall, Court Banker	1
His Excellency Count Alerin von Razumoffsky, Minister of Public Instruction	1
Mr. von Reissig, Privy Councilor and Professor	1
His Serene Highness Prince Repnin, General Major and Knight	1
His Highness Count von Rumanzoff, the Imperial Chancellor, Minister of Foreign Affairs, Knight of many Orders, etc.	1
His Excellency Franz von Schenk, Count of Castel-Dischingen, Royal Würtemberg Privy Councilor and the Extraordinary Ambassador at the Imperial Russian Court, Knight of several Orders	1

	No. of Copies
His Excellency, Baron von Schladen, the Minister Plenipotentiary of His Majesty, the King of Prussia, at the Imperial Russian Court	1
Mr. O. J. Schmidt	1
Mr. Schnackenburg	1
Mr. G. H. S. Severin, Commercial Councilor	1
Mr. von Staal, Colonel	1
Mr. von Tilesius, Privy Councilor and Member of the Imperial Academy of Sciences	1
Mr. von Turgenieff, Collegiate Councilor and Knight	1
Mr. H. D. Toussaint	1
His Excellency Mr. Uvaroff Serge, Fiscal Councilor, the Curator of the Pedagogical Institute and Educational Institutions for the District of St. Petersburg	1
Mr. Franz Waenker	1
His Serene Highness Prince Peter Volknosky, the General Adjutant, General Major and Knight	1
The District School for Wolmar	1
Piersal in Estonia	
Mr. Cornelius zur Mühlen	1
Reval	
Mr. Bornwasser	2
Mr. von Essen, the District Magistrate and Knight	1
Riga	
Mr. Libor. von Bergmann, Head Pastor	1
Mr. C. J. Gottfr. Hartmann, Bookseller	6
Baron von Liewen	1
His Excellency Mr. von Löwis, General Lieutenant	1
The Worthy Museum	1
Mr. von Reuter, Privy Councilor	1
Mr. Schmidt, Cornet	1
Mr. von Stakelberg, Baron von Ingensberg	1
Rügen in Livonia	
Mr. Gust. von Bergmann, the Head Consistorial Assessor and Pastor	1
Mr. von Holst, School Inspector	1
Sahten in Courland	
Mr. J. H. M. Bilterling, Pastor, Hereditary Owner of the Estates Kukschen	1
Strelna	
Mr. von Engelmann, Collegiate Councilor and Knight	1

	No. of Copies
Tver	
Mr. von Girard, Privy Councilor and Physician	1
Mr. Kalkau, Apothecary	1
Valck	
Mr. von Hagemeister, Collegiate Assessor	1
Venden (Wenden)	
hy Harmony Society	1
Vilna	
The Worthy University Library	1
Mr. von Boguslavski, Canonicus	1
Mr. von Bojanus, Privy Councilor and Professor	1
His Excellency Mr. von Knorring, General en Chef and Knight	1
Mr. von Liphardt, the District Magistrate at Rathshoff	1
Baron von Rosen	1
Mr. C. Friedr. Schwartze, Consistorial Councilor	1
His Excellency Count von Skorzewski	1
Baron von Taube, Artillery Captain and Knight	1
Mr. Wylezynski, Master of Philos.	1
Vitebsk	
Mr. von Trinius, Privy Councilor and Physician in Ordinary to His Royal Highness the Prince of Würtemberg	1
Tsarkoi-Selo	
Mr. von Hauenschild, Professor of German Literature at the Lyceum	1

In my announcement about this work I left it up to the subscribers to decide whether they desired it printed in German or Latin type and promised to proceed according to the wishes of the majority. The List of Subscribers shows that the majority of votes were for German type. Even in Russia, according to the information given by the author, only seventy requested Latin type. I therefore determined to print according to this principal and hope that all of the participants will not be displeased.

Frankfurt, February 15, 1812 Friedrich Wilmans

Notes

1. For additional information about titles and royalty see: *Burke's Royal Families of the World* (London: Burke's Peerage, Vol. I, 1977).

2. Only cities and areas with traditional English names still in use (Cologne, Prague, Moscow, Vienna, etc.) have been translated. With Langsdorff's transliterations from Russian, an English "v" has been substituted for the German "w" where it is pronounced "v." This preserves in the main Langsdorff's pronunciations and order.

EXPLANATION OF PLATES

1. *Northern Lights observed along the Norwegian Coast, September 19, 1803.*

2. *Clothing of the poorer inhabitants on Teneriffe.*

3. *The Interior of a Brazilian Dwelling.*

Two people are separating cotton from the seeds using a very unsatisfactory machine. One is seated on a typical stool for the area. Behind her is a water jug and two cuja along with straws. Next to the door is a net similar to one that served me well when hunting butterflies. Behind it is a bow for shooting clay balls rather than arrows. Fans are hanging next to the window on the wall. The accompanying sheet of music has on one side a Brazilian air and on the other music from Nukahiva.

4. *A View of the Island of Nukahiva.*

In the foreground a canoe from the Island. The black desolate cliffs with beautiful waterfalls lend the landscape a unique appearance. Mr. Orlowsky copied it from a sketch by Councilor Tilesius.

5. A second view of the Island of Nukahiva in the vicinity of the Harbor of Tayo-hoaë just when two shallops were being sent out to inspect it. Its entrance is behind the shallop with a sail.

6. *Jean Bapiste Cabri.*

7. *An inhabitant of the Island of Nukahiva.*

This and the next picture mainly illustrate the remarks in the text about tattooing. I drew both at the time in order to clarify the art of tattooing. This sketch is of an about 30-year-old on whom all of the tattoos are the clearest. Later, one figure is tattooed over another so that the lines blur greatly and the whole body takes on a negroid appearance as can be seen on the horizontal stripes over the stomach. This islander is holding a fan in one hand and a kind of battle club in the other that has a slain enemy's hair attached to the top.

8. *View of a young Nukahivan's back, which is completely tattooed.*

He is carrying, as proof of his heroic deed, a slain enemy's skull in one hand and a spear or lance in the other. Here and there you can see the outlines of the main individual figures, others are already finished. On the back of the head are two prominent glands which, as far as I know, have not been observed by any European anatomist. This man, as in the preceding etching, has all of his hair shaved off but for two small spots over his ears. The long hair has been bound up and almost looks like two horns.

9. *Representation of various main figures, several in actual size.*

Each figure has its own name. Most of them are intended for a particular part of the body. Figure 1 and 2 are intended for the inner side of the arm and ribs. The main figure is always the same but the details have their variations. Figures 3, 4, 5, 12, 13 and 14: *Enata* means man. Possibly this figure is mainly used when an enemy has been killed or eaten. In some figures there are several variations. In figures 5 and 13 with a bit of imagination you can see men with outstretched arms. At the bottom only one of the side lines is missing along with small squares to the side and a man would be standing on his legs.

Figures 6 and 7: *Niho-piata* — shark teeth. *Niho* means tooth. Sharks are actually called *mono* so it should be *niho-mono*. *Piata* is perhaps a particular species whose teeth produce the best cutting instruments for the islanders. This simple figure, as also the following one (Figure 8), is used here and there to decorate or fill in a hole and is put together with many variations.

Figure 9: *Matta comoe — matta* means the eye. Since the sign is of a human head and it is frequently used with *enata* (Figures 3, 5, 13, etc.), I suspect that it is a favorite sign of heroes. It usually is found on the chest, thighs and back (see Engravings 7 and 8).

Figures 10 and 11: *Kafe opogo* is a sign used right above the eyes and on the chest, etc. It is usually executed at a feast or when hogs are slaughtered.

Figures 12, 13 and 14: see Figures 3, 4 and 5.

Figure 15: *Tumu-ima*. The figure on the back of the head is found with little variations. The beauty and choice of a design depends upon the artist's taste and skill.

Figure 16: *Ehonu* — the turtle is used as an adornment between main figures. Depending upon taste, sometimes lizards and other animals are tattooed whose design and execution offer no great proof of the people's advancement in the art of drawing.

Figure 17. Queen Kätämuä's hand.

Figures 19, 20, 21. Adornments whose names and meanings were not explained to me. The names of several of their designs in the 7th and 8th engravings, which I consider superfluous to discuss, are: *Wibu*, a ring or bracelet; *Matta toï-toï*, the tattoo around the eye — like over Jean Baptist Cabri's — acquired at a pork feast (see the 6th engraving). *Uma hoka*, a breastplate; *Tua heu* and *kehu* — a wide stripe across the chest, shoulders, arms and stomach. This is the usual sign of an eating society. *Matta moë*, a wide stripe from the nose over the eyes to the ears.

10. *A view of an inhabited valley on Nukahiva.*

In the left foreground is a fenced-in tabu coconut tree whose trunk has coconuts tied to it from top to bottom which are being stored as provisions for a festival. On the next tree an islander, monkey-like with braced feet, is climbing up to get nuts. The representation of the dwelling built on a platform is sufficient to illustrate the text on page 87. Next to the house is a covered pit used to store a supply of *popoi* or fermented breadfruit.

11. Interior of a Nukahivan hut where a tattoo artist is sitting and practicing his art. A tabu person is entering the hut in order to present the artist with a gift of a pig's head.

12. *Nukahivan weapons and utensils.*

In the middle is a battle club decorated on the top with a slain enemy's braided hair. It has a feather decoration hanging from it that is used to adorn the hands and feet. Two delicately carved stilts — one from the front, the other from the back — are crossed. The trophy contains, in addition, a fish hook, a calabash or water vessel, a stone ax, a fan, an oar, slingshot, shell, a slain enemy's skull decorated with pig's teeth and a necklace. I am indebted to Mr. Orlowsky for the design and execution of this engraving.

13. *Plan and measurements of a Nukahivan canoe.*

(a) The canoe's bottom is made from a single tree trunk, the stern of which (b) is attached by means of a joint (c); the side boards used to make the canoe higher are attached; a thin slat covering the seam (d) between the bottom (a) and the side boards (c) used to prevent leaking. This slat is fastened on by strips of bark (e). The seams are filled in with moss and resin from the breadfruit tree. (f) A section at the back made from thin bamboo where one sits to guide the boat; (g) an elevation at the front where the eldest, the leaders or persons of rank sit; (h) balancing poles or outriggers placed straight across the boat along with a long pole (i), which touches the water and is fastened at (h) and often serves to prevent the motion or swaying from capsizing the boat; (k) the seats; (l) an oar; (m) a rudder for steering.

The boats are used in hostilities. Two of them are bound together and a platform of planks, about 12 to 14 *fuss* wide is built between them where the warriors stand for battle. These boats are extremely poorly built and cannot be used with a sail.

I owe this plan and the measurements of the canoe, as well as those of all of the other peoples' we observed along with their descriptions, to the generosity of Mr. Korukin, our shipwright and traveling companion, and I wish to thank him here publicly.

14. *A Canoe of the Sandwich Islanders.*

Bottom and side view of the canoe which is made from a single tree trunk (a); on the sides are placed thin boards (b) which are somewhat higher at the front and back where they come together; (c) outrigger or balance pole; (d) a small beam that touches the water and is fastened to the balance pole; (e) seats. The inhabitants sometimes use square sails made of grass or the inner bark of a tree. The mast is fastened to the foremost balance pole (f); (g) oar. These canoes are built with extraordinary assiduity and craftsmanship.

15. *View of Kaminosim, a landscape in the Harbor of Nangasaki.*

We were anchored a short distance away from the charming bay adorned with a beautiful little village. It is protected on all sides and serves many ships and vessels as protection in any wind. Its manifold objects offered us many a pleasant diversion. In the foreground is one of the vessels belonging to the Prince of Fisen's honor guard which guarded us. The closest mountain behind this vessel is called Lembon.

16. *A Japanese Fort.*

The house or enclosures are adorned with the Prince of Fisen's curtains or awnings and flags. We were told places and houses equipped and adorned in this manner were forts. We, however, never heard either a canon or gun fired from one of them and never saw one of the former. Thus, we do not know what is hidden behind the awnings. This fort is not far from a temple on a tongue of land at the entrance to the inner harbor of Nangasaki. In the foreground is a pleasure boat filled with curious women like several that came to observe our Russian ship from a distance.

17. *Ambassador von Resanoff's Dwelling at Megasaki.*

In the left foreground is part of the storehouse for the gifts we had brought along, then a water bearer with his back to the gate leading to land. Next to him are some of the officers' quarters and then the kitchen. In the middle is the main entrance to the Ambassador's quarters guarded by the Russian honor guard. To the right is the Ambassador's living room. Near it is the other gate leading to the water where the high bamboo fence begins. In the courtyard in front of the house is a group of Japanese officers and their entourage. In front of the Ambassador's room three people are conferring. In front of the main entrance several Japanese generals are greeting each other according to the country's custom by running the palm of their hands over their knees. Several men of rank or *great men* are standing in front of the kitchen. Behind one of them is a soldier carrying covered honor standards. A common servant has to set behind his master as soon as he stops. The one here is in this position holding his master's straw shoes. Major von Friederici drew most of this engraving for which I am gratefully indebted to him.

18. *One of the Prince of Omura's military officers taking up guard duty.*

In the foreground is the small spot where we were permitted to go for a walk toward the end of our stay in Megasaki. The guard is heading to the Ambassador's quarters. Behind the outer, lower bamboo fence can be seen the back wall of the storehouse. Only the officer is completely clothed. In front and behind him are two soldiers, then come military servants, one of whom is carrying his master's umbrella, and two others, several honor standards. The others are carrying baskets and chests of provisions, clothing, tobacco, utensils, etc. Finally, two soldiers lead the officer's horse. The officer may or may not decide to ride it. The horse has straw shoes on instead of iron ones. Our ship is surrounded by the small boats of the Japanese honor guard as in the Harbor of Nangasaki. Nearby is a Chinese junk. The view of the opposite shore is true to nature. The whole picture is based on sketches done by Mr. Mayr at that time and place.

19. *A Japanese Doctor.*

He is busy preparing medicine. His mortar is in front of him, it seems, in a sand bath; his retort and other vessels at his side. This engraving is based on a Japanese original woodblock print so that readers are able to judge somewhat that nation's taste and art of drawing.

20. Kakaminotschi *or New Year's gift given the Russian Ambassador von Resanoff by the governor of Nangasaki.*

It consisted of the following pieces (1) a new base made from thin slats. On it were put (2) green leaves and twigs, mainly of ferns; (3) a large rice cake with 6 small cakes on its top side; (4) another rice cake similar to the above with three rhombus-shaped cakes on top of it that were shoved together to form a six-sided figure. Then came (5) two long strips of seaweed with a diagonal stick fastened to the front end around which front and top some straw had been cleanly and neatly bound as shown in the engraving. (6 and 7) Two little packets of fine, white paper with colorful edges, evenly folded. One contained rice and the other salt; (8) a crab; (9) an orange in a (10) basket-like shaped piece of seaweed; (11) a fir twig wrapped in fine paper and around it a *Compliment* ribbon of colorful little strips of rolled together paper; (12) a little stick skewered with dried fruit wrapped in paper.

Just as we represent abundance with a cornucopia, the Japanese represent replenishment with this New Year's gift. Its head is made of straw, its tail of seaweed (*Fucus saccharinus Linn.*) and its body contains everything the body needs for nourishment. One wishes everyone one sends this gift abundance the whole year through.

21. *Landing in Nangasaki on the day of the audience. The Ambassador's solemn parade to the governor's house.*

In the foreground is the royal Fisen boat surrounded by several honor vessels. Next to them are the Ochatto steps leading to the open square hung with the Prince of Fisen's awnings. Opposite the Ochatto steps is the civilian guard post with a line of honor standards in front of it; on both sides are hanging large lanterns. Farther to the left are steps leading to the upper part of the town hung with imperial awnings because the building on the right and the steps belong to the Crown.

The Parade had the following order: first 40 people of various ranks, including several *banjos*, each of whom was followed by his servants. Then came 6 imperial soldiers with long poles instead of guns in their hands. They were followed by the norimon or portchaise, in which the Ambassador was carried. Immediately following came a Russian soldier with the Imperial Russian Standard, then 5 of the ambassadorial cavaliers on foot surrounded by a number of civil servants and interpreters. These were followed by 16 to 20 soldiers, also with poles instead of guns, along with an officer on horseback and finally a large number of civil servants, civil officers, interpreters, servants, etc. It had rained a little while before; thus, many people had umbrellas.

22. *Japanese in various costumes.*

On the left the first two figures show the front and back of a mendicant monk belonging to the Rokubo sect. He has a small copper bowl fastened over his abdomen on which he makes continual noise with a little stick he is carrying in his hand. He accompanies this music with a little bell he is holding in his left hand and usually also with song. His head is covered by a hat to protect him from rain and sun. The next figure is a typical civilian officer. Usually the interpreters and all civilian officers appeared in such costumes with two sabers. Next to them are some monks from various sects, the latter are called Oschiosan. The man with a saber was the gatekeeper at Megasaki who kept us under lock and key for 6 months.

23. *Japanese in various costumes.*

In the left foreground stands a Japanese in rain-wear, next to him 3 musicians, the right one with a tambourine (*saiko*), the second one with a copper cymbal (*schiang-schinag*) and the third one with a kind of *schlamay* (*schiamen*) that has 7 openings on its front side. Finally, the back and front views of a Japanese in ceremonial clothing.

24. *Japanese in various costumes.*

First to the left, one of the governor of Nangasaki's soldiers, then one of the Prince of Omura's. Next to him is standing the servant of the monk of bansen who is offering for sale letters of indulgence on the tray held by his servant. The last figure is a monk in summer clothing from a sect I do not know.

25. *Japanese in various costumes.*

The large figure in the foreground represents a man who sells whale meat. In addition he carries scales, a knife, a hook and an umbrella in his baskets. Like all Japanese, he has a belt around his hips with tobacco pipe and pouch attached to it. The next person shows a civilian officer from the back. Even though he has two sabers we can only see the longer one. A woman is shown from the front and back, thus illustrating how children of the poorer classes are carried. She is wearing in her hair as adornment various wide, long needles. The man in the house door is busy husking rice by means of a large wooden, hollowed out block which is almost filled to the top with rice. In its middle are put as many rings of the same size as are necessary to have the same height as the rice. The worker stamps or pounds with a heavy, long wooden hammer into the empty space formed by the rings causing with each blow some grains of rice to fall from the rice lying around the rings. From time to time the rice is sieved, cleaned and stored in a straw mat. The rings are changed according to the quantity of rice. Uncleaned rice is kept in a nearby wooden vessel or casks.

26. *Japanese in various costumes.*

The first figure on the left is a Japanese servant carrying some trifles. On the end of the pole resting on his shoulder hangs a pair of straw shoes. The second figure represents an imperial Japanese sailor. Next to him is a Japanese lady with a fan. On her back over her hips she has a large bow. This along with her white teeth is a sign that she is still unmarried. As soon as she is a wife the bow is tied in front and her teeth are blackened with a special stain. Her hairstyle is not unlike an old French one. Her hair stiffened with pomade has goid and silver hair pins with flowers and various kinds of sparkle stuck in it according to her station. On her shoulder is a round symbol. Since almost all Japanese of both sexes usually wear black or blue clothing and they often take off the top part like a jacket, almost all of them have a family coat of arms on them as a sign of ownership and to avoid mistakes. Behind the lady a servant is carrying a rich family's child on its shoulder. Small children usually have their heads shaved and wear red clothing or clothing decorated with many flowers. Red clothing is considered very healthy. Next is a poor worker who has a rain hat instead of an umbrella and instead of rain-wear a kind of straw coat that rather protects him against severe weather. Like all Japanese he has his tobacco pipe and pouch hanging at his side. Finally, a craftsman or common citizen in winter clothing. He has a cloth wound around his head to protect him from cold. In his underclothing over his waistband, like all of his fellow citizens, he is carrying his pocket book and in his waistband a fan, tabasco pouch, tabasco pipe and ink horn.

27. *A Boat from the Island of Tschoka.*

(a) The bottom sides of the boat which is made from a single tree trunk; (b) a strip fastened to the edge in which pegs have been placed (c). These strips have been fastened to the body of the boat with cords woven from bast; (c) pegs intended for oars above the plank. They are round on top and square at the bottom and fastened to the boat by cord (d); a plank with steps at the front of the canoe. One end of it is fastened to the bottom of the boat at (e) and the other sticks out in front. This plank serves for going from the boat onto land, especially at steep places where one cannot get too close to land; (f) benches and seats; (g) an oar, which has a hole in the middle at the top end so that it can be put on the peg. Islanders usually row with two oars, alternately rowing first on one side and then the other.

28. *View of St. George Island.*

This desolate and little known island is one of several inhabited by Russian hunters. They kill fur seals that gather on the coast in herds and prepare their skins for trade. The numbers of birds nesting on this island is so large that they form dark clouds when they fly up. The horizontally layered, rocky cliffs are made of black, loose, partially porous and charred kinds of rock.

On the horizon, I have pictured the island growing near Unalaska, as I observed it on August 18th.

29. *View of the Russian Settlement at Unalaska.*

The village of Illuluk lies on a small, low point of land. Next to the earthen huts resembling grave mounds are crosses erected in memory of several respected Russians who died on the Island. Next to them are racks used for drying fish.

In the foreground are several Aleuts in their leather canoes (baidarkas), who are launching their harpoons aided by launching boards. The small, longish figures in front of the huts on the shore are baidarkas turned upside down along the shore as they always are when not in use.

30. *A single-seated baidarka from the Island of Unalaska.*

(a) The keel; (b) lathes forming the front and back part of the keel and, at the same time, the frame of the boat; (c) the top fastening; (d) cross section of the framework; (e) thin lathes which are fastened lengthwise to the cross supports; (f) cross lathes which are fastened to the upper side lathes (c); (g) a long lathe which is fastened on top to the cross supports (f); (h) a ring the size of the seat hole. It is put on top of the horizontal lathes (f) and fastened to the sides with two supports (i) which are placed on the topmost side lathes (c) and are fastened to the seat ring; (k) the seat hole; (l) a small bone rod placed about seven zolls in from of the seat hole on the baidarka in two nails or little plates which have been ground concave. In stormy weather this little rod is supposed to help the baidarka very much and, if the leather boat is well made, always to turn it right side up; (m) the paddle.

All of the supports and lathes are fastened together with fish bones [whalebone or baleen?] or seal sinews. The entire frame, with the exception of the seat hole, is covered with sealskin.

The back cross-lathe of the seat hole (f) has to be firmly fastened to neighboring parts, the front one less firmly attached. The keel is made in three parts, of these the front-most one is five, the hindmost three and one-half English feet long. In the places where the various parts of the keel are fastened together (n) on the inside two crossed, flat, bone rods are put over each other (l). This special trick is kept secret from many others and a chief assured me that these bones are of great value in stormy seas because the baidarka is more elastic when hit by strong waves.

A good, freshly oiled, new leather boat in good calm weather or in very moderate wind can stay in the water continually for twelve to fourteen days without spoiling; in stormy weather, however, only six days at the most, since the seams will weaken and let in water. To keep a baidarka in good condition, it has to be taken out of the water after every trip and let dry. If a baidarka hits a rock or otherwise suddenly gets a tear, then a piece of seal meat or whale blubber, which the Aleuts always have along, is stuck into it. This is the best means of stopping a leak of that kind. In addition, as a matter of precaution, they take one or several needles with sinew thread along on every hunting excursion. The Aleuts often undertake long hunting trips on the open sea. They usually go in parties and always take along their rain garments made of bladder skins. If a storm comes up, they bind two or three baidarkas together and thus need not be afraid. The seat hole has a piece of leather which can be tightly tied around the body, thus preventing water from entering the baidarka.

31. *The main Russian Settlement on the Island of Kodiak.*

The largest building with the flagstaff serves as a casern. Next to it on the same hill is the storehouse. Next to the church, on the left, and between it and the casern are found the buildings used by the company for various kinds of work. Behind them is the house of the present manager Mr. Bander. To the right of the church is the new house Mr. von Lisiansky had built and next to it several little houses for craftsmen.

Just behind the foreground is a large, new storehouse. Next to it are Russian swings and a carousel which Mr. von Baranoff had built for the amusement of the inhabitants. To the left of the casern is the priests' house as well as the building intended for use as a school. Farther to the left in the distance is a large, round house used by all of the Aleuts living there.

32. *Three-seated baidarka from the Island of Kodiak.*

(a) The keel; (b) lathes on the front and back part of the keel which at the same time form the front and back part of the boat; (c) the top side bindings and fasteners; (d) supports for the skin or the lathes of the frame; (e) other lathes running the length of the vessel placed on the cross-lathes; (f) length-wise beam which closes the frame at the top and is fastened to the sides at (c); (g) a long lathe fastened on top of the beam (f) to strengthen it; (h) hoop which borders the seat hole. It is placed in front of and behind the beam (f) and on the side on two other beams (i) which are fastened to (f); (k) the seat skin; (l) the seat hole; (m) the paddle.

The whole frame and all the individual parts are fastened together by fish bone [whalebone or baleen?] or seal sinew. In the entire vessel there is neither a wooden nor an iron nail. When the frame is finished, it is covered with wet sealskin, which previously, like a dress, has been cut to fit the frame and then sewn together.

In my opinion, these baidarkas are the best means invented by man up to now to travel from one place to another on the shallowest as well as deepest water in the easiest, fastest and safest manner. I am not talking about long sea voyages, although the Aleuts are sent with their baidarkas from Kodiak to Sitcha, that is, from 57° north and 152° west to 56° north and 135° west longitude.

33. *View of the Russian-American Company's Outpost at Norfolk Sound or Sitcha.*

In the foreground is the fortification hill. At its foot, to the right, is a bath house along with housing for craftsmen. On the left, somewhat hidden by the hill, is part of the large fortified casern. Next to it, on a spit of land are the storehouses. In front of them is the small inlet used as the main landing spot for the outpost. Behind the hill along the shore are several buildings for the Aleuts, a kitchen, a smithy, the house of the locksmith as well as other men.

34. *The Kalusch in Sitcha dancing.*

They usually wear a simple blanket or clothes traded from the merchants of the United American Free States. They are holding the tails of bald eagles. Ermine fur on their heads and on their clothes also held sometimes in their hands is a sign of wealth and display. The dancer in front has a cane decorated with the teeth of sea otters that he uses to beat the rhythm. Several of them have powdered their heads with the white down of bald eagles. Their women sit in front of them and sing. Their expanded lower lips form their special national decoration.

35. *View of the Spanish settlement at San Francisco in New California.*

In the foreground is one of the boats the Indians of the area make out of bundled straw. The Spanish call them *valtsa*.

36. *Objects from New California and Norfolk Sound.*

(1) Indian head decoration in New California. (2) Another kind of Indian head decoration in New California. (3) An Indian basket in New California which is used instead of a soup bowl. (4 and 5) An Indian necklace from New California. (6 and 7) Strings of beads made from mussels in the manner of European glass beads and used by the Indians in New California as necklaces. (8 and 9) Bow and arrows of Indians in

New California. (10 and 11) Baskets made from straw and bark by the Kalusch or inhabitants of Norfolk Sound.

37. *An Indian Dance at the Mission of San Jose in New California.*

All of the figures are naked except for a covering over their genitals. Their facial features are rather accurate. Their hair is very strong, thick and stands erect. Several have powdered theirs with down. They have painted their bodies in various ways with cinders, chalk and red clay. The second to last dancer has covered himself with down, thus, making him resemble an ape. The last dancer had an original idea. He has painted his naked body so that he looks like a Spanish soldier in uniform with collar, cuffs, boots, stockings, breeches, etc. Next to the Indians at the foot of a tree is a fire. From time to time, the dancers take burning coals from it and swallow them.

38. *Objects from Alaksa and Unalaska.*

(1) A fishskin bag from Alaksa. (2) A finger covering of leather used instead of a thimble by the women of Alaska when sewing. (3) A rattle from Kodiak used at dances. It is made from the bills of auks. (4 and 5) Earrings made of tooth [dentalium?] shell, a mollusk shell. (6) An Aleut lip decoration in natural size. It is made from a piece of bone and beads and stuck in a hole cut under the lower lip. (7) An example of embroidery on leather with reindeer hair from Unalaska. (8) A cap made of ground squirrel from Alaksa. (9) A basket woven of straw from Unalaska. (10 and 11) Two purses woven of straw from Unalaska. (12) A richly embroidered cap only worn by the Aleuts at dances. The goat hairs flying around it are sewn and woven in for decoration.

39. *Baidara from the Peninsula of Alaksa.*

(a) The keel; (b) the back part which is fastened to the keel; (c) the board which rests on the front part of the keel; (d) cross-lathes which lie over the keel; (e) poles placed at the ends of the cross lathes; (f) the ribs over which the skin is stretched and which are fastened to the lower cross lathes (d); (g) the upper edge lathes which hold the skin; (h) lathes fastened on the inside on which the seats are placed; (i) the seats; (k) straps which are fastened under the seats in three or four places, so that the baidara does not fall apart in the waves. No nails are used. The pieces are fastened together with fish bones [whalebone or baleen?] or sinew. The entire frame or skeleton is finally covered with sealskin (l) that have been sewn together; (m) the paddle.

40. *A view of St. Peter and St. Paul in Kamtschatka.*

See Krascheninnikoff, No. 1; Steller, page 16; *Atlas* from la Pérouse, No. 56; Sarytscheff, Part I, p. 165; von Krusenstern's *Atlas*, Tab. 28.

All of these sources give a view from the houses at the Harbor of St. Peter and St. Paul toward the Awatscha Bay and the mouth of the Harbor. Major von Friederici, who was kind enough to make this sketch for me, chose the small spit of land, which is also shown in the other views, and is here in the foreground, as the base for his sketch, which gives a very faithful view of the actual town. In the background is the peak called Awatschinskaia Sopka. Among the largest buildings, the most important ones are the Crown storehouse, the commander's house and the Russian-American Company's buildings.

41. *Sketch and description of a Kamtschatkan sledge and dog harness with accessories.*

Figure 1. Cross section of a sledge.

Figure 2. Side view of a sledge.

The three main parts of a sledge are: Figure 1(F) and 2(F): Seat-basket (*reschotka*). Figure 3(C): Sledge feet (*lopulka*) in a cross view of the sledge and Figure 2(C) of the same from the side II sledge runners (*polosa*).

The seat-basket (Figure 2[F]) consists of five rods. Figure 3(a) shows them in cross view (two of them go through the sledge feet). In addition, small, thin, bent lathes (D) and finally straps (Figure 2[v]) are used to fasten the rods and lathes together.

(b) A cross-lathe (*properelschnaya*) used to hold together the sledge runner at the front of the sledge to which three strong rings (x) are fastened. The dog harness is hooked through holders (m).

(c) Figures 1 and 2: lathes (*potaski*) running the length of both sides of the sledge. Along with the three straps (e) (*nischnoie atuki*), a saddle bag which serves as a pad for dog food and other objects which are tied down on it; the two other straps (d) (*verchnoi atuki*) run upwards for the same purpose and at the same time give the seat-basket greater stability.

All of the parts taken together, i.e., b, c, d and e, constitute the front part of the sledge (*peredok*). The two back ends of the side lathes (e) together with the back part of the seat basket (f) constitute the back part of the sledge (*masadok*). It also serves as a spot to which small objects can be fastened. The holes (k) have strong straps drawn through them to fasten the sledge feet (c) to the sledge runners (E).

The following is to be noted when harnessing the dogs: (i) the shoulder strap (*alaki*), a wide, double, leather strap put over the dog's shoulders, that, while pulling, is more to the left of the dog on the right side in Figure 10 and more to the right on the dog on the left side in Figure 1 has a pull-strap (f) fastened to the shoulder strap (i). On its end there is a chain link with an iron pin (m), which is put in the ring (x), thus fastening the strap to the sledge *probeschek* (g), a strong strap that acts as a tongue. It is fastened to the sledge in the same way as the *alaki* (m and x). At the front of it is a set of chain links (h), whose back side-members serve to hold the dogs together in pairs by means of their collars. The front ring is used to extend the tongue strap, as well as to be hooked to the front of the *alaki*.

Similar chain harness is used for lengthening the team if 6 or more dogs are to be harnessed. If there is only one front or lead dog (Figure 10), then the link on the collar is fastened to a ring (z) on the top part of the *alaki*, so that the dog cannot slip out from the *alaki* and escape. The same thing would happen if the collar were not hooked into the rings on the set of rings (h).

Figure 4. A collar like the dogs wear all year round and helps greatly in harnessing them.

Figure 5. A stick (*doska*) usually made from bone or wood. At one end is an opening the size of the ring (x) and at the other a strap is fastened. These sticks are used for tying up the dogs at every stop. All travelers on winter trips take along as many of these sticks as they have dogs. Richer people use chains instead of sticks and straps.

Figure 6. *Ostall* or *ostoll*, a rod with rings and bells at its top and an iron point on its tip. Its rattle is used to urge the dogs on and its point to stop the sledge going down hill or at other times. The *ostoll* is driven into the snow or ice in front of the sledge runners.

Figure 7. A snowshoe, very necessary equipment when dog-sledding; (d) straps used to fasten the snowshoe to the foot.

Figure 8. Ice-shoe used for climbing glaciers.

Figure 9. *Posluki* or iron points fastened to the feet with straps, used for climbing mountain glaciers.

Figure 10. Harness of a front or lead dog.

42. *Sketch of a copper cannon, 1/12 of its actual size, which Lieutenant von Chwostoff took from the Japanese in 1807 on the 19th Kuril Island of Itureij in Schana Bay.*

(a) A little, removable cannon. For loading, it is removed and put back in its place after loading. In the holes (b) on both sides of the cannon, iron or wooden pins are put in so it cannot move; (c) sight for aiming; (d) on top of the cannon are Latin letters R. Co., which are cast. The letters are the reason for believing that the cannon is either an old Portuguese or Spanish one, since the Japanese do not use these letters at all.

During our six-month stay in Nangasaki, we saw no cannons and heard no Japanese cannon shot. The interpreters were evasive about the existence of Japanese cannons.

They know absolutely nothing about the use of a carriage. Instead, they drive four posts into the ground and put several poles between them. They put the cannon on the posts and tie it down so that it cannot move at all. They shoot lead balls filled with clay. They load the cannons and guns in the following manner: first they put powder in the barrel, then the ball on this and only then the plug. Their powder very much resembles our coarse cannon powder in form and size and is supposed to be very good. Filled with great fear, they fire their cannons by fastening the burning fuse on an extremely long pole. All of this betrays an ignorance and a dearth of knowledge about the use of firearms, especially of heavy cannons.

(1) View from the side. (2) Cross section of line AB. (3) View from above.

43. *View of an area along the Aldan River on the way to Irkutsk from Ochotsk.*

The cliffs on the left bank of the river are called Padjesobut.

44. *Brazilian Air.*

45. *Song of the Natives of Nukahiva.*

Volume One Frontispiece: Langsdorff.

Volume Two Frontispiece: Krusenstern.

Endpapers: Map of World showing Langsdorff's route.

INDEX

-W-

-Y-

-Z-

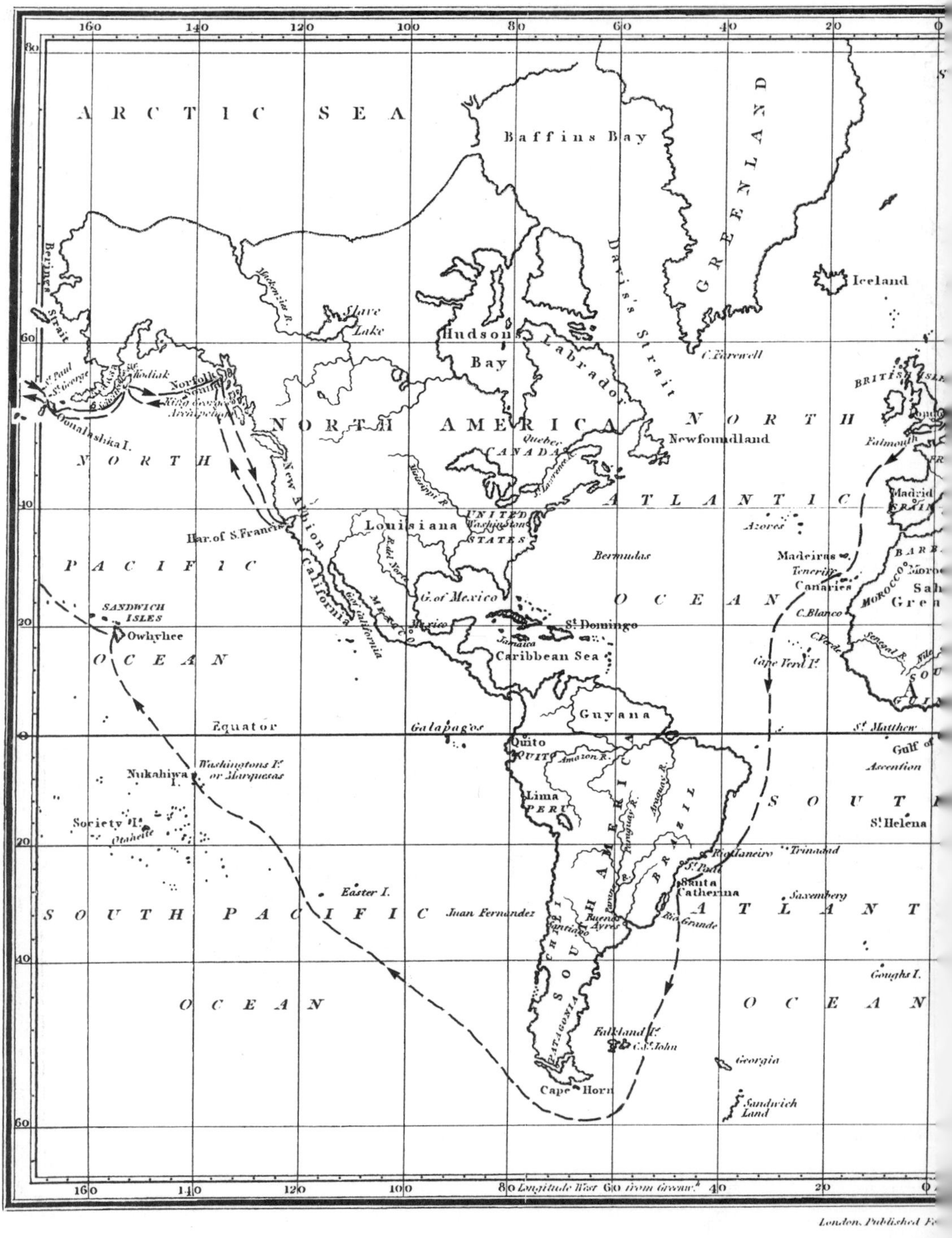
ARCTIC SEA
Baffins Bay
GREENLAND
Iceland
Davis's Strait
Hudsons Bay
Labrador
C. Farewell
Beerings Strait
Slave Lake
Mackenzie R.
St Paul
St George
Kodiak
Norfolk Sound
King Georges Archipelago
Oonalashka I.
NORTH AMERICA
Quebec
CANADA
St Lawrence R.
Newfoundland
NORTH ATLANTIC OCEAN
BRITISH ISLES
Falmouth
Madrid
SPAIN
New Albion
Har. of S. Francis
Louisiana
UNITED STATES
Washington
Mississippi R.
Azores
Bermudas
Madeiras
Teneriffe
Canaries
MOROCCO
C. Blanco
C. Verde
Senegal R.
Cape Verd Is
PACIFIC
California
MEXICO
Mexico
G. of Mexico
Gof California
St Domingo
Jamaica
Caribbean Sea
SANDWICH ISLES
Owhyhee
OCEAN
Equator
Galapagos
Guyana
Quito
Amazon R.
St Matthew
Gulf of Guinea
Ascention
Nukahiwa I.
Washingtons Is or Marquesas
Lima
PERU
BRAZIL
Araguay R.
Parana R.
Paraguay R.
SOUTH AMERICA
St Helena
Society Is
Otaheite
Rio Janeiro
Trinidad
St Paul
Santa Catherina
Saxemberg
Easter I.
SOUTH PACIFIC
Juan Fernandez
CHILI
Santiago
Buenos Ayres
Rio Grande
ATLANTIC
Goughs I.
OCEAN
PATAGONIA
Falkland Is
C. St John
Georgia
Cape Horn
Sandwich Land
160
140
120
100
80
60
40
20
0
Longitude West from Greenw.h
London, Published